Clinical Pharmacy Education, Practice and Research

Clinical Pharmacy Education, Practice and Research

Clinical Pharmacy, Drug Information, Pharmacovigilance, Pharmacoeconomics and Clinical Research

Edited by

Dixon Thomas

ELSEVIER

Elsevier
Radarweg 29, PO Box 211, 1000 AE Amsterdam, Netherlands
The Boulevard, Langford Lane, Kidlington, Oxford OX5 1GB, United Kingdom
50 Hampshire Street, 5th Floor, Cambridge, MA 02139, United States

Notices
Knowledge and best practice in this field are constantly changing. As new research and experience broaden our understanding, changes in research methods, professional practices, or medical treatment may become necessary.

Practitioners and researchers must always rely on their own experience and knowledge in evaluating and using any information, methods, compounds, or experiments described herein. In using such information or methods they should be mindful of their own safety and the safety of others, including parties for whom they have a professional responsibility.

To the fullest extent of the law, neither the Publisher nor the authors, contributors, or editors, assume any liability for any injury and/or damage to persons or property as a matter of products liability, negligence or otherwise, or from any use or operation of any methods, products, instructions, or ideas contained in the material herein.

Library of Congress Cataloging-in-Publication Data
A catalog record for this book is available from the Library of Congress

British Library Cataloguing-in-Publication Data
A catalogue record for this book is available from the British Library

ISBN: 978-0-12-814276-9

For information on all Elsevier publications visit our website at https://www.elsevier.com/books-and-journals

Working together
to grow libraries in
developing countries

www.elsevier.com • www.bookaid.org

Publisher: Andre Gerhard Wolff
Acquisition Editor: Erin Hill-Parks
Editorial Project Manager: Carlos Rodriguez
Production Project Manager: Swapna Srinivasan
Cover Designer: Mark Rogers

Typeset by TNQ Technologies

Contents

Section II
Drug Information

10. Medical Literature Evaluation and Biostatistics

*Christopher S. Wisniewski, Emily P. Jones,
Erin R. Weeda, Nicole A. Pilch and
Mary Frances Picone*

11. Evidence-Based Practice: Use in Answering Queries and Developing Systematic Reviews

*Emily Brennan, Jason C. Cooper and
Amanda Davis*

12. Clinical Guidelines for Decision-Making

Elangovan Gajraj and Leeza Osipenko

13. Drug Information Training for Pharmacists

*Dixon Thomas, Ivellise Costa de Sousa,
David J. Woods, Ronald A. Herman and
Danial E. Baker*

Section III
Pharmacoepidemiology and Pharmacovigilance

14. Essentials of Pharmacoepidemiology

Douglas T. Steinke

15. Pharmacovigilance Systems

Dixon Thomas and Christoph Klika

16. Adverse Drug Events, Medication Errors, and Drug Interactions

Vincent W.L. Tsui, Dixon Thomas, Shuhui Tian and Allen J. Vaida

Section IV
Pharmacoeconomics and Outcomes Research

17. Market Access, Pharmaceutical Pricing, and Healthcare Costs

Dixon Thomas, Denny John, Nermeen Ashoush, Federico Lega and Hong Li

18. Pharmacoeconomic Analyses and Modeling

Dixon Thomas, Mickael Hiligsmann, Denny John, Ola Ghaleb Al Ahdab and Hong Li

19. Interpreting Pharmacoeconomic Findings

*Piyameth Dilokthornsakul, Dixon Thomas,
Lawrence Brown and
Nathorn Chaiyakunapruk*

20. Outcomes Research

*Erin R. Weeda, Nicole A. Pilch and
Lieven Annemans*

21. Health Technology Assessment— Policy Objectives and Principles of System Design

Dávid Dankó

25. Stakeholders, Resources, and Documents in Clinical Research

Deepak C. Chilkoti

Section VI
Pharmacy Education

26. Quality Assurance in Pharmacy Education

Dawn G. Zarembski, Michael J. Rouse and Peter H. Vlasses

27. Adult Learning Theories in Pharmacy Education

Kashelle Lockman, Dixon Thomas and Lilian H. Hill

Section VII
Pharmacokinetics/ Pharmacogenomics/Nutrition

32. TPN Primer for the Pharmacist: Approach to Nutrition Therapy

Mark Decerbo

Section VIII
Conclusion

33. Advanced Clinical Pharmacy Practitioner

*Erick Sokn, Sam Calabrese,
Douglas Scheckelhoff, Dixon Thomas and
Jason A. Roberts*

List of Contributors

Ola Ghaleb Al Ahdab, Ministry of Health and Prevention, Abu Dhabi, United Arab Emirates

Alshabi Ali, Clinical Pharmacy Department, College of Pharmacy, Najran University, Najran, Saudi Arabia

Anna Birna Almarsdóttir, University of Copenhagen, Copenhagen, Denmark

Lieven Annemans, Ghent University, Ghent, Belgium

Nermeen Ashoush, The British University in Egypt, Cairo, Egypt

Danial E. Baker, Washington State University, Spokane, WA, United States

Anna Bryndis Blondal, University of Iceland, Reykjavik, Iceland

Emily Brennan, Medical University of South Carolina, Charleston, SC, United States

Lawrence Brown, Chapman University School of Pharmacy, Irvine, CA, United States

Daniel Buffington, University of South Florida, Tampa, FL, United States

Sam Calabrese, Cleveland Clinic, Cleveland, OH, United States

Nathorn Chaiyakunapruk, Monash University Malaysia, Selangor, Malaysia

Deepak C. Chilkoti, Consultant, Clinical Operations and Pharmacovigilance, Delhi, India

Wai Yee Choon, Monash University Malaysia, Bandar Sunway, Malaysia

Jason C. Cooper, Medical University of South Carolina, Charleston, SC, United States

Ivellise Costa de Sousa, University Hospital Professor Edgard Santos, Salvador, Brazil

Dávid Dankó, Ideas & Solutions, Budapest, Hungary

Amanda Davis, Medical University of South Carolina, Charleston, SC, United States

Mark Decerbo, Roseman University of Health Sciences, Henderson, NV, United States; University of Nevada School of Medicine, Reno, NV, United States

Brian S. Decker[†]

Piyameth Dilokthornsakul, Naresuan University, Phitsanulok, Thailand

Benny Efendie, Monash University Malaysia, Bandar Sunway, Malaysia

Firuz Gamal Feturi, University of Pittsburgh, Pittsburgh, PA, United States

Elangovan Gajraj, NICE Scientific Advice, NICE, London, United Kingdom

Manjiri Gharat, The Indian Pharmaceutical Association, Mumbai, India; Prin.K.M.Kundnani Pharmacy Polytechnic, Ulhasnagar, India

Anne Gerd Granas, University of Oslo, Norway

Ronald A. Herman, The University of Iowa, Iowa City, IA, United States

Mickael Hiligsmann, Maastricht University, Maastricht, The Netherlands

Angela Hill, University of South Florida, Tampa, FL, United States

Lilian H. Hill, The University of Southern Mississippi, Hattiesburg, MS, United States

Carrie Hoefer, Manchester University College of Pharmacy, Natural and Health Sciences, Fort Wayne, IN, United States

Denny John, Campbell Collaboration, New Delhi, India

Emily P. Jones, Medical University of South Carolina, Charleston, SC, United States

Siby Joseph, St. Joseph's College of Pharmacy, Cherthala, India

Sachita Joshi, National Medicines Laboratory, Department of Drug Administration, Ministry of Health, Nepal

Toluwalope Junaid, University of Pittsburgh, Pittsburgh, PA, United States

---

† Deceased.

Balkrishna Khakurel, USAID Nepal Global Health Supply Chain-Procurement and Supply Management, Kathmandu, Nepal

Sherief Khalifa, Gulf Medical University, Ajman, United Arab Emirates

David F. Kisor, Manchester University College of Pharmacy, Natural and Health Sciences, Fort Wayne, IN, United States

Christoph Klika, University of Duisburg-Essen, Duisburg, Germany

Johann Kruger, University of Pretoria, Pretoria, South Africa; EDNA Medical Distributors, Pretoria, South Africa

Kiran Kumar, Gulf Medical University, Ajman, United Arab Emirates

Shaun Wen Huey Lee, Monash University Malaysia, Bandar Sunway, Malaysia

Federico Lega, SDA Bocconi School of Management, Milan, Italy

Christine Leong, University of Manitoba, Winnipeg, MB, Canada

Hong Li, Shanghai Jiao-Tong University, Shanghai, China; University of Cincinnati, Cincinnati, OH, United States

Kashelle Lockman, The University of Iowa, Iowa City, IA, United States

S. Suresh Madhavan, West Virginia University School of Pharmacy, Morgantown, WV, United States

Lucinda L. Maine, American Association of Colleges of Pharmacy, Alexandria, VA, USA

Jennifer Marriott, Monash University, Faculty of Pharmacy and Pharmaceutical Science, VIC, Australia

Mohammad Kowser Miah, University of Pittsburgh, Pittsburgh, PA, United States

Saba Naeem, Gulf Medical University, Ajman, United Arab Emirates

James P. New, Medical University of South Carolina, Charleston, SC, United States

Leeza Osipenko, NICE Scientific Advice, NICE, London, United Kingdom

Ema Paulino, Pharmacy, Nuno Álvares, Almada, Portugal

Mary Frances Picone, Medical University of South Carolina, Charleston, SC, United States

Nicole A. Pilch, Medical University of South Carolina, Charleston, SC, United States

Nisha Rajendran, Azidus Laboratories Ltd., Chennai, India

Asawari Raut, Bharati Vidyapeeth, Pune, India

Mary E. Ray, The University of Iowa, Iowa City, IA, United States

Jason A. Roberts, The University of Queensland, Brisbane St Lucia, QLD, Australia; Royal Brisbane and Women's Hospital, Herston QLD, Australia

Michael J. Rouse, Accreditation Council for Pharmacy Education, Chicago, IL, United States

Gunasakaran Sambandan, Azidus Laboratories Ltd., Chennai, India

Douglas Scheckelhoff, American Society of Health-System Pharmacists, Bethesda, MD, United States

Imam Hussain Shaik, University of Pittsburgh, Pittsburgh, PA, United States

Rishav Shrestha, Nick Simons Institute, Kathmandu, Nepal

Erick Sokn, Cleveland Clinic, Cleveland, OH, United States

Douglas T. Steinke, University of Manchester, Manchester, Great Britain

Yen-Huei (Tony) Tarn, Kaohsiung Medical University, Kaohsiung, Taiwan

Harisudhan Thanukrishnan, University of Pittsburgh, Pittsburgh, PA, United States

Dixon Thomas, Gulf Medical University, Ajman, United Arab Emirates

Shuhui Tian, Beijing United Family Healthcare, Chaoyang District, Beijing, China

Vincent W.L. Tsui, Queen Elizabeth Hospital, Hong Kong

Adina Turcu-Stiolica, University of Medicine and Pharmacy of Craiova, Craiova, Romania

Rao Vadlamudi, The Indian Pharmaceutical Association, Mumbai, India

Allen J. Vaida, Institute for Safe Medication Practices, Horsham, PA, United States

Raj Vaidya, Hindu Pharmacy, Goa, India

Matthew P. Van Cuyk, Massachusetts General Hospital, Boston, MA, United States

Raman Venkataramanan, University of Pittsburgh, Pittsburgh, PA, United States; Thomas Starzl Transplantation Institute, University of Pittsburgh, Pittsburgh, PA, United States; University of Pittsburgh Medical Center, Pittsburgh, PA, United States

Peter H. Vlasses, Accreditation Council for Pharmacy Education, Chicago, IL, United States

Susan S. Vos, The University of Iowa, Iowa City, IA, United States

Erin R. Weeda, Medical University of South Carolina, Charleston, SC, United States

Christopher S. Wisniewski, Medical University of South Carolina, Charleston, SC, United States

David J. Woods, University of Otago, Dunedin, New Zealand

Xuemei Wu, University of Pittsburgh, Pittsburgh, PA, United States

Seeba Zachariah, Gulf Medical University, Ajman, United Arab Emirates

Dawn G. Zarembski, Accreditation Council for Pharmacy Education, Chicago, IL, United States

Preface

Clinical Pharmacy Education, Practice and Research is a resource to develop an integrated foundation in clinical aspects of pharmacy. Pharmacists are involved in direct patient care. Practice-based research could improve the quality of care. Incorporation of relevant and good-quality research findings assures the practice to be evidence based. Evidence-based pharmacy practice has patient and population dimensions. The relevant pharmacy and health topics are organized in this book to support the mission of pharmacists or pharmacy students in clinical/healthcare. It covers the basics of general clinical pharmacy, pharmacy management, drug information, evidence-based practice, pharmacoepidemiology, pharmacovigilance, pharmacoeconomics, outcomes research, health technology assessment, clinical research, pharmaceutical education, clinical pharmacokinetics, pharmacogenomics, and parenteral nutrition. It also serves as a reference for practicing pharmacists and pharmacy instructors to review the fundamentals of pharmacy education, practice, and research with a clinical focus. The organization of sciences is obvious, with easy-to-navigate learning objectives in the contents allowing readers to get their answers to focused areas, not necessarily reading through the full chapters. This book is designed to serve as a useful resource for undergraduate pharmacy students in various clinical/health courses.

Contributions from a variety of leading pharmacy professionals in different areas of education, practice, and research enrich the book. Though the authors are from different countries the concepts discussed are universal. Readers should be able to comprehend any scenarios, because the content revolves around the fundamentals of pharmacy. Changes happening to the profession have been incorporated, including both clinical and drug focus. Of note, "clinical" and "drug" are two important words used throughout this text.

Pharmacists are and should be considered clinical staff, similar to doctors, nurses, physiotherapists, and other health professionals, who provide direct patient care. "Clinical" usually refers to human patients and all those who seek healthcare. Clinical pharmacy is more of a concept than a setting, because clinical services could happen in hospitals, community pharmacies, or even in a patient's home. The majority of the time spent by pharmacists involves interactions with patients and other health professionals, the arrangement of practice sites, dispensing, documentation, and continuous professional development. Pharmacists often spend a significant amount of time preparing their pharmacy operations, layout, and services. However, pharmacy preparation time and dispensing time are decreasing with the help of pharmacy technicians and automation.

From a patient's viewpoint, pharmacists are primarily involved with supplying medications, providing instructions on how to take medications properly, and answering general questions. Pharmacists also educate their patients about relevant diseases and healthcare needs. In hospital pharmacies, decreased interaction with inpatients sometimes results in pharmacists being seen as nonclinical staff. Though a hospital pharmacist does not always directly interact with inpatients, checking the appropriateness of a drug, validating the dose, and assuring its correct administration to prevent drug-related problems are considered to be direct patient care activities. Subsequently, a pharmacist performs as a patient advocate within the healthcare team to contribute to the overall clinical decision-making process. Clinical pharmacists with advanced training can provide additional healthcare services at the bedside, but this does not mean that dispensing pharmacists are nonclinical. Dispensing pharmacists, while applying the expected competence in preventing drug-related problems (e.g., wrong dose, wrong route of administration, drug interactions), are contributing to direct patient care.

Clinical pharmacy practice in the community setting is of a more ambulatory nature. The professional services may be less complex than those involved in acute care medicine, depending on the location of their practice, but their importance to the overall health and well-being of the patient is just as important. Being the primary point of consultation and sometimes the only healthcare professional involved in direct patient care for a visit, community pharmacists need to apply their clinical skills. The clinical skills enable a pharmacist to collect patient information, perform physical assessment, interpret laboratory data, suggest appropriate intervention for a defined problem, and educate patients. Chronic care management is an important component of this practice.

An educational program that prepares graduates to be eligible for licensure as a pharmacist should have sufficient clinical components. The ability to provide direct patient care allows pharmacists to help their patients gain the most from their medication(s). Thus any pharmacist could provide clinical services irrespective of the practice setting. In this book, the concept of clinical pharmacy considers a broad perspective of direct patient care and health services, while not attempting to draw strict lines around "clinical pharmacy." Again, to reassure, clinical pharmacy is a concept that applies to all practice settings. Social, behavioral, and administrative sciences complement pharmacists' clinical activities. Overall, the approach is to integrate sciences that contribute to improved care provided by pharmacists.

Throughout this book, "drug" and "medicine" are used synonymously to represent the product (e.g., amoxicillin tablets). Some countries/agencies prefer the term medicine over drug mainly because consumers perceive drugs as substances of abuse. In this book, the term "drug" is commonly used; "medicine" is used especially in chapters mentioning the World Health Organization. The other related term is "medication," which refers to a drug for a particular patient.

Focusing on the clinical concepts does not undermine the focus on drugs. The role of the pharmacist as the drug expert requires knowledge of various drug-related information ranging from compounding (e.g., parenteral nutrition) to the creation of unique formulations (e.g., suspensions for pediatric patients) to the provision of clinical services. The business of pharmacy involves a blending of both product-oriented activities and patient management. Even though the information regarding specific drugs is important, this book focuses more on clinical services and skills, because more progress needs to happen in direct patient care areas.

Specific chapters on clinical trials and other forms of research guide pharmacists to perform or follow research. Pharmacists commonly perform "outcomes research." Following research is a commitment to continuing professional development. The evidence-based pharmacy practice requires a critical appraisal of information; just adopting the research findings without considering scientific rigor and applicability in local practice/patient care no good science or practice. Studying the process of development of systematic reviews and clinical guidelines will help in using them more logically. Informed decision making is an integrated approach that connects topics covered in this book for safe, effective, and affordable drug use.

The content in each chapter is organized under learning objectives and is easy to navigate. Hopefully, a well-read chapter, with further readings found in the references, will result in a good learning experience. At the end of each chapter, there are a few practice questions, cases, or other exercises. Case studies and a set of tools used in experiential education are found in the appendices. *Clinical Pharmacy Education, Practice and Research* is a good companion in the professional development of pharmacy students and pharmacists who wish to develop/refresh their clinical practice and research fundamentals.

Contributions of experts from different work settings and countries have enriched this resource as I mentioned before. The foundational concept that drives the pharmacy profession is its clinical focus. The collective wisdom of contributors to this book will guide readers to achieve the core mission of the pharmacy profession.

Dixon Thomas

Acknowledgments

I thank the publishing team and all contributors to this book both authors and reviewers; three special mentions are Jason C. Cooper, Hong Li, and Seeba Zachariah for their outstanding support.

Chapter 1

Introduction to Clinical Practice, Research, and Pharmacy Education

Dixon Thomas[1], Jennifer Marriott[2], Rao Vadlamudi[3], Benny Efendie[4] and Lucinda L. Maine[5]

[1]Gulf Medical University, Ajman, United Arab Emirates; [2]Monash University, Faculty of Pharmacy and Pharmaceutical Science, VIC, Australia; [3]The Indian Pharmaceutical Association, Mumbai, India; [4]Monash University Malaysia, Bandar Sunway, Malaysia; [5]American Association of Colleges of Pharmacy, Alexandria, VA, USA

Learning Objectives:

Objective 1.1 Describe salient features of clinical practice of pharmacists.
Objective 1.2 Address relevant concepts in pharmacy education leading to clinical practice.
Objective 1.3 Outline how research in pharmacy is improving patient outcomes.

OBJECTIVE 1.1. DESCRIBE SALIENT FEATURES OF CLINICAL PRACTICE OF PHARMACISTS

According to the *Oxford Dictionary of English*, the term "clinical" is used in various medical fields to mean that it relates to the treatment of actual patients. Pharmacists, regardless of where they are working, are clinical staff and healthcare professionals. In 2005, the American College of Clinical Pharmacy (ACCP) defined clinical pharmacy as

> *a health science discipline in which pharmacists provide patient care that optimizes medication therapy and promotes health, wellness, and disease prevention.*[1]

The practice of clinical pharmacy embraces the philosophy of pharmaceutical care[2]; it blends a caring orientation with specialized therapeutic knowledge, experience, and judgment to ensure optimal patient outcomes. All direct patient care activities such as patient counseling, medication reconciliation, medication therapy assessment, and any other patient care service are clinical services at the bedside or otherwise (Figs. 1.1 and 1.2). Practice-based research must contribute to the generation of new knowledge that improves practice and the quality of life of patients.[2]

Significant developments in the pharmacy profession have occurred since the introduction of the concept "pharmaceutical care" in the early 1990s.[2] Pharmacists provide a wide range of clinical services[3] irrespective of the setting in which they work.[4] Advising a patient to take an irritant drug with plenty of water will improve quality of life if the patient is adherent to the advice. The clinical expertise of a pharmacist helps to judge if the patient would use medicines appropriately. Tailoring advice or other supporting services to improve adherence of patients to therapy and actions to be taken to prevent adverse outcomes are clinical services. In some countries, pharmacists have also been granted independent or supplementary prescribing rights. Administration of certain vaccines is another such clinical service provided by pharmacists in many jurisdictions. Pharmacists have a long history of managing minor ailments with nonprescription products or just with lifestyle advice. All these activities involve clinical skills.

Pharmacy education has evolved to address the necessary clinical pharmacy competencies. Bachelors of pharmacy programs in many countries have less clinical education, though its importance is increasing. To develop expertise in clinical pharmacy means obtaining a specialized master's program. Although bachelors make pharmacists, masters in clinical pharmacy make clinical pharmacists. In the United States, Doctor of Pharmacy (PharmD) is the only program that makes pharmacists. Pharmacists are considered to have clinical expertise in community pharmacy, hospital pharmacy, or

Clinical Pharmacy Education, Practice and Research. https://doi.org/10.1016/B978-0-12-814276-9.00001-5

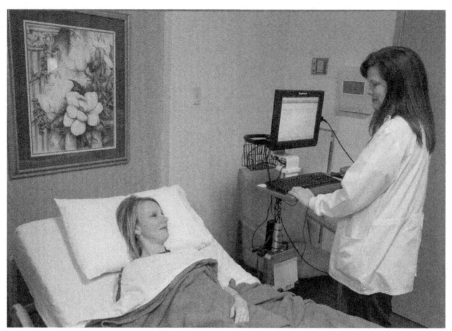

FIGURE 1.1 Clinical service at the bedside. *From Bob Nichols (photographer) https://commons.wikimedia.org/wiki/File:20130306-OC-RBN-3902_ (8575102773).jpg.*

FIGURE 1.2 Patient counseling at the pharmacy. *From Rhoda Baer (photographer) https://commons.wikimedia.org/wiki/File:Woman_consults_with_ pharmacist.jpg.*

other clinical pharmacy settings. Being a clinical pharmacist in a specialized area may require additional certification or residency.[5]

Community-based pharmacy practitioners are highly accessible healthcare professionals. Ambulatory patients and other consumers benefit from pharmacists' clinical care and supply of healthcare products. Timely access to quality drugs is important for the patient. Providing the right drug at the right time is part of a pharmacist's duty of care. Institutional pharmacists usually deliver more complex clinical services in addition to their nonclinical roles. Pharmacists have always responded clinically to people's health needs, improving their access to quality drugs and providing advice about drugs. Pharmacists with full-time clinical responsibilities provide their services mostly at the bedside.[6]

Pharmacists are well educated to interact with patients concerning their diseases and medication. Pharmacists possess in-depth knowledge of medications that integrates with a foundational understanding of the biomedical, pharmaceutical, sociobehavioral, and clinical sciences. To achieve the desired therapeutic goals, the pharmacist applies evidence-based therapeutic guidelines, evolving sciences, emerging technologies, and relevant legal, ethical, social, cultural, economic, and professional principles.

Accordingly, clinical pharmacists assume responsibility and accountability for managing medication therapy in direct patient care settings, whether practicing independently or in consultation/collaboration with other healthcare professionals. With increased patient care activities, it is likely that more pharmacists are involved in medication management and assume some level of prescribing or advising authority, as has already occurred in some countries.[7] The incidence of errors in pharmacist-written discharge medication orders in a study from the United Kingdom was found to be low.[8]

The clinical practice of pharmacists is evidence based. Pharmacists generate, disseminate, and apply new knowledge that contributes to improved health and quality of life. Pharmacists also supply evidence-based therapeutic advice to other healthcare professionals.[1]

To discuss as a model, the American Association of Colleges of Pharmacy (AACP) consistently tries to standardize the educational outcomes of pharmacy programs in association with other pharmacy organizations. Three important documents that explain the educational outcomes of pharmacy undergraduate programs in the United States are as follows:

- Center for the Advancement of Pharmacy Education 2013 Educational Outcomes (CAPE 2013)[9]
- Pharmacists' Patient Care Process (PPCP)[10]
- Entrustable Professional Activities (EPAs)[11]

AACP identified EPAs for pharmacy graduates. Core EPAs for New Pharmacy Graduates are discrete, essential activities and tasks that all new pharmacy graduates must be able to perform without direct supervision on entering practice or postgraduate training and operationalize the CAPE Educational Outcomes.[11] The 15 CAPE Educational Outcomes are relevant and consistent with emerging scientific and clinical developments and practitioner roles.[9] Continued development of practice-specific EPAs are necessary to extend the definition of what a pharmacist is and does beyond the new graduate. It also helps to improve the navigation of a clinician from one practice setting to another.[12]

PPCP is a consistent patient-centered care process that pharmacists use in collaboration with other healthcare providers, effective in communication and documentation to optimize patient health and medication outcomes.[10]

Competencies required for a clinical pharmacist are listed by ACCP in the following six domains:

- direct patient care,
- pharmacotherapy knowledge,
- systems-based care and population health,
- communication,
- professionalism, and
- continuing professional development.[13]

The International Pharmaceutical Federation (FIP) has developed pharmaceutical workforce development goals to establish the milestones for impactful global development of pharmacy professionals. The goals categorized under academy, professional development, and systems are used as benchmarks for quality improvement.[14] Many countries have similar guidelines to standardize pharmacy education and practice.

OBJECTIVE 1.2. ADDRESS RELEVANT CONCEPTS IN PHARMACY EDUCATION LEADING TO CLINICAL PRACTICE

Including more clinical components in pharmacy education is an increasing global trend. The traditional undergraduate pharmacy program has been revised in most institutions to include more clinical components. The PharmD program originally had a high focus on clinical sciences and experiential education. Standardization of pharmacy education systematically embeds essential competencies required in a pharmacist.[9,11] A key statement by FIP on pharmacy education is the "Nanjing Statement on Pharmacy and Pharmaceutical Sciences Education."[15] The statement describes the envisioned future for pharmaceutical education needed to enhance professional standards worldwide.[15] Pharmacy workforce development goals by FIP range from academics to early career to advancing further with continuing education.[16]

The number of pharmacy colleges/schools and pharmacy graduates has increased globally and has resulted in an increased need for experiential educational sites to provide clinical training and experienced educators with clinical expertise.

Educational outcomes of a pharmacy program are usually categorized into three generic domains such as knowledge, skill, and competence. The pharmacy workforce is developed with these predefined abilities. Knowledge includes recall and understanding; skills are cognitive and psychomotor; and competence is autonomy, responsibility, role in context, and self-development in the affective domain.[17]

Many adult learning methods are used in modern clinical pharmacy education curricula. Student centeredness—the importance of students in educational decision making—is now widely recognized; however, in many regions of the world, education remains teacher centered. The role of the teacher is shifting toward a facilitator, who supports the psychological and physical environment of the students to learn. Instead of students being the visitor of teachers' wisdom, the teacher visits the student's intellect and works on it with the student. Student centeredness should come next to patient centeredness. However, patient centeredness in clinical practice occurs faster than student centeredness in education. More importantly, students should accept patient centeredness even in didactic courses. Patients are the ultimate beneficiaries of pharmacy education that drives achievement of required patient care outcome educational competencies.[18]

Many modes are used for the delivery of course content. Blended learning uses a combination of face-to-face and online learning methods. It is also termed "the flipped classroom" as the lecture and supporting information are provided online before the class and assignments are completed in class—the reverse of traditional teaching methods. Blended learning requires the physical presence of both teacher and student, with some element of student control over time, place, path, or pace. Multiple delivery modes give students the freedom to choose their preferred mode of learning for a particular topic. Delivery modes may include lectures, videos, assignments, research, group discussions, and experiential placements, some or all of which may be optional. Blended learning should be planned considering the availability of technology support and training of teachers to be most useful for the students.[19] Learning is more efficient and interesting with the use of multiple modes of educational delivery. Multimodes of delivery help to reinforce learning. Use of prerequisites gives more time for slow learners to master the courses before they progress into more advanced courses.[20] Teachers should be trained well to perform as facilitators of appropriate modes of learning to their students.

Curriculum revisions to improve global health professional education are occurring to include elements such as integrated active learning, mastery learning, and early and extended clinical exposure. Changes in methods of course delivery encourage active learning, communication, and critical thinking. Some of the following approaches are used in pharmacy education to encourage the students to be more involved in their learning:

- Interactive lectures: A common criticism is that lectures are a passive method of learning. However, they are less expensive to deliver and more convenient than modern active learning methods. One method of making lectures more active is by including interactive sessions, preferably by the use of technology.[21] Other than lectures, methods with high faculty/student and student/student interactions provide active learning such as team-based and problem-based learning (PBL).

- Team-based learning (TBL): Psychologist Bruce Tuckman explained that teams have the following phases: forming, storming, norming, performing, and adjourning. In the stage of forming, a facilitator plays a dominant role as the team members have not yet identified their roles. In storming, the members resist working together. In norming, the members make compromises to work together in a team. In performing, the team is more productive. There are no clear boundaries between these phases. On any new task, the team may slip back to storming stage, especially in the presence of conflicts. Adjourning is a phase opposite to forming. The teams could be dissolved or rearranged at this stage. Many feel uncomfortable in the discontinuation of a good group with understandings of each other. The new teams may need to go through all the phases again.[22] TBL requires the student to be prepared before the class. Each individual student completes an assessment, the individual Readiness Assessment Test (iRAT). In the next step, individuals in small teams discuss and answer the same questions, the team Readiness Assessment Test (tRAT), with correct answers given after each attempt to influence a further decision-making process. Faculty should review the answers to questions students struggled with. Finally, the team discusses the relevance of the topic studied to real practice.[23] Peer learning happens in teams. Team dynamics affect the learning process. Identify and resolve the lack of coordination between teams and within team members to improve outcomes. It is important for team performance that students are accountable to themselves and the team. Frequent and timely feedback from the facilitator is important for learning to be directed toward the expected outcomes. Some pharmacy institutions have an integrated, team-based curriculum. TBL is equally, or sometimes more, beneficial than traditional learning methods in academic performance. The conversion of a part of a course or a group of courses in a program to TBL is commonplace in pharmacy education. In many cases, most students find it more satisfying educationally when trained faculty properly implements it. Faculty training is important to organize TBL systematically. However, students may not like the increased time spent in learning and the demand for more self-directed learning, especially when they change from a lecture to an activity session.[24]

- PBL: Students engage in a problem and a series of progressive disclosures (triggers) to identify the gaps in their understanding that need further self-directed learning. Students have chances to generate learning objectives.

Many trained facilitators are required to provide feedback to students for PBL sessions to be effective. PBL, when conducted properly, helps in problem-solving skills, self-directed learning, collaboration skills, and intrinsic motivation of students. Students learn to identify their knowledge gaps and determine methods to learn further. Use of real-life clinical cases equips students with potential practical skills in a given setting. Shifting from a traditional learning method to PBL is a major curriculum change. As in other healthcare professional education, the academic performance of pharmacy students has been found to be higher with PBL compared with traditional learning in some settings/course components.[25]

- Case-based learning (CBL): CBL is common in pharmacy education. Pharmacotherapy books include cases that lead to active learning. CBL is relatively more structured than PBL. The problem to be solved in CBL (guided inquiry) is provided in advance; however, in PBL (open inquiry), students need to determine the problem for themselves.[26]
- Simulation-based learning: Simulation in clinical experiential learning is common. Simulation, using standardized patients, virtual patients, and manikins, helps the student learn without the fear of causing harm to a real patient and decreases the anxiety of the patients who are being treated by students rather than by an experienced clinician. A standardized patient is a real person who is trained to act like a model patient. Such patients, through interactive virtual platforms, increase convenience and reduce costs. The manikin is used widely even in traditional lectures to demonstrate some course content. One of the most common uses of manikins is when learning basic life support in cardiopulmonary resuscitation. Simulation centers may also be called clinical skills laboratories, where pharmacy students can practice their patient physical assessment skills and provide certain pharmaceutical care services such as vaccinations, medication dosing, or dispensing. Virtual patient platforms are available to perform these tasks. Hybrid simulation is a combination of more than one method, e.g., a standardized patient and a task trainer demonstrating a procedure in a manikin. Simulation is an efficient method of developing practical skills if modeled properly. Simulation scenarios are adjustable to tailor the educational needs of a particular user. Simulation is especially useful in critical care to improve skills to manage patients in crisis situations.[27]

Integrated curriculum: Some level of integration of courses is an inherent component of the pharmacy curriculum. Biomedical and pharmaceutical courses provide a basis for learning clinical sciences. Medicinal chemistry, pharmaceutics, and pharmacology are prerequisites for pharmacotherapeutics, and it is integrated with clinical pharmacy services for better application to practice. In an integrated curriculum, these courses are studied together in modules to help students connect sciences better. Studying, e.g., medicinal chemistry, pathophysiology, pharmacology, pharmacotherapy, and the related pharmaceutics together provide horizontal integration. Horizontal integration brings together disciplines when studying. Horizontal integration is studying different basic sciences (medicinal chemistry, pharmaceutics, pharmacology, etc.) together as well as studying basic and clinical sciences together. Sometimes, the study of basic and clinical sciences together in a unit or year of study is also called horizontal integration. Basic and clinical sciences could be integrated both horizontally and vertically. Vertical integration has also been applied to spiral curricula. The topics are revisited in increasingly complex ways as the program progress. Grounding clinical sciences in the basic sciences or advanced clinical experience in the early clinical experience are examples of vertical integration. A scholarly pathway and a professional skills pathway across many units of study are examples of vertical integration. Early clinical exposure by introductory pharmacy practice experience and advanced experiential training toward the end of the program are other examples of vertical integration.[28,29] Adoption of horizontal and vertical integration at some level is becoming common in pharmacy education. The institution with an integrated pharmacy curriculum mostly has the core sciences in modules rather than in independent courses.[30]

Experiential learning: Students undergo at least two phases of their program: a didactic phase for the foundation courses and an experiential learning phase incorporating the clinical pharmacy education. The transition from didactic to experiential is not abrupt. In the foundation courses of biomedical and pharmaceutical sciences, students have some practical laboratory work. As well, there are didactic sessions in clinical pharmacy in the later years of study. Clinical experiential learning is often preceded by simulated learning that uses virtual patients, manikins, and role play. All these active learning and experiential trainings make students preceptor ready, team ready, and practice ready.

- Students who have sufficient knowledge, skills, and behavior to work in direct patient care areas are preceptor ready. Not only do the interns progress to practice independently, they are also able to precept junior students. This progress happens with peer mentoring of junior students within the pharmacy curriculum. Interns in advanced training mentor junior students in early practice exposure.
- Healthcare practice is teamwork. Abilities to work in teams improve the effectiveness of professionals. Interprofessional education and group-based active learning methods prepare students to be team ready.
- Practice readiness happens with experience. The graduates should be able to practice without supervision or minimal supervision.

The gradual transition from didactic learning methods to simulation to experiential learning results in less harm to patients. Some level of early experiential learning in real patient settings starts with introductory pharmacy practice experiences or clinical placements. Early experiential educational sessions in the pharmacy program help to relate what they are learning further to real practice settings. On completion of all didactic courses, students start their full-time clinical experiential learning, advanced experiential training, or internship or Advanced Pharmacy Experience. Advanced training makes the student fit for practice immediately following graduation. A junior practitioner is not exempted from practice competencies and is considered equally as responsible as an experienced practitioner. Experiential education bridges the transition from student to practitioner. Site capacity, preceptor development, and quality of training and assessment are common concerns faced in experiential education.[31]

Objective Structured Clinical Examination (OSCE): As the teaching of clinical practice in a skills laboratory and in experiential learning are significant curricular components, clinical performance examination is essential to assess clinical skills. Providing clinical services requires advanced clinical and communication skills. OSCEs are therefore becoming widely used to assess students' clinical and communication skills. OSCE has multiple stations that direct students to perform certain tasks to test their specific abilities. Critical thinking and problem-solving skills developed through active learning are best assessed using performance in clinical situations using OSCEs.[32,33]

Interprofessional education: Interprofessional education prepares health professionals to be team ready. Collaborative practice demands a high level of communication between different healthcare professionals. Interprofessional education is used to improve collaborative practice and interprofessional communication. Interactions of students with students of different healthcare professions provide a clear understanding of their roles and responsibilities in practice. Some pharmacy institutions have introduced departments or divisions for promoting interprofessional education.[6] The Inter-professional Education Collaborative (IPEC) was established in 2009 by six health professions with the AACP as a founding member. IPEC developed four core competencies and subcompetencies based on the concepts of patient and family centered and community and population oriented. The revised core competencies in 2016 are as follows:

- Work with other healthcare professionals to maintain a climate of mutual respect and shared values (values/ethics for interprofessional practice).
- Use the knowledge of one's role and those of other professions to assess and address the healthcare needs of patients appropriately and to promote and advance the health of populations (roles/responsibilities).
- Communicate with patients, families, communities, and professionals in health and other fields responsively and responsibly that supports a team approach to the promotion and maintenance of health and the prevention and treatment of disease (interprofessional communication).
- Apply relationship-building values and the principles of team dynamics to perform effectively in different team roles to plan, deliver, and evaluate patient/population-centered care and population health programs and policies that are safe, timely, efficient, effective, and equitable (teams and teamwork).[34]

OBJECTIVE 1.3. OUTLINE HOW RESEARCH IN PHARMACY IS IMPROVING PATIENT OUTCOMES

The practice of pharmacists is largely evidence based. Many pharmacists perform practice-based research. Pharmaceutical industries are highly research based. Pharmacy education focuses on preparing pharmacists and pharmaceutical scientists with research competencies. Pharmacy professionals who spend more of their time in research are pharmaceutical scientists. As per the FIP, "a pharmaceutical scientist is a qualified expert in aspects of the science and technology of medical products." It includes, but is not limited to, the discovery, development, manufacture, regulation, and utilization of medical products—embracing how drugs work, how safe and effective products are brought to the market, their impact on the body, and their effect on the prevention and treatment of disease.[35]

Pharmacists and pharmaceutical scientists perform research at different levels and types: practice-based research (action research), laboratory research, and clinical trials. Drug utilization research by pharmacists influences changes in drug use. Increased use of generic drugs and other rational approaches in drug use are examples of outcomes of pharmacy research. For example, the factors that could be studied for generic drug utilization are (1) patient-related factors, (2) formulary management or cost containment, (3) healthcare policies, (4) promotional activities, (5) educational initiatives, (6) technology, and (7) physician-related factors.[36] Pharmaceutical scientists participate in the innovation of new health technology.

Pharmaceutical scientists commonly perform research at pharmaceutical industries, universities, and governmental and nongovernmental agencies. Pharmaceutical industries produce drugs after comprehensive research. New drug development research for a product lasts longer than a decade, including many studies. Research continues for the marketed product on a larger population by the manufacturer and other agencies and healthcare professionals. Independent research adds value to existing information, and the drug may be withdrawn from the market if new findings are questioning or discouraging its use. Secondary research by combining clinical trials makes more reliable data through systematic reviews/meta-analysis. The sequence of generating and validating information through extensive research about drugs results in an abundant body of knowledge. Easy access, especially online access to such information and tools to filter information, provides clinicians with evidence to support practice. Clinical guidelines are considered on top of the evidence level as they are sets of practical recommendations reflecting the availability of primary and secondary research data.

New drugs and devices bring cures for diseases that were previously incurable and promote innovation in drug delivery to enhance effectiveness and safety. Newer drugs/devices provide a more patient-friendly treatment for conditions otherwise difficult to manage without serious safety concerns, e.g., complete oral regimen for hepatitis C.[37] Identifying responsible genes for diseases helps in targeting specific sites with specific drugs called personalized medicine. Personalized medicine is defined by the European Union as "the right patient with the right drug at the right dose at the right time." Pharmacogenomics is a part of personalized medicine. It is "the study of variations of DNA and RNA characteristics related to drug response." For certain drugs, pharmacists use pharmacogenomics information for ensuring effectiveness and safety in individual patients with affordable and convenient genetic tests. Some pharmacists work as practitioners in precision medicine, especially in cancer care. Pharmacogenomics has allowed for more tailored treatment of a wide range of health problems, including cancer, cardiovascular disease, and HIV/AIDS.[38]

Pharmacy professionals commonly research health outcomes too. Pharmacoeconomics and outcomes research studies affordability and value of pharmacy services and health technology. Economic, humanistic, or clinical outcomes are studied at clinical and societal levels. The evidence generated from these differs with different settings and perspectives.

It is essential for pharmacists to have research skills not just to generate evidence but also to read and understand research literature. Traditionally, pharmacists used their drug information and literature evaluation skills to incorporate best quality evidence into practice. Pharmacists specialized in drug information service are evidence support staff to other healthcare professionals. Pharmacists provide information support through their knowledge and skills in pharmacotherapy. These cognitive services provided by pharmacists need educational self-development investments and access to drug information resources. This improves evidence-based practice, and institutions should invest in such pharmacists and resources. A pharmacy workforce is developed to provide valuable services to patients and other healthcare professionals. Such services provided by pharmacists for the benefit of patients that result in quantifiable improvements in health outcomes and appropriate cost recovery are essential for sustainability.[39]

CONCLUSION

Pharmacists provide clinical services and research to achieve better patient outcomes. Clinical pharmacy is a concept of direct patient care, irrespective of the settings of practice. Preparing graduates for patient-centered, team-delivered clinical roles must be a priority for educators and agencies that oversee pharmacy workforce development. A pharmacist needs to undergo continuing education to enhance practice. A pharmaceutical scientist contributes to producing better drugs. Incorporation of evidence into practice and generation of practice-based knowledge demand research skills in pharmacists too.

PRACTICE QUESTIONS

1. What is clinical pharmacy, select the most appropriate statement?
   A. Direct patient care services by a pharmacist
   B. Procures medicines cheaper from trusted vendors
   C. Training junior pharmacists for continuous professional development
   D. Use of automation in dispensing
2. Which of the following is a consistent patient-centered care process that pharmacists use in collaboration with other healthcare providers, effective in communication and documentation to optimize patient health and medication outcomes?
   A. CAPE Educational Outcomes
   B. PPCP
   C. EPAs
   D. FIP workforce development goals

3. Match the most appropriate learning method to the following description: "students come prepared to the learning session and then work in teams to see the improvement in learning happening due to peer learning."
   A. PBL
   B. TBL
   C. CBL
   D. Activity-based learning
4. Select the ultimate aim of interprofessional education?
   A. Decreases the number of teachers as interprofessional education decreases the number of lectures
   B. Prepares healthcare students to be ready to work in multiprofessional teamwork in patient care
   C. Simplifies student posting at clinical practice sites
   D. Conducts exams in one step
5. Pharmacoeconomic study is a part of which research area?
   A. Bioequivalence
   B. Safety of drugs
   C. Precision pharmacy
   D. Outcomes science

REFERENCES

1. ACCP. The definition of clinical pharmacy. *Pharmacotherapy.* 2008;28(6):816—817. https://www.accp.com/docs/positions/commentaries/Clinpharmdefnfinal.pdf.
2. Hepler CD, Strand LM. Opportunities and responsibilities in pharmaceutical care. *Am J Hosp Pharm.* 1990;47(3):533—543. http://www.ncbi.nlm.nih.gov/pubmed/2316538.
3. Carter BL. Evolution of clinical pharmacy in the USA and future directions for patient care. *Drugs Aging.* 2016;33(3):169—177. https://doi.org/10.1007/s40266-016-0349-2.
4. Hughes E, Terry D, Huynh C, et al. Future enhanced clinical role of pharmacists in emergency departments in England: multi-site observational evaluation. *Int J Clin Pharm.* 2017;39(4):960—968. https://doi.org/10.1007/s11096-017-0497-4.
5. Knoer SJ, Eck AR, Lucas AJ. A review of American pharmacy: education, training, technology, and practice. *J Pharm Health care Sci.* 2016;2:32. https://doi.org/10.1186/s40780-016-0066-3.
6. ACCP. Standards of practice for clinical pharmacists. *Pharmacotherapy.* 2014;34(8):794—797. https://doi.org/10.1002/phar.1438.
7. Zellmer WA. Pharmacy forecast 2017: strategic planning advice for pharmacy departments in hospitals and health systems. *Am J Health Pharm.* 2016;73:e617—e643. https://doi.org/10.2146/sp170001.
8. Onatade R, Sawieres S, Veck A, Smith L, Gore S, Al-Azeib S. The incidence and severity of errors in pharmacist-written discharge medication orders. *Int J Clin Pharm.* 2017;39(4):722—728. https://doi.org/10.1007/s11096-017-0468-9.
9. Medina MS, Plaza CM, Stowe CD, et al. Center for the advancement of pharmacy education 2013 educational outcomes. *Am J Pharm Educ.* 2013;77(8):162. https://doi.org/10.5688/ajpe778162.
10. Joint Commission of Pharmacy Practitioners. *Pharmacists' Patient Care Process*; 2017. https://www.pharmacist.com/sites/default/files/files/PatientCareProcess.pdf.
11. Haines ST, Pittenger AL, Stolte SK, et al. Core entrustable professional activities for new pharmacy graduates. *Am J Pharm Educ.* 2017;81(1):S2. https://doi.org/10.5688/ajpe811S2.
12. Pittenger AL, Copeland DA, Lacroix MM, et al. Report of the 2016-17 academic affairs standing committee: entrustable professional activities implementation roadmap. *Am J Pharm Educ.* 2017;81(5):S4. https://doi.org/10.5688/ajpe815S4.
13. Saseen JJ, Ripley TL, Bondi D, et al. ACCP clinical pharmacist competencies. *Pharmacother J Hum Pharmacol Drug Ther.* 2017;37(5):630—636. https://doi.org/10.1002/phar.1923.
14. FIP. *Pharmaceutical Workforce Development Goals Presented at the Global Conference on Pharmacy and Pharmaceutical Sciences Education*; 2017. http://fip.org/files/fip/PharmacyEducation/Global_Conference_docs/WDGs_online_version.pdf.
15. FIP. *Nanjing Statements. Statements on Pharmacy and Pharmaceutical Sciences Education*; 2017. http://www.fip.org/files/fip/PharmacyEducation/Global_Conference_docs/Nanjing_Statements.pdf.
16. International Pharmaceutical Federation (FIP). *Transforming Pharmacy and Pharmaceutical Sciences Education in the Context of Workforce Development. The Hague*; 2017. https://fip.org/files/fip/publications/FIPEd_Nanjing_Report_2017_11.10.17.pdf.
17. Dennis VC, May DW, Kanmaz TJ, Reidt SL, Serres ML, Edwards HD. Pharmacy student learning during advanced pharmacy practice experiences in relation to the CAPE 2013 outcomes. *Am J Pharm Educ.* 2016;80(7):127. https://doi.org/10.5688/ajpe807127.
18. Holdford DA. Is a pharmacy student the customer or the product? *Am J Pharm Educ.* 2014;78(1):3. https://doi.org/10.5688/ajpe7813.
19. Margolis AR, Porter AL, Pitterle ME. Best practices for use of blended learning. *Am J Pharm Educ.* 2017;81(3):49. https://doi.org/10.5688/ajpe81349.
20. Sheng W Bin, Lifeng K. Mastery learning in the context of university education - NUS teaching academy. *J NUS Teach Acad.* 2012;2(3):206—222. http://www.nus.edu.sg/teachingacademy/article/mastery-learning-in-the-context-of-university-education-2/.

21. Abdel Meguid E, Collins M. Students' perceptions of lecturing approaches: traditional versus interactive teaching. *Adv Med Educ Pract.* 2017;8:229−241. https://doi.org/10.2147/AMEP.S131851.

22. Kumar S, Deshmukh V, Adhish VS. Building and leading teams. *Indian J Community Med.* 2014;39(4):208−213. https://doi.org/10.4103/0970-0218.143020.

23. Parmelee D, Michaelsen LK, Cook S, Hudes PD. Team-based learning: a practical guide: AMEE guide No. 65. *Med Teach.* 2012;34(5):e275−e287. https://doi.org/10.3109/0142159X.2012.651179.

24. Ofstad W, Brunner LJ. Team-based learning in pharmacy education. *Am J Pharm Educ.* 2013;77(4):70. https://doi.org/10.5688/ajpe77470.

25. Galvao TF, Silva MT, Neiva CS, Ribeiro LM, Pereira MG. Problem-based learning in pharmaceutical education: a systematic review and meta-analysis. *ScientificWorldJournal.* 2014;2014(578382). https://doi.org/10.1155/2014/578382.

26. Srinivasan M, Wilkes M, Stevenson F, Nguyen T, Slavin S. Comparing problem-based learning with case-based learning: effects of a major curricular shift at two institutions. *Acad Med.* 2007;82(1):74−82. https://doi.org/10.1097/01.ACM.0000249963.93776.aa.

27. Milkins L, Moore C, Spiteri J. *Simulation Based Education. Australia*; 2014. http://www.heti.nsw.gov.au/Global/NSSSimulation/Simulation BasedEducation_HETI.pdf.

28. Bradley P, Mattick K. *Integration of Basic and Clinical Sciences - AMEE 2008 what Is Integration? Why Do We Need Integration?* AMEE; 2008. https://amee.org/getattachment/Conferences/AMEE-Past-Conferences/AMEE-Conference-2008/Introduction-to-Medical-Education-Bradley-Mattick.pdf.

29. Pearson ML, Hubball HT. Curricular Integration in Pharmacy Education. *American Journal of Pharmaceutical Education.* 2012;76(10):204. https://www.ncbi.nlm.nih.gov/pmc/articles/PMC3530066/.

30. Regis University. *Active Learning through an Integrated Team-based Curriculum.* School of Pharmacy, Regis University; 2017. http://www.regis.edu/RHCHP/Schools/School-of-Pharmacy/Active-Learning.aspx.

31. Danielson J, Craddick K, Eccles D, Kwasnik A, O'Sullivan TA. A qualitative analysis of common concerns about challenges facing pharmacy experiential education programs. *Am J Pharm Educ.* 2015;79(1):6. https://doi.org/10.5688/ajpe79106.

32. Sturpe DA. Objective structured clinical examinations in doctor of pharmacy programs in the United States. *Am J Pharm Educ.* 2010;74(8):148. http://www.ncbi.nlm.nih.gov/pubmed/21179259.

33. Urteaga EM, Attridge RL, Tovar JM, Witte AP. Evaluation of clinical and communication skills of pharmacy students and pharmacists with an objective structured clinical examination. *Am J Pharm Educ.* 2015;79(8):122. https://doi.org/10.5688/ajpe798122.

34. Interprofessional Education Collaborative. *Core Competencies for Interprofessional Collaborative Practice: 2016 Update. Washington, DC*; 2016. https://ipecollaborative.org/uploads/IPEC-2016-Updated-Core-Competencies-Report__final_release_.PDF.

35. FIP. *What Is a Pharmaceutical Scientist? Pharmaceutical Sciences and the Special Interest Groups (SIGs)*; July 18, 2018. Accessed on http://www.fip.org/pharmaceutical_sciences.

36. Howard JN, Harris I, Frank G, Kiptanui Z, Qian J, Hansen R. Influencers of generic drug utilization: a systematic review. *Res Soc Adm Pharm.* August 2017. https://doi.org/10.1016/j.sapharm.2017.08.001.

37. US FDA. Hepatitis C Treatments Give Patients More Options. Consumer Updates. https://www.fda.gov/ForConsumers/ConsumerUpdates/ucm405642.htm.

38. US FDA. *Paving the Way for Personalized Medicine - FDA's Role in a New Era of Medical Product Development*; 2013. https://www.fda.gov/downloads/scienceresearch/specialtopics/personalizedmedicine/ucm372421.pdf.

39. Scott MA, Hitch WJ, Wilson CG, Lugo AM. Billing for pharmacists' cognitive services in physicians' offices: multiple methods of reimbursement. *J Am Pharm Assoc.* 2012;52(2):175−180. https://doi.org/10.1331/JAPhA.2012.11218.

ANSWERS TO PRACTICE QUESTIONS

1. A
2. B
3. B
4. B
5. D

Section I

General Clinical Pharmacy

Chapter 2

Evolution of the Pharmacy Profession and Public Health

Balkrishna Khakurel[1], Rishav Shrestha[2], Sachita Joshi[3] and Dixon Thomas[4]

[1]USAID Nepal Global Health Supply Chain-Procurement and Supply Management, Kathmandu, Nepal; [2]Nick Simons Institute, Kathmandu, Nepal; [3]National Medicines Laboratory, Department of Drug Administration, Ministry of Health, Nepal; [4]Gulf Medical University, Ajman, United Arab Emirates

Learning Objectives:

Objective 2.1 Outline historical developments in the pharmacy profession.
Objective 2.2 Overview eras of pharmaceutical industries and their jobs for pharmacy graduates.
Objective 2.3 Discuss policies and laws governing the pharmacy profession and public health.
Objective 2.4 Detail an overview of public health and disease prevention.

OBJECTIVE 2.1. OUTLINE HISTORICAL DEVELOPMENTS IN THE PHARMACY PROFESSION

Pharmacists are healthcare professionals whose responsibilities and accountabilities include ensuring that people derive maximum therapeutic benefit and minimum harm from their treatments with drugs. They also work in disease prevention with or without medical interventions. It requires pharmacists to keep abreast of developments in:

- Clinical practice and the pharmaceutical sciences.
- Professional standards and requirements.
- The laws governing pharmacy and drugs.
- Advances in knowledge and technology relating to the use of drugs and public health.

Pharmacists look out for lifestyle problems, disease outbreaks, and other emergency situations in society.[1] Many pharmacists visit institutions such as schools or communities to promote public health. In fact, the current work culture of pharmacists includes some of the following:

- Independent reviews of the treatment.
- Patient advocacy considering best interest of the patient.
- Educate patients about medication.
- Prevent drug-related problems and minimize harm.
- Ensure quality of drugs stored and dispensed and prevent pilferage and drug abuse, etc.

Pharmacists and pharmacies are widely recognized globally through the logo ℞, which is a contraction of an acronym for *recipere* (Latin, "you take") but often written as "℞" in typed text—a command at the beginning of a prescription.[2] An alternative belief is that the ℞ symbol evolved from the Eye of Horus, an ancient Egyptian god supposed to have healing powers.[3] Pharmacies are also recognized through symbols depicting the Bowl of Hygeia (Fig. 2.1), the Greek goddess of hygiene and the daughter of Asclepius (God of Medicine).[4] Other common symbols are the green cross or the mortar and pestle (Fig. 2.2).[5]

Pharmacy is a recognized part of medical practice dating at least as far back as the Sumerian civilization.[6] In ancient times, the physician and pharmacist were the same. The doctor-pharmacist would be needed to possess a thorough

Clinical Pharmacy Education, Practice and Research. https://doi.org/10.1016/B978-0-12-814276-9.00002-7

FIGURE 2.1 Bowl of Hygeia. *From David (developer). https://commons.wikimedia.org/wiki/File:Bowl_Of_Hygieia_by_David.svg.*

FIGURE 2.2 Mortar and pestle with ℞ symbol. *https://commons.wikimedia.org/wiki/File:PharmacistsMortar.svg.*

understanding of the different herbs and plants used as medications. In fact, training in pharmacy was an important component of ancient doctors. In the due course of time, the practice of medicine expanded and became increasingly complicated, necessitating specialization/separation. The first independent pharmacy was opened in Baghdad by the eighth century CE. This separation had formally been made in Europe by 1241 CE to prevent monopolies that could arise from collusion between prescriber and dispenser. Pharmacy being a full-time practice ensures the quality of medicinal plants grown and the drugs dispensed.[7] Compounders (or apothecaries) would prepare solutions, balms, tinctures, etc., extemporaneously (Latin, "at the very time") on prescription from the physician for a particular patient. As the knowledge regarding drugs and drug making became highly specialized and lucrative, more professionals started to enter the pharmacy profession.

In prehistoric times, drugs were mostly plant based. Preserved prescriptions from early civilizations include the following:

- the cuneiform tablets of the Sumerian times (around 2000 to 1500 BCE),
- the Ebers Papyrus (1550 BCE) and Edwin Smith Papyrus (16th century BCE) of the Egyptian civilization,
- the Sushruta Samhita (sixth century BCE) of the Indian Ayurveda, and
- the Shennong Bencao Jing (The Divine Farmer's Herb-Root Classic) compiled during the Han Dynasty China (first century CE).[6]

Most medieval drugs and pharmacy knowledge, however, came from the Greeks and the Romans. One of the pioneer pharmacists was Diocles of Carystus, a Greek physician whose "rhizotomoi" (400 BCE) was an early guide to the uses of medicinal plants. His other works on pharmacotherapeutics were the foundation for Pedanius Dioscorides (first century CE) who went on to write the famous five volume "De Materia Medica" (Concerning Medicinal Substances). It became a basic science for medieval European and Islamic medicine until the 16th century CE.[6]

Perhaps the most important medieval pharmacist was Galen (130–200 CE). Galen's work was instrumental in both pharmacy and medicine through his principles of preparing and compounding drugs by extracting a medicinal agent from plants (roots, rhizomes, leaves, flowers, and bark) and animals by mechanical means with water, alcohol, ether, or fatty oils. Such medications, called galenicals, include tinctures, infusions, extracts, medicinal waters, alcohols, syrups, soaps, plasters, and liniments. *Because of his contributions to the field, Galen is considered as the father of pharmacy.* These galenicals were the mainstay for nearly 1500 years, and many of his procedures have their counterparts in today's modern compounding laboratories and pharma industries as part of the pharmaceutical formulation.[8] Neogalenicals are the modern counterparts to galenicals, which are highly purified drugs that can be injected as well.[9]

Independent practice of the pharmacy was a revolutionary approach by the Arabs.[10] The Arabs separated the arts of pharmacist (or apothecary) and physician, establishing privately owned drug stores in Baghdad (Baghdad stores) by 750 CE (eighth century CE), which became state regulated by the ninth century CE. During this period, many advances were made in botany and chemistry by pioneers like Muhammad ibn ZakarīyaRāzi (Rhazes) who used chemicals as drugs (865−915) and Abu al-Qasim al-Zahrawi (Abulcasis) who used chemical processes such as sublimation and distillation for the synthesis of complex drugs from simpler chemicals (936−1013).[11] Al-Biruni's (973−1050) Kitab al-Saydalah (The Book of Drugs) and Ibn Sina's Avicenna (The Canon of Medicine) were important writings of this period. These influences reached Europe by the 1200s. In 1240, Frederic II issued a decree to separate the physician's and the apothecary's professions, called the edict of Salerno.[7] The first pharmacy in Europe (still working) was opened in 1241 in Trier, Germany. These pharmacies were called apothecary shops. Fig. 2.3 is published with permission from the New Orleans Pharmacy Museum; it shows the apothecary shop of America's first licensed pharmacist.

The 16th century marked the beginning of the city pharmacopoeias. Although many authors had written manuals/treatises in compounding (formularies), the "Dispensatorium" was the first pharmacopeia published in 1546 by Valerius Cordus under the authority of the Senate of Nuremberg.[12] These pharmacopeias had validity over certain cities only, but they helped delineate the legitimacy for pharmacopeias to be granted by a government or a medical or pharmaceutical society. Ironically, the term pharmacopeia (literally, drug making) was only introduced in 1561 by Anutius Foesius, in his book Pharmacopoeia Medicamentorum Omnium.[13] Other notable city pharmacopeias were the London Pharmacopoeia (first published 1621), the Pharmacopoeia Amstelredamensis (1636), Edinburgh Pharmacopoeia (1899), and the Dublin Pharmacopoeia (1807).

The chemical era started in the 1700s and was the forerunner of modern pharmaceuticals. Swede Carl Wilhelm Scheele (1742−86) made incalculable contributions to kick-start this era by discovering countless organic compounds as well as techniques to isolate organic plant acids. German Friedrich Wilhelm Adam Sertürner (1783−1841) discovered morphine and alkaloids. Pharmaceutical companies such as Merck, Hoffman-La Roche, Burroughs-Wellcome, etc., began as local apothecary shops in the mid-1800s. By the late 1880s, rudimentary methods in organic chemistry had been established by German dye manufacturers, and medicinal chemistry had started.[14] Retail pharmacies started popping up in the United States in 1729. The first attempts at standardizing drugs (or pharmaceuticals) started in 1852 through the foundation of the American Pharmaceutical Association. Instrumental in the association's formation and work was William Procter Jr. (1817−74). For his works, William Procter Jr. is considered as the father of American pharmacy.[15]

The late 1800s gave rise to the biological era and later the antibiotic era.[10] In 1894, Behring and Roux's demonstration of diphtheria antitoxin's effectiveness spurred its production by Parke, Davis & Company (1895) for vaccinating children. For the first time, biological products were used to save thousands of lives. In 1903, Parke-Davis received US Biological License No. 1. In 1955, poliomyelitis vaccine was produced. Another important event was Alexander Fleming's discovery of penicillin. This era also gave birth to modern pharmacology through the invention of the technique of drug discovery: screening for chemicals causing particular functional activity followed by receptor identification and biochemical understanding of involved protein and finally using medicinal chemistry to optimize a good drug.

FIGURE 2.3   Apothecary shop. *Published with permission from New Orleans Pharmacy Museum.*

Similar principles were used to optimize biological drugs. Biological drugs can help with a lot of different conditions in the body, such as monoclonal antibodies to fight cancer or filgrastim to boost white blood cells for a patient undergoing chemotherapy. The biosimilar is a generic version of the innovator biological drug.

Modern national pharmacopeias came out in the 1800s. By the late 1800s, it was realized that national agencies need to regulate pharmacopeias within the country. The British Pharmacopoeia[16] was the first national pharmacopeia. Although not the most popular at the onset, it paved the way for quality control in drug manufacturing. Similarly, the United States Pharmacopoeia[17] was another important pharmacopeia, which has become accepted worldwide. The International Pharmacopoeia is published by the World Health Organization (WHO) for adoption by the Member States and to help achieve a potentially global uniformity of quality specifications for selected pharmaceutical products, excipients, and dosage forms.[18]

The late 1950s observed a split of the pharmacy profession into the industrial pharmacy (pharmaceutical industry) and clinical pharmacy.[19] By the 1950s, as a result of advancements described above, the industrial pharmacy had replaced compounding pharmacy through standardized manufacturing of drugs (and other pharmaceuticals). Large-scale manufacturing of medicinal products in the pharmaceutical industry and the introduction of prescription-only legal status for most therapeutic agents limited the role of pharmacists to compounding. Pharmacies became retail outlets of pharmaceutical industries. This shift urged pharmacists to focus more on patient (clinical) services.

Clinical pharmacy, specifically hospital pharmacy, arose as a response to the rise of industrial pharmacy.[19] Until the 1960s, pharmacists were mostly product experts who compounded drugs. By the mid-1960s pharmacists had evolved toward a more patient care-oriented practice and developed the concept of providing clinically relevant expertise, especially in hospitals. It marked the beginning of a period of rapid transition that was characterized by closer interaction with physicians and other healthcare professionals.

The Ninth-Floor Pharmacy project delineated clinical pharmacy practice in the modern age.[20] With the rise in hospitals and improved needs for safe drug use, pharmacists began facing many difficulties managing drug distribution and dosage in the hospital pharmacies. The Ninth-Floor Pharmacy project, headed by William Smith at the University of California, San Francisco (UCSF) School of Pharmacy, was started at UCSF Medical Center on September 7, 1966. The project was to develop a hospital floor-based hospital pharmacy service that provided optimized drug use in hospitalized patients. In essence, the project created the modern clinical pharmacist by outlining their roles in patient care (provide and disseminate drug information, train pharmacy students, design and conduct studies in cooperation with clinicians within the framework of a team approach to patient care). The project also opened the way for drug information service and drug and therapeutics committees in hospitals.

The increased role of clinical pharmacists led to the pharmaceutical care era.[21] Hospital pharmacies eventually led to the birth of various forms of clinical pharmacy such as ambulatory care pharmacy, oncology pharmacy, pediatric pharmacy, pharmacotherapy, etc. Other pharmacies continued in operation as community pharmacy, veterinary pharmacy, mail-order pharmacy, or internet pharmacy. Developments in ambulatory care opened scopes for community pharmacists to provide pharmaceutical care services that used to be provided by clinical pharmacists. In 1990, Hepler and Strand and the WHO introduced the concept of pharmaceutical care as it was increasingly realized and established that pharmacists have an important role in patient care. Furthermore, pharmacists individually and as a profession have important roles to play in positively influencing drug policy, drug use, and outcomes, as well as other aspects of healthcare. In many instances, this will be through collaboration with other health professionals at a community level. Notably, pharmaceutical care has evolved in the United States as medication therapy management,[22] which is medical care provided by pharmacists aimed primarily at optimizing drug therapy and improving therapeutic outcomes for patients. An important development arising from pharmaceutical care is that of good pharmacy practice (GPP) to provide optimal evidence-based care. Another field that has emerged is pharmacovigilance. Pharmacovigilance constitutes safety monitoring of drugs (such as early detection of new adverse drug reactions and other drug-related problems) and is rapidly becoming an integral part of pharmaceutical care. Education and training of healthcare professionals on drug safety and effectiveness improved therapeutic outcomes. All these developments and activities have become more important as consumer-driven, not consumer-oriented practice; pharmaceutical care has emerged with consumers becoming more active, independent, informed, critical, and reflective of care.

Advancement in life sciences and pharmaceutical sciences has pushed pharmaceuticals and pharmacy practice to the era of genomics and personalized medicine/personalized pharmacy in the last three decades.[23] The omics revolution, especially genomics, has opened new horizons in healthcare. With genomics, the parts of the genome and the proteins responsible for diseases can be determined. It opens up the possibility of creating drugs that affect the genome and proteins, and more so in a tailored or personalized manner for each patient. Some drugs are indicated after quick genetic tests in the patients. Many pharmacists practice personalized pharmacy, especially in oncology. Although incredibly powerful, genomic drugs raise concerns of ethics and privacy. The integration of nanotechnology, biotechnology, and genomics in pharmaceuticals has further created new opportunities, exciting potential, and newer challenges to the pharmacy profession.

Many changes in pharmacy practice due to innovations in other fields have also occurred in the last few decades. Perhaps the most noticeable change is due to IT and related technologies. A case in point is the rise of internet pharmacies where one can purchase many drugs without prescription in most cases. Other changes are in the supply chain, with the use of pharmacy robots, smart packaging, and a "smart pill." Smart packaging is a blister pack containing a microchip that can monitor when doses are popped out of the package, with data transmitted to a mobile phone or tablet app. Because smart packaging cannot tell if the dose was taken, a smart pill is developed that has sensors that can provide information on dose, heart rate, and other variables once ingested by the patient. *A curious but not surprising case is the return of extemporaneous prescription compounding* for special cases such as dental care or customizing formulations or preparing drugs in new forms (e.g., a medicated lollipop containing the drug for patients who have difficulty in swallowing). Electronic prescribing (EP) systems automate prescribing, supply, and administration of drugs in hospitals, where they have been shown to reduce medication errors and have a high impact on patient safety. Barcode identification of drugs has been used with EP systems and has been shown to reduce medication administration errors, as well as improve the completeness of the medication history. In the United Kingdom, the Falsified Medicines Directive (2017) calls for unique identification of drugs at the point of dispensing to combat counterfeiting.[24] Telecare[25] and Remote Patient Management[26] are other technology applications in the pharmacy that use digital communications technology (audio and visual) to provide healthcare consultations and services and monitoring of patients remotely.

OBJECTIVE 2.2. OVERVIEW ERAS OF PHARMACEUTICAL INDUSTRIES AND THEIR JOBS FOR PHARMACY GRADUATES

The pharmaceutical industry had its origin in pharmacies and chemical companies.[14] The modern pharmaceutical industry traces its origin to

- apothecaries (Germany: Merck, Schering; Switzerland: Hoffmann-La Roche; United Kingdom: Burroughs-Wellcome; France: Etienne Poulenc; United States: Abbot, Smith Kline, Parke-Davis, Eli Lilly Squibb, Upjohn) that moved into wholesale production of drugs such as morphine, quinine, and strychnine in the middle of the 19th century, and
- dye and chemical companies (Agfa, Bayer, and Hoechst in Germany; Ciba, Geigy, and Sandoz in Switzerland; Imperial Chemical Industries in England; and Pfizer in the United States) that established research labs and discovered medical applications for their products starting in the 1880s.

A merger of these two types of firms took place with the emergence of pharmaceutical chemistry and pharmacology at the end of the 19th century. The remarkable thing was that pharmaceutical firms, first in Germany in the 1880s and later in the United States and England, established cooperative relationships with academic labs into a massive industrial research program that continues to the present.

Chemical era. By the early 19th century, chemists were able to extract and concentrate traditional plant-based remedies, giving rise to treatments such as morphine and quinine. By the early 20th century, similar methods applied to animal-based remedies resulted in the isolation of epinephrine, which was the first hormone to be used as a drug. German dye manufacturers, meanwhile, had already developed synthetic organic chemistry as an industrial discipline, especially in deriving dyes from coal tar. Chemists were soon able to modify raw dyes and their by-products to make them more effective as drugs, effectively beginning pharmaceutical and medicinal chemistry. One of the first chemically synthesized drugs, aspirin (1897) by the German pharmaceutical company Bayer, continues to be used and researched today.

Biological era and the beginning of regulation and mass production. The end of the 19th century also witnessed the development of several important vaccines, including those for tetanus and diphtheria. Similarly, the antisyphilitic organoarsenic compound salvarsan was developed as one of the first antimicrobial chemotherapeutic agents. In the early 20th century, the progressive role of chemical and life sciences began appearing. World War I blockades forced US chemists to replicate German processes for producing drugs such as aspirin, salvarsan, and veronal. As a result, the focus shifted to large-scale synthesis and newer drug discovery, including biologicals (or biologics) and small molecules. At the same time, regulations and laws began appearing to regulate pharmaceuticals. Regulations against secret recipes and fallacious claims were institutionalized. Professional bodies of physicians and pharmacists and national formularies set manufacturing standards. The development of diphtheria antitoxin in the 1890s and associated issues of inactive antitoxin forced the 1902 Biologics Control Act. The 1906 Food and Drugs Act in the United States and similar laws in several other countries prohibited adulteration. Manufacturers have to reveal ingredients on product labels.

After the expiry of the patent, generic versions of the drugs could be produced and marketed by any pharmaceutical companies. Patent expiry follows production by different manufacturers and improved access to drugs as the generic versions.

The biologics market is growing rapidly. Several biologics have sales of more than $1 billion annually. For example, in 2011, global sales were $7.19 billion for Remicade (infliximab) and $5.98 billion for Avastin (bevacizumab). In addition, many of these drugs when out of patent *biosimilars* (generic version of biologics) enter the market, e.g., Herceptin (trastuzumab), Humalog (insulin lispro), Rituxan (rituximab [MabThera in Australia]), Remicade, and Aranesp (darbepoetin alfa).[27,28] Furthermore, the opportunity exists, but unlike the generic market where market entry is fairly simple and well established, there are substantial barriers to entry into the biosimilar market.

Genomic era. Following an explosive growth, the pharmaceutical industry, which is always innovating, began looking at newer ways of therapy. With a better understanding of the disease and a more patient-centered approach, newer drugs, diagnostics, and lines of research emerged. The understanding of cellular processes, including the interaction of genes, proteins, and cellular machinery has given rise to targeted therapy and genomic drugs. An example is Benlysta (belimumab), which is a result of research through genomics and bioinformatics, and is the first new therapy for systemic lupus erythematosus in 50 years. Similarly, with the understanding that multiple cellular targets may be responsible for various forms of breast cancer, different targeted therapy is given that has transformed prognosis in breast cancer. Epigenetics has helped us target expression or silencing of select non-DNA genetic elements (such as siRNA, proteins) to change disease manifestation. Stem cell therapies, synthetic biology, and tissue engineering are providing newer approaches to treating diseases. Concepts like network medicine are improving understanding of the molecular relationships between apparently distinct manifestations of a disease. The pharmaceutical industry is undergoing an exciting revolution in the field of genomics.

Comparison of Financial Volume of Pharmaceutical Industries With Other Industries

The worldwide market for pharmaceuticals was projected to grow from around $1 trillion in 2015 to $1.3 trillion by 2020, representing an annual growth rate of 4.9%.[29] Several global demographic and economic trends are driving pharmaceutical consumption, including a rapidly aging world population and an associated rise in chronic diseases, increased urbanization and higher disposable incomes, greater government expenditure on healthcare, and growing demand for more effective treatments. The United States is a large pharmaceutical's market with a huge market size.[29] Developing country markets are relatively more heterogeneous with groups of high purchase power that spend more on innovation and groups of low purchase power that spend more on generics. Top markets for pharmaceutical products continue to be developed countries in North America, Western Europe, and East Asia with high per capita spending on healthcare, growing elderly populations, and advanced regulatory systems. Though ranked lower, there are growing opportunities in developing countries such as China and India as incomes and healthcare spending increase.

The pharmaceutical industry is known for its competitiveness, large employment, directly and indirectly, innovation as one of the most R&D-intensive industries (15%−20% of revenues to R&D activities in the United States), and fast-growing segment of biologics and generics.[29]

Global pharmaceutical, biotech, and medtech markets have shown a rising trend.[30] Although the pharmaceutical market is large, it is still a fraction of the chemical industry.[31]

Career Opportunities for Pharmacy Graduates in Pharmaceutical Industries

Pharmacy graduates have many career options in pharmaceutical industries. Traditionally, pharmacists have used their clinical knowledge in a variety of practice settings, including community pharmacies and hospitals. However, there are also many significant, alternative career opportunities within the pharmaceutical and biopharmaceutical industries. With advances in medical technology, the pharmaceutical and biopharmaceutical industries are constantly expanding efforts to discover, develop, and market new drugs, thereby creating more employment opportunities for pharmacists. The pharmacy professionals working on drug innovation and research are called pharmaceutical scientists. Some of the job areas in pharmaceutical industries include the following:

- clinical trials,
- pharmacovigilance,
- pharmaceutical formulation development,
- manufacture and supply,

- quality assurance,
- regulatory affairs,
- medical affairs,
- pharmacokinetics and drug metabolism,
- health economics and outcomes research,
- project management,
- commercial business development, and
- marketing and sales.

OBJECTIVE 2.3. DISCUSS POLICIES AND LAWS GOVERNING THE PHARMACY PROFESSION AND PUBLIC HEALTH

World Health Organization

International health policies often have influence to standardize and regulate the pharmacy profession. In this regard, policies set by the WHO have been significant in shaping pharmacy and other health professions globally. One of the most important international regulations set by the WHO has been the *right to health*, which was evident since the proposal of the WHO Constitution 1946 and the Universal Declaration of Human Rights 1948. The binding International Covenant on Economic, Social, and Cultural Rights of 1966 detailed realization of the right to health through bettering access to health facilities, goods, and services. The WHO introduced the concept of *Essential Medicines and National Drug Policy* in 1977 after the World Health Assembly 1975 in an attempt to make good quality modern drugs available and affordable.[32] National drug policies for ensuring essential drugs in member countries were considered to improve pharmaceutical care. Furthermore, the WHO in 1978, through the Declaration of Alma Ata, identified *provision of essential drugs* as one of the eight elements of primary healthcare. Declaration of Alma Ata by the WHO is one of the first of its kind to emphasize primary care.[32] Together, provision of essential drugs and national drug policies and various other WHO policies related to these have improved access to drugs and care in various WHO member countries. Going a step further, in 2000, WHO released the *WHO Model Formulary* to promote safe and cost-effective use of drugs and *WHO Model Quality Assurance (QA) System* for prequalification of vendors especially for UN agencies. The model formulary and model QA system provided important guidance to member countries developing their own formularies and QA systems. In 2000, the authoritative General Comment 14 (2000) also applied the principles of accessibility, availability, appropriateness, and assured quality to goods and services, which include essential drugs, to the right to health.[33] Through drug and therapeutic guidelines in association with the International Network for Rational Use of Drugs, rational prescribing guidelines have been released by the WHO.[34]

The International Pharmaceutical Federation (FIP) and WHO together developed GPP guidelines, first released in 1996, which ensure quality in pharmaceutical care.[35] In 1999, WHO released the *Counterfeit Drug Policy* guidelines to help member countries combat counterfeit drugs.[36] In the same year, the International Conference on Harmonisation (ICH) and WHO also released *Good Manufacturing Practice* (GMP): a system for ensuring that products are consistently produced and controlled according to quality standards minimizing the risks involved in any pharmaceutical production that cannot be eliminated through just testing the final product but by testing each step in the manufacturing process. Many countries have formulated their own requirements for GMP based on WHO GMP and others have harmonized their requirements through the Pharmaceutical Inspection Convention.[37,38]

WHO also improved health security through the International Health Regulations (IHR) 2005, a binding document between 196 countries including all WHO Member States.[39] IHR has been used as a guiding principle for many countries[40] and for coalitions like Global Health Securities Agenda for implementing health security, including pharmaceutical availability and stocking, for health emergencies and outbreaks.[41]

Apart from this, WHO has played a crucial role in drug utilization statistics with the aim of improving drug use. For this, WHO has defined the Anatomical Therapeutic Chemical (ATC[42]) system under which defined daily dose (DDD[43]), an assumed average maintenance dose per day for a drug used for its main indication in adults, is assigned. DDDs are assigned for drugs that are approved in at least one country. DDDs are not assigned for radiopharmaceuticals, appetite stimulants, anesthetics, blood substitutes, parenteral organic nitrates, many topical products, vaccines, antineoplastic agents, etc., due to high dose variation.[44] In the ATC classification system, the active substances are divided into different groups according to the organ or system on which they act and their therapeutic, pharmacological, and chemical properties. Like the International Classification of Diseases (ICD) that assign a unique codes for diseases, the ATC codes are unique to drugs based on anatomical therapeutic and chemical classification. It is possible for a drug to have more than one ATC code if it has more than one approved therapeutic indication. The ATC/DDD system is not exactly a therapeutic classification system and is for statistical studies regarding drug safety.[45]

WHO has pushed for standardization in the naming of drugs through the use of International Nonproprietary Names[46,47] (INN or generic names) globally over brand names since 1950. INN program gives a unique name to pharmaceutical substances or active pharmaceutical ingredients, which is globally recognized and is public property. INN is meant for pharmacopoeias, labeling, product information, etc. There were around 7000 names on the INN list in 2017, growing by some 120–150 names every year. INN has made naming of NDEs (new drug entities) that have complex IUPAC chemical names easier as the INN nomenclature follows a system for naming based on the IUPAC name and chemical structure, Chemicals Abstract Service registry number, as well as checking with previously existing INNs. INNs are published in the *WHO Drug Information*.

United States Drug Legislations

The US federal legislation—especially the FDC Act 1938, CSA 1970, PPMA 1970, PDMA 1970, OBRA-90, and HIPAA—has shaped pharmacy practice in the United States and globally.[48] Most of the federal legislation has been initiated in response to issues and concerns at certain points in time to protect the health, safety, and welfare of the patient from the potential risks of drug use or misuse. Most legislation has also imposed new requirements in such areas as record-keeping, counseling, and packaging of pharmaceuticals.

The Food, Drug, and Cosmetic (FDC) Act of 1938 provides the basis of quality control of drugs and penalties for spurious drugs. FDC Act of 1938 served as a replacement for the Food and Drug Act of 1906, which did not prohibit false therapeutic claims and, in some cases, even protected those claims. The 1906 law did not enforce labeling list ingredients, directions for use, or provide warnings. In 1937, more than 100 people, many of whom were children, died after a sulfa drug was administered that did not have proper labeling. As a result, FDC 1938 was passed, which brought cosmetics and medical devices under control and required proper labeling. It also mandated premarket approval of all new drugs, such that a manufacturer would have to prove that a drug was safe before it could be sold. FDC Act ensures the quality and safety of pharmaceuticals and regulates dispensing by the Durham–Humphrey Amendment to it (1951).[7] The FDC Act penalizes violations regarding drug products,[8] especially counterfeit or adulterated or misbranded drugs: the holding, dispensing, and sale of which are in violation of the Act.

The Comprehensive Drug Abuse Prevention and Control Act of 1970 or Controlled Substance Act (CSA) provides the basis against abuse of drugs. The CSA exerts more of a direct impact, as the law requires registration, specific record keeping, and rules regarding the dispensing of controlled substances. Penalties for the violation of the CSA are significantly more severe than a violation of the FDC Act.

The Poison Prevention Packaging Act (PPPA) of 1970 ensures safe packaging. The enactment of PPPA in 1970 reduced the oral prescription drug-related death rate of 1.4 deaths per million children under 5 years of age due to child-resistant packing, a reduction of up to 45%. Failure to comply with packaging requirements or any of the applicable regulations is considered a misbranding violation under the FDC Act.

The Prescription Drug Marketing Act of 1987 (PDMA), incorporated into the FDC Act, addresses the diversion of drugs into a secondary gray market commonly happening through drug-marketing practices. These marketing practices—including the distribution of free samples and the sale of deeply discounted drugs to hospitals and healthcare entities—have helped fuel a multimillion-dollar drug diversion market that provides a portal through which mislabeled, subpotent, adulterated, expired, and counterfeit drugs can enter the nation's drug distribution system. PDMA prohibits the act or offer of knowingly selling, purchasing, or trading a prescription drug sample. Another important portion of this extensive law that affects pharmacists prohibits the resale of any prescription drug that was previously purchased by a hospital or other "healthcare entity."

The Omnibus Budget Reconciliation Act of 1990 (OBRA-90) places expectations on the pharmacist in how to interact with the patient. Although the primary goal of OBRA-90 was to save the federal government money by improving therapeutic outcomes, the method to achieve these savings was implemented by imposing on the pharmacist counseling obligations, prospective drug utilization review (ProDUR) requirements, and record-keeping mandates. As part of the ProDUR, the following are areas for drug therapy problems that the pharmacist must screen for therapeutic duplication, drug–disease contraindications, drug–drug interactions, incorrect drug dosage, incorrect duration of treatment, drug–allergy interactions, and clinical abuse/misuse of medication. OBRA-90 overall resulted in standardized pharmaceutical care to all patients, although it was initially meant for Medicaid (one of the US health insurance program) patients.

The Health Insurance Portability and Accountability Act of 1996 (HIPAA) has been safeguarding the privacy of protected health information of patients since 2003. Pharmacies that maintain patient information in electronic format or conduct financial and administrative transactions electronically, such as billing and fund transfers, must comply with HIPAA. Although HIPAA places stringent requirements on pharmacies to adopt policies and procedures relating to the protection of patient protected health information (PHI), the law also gives important rights to patients. These rights include the right to access their information, the right to seek details of the disclosure of information, and the right to view the pharmacy's policies and procedures regarding confidential information. Typically, HIPAA restricts transmission and disclosure of PHI and strict adherence of the pharmacists/pharmacies to HIPAA. The pharmacy may disclose PHI to "business associates," which are billing services, claims processing, utilization review, or data analysis through stringent contractual agreements. HIPAA has security standards designed to protect the confidentiality of PHI that is threatened by the possibility of unauthorized access and an interception during electronic transmission.

HIPAA, through its different rules, indirectly forces healthcare organizations to comply with legislation. It is because HIPAA essentially enforces that all healthcare entities and organizations that use, store, maintain, or transmit patient health information ensure privacy, reduce fraudulent activity, and improve data systems. Accordingly, data regarding the use of drugs and health products are monitored by agencies to ensure use of drugs and health products that conform to FDC, CSA, PPMA, PDMA, and OBRA-90. By preventing security risks that could result in major compliance costs, HIPAA makes organizations focus on quality in drugs and health products as noncompliance results in massive fines.[49] Many countries have developed their policies and have taken inputs from the WHO and US policies and regulations (Table 2.1).

TABLE 2.1 An Overview of the Different Laws Governing Pharmacy Practice in Select Countries: United States,[48] United Kingdom,[50] Ireland,[51] India, and Nepal[52]

United States	United Kingdom	India
Pure Food and Drug Act of 1906	Pharmacy Order 2010 (Statutory Instrument 2010 No. 231) and the various sets of statutory rules made under the Order	Drug and Cosmetic Act,1940 and Rules, 1945
Harrison Narcotics Tax Act of 1914		The Narcotics Drug and Psychotropic Substances Act and Rules, 1985
Food, Drug, and Cosmetic Act of 1938		
Comprehensive Drug Abuse Prevention and Control Act of 1970 (with updates)	Medicines Act 1968	
Occupational Safety and Health Act of 1970	Poisons Act 1972	Drug Price Control Order, 1995
Poison Prevention Packaging Act of 1970		Consumer Protection Act, 1986
Medical Device Amendments of 1976		Infant Milk Substitutes, Feeding Bottles, and Infant Food Acts, 1992
Federal Anti-Tampering Act of 1983		
Orphan Drug Act of 1983		
Drug Price Competition and Patent-Term Restoration Act of 1984		Drug and Magic Remedies Act and Rules, 1954
Prescription Drug Marketing Act of 1987		Prevention of Food and Adulteration Act, 1954
Omnibus Budget Reconciliation Act of 1987		The Pharmacy Act, 1948
Anabolic Steroids Control Act of 1990		The Drugs and Magic Remedies (Objectionable Advertisement) Act, 1954
Omnibus Budget Reconciliation Act of 1990		
Dietary Supplement Health and Education Act of 1994		
Uruguay Round Agreements Act of 1994		
Health Insurance Portability and Accountability Act of 1996		
Food and Drug Administration Modernization Act of 1997		
2002 Best Pharmaceuticals for Children Act	**Ireland**	**Nepal**
Medicare Modernization Act of 2003		
Combat Methamphetamine Epidemic Act of 2005	Pharmacy Act 2007	Drug Act, 1978
Medicaid Tamper-Resistant Prescription Law of 2007	European Communities Regulations 2008	Nepal Pharmacy Council Act, 2000
Food and Drug Administration Amendments Act of 2007	European Union Regulations 2017	Narcotic Drugs (Control) Act, 1976
Elements of risk evaluation and mitigation strategies	Regulation of Retail Pharmacy Businesses Regulations 2008	Code for Manufacture of Drugs, 1986
Restricted drug programs	Health (Pricing and Supply of Medical Goods) Act 2013	
Thalidomide		Code for Sale and Distribution of Drugs
Clozapine	Health Act 2007 (Care and Welfare of Residents in Designated Centres for Older People) Regulations 2013	Code for Advertisement of Drugs
Buprenorphine		
Isotretinoin		
Patient Protection and Affordable Care Act of 2010		
Durham—Humphrey Amendment of 1951	Irish Medicines Board Act 1995	National Drug Control Policy, 1995
Kefauver—Harris Amendment of 1962	Medicinal Products Regulations 2007	Hospital Pharmacy Service Act
	Misuse of Drugs Regulations 1988	

International Pharmaceutical Federation or Fédération Internationale Pharmaceutique

FIP is the largest international pharmaceutical society that regularly contributes to the advancement of the pharmacy profession. Founded in 1912, FIP is a nongovernmental organization with its head office in the Netherlands. FIP coordinates observance of World Pharmacists Day on September 25th every year.[53] In 1912 the FIP was founded on September 25th.

It is important that modern pharmacists understand their increasingly complex role in light of complicated patient care guidelines, public health guidelines, a multitude of pharmaceuticals, and legal requirements. To aid in this process, the GPP guidelines and code of ethics (CoE) for pharmacists serve as a suitable starting point to provide professional pharmacy care.

Good Pharmacy Practice

Pharmacists are charged by their national or other appropriate (e.g., state or provincial) authorities with the management of the distribution of drugs to consumers and to engage in appropriate efforts to assure their safe and efficacious use. Not only that, pharmacists are increasingly accepting greater responsibility for the outcomes of drug use and are evolving their practices to provide patients with enhanced drug-use services. Increasingly complex and diverse nature of pharmacists' roles in the healthcare system demands that pharmacists follow GPP guidelines.[35] According to FIP/WHO, GPP is "the practice of pharmacy that responds to the needs of the people who use the pharmacists' services to provide optimal, evidence-based care. It is essential that there be an established national framework of quality standards and guidelines."

- A pharmacist's first concern in all settings is the welfare of patients;[54]
- The core of pharmacy activity is to help patients make the best use of drugs. Fundamental functions include the supply of medication and other healthcare products of assuring quality, the provision of appropriate information and advice to the patient, administration of medication, when required, and the monitoring of the effects of medication use;
- An integral part of the pharmacist's contribution is the promotion of rational and economic prescribing, as well as dispensing;
- The objective of each element of pharmacy service is relevant to the patient, is defined, and is effectively communicated to all those involved. Multidisciplinary collaboration among healthcare professionals is the key factor for successfully improving patient safety.

Necessary conditions to meet the GPP guidelines.[54] The following conditions are deemed necessary:

- The well-being of patients should be the main philosophy underlying practice, even though it is accepted that ethical and economic factors are also important.
- Pharmacists should have input into decisions about the use of drugs. A system should exist that enables pharmacists to report and to obtain feedback about adverse events, medication errors, misuse or drug abuse, defects in product quality, or detection of counterfeit products. This reporting may include information about drug use supplied by patients or health professionals.
- The relationship with other health professionals, particularly physicians, should be established as a therapeutic collaborative partnership that involves mutual trust and confidence in all matters relating to pharmacotherapy.
- The relationship between pharmacists should be one of the colleagues seeking to improve pharmacy service, rather than acting as competitors.
- In reality, organizations, group practices, and pharmacy managers should accept a share of responsibility for the definition, evaluation, and improvement of quality.
- The pharmacist should be aware of essential medical and pharmaceutical information (i.e., diagnosis, laboratory test results, and medical history) about each patient. Obtaining such information is made easier if the patient chooses to use only one pharmacy or if the patient's medication profile is available.
- The pharmacist needs evidence-based, unbiased, comprehensive, objective, and current information about therapeutics, drugs, and other healthcare products in use, including potential environmental hazards caused by disposal of drugs' waste.
- Pharmacists in each practice setting should accept personal responsibility for maintaining and assessing their competence throughout their professional working lives. Although self-monitoring is important, an element of assessment and monitoring by the national pharmacy professional organizations would also be relevant in ensuring that pharmacists maintain standards and comply with requirements for continuous professional development.
- Educational programs for entry into the profession should appropriately address both current and foreseeable changes in pharmacy practice.

- National standards of GPP should be specified and should be adhered to by practitioners.

Frameworks needed to implement GPP.[54] For GPP implementation, three frameworks are needed at the national or appropriate (e.g., state or provincial) level:

- A legal framework that ensures the integrity of supply chain and quality of drugs; defines who can practice pharmacy; and what the scope of pharmacy practice is.
- A workforce framework that defines personnel needed and ensures the competence of such staff through continuing professional development programs.
- An economic framework that provides sufficient resources and incentives to ensure the activities undertaken in GPP.

Code of Ethics in Pharmacy Practice

Laws and ethics of healthcare overlap considerably because both share the concern that the conduct of healthcare professionals should reflect respect for the well-being, dignity, and self-determination of the public. At the same time, there are situations in which the two domains of law and ethics may remain distinct and a CoE, while preparing with awareness of the law, is addressed to ethical obligations. Laws shall have their loopholes, and it cannot ensure fair practices without a CoE.

Although the specifics of CoE vary slightly country by country (influenced by cultures), most of them define and seek to clarify the obligations of the pharmacists to use their knowledge and skills for the benefit of others, to be fair and just in their service to the public, to minimize harm, and to respect patient autonomy. The CoE educates pharmacists about their ethical duties and obligations and serves as a tool for guiding pharmacists in relationships with patients, health professionals, and society, as well as for continued competence (via continuing education), self-evaluation, and peer review. Perhaps the best international CoE is that of points from FIP CoE (Table 2.2).[55]

Of course, the FIP CoE is more a guideline than a statute. Different countries and associations adopt their own CoEs.

International Patient Safety Goals

Joint Commission International accredited healthcare institutions insist on International Patient Safety Goals to improve patient safety.[65] The six goals are:

Goal 1: Identify patients correctly
Goal 2: Improve effective communication

TABLE 2.2 International Pharmaceutical Federation (FIP) Code of Ethics (2014)

FIP Code of Ethics for Pharmacists (2014)

- to act with honesty and integrity in their relationships with consumers, patients and carers, and other health professionals, including pharmacy practice colleagues, and not engage in any behavior or activity likely to bring the profession into disrepute or to undermine public confidence in the profession;
- to ensure that their priorities are the safety, well-being and the best interests of those to whom they provide professional services and that they act at all times as autonomous health professionals, recognizing the challenges posed by dividing loyalties and the potential in many settings for conflicts of interest that need careful management;
- to always act professionally, in accordance with scientific principles and professional standards, including those developed by the international pharmaceutical federation;
- to cooperate and collaborate with colleagues, other health professionals, consumers, patients, carers and other actors in the healthcare delivery system to ensure that the best possible quality of healthcare is provided both to individuals and the community at large, while always considering the limitations of available resources and the principles of equity and justice;
- to respect and protect the confidentiality of patient information acquired or accessed in the course of providing professional services and to ensure that such information is only disclosed with the informed consent of that individual or as allowed by applicable legislation and regulation;
- to respect patients' rights and recognize and respect the cultural differences, beliefs, and values of patients, carers and other healthcare professionals particularly in the event of a conflict with their own moral or religious beliefs;
- to ensure continuity of care for the patient in the event of a conflict with their own moral or religious beliefs, based on respect for patient autonomy;
- to comply with legislation and accepted codes and standards of practice in the provision of all professional services and pharmaceutical products and to ensure the integrity of the supply chain for drugs; and
- to ensure that they maintain competence through continuing professional development.

Goal 3: Improve the safety of high-alert medications
Goal 4: Ensure safe surgery
Goal 5: Reduce the risk of healthcare-associated infections
Goal 6: Reduce the risk of patient harm resulting from falls.

These patient safety goals are relevant to pharmacists in at least the following ways. Goal 1: Identifying patients correctly is essential to provide the right drug to the right patient. Goal 2: Improved effective communication focuses on patient counseling and medication reconciliation and to improve medication adherence. Goal 3: Improve safety of high-alert medication and consider other approaches to prevent adverse medication outcomes, especially of certain medications with expected immediate life-threatening events, e.g., adrenaline, insulin, etc. Goal 4: Ensure safe surgery concerns with proper use of anesthetics. Goal 5: Reduce the risk of healthcare-associated infections related to antimicrobial stewardship. Goal 6: Reduce the risk of patient harm resulting from falls as many drugs as associated with drowsiness.

OBJECTIVE 2.4. DETAIL AN OVERVIEW OF PUBLIC HEALTH AND DISEASE PREVENTION

Public health is the science and systems designed to protect and improve health at the community and population level. It includes efforts to improve health by preventing disease and promoting healthy behaviors.[56] These efforts include initiatives to educate the public about healthier choices, facilitating healthier lifestyles through community support, preventing outbreaks and the spread of infectious diseases, and ensuring safe food and water in communities. Public health includes the practices, procedures, institutions, and disciplines required to improve population health. Although the pharmacy practice needs to consider the impact it has on public health constantly, it must be increasingly recognized that public health activities, locally or globally, influence the decisions, roles, and scope of pharmacists. Therefore, pharmacists need to understand the public health picture and players to fulfill their increasingly complex role in maintaining individual and public health. Particular focus must be placed on the organizations involved in international public health as these organizations have affected local and national level public health initiatives and activities.

Organizations Involved in International Public Health

Apart from WHO, a large number of organizations of various sizes are involved in international public health. These are involved in either providing long-term healthcare or providing special aid to victims of war, famine, and natural disasters. Many have overlapping and crosscutting programs.

WHO has been the forefront organization in international public health since 1947.[57,58] WHO is an intergovernmental agency related to the United Nations, and its principal goal is "the attainment by all peoples of the highest possible level of health." WHO directs and coordinates international health activities by supplying technical assistance to member countries. It develops norms and standards, disseminates health information, promotes research, provides training in international health, collects and analyzes epidemiologic data, and develops systems for monitoring and evaluating health programs. WHO's scope of work includes health systems; noncommunicable diseases; communicable diseases; promoting health through life course; preparedness, surveillance, and response during emergencies; and corporate services to provide the enabling functions, tools, and resources for conducting its programs. An overview of the public health activities done by WHO is given in Table 2.3.

Organizations Providing Long-Term Healthcare.[60,61] The *World Bank* is another major intergovernmental agency related to the UN heavily involved in international health. The World Bank loans money to developing countries on advantageous terms not available in commercial markets, especially in health, nutrition, and education.

UN agencies such as UNICEF, UNFPA, and UNDP also provide public health aid. UNICEF focuses on children's healthcare (mostly in cooperation with WHO), especially that of the world's most vulnerable children younger than 5 years of age. UNICEF also provides aid on water supply and sanitation, child nutrition, and emergency relief. UNFPA spends on family planning programs, especially in high population growth and high poverty rate countries. UNDP spends on health, education, and employment. Its focus is on AIDS, maternal and child nutrition, and excessive maternal mortality. UNAIDS works for HIV/AIDS-related programs. UNITAID works on pharmaceutical supply chain programs in tuberculosis (TB), malaria, hepatitis C, etc. The Global Fund for AIDS, Malaria, and Tuberculosis works across crosscutting programs of AIDS, malaria, and TB in developing countries.

TABLE 2.3 WHO and Global Health: Historic Landmarks

1945	1946	1947	1948	1950
Diplomats decide on the need for a global organization overseeing global health and plan for the creation of WHO in San Francisco	WHO's constitution is drafted and then approved at the International Health Conference in New York City	WHO establishes the first ever global disease-tracking service, with information transmitted via telex	WHO's Constitution ratified on April 7—"World Health Day." Next two decades are focused on mass campaigns for communicable diseases[a]	WHO begins advising countries on the responsible use of antibiotics
1952–57	**1963**	**1969**	**1972**	**1974**
Mass global vaccination campaigns facilitation for polio eradication	Measles vaccination begins followed by mumps and rubella during the next 6 years	1st International Health Regulations are established	HRP[b] program is to research sexual and reproductive health and rights	WHO founds the Expanded Program on Immunization
1975	**1977**	**1978**	**1987**	**1988**
WHO founds TDR[c] program to combat diseases of poverty	The first essential drugs list is published	Alma Ata convention[d] sets the aspirational goal "Health for All" emphasizing Universal Health Coverage (UHC)	The first antiretroviral medication is licensed, prompting a shift in WHO's priorities to HIV/AIDS treatment	The Global Polio Eradication Initiative is established
1995	**1999**	**2000**	**2001**	**2003**
The DOTS strategy for reducing the toll of tuberculosis (TB) is launched	The Global Alliance for Vaccines and Immunization is formed	MDGs[e] are formed with specific goals for health. The WHO Global Outbreak Alert and Response Network is established	The Global Fund to fight AIDS, Tuberculosis, and Malaria is created	WHO Framework Convention on Tobacco Control is ratified. WHO launches the "3 by 5" initiative[f]
2004	**2005**	**2006**	**2008**	**2009**
Indian Ocean tsunami disaster: the Strategic Health Operations Centre is used for the first time to assist with global emergency coordination	The International Health Regulations are revised	The number of children who die before their fifth birthday declines below 10 million for the first time in recent history	The World Health Statistics report notes a global shift from infectious diseases to noncommunicable diseases (NCDs), and WHO begins to strengthen its focus on NCDs	First influenza pandemic since 1968 due to new H1N1 influenza virus; WHO works with partners to develop influenza vaccines in record time
2010	**2012**	**2014**	**2015**	**2016**
WHO issues opinions for raising sufficient resources and removing financial barriers to allow access to essential health services for UHC	For the first time, the WHO Member States set global targets to prevent and control NCDs	The biggest outbreak of Ebola virus disease ever experienced in the world strikes West Africa	2030 Sustainable Development Goals are put forth replace and supersede MDGs	Zika virus among pregnant women represents a Public Health Emergency of International Concern

[a]TB, malaria, yaws, syphilis, smallpox, and leprosy, etc.
[b]The Special Program of Research, Development, and Research Training in Human Reproduction
[c]Research and Training in Tropical Diseases; by 2016, five of eight targeted diseases are near elimination
[d]The International Conference on Primary Healthcare, in Alma Ata, Kazakhstan
[e]Millennium Development Goals
[f]Three by five initiative aims to bring treatment to 3 million people living with HIV by 2005
Adapted from World Health Organization. The Global Guardian of Public Health; 2016. http://www.who.int/about/what-we-do/global-guardian-of-public-health.pdf.

Bilateral agencies such as USAID, UKAID, and AusAID are also involved in population, health, and nutrition activities among others. Such programs are done on individual agreements between two governments.

Nongovernmental organizations (NGOs) work to complement governmental agencies. NGOs can be funded by various means—through grants or religious organizations or as partners of larger aid organizations—and they often run small but efficient programs. Examples of NGOs are OxFam, Bill and Melinda Gates Foundation, Clinton Foundation, Wellcome Trust, etc.

Refugee and Disaster Relief Organizations. In contrast to natural disasters, famines and refugee crises tend to develop slowly, often preceded by warning signs of the impending emergency, so that international agencies can coordinate relief efforts with national agencies in a timely fashion. The United Nations agencies are probably the most important of the international relief organizations, but there are several very large NGOs active in refugee and disaster relief. Two of these are the *International Committee of the Red Cross* and *Medecins Sans Frontieres* (commonly called doctors without borders).

Disease Prevention

A major goal of public health practice is prevention.[62] It includes a wide range of activities—known as "interventions"—aimed at reducing risks or threats to health or alters the adverse consequences of the natural history of the disease and health-related events. Such intervention can occur at any time during the natural history of the disease or health-related event.

To prevent disease, we must understand the natural history of the condition (Table 2.4), its distribution in the population, and how to detect early cases. The natural history begins with patients being susceptible to a disease, called the susceptible phase. Susceptible patients can undergo a biological onset of disease. The onset may lie undetected for a varying period called the preclinical phase. When symptoms appear, the patient typically seeks help, perhaps leading to a diagnosis. If therapy begins, this may alter the natural history, turning it into the clinical course of the condition. If there is no treatment, the natural history continues its course, ending in the cure, chronic condition, or decline (death).[63]

There are three identified levels of prevention that are aimed at different stages of disease.[62] Pharmacists have a role to play in all the different stages of prevention (Figs. 2.4 and 2.5).

Primary Prevention: Primary prevention interventions are aimed at individuals or communities in the susceptibility stage directed at reducing the risk of exposure to a risk factor or health determinant in an individual or the population. Immunization is a primary prevention measure. Primordial prevention is a type of primary prevention. Primordial prevention is defined as prevention of risk factors themselves, beginning with a change in social and environmental conditions

TABLE 2.4 An Overview of the Natural History of Diseases and Prevention Strategies to be Applied to Stages of Disease[62]

Stage	Susceptible	Preclinical	Clinical	Recovery, Disability, or Death
Characteristics	Risk factors and disease in the population	Exposure of individuals to risk factor or disease and early pathologic change	Signs and symptoms noted in individuals	Outcomes of clinical disease—death, disability, or recovery
Level of prevention	Primary	Secondary	Tertiary	–
Modes of intervention	Health promotion Specific protection	Screening Early diagnosis	Treatment and rehabilitation	–
Example	Immunization The family lives in adequate, affordable housing	Pap smear Blood pressure measurement in the clinic	Prophylactic medication to prevent myocardial infarction (MI)/prompt administration of thrombolytic therapy following MI	Speech therapy following a cerebro-vascular accident

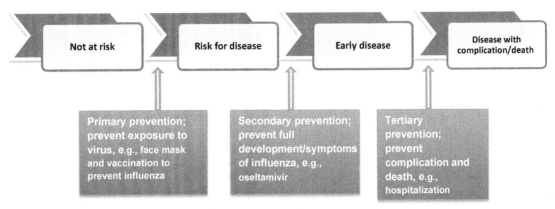

FIGURE 2.4   Levels of disease prevention (e.g., influenza).

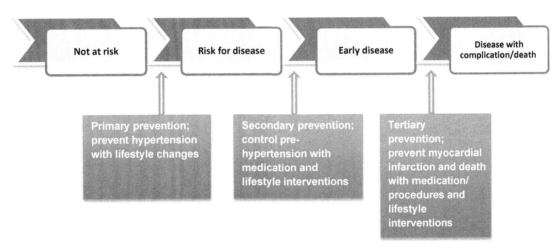

FIGURE 2.5   Levels of disease prevention (e.g., myocardial infarction).

in which these factors are observed to develop and continuing for high-risk children, adolescents, and young adults. Wearing a face mask to avoid exposure to influenza virus is primordial prevention.

Secondary Prevention: Secondary prevention interventions focus on the subclinical stage and the early clinical stage to enable early detection and prompt, effective intervention to correct departures from a state of health. Screening programs such as Pap smears for early diagnosis of cancer of the cervix and mammography for early diagnosis of breast cancer are all examples of secondary prevention. Secondary prevention prevents full development of the disease with symptoms mitigated.

Tertiary Prevention. Tertiary prevention interventions prevent disability or death—although they are used to some extent in any clinical stage. The purpose is to reduce or eliminate suffering, long-term impairments and disabilities, optimize function, assist in adjusting to disease-related limitations in health and function, and extend survival. Examples include prevention of complications and death due to diseases (Figs. 2.4 and 2.5).

Pharmacist's roles in public health continue to evolve. Encouragingly, the American Public Health Association has supported the pharmacist's role in public health as a policy statement.[64]

CONCLUSION

The pharmacy profession developed through identifying, making, and advising how to use drugs. Pharmacists work in a variety of settings such as community pharmacies, healthcare institutions, industries, healthcare agencies, and as consultants. The profession is highly regulated by laws, guidelines, and CoE. The scope of practice has expanded from pharmacy management to additional clinical services to broader public health functions.

PRACTICE QUESTIONS

1. Where was the first apothecary shop opened in the late eighth century separating the practice of pharmacy from medicine?
   A. Milan
   B. London
   C. Baghdad
   D. Brazil

2. Which of the following is used as a symbol of pharmacy?
   A. Bowl of Hygeia
   B. Rx
   C. Mortar and pestle
   D. All of the above

3. The original definition of pharmaceutical care in 1990 was created by?
   A. Hepler and Strand
   B. William Procter
   C. William Smith
   D. David and Edwards

4. What is biosimilar?
   A. Pharmaceutical device
   B. Generic version of biologicals
   C. Bioequivalent drugs
   D. Genomic products

5. Unique identification code for a drug given by WHO is?
   A. DDD
   B. ICD
   C. ABC
   D. ATC

6. Tertiary disease prevention is to prevent?
   A. Permanent disability due to disease
   B. Exposure to disease
   C. Development of disease
   D. Spread of disease

7. Which of the following is part of public health?
   A. Health education
   B. Nutrition
   C. Vaccination
   D. All of the above

REFERENCES

1. International Pharmaceutical Federation. *Military and Emergency Pharmacy Section*; 2017. http://www.fip.org/military_emergency_pharmacy.
2. World Health Organization. Chapter 9. Step 4: write a prescription. In: *Guide to Good Prescribing - A Practical Manual*; 1994. http://apps.who.int/medicinedocs/en/d/Jwhozip23e/5.4.html.
3. Walker C. Rx—the eye of horus. *J R Coll Phys Lond*. 1992;26(1):102.
4. Okuda J, Kiyokawa R. Snake as a symbol in medicine and pharmacy - a historical study. *Yakushigaku Zasshi*. 2000;35(1):25—40.
5. College of Pharmacy - University of Arizona. *Mortars & Pestles*; 2017. http://www.pharmacy.arizona.edu/print/2748.
6. Coyne College. *History of Pharmacy*; 2017. www.coynecollege.edu/news-events/history-pharmacy.
7. Dukes G, Braithwaite J, Moloney JP. *Pharmaceuticals, Corporate Crime and Public Health*. Edward Elgar Publishing; 2014.
8. Capasso F, Gaginella TS, Grandolini G, Izzo AA. Therapeutic overview of galenical preparations. In: *Phytotherapy*. Berlin, Heidelberg: Springer; 2003:45—60. https://doi.org/10.1007/978-3-642-55528-2_9.
9. Sladkova Anastasya, Loginova Natalya. Terminology of drugs. In: *Presented at the: Drug Chemistry and Technology Basics, Cleaner Production and Mega - Trends in Pharmaceutical Industry*; 2017. http://im.bsu.by/docs/prasintation/L%202%20Terminology%20of%20Drugs.pdf.
10. Thom RA. *Great Moments in Pharmacy*; 2017. https://www.pharmacist.com/sites/default/files/Great_Moments_in_Pharmacy.pdf.
11. Pormann PE. The formation of the Arabic pharmacology between tradition and innovation. *Ann Sci*. 2011;68(4):493—515. https://doi.org/10.1080/00033790.2011.594619.

12. Sprague TA, Sprague MS. The herbal of Valerius Cordus. *J Linn Soc Lond Bot*. 1939;52(341):1−113. https://doi.org/10.1111/j.1095-8339.1939.tb01598.x.
13. Foesius A. *Pharmacopœia Medicamentorum Omnium, Quæ Hodie... Officinis Extant, Etc*. 1561.
14. Daemmrich Arthur, Bowden Mary Ellen. A rising drug industry. *Chem Eng News*. 2005;83(25):28−42.
15. Worthen DB. William Procter Jr. (1817−1874). J Am Pharm Assoc. 2002;42(2):363−364. https://doi.org/10.1331/108658002763508623.
16. Dunlop DM, Denston TC. The history and development of the "British pharmacopoeia". *Br Med J*. 1958;2(5107):1250−1252.
17. *The United States Pharmacopeial Convention. USP*; 2017. http://www.usp.org/.
18. World Health Organization. *International Meeting of World Pharmacopoeias*; 2012. http://www.who.int/medicines/areas/quality_safety/quality_assurance/resources/InternationalMeetingWorldPharmacopoeias_QAS13-512Rev1_25032013.pdf.
19. Carter BL. Evolution of clinical pharmacy in the us and future directions for patient care. *Drugs Aging*. 2016;33(3):169−177. https://doi.org/10.1007/s40266-016-0349-2.
20. School of Pharmacy UCSF. *The Ninth Floor Pharmacy Project*. History of the Department of Clinical Pharmacy, UCSF; 1965−1972. https://pharm.ucsf.edu/history-cp/1965-1972.
21. World Health Organization. *The Role of the Pharmacist in the Health Care System*; 2017. http://apps.who.int/medicinedocs/en/d/Jh2995e/.
22. American Pharmacists Association. National association of chain drug stores foundation. In: *Medication Therapy Management in Pharmacy Practice: Core Elements of an MTM Service Model*; 2008. http://www.pharmacist.com/sites/default/files/files/core_elements_of_an_mtm_practice.pdf.
23. Porteus MH. Towards a new era in medicine: therapeutic genome editing. *Genome Biol*. 2015;16:286. https://doi.org/10.1186/s13059-015-0859-y.
24. Carlisle Daloni. Falsified medicines directive: opportunity or obstacle? *Pharm J*; 2017. https://www.pharmaceutical-journal.com/news-and-analysis/features/falsified-medicines-directive-opportunity-or-obstacle/20202646.article.
25. The Pharmaceutical Journal. Telecare management proves helpful in patients with chronic pain. *Pharm J*; 2017. https://www.pharmaceutical-journal.com/news-and-analysis/research-briefing/telecare-management-proves-helpful-in-patients-with-chronic-pain/20065942.article.
26. Badowski ME, Michienzi S, Robles M. Examining the implications of analytical and remote monitoring in pharmacy practice. *Pharm J*; 2017. https://www.pharmaceutical-journal.com/research/examining-the-implications-of-analytical-and-remote-monitoring-in-pharmacy-practice/20202516.article.
27. Silver Steven. *Industry Surveys: Biotechnology*. Standard & Poor's; 2013.
28. Blackstone EA, Joseph PF. The economics of biosimilars. *Am Health Drug Benefits*. 2013;6(8):469−478.
29. PWC. *From Vision to Decision Pharma 2020*; 2017. http://www.pwc.com/gx/en/pharma-life-sciences/pharma2020/assets/pwc-pharma-success-strategies.pdf.
30. Deloitte Global. *Global Life Sciences Outlook | Moving Forward with Cautious Optimism*; 2016. https://www2.deloitte.com/content/dam/Deloitte/global/Documents/Life-Sciences-Health-Care/gx-lshc-2016-life-sciences-outlook.pdf.
31. Statista. *Global Chemical Industry Revenue*. Statista; 2002−2015. https://www.statista.com/statistics/302081/revenue-of-global-chemical-industry/.
32. World Health Organization. Essential drugs monitor No. 032. In: *Access to Essential Medicines: A Global Necessity*; 2003. http://apps.who.int/medicinedocs/en/d/Js4940e/8.html#Js4940e.8.
33. World Health Organization. Essential drugs monitor No. 033. In: *Access: Access to Essential Medicines as a Human Right*; 2003. http://apps.who.int/medicinedocs/en/d/Js4941e/5.1.html#Js4941e.5.1.
34. World Health Organization. *Drug and Therapeutics Committees - A Practical Guide*; 2017. http://apps.who.int/medicinedocs/en/d/Js4882e/.
35. International Pharmaceutical Federation. *Good Pharmacy Practice (GPP) in Developing Countries Recommendations for Step-wise Implementation*; 2017. http://www.fip.org/files/fip/Statements/GPP%20recommendations.pdf.
36. World Health Organization. *Counterfeit Drugs. Guidelines for the Development of Measures to Combat Counterfeit Drugs*; 2017. http://apps.who.int/medicinedocs/en/d/Jh1456e/.
37. WHO. *GMP Question and Answers*. WHO. http://www.who.int/medicines/areas/quality_safety/quality_assurance/gmp/en/.
38. World Health Organization. *WHO Good Manufacturing Practices for Pharmaceutical Products: Main Principles*. World Health Organization; 2014. http://www.who.int/medicines/areas/quality_safety/quality_assurance/TRS986annex2.pdf.
39. World Health Organization. *International Health Regulations*; 2005. http://apps.who.int/iris/bitstream/10665/246107/1/9789241580496-eng.pdf?ua=1.
40. Wilson K, von Tigerstrom B, McDougall C. Protecting global health security through the international health regulations: requirements and challenges. *CMAJ Can Med Assoc J*. 2008;179(1):44−48. https://doi.org/10.1503/cmaj.080516.
41. Marinissen MJ, Barna L, Meyers M, Sherman SE. Strengthening global health security by developing capacities to deploy medical countermeasures internationally. *Biosecur Bioterror Biodef Strateg Pract Sc*. 2014;12(5):284−291. https://doi.org/10.1089/bsp.2014.0049.
42. *WHO Collaborating Centre for Drug Statistics Methodology. ATC*; 2017. https://www.whocc.no/atc/structure_and_principles/.
43. *WHO Collaborating Centre for Drug Statistics Methodology. DDD*; 2017. https://www.whocc.no/ddd/definition_and_general_considera/.
44. WHO Collaborating Centre for Drug Statistics Methodology. *Guidelines for ATC Classification and DDD Assignment.*; 2012. https://www.whocc.no/filearchive/publications/1_2013guidelines.pdf.
45. *WHOCC - Use of ATC/DDD*; 2017. https://www.whocc.no/use_of_atc_ddd/.
46. World Health Organization. *International Nonproprietary Names*. WHO. http://www.who.int/medicines/services/inn/en/.
47. World Health Organization. *Guidance on the Use of International Nonproprietary Names (INNs) for Pharmaceutical Substances*; 2017. http://www.who.int/medicines/services/inn/FINAL_WHO_PHARM_S_NOM_1570_web.pdf?ua=1.

48. Van Dusen Virgil, Spies Alan R. *A Review of Federal Legislation Affecting Pharmacy Practice*; 2006. http://www.pharmacytimes.com/publications/issue/2006/2006-12/2006-12-6154.

49. Nass SJ, Levit LA, Gostin LO. *Rule I of M (US) C on HR and the P of HITHP. HIPAA, the Privacy Rule, and Its Application to Health Research*. National Academies Press (US); 2009. https://www.ncbi.nlm.nih.gov/books/NBK9573/.

50. UK Legislation. *The Pharmacy Order*; 2010. http://www.legislation.gov.uk/ukdsi/2010/9780111487358/contents.

51. The Pharmaceutical Society of Ireland. *Legislation Governing the Practice of Pharmacy in Ireland*; 2017. http://www.thepsi.ie/gns/inspection-enforcement/enforcement/legislation.aspx.

52. Ministry of Health Nepal. *Acts & Rules*; 2017. http://www.mohp.gov.np/content/acts-rules.

53. FIP - International Pharmaceutical Federation. *World Pharmacists Day*; 2018. http://www.fip.org/www/index.php?page=news_publications&news=newsitem&newsitem=117.

54. Joint FIP/WHO guidelines on good pharmacy practice: standards for quality of pharmacy services. In: *WHO Technical Report. WHO Technical Report*. World Health Organization; 2011:310–323. http://apps.who.int/medicinedocs/documents/s18676en/s18676en.pdf.

55. FIP - International Pharmaceutical Federation. *FIP Statement of Professional Standards - Code of Ethics for Pharmacist*; 2017. http://apps.who.int/medicinedocs/en/d/Js19757en/.

56. National Conference of State Legislatures. *State Public Health Initiatives to Improve Community Health*; 2017. http://www.ncsl.org/research/health/public-health-and-prevention.aspx.

57. World Health Organization. *History of WHO*. WHO. http://www.who.int/about/history/en/.

58. World Health Organization. *What We Do*. WHO. http://www.who.int/about/what-we-do/en/.

59. World Health Organization. *The Global Guardian of Public Health*; 2016. http://www.who.int/about/what-we-do/global-guardian-of-public-health.pdf.

60. International Medical Volunteers Association. *The Major International Health Organizations*; 2017. http://www.imva.org/pages/orgfrm.htm.

61. Fogarty International Center at NIH. *Nongovernmental Organizations (NGOs) Working in Global Health Research*; 2017. https://www.fic.nih.gov/Global/Pages/NGOs.aspx.

62. Virtual Campus of Public Health. *Types of Prevention*; 2017. https://cursos.campusvirtualsp.org/mod/tab/view.php?id=23157.

63. University of Ottawa Faculty of Medicine. *Public Health and Preventive Medicine*; 2018. https://www.med.uottawa.ca/sim/data/Pub_PublicH_Prevention_e.htm. Accessed on July 18, 2018.

64. American Public Health Association. *The Role of the Pharmacist in Public Health*; 2017. https://www.apha.org/policies-and-advocacy/public-health-policy-statements/policy-database/2014/07/07/13/05/the-role-of-the-pharmacist-in-public-health.

65. JCI. International Patient Safety Goals. https://www.jointcommissioninternational.org/improve/international-patient-safety-goals/. Accessed on July 28, 2018

ANSWERS TO PRACTICE QUESTIONS

1. C
2. D
3. A
4. B
5. D
6. A
7. D

Chapter 3

Clinical and Social Perspectives on Pharmacy Services

Anna Birna Almarsdóttir[1], Anne Gerd Granas[2] and Anna Bryndis Blondal[3]

[1]University of Copenhagen, Copenhagen, Denmark; [2]University of Oslo, Norway;
[3]University of Iceland, Reykjavik, Iceland

Learning Objectives

Objective 3.1   Position pharmacists in the healthcare system.
Objective 3.2   Describe the patient viewpoints on clinical pharmacy services.
Objective 3.3   Highlight the pharmacist perspective on clinical pharmacy services.
Objective 3.4   Describe the institutional and societal viewpoints on clinical pharmacy services.

OBJECTIVE 3.1. POSITION PHARMACISTS IN THE HEALTHCARE SYSTEM

During the past decades, the practice of pharmacists has lost two of the three main pillars of practice to the pharmaceutical industry: procuring and storing raw materials and producing drugs for each patient. The third pillar, the supply function of drugs, is not a viable lone pillar to build the future of pharmacy. The pharmacy profession, therefore, started the process to widen its scope to clinical pharmacy in the 1970s and to take a more active role in patient care.[1]

There is a difference in terminology across Europe, Great Britain, and North America regarding the concepts pharmacy practice and clinical pharmacy. In Great Britain, university departments that teach and research on pharmacy within healthcare in the broadest sense are often called *Pharmacy Practice*. In North America, Pharmacy Practice is the common name for the departments, but some of it is being renamed as *Pharmacotherapy and Outcomes Science or similar*. Countries in Northern Europe use the term *clinical pharmacy or social pharmacy*. One can, therefore, say that pharmacy practice is a broader concept than clinical pharmacy in that it both focuses on the clinical work of pharmacists with patients and on the social environment in which pharmacists work.

Knowledge of pharmacotherapy on its own is not enough to establish clinical pharmacy within the healthcare system. Understanding the broader field of social pharmacy is necessary for pharmacists to take on the responsibilities of providing patient care and clinical pharmacy services. Authors from Denmark and the United States define social pharmacy as a field dealing with the medical sector from the social scientific and humanistic perspectives.[2]

Topics relevant to social pharmacy consist of all the social factors that influence drug use, such as drug- and health-related beliefs, attitudes, rules, relationships, and processes.[2]

The terms used to define social pharmacy vary between countries. The United Kingdom tends to include the clinical pharmacy, pharmaceutical policy, and social pharmacy within the term *pharmacy practice*. In the United States pharmacoepidemiology, pharmacoeconomics, and pharmaceutical policy—all considered as parts of social pharmacy in Europe—are seen as separate fields from pharmacy practice and clinical pharmacy.[3] The knowledge from social pharmacy about the function that various stakeholders have in the healthcare system, and knowledge of pharmacoepidemiology, pharmacoeconomics, and pharmaceutical policy, is needed for pharmacists to establish themselves as distinct clinical practitioners.

Clinical pharmacy deals with caring for patients' pharmacotherapy and with rational drug use. Clinical pharmacy has been defined in various ways by professional organizations and academics across the world. The most used definitions are by the European Society of Clinical Pharmacy[4] and the American College of Clinical Pharmacy[5] (see Table 3.1).

When comparing these definitions, they overlap on three important issues.

Firstly, the focus of clinical pharmacy is on the pharmacist's role in patient care. Pharmacists' patient care services are expanding with prescribing and immunization services.

Secondly, clinical pharmacy has a focus on ensuring the rational and appropriate use of drugs. The World Health Organization defines the rational drugs use as follows:

> *The rational use of drugs requires that patients receive medications appropriate to their clinical needs, in doses that meet their requirements, for an adequate period and at the lowest cost to them and their community.*[6]

Thirdly, clinical pharmacy can be practiced in a wide variety of settings at different levels of care. Approaches of pharmacists to provide clinical services vary from setting to setting. In a tertiary level, care facility pharmacists could provide full-time clinical pharmacy service at the bedside. Advanced level of patient care services is provided by clinical pharmacists in collaboration with other healthcare professionals. These pharmacists are called clinical pharmacists as they are mainly providing direct patient care services. A community pharmacist spends the vast majority of their time on drug supply and other pharmacy management responsibilities. It does, however, not exclude provision of clinical services. All the cognitive services provided by a community pharmacist are clinical when they involve in direct patient care.

Community pharmacies and other primary care services are often the first point of call for both chronically ill patients and those seeking advice for the first time. Initiatives have been taken to involve pharmacists more actively in patient care away from the dispensing counter in pharmacies. An example is home care services offered by the Australian Home Medication Review service, where pharmacists make domiciliary visits to chronically ill patients and provide pharmaceutical care.[7]

In addition, the pharmacists should engage in research to generate new knowledge on how clinical pharmacy services advance human health and improve quality of life. It is important that pharmacists do research on the implementation and explore the impact of their services. Pharmacists provide clinical services to achieve definite health outcomes. They are well positioned in the society to cater to healthcare needs of patients and other consumers of healthcare.

TABLE 3.1 Definitions of Clinical Pharmacy

European Society of Clinical Pharmacy (ESCP)

Clinical Pharmacy is a health specialty, which describes the activities and services of the clinical pharmacist to develop and promote the rational and appropriate use of medicinal products and devices.

Clinical Pharmacy includes all the services performed by pharmacists practicing in hospitals, community pharmacies, nursing homes, home-based care services, clinics and any other setting where medicines are prescribed and used.

The term "clinical" does not necessarily imply an activity implemented in a hospital setting. It describes that the type of activity is *related to the health of the patient(s)*. This implies that community pharmacists and hospital pharmacists both can perform clinical pharmacy activities.[4]

The American College of Clinical Pharmacy (AACP)—Abridged Definition

Clinical Pharmacy is that area of pharmacy concerned with the science and practice of rational medication use.[5]

The American College of Clinical Pharmacy (AACP)—Unabridged Definition

Clinical Pharmacy is a health science discipline in which pharmacists provide patient care that optimizes medication therapy and promotes health, wellness, and disease prevention. The practice of clinical pharmacy embraces the philosophy of pharmaceutical care; it blends a caring orientation with specialized therapeutic knowledge, experience, and judgment for the purpose of ensuring optimal patient outcomes. As a discipline, clinical pharmacy also has an obligation to contribute to the generation of new knowledge that advances health and quality of life.

Clinical pharmacists care for patients in all healthcare settings. They possess in-depth knowledge of medications that is integrated with a foundational understanding of the biomedical, pharmaceutical, sociobehavioral, and clinical sciences. To achieve desired therapeutic goals, the clinical pharmacist applies evidence-based therapeutic guidelines, evolving sciences, emerging technologies, and relevant legal, ethical, social, cultural, economic and professional principles. Accordingly, clinical pharmacists assume responsibility and accountability for managing medication therapy in direct patient-care settings, whether practicing independently or in consultation/collaboration with other healthcare professionals. Clinical pharmacist researchers generate, disseminate, and apply new knowledge that contributes to improved health and quality of life.

Within the system of healthcare, clinical pharmacists are experts in the therapeutic use of medications. They routinely provide medication therapy evaluations and recommendations to patients and healthcare professionals. Clinical pharmacists are a primary source of scientifically valid information and advice regarding the safe, appropriate, and cost-effective use of medications.[5]

OBJECTIVE 3.2. DESCRIBE THE PATIENT VIEWPOINTS ON CLINICAL PHARMACY SERVICES

Clinical pharmacy emerged based on the need to improve pharmacotherapy of patients to maximize the health outcomes and to minimize the costs and risks associated with the irrational use of drugs. Pharmacists can take on a significant role in improving drug use and lowering the risk to patients.

Two challenges are important for pharmacists to consider. The first is that a high proportion of patients use many drugs concomitantly, some of them being unnecessary—also called polypharmacy. Another important challenge is that patients have their rationales and perceptions of drugs' use, which affects adherence, and therefore need to be understood and taken into account when providing drug information or counseling.

Polypharmacy and Inappropriate Drug Use

Treatment with drugs has many positive effects on the health and quality of life at all ages by preventing and treating various diseases. The health gains with drugs should, however, be greater than the troublesome side effects and other unwanted effects. Inappropriate prescribing occurs when potential risks are greater than the benefits of drug treatment. The concomitant use of many drugs is called *polypharmacy*—defined by different authors as taking a minimum of 4—10 drugs at the same time.[8] The number of drugs as such has no direct connection with neither pharmacodynamic or pharmacokinetic challenges, nor does it mean that some of the drugs are unnecessary. It is, however, proven that the number of drugs increases the risk for drug therapy problems, such as drug—drug interactions, side effects, inappropriate medications, or inappropriate dosages. It is also well known that old age affects the pharmacokinetics and efficacy of drugs because of physiological decline.[9]

A linear relationship exists between the number of drugs taken and the risk of having an adverse drug reaction (ADR), where each additional drug increases the risk of ADRs by 8.6% as per a study.[10] *Deprescribing* is defined as "the process of withdrawal of an inappropriate medication, supervised by a healthcare professional with the goal of managing polypharmacy and improving outcomes."[11] Scott et al. define deprescribing as "the systematic process of identifying and discontinuing drugs in instances in which existing or potential harms outweigh existing or potential benefits within the context of an individual patient's care goals, current level of functioning, life expectancy, values, and preferences."[12] Research has shown that doctors are reluctant to deprescribe drugs because of various reasons,[13] and here pharmacists are needed to support these efforts.

Rational use of drugs is at large about patients taking drugs appropriately to treat their clinical needs, in appropriate dosages. A related concept is the Goldilocks Principle, which means that the patient gets the right number of drugs—neither too much nor too little—just the right number and dose to treat the diseases.

The problems associated with polypharmacy and inappropriate drug use are not easy to solve. A systematic review and metaanalysis of whether pharmacist-led medication review can help to reduce hospital admissions and deaths in older people was in fact inconclusive. Pharmacist-led medication review suggested that interventions could improve knowledge and adherence and, in some studies, reduce the number of prescribed drugs, but had little, if any, effect on reducing mortality or hospital admission in older people.[14] The role of pharmacists in deprescribing should be reducing the number of (potentially) inappropriate medications and minimizing risks and maximizing outcomes of drug use.[15]

Nonadherence to Pharmacotherapy—The Patients' Perspective on Taking Drugs

The term adherence to medication is defined as "the process by which patients take their medications as prescribed."[16] Giving patients clear and concise instructions on how to take their drugs is no guarantee for that they will take it as instructed. In fact, roughly half of medications prescribed for long-term conditions are not taken appropriately by the patients. As a result, neither the patient nor the society has optimal outcomes from the drugs.[17,18]

Most would agree that our attitudes or understanding of any given subject affects our behavior. To explain nonadherence, one must take into account that all patients have their rationales and perception of drugs.[19] For pharmacists and other health personnel, it is important to develop an understanding of how patients' perspective on taking drugs directly or indirectly affects adherence. There is no single "solution" to rectify nonadherence, be it intentional or unintentional from the patients' perspective. Horne and Weinman[20] made a model on the beliefs about drugs, which has been used by many to study how patients are taking drugs. On one hand, patients have *necessity beliefs* on why they need to take drugs. On the other hand, patients have *concerns* about a range of potential adverse events from drug treatment. This balance, depending on whether concerns are stronger than the necessity or vice versa, directly affects adherence to drugs. So why do patients take less medicines and dosages than prescribed?

Intentional nonadherence occurs when patients make an active decision not to follow the instructions for a particular treatment. This behavior is best understood by patients' beliefs about drugs and the preferences people have for one kind of drug or treatment option compared with another. Intentional nonadherence is also influenced by previous experiences with a drug or disease, and this directly influences their motivation to start, carry on, or stop taking a drug.

Unintentional nonadherence, on the other hand, occurs for instance when patients have a desire to adhere to the treatment but are unable to do so. Unintentional nonadherence is often related to practical aspects of taking medicines: the information on how to take the drug is not understood, patients find it difficult to remember to take it, or it is difficult to administer.

A range of other factors additionally affect adherence. These are, for instance, the socioeconomic group one belongs to, cultural perceptions of illness and health, availability to healthcare services, or the disease itself. Pharmacists and other health personnel must tailor drug information and guidance on how to take drugs. They should openly discuss patients' intention to adhere to treatment. Research supports patient-centeredness in clinical decisions to improve adherence. Patients should be involved in the choice of drugs to clarify their responsibility and awareness of effects and side effects. For further reference, the NICE Medicines Adherence Guideline provides an overview of interventions to enhance adherence and insight into studies of patients' nonadherence.[17]

OBJECTIVE 3.3. HIGHLIGHT THE PHARMACIST PERSPECTIVE ON CLINICAL PHARMACY SERVICES

Pharmaceutical Care—A Central Concept in Patient Care

Pharmaceutical care as a concept has moved the pharmacy profession from primarily focusing on the product (the drug itself) to the patient's drug therapy and how it should be optimized for the individual patient.

The original definition of the concept of pharmaceutical care was published by Hepler and Strand in 1990 as follows "Pharmaceutical care is the responsible provision of drug therapy for the purpose of achieving definite outcomes that improve a patient's quality of life."[21] However, new definitions have emerged. The definition from a group in Minnesota, USA, which has been the most instrumental originally dating from 1998, is patient-centered and underlines that the practitioner (usually a pharmacist) is responsible for the patient's drug therapy:

> *Pharmaceutical care is a practice in which the practitioner takes responsibility for a patient's drug-related needs, and is held accountable for this commitment. In the course of this practice, responsible drug therapy is provided for the purpose of achieving positive patient outcomes.[22]*

A more recent definition by the Pharmaceutical Care Network Europe (PCNE), specifying pharmaceutical care as a service provided by pharmacists, states that:

> *Pharmaceutical Care is the pharmacist's contribution to the care of individuals in order to optimize medicines use and improve health outcomes.[23]*

According to Cipolle et al., the philosophy of pharmaceutical care practice consists of four elements. First, the social need to reduce drug-related morbidity and mortality associated with medication use. Second, the social need is met by the practitioners' responsibility to identify, resolve, and prevent drug therapy problems. Third, this service is provided in a patient-centered context, which means that the practitioner is working for the patient directly. The last part is caring, which means that the practitioner takes the time to assess, make a care plan, and follow up on the patient.[24]

In the United Kingdom or the United States, pharmacists often refer to providing *medication management* when optimizing patients' medication therapy[25] and not to the concept of *pharmaceutical care*. Interestingly, the new concept of Pharmacists' patient care process[26] has been introduced in the United States, which represents the care process delivered by pharmacists. It was developed by examining some key source documents on pharmaceutical care and medication therapy management.

Medication Reviews and Drug Therapy Problems

According to PCNE, a medication review is "a structured evaluation of patient's medication with the aim of optimizing drugs use and improving health outcomes. It entails detecting drug-related problems and recommending interventions."[27] Medication reviews require knowledge of pharmacotherapy and an ability to apply this knowledge to the individual patient. It is widely accepted that there are different levels of medication review depending on which information sources are available and whether the patient is involved in the review process.[28,29] The levels of a medication review range from addressing technical issues based merely on prescription information to the advanced level of medication reviews. In medication reviews, details of the drug and the clinical conditions are discussed with the patient and a multiprofessional team.[28,29]

However, deep knowledge and skills in pharmacotherapy are not enough for a pharmacist to tackle the problems of inappropriate drug use. As Strand and Cipolle stated back in 1989:

Pharmacists must define their professional function from the perspective of the whole patient, the biopsychosocial sense, and not primarily from that of the pharmaceutical agent (e.g., gentamicin, theophylline) or the technical instrument employed (e.g., pharmacokinetic dosing, cholesterol measurement, blood pressure monitoring, nutritional protocol development).[30]

The ability to work in multidisciplinary teams is also important for pharmacists to bring their knowledge and skills to bear on the patients' drug therapy and ultimately impact their quality of life.[31]

Cognitive Pharmaceutical Services

Pharmacist cognitive services are a range of healthcare-related activities provided by the pharmacist in all settings of care. Cognitive pharmaceutical services are strategies and actions to improve the patients' drug therapy by using pharmacists to the fullest extent of their training and education as medication experts.[32] Cognitive pharmaceutical services have been defined as follows:

Professional services provided by pharmacists, who use their skills and knowledge to take an active role in patient health, through effective interaction with both patients and other health professionals.[33]

Examples of pharmacist cognitive services are within the realm of healthcare promotion, disease management and prevention, and services regarding drug therapy issues such as medication review. Fig. 3.1 shows how wide-ranging pharmacist cognitive services can be, but they can be roughly divided into activities related to health promotion, preventive and disease management, drug therapy issues, and prescribing.

Sometimes all pharmacists' services beyond dispensing drugs, have been referred to as pharmaceutical care service.[32,38] As seen in Fig. 3.1, pharmaceutical care is listed as one type of cognitive service. There are many types of services listed under the heading of Drug Therapy Issues in Fig. 3.1 that are related to and sometimes the components of pharmaceutical care, such as medication review, changing drugs/dosages, and patient education and monitoring. Many of these services can be provided in conjunction with dispensing in community pharmacies and then add a clinical dimension to the work of the pharmacist. However, pharmaceutical care is defined by Cipolle et al. as larger than all the other cognitive services because it states that the pharmacist takes the time to assess, make a care plan, and follow up on the patient. This service is, therefore, less suited in conjunction with dispensing because it encompasses reviewing and evaluating the patient's medications in a dialog with the patient and through this taking responsibility for the patient's whole medication therapy being appropriate, safe, and effective.

OBJECTIVE 3.4. DESCRIBE THE INSTITUTIONAL AND SOCIETAL VIEWPOINTS ON CLINICAL PHARMACY SERVICES

Clinical pharmacy services are often thought of as those where the pharmacist discusses medication therapy with the patient and other healthcare professionals. However, pharmacists also give structural support to health personnel. In hospitals they for example run drug information centers that primarily assist nurses and doctors with medication-related queries. Pharmacists also contribute to drug formularies in hospitals, with immense economic implications for the organization. Here the pharmacists contribute to rational drug prescribing and cost containment with implications to the institution and more broadly to the society.

There are evident challenges in society regarding the use of drugs, some of which will be highlighted here. Large proportions (1.4% in the OECD countries) of country's gross domestic product are spent on healthcare, and for most countries, medication expenditures constitute about one-fifth of total healthcare spending in OECD countries.[39] Taking drugs also involves risk of side effects and drug-related morbidity and mortality. In addition to incurring pain and loss, these risks have also been quantified into economic costs. As an example, it was found that in Germany the costs of drug-related morbidity could be as high as 816 million Euros in 2007.[40] Governments seek to contain these costs through a variety of measures.

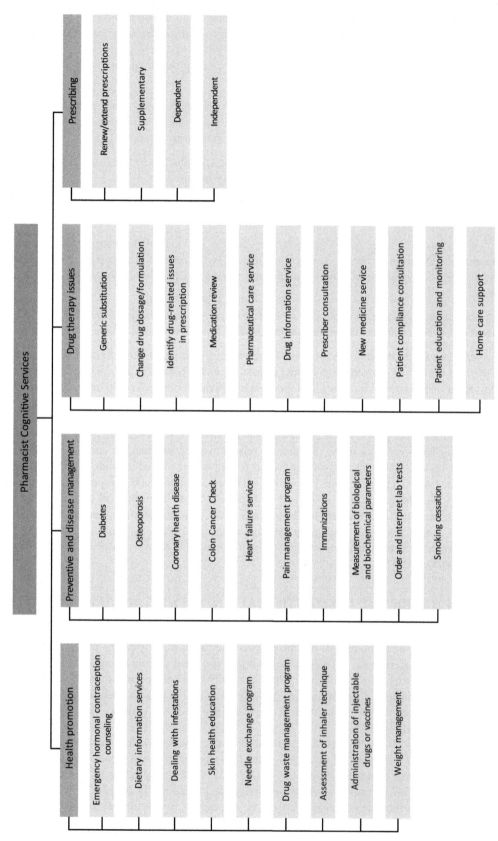

FIGURE 3.1   Examples of pharmacist cognitive services compiled from the cited articles.[34–37]

Barriers and Facilitators for Implementing Clinical Pharmacy Services

Providing additional clinical pharmacy services such as medication review and detailed counseling is not common within community pharmacies[36,38] or primary care.[37] It has been shown to be difficult to implement pharmacist services in community pharmacies beyond dispensing, probably because managing a pharmacy and dispensing drugs is a full-time job in its own right. Providing additional cognitive services needs more staff with limited or no dispensing roles. Pharmacies ought to have separate consulting rooms dedicated to the more intimate patient assessments such as to diagnose minor ailments, counseling sessions, address nonadherence behavior, or to administer vaccines, etc. Many pharmacies offer services such as monitoring body mass index, blood pressure, blood sugar, etc. Although barriers to new pharmacy services differ across countries,[41] they can be categorized into three domains: resources, attitude and opinion, and lack of education and skills.[42–44] It is likely that community pharmacies in different countries will differ even more in the years to come, depending on strategies chosen on which roles pharmacists should have in the healthcare system.

Clinical pharmacy services have been making inroads into practice in hospitals where pharmacists often provide cognitive services such as pharmaceutical care directly to patients. Hospital pharmacists still meet barriers limiting direct patient care in hospitals.

A pharmacist needs to have good rapport and connections with doctors (GPs and other medical specialists) and other healthcare personnel to provide pharmaceutical care.[24] Clinical pharmacy service often involves collaborative practice with doctors, especially for prescription drugs.[45] A model by McDonough and Doucette[46] describes the collaboration stages between doctors and pharmacists for successful collaboration, ranging from "Professional awareness" to "Commitment to the Collaborative Working Relationship." Although the collaborative practice has its advantages, pharmaceutical care could also be given by pharmacists without consulting other healthcare professionals as allowed by law in many countries. Changes in pharmacy education in some countries (e.g., the United States) are making pharmacists highly competent in the patient care process.[26,47] However, in some countries—such as the Nordic countries—the development has been much slower within academic institutions training pharmacists, and there exists a large gap between the visions for patient-centered care and a reality where pharmacy has a traditional focus on dispensing drug products.[48,49]

The American Pharmaceutical Association has set out prerequisites for introducing pharmaceutical care. They include an emphasis on establishing and maintaining a professional relationship; keeping patient-specific medical information; evaluating patient-specific medical information and developing a drug therapy plan with the patient; assuring that the patient has all information and knowledge necessary to carry out the drug therapy plan; and reviewing, monitoring, and modifying the therapeutic plan as necessary and appropriate, in concert with the patient and healthcare team.[50]

Reaching clinical consensus on pharmacotherapy and drug therapy changes is challenging. As per an article, the acceptance rate of pharmacists' interventions by other healthcare professionals ranges from 17% to 86% depending on the study design and care settings.[51] For pharmacists to increase the acceptance from doctors, they as professionals have to fulfill as many as possible of the following criteria. They need to

- have sufficient clinical experience,
- have evidence-based practice,
- have close and established collaboration with the doctor,
- have access to the patient's medical records,
- have access to quality drug information resources,
- be able to interview patients, and
- have patients referred for counseling with the pharmacist.

When doctor's involvement is needed, there should be a face-to-face communication between the doctor and the pharmacist about the drug therapy problems and possible solutions, and the pharmacists should be able to give clear suggestions for actions to be taken, and follow-up systems must be in place.

There are other societal pressures such as hospital accreditation, increased patient safety requirements, and demands of professional agencies and patient right movements for more rational use of drugs. These pressures may, in fact, support the establishment and growth of pharmaceutical care service. At the same time, these factors increase the demands on pharmacists to provide higher quality clinical services. As pharmacists become more accepted as an important profession in patient care, they are expected to meet quality standards and take responsibility for the care provided.

UNDERSTANDING THE ENVIRONMENT AND STRUCTURE OF HEALTHCARE

A pharmacist can either work independently with patients and other professionals or work in multiprofessional team caring for patients. It is paramount that the pharmacist understands how other professions define their role in patient care and where the roles with the pharmacist may overlap. Social pharmacy as an academic discipline can complement the clinical pharmacy discipline and vice versa.

One example: Clinical pharmacists have in some countries expanded their role as independent prescribers. But can pharmacists be trusted as independent prescribers? If the same professional diagnoses the disease and dispenses the drugs, chances are higher for financial bias. This fact triggered the split between the pharmacy profession and the medical profession in the middle ages. A review of the physicians' prescription by an independent pharmacist reassures the patient that the therapy is appropriate, and that the person prescribing the drug is not a financial beneficiary of the sale.

Another example: The pharmacist cannot assume that the other professions or patients know what pharmacist can add to the other profession's expertise. To succeed in interprofessional healthcare teams, pharmacists must be complementary, rather than replacing the needed services of other healthcare professions.[52]

Pharmacists need to better understand the system they work within and how to interact with the system—a field mostly researched in social pharmacy. Clinical pharmacists must work interprofessionally to improve rational drug use and patient safety. They must, however, strengthen their understanding of the environment and structure of healthcare to succeed in an extended role in patient care.

CONCLUSION

Pharmacy practice is a broader concept than clinical pharmacy in that it focuses both on the clinical work of pharmacists with patients and on the social environment within which pharmacists work. Globally, pharmacists increasingly provide more clinical patient-centered services, either in the community pharmacies or other healthcare institutions. Pharmacists are increasingly spending more time in direct patient care or for its preparation. It is important for pharmacists to have a common understanding of pharmaceutical care, and that they expand their role to include research on future clinical pharmacy services with high social and economic impacts. Recognition of pharmacists as a healthcare professional needs strategic approaches. Pharmacists need to engage with the health organizations, other healthcare professions and the patients with more clinical approaches. Social pharmacy provides this helicopter perspective on the healthcare sector and provides a deeper insight into how the actors in the sector think and act.

PRACTICE QUESTIONS

The following are exercises that help to reflect on clinical pharmacy:

1. Ask three clinical pharmacists these questions:
   A. What their job setting is and what their job contains?
   B. Which strategies, if any, they use to introduce a new service or new way of working within their job setting?
2. What do your closest family or friends worry the most about when they:
   A. Start to take a new medicine?
   B. Have to take medicines long term?

REFERENCES

1. Brodie DC, Parish PA, Poston JW. Societal needs for drugs and drug-related services. *Am J Pharm Educ*. 1980;44(3):276−278.
2. Sørensen EW, Mount JK, Christensen ST. The concept of social pharmacy. 2003;(7):8−11. http://www.mcppnet.org/publications/issue07-3.pdf.
3. Almarsdottir AB, Kaae S, Traulsen JM. Opportunities and challenges in social pharmacy and pharmacy practice research. *Res Social Adm Pharm*. 2014;10(1):252−255.
4. European Society of Clinical Pharmacy. *What Is Clinical Pharmacy?*; 2017. http://www.escpweb.org/content/escp-mission-vision.
5. American College of Clinical Pharmacy. *Clinical Pharmacy Defined*; 2017. https://www.accp.com/about/clinicalPharmacyDefined.aspx.
6. World Health Organization. *How to Develop and Implement a National Drug Policy*. 2nd ed. Geneva: World Health Organization; 2001.
7. Chen TF. Pharmacist-led home medicines review and residential medication management review: the Australian model. *Drugs Aging*. 2016;33(3):199−204.
8. Jokanovic N, Tan EC, Dooley MJ, Kirkpatrick CM, Bell JS. Prevalence and factors associated with polypharmacy in long-term care facilities: a systematic review. *J Am Med Dir Assoc*. 2015;16(6), 535.e531−512.
9. Turnheim K. Drug therapy in the elderly. *Exp Gerontol*. 2004;39(11−12):1731−1738.

10. Viktil KK, Blix HS, Moger TA, Reikvam A. Polypharmacy as commonly defined is an indicator of limited value in the assessment of drug-related problems. *Br J Clin Pharmacol*. 2007;63(2):187—195.

11. Reeve E, Gnjidic D, Long J, Hilmer S. A systematic review of the emerging de fi nition of 'deprescribing' with network analysis: implications for future research and clinical practice. *Br J Clin Pharmacol*. 2015;80(6):1254—1268.

12. Scott IA, Hilmer SN, Reeve E, et al. Reducing inappropriate polypharmacy: the process of deprescribing. *JAMA Intern Med*. 2015;175(5):827—834.

13. Nixon M, Kousgaard MB. Organising medication discontinuation: a qualitative study exploring the views of general practitioners toward discontinuing statins. *BMC Health Serv Res*. 2016;16:226.

14. Holland R, Desborough J, Goodyer L, Hall S, Wright D, Loke YK. Does pharmacist-led medication review help to reduce hospital admissions and deaths in older people? A systematic review and meta-analysis. *Br J Clin Pharmacol*. 2008;65(3):303—316.

15. Granas AG, Stendal Bakken M, Ruths S, Taxis K. Deprescribing for frail older people - learning from the case of Mrs. *Hansen Res Social Adm Pharm*. 2017:1—5.

16. Vrijens B. An introduction to adherence research. In: *Drug Utilization Research: Methods and Applications*. Chichester Wiley-Blackwell; 2016:355—360.

17. National Institute for Health and Care Excellence. *Medicines Adherence: Involving Patients in Decisions about Prescribed Medicines and Supporting Adherence*; 2009. https://www.nice.org.uk/guidance/cg76/resources/medicines-adherence-involving-patients-in-decisions-about-prescribed-medicines-and-supporting-adherence-pdf-975631782085.

18. World Health Organization. Adherence to long-term therapies. In: *Evidence for Action*. Geneve: World Health Organization; 2003.

19. Granas AG, Bates I. Patients' understanding and management of their illnesses and prescribed medicines - a descriptive study. *Pharm World Sci*. 2005;27(4):321—328.

20. Horne R, Weinman J. Patients' beliefs about prescribed medicines and their role in adherence to treatment in chronic physical illness. *J Psychosom Res*. 1999;47(6):555—567.

21. Hepler CD, Strand LM. Opportunities and responsibilities in pharmaceutical care. *Am J Hosp Pharm*. 1990;47(3):533—543.

22. Cipolle RJ, Strand L, Morley P. *Pharmaceutical Care Practice*. New York: McGraw-Hill; 1998.

23. Allemann SS, van Mil JW, Botermann L, Berger K, Griese N, Hersberger KE. Pharmaceutical care: the PCNE definition 2013. *Int J Clin Pharm*. 2014;36(3):544—555.

24. Cipolle RJ, Strand L, Morley P. *Pharmaceutical Care Practice: The Patient-Centered Approach to Medication Management Services*. Vol. 3. New York: McGraw-Hill; 2012.

25. Barber N. Pharmaceutical care and medicines management—is there a difference? *Pharm World Sci*. 2001;23(6):210—211.

26. Joint Commission of Pharmacy Practitioners. *Pharmacists' Patient Care Process*; 2014. https://jcpp.net/wp-content/uploads/2016/03/PatientCareProcess-with-supporting-organizations.pdf.

27. Pharmaceutical Care Network Europe. *Medication Review Definition Approved - Pharmaceutical Care Network Europe*; 2017. http://www.pcne.org/news/35/medication-review-definition-approved.

28. Clyne W, Blenkinsopp A, Seal R. In: *A Guide to Medication Review*. National Prescribing Centre (NPC); 2008. http://www.sefap.org/media/upload/arxius/formacion/aula_fap_2010/bibliografia/guide_medication_review_2008.pdf.

29. Pharmaceutical Care Network Europe. *What Activities Are Part of the Different PCNE Types of Medication Review*; 2013. http://www.pcne.org/upload/wc2013/Workshops/WS%201%20PCNE%20Types%20and%20Activities.pdf.

30. Morley P, Strand L. Critical reflections on therapeutic drug monitoring. *J Pharm Pract*. 1989;2(6):327—334.

31. Halvorsen KH, Ruths S, Granas AG, Viktil KK. Multidisciplinary intervention to identify and resolve drug-related problems in Norwegian nursing homes. *Scand J Prim Health Care*. 2010;28(2):82—88.

32. Moullin JC, Sabater-Hernandez D, Fernandez-Llimos F, Benrimoj SI. Defining professional pharmacy services in community pharmacy. *Res Social Adm Pharm*. 2013;9(6):989—995.

33. Roberts AS, Benrimoj SI, Chen TF, Williams KA, Aslani P. Implementing cognitive services in community pharmacy: a review of facilitators used in practice change. *Int J Pharm Pract*. 2006;14(3):163—170.

34. Basak SC. *Pharmaceutical Cognitive Services in Community Pharmacy*; 2013. http://www.pharmabiz.com/NewsDetails.aspx?aid=74495&sid=9.

35. Bulajeva A, Labberton L, Leikola S, et al. Medication review practices in European countries. *Res Social Adm Pharm*. 2014;10(5):731—740.

36. Martins SF, van Mil JW, da Costa FA. The organizational framework of community pharmacies in Europe. *Int J Clin Pharm*. 2015;37(5):896—905.

37. Tan EC, Stewart K, Elliott RA, George J. Pharmacist services provided in general practice clinics: a systematic review and meta-analysis. *Res Social Adm Pharm*. 2014;10(4):608—622.

38. Costa FA, Scullin C, Al-Taani G, et al. Provision of pharmaceutical care by community pharmacists across Europe: is it developing and spreading? *J Eval Clin Pract*. 2017;23(6):1336—1347.

39. OECD. *Health at a Glance 2015*; 2015. http://www.oecd-ilibrary.org/social-issues-migration-health/health-at-a-glance-2015_health_glance-2015-en.

40. Stark RG, John J, Leidl R. Health care use and costs of adverse drug events emerging from outpatient treatment in Germany: a modelling approach. *BMC Health Serv Res*. 2011;11:9.

41. Farris KB, Fernandez-Llimos F, Benrimoj SI. Pharmaceutical care in community pharmacies: practice and research from around the world. *Ann Pharmacother*. 2005;39(9):1539—1541.

42. Aburuz S, Al-Ghazawi M, Snyder A. Pharmaceutical care in a community-based practice setting in Jordan: where are we now with our attitudes and perceived barriers? *Int J Pharm Pract*. 2012;20(2):71—79.

43. Blake KB, Madhavan SS. Perceived barriers to provision of medication therapy management services (MTMS) and the likelihood of a pharmacist to work in a pharmacy that provides MTMS. *Ann Pharmacother.* 2010;44(3):424–431.

44. Mehralian G, Rangchian M, Javadi A, Peiravian F. Investigation on barriers to pharmaceutical care in community pharmacies: a structural equation model. *Int J Clin Pharm.* 2014;36(5):1087–1094.

45. Bradley F, Elvey R, Ashcroft DM, et al. The challenge of integrating community pharmacists into the primary health care team: a case study of local pharmaceutical services (LPS) pilots and interprofessional collaboration. *J Interprof Care.* 2008;22(4):387–398.

46. McDonough RP, Doucette W. Developing collaborative working relationships between pharmacists and physicians. 2001;41(5):682–692.

47. Medina MS, Plaza CM, Stowe CD, et al. Center for the advancement of pharmacy education 2013 educational outcomes. *Am J Pharm Educ.* 2013;77(8):162.

48. Svensberg K, Bjornsdottir I, Wallman A, Sporrong SK. Nordic pharmacy schools' experience in communication skills training. *Am J Pharm Educ.* 2017;81(9):6005.

49. Svensberg K, Kalvemark Sporrong S, Hakonsen H, Toverud EL. 'Because of the circumstances, we cannot develop our role': Norwegian community pharmacists' perceived responsibility in role development. *Int J Pharm Pract.* 2014.

50. American Pharmacists Association. *Principles of Practice for Pharmaceutical Care*; 2012. https://www.pharmacist.com/principles-practice-pharmaceutical-care.

51. Kwint HF, Bermingham L, Faber A, Gussekloo J, Bouvy ML. The relationship between the extent of collaboration of general practitioners and pharmacists and the implementation of recommendations arising from medication review: a systematic review. *Drugs Aging.* 2013;30(2):91–102.

52. Almarsdottir AB, Granas AG. Social pharmacy and clinical pharmacy-joining forces. *Pharm (Basel, Switz).* 2015;4(1).

Chapter 4

Pharmacy Management

Johann Kruger[1,2], Raj Vaidya[3] and Erick Sokn[4]

[1]University of Pretoria, Pretoria, South Africa; [2]EDNA Medical Distributors, Pretoria, South Africa; [3]Hindu Pharmacy, Goa, India; [4]Cleveland Clinic, Cleveland, OH, United States

Learning Objectives

Objective 4.1 Outline the major principles in managing a pharmacy.
Objective 4.2 Overview the purchase, inventory control, storage, drug distribution, compounding, and disposal of drugs and related products.
Objective 4.3 Illustrate a model pharmacy and detail the facilities required.
Objective 4.4 Overview pharmacy practice setting and responsibilities of professionals.
Objective 4.5 Explain advantages and limitations of pharmacy automation.

OBJECTIVE 4.1. OUTLINE THE MAJOR PRINCIPLES IN MANAGING A PHARMACY

The effective management of a pharmacy requires much more than what is normally seen as the task a pharmacist performs, namely dispensing drugs and consulting patients or providers. It requires skills to effectively manage personnel, inventory, and various licensing formalities including documentation, finances, and facilities. Pharmacists are required to know how to manage stock levels, make provisions for alternatives, know how to budget and manage the finances of a pharmacy, and, above all, ensure patient safety and drug optimization.[1]

It is well known that healthcare costs are a significant and rising expense for countries throughout the world. In the United States, costs of care are particularly worrisome, as some predict healthcare spending will account for 19.7% of the economy by 2026.[2] The same authors estimate that medications will account for nearly 11% of healthcare spending by 2026,[2] reinforcing the need for the cost-effective use of medications. For many health systems, pharmacy departments are being asked to evaluate and address rising healthcare costs through the judicious use of medications.[3] To be effective in this environment, pharmacy leaders must have a firm understanding of basic management principles and must develop and implement pharmacy services with highly trained personnel to help improve affordability and quality.

The major principles in managing a pharmacy are financial management, personnel management, and regulatory compliance.

Financial Management

Besides being a patient care location, pharmacies are also businesses and need to manage financial resources effectively. Financial management for a given period at its most basic consists of balancing revenue against costs by developing and implementing a budget or financial plan. Sustainable pharmacies must take in at least as much money as they spend. In some countries, hospitals are state-run, and revenue-generating business practices may not apply. Instead, hospital pharmacies often resemble cost centers and as such need to apply business principles to utilize resources such as drugs, staff, and utilities efficiently and within budget restrictions.

Costs for pharmacy managers come from many sources (Table 4.1). Some of these costs (such as utilities) are budgeted separately in hospitals and retail pharmacy stores, and the pharmacy manager may not have specific budgets to consider for lighting and temperature. The pharmacy manager, however, is responsible for drug costs, personnel, and revenue cycle management. Drug costs represent the highest budgeted expense for a pharmacy of all potential categories. Managing drug inventory has a significant impact on how effectively one manages drug costs and is discussed below.

Clinical Pharmacy Education, Practice and Research. https://doi.org/10.1016/B978-0-12-814276-9.00004-0

TABLE 4.1 Common Costs for Pharmacies

Medication costs	• Cost to purchase medications from manufacturers or wholesalers
Personnel costs	• Salary • Benefits (health insurance, life insurance, dental/vision insurance, vacation time, disability, protected medical or family leave, etc.)
Automation/technology	• Purchase and maintenance fees for computers, automated dispensing cabinets, dispensing carousels, intravenous admixture robotics, medication repackaging machines, pill counters
Utilities/infrastructure	• Lighting • Heat/air conditioning • Water/sewer • Rent • Telephone/Internet
Regulatory	• Licensing and accreditation fees • Liability insurance for employees
Supplies	• Medication labels • Pill bottles/caps • Bags • Pens/paper • Desks/chairs • Syringes/needles • Scales • Compounding supplies

Other sources of expense for a pharmacy include various automation and technology expenses. Today, the use of electronic health records, computerized dispensing software, and vast amounts of medical data and references has rendered Internet and computer resources a necessity for effective and efficient practice. In some hospitals, the use of technology is so pervasive that pharmacists are provided individual laptops or mobile workstations to be more effective while rounding through patient care areas. Additionally, pharmacists in larger hospitals are often provided some type of paging device or telephone at which they could be easily reached for urgent communications. Each of these resources has an initial purchasing price and in many cases a monthly fee, either for maintenance or continued access and use of the system.

On a larger scale, dispensing automation represents a significant expense for some pharmacies. With purchase prices ranging from thousands to hundreds of thousands of dollars, automation ranging from pill counters to sterile compounding robots to automated dispensing cabinets to medication storage carousels requires significant planning and preparation to yield benefit. In most cases, the technology is justified financially by improving dispensing accuracy, safety, decreasing the footprint required for medication storage by taking up less total space, meeting regulatory requirements for secure storage of medications, or improving the efficiency of the dispensing process (thereby saving salary cost). A pharmacy manager must carefully assess the medication use process to determine where a piece of automation may provide benefit and assess and manage costs associated with purchase and maintenance of such a device.

Computers and automation or technology are generally simple expenses to plan for—purchase prices are known in advance, and costs do not change based on how much or how little each component is used. Such expenses are considered "fixed." Expenses such as medications and any supplies needed for dispensing (pill bottles, labels, printer ink, bags, etc.) are considered "variable", as the total amount spent by the pharmacy will vary with the number of prescriptions dispensed or medication orders processed. Both types of expenses must be considered by a pharmacy manager when planning annual budgets.

Revenue

Although all pharmacies must address costs, not all pharmacies generate revenue directly. In many outpatient models, pharmacies may charge patients a fee based on the type and quantity of medication being dispensed. This practice varies substantially across the world, with some countries providing medication coverage, whereas others, such as the United States, utilize public and private insurance companies to cover a portion of the expense, with the remainder paid for by the patient. Depending on the practice setting, pharmacy managers may have some ability to set or negotiate pricing with various payers. In private-pay situations, where the patient is responsible for the whole expense, pharmacies have significant flexibility in setting prices. In settings where insurance companies or government payers handle payment, there is generally more limited opportunity for a pharmacy to negotiate prices and less flexibility in adjusting those prices outside of the contract period. For example, in the United States, it is common for a medical insurance company to negotiate reimbursement for pharmacist services. These services include some accounting for the cost of the medication plus a set fee for the time of the pharmacist and support personnel (often called a "dispensing fee"). The collection of these fees, whether negotiated with insurance companies or set independently by the pharmacist, represents the source of revenue for the pharmacy and thus a process that needs scrutiny by the pharmacy manager.

In hospital pharmacies, there is less opportunity to generate revenue. In many countries, including the United States, inpatient pharmacy services are considered a component of the hospital stay and are thus billed and reimbursed as a component of overall care. Using more expensive drugs without achieving better outcomes decreases available funds for the health system. Pharmacy departments are responsible for assuring cost-effective use of medications to maximize the amount of revenue available for use in improving or expanding hospital services. This goal is achieved through the judicious application of pharmacist training and experience to guide prescribing practices toward the most cost-effective therapy.[4] The role of pharmacist position design, recruitment, and management is an important one for the pharmacy manager and is discussed more fully below.

Budgeting

As mentioned previously, a significant role for the pharmacy manager is planning for expenses and revenues to ensure the appropriate financial performance of the pharmacy. Budgeting is the process of planning expenses and revenues for an upcoming period. As many variables impacting pharmacy expenses and revenues change over time, budgeting is often completed annually through a "budget cycle" (Fig. 4.1). The basic components of a budget cycle include planning, review and approval, implementation, and evaluation.

Planning

Budgeting for healthcare services is commonly achieved through an incremental budgeting process, wherein the budget from the prior budget cycle is reviewed and revised to reflect anticipated trends, new services, or other changes. To begin the budgeting cycle, a pharmacy manager reviews the evaluation from the prior budget cycle and considers emerging trends (new medication approvals, new studies influencing use of existing medications, new reimbursement models affecting the pharmacy, new generic medication availability, ending technology service contracts) and service gaps (opportunities to add services [and thereby workload and potentially personnel expense]). Additionally, pharmacy managers must consider whether the volume of existing work might change (either through the emergence of new technology or through increased patient volumes such as the addition of a new wing of a hospital or a new insurer contract with a retail pharmacy system). Once the pharmacy manager has considered emerging trends, he or she must estimate the impact on workload, expense, and revenue and account for these changes in the budget.

FIGURE 4.1 Basic budget cycle.

One challenging opportunity with high potential risk and reward is the addition of pharmacy personnel to begin new service. As described above, the changing landscape of healthcare away from a fee-for-service design to an outcomes-driven reimbursement model opens new doors for pharmacist involvement and ownership of the medication use process, including prescribing of medications. During the budget cycle, a pharmacy manager must assess which new services could be used to achieve improved outcomes and reimbursement for the organization, preparing a business case that outlines the role of such services, the quality impact, and resulting financial impact. These cases are designed to describe the return on investment (ROI) of a pharmacist (for every dollar spent on the pharmacist, how many dollars does the system save or gain over a defined period) (Table 4.2). Once the budget is described and any new services have an accompanying business case, the budget is submitted for review and approval.

Review and Approval

The review and approval process of a pharmacy budget will vary significantly by practice setting. In a large health system, for example, budgets from all disciplines (pharmacy, nursing, physicians, respiratory therapists, etc.) are reviewed alongside one another. The first priority for approval is given to maintaining current services and addressing increased visit volumes by patients. Once this review is completed, the team reviews new business case opportunities (such as those submitted for new pharmacy services). There are two common calculations used to help compare cases: ROI and breakeven. While ROI focuses on the amount of financial gains or savings achieved through the investment, breakeven focuses on how quickly initial start-up costs are recovered through those gains or savings. Business cases with high ROI, fast breakeven, and low overall risk have the strongest chance of approval. Once approved, final budgets are distributed back to the manager for implementation.

TABLE 4.2 Example of a Pharmacy Business Case Template

Example Business Case Template

1. Executive summary
   a. Proposal
   b. Background
   c. Benefits
   d. Financial impact
   e. Conclusion
   f. Return on investment (ROI) table (brief)
2. Background
   a. Description of problem
   b. Evidence of current state
   c. Solutions implemented elsewhere
3. Proposal
   a. Full-time equivalent/resource needs
   b. Benefits
4. Potential impact
   a. Financial impact
   b. Nonquantifiable benefits
5. Alternatives (with financial impact and pros/cons list)—*often removed in final case*
   a. Brief review of other solutions considered and key reasons they are not preferred
6. Implementation plan
   a. Who does what and when
7. Assumptions
   a. Describe trends or values assumed static in benefit/risk calculations
8. Sensitivity analysis—*often removed in the final case or embedded in the description*
   a. Pick assumptions that have the greatest impact on ROI and some risk of variability. Assume worst-case scenario and evaluate benefit/risk in these cases. Alternatively, if worst case is unknown, select values representing minimum necessary for benefits to equal risks and determine the likelihood of worse performance.
9. Risks and mitigation plans
   a. If the significant risk is identified during sensitivity analysis, describe monitoring plan to detect early and steps to take to mitigate risk if detected.
10. Exit Strategy
   a. If risk comes true, how to minimize adverse impact on the organization

Implementation

The manager is responsible for implementing the budget as outlined and assuring appropriate resource management throughout the budget year to stay on target. Budgets represent financial plans for an organization, providing a guidance on decisions impacting financial performance. During implementation, managers can begin to hire employees for newly approved positions, can schedule and complete needed renovations, or purchase and implement new automation or technology.

Evaluation

Budgets represent a plan of action for the pharmacy department, and both overestimation and underestimation of expenses and revenues create lost opportunity. Although one can easily see how spending more than planned is negative (the pharmacy or hospital may or may not have sufficient money on hand to handle significant underestimations of expenses in a budget), overestimating expenses can lead to lost opportunity by tying up funding in planned expenses that never gets spent. In such cases, opportunities to improve facilities or automation and technology or add a new service may be set aside, creating a delay in quality or efficiency advancements. To safeguard against this potential, managers frequently assess variance from the budget and identify causes. For example, a manager may review monthly productivity reports and identify staff is completing far more work than planned, leading to potential overtime expenses and burnout. Identifying the cause (perhaps increased admissions above what had been anticipated) can help identify solutions to head off negative consequences of the budget deviation. Managers often document these deviations in "variance reports," which are used to help explain why or why not a budget was accurate, offering the opportunity to improve accuracy during the next budget cycle.

Personnel Management

Another common source of expense for a pharmacy is staff salaries. Pharmacies may employ a wide array of positions, including pharmacists, pharmacy technicians, clerical staff, administrative support staff, data analysts, and informatics personnel. Salaries may be paid out at a set amount regardless of hour worked (called "salaried" employees) or at a set amount per hour of work (called "hourly" employees).

Management strategies for salaried and hourly employees generally revolve around the principle of a full-time equivalent, or FTE, representing a standard 40-h work week in the United States. Pharmacy managers must decide whether a particular position is most appropriately hourly or salaried. Many pharmacist positions are considered salaried especially when responsibility is assigned for a particular group of patients. For example, an infectious disease pharmacist may participate in patient care rounds with the infectious disease consult service. This pharmacist may be staffed as a salaried employee because the volume of patients seen may require more than a typical 8-hour day in some cases and may require a bit less in others. This variable work schedule lends itself well to a salaried role because the pharmacy manager still may accurately predict (and therefore budget) the salary. In an hourly position, such accuracy is obtained through use of scheduled shifts. For example, an employee may start work at 07.00 and finish at 15.30 daily. Paid at an hourly rate, this schedule yields a consistent expense the pharmacy manager can predict and plan for. If the workload was highly variable, additional shifts may be needed (for example, 07.00−15.30 and 14.30−23.00). To determine which schedules are needed to address the workload, pharmacy managers rely on productivity monitoring and benchmarking.

Productivity

As pharmacists work to improve the care of their patients, pharmacy leaders work to ensure the availability of pharmacists to meet patients' needs. To do so, pharmacy leaders rely on information about the productivity of the pharmacists. Productivity is a ratio of outputs (work done) to inputs (pharmacist time). Outputs in pharmacy practice can be expressed in many ways, ranging from the number of orders verified by the number of patients seen in an ambulatory clinic in the volume of pharmacokinetic monitoring completed. Other measures of outputs serve as surrogates for total pharmacy practice. For example, many productivity calculations include the number of patient admissions or ambulatory visits or the severity of illness of patients the pharmacist cares for.[5] As these surrogate measures increase or decrease, pharmacy managers anticipate an increase or decrease in total work done to provide care. Inputs for productivity assessments are often expressed as some function of time. Time could be expressed as total pharmacist hours worked or as pharmacist FTE (the number of pharmacists that could be hired if all worked 40 h per week). In one way or another, inputs in pharmacist productivity calculations represent an expense for the healthcare organization, with the outputs representing the value or benefit resulting from that expense. For healthcare organizations to be successful, they must find a sustainable balance between outputs and inputs.

Pharmacy leaders and governments pay close attention to pharmacist productivity, as it directly impacts their goal to ensure availability of pharmacists for patient care needs. If productivity decreases, the healthcare organization may conclude that there is insufficient work to justify hiring more pharmacists and may even choose to reduce the total number of pharmacists it employs. If productivity increases, it may represent the increasing workload for pharmacists, creating additional pressure to complete all the necessary work in a shorter amount of time—eventually, this trade-off could lead to less effective pharmacy practice. To help identify reasonable expectations for productivity, pharmacy leaders benchmark productivity calculations against other pharmacy teams in the health system (internal benchmarking) or other pharmacy teams outside the health system (external benchmarking).[5] The success of benchmarking relies on comparing similar processes—if two pharmacy teams have very different approaches to patient care, benchmarking one against the other will not yield useful information. Although there is no gold standard for reporting productivity, some common methods are used to help ensure comparisons are made similarly across institutions.

Because much of what advanced pharmacy practitioners do is a cognitive service instead of a discretely identifiable action, measuring pharmacist productivity is challenging. Common productivity reporting and benchmarking systems may not adequately reflect specific clinical functions of interest to health system leaders. Early reports evaluated clinical pharmacist activities, including patient care rounding, chart reviews, responding to drug information requests, and performing literature searches. Some assessments also included distributive functions such as obtaining first doses from a central pharmacist, ordering medications, and checking unit-dose carts. Given the capabilities of health information systems at the time, simplifying calculations made quantifying clinical pharmacist activity feasible. As the speed and efficiency of electronic data collection and analysis have increased, pharmacists can apply more complex productivity assessment techniques.

Work productivity of pharmacists is studied in medical and surgical patients, high- and low-risk patients, orders for specific medication classes, emergency resuscitation, and medication cost management.[6–8] In comparing time needs for medical and surgical patients and high- and low-complexity patients (identified through diagnosis-related groups), a significant difference was noted between high- and low-complexity patients for all documented activities except drug information request. Significantly more time was required for medical patient care than surgical patient care.[6] In separate studies, pharmacy teams utilized input from pharmacists to weigh various pharmacist actions (order verification, code response, etc.) based on the perceived complexity of cognitive assessments needed to complete the action.[7,8] More complex activities were assigned higher values to adjust for the time needed to assess available information appropriately.

Because productivity monitoring has an indirect effect on patient care, all pharmacists should have a basic understanding of how productivity is measured and how it is used to make decisions about assigning available pharmacist services. To ensure success, pharmacists should review productivity measures used by their employers to determine appropriate staffing levels and provide feedback to identify the most accurate assessment possible in a given health system. Only by understanding and influencing productivity assessment can one be sure that sufficient time is protected to achieve the outcomes discussed previously.

Job Design

In developing a new position or service, a pharmacy manager must consider more than salary to manage the team effectively. A pharmacy manager also has responsibility for job design, recruitment, training, schedules, and performance management.

One component of pharmacy management is consideration of the job design of the various pharmacy employees to ensure that the overall structure of the department of pharmacy meets the needs of patients, providers, and other customers. Although there are many ways to organize thoughts around a new position, one method includes working backward through the Donabedian model (Fig. 4.2).[9] Beginning with outcomes of interest, the pharmacy manager identifies as clearly as possible what the role should achieve, then outlines how the pharmacist would go about achieving those objectives and considers what core structural elements the position requires (such as training, licensure, advanced certifications, and years of experience). These concepts come together as a position description, which is used to set expectations of job performance and as a communication tool during recruitment.

Recruitment

When a position becomes available, the pharmacy manager must oversee recruitment and hiring of a new employee. Applications are received and candidates are screened to ensure they meet minimum requirements outlined in the position

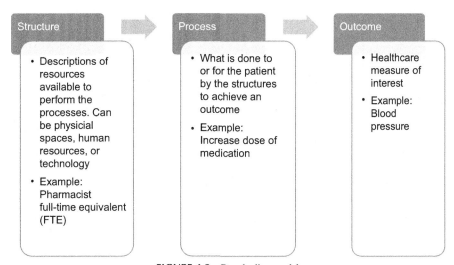

FIGURE 4.2 Donabedian model.

description. Appropriate candidates are contacted, and an interview is scheduled. Managers utilize some interview techniques to determine which candidate seems to be a great fit for the needs of the role. Managers use combinations of behavioral and situational questions to determine how the candidate will likely respond to various scenarios they are likely to encounter in the position. Behavior-based interviewing focuses on how the candidate responded to similar scenarios in the past ("tell me about a time when …."), anticipating future behavior to mirror previous behavior. Situational questions are used when the candidate may not have had specific experiences as they would encounter in the role. These questions are future-focused ("how would you respond if …"). Interviewing is such a complex skill to develop that several popular publications exist around the topic.[10]

Training

Once a job offer has been made and accepted, the manager must oversee the initial training period for the new employee. This period covers a large number of policies and procedures, instructing the new pharmacist on how the current team ensures compliance with applicable laws and regulations, as well as how care is delivered and documented. The pharmacist is taught how to use the specific electronic health record and other automation or technology the pharmacy may utilize, and gradually the employee becomes familiar with the various roles and functions within the team.

Performance Management

During orientation, pharmacists should also have clear expectations of performance set. In many cases, performance management for pharmacist presents significant challenges. Although performance management practices is another large and complex topic, many managers have found the concept of a "balanced scorecard"[11] to be an effective strategy for developing a well-rounded set of performance expectations for pharmacists. As described by Kaplan and Norton, the balanced scorecard outlines performance measures from the financial, business, innovation/learning, and customer perspectives. In healthcare, this model can be adapted to include measures of drug cost and revenue, productivity, education and research, and patient or healthcare worker satisfaction (Fig. 4.3). Developing objective and effective performance measures is a challenge in pharmacy, as much of the service is completed as a cognitive function (challenging to measure) and outcomes are not always available to measure (such as prevention of adverse effects by adjusting a dose or decreasing mortality by adding or revising a medication regimen). Nonetheless, a major role of a pharmacy manager is evaluating performance and providing feedback to employees to help improve effectiveness and efficiency. Pharmacy managers utilize available objective data combined with subjective input from coworkers, technicians, and other medical professionals. This type of all-around review is known as a 360-degree evaluation.[12]

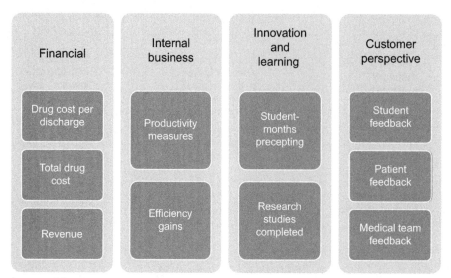

FIGURE 4.3 Balanced scorecard for pharmacist performance. *Adapted from Kaplan RS, Norton DP. The balanced scorecard—measures that drive performance.* Harv Bus Rev. *1992;70(1):71–79. http://www.ncbi.nlm.nih.gov/pubmed/10119714.*

Regulatory Compliance

Another important role of the pharmacy manager is to ensure compliance with applicable laws and regulations. In the United States, a myriad of regulatory bodies oversees the structure and function of a pharmacy team. At the federal level, the Food and Drug Administration in the United States oversees which pharmaceutical agents can be bought and sold for patient use and what labeling must be included. Accrediting bodies such as the Centers for Medicare and Medicaid Services utilize their status as a major payer to enforce process and quality requirements. The Drug Enforcement Agency also has specific requirements around prescribing, purchasing, storing, and dispensing controlled substances with abuse potential. Each state has its own Board of Pharmacy, which can enact rules governing how pharmacists practice. There are many more examples of local, state, and federal agencies with authority to govern pharmacy practice, leading to small but important distinctions across the United States. These groups will provide periodic inspection of pharmacy practice areas to ensure compliance with the applicable rules. If a pharmacy is found to not comply with various requirements, punishments can range from fines to revocation of license, essentially shutting down the pharmacy and potentially removing the ability for the pharmacy manager to practice or operate a pharmacy again. As such, pharmacy managers must remain knowledgeable on statutes and rules affecting pharmacy practice and must enact policies and procedures for staff to follow, ensuring compliance with the law and continuation of the practice.

OBJECTIVE 4.2. OVERVIEW THE PURCHASE, INVENTORY CONTROL, STORAGE, DRUG DISTRIBUTION, COMPOUNDING, AND DISPOSAL OF DRUGS AND RELATED PRODUCTS

The pharmaceutical industry manufactures drugs and other healthcare products. They are distributed to the retail community or hospital pharmacies through pharmaceutical distribution channels. The integrity of these distribution systems is important to avoid infiltration of counterfeit products in the supply chain, as well as to maintain the correct transport and storage conditions.[13] The pharmacy manager is also responsible for oversight of the pharmacy's purchasing practices. Here, we will review basic principles of inventory management.

Methods in inventory control such as ABC analysis and VED analysis are important measures in maintaining optimum stock levels. ABC analysis, otherwise known as "Always Better Control," is a method of controlling stock according to Pareto's principle of "vital few and trivial many." This principle states that approximately 10% of hospital medications are responsible for 70% of the budget (A). The next 20% (B) consume 20% of the budget, whereas the remaining 70% of the products (C) account for the last 10% of the budget. It is therefore extremely important to manage the 10% of medications responsible for 70% of the budget (A) (Table 4.3).[14]

TABLE 4.3 ABC Analysis

Item	Items (%)	Money Value (%)
A	10	70
B	20	20
C	70	10

VED analysis is based on the criticality of the product, where "V" determines the items that are vital to the hospital's system without which they cannot function, and "E" are the essential items without which the hospital's quality of service might be affected. "D" stands for the desirable items which, if not available, will not affect the functioning of the hospital.

If one combines the two types of analyses, the results will fall between having a very expensive but desirable drug (which is best avoided) to an ideal, vital product. The balance of the rest of the products falls on a continuum of the above categories.

In retail community pharmacy, stock control is different from hospital pharmacies and will vary from pharmacy to pharmacy. Factors that influence stock holding and control will be related to the following:

- Seasonal factors (e.g., winter vs. summer, rainy season in the tropics, cyclic illnesses/infections)
- Doctors' prescribing habits in the vicinity (e.g., there could be an oncology practice or pain clinic or a dermatologist nearby that could influence the type and quantity of drugs held in stock).
- The size and stock turnover of the pharmacy
- The area that the pharmacy serves (e.g., population ethnicity, affluent/poor) might also affect the price and sale of products held in stock.

Proper storage of goods ensures that the patient receives the highest quality of drug that they deserve. Maintaining the cold chain during transportation, using light-resistant containers, pilfer-proof lids, and securing are all physical measures that pharmacists should implement as part of inventory control measures.

Drugs that should be stored at room temperature means between 15 and 25 or up to 30°C; cool temperature means between 8 and 15°C; refrigeration means between 2 and 8°C; and freezing temperature means −10 to −25°C. Different countries have different room temperatures and definitions of cool temperatures.[15]

Drug distribution in a hospital, from main pharmacies to satellite pharmacies, should be one of the most critical elements of inventory management. Too much stock leads to the risk of wastage and pilferage, and too little may cause patients to experience potentially life-threatening conditions untreated. Different methods of inventory control can be employed, such as the following:[16]

1. Floor stock system—drugs are given to patients through nursing stations; patients are charged for them on administration,
2. Individual prescription or separate billing system—drugs prescribed are billed separately on the patient's unique hospital administration record. Common drugs (e.g., aspirin, acetaminophen) may be included in the hospital room charges.
3. Mobile dispensary or drug cabinet system—a standard list of drugs is kept within dispensing cabinets within the unit and administered to patients on a doctor's order. The charge is recorded by the automated system and is charged to the patient's profile and hospital/ward encounter.
4. A centralized unit-dose drug distribution system—all inpatient drugs are dispensed in unit doses from a central pharmacy. Medications may be dispensed at the time the dose is due to be given to the patient or more likely, in timed batches delivered to the unit prior to the scheduled dose.
5. Decentralized unit-dose dispensing—operated through small satellite pharmacies located on different levels of the hospital. The prescription is sent directly to the pharmacist and then entered in the patient's profile. The pharmacist checks the medication order and technicians fill the prescription; the drugs are then sent to the ward for the nurse to administer the medication.

It should be clear which method(s) is(are) followed, and a standard operating procedure (SOP) should be written in the precise and unambiguous language for everyone to understand, implement, and follow correctly.

Some hospitals have a pneumatic conveyer system for easy distribution of drugs and products to units. The system, if used correctly, can be of great benefit and save many person-hours of staff running between the hospital pharmacy and wards to collect and deliver drugs to the patient. Pharmacy technicians supplying drugs to nursing stations and storing drugs in locked drug cabinets can decrease wastage and theft. In some hospitals, all unit doses are packed in the pharmacy and supplied to the clinics which avoid drug wastage, but this increases labor costs. Software programs available to enhance these processes are helpful, as nurses can see the drug distribution firsthand by tracking each medication order on their computers to have an idea of approximately when they will receive the drugs for their patients.[17]

Drugs that are not available from suppliers because of stock-outs or drugs that are discontinued because of lower demand can then be compounded in the pharmacy. It may also be necessary to compound a drug for a specific patient's need. Fewer products are compounded nowadays, and in some countries, very little compounding is performed as it is difficult to control quality during compounding. The other potential issue is that the compounded product usually has a very short shelf life. Expiration dates on compounded drugs vary because of the content (e.g., 1 day for water-based injectables to 360 days for solid preparations). The volatility of the constituents and the water content plays a big role in the shelf life of the product. The pharmacists can send their product for stability testing to an accredited laboratory if unsure.

Checking expiry dates and proper disposal of drugs are two other important tasks pharmacists are responsible for (e.g., disposal without contaminating groundwater, flushing drugs in the toilet). One of the consequences of flushing hormone tablets down the toilet is that fish in the river could absorb significant amounts of estrogen. Some expired products can be sent back to the supplier, and they, the manufacturers, or the hospital will destroy them in the correct environmentally friendly manner. The concentration of active ingredients in expired drugs will reach a level below which they are deemed ineffective beyond their expiry date, and some might even become toxic (e.g., tetracycline—Fanconi syndrome). The principle of first expired, first out (FEFO) should always be followed when packing stock in shelves (i.e., rotation of stock). The stock should be checked regularly, as well as during dispensing, and if found within 3 months of expiration, it is removed from the shelves and sent back for credit if possible to the supplier or manufacturer.[18]

Organization (Arrangement) of Products in a Hospital Pharmacy

The financial system is of utmost importance in assisting the smooth running of making and receiving payments. It will have to make provisions for issuing invoices for sales, receipts for payments, credit notes, and keeping records for debtors and creditors, all the while being integrated with inventory and dispensing systems.

An inventory/stock control system assists with keeping an optimal level of stock as medication levels are depleted and automatically reorders stock. It should be equipped and programmed to assess, minimum stock levels, lead times (i.e., the time it takes from ordering the stock until it arrives at the pharmacy) and even seasonal trends (e.g., ordering more flu drug in winter) when considering appropriate medication levels for that particular pharmacy.

The correct organization of products in any business is critical to the financial success of the business and is even more important in community pharmacy because drugs have the extra burden of relatively short shelf lives. Correct organization of products is important so that pharmacy staff and consumers can easily and quickly access them.

The front portion of the pharmacy, which is accessible to consumers, will have a different arrangement of products than those in the dispensary. The criteria that apply to the front of the pharmacy shop will have more to do with economics and will take into consideration consumers' shopping patterns (i.e., turning right when entering a store and noticing products that are displayed at eye level first). The market leader in a product category will thus be displayed at eye level with a competitor's products arranged around it; similar products can then be displayed in the same area. A good example is toothpaste, which typically will have mouthwash products, as well as floss and toothbrushes arranged in the same area. Gondola ends (shelf ends) is always regarded as the optimum display, as products are noticed more often by consumers than when these same products are displayed elsewhere. Additionally, companies often pay retailers to have their products displayed in those pharmacy areas fairly large in size.

Having sufficient stock creates the image that the consumer has a wide choice and improves sales. Keeping displays neat and tidy is very important, as well as the fact that the stock rotation needs to happen regularly to keep the consumers' attention—especially the regular visitors—when browsing through the aisles. It is of course just as bad to be overstocked as understocked. A good stock management system, whether it be a computerized model or even a manual system that reflects the number of items sold per period (day/week/month) and the lead times (time from order to delivery), is of critical financial importance. The arrangement of the products should be what the average consumer will expect to find. For instance, all over-the-counter (OTC) products that have to do with colds/flu or stomach conditions need to be clearly identified by signs to assist consumers/patients with ease of purchases. Systematically identifying and organizing the different categories of medications plays a major role in the financial success of the pharmacy.

The arrangement in the dispensary usually is different as it is not accessible to the consumer/patient and has to do more with the ease of dispensing for the pharmacists and technicians. There are different systems implemented that are sometime alphabetical for all drugs or the therapeutic categories (again arranged alphabetically within the category). Drugs arranged in a specific therapeutic category (e.g., antimicrobials, cardiovascular drugs, antidiabetic drugs, contraceptives, etc.) in one place reduces dispensing errors. All antihypertensives are in one place and a look-alike drug from another therapeutic category is not dispensed by mistake as the pharmacist is concious about the therapeutic category. Drugs are also grouped together by dosage form. Each pharmacy decides what is most convenient for them and in many cases a combinaton of methods are used.

Hospital pharmacist has over the years been the purchasers of drugs and medical devices in the hospital. This role has in many instances been taken over by strategic purchasing units in the hospital that use standardized treatment regimens and use standardized formularies. The pharmacist, however, still has a big role to play in increasing efficiencies in drug utilization and management. In most hospitals, pharmacists are part of the Drug/Pharmacy and Therapeutics Committee for the hospital where they can participate in discussions regarding formulary management systems applicable to that specific hospital, taking into consideration scientific and pharmacoeconomic data.

Hospital drugs are usually arranged for unit stock, outpatient stock, and drugs for the emergency department; often the hospital is also the supplier of stock for nearby primary health clinics. This whole process needs careful planning and follows up to ensure a safe and consistent supply of drugs to patients. The hospital pharmacist is not only expected to be the expert in clinical pharmacy matters but is also responsible for the negotiation, drug management, and budget control, as well as personnel management.[19]

OBJECTIVE 4.3. ILLUSTRATE A MODEL PHARMACY AND DETAIL THE FACILITIES REQUIRED

The main components of a pharmacy care clinic are a pharmacy, a lab, a few consultation rooms for doctors and clinical pharmacists, a nursing unit, and a few ambulatory beds for evaluation or procedures (Fig. 4.4). Patients, typically, would enter through the pharmacy, and if referred to a doctor or clinical pharmacist, enter the clinic area and report to the reception desk. Their information is being recorded, and then they would be assessed by a skilled nurse practitioner and sent to the doctor, clinical pharmacist, or the examination room. The doctor can then take care of the patient either by consultation in his/her room, treat the patient in the procedure room, or assess the patient in the examination room. If blood samples need to be taken, the patient will go to the phlebotomy area; blood or any other samples would be analyzed in the laboratory. Then, the clinical pharmacist assesses the patient's needs and adjusts the treatment, if necessary. The clinic should also have a kitchen for staff and a storage area for use by the pharmacy and the clinic.[20]

A community pharmacy should include a small compounding area; however, it may also be located near/within a hospital pharmacy with a small manufacturing unit (e.g., topical preparations, capsule filling, small tablet punching, parenteral nutrition, IV fluids, ampoule sealing). Some hospital pharmacies have such manufacturing units as an extension to a pharmacy.

Patients have the right to professional treatment by the pharmacist, including the right to privacy. An ideal pharmacy would have a semiprivate consultation area where patients receive information regarding the correct use of their medication and provide the pharmacist personal information necessary for the dispensing of their medication. These semiprivate consultation areas are usually located as part of the dispensing area (Fig. 4.5).[19]

Whenever the situation necessitates, consultations of a more private nature need to take place in a separate private area where confidential information (e.g., HIV status, pregnancy) can be discussed openly with the pharmacist without anyone else (e.g., staff, other clients in the pharmacy) overhearing the discussion. This area usually adjoins the dispensing area. Provisions should also be made for a waiting area for patients, as well as a desk where the pharmacist can be seated for writing purposes, if necessary, and at least two comfortable chairs that can accommodate the elderly and young children (Fig. 4.6).

The third area will be the consultation area which can also serve as the clinic area. This needs to be properly equipped to enable the pharmacist or clinician to perform limited clinical procedures as their respective scope of practice dictates. This area needs an examination couch, a washbasin, and a portable cart with equipment (e.g., stethoscope with baumanometer, otoscope, syringes, needles). There should also be a trauma tray and equipment for the treatment of allergies and other types of minor emergencies. Figs. 4.7 and 4.8 show fully furnished pharmacy areas.

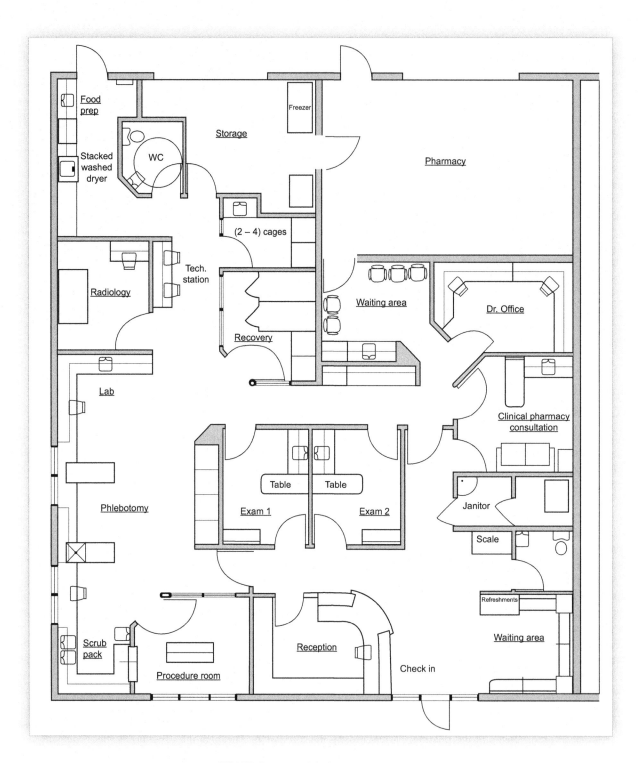

FIGURE 4.4 A model of pharmacy in a clinic.

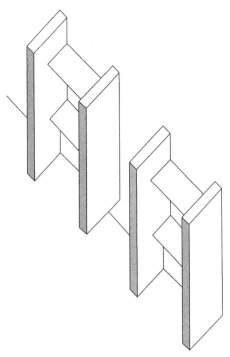

FIGURE 4.5 Semiprivate consultation area.

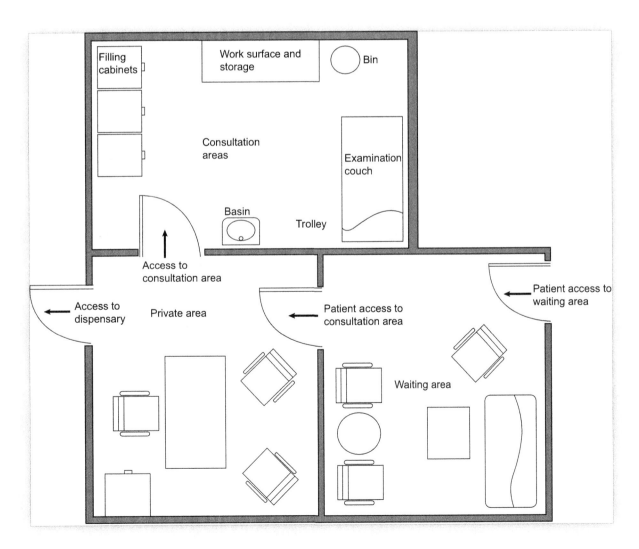

FIGURE 4.6 Private area and consultation room in a pharmacy with large clinical area.

FIGURE 4.7 Inside a pharmacy.

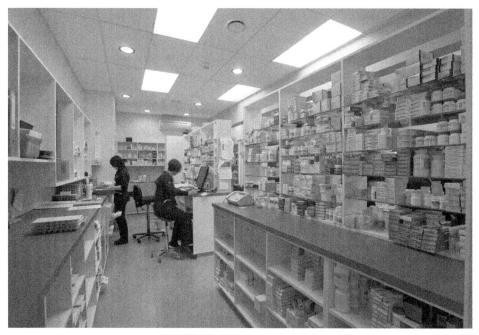

FIGURE 4.8 Pharmacy workstation.

OBJECTIVE 4.4. OVERVIEW PHARMACY PRACTICE SETTING AND RESPONSIBILITIES OF PROFESSIONALS

Pharmacists practice in different work settings, which are popularly known as the following[21−23]:

1. Community pharmacy

   These settings involve improving access to quality drugs and related products to the community it serves. In many countries, still, pharmacists focus heavily on the supply of products and provide little clinical services. This process is changing globally by providing clinical services appropriate for ambulatory settings. Sometimes called as ambulatory care pharmacies, pharmacists with advanced knowledge and expertise focus on to provide detailed medication consultation. Patients who may have concurrent illnesses and are taking multiple medications either via self-administration or with the help of caregivers need a pharmacist consultation to achieve appropriate clinical outcomes. When not hospitalized and have inconveniences in visiting their treating hospital often, patients prefer to consult pharmacists in community pharmacies. However, the pharmacists should be competent enough to advice in coordination with existing medical care and refer to the hospital if further care is essential. Performing drug interaction screens, as well as medication reconciliations to make sure that the patient's medication list is complete and current is a standard service by the pharmacist. Anticipating adverse outcomes and identifying drug-related problems improves safety of patients. Community pharmacist also treats minor ailments with over-the-counter products, lifestyle modification or with their limited prescribing authority. Thus community pharmacy provides both advanced care in communication with other healthcare faiclities and primary healthcare services independently.

2. Hospital pharmacy (Institutional)
   a. Inpatient pharmacy
      The inpatient pharmacy in a hospital supplies the medicinal needs of patients who have been admitted to the hospital, as well as the drugs that are used during operations and, in most cases, the stock used in the surgery wards, intensive care units, and theatres. It also supplies drug to the general units/wards that are kept as backup stock, or when the pharmacy is closed, it could also be the source of drugs to outlying clinics.
   b. Outpatient pharmacy
      Patients that have been discharged from the hospital, but still need ongoing therapy, are usually supplied by the outpatient pharmacy. They could be patients on chronic medication or supportive medication after treatment (e.g., antibiotics, pain medications, antiinflammatory drugs). Services for outpatients are ambulatory care. Ambulatory care include services for patients not admitted to a healthcare institutions, literally meaning walking patient.

3. Clinical pharmacists
   Clinical pharmacy is a concept that means providing direct patient care services. Irrespective of the site of practice, all pharmacists provide clinical services, such as counseling, prevention of drug-related problems, etc. The pharmacists who work exclusively to provide clinical services are called clinical pharmacists. Clinical pharmacists work in inpatient and ambulatory settings, spending most of their time providing direct patient care but not direct pharmacy dispensing activities. They collaborate with other healthcare professionals to optimize the outcome of drugs in patients. Pharmacy technicians are mostly filling the prescription and the pharmacists are providing exclusive clinical services with dispensing. Pharmacy managers takes care of inventory control. As pharmacy managers and pharmacy technicians performs non-clinical functions of pharmacy, pharmacists could focus fully on clinical services. In this ideal situation, patients are benefited with a full pharmacist interaction that they deserve.

4. Consulting pharmacist
   A consultant pharmacist can operate his/her business by offering a wide range of services visiting the patients. It can range from consulting with senior citizens where the health and medication needs of elderly patients are looked after. In consulting pharmacy, pharmacists visit where the patient lives, especially the old age homes. They differ from other pharmacists who are stationed at a hospital or pharmacy.

5. Managed care pharmacy
   These pharmacies and the pharmacists that work in them are usually attached to health plans and pharmacy benefit management firms. They operate through evidence-based strategies and practices that optimize drug use for their members. They achieve their objective by looking at the most cost-effective treatment for different types of patients primarily by means of drug therapy.

Responsibilities of Personnel Involved in Pharmacy Operations

Apart from the classical categories of pharmacists listed above, there are also the hierarchical categories involved in pharmacy and the ancillary staff involved in a pharmacy.

In a typical hospital pharmacy (and even in community pharmacy) one would also find these different categories of pharmacy staff[19,21,24]:

1. Pharmacy/hospital administrator: To qualify for such a position, pharmacists would usually be required to have at least a Master's degree in Pharmacy or a Master's in Business leadership (or both).

2. Chief pharmacist: This person sees to the proper running of all aspects of the pharmacy (e.g., stock levels, sufficient staff members, organizing staff work schedules); they would have to have a minimum of a Bachelor, Master's degree in Pharmacy, or PharmD. Often, this position is given to a pharmacist who has a significant amount of experience in that particular pharmacy area.

3. Compounding pharmacist: This pharmacist does the specialized compounding required by doctors or hospital staff. They can have specialized training or have received in-house training. A minimum requirement regarding their qualification would need to be a Bachelor in Pharmacy or PharmD.

4. Dispensing pharmacist: This is the most common type of pharmacist found in all areas of pharmacy. They perform all the functions related to the correct dispensing of a prescribed product to a patient including verifying the legality of the prescription, assessing drug–drug, drug–food, or drug–disease interactions, selecting the appropriate drug, and checking for final correctness and expiration dates before handing over the medication to the counseling pharmacist or another clinician. Such pharmacists would need to have a Bachelor in Pharmacy or PharmD as a qualification for this position.

5. Counseling/clinical pharmacist: Their day-to-day tasks can differ from counseling a patient on the correct use of a medication to doing unit/ward rounds with physicians advising on correct regimes, dosages, and contraindications of therapy. These pharmacists are called pharmacotherapy (or clinical) pharmacists, and their training involves a postgraduate course in clinical pharmacy (i.e., PharmD with residency training).

6. Pharmacy intern: These are pharmacy students performing their experiential learning in the hospital/community pharmacy after/during completion of their Bachelor of Pharmacy or PharmD degrees before they can be licensed as pharmacists. They rotate between the different departments of the pharmacy and assist in pharmacy-related tasks allocated to them by their preceptors.

7. Pharmacy technician: This essential personnel performs the technical tasks involved in dispensing medications such as packing medications in their correct places, stocking shelves, and automated cabinets, and general medication preparation tasks freeing the pharmacist to perform other functions of order-entry, verification, and dispensing to ensure patient compliance and medication adherence. In most countries, technicians have to complete a 2-year course at an accredited institution.

8. Administrative/management assistants: These employees see to it that important documentation (e.g., receiving stock, billing to patient records, staff work schedule) and record keeping of SOPs are being done and regularly adhered to. This personnel is usually trained in-house or have a qualification in finances and/or administration.

OBJECTIVE 4.5. EXPLAIN ADVANTAGES AND LIMITATIONS OF PHARMACY AUTOMATION

Automation in pharmacies may decrease the required number of pharmacy technicians and supporting staff, but not necessarily pharmacists. For example, an automatic pill counter improves output and helps to minimize dispensing errors. The same can be said about dispensers, robots, and automated remote dispensers (robots that are controlled from a remote site). Despite their availability, medication error checking and clinical decisions by a pharmacist is considered to be superior to any software. Add to that the counseling of the patient by the pharmacist, as well as other regular tasks performed to decrease medication errors and adverse drug reactions, and automation can be seen as an overall method of improving output by the pharmacist but not replacing them. Compare such advances of automation in other fields that have shown a similar benefit—airplanes have an autopilot, but pilots are still required, and doctors have robots that assist with operations, but it cannot perform the task without being programmed or guided.[21,25]

The advantages of this type of automation are that pharmacy unit-dose dispensing can make a significant impact on the budget/economy within an institution or pharmacy. Automation can assist in compounding/manufacturing, dispensing, and distributing drugs. However, they are costly to acquire, and pricing could be difficult to manage in resource-limited settings.

Pharmacies all over the world make use of computer software to operate dispensing procedures, storage of prescriptions on individual patient profiles, assessment of drug–drug interactions, and evaluate patient-allergic reactions to certain drugs. Software systems can also be used to automatically generate refill prescriptions and communicate with patients regarding the readiness of such refills, as well as provide relevant medical information to the patient (Fig. 4.9).[26]

FIGURE 4.9   Pharmacy automation. *Picture credit: Swisslog Healthcare.*

CONCLUSION

Managing pharmacy needs special skills to manage products, facilities, patients, and staff. Effectively managed pharmacy facilitates access to safe, effective, and affordable drugs and other services by pharmacists. With increased responsibilities to provide patient-based services, it takes more staff time, counseling rooms, and comfort areas for the customers.

PRACTICE QUESTIONS

1. In a hospital pharmacy budget, overestimating expenses and not spending for improvement actions is a type of?
   A. Direct medical cost
   B. Indirect medical cost
   C. Nonmedical cost
   D. Opportunity cost
2. ABC system is for?
   A. Inventory management
   B. Dispensing protocol
   C. Drug administration SOP
   D. Storage conditions
3. Major reasons for the shorter shelf life of compounded products are?
   A. Nonavailability of raw materials
   B. Not prepared in bulk and packed in suboptimally filled containers
   C. Volatility of the constituents and the water content
   D. Possible contamination with microbes and heavy metals

REFERENCES

1. Royal Pharmaceutical Society. *Improving the Quality of Medicines Reconciliation a Best Practice Resource and Toolkit*; 2015. https://www.sps.nhs. uk/wp-content/uploads/2015/06/Medicines_Reconciliation_Best_Practice_Standards_Toolkit.pdf.
2. Cuckler GA, Sisko AM, Poisal JA, et al. National health expenditure projections, 2017−26: despite uncertainty, fundamentals primarily drive spending growth. *Health Aff.* 2018;37(3):482−492. https://doi.org/10.1377/hlthaff.2017.1655.
3. Millonig MK. *Rising Drug Prices: Impact on Patients and Pharmacy.* Wolters Kluwer Clinical Drug Information; 2016. http://www. wolterskluwercdi.com/blog/rising-drug-prices-impact-patients-and-pharmacy/.
4. Vega A, Meola P, Barcelo J, Ruiz H, Oh S, Ho T. Commentary on current trends in rising drug costs and reimbursement below cost. *Manag Care*; 2016. https://www.managedcaremag.com/archives/2016/4/commentary-current-trends-rising-drug-costs-and-reimbursement-below-cost.
5. Rough SS, McDaniel M, Rinehart JR. Effective use of workload and productivity monitoring tools in health-system pharmacy, part 1. *Am J Health Pharm.* 2010;67(4):300−311. https://doi.org/10.2146/ajhp090217.p1.

6. Stuchbery P, Kong DCM, DeSantis GN, Lo SK. Clinical pharmacy workload in medical and surgical patients: effect of patient partition, disease complexity and major disease category. *Int J Pharm Pract*. 2010;18(3):159−166. http://www.ncbi.nlm.nih.gov/pubmed/20509349.

7. Pawloski P, Cusick D, Amborn L. Development of clinical pharmacy productivity metrics. *Am J Health Pharm*. 2012;69(1):49−54. https://doi.org/10.2146/ajhp110126.

8. Granko RP, Poppe LB, Savage SW, Daniels R, Smith EA, Leese P. Method to determine allocation of clinical pharmacist resources. *Am J Health Pharm*. 2012;69(16):1398−1404. https://doi.org/10.2146/ajhp110510.

9. Donabedian A. Evaluating the quality of medical care. Reprinted 1966 article *Milbank Q*. 2005;83(4):691−729. https://doi.org/10.1111/j.1468-0009.2005.00397.x.

10. Fernández-Aráoz C, Groysberg B, Nohria N. The definitive guide to recruiting in good times and bad. *Harv Bus Rev*; 2009. https://www.hbs.edu/faculty/Pages/item.aspx?num=36014.

11. Kaplan RS, Norton DP. The balanced scorecard−measures that drive performance. *Harv Bus Rev*. 1992;70(1):71−79. http://www.ncbi.nlm.nih.gov/pubmed/10119714.

12. Peiperl MA. Getting 360 degrees feedback right. *Harv Bus Rev*. 2001;79(1):142−147, 177 http://www.ncbi.nlm.nih.gov/pubmed/11189458.

13. Chambliss WG, Carroll WA, Kennedy D, et al. Role of the pharmacist in preventing distribution of counterfeit medications. *J Am Pharm Assoc*. 2012;52(2):195−199. https://doi.org/10.1331/JAPhA.2012.11085.

14. Kumar S, Chakravarty A. ABC-VED analysis of expendable medical stores at a tertiary care hospital. *Med J Armed Forces India*. 2015;71(1):24−27. https://doi.org/10.1016/j.mjafi.2014.07.002.

15. JohnSnow/DELIVER. *Guidelines for the Storage of Essential Medicines and Other Health Commodities*. John Snow/DELIVER & WHO; 2003. http://apps.who.int/medicinedocs/pdf/s4885e/s4885e.pdf.

16. ASHP. *Drug Distribution and Control*. ASHP; 2017. https://www.ashp.org/Pharmacy-Practice/Policy-Positions-and-Guidelines/Browse-by-Topic/Drug-Distribution-and-Control.

17. Cousein E, Mareville J, Lerooy A, et al. Effect of automated drug distribution systems on medication error rates in a short-stay geriatric unit. *J Eval Clin Pract*. 2014;20(5):678−684. https://doi.org/10.1111/jep.12202.

18. Holloway K, Carandang E, Hogerzeil H, et al. *Drug and Therapeutics Committees a Practical Guide*; 2003. http://apps.who.int/medicinedocs/pdf/s4882e/s4882e.pdf.

19. Wiedenmayer K, Summers RS, Mackie CA, Gous AGS, Everard M. *Developing Pharmacy Practice a Focus on Patient Care Handbook − 2006 Edition*; 2006. https://www.fip.org/files/fip/publications/DevelopingPharmacyPractice/DevelopingPharmacyPracticeEN.pdf.

20. Hepler CD, Strand LM. Opportunities and responsibilities in pharmaceutical care. *Am J Hosp Pharm*. 1990;47(3):533−543. http://www.ncbi.nlm.nih.gov/pubmed/2316538.

21. Allen SJ, Zellmer WA, Knoer SJ, et al. ASHP foundation pharmacy forecast 2017: strategic planning advice for pharmacy departments in hospitals and health systems. *Am J Health Syst Pharm*. 2017;74(2):27−53. https://doi.org/10.2146/sp170001.

22. Elliott RA, Lee CY, Beanland C, et al. Development of a clinical pharmacy model within an Australian home nursing service using co-creation and participatory action research: the visiting pharmacist (ViP) study. *BMJ Open*. 2017;7(11):e018722. https://doi.org/10.1136/bmjopen-2017-018722.

23. Blouin RA, Adams ML. The role of the pharmacist in health care. *N C Med J*. 2017;78(3):165−167. https://doi.org/10.18043/ncm.78.3.165.

24. Braund R, Chesney KM, Keast EP, et al. Are all pharmacy staff interested in potential future roles? *Int J Pharm Pract*. 2012;20(6):417−421. https://doi.org/10.1111/j.2042-7174.2012.00216.x.

25. Fung E, Leung B, Hamilton D, Hope J. Do automated dispensing machines improve patient safety? *Can J Hosp Pharm*. 2009;62(6):516−519. http://www.ncbi.nlm.nih.gov/pubmed/22478942.

26. Yu KH, Sweidan M, Williamson M, Fraser A. Drug interaction alerts in software−what do general practitioners and pharmacists want? *Med J Aust*. 2011;195(11−12):676−680. http://www.ncbi.nlm.nih.gov/pubmed/22171864.

ANSWERS TO PRACTICE QUESTIONS

1. D

2. A

3. C

Chapter 5

Rational Drug Use, Formulary Management, Pharmaceutical Care/ Medication Therapy Management/ Pharmacists' Patient Care Process

Seeba Zachariah[1], Angela Hill[2], Dixon Thomas[1], Ola Ghaleb Al Ahdab[3] and Daniel Buffington[2]

[1]Gulf Medical University, Ajman, United Arab Emirates; [2]University of South Florida, Tampa, FL, United States;
[3]Ministry of Health and Prevention, Abu Dhabi, United Arab Emirates

Learning Objectives:

Objective 5.1 Define drug/medicine, medication, and health technology.
Objective 5.2 Overview rational drug use in clinical practice.
Objective 5.3 Detail the constitution and functions of a drug and therapeutics committee.
Objective 5.4 Discuss essential medicines policy and formulary management.
Objective 5.5 Explain methods in drug use evaluation (drug utilization review).
Objective 5.6 Explain methods to standardize pharmacy education and practice: pharmaceutical care, medication therapy management, CAPE educational outcomes, Nanjing Statement, pharmacists' patient care process, and entrustable professional activities.

OBJECTIVE 5.1. DEFINE DRUG/MEDICINE, MEDICATION, AND HEALTH TECHNOLOGY

A drug is defined with slight differences in each country's drug laws. For healthcare professionals, drug is synonymous with medicine. Especially as "medicine" is also used to represent the practice of physicians, use of "drug" is preferred for pharmacists in professional communications. For the public, the term "drug" is commonly used as a substance of abuse; use of the term "medicine" is preferred for pharmacists while communicating with the public. Many agencies, including the World Health Organization (WHO), recommend using the term medicine. In healthcare regulations of many countries, the term drug is still commonly used for medicinal products. In the United States, the drug regulatory agency is called the Food and Drug Administration (FDA), whereas in the European Union, it is called the European Medicines Agency.

The US FDA defines a drug as follows:

- A substance recognized by an official pharmacopeia or formulary.
- A substance intended for use in the diagnosis, cure, mitigation, treatment, or prevention of disease.
- A substance (other than food) intended to affect the structure or any function of the body.
- A substance intended for use as a component of a drug but not a device or a component, part or accessory of a device.
- Biological products are included within this definition and are covered by the same laws and regulations, but differences exist regarding their manufacturing processes (chemical process vs. biological process).[1]

A newer way of defining all pharmaceutical products together is by calling them "health technology." This includes drugs and medical devices. WHO defines a medical device as any instrument, apparatus, implement, machine, appliance, implant, reagent for in vitro use, software, material, or other similar or related article, intended by the manufacturer to be used, alone or in combination, for human beings, for one or more of the specific medical purpose(s) of:

- diagnosis, prevention, monitoring, treatment, or alleviation of disease,
- diagnosis, monitoring, treatment, alleviation of, or compensation for an injury,
- investigation, replacement, modification, or support of the anatomy or of a physiological process,
- supporting or sustaining life,
- control of conception,
- disinfection of medical devices,
- providing information by means of in vitro examination of specimens derived from the human body.

Moreover, device does not achieve its primary intended action by pharmacological, immunological, or metabolic means, in or on the human body, but may be assisted in its intended function by such means.

Note: Products that may be considered to be medical devices in some jurisdictions but not in others include the following:

- disinfection substances,
- aids for persons with disabilities,
- devices incorporating animal and human tissues, and
- devices for in vitro fertilization or assisted reproduction technologies.[2]

Drug Names

Drugs have generic names and brand names. For example, atorvastatin is the generic name and Lipitor is a brand name. Brand names are assigned by the pharmaceutical companies, and the generic name is selected by WHO. Pharmaceutical companies keep both brand and generic names on the product labels. The brand name is also called a proprietary name, and the generic name is an International Nonproprietary Name.[3] When a company develops and releases a new drug into the market, they will have market exclusivity protected by patent law. Once the patent expires, generic or branded versions of the same bioequivalent product could be released by any companies following approval by an appropriate regulatory agency. If a drug is marketed by the generic name, without a brand name, it is called as a generic product. The generic version of a biological product is called a biosimilar.[4] When we write these names within a sentence, a brand name starts with a capital letter and generic names start with a small letter. Another unique name for the pharmacological product is International Union of Pure and Applied Chemistry (IUPAC) name, a detailed chemical name.[5] Aspirin was originally the brand name of acetylsalicylic acid, but it is now commonly used as its generic name. The generic name is the same for most drugs throughout the world. However, there are exceptions. In the United States, the generic name for paracetamol is acetaminophen, salbutamol is called albuterol, and pethidine is meperidine. The problem does not stop here. In different languages such as German, Spanish, etc., the names are spelled and pronounced differently. To solve this problem, WHO assign a unique international code for each drug as per the Anatomical Therapeutic and Chemical (ATC) classification system. Some drugs may have more than one ATC code for their different therapeutic uses. For ibuprofen, the ATC code is "M01AE01." "M" stands for the musculoskeletal anatomical system, "01A" stands for nonsteroidal antiinflammatory and antirheumatic therapeutic class, "E" stands for propionic acid derivative chemical class, and the last number "01" stands for ibuprofen differentiating it from other nonsteroidal antiinflammatory drugs (NSAIDs) in the class.[6]

OBJECTIVE 5.2. OVERVIEW RATIONAL DRUG USE IN CLINICAL PRACTICE

Rational use of drugs is defined by WHO as "patients receive medications appropriate to their clinical needs, in doses that meet their own individual requirements, for an adequate period of time, and at the lowest cost to them and their community."[7]

Some of the WHO/International Network for the Rational Use of Drug (INRUD) drug use indicators for primary healthcare facilities (WHO, 1993) are as follows:

Prescribing indicators:

- Average number of drugs prescribed per patient encounter
- % drugs prescribed by generic name
- % encounters with an antibiotic prescribed
- % encounters with an injection prescribed
- % drugs prescribed from an essential drugs list or formulary

Patient care indicators:

- Average consultation time
- Average dispensing time
- % drugs actually dispensed
- % drugs adequately labeled
- % patients with knowledge of correct doses

Facility indicators:

- Availability of essential drugs list or formulary to practitioners
- Availability of clinical guidelines
- % key drugs available

Complementary drug use indicators:

- Average drug cost per encounter
- % prescriptions in accordance with clinical guidelines.[7]

These indicators are usually assessed by drug use evaluations (DUEs). Irrational drug use may be any clinically significant inappropriate use of drugs such as no drugs when required, unnecessary drugs, overuse, underuse, ineffective drugs, unsafe drugs, etc. Irrational drug use can be identified, prevented, or managed by the methods developed through pharmacy practice. A drug and therapeutics committee (DTC) could function to improve the rational use of drugs in a hospital.

WHO advocated 12 key interventions to promote more rational use:

- Establishment of a multidisciplinary national body to coordinate policies on drug use
- Use of clinical guidelines
- Development and use of a national essential drugs list
- Establishment of drug and therapeutics committees in districts and hospitals
- Inclusion of problem-based pharmacotherapy training in undergraduate curricula
- Continuing in-service medical education as a licensure requirement
- Supervision, audit, and feedback
- Use of independent information on drugs
- Public education about medicines
- Avoidance of perverse financial incentives
- Use of appropriate and enforced regulation
- Sufficient government expenditure to ensure availability of drugs and staff.[7]

OBJECTIVE 5.3. DETAIL THE CONSTITUTION AND FUNCTIONS OF A DRUG AND THERAPEUTICS COMMITTEE

DTC, also known as pharmacy and therapeutics committee (PTC), functions typically in institutional (hospital) settings. Similar committees could also work at public health (governmental and nongovernmental agencies) levels to develop state/national formularies and advice on the rational management of drugs in the region. DTC formulates policies and guidelines for the rational use of drugs and other pharmaceutical products. WHO uses the term DTC, whereas in the United States PTC is more commonly used.

According to WHO, goals and objectives of the DTC are as follows:

The goal of a DTC is to ensure that patients are provided with the best possible cost-effective and quality of care through determining what drugs will be available, at what cost, and how they will be used.

To achieve this goal, a DTC will have the following objectives:

- to develop and implement an efficient and cost-effective formulary system that includes consistent standard treatment protocols, a formulary list, and formulary manual
- to ensure that only efficacious, safe, cost-effective, and best quality drugs are used

- to ensure the best possible drug safety through monitoring, evaluating, and thereby preventing, as far as possible, adverse drug reactions (ADRs) and medication errors
- to develop and implement interventions to improve drug use by prescribers, dispensers, and patients; this will require the investigation and monitoring of drug use.[8]

Constitution of Drug and Therapeutics Committee

The DTC is usually constituted with expected competency to perform its duties. Any committee could have odd numbers of members with voting powers that help in avoiding a draw. A DTC should include stakeholders from major clinical specialty departments, administrations, and pharmacies. A small committee could be formed with a minimum of seven members (2—3 doctors, 1—2 pharmacists, 1 nurse, 1 administrator, and another member as per the hospital's requirement, preferably a medical IT specialist). The number shall vary based on the hospital's organizational structure. The following points should be considered to decide the committee to be small or large. For a small hospital, a small committee might be suitable. Small committees are less expensive and more easily reach consensus decisions.

Large committees are suitable for large hospitals with extensive pharmacy operations:

- Greater expertise by adding professionals with different backgrounds.
- Less workload for each member.
- Involving more of the hospital staff helps with the implementation of decisions.

The following members could be included based on defined responsibilities:

- a representative clinician from each major specialty, including surgery, obstetrics and gynecology, internal medicine, pediatrics, infectious diseases, and general practice (to represent the community)
- a clinical pharmacist
- a nurse, usually the senior infection control nurse, or nursing superintendent
- a pharmacist (usually the chief or deputy chief pharmacist) or a pharmacy technician where there is no pharmacist
- an administrator, representing the hospital administration and finance department
- a clinical microbiologist or a laboratory technician where there is no microbiologist
- a member of the hospital records department.[8]

Some DTCs also include drug information pharmacists, trainees, consumer representatives, etc.

Common subcommittees of DTC are the infection control committee, procurement committee, patient safety committee, etc.

Functions of Drug and Therapeutics Committee

DTC teams up with other committees and professionals in the hospital to manage the purchase, inventory, distribution, rational use, and disposal of pharmaceutical products in the hospital. DTC's functions are mostly advisory. It also develops policies and guidelines and plans strategies to implement change. Direct patient care is the responsibility of clinical staff and the DTC only monitors and suggests how to improve it. Some of the key functions of DTC are as follows:

- Advice healthcare professionals, administrators, and other committees on any issues related to pharmaceutical products. DTC has a pool of experts with technical expertise that could prepare guidance documents combining evidence, local experience, patient values, and technological support available. DTC promotes evidence-based clinical practices.
- Develop drug policies and plan strategies to implement new policies. The policies addressed generally include purchase, inventory, distribution, rational use, and disposal of pharmaceutical products. Examples of some specific policies include reduce the drug budget, procure drugs only from manufacturers that follow good manufacturing practices and holding the WHO prequalification certificate, hospital formulary management, prescribe only from the hospital formulary and in generic names of drugs, pharmacovigilance practices, safety culture, medical reconciliation in transitions of care, return or dispose expired drugs without polluting groundwater or air, etc.
- Prepare essential drugs list/hospital formulary and standard treatment guidelines (STGs)/clinical protocols.
- Perform DUE studies of drug-related problems such as medication errors and ADRs and suggest improving better utilization of resources for rational drug use.
- Conduct pharmacoeconomics evaluations to assure cost-effective and affordable drug use in the hospital.

- Monitor information management system in the hospital to protect patient privacy and confidentiality in the system. The DTC could also monitor potential legal and ethical violations in clinical practice in collaboration with other bodies in the hospital.
- The DTC also works with the quality assurance committee to ensure the hospital follows international patient safety goals and accreditation standards. It also self-evaluates its performance to deliver better services to the hospital and the community.[8]

For a DTC to function, it should have a multidisciplinary, transparent approach, technical competence, and an official mandate. Being multidisciplinary reflects different professionals and departments that have the competency to advise other professionals or bodies in the hospital. A collaborative clinical practice work environment requires teamwork between different healthcare professionals. The transparent approach is essential for providing a clear understanding of the situation by unbiased assessment and decision making. Finally, the official mandate is essential to implement a change. Otherwise, advice shall be ignored by the workforce. (E.g., if the prescribers ignore the advice to prescribe in generic names, the committee should have the support of the hospital administrator to warn or impose the advice as a rule.) The committee is for this reason inclusive of administrative staff. This does not mean the committee is adamant on its decisions but is sensitive to recognize practice difficulties and suggest relaxations of or revisions to the advice.

OBJECTIVE 5.4. DISCUSS ESSENTIAL MEDICINES POLICY AND FORMULARY MANAGEMENT

In this section, to have consistency the term medicine is used under this objective instead of drug. Essential medicines policy and formulary management principles and procedures are promoted by WHO. WHO defines essential medicines as those that satisfy the priority healthcare needs of the population. The essential medicines list is also called a formulary list. They are selected with due regard to public health relevance, evidence on efficacy and safety, and comparative cost-effectiveness. Essential medicines are intended to be available within the context of functioning health systems at all times in adequate amounts, in the appropriate dosage forms, with assured quality and adequate information, and at a price the individual and the community can afford.

The implementation of the concept of essential medicines is intended to be flexible and adaptable to many different situations; exactly which medicines are regarded as essential remains a national responsibility. WHO essential medicines list is a model that countries use in making their essential list. Hospital formularies are made by hospitals referring to the state/country/WHO formularies. For a hospital, the more relevant list of medicines is the hospital formulary that is made to address the healthcare needs of the majority population that the hospital serves. Regional variations and nature of hospital policies (corporate, not-for-profit, etc.) shall result in significant variations in the population availing its services. A corporate and charity hospital in the same city shall have a significantly different essential medicines list or formulary.

It is difficult to achieve efficiency in the hospital pharmaceutical system if there are too many medicines. All aspects of medicines management, including procurement, storage, distribution, and use, are easier if fewer items are managed.

The WHO Model List of Essential Medicine (EML), which serves as a guide for the development of national and institutional essential medicine lists, is updated and revised every 2 years by the WHO Expert Committee on Selection and Use of Medicines. The EML was first published in 1977 and the Model List of Essential Medicines for Children (EMLc) was first published in 2007.[9]

The 20th EML and sixth EMLc, published on June 6, 2017, mark the 40th anniversary of this flagship WHO tool to expand access to medicines. The 20th EML adds 30 medicines for adults and 25 for children and specifies new uses for 9 already-listed products, bringing the total to 433 medicines deemed essential for addressing the most important public health needs globally.[10]

Most countries have national lists, and some have provincial or state lists as well. National lists of essential medicines guide the procurement and supply of medicines in the public sector, schemes that reimburse medicine costs, medicine donations, and local medicine production.

WHO Criteria for Selection of Essential Medicines

The WHO Expert Committee on Selection and Use of Essential Medicines meets every 2 years to review the latest scientific evidence on the efficacy, safety, and cost-effectiveness of medicines to revise and update the WHO EML and EMLc. Committee members are selected from WHO Expert Advisory Panels based on equitable geographical representation, gender balance, and professional competencies to provide a representation of different approaches and practical experience from all regions of the world.

Essential medicines are selected with due regard to disease prevalence and public health relevance, evidence of clinical efficacy and safety, and comparative costs and cost-effectiveness.

Which treatment is recommended and which medicines are selected depend on many factors, such as the pattern of prevalent diseases, treatment facilities, the training and experience of available personnel, financial resources, and genetic, demographic, and environmental factors. The following criteria are used by the WHO Expert Committee on the Selection and Use of Essential Medicines:

- Only medicines for which sound and adequate evidence of efficacy and safety in a variety of settings is available should be selected
- Relative cost-effectiveness is a major consideration for choosing medicines within the same therapeutic category. In comparisons between medicines, the total cost of the treatment—not only the unit cost of the medicine—must be considered and compared with its efficacy
- In some cases, the choice may also be influenced by other factors such as pharmacokinetic properties or by local considerations such as the availability of facilities for manufacture or storage
- Each medicine selected must be available in a form in which adequate quality, including bioavailability, can be ensured; its stability under the anticipated conditions of storage and use must be determined
- Most essential medicines should be formulated as single compounds. Fixed dose combination products are selected only when the combination has a proven advantage in therapeutic effect, safety, adherence, or in decreasing the emergence of drug resistance in malaria, tuberculosis (TB), and HIV/AIDS.[10]

Formulary

As per definition, a *formulary list* and essential medicines list convey the same meaning. They are the medicines that satisfy the priority healthcare needs of the population. The *formulary manual* (e.g., WHO Model Formulary, British National Formulary, hospital formulary) is usually published as a small book that has the essential medicines list with short clinical profiles of each medicine. It serves as a medicines information resource for the healthcare professionals in their clinical practice.

The formulary process or formulary system is the cornerstone of good pharmaceutical management and rational medicine use. It consists of preparing, using, and updating a formulary list (essential medicines list, EML also known as essential drug list, EDL), a formulary manual (providing information on medicines in the formulary list), and STGs. Choosing the most appropriate therapies and selecting the most cost-effective good-quality medicines lead to better quality of care and more efficient, equitable use of resources.[8]

Since its first publication in 2002, the WHO Model Formulary has become a source of independent information on essential medicines for pharmaceutical policy-makers and prescribers worldwide. For each medicine, the formulary provides information on use, dosage, adverse effects, contraindications, and warnings, supplemented by guidance on selecting the right medicine for a range of conditions.[11]

OBJECTIVE 5.5. EXPLAIN METHODS IN DRUG USE EVALUATION (DRUG UTILIZATION REVIEW)

DUE (also known as drug utilization review or drug utilization research) tries to interpret the quality and quantity indicators to understand and improve the use of pharmaceuticals at a clinical level to international levels in healthcare system management. DUE is one of the fundamental research activities in pharmacy practice, and most of the research performed in pharmacy practice refers to DUE. Advanced research fields such as pharmacoepidemiology, pharmacovigilance, pharmacoeconomics, outcomes research, etc., claim to produce more useful knowledge compared with DUE. These newer fields of research evolved from DUE, and they use some DUE methods at least in part. The DUE studies by itself are still commonly used as healthcare system indicators locally and internationally.

Practice-based data can be used to check the quality of prescribing, dispensing, administering, etc., and quantities of pharmaceutical use in a healthcare system (hospital, community, country, etc.). Prescribing patterns are commonly used methods to check adherence of prescribers to standard treatment guidelines and the rational or good prescribing practices in general. Qualities of drug dispensing procedures and pharmacist interventions that prevent medication errors at the prescriber, nurse, patient, or pharmacist level can be assessed by DUE research. Hospital administrators or governmental health authorities might need to know the usage patterns of drugs that are subsidized or reimbursed. Economic aspects, including the drug budget management, are largely conducted as pharmacoeconomic studies. DUEs are commonly used in resource-limited settings in budget planning and assessments. In hospitals, the DTC typically organizes DUEs for the formulary management.

Defined daily dose (DDD) is the most regarded drug utilization metric. It was developed as a universal measure of drug consumption. Expression of consumption regarding cost or numbers is not comparable between countries. DU90% is another metric used to identify the most commonly used drugs. It measures the number of drugs accounting for 90% of the use in DDDs. An antimicrobial day (also known as Day Of Therapy-DOT) is defined by any amount of a specific antimicrobial agent administered in a calendar day to a particular hospitalized patient. DOT is a useful measure in antimicrobial stewardship.

DDD is defined as *the assumed average maintenance dose per day for a drug used for its main indication in adults.* DDDs are assigned to drugs that have an ATC code.[12] DDDs are assigned for drugs that are approved in at least one country. DDDs are not assigned for radiopharmaceuticals, appetite stimulants, anesthetics, blood substitutes, parenteral organic nitrates, many topical products, vaccines, antineoplastic agents, etc., due to high dose variation. The DDD is a unit of measurement and does not necessarily correspond to the recommended or prescribed daily dose. Drug utilization data expressed using DDDs are a rough estimate of drug use that could vary in different patient populations with comorbidities.[13]

DDDs are assigned by the WHO Collaborating Centre for Drug Statistics Methodology in the Norwegian Institute of Public Health and funded by the Norwegian government. An assigned DDD may be revised after 3 years. Drug utilization figures should ideally be presented using a relevant denominator in the health context, such as numbers of DDDs per 1000 inhabitants per day, DDDs per inhabitant per year, or as DDDs per 100 bed days.

For a patient, the actual dose used is the *DDD*. If numbers of days in that treatment period also need to be noted, the *DDD/patient* could be used. Once the WHO-assigned DDD is available for a drug, use of that drug by an individual regarding DDD could be calculated as follows:

$$\text{Drug usage (DDD) for a patient} = \frac{(\text{Item issues} \times \text{amount of drug per item})}{\text{DDD}}$$

DDDs per 1000 inhabitants per day: Sales or prescription data presented in DDDs per 1000 inhabitants per day may provide a rough estimate of the proportion of the study population treated daily with a particular drug or group of drugs.

DDDs per 100 bed days: The DDDs per 100 bed days may be applied when drug use by inpatients is considered. The common definition of a bed day is "*a day during which a person is confined to a bed and in which the patient stays overnight in a hospital.*"[14]

OBJECTIVE 5.6. EXPLAIN METHODS TO STANDARDIZE PHARMACY EDUCATION AND PRACTICE: PHARMACEUTICAL CARE, MEDICATION THERAPY MANAGEMENT, CAPE EDUCATIONAL OUTCOMES, NANJING STATEMENT, PHARMACISTS' PATIENT CARE PROCESS, AND ENTRUSTABLE PROFESSIONAL ACTIVITIES

Pharmaceutical Care

The pharmaceutical care concept revolutionized the practice of pharmacists toward delivering more services to patients in addition to the traditional dispensing of medication. The concept emerged in the mid-1970s. Globally, pharmaceutical care services are provided by pharmacists in different forms.

Pharmaceutical care is the leading term used globally to represent overall patient care services, including the WHO and the International Pharmaceutical Federation (FIP). In Australia, the related term is Quality Use of Medicines (QUM). QUM is one of the central objectives of Australia's National Medicines Policy. QUM means selecting management options wisely, choosing a suitable medicine if a medicine is considered necessary, and using medicines safely and effectively. QUM applies to medicines used at both patient and population levels.[15]

In the United States the term used mostly is medication therapy management (MTM), but pharmaceutical care is also used. One of the biggest problems of pharmaceutical care or MTM is that it is not standardized; many define and use it in different ways. In 2014, in the United States, a collaborative effort of leading pharmacy organizations resulted in a standardized method to deliver care services called the pharmacists' patient care process (PPCP). PPCP combined principles of pharmaceutical care and MTM.[16]

Definitions of Pharmaceutical Care

The original and most popular definition of pharmaceutical care was developed by Charles D. Hepler and Linda M. Strand in 1990. The Hepler and Strand definition is:

> *Pharmaceutical care is the responsible provision of drug therapy for the purpose of achieving definite outcomes that improve a patient's quality of life.*

These outcomes are as follows:

- curing a disease,
- eliminating or reducing a patient's symptomatology,
- arresting or slowing down a disease process, or
- preventing a disease or symptomatology.

Three major functions of pharmaceutical care are to

- identify potential and actual drug-related problems
- resolve actual drug-related problems, and
- prevent drug-related problems.[17]

In 1992, the American Society for Health-System (ASHP) Pharmacists adopted the Hepler and Strand definition with two changes. The ASHP definition is:

Pharmaceutical care is the direct, responsible provision of medication-related care for the purpose of achieving definite outcomes that improve a patient's quality of life.[18]

In 1998, the FIP adopted the Hepler and Strand definition with a little modification:

Pharmaceutical care is the responsible provision of drug therapy for the purpose of achieving definite outcomes that improve or maintain a patient's quality of life.[19]

The addition to *maintain* a patient's quality of life is significant when improvement is not possible. Pharmacists, in collaboration with other healthcare professionals, aim to at least maintain individuals' quality of life. Suffering could be decreased even if a cure is not possible.

Another significant effort came from the Pharmaceutical Care Network Europe (PCNE) in 2013. The PCNE definition is:

Pharmaceutical Care is the pharmacist's contribution to the care of individuals in order to optimize medicines use and improve health outcomes.[20]

Pharmaceutical care practice consists of three major components: a philosophy of practice, a patient care process, and a practice management system.

The philosophy of pharmaceutical care practice consists of

- a description of the social need for the practice,
- a clear statement of individual practitioner responsibilities to meet this social need,
- the expectation to be patient centered, and
- the requirement to function within the caring paradigm.

These four constructs, social need, practitioner responsibilities, patient-centered approach, and caring paradigm, formulate professionalism for pharmacists.[21]

Steps in pharmaceutical care vary widely. Many develop their suitable models of the care process. What is common in the process is to collect relevant information, assess the information for healthcare needs and drug therapy problems, prepare a care plan, and evaluate the outcomes. Alternatively, it can be identify, assess, resolve, and monitor drug-related problems. Repeat the process if required. Some of the common formats to report a pharmaceutical care intervention are SOAP (subjective, objective, assessment, plan), TITIRS (title, introduction, text, recommendation, signature), and FARM (findings, assessment, recommendations/resolutions, management). Among these, SOAP notes are the most common.[22]

Hepler, who originally defined pharmaceutical care, suggested eight steps in the pharmaceutical care process:

1. Record and interpret relevant patient information.
   What do we need to know about this patient?
2. Document Therapeutic Plan and Desired Therapeutic Objectives for the Patient.
   What do we intend to achieve with this therapy in this patient?
3. Evaluate a Therapeutic Plan.
   Is this an acceptable plan to achieve those objectives for this patient?
4. Design a Monitoring Plan.
   What evidence will we need to assess the progress of therapy?

5. Dispense, Drug Products, Advise Patient.
   Can this patient (or family caregiver, etc.) now make the best use of this drug?
6. Implement the Monitoring Plan.
   What evidence do I need to assist in evaluating this patient's progress?
7. Identify Possible Drug Therapy Problems.
   Is this patient progressing toward therapeutic objectives? Are there indicators of drug therapy problems?
8. Respond to Problems.
   What action should I take now?[23]

ASHP categorized drug therapy problems into 11 types for the national skills competition in 2012:

1. Correlation between drug therapy and medical problems
2. Appropriate drug selection
3. Drug regimen
4. Therapeutic duplication
5. Drug allergy or intolerance
6. Adverse drug events
7. Interactions: drug—drug, drug—disease, drug—nutrient, and drug—laboratory test
8. Social or recreational drug use
9. Failure to receive therapy
10. Financial impact
11. Patient knowledge of drug therapy

As per PCNE, a drug-related problem is an event or circumstance involving drug therapy that actually or potentially interferes with desired health outcomes. PCNE drug-related problems are classified in Table 5.1.

Medication Therapy Management

Following the late 2003 passage of the Medicare Prescription Drug Improvement and Modernization Act, a unanimous definition of MTM was required in the United States. Eleven pharmacy organizations in the US coordinated by the American Pharmacists Association (APhA) approved a definition in 2004.[25] The MTM definition is:

> *MTM is a service or group of services that optimize therapeutic outcomes for individual patients. MTM services include medication therapy reviews, pharmacotherapy consults, anticoagulation management, immunizations, health and wellness programs and many other clinical services. Pharmacists provide MTM to help patients get the best benefits from their medications by actively managing drug therapy and by identifying, preventing and resolving medication-related problems.*[26]

MTM is a distinct service or group of services that optimizes therapeutic outcomes for individual patients.
MTM services are independent of, but can occur in conjunction with, the provision of a medical product.
MTM encompasses a broad range of professional activities and responsibilities within the licensed pharmacist's, or other qualified healthcare provider's, scope of practice. These services include, but are not limited to, the following, according to the individual needs of the patient:

- Performing or obtaining necessary assessments of the patient's health status
- Formulating a medication treatment plan
- Selecting, initiating, modifying, or administering medication therapy
- Monitoring and evaluating the patient's response to therapy, including safety and effectiveness
- Performing a comprehensive medication review to identify, resolve, and prevent medication-related problems, including adverse drug events
- Documenting the care delivered and communicating essential information to the patient's other primary care providers
- Providing verbal education and training designed to enhance patient understanding and appropriate use of his/her medications
- Providing information, support services, and resources designed to enhance patient adherence to his/her therapeutic regimens
- Coordinating and integrating medication therapy management services within the broader healthcare management services being provided to the patient.[27]

TABLE 5.1 Pharmaceutical Care Network Europe Classified Drug-Related Problems (DRPs), Causes, Interventions, and Outcomes V8.0[24]; the Basic Classification

	Code V8.0	Primary Domains
Problems (also potential)	P1	**Treatment effectiveness** There is a (potential) problem with the (lack of) effect of the pharmacotherapy
	P2	**Treatment safety** Patient suffers, or could suffer, from an adverse drug event
	P3	**Others**
Causes (including possible causes for potential problems)	C1	**Drug selection** The cause of the DRP can be related to the selection of the drug
	C2	**Drug form** The cause of the DRP is related to the selection of the drug form
	C3	**Dose selection** The cause of the DRP can be related to the selection of the dosage schedule
	C4	**Treatment duration** The cause of the DRP is related to the duration of treatment
	C5	**Dispensing** The cause of the DRP can be related to the logistics of the prescribing and dispensing process
	C6	**Drug use/process** The cause of the DRP is related to the way the patient gets the drug administered by a health professional or carer, in spite of proper instructions (on the label)
	C7	**Patient related** The cause of the DRP can be related to the patient and his/her behavior (intentional or nonintentional)
	C8	**Other**
Planned interventions	I0	**No intervention**
	I1	**At prescriber level**
	I2	**At patient level**
	I3	**At drug level**
	I4	**Other**
Intervention acceptance	A1	**Intervention accepted**
	A2	**Intervention not accepted**
	A3	**Other**
Status of the DRP	O0	**Problem status unknown**
	O1	**Problem solved**
	O2	**Problem partially solved**
	O3	**Problem not solved**

As per APhA, a program that provides coverage for MTM services shall include:

1. Patient-specific and individualized services or sets of services provided directly by a pharmacist to the patient. These services are distinct from formulary development and use, generalized patient education and information activities, and other population-focused quality-assurance measures for medication use.

2. Face-to-face interaction between the patient and the pharmacist as the preferred method of delivery. When patient-specific barriers to face-to-face communication exist, patients shall have equal access to appropriate alternative delivery methods. MTM programs shall include structures supporting the establishment and maintenance of the patient/pharmacist relationship.
3. Opportunities for pharmacists and other qualified healthcare providers to identify patients who should receive MTM services.
4. Payment for MTM services consistent with contemporary provider payment rates that are based on the time, clinical intensity, and resources required to provide services.
5. Processes to improve continuity of care, outcomes, and outcome measures.[28]

Core Elements of an MTM Service Model in Pharmacy Practice

The MTM service model in pharmacy practice includes the following five core elements:

- Medication therapy review
- Personal medication record
- Medication-related action plan
- Intervention and/or referral
- Documentation and follow-up[28]

A variety of direct patient care services offered by pharmacists through MTM services include comprehensive medication reviews (CMRs) and targeted medication reviews (TMRs). CMRs consist of a full review of all medications and past medication history. Following a CMR and when a medication-related problem is identified, a TMR can be provided to resolve the specific finding. CMRs and TMRs are services delivered by pharmacists to optimize patient-specific medication regimens to improve patient outcomes and reduce treatment-related harm.

MTM services are provided to patients in a variety of clinical practice settings (i.e., inpatient, ambulatory care, managed care, long-term care, and telehealth). However, MTM services are frequently not billed or reimbursed and are related to numerous factors, including practice model limitations, lack of integrated billing support services, or payer-based confusion regarding benefit coverage. The shift from fee-for-service payment models to quality outcome-driven models as well struggles to include pharmacist providers within the standard scope of providers at the federal level are key factors that limit the full utilization of MTM services. Functional payment models for MTM services are essential to ensure the ability to achieve improvements in patient-specific and population-based health outcomes. Commercial insurers and government payers are not universally reimbursed for MTM services despite the fact that these services demonstrate a strong return-on-investment based on improving quality of health outcomes, improved treatment adherence, reduced adverse side effects, and other medication-related problems. Some payers, such as Kaiser Permanente, are implementing "at-risk" contracts in bundled practice models like Accountable Care Organizations to ensure improved provider engagement and economic performance.

Despite the overwhelming success of numerous demonstration projects, research studies, and practice model initiatives, including the Asheville Project, Ten Cities Challenge, Project Impact, and multiple others, viable reimbursement mechanisms remain one of the key barriers to nationwide MTM implementation and sustainability.

Rosenthal et al. describe MTM services in three definable levels of intensity. Level 1 (low intensity) involves adherence management, Level 2 (mid-level) involves drug-related problems, and Level 3 (high intensity) involves disease state management. Although Level 3 may be described as the ideal performance level, MTM services should be tailored to meet the needs of each specific patient, family, or caregiver. Table 5.2 describes the goals of these three levels of performance.[29,30]

Just as in medical practice, recognizing differences in pharmacist practitioners' level of training, clinical proficiencies, practice experience, and credentialing may also help in driving optimal levels of performance for targeted patient populations.[31]

A broader array of clinical service coding billing methods will assist in improving future reimbursement rates for pharmacists' services.[32] There will always be opportunities for future innovation and practice enhancement at both the state and federal levels to improve the utilization of pharmacists' patient care services. Pharmacists remain diligent and committed to expanding collaboration with other healthcare providers to ensure optimization of medication therapy to improve the quality of health outcomes, patient safety, and cost-effectiveness of future healthcare delivery models.[33]

TABLE 5.2 Performance Levels of Medication Therapy Management

Performance Level	Goals
Level 1	Adherence management
Level 2	Interventions in drug-related problems
Level 3	Disease state management

Nanjing Statements

The FIP's Nanjing Statements were released in 2017. The Nanjing Statements are intended for education providers, including Schools of Pharmacy and providers of Continuing Professional Development and Continuing Education. They are to be used for self-assessment and monitoring (at the country level or the education provider level), identification of gaps and strategic planning, and improving the process of education. The statements have eight clusters as follows:[34]

- Shared Global Vision: A shared global vision promotes workforce development in the context of pharmaceutical education and training. This global vision should help professional leadership bodies, educators, and regulators in developing a national or regional vision based on the priorities and resources of the country or region, with the aim of developing new drugs and improving their use for better health.
- Professional Skills Mix: Pharmacists in all settings and pharmaceutical scientists need competence, skills, knowledge, and attitudes to meet the needs of the public and interact with other healthcare professionals.
- Recruitment of Students: Recruiting students who have a profile that fits the requirements of the school and are aligned with the profile of pharmacists desired for the country.
- Foundation Training and Leadership: Foundation training includes the process of education and leadership development for students and new graduates in pharmacy and the pharmaceutical sciences with a priority on developing the next generation of clinical, scientific, academic, and professional leaders.
- Experiential Education: Experiential education programs are where students incrementally develop their pharmacy practice and science skills in a wide variety of real-life settings.
- Resources and Academic Staff: Resources and academic staff refer to equipment, finances, technology, and human resources needed to prepare pharmacists and pharmaceutical scientists properly.
- Quality Assurance: Quality assurance refers to the key aspects and mechanisms to identify opportunities for and make improvement in pharmacy and pharmaceutical sciences education to ensure a good, sustainable performance and suitable competencies of the future workforce.
- Continuing Professional Development: Continuing professional development (CPD) refers to building on previous education as a pharmacist and pharmaceutical scientist.[34]

CAPE Educational Outcomes

Center for the Advancement of Pharmacy Education (CAPE) Educational Outcomes is a model used to plan pharmacy curricula. The CAPE Educational Outcomes could be used as a basis to develop learning objectives of the pharmacy undergraduate program.[35] The CAPE Educational Outcomes 2013 consists of the following:

Domain 1—Foundational Knowledge
1.1. Learner (Learner)
Domain 2—Essentials for Practice and Care
2.1. Patient-centered care (Caregiver)
2.2. Medication use systems management (Manager)
2.3. Health and wellness (Promoter)
2.4. Population-based care (Provider)

Domain 3—Approach to Practice and Care
3.1. Problem-solving (Problem solver)
3.2. Educator (Educator)
3.3. Patient advocacy (Advocate)
3.4. Interprofessional collaboration (Collaborator)
3.5. Cultural sensitivity (Includer)
3.6. Communication (Communicator)
Domain 4—Personal and Professional Development
4.1. Self-awareness (Self-aware)
4.2. Leadership (Leader)
4.3. Innovation and entrepreneurship (Innovator)
4.4. Professionalism (Professional)

Pharmacists' Patient Care Process

PPCP is a newer care process that combines pharmaceutical care and MTM. The Joint Commission of Pharmacy Practitioners (JCPP) is a forum of leading pharmacy organizations in the United States. PPCP was a group effort of these agencies in producing a standardized patient care process by pharmacists for pharmacists. It is a comprehensive approach to patient-centered care delivered by pharmacists in collaboration with other healthcare professionals. PPCP is based on the existing evidence of pharmaceutical care and MTM. It tries to incorporate the following concepts into patient care provided by the pharmacists:

- Quality care: Assuring quality in the healthcare products and services. Providing drugs of good quality and caring to prevent and manage any drug-related problems. Pharmacists regularly deliver evidence-based recommendations to healthcare professionals and patients.
- Access to healthcare: Being one of the most accessible healthcare professionals, pharmacists improve the patients' access to healthcare interventions.
- Cost-effective outcomes: Assuring value for money spent in achieving measurable clinical outcomes.
- Collaborative practice: Collaborating with physicians and other pharmacists to provide coordinated care.
- Patient-centered care: Giving importance to the role of patients in the clinical decision-making process (Fig. 5.1).

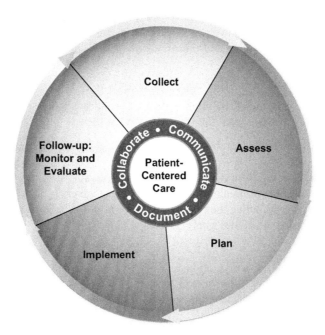

FIGURE 5.1   Pharmacists' patient care process (Joint Commission of Pharmacy Practitioners).[16]

As per the JCPP guidance, using principles of evidence-based practice, pharmacists perform the following:

Collect

The pharmacist assures the collection of necessary subjective and objective information about the patient to understand the relevant medical/medication history and clinical status of the patient. Information may be gathered and verified from multiple sources, including existing patient records, the patient, and other healthcare professionals. This process includes collecting

- A current medication list and medication use history for prescription and nonprescription medications, herbal products, and other dietary supplements.
- Relevant health data may include medical history, health and wellness information, biometric test results, and physical assessment findings.
- Patient lifestyle habits, preferences and beliefs, health and functional goals, and socioeconomic factors that affect access to medications and other aspects of care.

Assess

The pharmacist assesses the information collected and analyzes the clinical effects of the patient's therapy in the context of the patient's overall health goals to identify and prioritize problems and achieve optimal care. This process includes assessing

- Each medication for appropriateness, effectiveness, safety, and patient adherence.
- Health and functional status, risk factors, health data, cultural factors, health literacy, and access to medications or other aspects of care.
- Immunization status and the need for preventive care and other healthcare services, where appropriate.

Plan

The pharmacist develops an individualized patient-centered care plan in collaboration with other healthcare professionals and the patient or caregiver who is evidence based and cost-effective. This process includes establishing a care plan that

- Addresses medication-related problems and optimizes medication therapy.
- Sets goals of therapy for achieving clinical outcomes in the context of the patient's overall healthcare goals and access to care.
- Engages the patient through education, empowerment, and self-management.
- Supports care continuity, including follow-up and transitions of care as appropriate.

Implement

The pharmacist implements the care plan in collaboration with other healthcare professionals and the patient or caregiver. During the process of implementing the care plan, the pharmacist

- Addresses medication- and health-related problems and engages in preventive care strategies, including vaccine administration.
- Initiates, modifies, discontinues, or administers medication therapy as authorized.
- Provides education and self-management training to the patient or caregiver.
- Contributes to coordination of care, including the referral or transition of the patient to another healthcare professional.
- Schedules follow-up care as needed to achieve goals of therapy.

Follow-Up: Monitor and Evaluate

The pharmacist monitors and evaluates the effectiveness of the care plan and modifies the plan in collaboration with other healthcare professionals and the patient or caregiver as needed. This process includes the continuous monitoring and evaluation of

- Medication appropriateness, effectiveness, and safety and patient adherence through available health data, biometric test results, and patient feedback.

- Clinical endpoints that contribute to the patient's overall health.
- Outcomes of care, including progress toward or the achievement of goals of therapy.[16]

Core Entrustable Professional Activities

Core Entrustable Professional Activities (EPAs) for New Pharmacy Graduates are discrete, essential activities and tasks that all new pharmacy graduates must be able to perform without direct supervision on entering practice or postgraduate training. These statements were labeled as "core" to denote that these EPAs are expected of all graduates independent of practice setting. They serve as a baseline, not a ceiling.[36] The EPA Statements for New Pharmacy Graduates are as follows (Table 5.3):

TABLE 5.3 Core Entrustable Professional Activities for New Pharmacy Graduates[36]

Patient Care Provider Domain	Example Supporting Tasks
Collect information to identify a patient's medication-related problems and health-related needs.	- Collect a medical history from a patient or caregiver. - Collect a medication history from a patient or caregiver. - Discuss a patient's experience with medication. - Determine a patient's medication adherence. - Use health records to determine a patient's health-related needs relevant to the setting of care and the purpose of the encounter.
Analyze information to determine the effects of medication therapy, identify medication-related problems, and prioritize health-related needs.	- Assess a patient's signs and symptoms to determine whether the patient can be treated within the scope of practice or requires a referral. - Measure an adult patient's vital signs and interpret the results (e.g., body temperature, pulse rate, respiration rate, and blood pressure). - Interpret laboratory test results. - Identify drug interactions. - Perform a comprehensive medication review (CMR) for a patient. - Assess a patient's health literacy using a validated screening tool. - Compile a prioritized health-related problem list for a patient. - Evaluate an existing drug therapy regimen.
Establish patient-centered goals and create a care plan for a patient in collaboration with the patient, caregiver(s), and other health professionals that are evidence based and cost-effective.	- Follow an evidence-based disease management protocol. - Develop a treatment plan with a patient. - Manage drug interactions. - Select monitoring parameters to determine the therapeutic and adverse effects related to the treatment plan. - Determine the appropriate time interval(s) to collect monitoring data. - Create a patient-specific education plan.
Implement a care plan in collaboration with the patient, caregivers, and other health professionals.	- Write a note that documents the findings, recommendations, and plan from a patient encounter. - Educate a patient regarding the appropriate use of a new medication, device to administer a medication, or self-monitoring test. - Educate a patient on the use of medication adherence aids. - Assist a patient with behavior change (e.g., use shared decision-making and motivational strategies).
Follow-up and monitor a care plan.	- Collect monitoring data at the appropriate time interval(s). - Evaluate the selected monitoring parameters to determine the therapeutic and adverse effects related to the treatment plan.

Continued

TABLE 5.3 Core Entrustable Professional Activities for New Pharmacy Graduates[36]—cont'd

	• Recommend modifications or adjustments to an existing medication therapy regimen based on patient response. • Present a patient case to a colleague during a handoff or transition of care.
Interprofessional Team Member Domain:	**Example Supporting Tasks:**
Collaborate as a member of an interprofessional team.	• Contribute medication-related expertise to the team's work. • Explain to a patient, caregiver, or professional colleague each team member's role and responsibilities. • Communicate a patient's medication-related problem(s) to another health professional. • Use setting-appropriate communication skills when interacting with others. • Use consensus-building strategies to develop a shared plan of action.
Population Health Promoter Domain:	**Example Supporting Tasks:**
Identify patients at risk for prevalent diseases in a population.	• Perform a screening assessment to identify patients at risk for prevalent diseases in a population (e.g., hypertension, diabetes, depression).
Minimize adverse drug events and medication errors.	• Assist in the identification of underlying system-associated causes of errors. • Report adverse drug events and medication errors to stakeholders.
Maximize the appropriate use of medications in a population.	• Perform a medication use evaluation. • Apply cost–benefit, formulary, and/or epidemiology principles to medication-related decisions.
Ensure that patients have been immunized against vaccine-preventable diseases.	• Determine whether a patient is eligible for and has received recommended immunizations. • Administer and document recommended immunizations to an adult patient. • Perform basic life support.
Information Master Domain:	**Example Supporting Tasks:**
Educate patients and professional colleagues regarding the appropriate use of medications.	• Lead a discussion regarding a recently published research manuscript and its application to patient care. • Develop and deliver a brief (less than 1 h) educational program regarding medication therapy to health professional(s) or lay audiences.
Use evidence-based information to advance patient care.	• Retrieve and analyze scientific literature to make a patient-specific recommendation. • Retrieve and analyze scientific literature to answer a drug information question.
Practice Manager Domain:	**Example Supporting Tasks:**
Oversee the pharmacy operations for an assigned work shift.	• Implement pharmacy policies and procedures. • Supervise and coordinate the activities of pharmacy technicians and other support staff. • Assist in training pharmacy technicians and other support staff. • Assist in the evaluation of pharmacy technicians and other support staff. • Identify pharmacy service problems and/or medication safety issues. • Maintain the pharmacy inventory. • Assist in the management of a pharmacy budget. • Interpret pharmacy quality and productivity indicators using continuous improvement quality techniques. • Assist in the preparation for regulatory visits and inspections.

Continued

TABLE 5.3 Core Entrustable Professional Activities for New Pharmacy Graduates[36]—cont'd

Fulfill a medication order.	<ul><li>Enter patient-specific information into an electronic health or pharmacy record system.</li><li>Prepare commonly prescribed medications that require basic sterile compounding or basic nonsterile compounding prior to patient use.</li><li>Determine if a medication is contraindicated for a patient.</li><li>Identify and manage drug interactions.</li><li>Determine the patient co-pay or price for a prescription. Ensure that formulary preferred medications are used when clinically appropriate.</li><li>Obtain authorization for a nonpreferred medication when clinically appropriate.</li><li>Assist a patient to acquire medication(s) through support programs.</li></ul>
Self-Developer Domain:	**Example Supporting Tasks:**
Create a written plan for continuous professional development.	<ul><li>Create and update a curriculum vitae, resume, and/or professional portfolio.</li><li>Perform a self-evaluation to identify professional strengths and weaknesses.</li></ul>

Adapted with permission from the American Association of Colleges of Pharmacy. The full report is available at http://www.aacp.org/resources/education/cape/Pages/EPAs.aspx.

CONCLUSION

Services provided by the pharmacists are heavily based on rational drug use and other WHO guidance. Standards for improving practice and education of pharmacists are in place. Good examples of practice standards are PCNE classification of drug-related problems in Europe and PPCP in the United States.

PRACTICE QUESTIONS

1. Azithromycin is a/an?
   A. Proprietary name
   B. Nonproprietary name
   C. IUPAC name
   D. ATC code
2. As per the WHO definition, which of the following is a device?
   A. NSAID
   B. Oral contraceptive
   C. Injection
   D. Implant
3. DDD is a?
   A. Universal unit of drug consumption
   B. Dose approved by a regulatory agency
   C. Days of drug use affecting the dose
   D. Dose mentioned on a product label
4. The center point of PPCP is?
   A. Patient-centered care: Collaborate, Communicate, Document
   B. Patient-centered care: Follow-up, Monitor, Evaluate
   C. Patient-centered care: Collect information
   D. Patient-centered care: Prepare pharmaceutical care plan

REFERENCES

1. US FDA. *Glossary of Terms. Drug Approvals and Databases*; 2017. Drugs@FDA. https://www.fda.gov/drugs/informationondrugs/ucm079436.htm.
2. WHO. *Medical Device – Full Definition*. World Health Organisation. http://www.who.int/medical_devices/full_deffinition/en/. Accessed on July 21, 2018.
3. WHO. *International Nonproprietary Names. Essential Medicines and Health Products*. WHO. http://www.who.int/medicines/services/inn/en/. Accessed on July 21, 2018.
4. US FDA. *Information on Biosimilars*. US FDA; 2017. https://www.fda.gov/drugs/developmentapprovalprocess/howdrugsaredevelopedandapproved/approvalapplications/therapeuticbiologicapplications/biosimilars/default.htm.
5. IUPAC Nomenclature. *International Union of Pure and Applied Chemistry*. https://iupac.org/what-we-do/nomenclature/. Accessed on July 21, 2018.
6. WHO. ATC/DDD Index. *WHO Collaborating Centre for Drug Statistics Methodology*; 2017. https://www.whocc.no/atc_ddd_index/.
7. WHO. *Promoting Rational Use of Medicines: Core Components - WHO Policy Perspectives on Medicines. Essential Medicines and Health Products Information Portal*; 2002. http://apps.who.int/medicinedocs/en/d/Jh3011e/.
8. Holloway K, Green T. *Drugs and Therapeutics Committee - A Practical Guide*. WHO/MSH; 2003. http://apps.who.int/medicinedocs/en/d/Js4882e/.
9. WHO. *Model Lists of Essential Medicines. Essential Medicines and Health Products*. WHO; 2017. http://www.who.int/medicines/publications/essentialmedicines/en/.
10. WHO. *The Selection of Essential Medicines*. Geneva: WHO; 2002. http://apps.who.int/medicinedocs/pdf/s2296e/s2296e.pdf.
11. WHO. *Essential Medicines and Health Products Information Portal*. WHO Model Formulary; 2008. http://apps.who.int/medicinedocs/en/d/Js16879e/.
12. WHO. *Defined Daily Dose (DDD). Essential Medicines and Health Products*. http://www.who.int/medicines/regulation/medicines-safety/toolkit_ddd/en/. Accessed on July 21, 2018.
13. WHO. *Definition and General Considerations. WHO Collaborating Centre for Drug Statistics Methodology*; 2017. https://www.whocc.no/ddd/definition_and_general_considera/.
14. WHO. *DDD Indicators. Essential Medicines and Health Products*. http://www.who.int/medicines/regulation/medicines-safety/toolkit_indicators/en/. Accessed on July 21, 2018.
15. Australian Government Department of Health and Ageing Pharmaceutical Benefits Branch. *Quality Use of Medicines (QUM)*. Department of Health - Australian Government; 2011. http://www.health.gov.au/internet/main/publishing.nsf/content/nmp-quality.htm.
16. Joint Commission of Pharmacy Practitioners. *Pharmacists' Patient Care Process*; 2014. https://www.pharmacist.com/sites/default/files/files/PatientCareProcess.pdf.
17. Hepler CD, Strand LM. Opportunities and responsibilities in pharmaceutical care. *Am J Hosp Pharm*. 1990;47(3):533–543. http://www.ncbi.nlm.nih.gov/pubmed/2316538.
18. American Society of Hospital Pharmacists. ASHP statement on pharmaceutical care. *Am J Hosp Pharm*. 1993;50:1720–1723.
19. Wiedenmayer K, Summers S, Mackie A, Gous S, Everard M, Dick T. *Developing Pharmacy Practice a Focus on Patient Care*. 2006.
20. Allemann SS, van Mil JWF, Botermann L, Berger K, Griese N, Hersberger KE. Pharmaceutical care: the PCNE definition 2013. *Int J Clin Pharm*. 2014;36(3):544–555. https://doi.org/10.1007/s11096-014-9933-x.
21. Cipolle R, Strand L, Morley P. Chapter 2. Pharmaceutical care as the professional practice for patient-centered medication management services. In: *Pharmaceutical Care Practice: The Patient-Centered Approach to Medication Management Services*. 3rd ed. New York: McGraw-Hill Medical; 2012. Accesss Pharmacy.
22. American Pharmacists Association. *Medication Therapy Management Services. Baltimore*. 2007.
23. Hepler CD. *Pharmaceutical Care Principles and Processes*. University of Florida; 2010.
24. PCNE. *Pharmaceutical Care Network Europe - Classification of Drug Related Problems V 8.01. The Netherlands*. 2017.
25. Bluml BM. Definition of medication therapy management: development of professionwide consensus. *J Am Pharm Assoc JAPhA*. 2005;45(5):566–572.
26. APhA MTM Central. American Pharmacists Association.
27. Joint Commission of Pharmacy Practitioners. *Medication Therapy Management Services - Definition and Program Criteria*. American Pharmaceutical Association; 2004.
28. Medication therapy management in pharmacy practice: core elements of an MTM service model (version 2.0). *J Am Pharm Assoc JAPhA*. 2008;48(3):341–353. https://doi.org/10.1331/JAPhA.2008.08514.
29. Rosenthal M, Holmes E, Banahan B. Making MTM implementable and sustainable in community pharmacy: is it time for a different game plan? *Res Soc Adm Pharm*. 2016;12(3):523–528. https://doi.org/10.1016/j.sapharm.2015.07.006.
30. Koenigsfeld CF, Horning KK, Logemann CD, Schmidt GA. Medication therapy management in the primary care setting. *J Pharm Pract*. 2012;25(1):89–95. https://doi.org/10.1177/0897190011416671.
31. Stafford R, Thomas J, Payakachat N, et al. Using an array of implementation strategies to improve success rates of pharmacist-initiated medication therapy management services in community pharmacies. *Res Soc Adm Pharm*. 2017;13(5):938–946. https://doi.org/10.1016/j.sapharm.2017.04.006.
32. Scott MA, Hitch WJ, Wilson CG, Lugo AM. Billing for pharmacists' cognitive services in physicians' offices: multiple methods of reimbursement. *J Am Pharm Assoc*. 2012;52(2):175–180. https://doi.org/10.1331/JAPhA.2012.11218.
33. Butler A, Dehner M, Gates RJ, et al. Comprehensive medication management programs: 2015 status in southern California. *Res Soc Adm Pharm*. 2017;13(1):63–87. https://doi.org/10.1016/j.sapharm.2016.02.003.

34. FIP. *Nanjing Statements. Statements on Pharmacy and Pharmaceutical Sciences Education*; 2017. http://www.fip.org/files/fip/PharmacyEducation/Global_Conference_docs/Nanjing_Statements.pdf.

35. Medina MS, Plaza CM, Stowe CD, et al. Center for the advancement of pharmacy education 2013 educational outcomes. *Am J Pharm Educ.* 2013;77(8):162. https://doi.org/10.5688/ajpe778162.

36. Haines ST, Pittenger AL, Stolte SK, et al. Core entrustable professional activities for new pharmacy graduates. *Am J Pharm Educ.* 2017;81(1):S2. https://doi.org/10.5688/ajpe811S2.

ANSWERS TO PRACTICE QUESTIONS

1. B
2. D
3. A
4. A

Chapter 6

Communication Skills and Patient History Interview

Shaun Wen Huey Lee[1], Dixon Thomas[2], Seeba Zachariah[2] and Jason C. Cooper[3]

[1]Monash University Malaysia, Bandar Sunway, Malaysia; [2]Gulf Medical University, Ajman, United Arab Emirates; [3]Medical University of South Carolina, Charleston, SC, United States

Learning Objectives

Objective 6.1 Explain why communication skills are essential for pharmacists.
Objective 6.2 Detail the elements of professional communication.
Objective 6.3 Identify barriers to communication and suggest how to overcome them.
Objective 6.4 Discuss the characteristics and process of the patient history interview.

OBJECTIVE 6.1. EXPLAIN WHY COMMUNICATION SKILLS ARE ESSENTIAL FOR PHARMACISTS

Good communication plays an important role in patient-centered care and collaborative practice. While considering communication as a skill in both clinical practice and life, it takes time and effort before one becomes comfortable and proficient. As such, one should take time to reflect after an interaction about what went well, what did not, and what contributed to the success/failure of the communication. It can help the pharmacist to identify further aspects that can be strengthened, as well as being an extremely powerful developmental exercise. Ideally, the development of communication skills should happen in a comfortable setting, such as with family/friends or in educational settings. Pharmacists who do not possess sufficient communication skills will find it difficult to work effectively.[1–5]

Pharmacists should have good reading, listening, speaking, and written communication skills. The order given here is intentional. Traditionally, pharmacists are known for their skills to read prescriptions and interpret their meaning into action. Reading and deciphering medical records requires the application of pathophysiology and pharmacotherapy knowledge. Reading skills are also essential in evidence-based practice to read and interpret clinical literature. Listening involves hearing from patients, other consumers, caregivers, healthcare professionals, and administrators. In a typical counseling session, the pharmacist listens for more time than he/she speaks. Collecting appropriate information happens only when the pharmacist listens to and observes all signals from medical records, patient explanations, signs/symptoms, and patient behavior. Speaking is a way of giving advice. Such guidance should be trustworthy, assertive enough to change wrong practice, and empathic enough to be accepted. Written skills are especially important when providing drug information, writing in medical records, and other clinical communications. The combination of these important communication skills will result in better patient adherence and outcomes, prevention of medication errors, and an efficient healthcare system.

The scope of pharmacy practice now also includes patient-centered processes such as providing drug information and direct patient counseling, as well as technical aspects of pharmaceutical care such as medication reconciliation. Collection of information from patients as part of pharmaceutical care or the newer term pharmacists' patient care process (PPCP) requires improved communication skills. As such, it is essential that pharmacists become an effective healthcare team member and possess the skills and attitudes to enable them to assume their roles appropriately. Indeed, this has been highlighted by several organizations including the Joint Commission International, which identified in their patient safety goals for the need to "improve effective communication."[6] This has been similarly endorsed by the World Health Organization, in which a pharmacist has been identified as the communicator or the link between patient and other healthcare professionals.[7] As per the Center for the Advancement of Pharmacy Education (CAPE) communicator is an educational outcome.[8] Pharmacy programs include communication as a core element of their curriculum.

Pharmacists' Communication Skills Relevant to Consumers

Pharmacists regularly communicate with consumers and healthcare professionals. Application of relevant communication skills helps consumers to understand what they should know. Understanding the audience or whom we are interacting with about their likes and dislikes, and information needs is a foundation in professional communication. For example, a patient may swallow a suppository if the route of administration is not communicated well. Studies show that communication gaps result in medication errors; subsequently, the healthcare system fails to produce optimal outcomes.[2] Strong communication skills improve pharmacist–consumer interactions by

- Being a highly accessible healthcare professional.
- Establishing the necessary rapport to build a trusting relationship.
- Being a trusted consultant in the use of over-the-counter (OTC) as well as complementary alternative medicine products.
- Persuading consumers to adhere to their medication.
- Communicating essential information that guides consumers on the safe use of their medications.
- Tailoring and directing the communication process as the situation demands.
- Providing advice on other healthcare needs, such as preventive health (e.g., vaccinations, health screenings, physicals).

Pharmacists' Communication Skills Relevant to Other Healthcare Professionals

Communicating to healthcare professionals are in professional language expressing pathophysiological and pharmacotherapy knowledge in technical terms for exchanging deep scientific information. Clinicians appreciate evidence-based information to develop or modify patient care decisions while patients appreciate if pharmacists communicate same concepts in lay language. Developing and implementing pharmaceutical care plans requires efficient teamwork. Teamwork based on effective communication is the cornerstone of today's collaborative practice. Interprofessional communication is promoted in healthcare education, practice, and research.[9] Phases of team performance described by Psychologist, Bruce Tuckman, is well known. According to him, a group goes through the following phases to perform[10]:

- Forming
- Storming
- Norming
- Performing

Rightly said, when a healthcare professional team is under development, the communication gaps between doctors, nurses, and pharmacists are experienced by all. In the storming stage, criticism may arise regarding what is going wrong. Later, when rapport is established, professionals understand the shared responsibility and work in harmony (i.e., normalization). As a result, patients greatly benefit from the enhanced performance of multiprofessional healthcare teams as efficient teamwork is found to reduce medication errors and other drug-related problems.[2,11,12]

OBJECTIVE 6.2. DETAIL THE ELEMENTS OF PROFESSIONAL COMMUNICATION

Interpersonal communication is a fundamental aspect of clinical practice. It is a two-way process where both the patient and pharmacist can give information through verbal and nonverbal messages. The interpersonal communication model comprises five key elements (Fig. 6.1):

- Sender—person conveying the message
- Message—information conveyed (verbal and nonverbal)
- Receiver—the person receiving the message
- Feedback—receiver communicates their understanding of the sender's message
- Barrier—any interference with the expression or understanding of the message

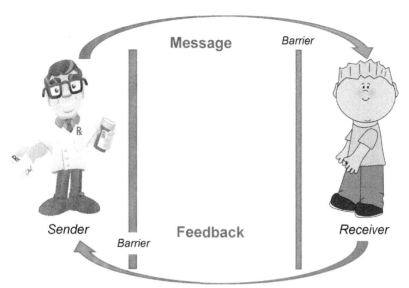

FIGURE 6.1   Interpersonal communication model. *Adapted from Beardsley RS, Kimberlin CL, Tindall WN.* Communication Skills in Pharmacy Practice: A Practical Guide for Students and Practitioners. *Lippincott Williams & Wilkins; 2012.*

Key Communication Skills

Research suggests that a message is communicated via three methods, namely words, the tone of voice, and body language. The factors facilitating the communication or its barriers are not always physical, it might be behavioral or situational too. Details of these key components are described further (Fig. 6.2).[14]

Body Language or Nonverbal Language

Body gestures, facial expressions, and eyes can speak a thousand words. As such, being able to interpret body language helps us to know how a patient feels during their consultation and the extent to which they are comfortable during the conversation.
  Body language is the transmission and interpretation of one's feeling, attitudes, and moods via the following:

- Body posture, movement, position, and relationship to other objects and surroundings
- Facial expression and eye movement

  As such, it is important to understand a patient's body language, as this will help identify points in the consultation where the patient may feel uncomfortable, confused, or disagree with something said. For example, a patient may have

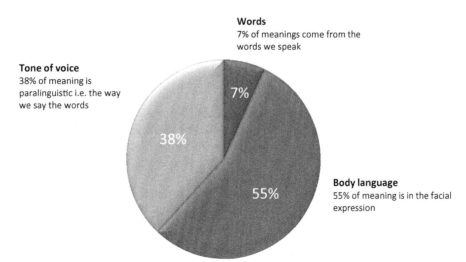

FIGURE 6.2   Components on how messages are communicated. *Adapted from Mehrabian A.* Silent Messages: Implicit Communication of Emotions and Attitudes. *2nd ed. Belmont, California: Wadsworth Publishing Company; 1981.*

certain beliefs about their medication (e.g., that the medication may result in side effects, or that it is not "natural", many are scared of chemical or genetically engineered products), which may affect their adherence. They will usually not offer this information, as they may feel their opinions will be brushed aside or misunderstood. Subsequently, it is important for a pharmacist to be able to identify some of the nonverbal cues associated with a patient's beliefs, including crossing their arms or hands during a consultation, showing a reluctance to listen, or trying to rush off during the consultation.

Verbal Language

Language is important in any consultation, either in the choice of words used or how information is being conveyed. One general rule of thumb is to avoid medical jargon and terminology, as this helps give the assurance that messages are communicated effectively. However, there is also a strong need to reflect the language and manner in which the patient speaks. For example, if the patient uses medical words during the consultation, choosing to respond in layman's terms may send out the wrong signals, as either they are not being listened to or the patient's knowledge is not being respected. As such, language and the way a patient uses language to communicate in a context is important; ultimately, this will help build rapport between the pharmacist and the patient.

In our increasingly diverse communities, it is also important to consider whether the pharmacist knows the language spoken by the patient. If not, steps should be taken to ensure that essential information can be provided by and to the patient either through a family member, another member of the pharmacy staff who speaks the patient's language, or an interpreter, if available.

Tone of Voice

The tone of voice, inflection, or nuance can help contextualize a message. An example is saying "no" in a firm tone when disagreeing with something, suggesting that the patient is adamant that this should not be done. The tone of voice will also produce different effects although the identical words may be spoken. For example, a sarcastic or threatening tone will produce different effects/emotions when compared with an empathetic tone.

Reflective Exercise

Have you ever considered assessing your own communication styles (e.g., body language, the tone of voice, and verbal language)? Try asking a family member or friend to take a video of yourself when you are in conversation with others. Watch this video and make notes on the language you portray. What changes will you make so that your communication is more effective?

Active Listening

One of the key components of effective communication is active listening. Listening is an approach to know the audience. Any communication will not be as effective without understanding the person, situaton and needs to be addressed through communication. It involves not only using the ears but also consists of a conscious effort to pay complete attention to the facial expression, body language, and verbal tone of the patient. It also involves active participation by the pharmacist (i.e., it is necessary to respond to the patient in a manner that demonstrates that the patient has both been heard and understood). In this manner, any responses can also serve to clarify the accuracy of understanding. In general, there are several types of responses which can be given.

- Paraphrasing: A response that repeats the words heard, as well as some superficial recognition of the patient's attitude or feeling. This is best used in the initial stages of patient interaction by restating phrases to reassure the patient that they are being listened to and to encourage them to continue communicating. For example, to check for the accuracy of their statement, reword the information provided in the form of a question back to the patient (i.e., "Are you saying … ?").
- Summarizing: A response that concisely reiterates the main points of interaction or consultation. Highlight any key critical points and allow the patient to add any new information that they may have forgotten. This type of response is most important to identify any misunderstandings that may exist, especially if there are barriers to communication (e.g., language barriers). Take this opportunity to form an agreement with the patient regarding the information discussed.

- Reflection: A response that verbalizes both the content presented and the feelings of the patient. It has the advantage of showing the patient that the pharmacist is paying attention to verbalizing words/information, as well as the emotions behind them. Usually, responses often begin with phrases such as "It sounds like you are experiencing ..." or "You seem to be feeling ....". By communicating back to the patient that their feelings or concerns have been understood and are valid, a caring trusting relationship can be established.
- Clarifying: A response which questions or restates the content and feeling of the information presented. It can also be used to summarize the patient's statements into a clear, concise account. This response can begin with a phrase such as "As I understand it, you ...". These statements allow for the patient to correct or reframe their understanding, if necessary.

Empathy

Empathy is the process of communicating with patients that the pharmacist understands the patient's perspective about their disease,[15] medications, and overall health. In simpler terms, this is considered "putting one's self in the patient's shoes." It is a core ingredient in any healthcare provider–patient relationship.[16] Empathy can be learned and requires that the pharmacist place importance on developing a caring response with the patient. This term should not be confused with sympathy. Sympathizing is feeling sorry for but many patients do not like showing a feeling of pity. Empathy is a more sharing approach feel the difficulty together with respect to autonomy. In empathy, the pharmacist needs to demonstrate how they respond to patients, both verbally and nonverbally. It does not necessarily require the pharmacist to experience the particular incident but will require the pharmacist to be open and able to acknowledge the feelings of the patient.

Demonstrating empathy through verbal responses means choosing words that do not judge, give advice, quiz, or placate. Rather, the words chosen should demonstrate understanding and acceptance of the patient. It should be acknowledged appropriately. For example, "I can see this is difficult for you to discuss ..." or "It must be difficult for you to manage these new medicines with no one at home to help you ...."

Reflective Exercise

Empathy is showing a response that demonstrates you share or acknowledge a person's feelings. Think about an occasion when someone you cared for shared some good news. What was your reaction as you shared their joy? Did any words convey your excitement, encouragement, or congratulations?

OBJECTIVE 6.3. IDENTIFY BARRIERS TO COMMUNICATION AND SUGGEST HOW TO OVERCOME THEM

In many situations, there are times when a consultation does not go as expected. These could be due to several reasons:

- Lack of skills and understanding of the structures of discussion and conversation.
- Inadequate knowledge of other forms of communication skills, such as body language.
- Lack of personal insight into other people's communication difficulties.
- Personal barriers, including stress, lethargy, shyness, and lack of time, to engage in meaningful discussion.
- Language barriers, including difficulty in speaking the language that patient understands, or cultural differences.
- Physical barriers, including lack of counseling rooms, cluttered desk, and noisy environments.
- Personal barriers (patient), including anxiety about their health or anger toward a previous incident (e.g., error in dispensing).
- Lack of knowledge by the pharmacist regarding medications prescribed or patient history.

As such, identifying these barriers are key steps to overcoming them. Once these barriers are identified, a pharmacist can then create and implement a solution. Some suggestions that could be used to reduce these communication barriers include the following:

- Reduce clutter and the number of products on sale near the counseling area.
- Use support staff, such as technicians and assistants, for other roles to effectively free-up time to speak with patients.
- Supplement patient counseling with print materials to increase understanding of information.
- Maintain eye contact with the patient. It will help the pharmacist to watch for any nonverbal cues that indicate a lack of understanding or concern.

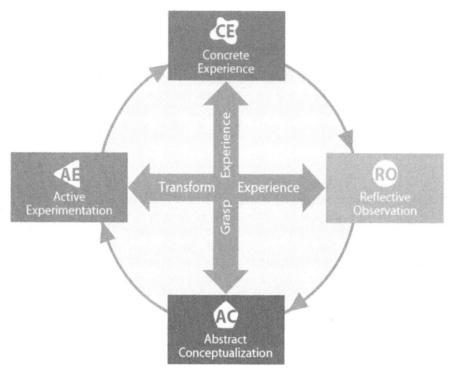

FIGURE 6.3 The experimental learning style. *Courtesy of Experience Based Learning Systems, Inc. Alice & David Kolb.* The Experiential Educator: Principles and Practices of Experiential Learning. *Kaunakakai, HI: EBLS Press; 2017.*

- Encourage patients to ask questions and thoughtfully respond to them.
- Wear clothing that is reflective of the healthcare status, including the use of name tags.
- Develop an effective patient interview style to ensure the ability to gather all the information before providing patient care.

Knowing Kolb's learning styles will help categorize the patient learner type in tailoring the approach by the pharmacist. In 1984, Kolb described different learning styles as to how an individual learns (Fig. 6.3).[17] An understanding of how individuals learn can help pharmacists be more effective in their communication skills and also how they can best approach the patient, especially concerning patient education. As there is a tendency for everyone to teach using their style, it is helpful to know what styles can be consciously incorporated when educating patients about their medications and health. Briefly, this can be categorized into four different learning styles:

Divergers
- Prefer doing and experiencing
- Focus on generating ideas and solutions
- Value harmony, listen with an open mind

Assimilators
- Prefer observation and reflection
- Focus on ideas and concepts over individual needs; requires time to reflect before responding to questions or situations
- Value logic and has strong organizational skills

Convergers
- Prefer to begin with understanding reasons and concepts
- Prefer to focus on finding practical solutions; can be unemotional
- Value quick decision-making and leadership

Accommodators
- Prefer to dive in and trying things out
- Focus on efficient time and energy; enjoy finding useful, convenient solutions
- Value a direct approach when dealing with people and situations

Reflective Exercise

Which learning style most closely applies to you? Think how you would tailor the way you would teach others about their medications or health conditions when their learning preference may be different from your own?

Always demonstrate an open body stance. Some additional tips to ensure success include the following:

- Maintain a confident but empathic behavior that gives warmth to the patient and colleagues, versus an assertive behavior.
- Make sure the arms and legs are uncrossed, as folded arms may look defensive or imply decreased interest.
- Lean forward slightly when providing key facts to demonstrate active listening.

Many factors contribute to miscommunication in healthcare. Identifying these barriers and solving them are key to preventing harm.

OBJECTIVE 6.4. DISCUSS THE CHARACTERISTICS AND PROCESS OF THE PATIENT HISTORY INTERVIEW

Collecting subjective and objective information from the patient is one of the first steps in pharmaceutical care or the newer PPCP model. The first step is to collect. It is not easy to collect subjective information from a noncooperating patient. Especially with limited objective evidence, collecting accurate history uses effective communication skills, influence, diagnosis, and prognosis.

A patient history should be a comfortable discussion for the patient, but it should be skillfully directed by the pharmacist to collect important information. The patient should not feel like they are being interrogated. In addition, any admonishment of the patient from doing something wrong and suggesting that they may end up with a disease will likely result in less cooperation from the patient (e.g., diabetes from poor dietary habits). The interview session should be warm and encouraging to reveal helpful information about the patient. It should be as short as possible, except in some cases when the diagnosis or prognosis is significantly based on history interview.

Pharmacist—patient interactions involve usually no history taking while dispensing medication. History taking is performed when required. Some may need to conduct a detailed, structured interview, whereas in most other cases, a few short questions will do. Taking a relevant medical and medication history helps in deciding on the next appropriate steps, such as further assessment or referral to another healthcare professional.[18]

Involve the Patient in the Care Process

One of the key features in taking any patient history is the involvement of the patient as a stakeholder in clinical practice decisions. The patient history interview is a chance for the patient to discuss his/her health problems with a trusted partner in healthcare. It can also provide significant emotional support to the patient. A proper patient history interview results in a common understanding of the health condition of the patient. Early engagement of patients in contributing to clinical decisions may motivate them to be more of an active participant in their own self-care. An informed patient has higher chances of being adherent to therapy. The interviewer should not be judgmental, as expressions that communicate wrongdoing or disagreement in their overall health may demotivate patients to stay involved. Even when some items that patients say may be irrelevant to the current situation, the conversation should eventually be diverted back to what is significant.[18,19]

History Interview for Clinical Diagnosis

To tailor individualized therapy, perform a detailed patient history interview. In the complexity of atypical presentations of illness, patient assessment is highly supported with a proper interview. The patient history interview is important to rule out certain suspected conditions in the differential diagnosis. Many times, with accurate patient history interviews, the proper diagnosis can be made without inconvenient lab tests for the patients. The growth of newer technological support regarding diagnosis, however, has not decreased the value of the patient history interview. Many times, a combination of the patient history interview, physical assessment, diagnostic tests, and other technical support is required to arrive at a correct diagnosis.

The Patient History Interview Should Be Ethical

Cultural dimensions of the patients should be observed during the interview. Being interviewed by the person of opposite gender can also be a barrier for patients to open up completely. Such inhibition is extremely high in certain cultures, and collecting information about religiously or culturally restricted activities can be tricky. Asking questions about sexual practices or alcohol consumption is usually not well received by patients in some cultures but are sometimes important questions to ask. Sensitive issues should be handled carefully only if the interviewer feels they have the competence to manage certain situations; otherwise, such questions may need to be omitted for the time being, or another person of the same gender or a highly competent interviewer could be arranged to collect such information.

It is not just the information that is sensitive, but also, some patients may be sensitive themselves, especially following trauma or a psychiatric event. A competent psychologist may be needed to interview such patients without causing further psychological harm.[20]

The Information Collected Should Be Reliable

Patients should be encouraged to detail what they think is true about their conditions. Still, such information may be incorrect, as they are not experts in perceiving disease symptoms or making diagnoses. Many patients may intentionally lie to please the interviewer; they may underreport things that are bad for their health (e.g., smoking tobacco) and overreport things that are good for health (e.g., fruits, vegetables, exercise). If the patient does not like the way they are being interviewed, they may try to falsify or omit information as a part of being resistant. The interviewer should have appropriate communication skills to detect and prevent such intentional or unintentional wrong data being given. Clinicians can verify information collected from the interview with lab tests (e.g., diet control with blood glucose/hemoglobin A1C levels in diabetics). As one strategy alone is insufficient to diagnose and prognose the conditions accurately, a combination of subjective (e.g., observation, history interview) and objective (e.g., lab tests, scans, physical examination) methods may be adopted.

Some patient history interviews require the help of a third person:

- Parents to provide information about a pediatric patient.
- Interpreters to collect information about a patient who speaks a different language.
- Caregivers to collect information about a patient with sensory impairments.
- Caregivers or aid workers to collect information about patients with impaired cognition (e.g., psychiatric and neurologically disabled).[20]

Steps in the Patient History Interview

Many formats of a structured history interview are used by different healthcare providers. For example, the Calgary Cambridge model provides a good guide to the medical interview and communication process. It explains a systematic method of obtaining a patient history interview.[21] A summary of the common steps used in most patient history interviews are given below:

1. Collect appropriate background information
   Read about the patient if any information is available, as some patients might have already undergone a detailed history interview in the past. It is unnecessary to repeat questions on historical information unless further clarification is needed. Remember that the history interview is not a counseling session. Its main aim is to collect all the relevant information from the patient. Therefore, the patient should speak more than the interviewer.
2. Plan for the interview
   When a patient makes an appointment, it is important to tell them to bring a written list of problems they are facing, as well as the medicines (prescription/OTC) and herbal products they are taking. It will greatly help in identifying the patient's current medicines, because many patients do not remember the names of all the drugs they are taking. Such early engagement of the patient is likely to make them more actively involved in the care process. Depending on the information available, make plans as to how to start, conduct, and end the interview. Changes might be required to the original plan depending on how the interview goes. However, having an initial plan will greatly influence the outcome of the interview, as well as improve the skills of interviewer over time.
3. Try to know the patient
   Getting to know the patient is important in providing individualized care. The patient's behavior might not be the same since the last visit. As such, always take a moment to focus on the patient and task at hand. Always greet them by their name and remind them who you are. If possible, try to take a few moments to screen through and read any previous

encounters with the patient (e.g., dispensing records). Ask the patient to describe their problem, as this gives them the opportunity and time to talk about their situation. This can also help uncover problems that the patient has not acknowledged themselves, such as depression or anxiety. It also helps to develop a good relationship between the pharmacist and patient and promotes empathy and understanding. Understanding the cooperation level is important. Patients should be prepared to receive questions and be ready to answer.

4. Gather information

   This is the step mainly to gather and record the information. If some of the information has already been stated, do not repeat such questions. Gather all required information such as the following:

   a. Social and family history: Some conditions have a familial relationship, whereas ethnic background may be another predisposing factor. Some conditions also may be epidemic in the society (e.g., influenza).

   b. Vaccination and childhood illness history: This information can rule out risks for certain vaccine-preventable diseases, but the success rate of vaccines in preventing such diseases should also be considered. If some viral infections happened in childhood, the likelihood of recurrence is less. The reverse is also possible, as some childhood illnesses could have lingering effects. For example, children who are infected with the respiratory virus when they were young have a higher risk of wheezing and other signs of respiratory distress at a younger age.[22]

   c. Medical and surgical history: It is important to obtain a history of diseases, both cured and ongoing. Medical procedures and surgeries undertaken shall also need to be documented.

   d. Medication and diet history: List key medicines the patient has previously taken and those that are currently being taken, including prescription, OTC, supplements, and herbal products. Note adverse drug reactions to medications, as well as the time of occurrence, management, and outcome. Ask about drug and food allergies and food habits, which may previously suggest disease-specific diets.

   e. History of present illness: Detail symptoms of the current illness that are bothering the patient. Obtain information about the occurrence and nature of the illness (e.g., how often does it occur, does it reoccur at a specific time).

   f. Patient/social lifestyle: Ask about daily habits of the patient, including relevant hobbies, physical activity, alcohol, tobacco, and recreational drug use. Breach the subject of sexual activity, if necessary.

   g. Adherence history: Document levels of patient adherence to previously prescribed therapy.

   h. Review of systems/conclusion of the interview: Request the patient to think from head-to-toe, as well as through each organ system, to recall of any symptoms they missed for the final report.

5. Be aware of limitations

   Collecting information from the patient is a skillful activity. It is sometimes called an art. Some patients may be difficult to interview. Talkative, silent, depressed, confused, aggressive, or crying patients will need different approaches. For example, a talkative patient may need to be directed to focus and describe their problems, whereas a confused patient may need to be probed further. In addition, there will be culturally sensitive issues which need to be asked sensibly, such as dietary habits or alcohol use.[23] It is better to skip certain questions that complicate the situation; a noncooperating patient should not be asked questions that worsen the situation.

6. Answer the questions

   The patient's questions should be answered appropriately, as a diagnosis may not have been confirmed or misunderstood. Sometimes patients might gauge how the interviewer feels about the prognosis of their condition. Being genuine in addressing and acknowledging their problems and encouraging the patient to wait for a conclusion/clinical diagnosis, is a good strategy.

7. Develop a common empirical understanding of the condition

   Patients often seek a consultation to understand their condition. They need the expertise of a clinician to help them understand it. Development of a common understanding of the conditions will help both the patient and clinicians to plan an effective and feasible solution.

8. Prepare the patient for the next task and close the interview

   If necessary, the patient should be made aware why further examinations (e.g., lab tests) are required. Of course, they should be advised on how to solve their health problem, if a direct course of action is known. If the interview is not closed well, the patient may feel the session was performed incompletely. It will affect patient satisfaction during the care process.[18,19]

   Preferably the patient history interview should be performed exclusively. If not enough time is available, some clinicians may start with the interview and continue it while performing a physical assessment. However, such an approach may be only applicable to more experienced interviewers who are good at multitasking. Remember not to ask too many questions unless necessary. Short interventions should be linked to short history taking.

For those who like mnemonics, some of the classic mnemonics used in the patient history interview are as follows:

- Eight dimensions of a medical problem to collect the history of present illness; **OLDCARTS**—**O**nset, **L**ocation and/or radiation, **D**uration, **C**haracteristics (e.g., what does it feel like?), **A**ggravating and/or relieving factors, **R**elated symptoms, **T**reatments tried (including the patient's response), and **S**everity (usually on a scale of 0−10).
- Specifically for a patient complaining of pain, consider using **OPQRST**—**O**nset, **P**rovocation and palliation, **Q**uality of pain (e.g., what does it feel like?), **R**egion and radiation, **S**everity, and **T**iming (e.g., constant, intermittent, duration, time of day).
- **SOCRATES**—**S**ite, **O**nset, **C**haracteristics, **R**adiating, **A**lleviating, **T**iming, **E**xacerbating factors, and **S**everity.[18]

Some of these tools are linked to the provision of a service or are more specific for medication history taking. To make the best of these tools, a pharmacist should become familiar with their content and use them as a guide rather than as a formal, prescriptive method of history taking, as each patient is an individual with different needs.

Reflective Exercise

Prepare two checklists: (1) the steps of patient history interview (i.e., #1 through #8) and (2) OLDCARTS. Practice and perform a patient history interview with each method. Have your supervisor or peer check off each section as you progress systematically through the history-taking process. In addition, do not forget to tailor the session as a natural and convenient conversation for the patient.

CONCLUSION

Communication skills are essential for pharmacists to deliver their services to healthcare professionals and consumers successfully. It is a core competency which pharmacy students should develop through education. Communication skills are evident in the practice of professionals regarding their knowledge transfer, utilization, and behavior. Accreditation standards for healthcare facilities aim to decrease medication errors by effective communication. Appropriate healthcare practice involves teamwork and communication, which are essential to developing and implementing clinical decisions via consensus. Patient history interviews need high levels of communication skills to collect important information. Collecting vital information from all patients, including noncooperating ones, is essential in proper diagnosis and prognosis when objective evidence is limited.

PRACTICE QUESTIONS

1. The ultimate reason why pharmacists would want to improve their communication skills is to:
   A. increase the number of prescriptions received and dispensed
   B. increase personal job scope and salary
   C. improve patient adherence to medication
   D. reduce pharmacy automation
2. Most of the messages we communicate occur via:
   A. words we say
   B. way we say things
   C. gestures and body movement
   D. written information given to patients
3. Which of the following is an example of physical barriers to communications?
   A. Busy pharmacy with many patients
   B. Cluttered dispensing desk
   C. Lack of counseling room
   D. All of the above

REFERENCES

1. Hammarlund ER, Ostrom JR, Kethley AJ. The effects of drug counseling and other educational strategies on drug utilization of the elderly. *Med Care*. 1985:165—170.
2. Chua SS, Kok LC, Yusof FAM, et al. Pharmaceutical care issues identified by pharmacists in patients with diabetes, hypertension or hyperlipidemia in primary care settings. *BMC Health Serv Res*. 2012;12(1):388.
3. Lee JK, Grace KA, Taylor AJ. Effect of a pharmacy care program on medication adherence and persistence, blood pressure, and low-density lipoprotein cholesterol: a randomized controlled trial. *JAMA*. 2006:296.
4. Lee JY, Chan CKY, Chua SS, et al. Intervention for Diabetes with Education, Advancement and Support (IDEAS) study: protocol for a cluster randomized controlled trial. *BMC Health Serv Res*. 2016;16(1):524.
5. Lee SWH, Mak VSL. Changing demographics in Asia: a case for enhanced pharmacy services to be provided to nursing homes. *J Pharm Pract Res*. 2016;46(2):152—155.
6. Joint Commission International. *International Patient Safety Goals*; 2018. https://www.jointcommissioninternational.org/improve/international-patient-safety-goals/.
7. The Role of the Pharmacist in the Health Care System. *Preparing the Future Pharmacist: Curricular Development. Report of the Third WHO Consultative Group on the Role of the Pharmacist, Vancouver, Canada, 27—29 August 1997*. WHO/PHARM/97/599; 1997. http://apps.who.int/medicinedocs/en/d/Js2214e/1.html.
8. Medina MS, Plaza CM, Stowe CD, et al. Center for the advancement of pharmacy education 2013 educational outcomes. *Am J Pharm Educ*. 2013;77(8):162.
9. Muller BA, McDanel DL. Enhancing quality and safety through physician—pharmacist collaboration. *Am J Health Syst Pharm*. 2006;63(11):996—997.
10. Tuckman BW. Developmental sequence in small groups. *Psychol Bull*. 1965;63(6):384.
11. Cohen LB, Taveira TH, Khatana SAM, Dooley AG, Pirraglia PA, Wu W-C. Pharmacist-led shared medical appointments for multiple cardiovascular risk reduction in patients with type 2 diabetes. *Diabetes Educ*. 2011:37.
12. Davidson MB, Karlan VJ, Hair TL. Effect of a pharmacist-managed diabetes care program in a free medical clinic. *Am J Med Qual*. 2000:15.
13. Beardsley RS, Kimberlin CL, Tindall WN. *Communication Skills in Pharmacy Practice: A Practical Guide for Students and Practitioners*. Lippincott Williams & Wilkins; 2012.
14. Mehrabian A. *Silent Messages: Implicit Communication of Emotions and Attitudes*. 2nd ed. Belmont, California: Wadsworth Publishing Company; 1981.
15. Riess H. Empathy in medicine—a neurobiological perspective. *JAMA*. 2010;304(14):1604—1605.
16. DiMatteo MR, Hays RD, Prince LM. Relationship of physicians' nonverbal communication skill to patient satisfaction, appointment noncompliance, and physician workload. *Health Psychol*. 1986;5(6):581—594.
17. Alice & David Kolb. *The Experiential Educator: Principles and Practices of Experiential Learning*. Kaunakakai, HI: EBLS Press; 2017.
18. Interviewing and the Health History. In: Bickley LS, Szilagyi PG, Bates B, eds. *Bates' Guide to Physical Examination and History Taking*. 11th ed. Philadelphia: Wolters Kluwer Health/Lippincott Williams & Wilkins; 2013:55—96.
19. Srivastava SB. The patient interview. In: Lauster CD, Srivastava SB, eds. *Fundamental Skills for Patient Care in Pharmacy Practice*. Jones & Bartlett Learning, LLC; 2013.
20. US Department of Health and Human Resources Centers for Disease Control and Prevention. *A Guide to Taking a Sexual History*; 2018. https://www.cdc.gov/std/treatment/sexualhistory.pdf.
21. *Calgary Cambridge Guide to the Medical Interview - Communication Process*; 2017. http://www.gp-training.net/training/communication_skills/calgary/guide.htm.
22. Illi S, von Mutius E, Lau S, Niggemann B, Grüber C, Wahn U. Perennial allergen sensitization early in life and chronic asthma in children: a birth cohort study. *The Lancet*. 2006;368(9537):763—770.
23. Lee JY, Wong CP, Tan CSS, Nasir NH, Lee SWH. Type 2 diabetes patient's perspective on Ramadan fasting: a qualitative study. *BMJ Open Diabetes Res Care*. 2017;5(1).

ANSWERS TO PRACTICE QUESTIONS

1. C
2. C
3. D

Chapter 7

Interpretation of Laboratory Data and General Physical Examination by Pharmacists

Seeba Zachariah[1], Kiran Kumar[1], Shaun Wen Huey Lee[2], Wai Yee Choon[2], Saba Naeem[1] and Christine Leong[3]

[1]Gulf Medical University, Ajman, United Arab Emirates; [2]Monash University Malaysia, Bandar Sunway, Malaysia; [3]University of Manitoba, Winnipeg, MB, Canada

Learning Objectives:

Objective 7.1 Describe common laboratory tests and interpret their clinical significance to the practice of pharmacists.
Objective 7.2 Discuss the scope of general physical examination by pharmacists.
Objective 7.3 Explain how to measure and interpret vital signs.
Objective 7.4 Perform a detailed head-to-toe physical examination and explain possible findings.

OBJECTIVE 7.1. DESCRIBE COMMON LABORATORY TESTS AND INTERPRET THEIR CLINICAL SIGNIFICANCE TO THE PRACTICE OF PHARMACISTS

Laboratory tests can provide useful information for clinicians for the diagnosis of a medical condition and for the monitoring of drug therapy (e.g., effect of an antibiotic therapy for a bacterial infection[1]). As a pharmacist, laboratory values can help select the most safe and appropriate therapy for patients, in addition to aid in the monitoring of the selected therapy. For instance, serum creatinine is a laboratory value used to estimate the patient's renal function by calculating creatinine clearance. This information is useful for adjusting the dose of certain medications cleared through the kidneys, such as digoxin. In patients with renal insufficiency, decreased renal excretion of digoxin can lead to increased risk of digoxin toxicity, and as a result, patients may benefit from a dose reduction of digoxin based on creatinine clearance.[2]

The following caution is required while interpreting laboratory values:

- Although laboratory errors are fairly uncommon, they do occur. Potential causes could include technical errors, sample contamination, timing in which the lab value was taken, i.e. trough levels should be drawn just prior to the next dose, and medication interference, i.e. Dopamine and dobutamine influence methods which use the Trinder reaction, thus affecting determination of glucose, cholesterol, and other tests.[41] If any laboratory error is suspected, the test should be repeated.
- Values shown in mmol/L units are equivalent to mEq/L units for some ions when valence is 1, like Hydrogen and Potassium. Otherwise mEq/L could be converted by multiplying mmol/L with valence.
- Always treat the patient, never the laboratory value!

The following are common laboratory tests:

Electrolytes

Electrolytes and blood chemistries are important for maintaining acid-base and fluid balance. They also play a vital role in nerve and muscle functioning. These usually comprise of sodium, potassium, chloride, calcium, magnesium, and phosphate.[1–4]

Sodium

Sodium is the most prevalent extracellular cation in the body. Its primary function is to regulate the serum osmolality, fluid balance, and acid–base balance. Measuring serum sodium values helps in assessing the patient's electrolyte, water, and acid–base balance. It also helps assess their renal function.[1,5]
  Normal values: 135–145 mEq/L.

Clinical Significance An increased level of sodium (hypernatremia) often occurs as a result of dehydration or fluid loss, which could be due to conditions such as gastroenteritis, diarrhea, or Cushing's syndrome.[6] Conversely, hyponatremia is often due to edema from a relative increase in free body water. Certain drugs, like tricyclic antidepressants and loop diuretics, could potentially cause hyponatremia.[6,7]

Potassium

Potassium is the main intracellular cation and plays a key role in many bodily functions including nerve excitability, acid–base balance, and muscle function.[1,8]
  Normal values: 3.5–5 mEq/L.

Clinical Significance An increase in potassium (hyperkalemia) could be due to metabolic or respiratory acidosis, or renal failure. Certain drugs, like angiotensin converting enzyme inhibitors (ACEIs) and potassium sparing diuretics, may elevate potassium. Potassium is typically monitored at baseline, and after a few weeks of starting therapy. Meanwhile, the reasons for hypokalemia could include severe diarrhea, respiratory alkalosis, and use of drugs, such as loop and thiazide diuretics as well as osmotic diuretics, like mannitol.[9]

Chloride

Chloride is the principal extracellular anion which functions to serve a passive role in the maintenance of fluid balance and acid–base balance, by having an inverse relationship with bicarbonate.[8,10]
  Normal values: 96–106 mEq/L.

Clinical Significance Any deviations in normal values are a sign of fluid or acid–base balance disorder, such as metabolic acidosis, respiratory alkalosis, or prolonged vomiting.[10]

Blood Gas

Carbon dioxide

The majority of carbon dioxide in the plasma is present as bicarbonate ions. However, a small percentage is present in the form of dissolved carbon dioxide. Both carbon dioxide and bicarbonate are extremely important in regulating physiological pH.[11]
  Normal values: Bicarbonate ions: 22–28 mEq/L.
  Partial Pressure of CO_2 (P_aCO_2): 38–42 mmHg (5.1–5.6 kPa).

Clinical Significance The increase in serum CO_2 levels is seen in metabolic alkalosis, whereas decreasing levels are seen in metabolic acidosis (due to deep breaths to decrease acidosis). Some common causes include the use of diuretic therapy, lactic acidosis, and renal failure.

Blood Glucose

Glucose

Glucose is an important source of energy for most cellular functions, and its regulation is achieved through a complex mechanism comprising insulin, glucagon, cortisol, adrenaline, and other hormones.[12]

Normal values: Fasting blood glucose: 3.9–5.5 mmol/L (70–99 mg/dL).

Clinical Significance High levels of glucose may be detected in patients with Type I, Type II, or gestational diabetes, and are commonly used as a diagnosis of diabetes or pre-diabetes. It is also used as a monitoring tool to monitor the diabetic control of a patient, both for routine monitoring and self-monitoring.[12,13]

Hematology

Full Blood Count

The full blood count provides values for hemoglobin (Hb) and hematocrit (Hct) (to detect anemia), red blood cell (RBC) count, white blood cell (WBC) count, WBC differential count, and RBC morphology.[3,5,14] There are some subtle differences in values between males and females for these measurements, and these need to be taken into consideration when interpreting the values.

Hemoglobin

Hemoglobin is the oxygen-carrying compound in the RBCs and is a direct indicator of the oxygen-carrying capacity of blood.[2,5,15]

Normal values:

Male: 14–18 g/dL or 8.7–11.2 mEq/L.
Female: 12–16 g/dL or 7.4–9.9 mEq/L.

Clinical Significance Increased Hb levels can be due to diseases such as chronic pulmonary lung disease or polycythemia vera. It may also be increased in chronic smokers, those who live at high altitudes (due to low oxygen in air at higher altitudes), and those who engage in regular exercise. The high carbon monoxide content in cigarette smoke prevents oxygen from binding to Hb, making the body interpret low Hb levels, and signal for increased RBCs production. Conversely, lower levels are an indication of anemia or hemorrhage.[15]

Hematocrit

Hematocrit, also known as packed cell volume, describes the volume of blood occupied by RBCs. It can also be used as an indicator of Hb, as hematocrit values are usually three times the value of Hb.[8,11,16]

Normal values:

Male: 39%–49%
Female: 33%–43%

Clinical Significance Similar to Hb, decreased values are an indication of anemia or hemorrhage. The hematocrit can indicate if there is a problem with RBCs, but it cannot determine the underlying cause.

Red Blood Cell Count

RBCs serve to transport oxygen from the lungs to the body tissues. They have a life span of approximately 120 days, before being cleared by the reticuloendothelial system.[17] In most laboratory reports, the results will examine the number of cells per cubic mm, size, shape, color, maturation, and content. These can then be used to classify different types of anemia to pinpoint the etiology. In general, they can be classified by the following:

- RBC size or mean corpuscular volume (indicating average RBC size).
- RBC color or mean corpuscular Hb concentration, which can be hypochromic, hyperchromic, and normochromic.

For example, microcytic, hypochromic anemia could be due to iron deficiency.
Normal values:

Male: $4.3-5.9 \times 106$ cells/mm^3 or $4.3-5.9 \times 10^{12}$ cells/L.
Female: $3.5-5.0 \times 106$ cells/mm^3 or $3.5-5.0 \times 10^{12}$ cells/L.

Clinical Significance An increased level of RBCs is usually associated with polycythemia vera, stress, chronic smoking, and living at high altitudes.[8,17] Low RBC counts can be due to anemia, hemorrhage, or chronic renal failure. Low levels of iron causes iron deficiency anemia, folic acid deficiency causes megaloblastic anemia, B-12 vitamin deficiency causes pernicious anemia, and pyridoxine or copper deficiency causes sideroblastic anemia. Long term use of the oral hypoglycemic agent, metformin, has been linked with vitamin B12 deficiency.

White Blood Cell Count

WBCs, or leukocytes, consist of five main types: neutrophils, lymphocytes, monocytes, eosinophils, and basophils. The WBC count is usually given with a breakdown of the percentage of each WBC type. WBCs protect the body against foreign bodies and infection. Neutrophils are the most abundant WBCs.
Normal values: $3.2-11.3 \times 10^9$ cells/L.

Clinical Significance An increase in WBC count (leukocytosis) is suggestive of an invading organism. In general, the most commonly observed readings are the lymphocyte counts, as these are usually an indicator of viral infections. Meanwhile, an increase in eosinophil levels is taken to be associated with allergic reactions and parasitic infections.[18] Neutrophil levels may rise due to drugs like steroids, infection, or intense exercise.

Platelets

Platelets are a critical element of blood clot formation. They bind together when damaged blood vessels are recognized.[19,20]
Normal values: 150,000−450,000/μL.

Clinical Significance High levels of platelets (thrombocytosis) can be caused by infections and chronic inflammatory disorders, as well as iron deficiency anemia. Decreased platelet counts (thrombocytopenia) may occur in patients with an autoimmune disorder, or while under chemotherapy, due to bone marrow suppression. Heparin can also cause an idiosyncratic reaction of low platelet counts called heparin-induced thrombocytopenia.[21]

Prothrombin Time

A fundamental understanding of the coagulation pathway is imperative in interpreting prothrombin time (PT). The PT is a measure of the integrity of the extrinsic and final common pathways of the coagulation cascade. It consists of tissue factor and factors II (i.e., prothrombin), V, VII, X, and fibrinogen. The test is performed by the addition of calcium and thromboplast, an activator of the extrinsic pathway, to the blood sample; then, the time (in seconds) is measured for the formation of fibrin clot.[22]
Normal values: 9.5−13.5 seconds.

International Normalized Ratio

The international normalized ratio (INR) is a standardized method of reporting the effects of oral anticoagulants, such as warfarin, on blood clotting. This test is commonly performed in individuals receiving warfarin, to ensure the dose is sufficient to prevent thrombosis, and to minimize the risk of bleeding.
Normal values: The reference range for INR should be less than 1.3.[23] An INR range of 2.0−3.0 is the target therapeutic range for most patients on anticoagulant therapy.[24]

Clinical Significance There are various conditions that may affect PT and INR. Some of the causes of a prolonged PT include anticoagulant therapy (e.g., warfarin). Vitamin K deficiency can elevate the INR, and may occur due to malnutrition, biliary obstruction, malabsorption, use of certain broad-spectrum antibiotics, liver diseases (i.e., synthesis of clotting factors is diminished), fibrinogen abnormalities (e.g., hypofibrinogenemia, afibrinogenemia, dysfibrinogenemia), or dilution of plasma clotting proteins after a blood transfusion. Examples of antibiotics that may interact with warfarin, and alter the INR, include cephalosporins, metronidazole, macrolides, fluoroquinolones, penicillins, sulfonamides, and tetracyclines. Furthermore, azole antifungals are most likely to increase bleeding risk in older continuous users of warfarin.[42] It is worth repeating the test to rule out an error if a prolonged PT and INR is observed in patients who are not on anticoagulant therapy or no history of medical problems can explain the abnormal finding. A decreased PT can be caused by vitamin K supplementation, high intake of food containing vitamin K (e.g., liver, broccoli, kale), estrogen-containing drugs (e.g., contraceptive pills, hormone replacement therapy), and freshly frozen plasma transfusion. Patients on warfarin therapy should be counseled regarding major changes in vitamin K rich food, like green leafy vegetables, and its affect on PT/INR.

Partial Thromboplastin Time and Activated Partial Thromboplastin Time

A test similar to the PT, the partial thromboplastin time (PTT) and activated partial thromboplastin time (aPTT), is performed to detect clotting abnormalities. The aPTT is similar to PTT, but an activator is added to speed up the clotting time, thus rendering it more sensitive than PTT due to the narrow range.

Normal values: 60−70 seconds for PTT; 30−45 seconds for aPTT (depending on methods).

Clinical Significance A prolonged PTT or aPTT may indicate congenital deficiencies of intrinsic system clotting factors such as factors VIII, IX, XI, and XII including hemophilia A and hemophilia B (Christmas disease), an inherited bleeding disorder, Von Willebrand disease (which affects platelet function owing to decreased Von Willebrand factor activity). Liver cirrhosis, vitamin K deficiency, and heparin therapy may also prolong PTT or aPTT (in a new sentence). Early stages of disseminated intravascular coagulation, extensive cancer, such as ovarian, pancreatic, or colon cancer, or an acute-phase response leading to high factor VIII levels, may lead to a decreased PTT or aPTT.

There are also some factors that may interfere with the aPTT test. These could be a drug, such as antihistamines, chlorpromazine, heparin, and salicylates, or other factors such as erroneous blood-to-citrate ratio and blood samples drawn from the heparin lock or a heparinized catheter. It is worth considering the confirmation of the test value with subsequent samples to rule out any abnormal results.

Renal Function

The kidneys are responsible for maintaining the homeostasis within the body, through the excretion of solutes and water. The kidney function is affected by the cardiovascular, endocrine, pulmonary, and central nervous systems. Therefore, any abnormalities in these systems may be reflected in renal or urine tests.

Serum Creatinine and Creatinine Clearance

Creatinine is a metabolic product of the dephosphorylation of creatine phosphate from the muscle. It occurs at a relatively constant rate (assuming stable muscle mass) and is excreted primarily by the kidneys. As such, any increase in serum creatinine can be used as a marker to identify patients with renal dysfunction, as it indicates a diminished ability of the kidneys to filter creatinine. In most laboratory reports, the creatinine clearance is also provided, as it is a better indication of kidney function compared to serum creatinine alone. However, a full, true measurement of creatinine excreted by the kidneys requires the collection of urine for 24 h. Alternatively, the creatinine clearance is commonly estimated from the serum creatinine using the Cockroft−Gault formula. Glomerular filtration rate (GFR) calculations also use serum creatinine values. Chronic Kidney Disease Epidemiology Collaboration (CKD-EPI) equation and Modification of Diet in Renal Disease (MDRD) are common formulas to calculate GFR.

Normal values of serum creatinine: 53−106 μmol/L or 0.5−1.5 mg/dL.

Clinical Significance As mentioned previously, high levels of serum creatinine can be used 'to indicate' (or) 'as a marker' would sound better that the kidneys are not functioning optimally. Underlying causes for this could include kidney damage, dehydration, or an obstructed urinary tract. In addition, decreased kidney function can be a microvascular complication of diabetes or can be due to the use of nephrotoxic drugs, such as nonsteroidal antiinflammatory drugs, vancomycin, or contrast media.[25]

Blood Urea Nitrogen

Blood Urea Nitrogen (BUN) measures the amount of urea nitrogen in the blood. Urea nitrogen is excreted from the blood by the kidneys, thus high BUN levels could indicate kidney damage. However, it is a less sensitive marker of renal failure, as it can be affected by hydration, as well as dietary protein intake and protein catabolic rate.

Normal values: 2.1–7.1 mEq/L.

Clinical Significance BUN levels may be high due to heart failure, dehydration, or a high protein diet. Low BUN levels could be due to liver disease. However, it is normal for a pregnant woman to have low BUN levels in the second or third trimester. Blood urea nitrogen to creatinine ratio is used as an indicator of renal function.

Urinalysis

Urinalysis is a useful laboratory test that enables a clinician to identify patients with a wide variety of disorders, especially those associated with the renal system. It is an inexpensive and noninvasive procedure. In general, the test provides a report on the gross examination (e.g., color, clarity), pH, specific gravity, and the presence of protein, glucose, ketones, blood, bilirubin, leukocyte, or nitrates in the urine. Normal urine color should range from clear to dark yellow, with some cloudiness due to the presence of phosphates or urates. If urine is reddish orange, this may indicate the presence of blood or be due to drugs such as rifampicin. Other drugs that may cause urine discoloration include, amitriptylline, which can cause a blue-green color, and chloroquine and metronidazole which can cause brown discoloration of urine. [6]

The kidney normally prevents larger protein molecules from escaping into the urine. Small traces of protein are a common clinical finding, and have no implications. However, the presence of protein (proteinuria) greater than 150 mg/day indicates dysfunction or renal disease. Normally, glucose is actively reabsorbed into the body by the kidney up to a maximum threshold (approximately 180 mg/dL blood glucose). As such, a high level of glucose in the urine is an indication of diabetes mellitus or the need for improved glucose control.[12]

Liver Function

The liver is the largest solid organ in the human body. It plays a central role in all of the body's biochemistry. Thus, liver function tests can give a clearer picture of any of the functions of the liver: synthesis, excretion, or detoxification. These tests can also help indicate liver injury.[1] Elevations in serum transaminases are also seen in patients with myocardial infarction.

Serum Bilirubin

Bilirubin is a reddish-yellow pigment which is produced during the normal breakdown of RBC. It is excreted bile, into the duodenum. Bilirubin circulates in the bloodstream in two forms:

1. Indirect (unconjugated) bilirubin, which does not dissolve in water, and thus cannot be measured. As such, it is derived from both the total and direct bilirubin measurements. It travels through the blood to the liver, where it is changed into a soluble form.
2. Direct (or conjugated) bilirubin, which is the conjugated form of bilirubin. The levels can be measured directly from the blood.

Normal values:

Total bilirubin: 1.7–17.1 μmol/L.
Indirect bilirubin: 3.4–12 μmol/L.
Direct bilirubin: 0–3.4 μmol/L.

Clinical Significance Because of the properties of bilirubin, the levels of serum bilirubin can help clinicians identify liver cell damage in a patient.[26] For example, if there was an increase in total bilirubin and indirect bilirubin, but not direct bilirubin, this could be an indication of RBC hemolysis, because the liver produces direct bilirubin, which is unaffected.

Meanwhile, elevated levels of direct bilirubin may be associated with hepatocellular diseases. In cases where there is excessive total bilirubin, patients will exhibit signs of jaundice, which could result in kernicterus in infants and children.

Urine Bilirubin and Bilirubinogen

As discussed previously, conjugated bilirubin is excreted with the bile into the duodenum, where the conjugated bilirubin is converted by bacteria into urobilinogen. Most of the urobilinogen is excreted in the feces, but some is reabsorbed into the blood and goes either into the liver for reexcretion in the bile, or the urine. In patients with complete bile duct obstruction, no urobilinogen is formed. Therefore, the stools will become gray—white or clay-colored due to the lack of bilirubin. In addition, as conjugated bilirubin cannot be excreted into bile, it will be reabsorbed into the bloodstream and thus spilled into the urine, resulting in high levels of direct bilirubin in the blood.[1] Nevertheless, false-positive results may occur in patients is taking phenazopyridine or phenothiazines. Thus, it is important for pharmacists to note this, since both the drugs, and bile pigments in urine can cause an orange discoloration.

Alkaline Phosphatase

Alkaline phosphatase (ALP) is an enzyme produced mainly in the liver and bone, but can also be found in the kidneys, intestines, and placenta. It is excreted by the liver into the bile, and thus, it is a sensitive indicator of biliary obstruction.

Normal values: 30—120 U/L (depending on age and assay).

Clinical Significance Increased concentrations of alkaline phosphatase may indicate hepatitis, liver cirrhosis, hepatic cancer, or gallstones and high ALP levels may indicate an overreactive parathyroid gland, rickets, Paget's disease, or bone cancer.

Aminotransferases: Aspartate Aminotransferase and Alanine Aminotransferase

These enzymes are located inside the hepatocytes, and function primarily to assist with various metabolic pathways. Any injury to these tissues will release the aminotransferases into the systemic circulation and result in their elevation. Of the two enzymes, alanine aminotransferase is considered a more specific marker of liver disease than aspartate aminotransferase. As such, they are commonly used to assess for hepatocellular injuries, such as hepatitis.

Normal values: 0—35 U/L (depending on age and assay).

Clinical Significance Increased concentrations are associated with hepatitis, and alcoholic liver diseases. Elevated levels could also be seen with drug toxicity or interference with drugs such as acetaminophen, erythromycin, or levodopa.

Thyroid Function

The thyroid is a small, butterfly-shaped gland found in the lower-front part of the neck. This hormonal gland plays a role in regulating many of the body's processes such as metabolism, growth, and maturation of the body.[1] The production of hormones is regulated based on the need of the body. The gland produces three hormones, namely:

1. Triiodothyronine or T3
2. Tetraiodothyronine also called thyroxine or T4
3. Calcitonin

The two main hormones are T3 and T4, produced in the follicular epithelial cells of the thyroid, with iodine being one of the major components of both hormones.

Thyroid-Stimulating Hormone

The thyroid-stimulating hormone (TSH) test, and the T4 test, are the most common thyroid function tests. The TSH test measures the level of circulating TSH, and is used to screen for, and diagnose thyroid disorders. It is also used for routine monitoring during hypothyroidism treatment.

Normal values: 0.3–5 mIU/L.

Clinical Significance If the thyroid gland fails to produce a sufficient amount of these hormones, patients may develop a condition known as hypothyroidism; subsequently, they may experience symptoms such as weight gain, lack of energy, and depression. On the contrary, if the thyroid gland produces too much of these hormones, (i.e., hyperthyroidism) patients may experience weight loss, high levels of anxiety, and tremors. When the thyroid gland is enlarged, it becomes visible as a "goiter," and patients may experience a sense of pressure in the neck, and difficulty in swallowing. If the thyroid becomes even bigger, the tissue enlarges downward, due to restrictions of space. When this occurs, it may lead to more serious effects, such as constriction of the windpipe, causing difficulty in breathing.

Triiodothyronine

T3 is the more potent form of circulating thyroid hormone. It is usually used in the diagnosis of hyperthyroidism.

Normal values: 1.2–3.1 mIU/L.

Clinical Significance High levels of T3 are usually seen in patients with hyperthyroidism, as well as in those with Graves' disease. Conversely, decreased T3 levels are associated with hypothyroidism and/or malnutrition. Some drugs, such as corticosteroids and propranolol, which decrease the conversion of T4 to T3, may result in reduced levels of T3. It is important to take into consideration the effect of amiodarone on thyroid function. Amiodarone, due to its high iodine content, may induce hypothyroidism or thyrotoxicosis. Thus amiodarone should be avoided in patients on medications to manage thyroid abnormalities.[43]

Lipid Profile

The lipid profile is commonly used as part of a cardiac risk assessment, to determine an individual's likelihood of heart disease, and to assist in decision-making on what treatment may be best. When a lipid profile is called for, it primarily comprises the measurement of total cholesterol (TC), high-density lipoprotein cholesterol (HDL-C), low-density lipoprotein cholesterol (LDL-C), and triglycerides (TGs). It is recommended that healthy adults with no other risk factors for heart disease be tested with a fasting lipid profile once every 4 to 6 years.[27] If there are other risk factors, or if a high cholesterol level was detected in the previous testing, more frequent testing with a full lipid profile is recommended. Some of the risk factors other than high LDL-C are cigarette smoking, sedentary lifestyle, being overweight or obese, hypertension, diabetes or prediabetes, and preexisting heart disease.[27,28]

As the level of cholesterol and TGs are commonly reported either in mmol/L or mg/dL, the following conversion factors should be used:

mg/dL cholesterol = mmol/L × 38.6.
mg/dL triglycerides = mmol/L × 88.5.

Low-Density Lipoprotein Cholesterol

Approximately 60%–70% of cholesterol in the body is carried as LDL-C in the blood. Lipoproteins are essential for the transportation of cholesterol, which in turn is vital for the biosynthesis of bile acids, vitamin D, and steroid hormones. Dietary intake and endogenous hepatic production are the two primary sources of cholesterol. Metabolism of ingested cholesterol produces very low-density lipoprotein (VLDL) and intermediate-density lipoprotein. Subsequent metabolism of the VLDL produces LDL, which is one of the major components in the development of an atherosclerotic plaque. Most clinicians monitor LDL levels to prevent the progression of coronary artery disease (CAD). The Friedewald formula, used to calculate the LDL level in the blood, is as follows:

LDL = Total cholesterol − HDL − (Triglycerides/5)

However, it is important to bear in mind that the Friedewald formula for estimating LDL is invalid in the following three conditions:

1. presence of chylomicrons,
2. TGs greater than 400 mg/dL, and
3. presence of dysbetalipoproteinemia (type III hyperlipidemia).

These three conditions lead to an underestimated LDL, and in such cases, a direct level is warranted.[29]

Normal values: Values for LDL-C can be divided into several categories:
Optimal: <100 mg/dL or < 2.6 mmol/L.
Near optimal/above optimal: 100−129 mg/dL or 2.6−3.3 mmol/L.
Borderline high: 130−159 mg/dL or 3.4−4.1 mmol/L.
High: 160−189 mg/dL or 3.1−4.9 mmol/L.
Very high: >190 mg/dL or > 4.9 mmol/L.

Clinical Significance The target LDL for the prevention of atherosclerotic plaque formation is between 50 and 70 mg/dL (1.3−1.8 mmol/L).[27,28] A higher value is associated with an increased risk for the development of CAD, and intervention may be needed. It is based on the Framingham Heart Study, which was the first study to reveal a positive association between TC and CAD. A target LDL value of less than 100 mg/dL is particularly imperative in patients with other risk factors, such as cigarette smoking, hypertension, low HDL, and a family history of CAD, as these will accelerate the development of CAD.

High-Density Lipoprotein Cholesterol

HDL-C is produced and secreted by the liver and intestine. It consists mostly of cholesterol, phospholipid, and protein. HDL-C acts as transporters for cholesterol from tissues to the liver. Owing to the reverse cholesterol transport process, it confers a "clean-up" function. This process is called reverse cholesterol transport, because cholesterol synthesized in peripheral tissues is ultimately returned to the liver to be disposed from the body. High levels of HDL-C are deemed desirable due to their inverse relation with coronary risk. Hence, HDL-C is commonly called "good cholesterol". Because of this inverse relation with the incidence of atherosclerosis.
Normal values:

Low: <40 mg/dL or < 1.3 mmol/L.
Optimal: >60 mg/dL or > 1.5 mmol/L.

Clinical Significance In general, elevated HDL levels are ideal, because they are associated with a decreased risk for cardiovascular diseases. HDL levels can be decreased in association with recent illness, starvation, stress, smoking, obesity, lack of exercise, hypertriglyceridemia, or may be due to some medications (e.g., thiazide diuretics, steroids, beta blockers), and regular aerobic exercise, smoking cessation, a decrease in body mass index, and mild therapy with HMG-CoA reductase inhibitors (i.e., statins), may increase HDL-C levels. The slight rise in HDL-C levels from these drugs may be attributable to inhibition of Rho-signaling pathways, with activation of peroxisome proliferator-activated receptor alpha. Increases in HDL-C levels may also be seen due to decreasing plasma cholesteryl ester transfer protein activity by statins.[27,28]

Triglycerides

TGs are lipid compounds made up of a glycerol, which is esterified to three fatty acid chains of varying length and composition. It is the most abundant dietary lipid compound found in the daily diet.
Normal values: There are currently no targets for serum TG levels, but levels below 150 mg/dL <1.7 mmol/L are considered desirable.

Clinical Significance Some substances and drugs that may account for TG elevation are ethanol, corticosteroids, non-cardioselective beta blockers, thiazide diuretics, bile-binding resins, oral estrogens, progestins, tamoxifen, and antiretroviral therapy. Patients who are at risk for developing secondary hypertriglyceridemia in the setting of CAD, diabetes, disease states secondarily elevating TGs, or another CAD? should receive routine screening. Patients who have consumed a meal high in lipids, and have not fasted for 8 hours before a cholesterol test, may show false-positive highTG levels. In addition, patients who have recently consumed ethanol may show an elevation of TGs that may not certainly be indicative of baseline levels.

Cardiac Enzymes

Creatinine Kinase

Formerly known as creatinine phosphokinase, creatinine kinase (CK) is a key protein enzyme in catalyzing the reversible phosphorylation reaction. CK levels can be further divided into its isoenzymes, depending on where they originate from; muscle (CK-MM), brain (CK-BB), and cardiac tissue (CK-MB). Making up 15%−30% of the total CK in the heart muscle, CK-MB is found mostly in the myocardium, whereas a much smaller proportion is found in the skeletal muscle. CK-MB is sensitive and very specific to myocardial injury.

Normal values: The normal range of CK-MB is 3%−5% of total CK.

Clinical Significance Following the onset of acute myocardial injury, CK-MB begins to rise in 4−6 h, and returns to baseline level after 36−48 h. Therefore, CK-MB is also a good marker of acute myocardial injury, reinfarction, or infarct extension. CK-MB can be used to indicate successful reperfusion after fibrinolysis, estimate infarct size, and predict infarct-related mortality.

Troponin

Troponins are protein molecules, and are part of the cardiac and skeletal muscle. Without cardiac myocyte damage, cardiac troponin levels do not increase in the presence of skeletal damage. It is unlike CK-MB, which can be increased on injury to these tissues, potentially leading to false-positive results. Hence, troponin testing is more reliable than CK-MB testing in that sense.

Clinical Significance Troponin values are usually assessed on clinical suspicion of myocardial infarction (MI). In healthy patients, troponins are undetectable, although this may not be the case as more sensitive assays become available. In a patient with presentations such as chest pain and possible MI, an abnormal value is that above the 99th percentile of the healthy population. In patients with MI, a time lag is seen before troponin elevations can be detected. Therefore, the markers should be serially monitored, should there be suspicion for the acute coronary syndrome. Normally three sets of cardiac enzymes are checked. The initial recommendation is to assess the markers every 3 hours until the expected peak is reached.[30]

It is important to note some of the analytical interfering factors that may lead to falsely elevated troponin results. Examples of such items include a specimen with incomplete clotting (often seen in patients with coagulopathy or those on anticoagulant therapy), elevated bilirubin levels, markedly elevated alkaline phosphatase levels, immunocomplex formation, and analyzer malfunction.

Information obtained from lab tests can help pharmacists make informed decisions by individualizing therapy depending on the patient's current conditions. Therapy can be monitored throughout the course of treatment, and alterations can be made to give the appropriate drug regimen.

OBJECTIVE 7.2. DISCUSS THE SCOPE OF GENERAL PHYSICAL EXAMINATION BY PHARMACISTS

The general physical examination is a systematic process by which the clinician uses his/her sensory skills to evaluate physical signs pertaining to a patient's clinical condition, and then correlates that information with previous patient history for the formulation of a clinical diagnosis.[31] It is essential that the examiner has a sound knowledge of anatomy, physiology, and pathophysiology to identify and evaluate clinical signs and symptoms.

Integrating physical assessment skills into pharmacy practice is important for improving the quality of patient care. Data obtained from a physical assessment can allow the pharmacist to monitor and optimize medication management, to determine whether a medication is appropriate, effective, and safe. Information from a physical assessment will also allow a clinician to screen patients at risk for chronic conditions, such as hypertension, and help set the direction of the therapeutic plan. Practicing physical assessment skills will also promote better communication among healthcare practitioners and improve our understanding of patient care.

Context

The clinical examination should be part of a process wherein the clinician has the patient's basic history available at his or her disposal. The goal of such an assessment is to gather pertinent information to identify underlying clinical conditions and set the direction of a therapeutic plan. The clinical examination begins well before talking to the patient. A mere look at the patient by observing gait, level of consciousness, skin color and obvious lesions, grooming, facial expression, body odors, behavior, speech, and overall presentation would help identify many important findings.[31,32] A further detailed evaluation would systematically focus on every organ system to identify the clinical processes occurring beneath the surface.

There are four techniques that are typically used during a physical assessment: (1) inspection, in which each body system is assessed for any deviations using vision, smell and hearing, (2) palpation, in which you need to use different parts of your hands in varying degrees of pressure to touch the patient, (3) percussion, in which you sharply and quickly tap your fingers or hand against specific body parts of the patient, and (4) auscultation, in which a stethoscope is used to listen to various organ sounds.[32]

Inspection is also known as "concentrated watching," and it involves observing the patient for physical signs. For instance, yellowing of the skin can be a sign of jaundice. The inspection begins the moment the patient is introduced; good lighting is important for this first step. The patient can be used as his or her control by comparing the right and left sides of the body.

Palpation involves using the sense of touch to collect information. For example, the radial pulse can be determined by palpating the radial artery. The fingertips are best for detecting fine tactile discrimination such as skin texture. The fingers and thumbs can be used to grasp and detect organ position, shape, and consistency. The backs of the hands and fingers are best for determining skin temperature, and the base of the fingers or ulnar surface of the hand can be used for detecting vibrations.

Percussion involves tapping the patient's skin with short and sharp strokes to assess the density of structures 4–5 cm below the skin. These strokes result in vibrations that can produce a characteristic sound to map the location and size of the organ and to determine whether air, fluid, or a mass exists beneath the surface. For instance, the disappearance of a dull sound (indicating fluid accumulation) over the lung can indicate a sign of antibiotic effectiveness.

Finally, auscultation can be performed to assess sounds originating within the organ or body cavity, such as heart sounds, bowel sounds, etc. A stethoscope is required to perform auscultation.

Pharmacist–Patient Interaction

For a clinician, a medical examination is a learned behavior. However, for a patient, it is a first-time experience, where someone is handling his or her body systems. It is highly essential that the clinician generates trust and confidence of the patient to avoid any embarrassment to the patient, and also to help bring out the clinical signs. It is essential that the patient be made as comfortable as possible. The clinician has to be polite and genuinely compassionate when approaching the patient. There should be a continuous conversation during the examination to relieve any anxiety the patient might have during the process. A brief description of the findings to the patient will help him/her understand the physical examination process and to participate in the clinical management plan.

Prerequisites

A trained and knowledgeable mind is the most important prerequisite for a good clinical examination. Some basic equipment, if made available, will facilitate detailed assessment. This would include, and is not limited to, a light/torch, measuring tape, blood pressure monitoring device, tongue depressor, cotton, stethoscope, otoscope, fundoscopy, gloves, magnifying glass, thermometer, and a tuning fork.

As the environment affects the quality of the physical examination, it is wise to arrange for a quiet area for privacy, darkening the room for parts of the examination, and providing comfort for the patient and examiner. Although there is no right or wrong sequence, it is important to follow a systematic approach to ensure full completeness of the examination. As a convention, the examiner would stand on the right side as the patient is lying on a couch. In the sitting position, it is appropriate to stand in front of the patient and move around with various steps of examination.

OBJECTIVE 7.3. EXPLAIN HOW TO MEASURE AND INTERPRET VITAL SIGNS

Body Temperature

Body temperature is regulated by the hypothalamus to maintain the core temperature of approximately 37°C (98.6°F).[31,32] Body temperature can be affected by diurnal fluctuations throughout the day (e.g., lowest in the morning, highest in the late afternoon to early evening), hormones, exercise, smoking, consumption of hot or cold beverages, and age.[32] Measurement of body temperature can be obtained by an oral, rectal, axillary, or tympanic thermometer.

An oral thermometer is ideal for alert patients. The body temperature can be obtained by placing the oral thermometer under the tongue in either of the sublingual pockets with the lips closed. Hot or cold liquids and smoking can alter the temperature reading. As such, it is advised to delay the temperature measurement by 10–15 min after consuming beverages or smoking. The rectal thermometer may be considered in comatose patients or patients who are unable to close their mouth (e.g., intubation, wired mandible, facial surgery). The temperature reading through the rectal route may be 0.5°C (0.9°F) higher than the oral reading. The axillary route may be ideal for infants and small children. This reading may be 0.5°C (0.9°F) lower than the oral route, and it is obtained by placing the thermometer under the arm into the center of the axilla with the patient's arm folded over the chest to keep it in place for 5–10 min. A tympanic thermometer can be considered for unconscious patients, emergency departments, and labor and delivery units. These readings may be 0.8°C (1.4°F) higher than the oral route. Temperature readings are obtained by gently pulling the ear up and back to straighten the ear canal (if under 3-years old, the ear is pulled downward and back) and placing the probe into the ear canal. Most digital tympanic thermometers can provide a reading in 2–3 s. Additionally, noncontact forehead thermometers are also available and may be more advantageous for reading temperatures in children.[33,34]

A normal body temperature reading is 35.8–37.3°C (96.4°F to 99.14°F).[31,32] A higher than normal temperature reading can be a result of pyrexia (i.e., fever) caused by infection, tissue breakdown (e.g., MI), or neurological (e.g., brain tumor). A high-temperature reading can also be a result of hyperthermia, in which heat production or external heat exposure exceeds heat loss, and the body is unable to thermoregulate. This can occur due to heat stroke, drugs (e.g., serotonin syndrome), and hyperthyroidism. A lower than normal temperature reading can be a result of hypothermia in which heat loss exceeds heat production. This can occur due to prolonged exposure to cold or intentional induction (e.g., cardiovascular surgery).

Peripheral Pulses

A quick assessment of all peripheral pulses would help assess heart rate, rhythm, and force. Peripheral pulses include radial, brachial, carotid, popliteal, posterior tibial, and dorsalis pedis pulses. The peripheral pulse is felt by the gentle compression of the artery against the underlying structures such as bone or the soft tissues. The radial pulse is felt by palpating the artery at the lower end of the radius bone anteriorly. The brachial artery can be felt at the cubital fossa just medial to the biceps tendon. A posterior tibial pulse is felt 1 inch below and behind the medial malleoli, against the body of calcaneum, in the groove between the medial malleolus and the Achilles tendon. Dorsalis pedis pulses are felt at the ankle in the first interosseous space of the feet, medial to the external hallucis tendon. While examining the peripheral pulse, it is necessary to appreciate the rate, rhythm (regular vs. irregular), and character (normal vs. weak vs. bounding) of the sound, as well as the condition of the vessel wall (e.g., calcified arteries in elderly can feel like fibrous cords). It is also a good practice to feel both radial pulses simultaneously to appreciate any radio-radial delay (e.g., aortic dissection) and the radial and femoral pulses to appreciate radio-femoral delay (e.g., coarctation of the aorta).

To obtain an accurate reading of the radial pulse, the clinician can count the number of beats in 30 s; if the beats are regular, multiply this number by two to obtain the number of beats per minute (bpm). However, if the beats are irregular, it is recommended to count the number of beats for the full minute. The normal heart rate for adults is 60–100 bpm. Children are expected to have higher heart rate ranges (e.g., newborns: 70–170 bpm, 1- to 6-year-olds: 75–160 bpm, 6- to 12-year-olds: 80 to 120 bpm).

Respiration Rate

The respiratory rate should be measured without the patient's knowledge, as the rate can change as soon as the person is aware that it is being done. To measure the respiratory rate, maintain the position of a radial pulse measurement and observe the patient's chest or abdomen for respiration. One respiration is inhalation and exhalation. To obtain the respirations per minute (rpm), count the number of respirations in 30 s; if the rhythm is regular, multiply this number by 2. However, if the rhythm is irregular, the number of respirations should be counted for the full minute. In adults, the normal respiration rate is 12—20 rpm, whereas the normal respiration rate for children is between 20 and 30 rpm. A lower than the normal respiratory rate is termed bradypnea, and a higher than the normal respiratory rate is termed tachypnea.

Blood Pressure

Blood pressure is measured in millimeters of mercury (mmHg) and comprises two components: (1) systolic blood pressure and (2) diastolic blood pressure. The systolic blood pressure is the highest pressure that is felt in the arteries, and it occurs when the ventricles contract.[18] The diastolic blood pressure is the lowest or resting pressure that occurs when the ventricles relax. A blood pressure reading can be obtained using an oscillometric (electronic) automated monitoring, or an auscultatory (manual) reading with a mercury or aneroid sphygmomanometer. An ideal oscillometric blood pressure device takes six consecutive readings at one- to two-min intervals.[35] The clinician would attend the first reading to ensure the patient is in the proper position and that the monitor is operating properly. The patient is then left alone for the subsequent readings. The device then discards the first reading and averages the next five measurements to obtain the blood pressure reading. If necessary, an ambulatory (out-of-office) blood pressure device can be worn by the patient to record blood pressure readings over a 24-h period at half-hour to one-hour intervals.[36,37] This allows the blood pressure to be monitored for fluctuations throughout the day based on activity and medications. It also helps rule-out white coat hypertension in clinical settings.

An automated home blood pressure machine can be purchased for patients to use at home. Although these machines are typically easy and convenient to use, the accuracy of the measurement depends on the proper positioning of the patient and placement of the cuff. Moreover, readings can be inaccurate if the heart rate is irregular and if there is physical movement (e.g., shivering).

It is advised to use an automated blood pressure device that has been validated and endorsed by a regulating body.[38] The aneroid and mercury sphygmomanometers have traditionally been used in practice to obtain a manual blood pressure reading. Accuracy depends on the proper standardized technique and calibration of the device.

To obtain an accurate blood pressure measurement, it is important that the patient be seated and comfortable. Ideally, the patient should be well rested for at least 5 min before the blood pressure measurement. As such, the pharmacists could conduct a medication history with the patient during this period. The patient should also not have smoked at least 30 minutes before getting their blood pressure monitored. The patient should subsequently be seated with back supported, feet flat on the floor, and arm slightly bent, palm up, and supported at heart level.[31,39] Next, the appropriate cuff size should be selected. The cuff size can be determined by ensuring the bladder width is approximately 40% of the arm circumference and the bladder length is approximately 80% of the arm circumference. Once an appropriate cuff size has been selected, the center of the cuff bladder can be placed over the brachial artery. The cuff should be wrapped smoothly and snuggly around the arm approximately 2.5 cm above the crease of the elbow. The patient is now ready to have a blood pressure measurement.

An automated device will typically take a measurement after being activated and display the blood pressure reading digitally. However, if using a manual cuff, the manometer should be in direct line of eye site to allow for an accurate reading.

With a manual cuff, it is recommended to estimate the systolic blood pressure first, to determine how high to raise the cuff pressure to prevent discomfort to the patient and to prevent error caused by an auscultatory gap. To estimate the systolic pressure, the clinician palpates the radial pulse and then inflates the cuff to a point at which the radial pulse can no longer be felt. The clinician then adds 30 mmHg to this reading to obtain an estimated systolic blood pressure. After the systolic blood pressure is estimated, the clinician can use the stethoscope, placing the bell of the stethoscope lightly over the brachial artery site, but in a position to make a tight seal with the patient's skin. The clinician inflates the cuff again to the estimated systolic blood pressure, and then slowly deflates the cuff at a steady rate of 2—3 mmHg/s. While the cuff is deflating, the clinician is listening for Korotkoff sounds with the stethoscope. The pressure at which the first of two consecutive beats are heard (Korotkoff Phase I), is the systolic blood pressure. The pressure at which the last beat is heard (Korotkoff Phase V), is the diastolic blood pressure.[31,32] It is recommended to continue listening until 20 mmHg below the diastolic blood pressure, and then rapidly and completely deflate the cuff. The clinician should then wait 2 minutes and repeat the reading. It is recommended to take three readings on the same arm, and average only the last two readings.

Common mistakes while taking a blood pressure reading include using an incorrect cuff size (e.g., if it is too small for the patient it can overestimate the blood pressure reading) and the patient's positioning (e.g., if the patient's arm is below heart level, or if the patient is not rested or comfortable, it can overestimate the reading). Other common mistakes while using a manual device for measuring blood pressure include stopping during deflation or reinflating the cuff too soon/deflating too quickly to allow enough time to hear the Korotkoff sounds.[37] A cuff deflation rate of 2 mmHg per beat is necessary for accurate blood pressure measurement.

There are also several factors that can influence blood pressure. Factors that can raise blood pressure include nicotine or caffeine consumption in the last 30 min, certain drugs (e.g., decongestants, corticosteroids, NSAIDs), exercise, anxiety, full bladder, room temperature, patient talking during a reading, or tight clothing around the forearm. Factors that can lower blood pressure include fasting or certain drugs (e.g., depressants). Some patients have an auscultatory gap, which is a silent interval between the systolic and diastolic pressures caused by arterial stiffness and atherosclerotic disease.[1] It can result in an underestimation of the systolic blood pressure or an overestimation of the diastolic blood pressure.

OBJECTIVE 7.4. PERFORM A DETAILED HEAD-TO-TOE PHYSICAL EXAMINATION AND EXPLAIN POSSIBLE FINDINGS

The entire process of general physical examination will involve inspection and palpation. A general head-to-toe survey is useful to find out any obvious abnormalities. It could include any patient concerns such as pain/discomfort, respiratory distress, skin and pigment changes, abnormal posture of extremities, and the general look of the patient. It is followed by a detailed head-to-toe examination.

Head and Neck

The examination will systematically look for signs in the head and neck, and will try to correlate with anatomic and pathophysiologic processes. A general look at the scalp and facial hair will help in assessing the types of alopecia; the common ones are male- and female-type baldness, alopecia areata, scarring, and anagen and telogen effluvium. Excess of facial hairs in females (hirsuitism) is a sign of androgen excess and can suggest the presence of polycystic ovarian syndrome (more likely) or ovarian/adrenal neoplasms (less likely). Malar rash over the bridge of the nose and cheek are suggestive of immunologic disorders such as systemic lupus erythematosus (SLE). Other abnormalities in the face include scars, chloasma, moles, and acne.

Eyes

A quick look at the eyes is a great source of information about a patient's general health. The presence of pale palpebral conjunctiva signifies anemia. It can be substantiated by examining the tongue, nail beds, or palms for evidence of pallor. Any cause of anemia would produce pallor.

Examination of the bulbar conjunctiva in daylight will help identify any yellowish tinge/discoloration which may signify jaundice. Sometimes, people who have had chronic exposure to sunlight and dust tend to have muddy conjunctiva which can be mistaken for jaundice. In mild jaundice, the lemon yellow tinge is usually visualized only in the eyes and in oral mucosa, in the floor of mouth, after asking the patient to elevate their tongue. In marked elevations of bilirubin, a yellowish tinge can be visualized on the skin, as well as the patient's palms and soles. Patients with obstructive jaundice tend to have a deep yellow icterus and scratch marks over the body due to excess itching, which arises as a result of elevations of bile acids.

Other ocular findings which one must be aware of are subconjunctival hemorrhages (usually self-limiting), Kayser–Fleischer rings (i.e., brownish-yellow rings visible around the corneoscleral junction in Wilson's disease), and conjunctivitis. Drooping of the eyelid can signify oculomotor nerve (i.e., cranial nerve III) palsy. Extraocular movements can be assessed to check the integrity of cranial nerves III, IV (i.e., the trochlear nerve which innervates the superior oblique muscle), and VI (i.e., abducens which innervates the lateral rectus muscle). It is important to take proper medication history, since drugs like ethambutol may cause vision problems ranging from blurred vision to red-green blindness. Sildenafil may cause a mild and transient blue tinge to vision.[44]

Face

Check for any facial asymmetry which can be congenital, due to developmental abnormalities, or acquired, due to facial nerve palsy on one side (e.g., reduced wrinkles, inability to close eyes and flattening of nasolabial folds on the affected side, deviation of angle of mouth to the opposite side). Masked facies is associated with Parkinson's disease, in which facial expressions are lost.

Oral Cavity

After checking for pallor and icterus, evaluate general dental hygiene by looking for any caries or infection. Any oral pigmentation may be a cause of concern, as it could suggest a serious condition, such as melanoma or Peutz–Jeghers syndrome.

Common lesions may also be due to smoking or could be benign nevi. The moistness of the tongue and mucous membrane is a sign of hydration status of the patient and is helpful in assessing the need for fluid in a patient with acute illnesses. Presence of white patches in the oral cavity may indicate oral candidiasis, which could be due to antibiotics or inhaled corticosteroids. In the latter case, the patient should be advised to rinse their mouth after using the corticosteroid.

Neck

Examination of the neck should proceed systematically. The neck should be inspected from the front and sides for any obvious swelling/masses. Common swellings include thyroid enlargement (e.g., diffuse in Graves' disease and nodular in nodular goiter). The patient should be asked to swallow saliva or be given a glass of water to drink, and movement of thyroid upward should be observed which confirms the thyroid swelling. Thyroglossal cyst is also a midline cystic swelling in the region or slightly above the thyroid gland. Such swelling will move up on protrusion of the tongue, whereas thyroid swelling will not. Other common neck swellings can include lymph nodal masses, which can be detected by submandibular gland enlargement just below the mandible, and parotid gland enlargement just under the earlobe. As a convention, it is recommended to palpate the neck with the patient sitting on a chair and the examiner standing behind the patient. Fingertips are used to palpate the neck looking for any lymph nodes in the submental and submandibular region, anterior and posterior triangle of the neck, and supraclavicular fossa. Thyroid gland should be palpated from behind, and movement assessed with swallowing.

With two fingers, careful palpation of the carotid arteries can be done by moving lateral to the thyroid cartilage, and in the groove between the trachea and sternocleidomastoid muscle. Care should be taken not to palpate both the arteries simultaneously. Also in elderly patients, undue pressure should be avoided as it can stimulate carotid sinus and lead to bradycardia and syncope, or can dislodge an atherosclerotic plaque, leading to a cerebrovascular accident. With the patient in 45-degree position, the neck should be examined for a jugular venous pulse, which can be elevated in a patient with congestive cardiac failure and right heart dysfunction. Engorged neck veins such as the external jugular vein is also a sign of right heart dysfunction and biventricular failure.

Upper Limbs and Hands

It is usually recommended that the whole upper extremity be observed at once. Any obvious drooping of the shoulder can be picked up on by examining the patient from behind while they are standing. Any swelling, deformities, and congenital abnormalities should be recorded. A patient can have generalized swelling, which indicates circulatory issues, or localized swelling which suggests fractures, infections, tumors, and tendon abnormalities. Observe the skin color of the hands and fingers. Hyperemia is usually a result of bacterial infection. Dry and shiny skin may occur with systemic diseases such as scleroderma; punctate digital ulcers and nail atrophy are seen in Raynaud's disease. Hypo/hyperpigmentation plus hypertrichosis and dry skin may be signs of neuropathy.

Inspection of the fingernails can also provide information about systemic disorders. Flattening (platonychia) and spooning (koilonychia) are suggestive of severe iron deficiency anemia. Clubbing is usually a sign of a lung disorder, but can also be seen in inflammatory bowel diseases, cirrhosis, cyanotic congenital heart disease, and lung cancers. Half-and-half nail syndrome is a condition in which the proximal portion of the nail bed is white, and the distal portion is dark (e.g., usually brown); this may signify advanced renal disease. It is also seen with advanced HIV infection and lymphomas. Terry's nail is a condition where the proximal 80% of the nail bed is white, and the distal 20% are normal/pink; this is usually seen with circulatory insufficiency. Other abnormalities which can be seen include Mees' lines (i.e., transverse white lines suggestive of arsenic poisoning), Beau's lines (i.e., transverse ridge/depressions due to intermittent cessation of nail growth in systemic illness/trauma/zinc deficiency), blue nails (e.g., drugs—zidovudine), fungal infections, nail pitting due to psoriasis, and splinter hemorrhages due to bacterial endocarditis.

Two distinct nodular swellings are found on the fingers of patients with osteoarthritis. Posterolateral swelling of distal interphalangeal (DIP) joints are called Heberden's nodes, and swelling of proximal interphalangeal (PIP) joints is called Bouchard's nodes.

The patient can also have swelling of the small joints of hands. The swelling is usually associated with stiffness in the fingers on flexion, especially during the early morning, and is usually associated with tenderness on palpation. It is suggestive of polyarthritis which can be due to various causes. The pattern of involvement of the small joint of the hands is quite suggestive of the etiology. Bilateral symmetrical involvement of metacarpophalangeal (MCP) and PIP joints are common with rheumatoid arthritis. Duration of morning stiffness can help distinguish the type of arthritis. Morning stiffness typically lasts < 30 minutes in osteoarthritis, compared to rheumatoid arthritis. Conditions preferentially affecting the DIP joints include osteoarthritis, psoriatic arthritis, SLE, and reactive arthritis. Arthritis of the first carpometacarpal joint is also seen typically in osteoarthritis; nowadays, with the advent of smartphones, these are more commonly seen even in younger individuals.[40] Deformities of the small joint of the fingers can produce characteristic morphology. This is common in advanced rheumatoid arthritis, which can lead to swan-neck deformity (i.e., flexion of MCP and DIP joints and hyperextension of PIP joints) and Boutonniere deformity (i.e., flexion of proximal interphalangeal PIP joints, an extension of the DIP joint of the fingers, and flexion of the MCP joint. A note should be made of any missing digits due to amputations. Other congenital abnormality such as polydactyly or syndactyly should be noted.

Lower Limbs

On examination, the lower limbs should preferably be exposed to the groin region. Privacy needs to be addressed, and patient consent is mandatory. The limbs should be examined for any obvious deformities, swelling, and signs of inflammation such as redness. Gentle pressure over bony prominences, such as the shin or the malleoli for a few seconds will elicit the presence of pitting pedal edema. This is usually seen in both lower limbs in conditions with an overall increase in total body water (e.g., hypoalbuminemia, CHF, cirrhosis, and nephrotic syndrome), and unilaterally in infections and venous thrombosis. Drugs like thiazolidinediones, estrogens, and amlodipine may cause pedal edema. The health of the toenails also has similar significance as upper limb nails. The inter-digital areas should be examined for the presence of whitish/reddish lesions suggestive of infections (e.g., tinea pedis). Special attention should be paid at the feet of diabetic patients; look for sores, blisters or wounds. Watch out for any staining on socks, and check for numbness or loss of sensation.

CONCLUSION

Confidence in clinical skills like interpretation of laboratory data, patient history interview, and physical assessment, is vital for pharmacists. Clinical significance of laboratory tests indicate relevant pathological and drug-induced changes in biochemistry. A trained and knowledgeable pharmacist is able to comfortably engage with a patient to gather basic history, while screening for signs of chronic disease or medication side effects. A pharmacist can provide optimal patient care by using the right techniques to measure vital signs, and performing a detailed head-to-toe physical examination. Knowledge about the possible findings helps the pharmacist identify the root cause, and provide the best drug therapy. All these skills are practiced with the ultimate goal of improving patient care outcomes. Doesn't fit in Repetition.

PRACTICE QUESTIONS

1. Blood glucose results are correctly reported in:
   A. g/mmol
   B. mg/dL
   C. g/L
   D. g/ml
2. Although common method of estimation of creatinine clearance is by using Cockroft–Gault equation, more accurate creatinine clearance (inconvenient) could be found when necessary by?
   A. is a liver function test
   B. requires timed blood samples to be drawn
   C. requires both serum and a 24-h urine sample
   D. requires the patient to be fasting at the onset of testing
3. Which of the following test can be used to determine for a patient's kidney function?
   A. blood urea nitrogen
   B. creatinine clearance
   C. electrolyte profile
   D. all of the above
4. Which of the following is NOT a test ordered in a cardiac enzyme profile:
   A. CK
   B. CK-MB
   C. Serum creatinine
   D. Troponin

5. What is the normal heart rate beats per minute (bpm) of a 7 year old child?
   A. 70–170 bpm
   B. 75–160 bpm
   C. 80–120 bpm
   D. 60–100 bpm
6. On physical examination, pallor is observed for identifying anemia on,
   A. Conjunctiva
   B. Tongue
   C. Nail beds
   D. All of the above

REFERENCES

1. Alldredge BK, Koda-Kimble MA. *Koda-kimble and Young's Applied Therapeutics: The Clinical Use of Drugs.* Lippincott Williams & Wilkins; 2013.
2. Fischbach FT, Dunning MB. *A Manual of Laboratory and Diagnostic Tests.* Lippincott Williams & Wilkins; 2009.
3. Lee M. *Basic Skills in Interpreting Laboratory Data.* ASHP; 2009.
4. Schmidt J, Wierczorkiewicz J. *Interpreting Laboratory Data: A Point-of-Care Guide.* ASHP; 2011.
5. Garrels M. *Laboratory and Diagnostic Testing in Ambulatory Care - E-book: A Guide for Health Care Professionals.* Elsevier Health Sciences; 2014.
6. Lewis J. Hypernatremia - electrolyte disorder: endocrine and metabolic disorder. In: *The Merck Manual;* 2016. Online [Internet] Available from: http://www.merckmanuals.com/en-ca/professional/endocrine-and-metabolic-disorders/electrolyte-disorders/hypernatremia.
7. Sahay M, Sahay R. Hyponatremia: a practical approach. *Indian J Endocrinol Metab.* 2014;18(6):760.
8. Burtis CA, Bruns DE. *Tietz Fundamentals of Clinical Chemistry and Molecular Diagnostics.* 7th ed. Elsevier Health Sciences; 2015.
9. Kang KP, Lee S, Lee KH, Kang SK. Mannitol-induced metabolic alkalosis. *Electrolytes Blood Press.* 2006;4(2):61–65.
10. Morrison G. Serum chloride. In: *Clinical Methods, the History, Physical, and Laboratory Examinations.* Stoneham, MA: Butterworth Publishers; 1990 [Internet] Available from: https://www.ncbi.nlm.nih.gov/books/NBK309/.
11. Chernecky CC, Berger BJ. Blood gases, arterial blood. In: Chernecky CC, Berger BJ, eds. *Laboratory Tests and Diagnostic Procedures.* 6th ed. Philadelphia, PA: Elsevier Health Sciences; 2013:208–213.
12. Association AD. Classification and diagnosis of diabetes: standards of medical care in Diabetes—2018. *Diabetes Care.* 2018;41(Suppl. 1):S13–S27.
13. Alberti KGMM, Zimmet Pf. Definition, diagnosis and classification of diabetes mellitus and its complications. Part 1: diagnosis and classification of diabetes mellitus. Provisional report of a WHO consultation. *Diabet Med.* 1998;15(7):539–553.
14. Wintrobe MM. *Wintrobe's Clinical Hematology.* Lippincott Williams & Wilkins; 2009.
15. Pittman RN, ed. *Regulation of Tissue Oxygenation. Colloquium Series on Integrated Systems Physiology: From Molecule to Function.* Morgan & Claypool Life Sciences; 2011.
16. Ferri F. In: Ferri FF, ed. *Laboratory Values and Interpretation of Results.* Vancouver, PA: Elservier Health; 2015.
17. Arias CF, Arias CF. How do red blood cells know when to die? *R Soc Open Sci.* 2017;4(4):160850.
18. Barrett KE, Barman SM, Boitano S, Brooks H. *Ganong's Review of Medical Physiology.* New York: McGraw-Hill Medical; 2009.
19. Ware JA, Heistad DD. Platelet-endothelium interactions. *N Engl J Med.* 1993;328(9):628–635.
20. Ruggeri ZM. Platelets in atherothrombosis. *Nat Med.* 2002;8:1227.
21. Warkentin TE. Heparin-induced thrombocytopenia. *Circulation.* 2004;110(18):e454–e458.
22. Moake J. Overview of coagulation disorders. In: *The Merck Manual Online;* 2016 [Internet] Available from: http://www.merckmanuals.com/en-ca/professional/endocrine-and-metabolic-disorders/electrolyte-disorders/hypernatremia.
23. Hirsh J, Poller L. The international normalized ratio. *Arch Intern Med.* 1994;154:282–288.
24. Sheth S, DiCicco R, Hursting M, Montague T, Jorkasky D. Interpreting the International Normalized Ratio (INR) in individuals receiving argatroban and warfarin. *Thromb Haemost.* 2001;86(03):435–440.
25. Bamgbola O. Review of vancomycin-induced renal toxicity: an update. *Ther Adv Endocrinol Metab.* 2016;7(3):136–147.
26. Hoekstra LT, de Graaf W, Nibourg GA, et al. Physiological and biochemical basis of clinical liver function tests: a review. *Ann Surg.* 2013;257(1):27–36.
27. Catapano AL, Graham I, De Backer G, et al. 2016 ESC/EAS guidelines for the management of dyslipidaemias. *Eur Heart J.* 2016;37(39):2999–3058.
28. Jellinger PS, Handelsman Y, Rosenblit PD, et al. American association of clinical endocrinologists and American College of Endocrinology guidelines for management of dyslipidemia and prevention of cardiovascular disease. *Endocr Pract.* 2017;23(s2):1–87.
29. Warnick GR, Knopp RH, Fitzpatrick V, Branson L. Estimating low-density lipoprotein cholesterol by the Friedewald equation is adequate for classifying patients on the basis of nationally recommended cutpoints. *Clin Chem.* 1990;36(1):15–19.
30. Thygesen K, Alpert JS, Jaffe AS, et al. Third universal definition of myocardial infarction. *Eur Heart J.* 2012;33(20):2551–2567.
31. Bickley L, Szilagyi PG. *Bates' Guide to Physical Examination and History-Taking.* 12th ed. Lippincott Williams & Wilkins; 2016.
32. Jarvis C. *Physical Examination and Health Assessment.* 7th ed. Elsevier Health Sciences; 2015.
33. Batra P, Saha A, Faridi MMA. Thermometry in children. *J Emerg Trauma Shock.* 2012;5(3):246.

34. Non-Contact Thermometers for Detecting Fever. *A Review of Clinical Effectiveness Ottawa (ON)*. Canadian Agency for Drugs and Technologies in Health; 2014. Available from: https://www.ncbi.nlm.nih.gov/books/NBK263237/.

35. Wan Y, Heneghan C, Stevens R, et al. Determining which automatic digital blood pressure device performs adequately: a systematic review. *J Hum Hypertens*. 2010;24(7):431.

36. O'brien E, Coats A, Owens P, et al. Use and interpretation of ambulatory blood pressure monitoring: recommendations of the British Hypertension Society. *BMJ Br Med J*. 2000;320(7242):1128.

37. O'brien E, Atkins N, Stergiou G, et al. European society of hypertension international protocol revision 2010 for the validation of blood pressure measuring devices in adults. *Blood Press Monit*. 2010;15(1):23−38.

38. Dasgupta K, Quinn RR, Zarnke KB, et al. The 2014 Canadian Hypertension Education Program recommendations for blood pressure measurement, diagnosis, assessment of risk, prevention, and treatment of hypertension. *Can J Cardiol*. 2014;30(5):485−501.

39. Whelton PK, Carey RM, Aronow WS, et al. ACC/AHA/AAPA/ABC/ACPM/AGS/APhA/ASH/ASPC/NMA/PCNA guideline for the prevention, detection, evaluation, and management of high blood pressure in adults. In: *A Report of the American College of Cardiology/American Heart Association Task Force on Clinical Practice Guidelines. 2017*. 2017.

40. Gustafsson E, Thomee S, Grimby-Ekman A, Hagberg MM. Texting on mobile phones and musculoskeletal disorders in young adults: A five-year cohort study. *Applied Ergonomics*. 2017;58:208−214.

41. Martha V, Nemeth Csoka, Naszlady A. The interference of drugs with clinical laboratory test results. http://www.mldt.hu/upload/labor/document/labor_medicina/valyon_marta_cikk.htm.

42. Baillargeon J, Holmes HM, Lin Y, Raji MA, Sharma G, Kuo Y. Concurrent use of warfarin and antibiotics and the risk of bleeding in older adults. *Am J Med*. 2013;125(2):183−189.

43. Loh K. Amiodarone-induced clinical disorders: a clinical review. *Postgraduate Medical Journal*. 2000;76:133−140.

44. Laties A, Zrenner E. Viagra (sildenafil citrate) and ophthalmology. *Prog Retin Eye Res*. 2002;25(5):485−506.

ANSWERS TO PRACTICE QUESTIONS

1. B
2. C
3. D
4. C
5. C
6. D

Chapter 8

Dispensing Process, Medication Reconciliation, Patient Counseling, and Medication Adherence

Ema Paulino[1], Dixon Thomas[2], Shaun Wen Huey Lee[3] and Jason C. Cooper[4]

[1]Pharmacy, Nuno Álvares, Almada, Portugal; [2]Gulf Medical University, Ajman, United Arab Emirates; [3]Monash University Malaysia, Bandar Sunway, Malaysia; [4]Medical University of South Carolina, Charleston, SC, United States

Learning Objectives

Objective 8.1 List steps in the dispensing process.
Objective 8.2 Detail methods in medication reconciliation to prevent errors.
Objective 8.3 Explain approaches to patient counseling.
Objective 8.4 Outline strategies to improve medication adherence.

OBJECTIVE 8.1. LIST STEPS IN THE DISPENSING PROCESS

Good dispensing practices ensure that an effective form of the correct drug is delivered to the right patient, in the correct dosage and quantity, with clear instructions, and in a package that maintains the potency of the drug. Dispensing also includes all of the activities that occur between the time the prescription is presented to the pharmacy and the time the drug or other prescribed items are issued to the patient.[1]

Dispensing is a fundamental service that pharmacists have been traditionally providing. Although non-prescription drugs and products can be dispensed following a short interview or physical assessment of the patient, prescription-only drugs are mostly dispensed as per prescriber's instructions. Besides community pharmacies, certain prescription-only drugs may be dispensed by hospital pharmacy outpatient services in a significant number of countries.[2] In fact, in some countries, especially in Asia, prescription-only drugs are mainly dispensed by hospital pharmacies, as is the case in China, Indonesia, or Taiwan. In some jurisdictions, pharmacists are allowed to independently prescribe and dispense from a limited list of drugs. Most jurisdictions reserve the right and responsibility to dispense drugs exclusively to pharmacists, whereas some grant dispensing privileges to doctors and/or nurses.

Supply chain systems aim to promote the continuous availability of the right drug, at the right time, to the right patient. To that end, supply chain integrity and efficiency is ensured by several stakeholders throughout the distribution pathway, including manufacturers, wholesalers, and pharmacies.

Substandard and falsified drugs threaten patient safety by, at best, causing no improvement or, worse, causing added burden of disease and even death; endangering public health by increasing the risk of antimicrobial resistance; and eroding patients' trust in health professionals and health systems. As part of the healthcare system, pharmacists and other healthcare professionals have a shared responsibility to avoid penetration of such drugs within the legitimate pharmaceutical supply chain. The International Pharmaceutical Federation (FIP), in cooperation with the Indian Pharmaceutical Association, has developed a handbook for healthcare professionals entitled *All You Need to Know about Spurious Medicines*, which contains tips on preventing and detecting substandard and falsified drugs; additionally, it contains advice on how to minimize the threat and change behaviors.[3] This handbook was launched as part of a World Health Professions Alliance campaign and aimed to raise awareness and develop competencies of healthcare professionals in the prevention of substandard and falsified drugs in the supply chain. It also serves to enhance the detection of and the ability to communicate such issues to patients and other stakeholders.

For instance, to address the concerns about increasing falsified drugs, the European Union amended the Directive 2001/83/EC by implementing measures to prevent the entry into the legal supply chain of falsified drugs. Such requirements involved a unique identifier and an anti-tampering device on the package of drugs for human use. This system consists of an end-to-end verification of those drugs, which means that pharmacists have to scan the box and verify the product against a central database at the point of dispensing. If located within the system, that product is then recognized and considered legitimate.

To avoid issues around the quality of drugs that are dispensed, guaranteeing that the right storage conditions are kept is of utmost importance. Pharmacies also often hold obligations in reverse logistics, ensuring a safe medication waste-management program and, if necessary, recall and withdrawal operations in case the pharmacist identifies a medical product that may be substandard or falsified. In the latter example, pharmacists often hold the obligation to report this to the relevant authorities and should do so even when this obligation is not in place.

Dispensing of controlled drugs requires more documentation and accountability to prevent drug diversion and potential abuse. Opioid overdose-related deaths are increasing; therefore, pharmacists' interventions are required on appropriate opioid use, with special provisions related to narcotic/opioid dispensing regulations implemented worldwide. Opioid stewardship programs are also in place to ensure judicious use of opioids.[4,5]

Antimicrobial stewardship programs require prudent prescribing and dispensing of antimicrobials. Overprescribing, inappropriate use, and dispensing without a prescription are reasons for unnecessary use of antibiotics that eventually lead to increased antimicrobial resistance. Healthcare—associated infections are often caused by resistant microorganisms. Optimizing prescribing and dispensing practices decreases antimicrobial misuse, which results in better patient outcomes at a lower cost for the individual and the healthcare system.[6,7] Specific emphasis should be given to collaborative approaches as part of interprofessional teams or interdisciplinary management of antimicrobial strategies along with stakeholder engagement.[8]

Pharmacists are responsible for ensuring that appropriate medications are prescribed, dispensed, and administered to the patient or their carer.[9] The steps involved in the dispensing of drugs are described in Fig. 8.1.[1,10] This should be consistent with the relevant national drug policy of the respective country. Good Pharmacy Practice guidelines describe in further detail the best practices in dispensing.[11]

In dispensing, a systematic approach is required, preferably following a written protocol; thus, there is a need for clear documentation and risk management procedures to minimize the possibility of any error that can arise during any stage of the dispensing process.

Receive and Validate the Prescription

The first step in dispensing is to validate the prescription. This is needed to ensure that

- details are accurate and complete, including the patient's name;
- legal and regulatory requirements are satisfied.

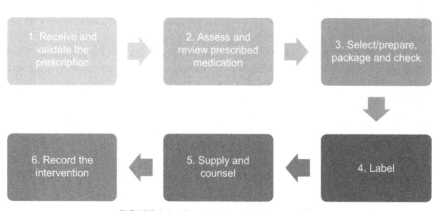

FIGURE 8.1 Steps in dispensing drugs safely.

Assess and Review the Prescribed Drugs

In this step, pharmacists assess the prescription, interpret the prescribed drug, and check whether the dose, frequency, route, and quantity are appropriate for the intended patient. The pharmacist also quickly assesses the patient and should adapt his/her intervention accordingly.

While assessing the prescription, a pharmacist should systematically collect and accurately record any relevant information (e.g., comorbidities, allergies, use of complementary medications). This is especially important in groups of people who are at risk of medication-related issues, including those patients[12,13]

- recently discharged from the hospital or with multiple transitions of care;
- taking multiple drugs (five or more);
- with complex chronic conditions;
- taking drugs with a narrow therapeutic index;
- taking drugs that have increased potential to interact with other drugs.

The pharmacist should further consider the appropriateness of the prescribed drug, considering the patient's clinical record and dispensing history based on the following principles:

- medication safety and efficacy, considering patient-specific factors such as age, allergies, other health conditions, and pregnancy/lactation;
- dosage regimen;
- dosage form;
- potential interactions;
- contraindications;
- precautions;
- patient's medication experience, needs, and adherence to the prescribed regimen, including misuse and abuse issues (which may be intentional or unintentional).

In particular, some medications have a high risk of causing death or harm. These include drugs with a narrow therapeutic index. Dosing errors with these medications can result in serious consequences. These drugs are often represented by the acronym APINCH[14]:

- **A**nti-infective;
- **P**otassium and other electrolytes;
- **I**nsulin;
- **N**arcotics and other sedatives;
- **C**hemotherapeutic agents;
- **H**eparin and other anticoagulants.

Although this list is nonexhaustive, it can be a good guide to alert pharmacists for some of the more commonly prescribed drugs, which may present an increased risk for harm.

The prescriber should be contacted whenever there is a need to discuss the patient's prescription or therapeutic regimen. This is also an opportunity to collaborate with the prescriber and contribute to clinical decision-making. Some common issues a pharmacist would contact a prescriber include the following:

- concern about the suitability of the drug;
- concern about the potential for medication-related problems;
- doubt about the legality or validity of the prescription;
- uncertainty about the prescriber's intentions.

It is important that pharmacists prioritize and list some of the key concerns during the discussion. In addition, the pharmacist can offer evidence-based strategies or solutions to the prescriber to promote optimal medication use. Always document any outcome of the discussion with the prescriber and inform the patient of the result of the discussion. In the event that the prescriber is unavailable, or unwilling to accept the pharmacist's advice, use professional judgment to determine the most appropriate action to take to satisfy the duty of care to the consumer.

Select/Prepare, Package, and Check Against the Original Prescription

In this step, pharmacists select the appropriate drug, brand, strength, form, and quantity. In countries where this applies, the pharmacist may need to repack. When applicable, the pharmacist should prepare the drug, which may include reconstituting (e.g., antibiotics) or compounding from raw materials.

In some instances, the pharmacist might have to deal with requests for out-of-stock drugs. Medication shortages have become a global issue, putting patient lives at risk and creating difficulties for healthcare professionals.[15] The causes of these shortages are multidimensional in the context of a complex global supply chain and thus require a holistic approach. In some jurisdictions, pharmacists may be able to independently substitute for a therapeutic alternative. When this is not the case, the pharmacist should contact the prescriber to ensure that the patient receives the medication needed. In addition, when faced with a shortage, pharmacists should report this to the competent authority or the appropriate organization, such as the American Society of Health-System Pharmacists in the United States. Reporting shortages is important to support public health decisions, provide guidance and information to enable all healthcare professionals to limit the impact of such shortages, and offer data to monitor the impact of public health policies that aim to curb this issue.[15]

Pharmacists should, at this stage, make a visual inspection of the drug. This visual inspection allows for the pharmacist to detect signs of potential falsified drugs such as improper packaging, labeling, and description of dosage, and to check whether the product is in good dispensing conditions (e.g., expiry date, integrity of the container/box). FIP, together with the US Pharmacopeia and the International Council of Nurses, developed a checklist for a visual inspection of drugs to help identifying suspicious products for further examination.[3]

This is also a good opportunity for the pharmacist to discuss with the patient any generic substitution. It is important for the pharmacist to clarify with the patient on their knowledge, attitudes, and preferences toward the use of a generic product versus the brand-name medication. This can be an opportunity for the pharmacist to identify any real or potential confusion related to generic/brand substitution.[16]

The final portion of this step should include a dispensing check against the original prescription. This should involve a visual check or a scan of the drug barcode, if available. Scanning the barcode also allows for documentation of the dispensing.

Label Drugs

Always prepare and attach any dispensing and cautionary advisory labels in a way that best meets the needs of the patient. Some considerations include the following:

- medical conditions;
- eyesight;
- health literacy.

Always ensure that the drug labeling is accurate, unambiguous, legible, and complete, as any misunderstandings can lead to unintentional misuse and poor health outcomes. Always follow the best practice for labeling drug containers[17]:

- Use dark print and a suitably sized font;
- Attach dispensing labels and appropriate cautionary advisory labels to the primary container (e.g., bottle or inhaler) to ensure that the directions are readily available;
- Comply with relevant legislation and guidelines;
- Attach labels to flat surfaces (i.e., not over the edge of the box);
- Use purpose-designed tags or "winged" labels if the primary container is very small;
- Ensure that the dosage and name of the active ingredient(s) are visible;
- Ensure that the batch number, expiry date, and storage requirements are visible;
- Avoid placing labels over barcodes or seals.

Supply and Provide Counseling

Counseling is a vital step in the dispensing process. This is to ensure that the patient will have sufficient information to understand their drugs and intended therapeutic effects. Always give the patient the opportunity to ask any questions and clarify any information. In counseling, discuss the following:

- what the drug is used for;
- how the drug works;
- how to take drug, use devices, and measure doses;
- when to take the drug;
- how long to continue taking the drug;

- what to do if a dose is missed;
- what to do if a dosing error or overdose occur;
- how to recognize adverse effects and what to do if they occur;
- how to store or dispose of the drug;
- lifestyle advice relevant to the condition or disease (e.g., smoking, alcohol);
- potential interactions with other drugs, complementary drugs, or foods.

Please bear in mind that different patients may have different informational needs; the intervention should be customized accordingly.

Always highlight any drugs and brands that are new to the patient using an appropriate language. Written information can be useful to supplement verbal counseling.

Record the Intervention

Pharmacists should keep a record of the prescribed and dispensed medication, as well as of any interventions undertaken by the pharmacist.

This record of drugs dispensed may be constructed automatically through scanning the drug box or barcode, which also allows for correct billing.

When patient records are available, the possibility to create and maintain the medication history of that specific patient has several benefits, including the ability to intervene and prevent polypharmacy, drug interactions, and/or medication errors.

OBJECTIVE 8.2. DETAIL METHODS IN MEDICATION RECONCILIATION TO PREVENT ERRORS

It is important for a pharmacist to reconcile a patient's current prescription with the medication history obtained. This usually involves comparing the prescribed medication with medication history, identifying and resolving any discrepancies that may arise, and documenting the changes in the medication regimen. Prescribing, dispensing, and administration of new drugs should be performed after proper reconciliation, as an accurate medication history is essential to avoid medication errors.[18] It has been found that availability of an electronic database, which includes patient medication history, enhances on-admission medication reconciliation process.[19]

Studies have shown that poor, or lack of, medication reconciliation constitutes a significant risk for medication discrepancies, errors, and adverse drug reactions that can result in adverse events, particularly when transitions of care occur.[20,21] In a systematic review and metaanalysis published in 2016, pharmacy-led medication reconciliation interventions were found to be an effective strategy to reduce medication discrepancies and had a greater impact when conducted at either admission or discharge.[22]

Medication reconciliation is not only relevant at transitions between different levels of care but also in the transfer of care within the hospital. Medication errors increase when intensive care unit (ICU) transfers are high. Pharmacists' medication reconciliation was found to decrease medication transfer errors at ICU admission and prior to ICU discharge.[23] In addition, pharmacists demonstrate their advocacy roles throughout the transition of care on behalf of the patient. Pharmacists are empowered with patient advocacy skills to prevent medication errors through medication reconciliation. Fig. 8.2 shows a pharmacist verifying a medication order.[24]

A standard operating protocol (SOP) for medication reconciliation was developed, tested, and refined for use within the context of the WHO Action on Patient Safety ("High 5s") initiative. This is an internationally coordinated, limited participation activity for testing the feasibility of implementing standardized patient safety protocols and determining the impact of the implementation on certain specified patient safety outcomes.[25] It applies to the acute hospital setting and covers implementing medication reconciliation on admission, at internal transfer, and on discharge from hospital. This SOP established guiding principles for implementation of this process, namely:

1. An up-to-date and accurate patient medication list is essential to ensure safe prescribing in any setting;
2. A formal structured process for reconciling medications should be in place across all interfaces of care;
3. Medication reconciliation upon admission is the foundation for reconciliation throughout the episode of care;

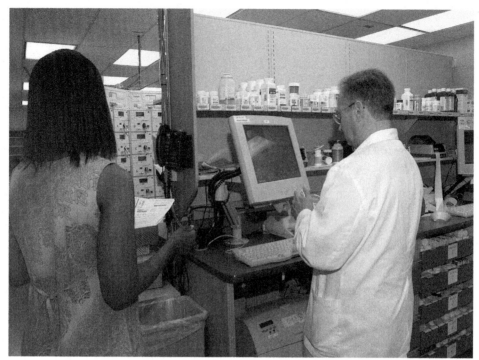

FIGURE 8.2 Pharmacist verifying a prescription. *Courtesy https://commons.wikimedia.org/wiki/File:US_Navy_030819-N-9593R-082_Pharmacist_Randal_Heller,right_verifies_the_dosage_and_medication_of_a_prescription_at_the_National_Naval_Medical_Center_in_Bethesda,_Maryland.jpg.*

4. Medication reconciliation is integrated into existing processes for medication management and patient flow;
5. The process of medication reconciliation is one of shared accountability with staff being aware of their roles and responsibilities;
6. Patients and families are involved in medication reconciliation;
7. Staff responsible for reconciling medications are trained to take a patient's list of current medications and reconcile with previous drugs/regimens.

Medication reconciliation also occurs in community pharmacies and is especially important for patients who are discharged from hospitals or other healthcare facilities and/or who are visiting more than one physician.[26–28] Further research on clinical relevance of discrepancies and potential benefits on reducing healthcare team workload should be undertaken.[29]

OBJECTIVE 8.3. EXPLAIN APPROACHES TO PATIENT COUNSELING

The community pharmacy is often the first point of contact between patients and the healthcare system. Pharmacists provide education and pharmaceutical care to help patients to understand and use drugs responsibly.[30] Counseling is part of the dispensing process and includes instructions on how to administer medications and what to do if something goes wrong.[9]

Patient education is usually a broader term and has been described as an element of patient empowerment. This can be achieved by teaching patients about their illnesses/conditions and encouraging greater involvement in decisions related to ongoing care and treatment.[31]

The primary purpose of offering drug information to patients is to improve public health literacy and to empower and assist citizens in achieving safe, effective, and appropriate use of drugs. This includes providing information that allows users of drugs to make informed decisions about their healthcare.[32] Users of drugs value accurate, comprehensible, appropriate, objective, independent, up-to-date, and relevant information, which can adequately inform and assist them in safe, effective, and appropriate self-management.

Pharmacists influence drug therapy, public health, and disease prevention through counseling. Specialized disease counseling improves patient outcomes. Although outcomes may vary in different health systems and individual patients, counseling has been found to be effective.[33,34]

Patient Counseling on Over-The-Counter medication. *Courtesy https://commons.wikimedia.org/wiki/File:Pharmacist_assisting_a_customer_at_Terry_White_Chemists.jpg.*

Pharmacists also counsel consumers on health promotion and disease prevention, even when a drug is not dispensed. Depending on practice settings, job description, and patient needs, counseling provided by pharmacists may vary. In fact, there is much evidence demonstrating that pharmacist input into self-care is highly effective. The value of this pharmacist input derives from[35]

- Professional competency: The ability to safely assess minor illnesses effectively and distinguish them from major disease;
- Economic factors: The ability to support self-care efficiently by reducing health costs, both in terms of drug and salary costs and through indirect costs (e.g., enabling people to remain at work, minimizing time off work);
- Integration factors: The ability to ensure continuity of care; and
- Communication and access factors: The ability to interact effectively with the public.

Whenever counseling is used as an intervention (e.g., to improve awareness and medication adherence), pharmacists ideally use the five-step approach in Pharmacists' Patient Care Process:[36]

1. Information is collected on nonadherence of patient to the medication;
2. The pharmacist assesses the reasons for the nonadherence;
3. Together, with the patient and other pertinent healthcare professionals, the pharmacist prepares a care plan, which in the case of nonadherence, may be to clarify doubts related to medication use;
4. The pharmacist implements the care plan in collaboration with other healthcare professionals and the patient or caregiver;
5. The pharmacist monitors changes in adherence patterns and evaluates the effectiveness of the intervention.

Counseling in acute and chronic disease conditions is different. Counseling in certain diseases needs special training (e.g., diabetes, HIV/AIDS, psychiatric). For instance, chronic conditions are prone for deviations in medication adherence patterns due to many factors. Conditions with social stigma require a private and comfortable counseling environment.[37] Care should be taken while counseling patients with dementia or sensory impairments. Appropriate counseling aids may be required to effectively communicate the message.[38]

Counseling for specific populations also needs a varied approach. The approach to pediatric, geriatric, or pregnant populations should be different according to common issues and concerns within that population. For instance, when drugs are intended for children, their caregiver should be involved, as nonadherence to drugs is an important issue for pediatric patients. To ensure compliance, the pharmacist must optimize a child's therapy regimen by partnering with the family to identify barriers to compliance, provide education on the importance of compliance, provide strategies to help children take their medications, and offer ongoing support and assistance. By involving the child in this process, the pharmacist must communicate in an age-appropriate manner, utilizing appropriate aids when necessary.[39]

Geriatric patients can pose significant challenges to counseling by the pharmacist. Complex medication regimens, physical limitations, cognitive impairment, economic issues, adherence, and attitudes toward sickness and medications should be addressed. This may necessitate the counseling process to occur with a caregiver or family member.[40]

Pregnant and lactating mothers are concerned about the safety of their fetus/infant. Addressing the probability of harm for each drug is therefore paramount. Specialized references (e.g., *Briggs Pregnancy and Lactation*) should be consulted to provide accurate information.

Extremely careful strategies are required while counseling a noncooperating, angry, or frustrated patient. The pharmacist should apply active listening techniques and address patients' concerns and causes for frustration in a professional, assertive, but empathic manner. If a patient refuses counseling, the pharmacist should ascertain whether this refusal is based on the patient's conviction that they already know how to handle their medication. In this case, asking how the patient has been taking their drugs and how they are feeling might provide the opportunity to identify any knowledge gaps and address those in a constructive manner.

It is important to acknowledge that patients have the right to accept or deny advice and counseling. Counseling should not be imposed but offered. It should be provided at the right extent through an approach that is acceptable to consumers. Understanding cultural sensitivity is essential; a comment that negatively addresses culture or beliefs could result in nonadherence. Studying and practicing in a community with diversity is associated with better outcomes. The Institute of Medicine has stated that greater diversity within healthcare professionals leads to improved patient outcomes.[41]

Steps in the patient education and counseling process may vary according to needs of the individual, environment, and practice setting. The following is a generalized list of things to remember when counseling patients[40,42]:

- Establish a relationship that will maximize effective communication by demonstrating genuine interest, acceptance, and rapport.
- Address people using their preferred name.
- Introduce yourself as a pharmacist, explain the purpose and expected length of the session, and obtain the patient's agreement to participate.
- Determine patient-specific barriers to communication and implement a strategy to overcome barriers.
- Assess the patient's knowledge about health problems and medications, physical and mental capability to use the medications appropriately, and attitude toward the health problems and medications used.
- Provide information orally and use visual aids or demonstrations to fill the patient's gap in knowledge and understanding. Show the patient the colors, sizes, shapes, and markings on oral solids. For oral liquids and injectable drugs, show patients the dosage marks on measuring devices. Demonstrate the assembly and use of administration devices such as nasal and oral inhalers. As a supplement to face-to-face oral communication, provide written handouts to help the patient recall the information.
- Use active listening skills, good eye contact, and gestures when appropriate.
- Observe nonverbal cues such as body language, behavior or facial expression, for reactions.
- Give support, encouragement, and feedback.

When dealing with complaints, the method used by Starbucks employees is worth mentioning, LATTE. LATTE stands for "We **Listen** to the customer, **Acknowledge** their complaint, **Take** action by solving the problem, **Thank** them, and then **Explain** why the problem occurred."[43]

OBJECTIVE 8.4. OUTLINE STRATEGIES TO IMPROVE MEDICATION ADHERENCE

Nonadherence occurs when patients do not take their drugs appropriately or at all. Studies have shown that approximately 50% of patients do not take medications as prescribed.[44] Nonadherence is driven by a combination of factors versus just one. These include lack of affordability; unintended patient-related factors such as forgetfulness or an unsupportive patient and healthcare professional relationship; or inappropriate patient–product suitability such as packaging/device, complexity of medication regimen, and adverse drug reactions. All of these affect patient responsiveness and drug use.[44,45]

Poor adherence can impair the efficacy and safety of drugs, reduce the full benefits of treatment, and lead to unnecessary adverse events and hospitalization. This usually results in costly complications, which are often more expensive than drugs, and poorer health outcomes.[46]

Some authors argue that the terms compliance and adherence have differences, whereas some use it interchangeably.[44] Compliance is the extent to which the patient's behavior matches the prescriber's recommendations. Adherence is the extent to which the patient's behavior matches the agreed-on recommendations from the prescriber. Many prefer to use the term adherence over compliance, because this later implies patient passivity. Concordance is a similar but broader term that stresses patient support in drug taking. Generally, the goal is achieved if the patient takes the medication as recommended to achieve maximum therapeutic benefit.[47] Adherence is the more popular term used.

Improving medication adherence is a challenge. Pharmacists are not in control of many factors that decrease medication adherence. However, being a drug expert and the last professional in the patient care process, pharmacists have leading responsibilities to implement strategies and services which enhance medication adherence.

Initial medication adherence (IMA) and persistence are different in certain aspects. IMA is defined as the patient obtaining, for the first time, a new prescription medication. Difficulties in access to a prescribed drug due to nonavailability in the pharmacy or the drug being too costly are issues leading to nonadherence. More complex patient factors may exist, however, as many patients may not use their medications from the very beginning for a variety of reasons.[48] Medication persistence has been defined as "the duration of time from initiation to discontinuation of therapy."[49] Persistence is particularly relevant in the context of chronic diseases and may require tailored interventions, as adherence changes over time.

Counseling and providing instructions with assertiveness is important to win the trust of patients and to motivate them to take their drugs as instructed. Pharmacists should not contradict prescriber's instructions, as this may decrease trust between the healthcare provider and patient. Any intervention to modify the prescription should be made in collaboration with the prescriber, to avoid losing the trust of the patient.

Many methods are in place to improve medication adherence, and these relate to the reasons for nonadherence.[44] To identify the best strategy or service for a given situation, it is important to determine if the nonadherence is intentional or unintentional.[50] Unintentional nonadherence (e.g., poor memory, work restrictions, mental illness) is usually more easily resolved and could involve simple adjustments to the medication regimen or even providing certain services such as medication administration aids (e.g., medication calendars, pill organizers).

Intentional nonadherence requires a more structured approach, as reasons usually involve patients' beliefs, concerns, or issues related to side effects of drugs, fear of dependency, or mistrust in the benefit.

It is important to create a "shame-free" environment to address poor health literacy and ask questions in the affirmative.[44,50] Patients should not feel ashamed or feel that they have done something wrong. Otherwise, they might stop revealing nonadherence issues with the pharmacist, with fear that there is an unpleasant response.

A health coaching or motivational interviewing approach is usually most suitable for a patient counseling session. This takes into account not only the pharmacist being an expert in medication use but the patient also being an expert on their health and personal circumstances which can influence medication decisions.

The pharmacist could adopt the following approach for a counseling session:[44,51−53]

1. Explore the patient's perspective;
2. Address any beliefs and concerns the patient may have which resulted in the nonadherence;
3. Explain key information when prescribing/dispensing a drug, including key information about the drug;
4. Share and discuss the advantages and disadvantages of different drugs options, including common side effects;
5. Reach a shared understanding about the issues that affect adherence;
6. Use, when applicable, medication adherence-improving aids, such as medication calendars or schedules that specify the time to take medications, drug cards, medication charts; drug-related information sheets; or specific packaging strategies such as pill boxes, "unit-of-use" packaging, and special containers indicating the time of dose;
7. Provide behavioral support to incorporate the medication regimen into the patient's daily regimen;
8. Negotiate, agree, and record the plan;
9. Schedule appropriate follow-up to assess the medication adherence and identify further difficulties and barriers to be addressed.

There are several methods to measure adherence, which can be broken down into direct and indirect methods of measurement.[44,52] Direct methods include direct observed therapy, measurement of the level of a drug or its metabolite in blood or urine, and detection or measurement of a biological marker added to the drug formulation. Direct approaches are most accurate but are more expensive. Indirect methods include patient questionnaires, patient and caregivers' self-reports, pill counts, rates of prescription refills, assessment of patient's clinical response, electronic medication monitors, measurement of physiologic markers, and patient diaries.

A recent systematic review addressing the effectiveness of interventions by community pharmacists to improve patient adherence to chronic medications concluded that, although counseling, monitoring, and education during weekly or monthly appointments showed some effect, it was impossible to identify an overall successful adherence-improving strategy performed by pharmacists.[54] The authors concluded that more well-designed and well-conducted studies need to be performed.

However, there has been evidence of initiatives which have been successful. An example is the New Medicine Service (NMS), which was introduced in 2011 by community pharmacists in England, and is performed 1 to 2 weeks after a patient is prescribed a new drug for a chronic disease. The pharmacist talks to the patient to find out whether they are taking the drug, if they consider it to be working, and if they are experiencing side effects. An appropriate intervention can then be recommended.[55] An evaluation of the NMS published in August 2016 found that such efforts the number of patients who are adherent to their treatment by about 10%. There was also a general trend to reduced healthcare costs.[56]

CONCLUSION

The core responsibility of a pharmacist is to facilitate access to quality drugs in such conditions that they are the most effective, safe, and affordable for the patient. Dispensing is a fundamental service provided by pharmacists which aims to ensure that patients will derive maximum clinical benefit from drugs with no harm. Optimal patient adherence to therapy remains a challenge. Pharmacists are instrumental in improving patient medication adherence by implementing a range of pharmaceutical services that should be tailored to patient needs and expectations.

PRACTICE QUESTIONS

1. An opioid stewardship program is designed to improve:
   A. Prescribing
   B. Dispensing
   C. Administration
   D. All of the above
2. Medication reconciliation is important for which of the following situations:
   A. New admission to hospital
   B. Admission to the ICU
   C. Discharge from ICU
   D. All of the above
3. Counseling and providing proper medication instruction with the patient is a strategy to:
   A. Decrease medication shortage
   B. Improve medication inventory
   C. Improve medication adherence
   D. All of the above

REFERENCES

1. World Health Organization. Ensuring good dispensing practices. In: *MDS-3: Managing Access to Medicines and Health Technologies*. WHO/MSH; 2012. http://apps.who.int/medicinedocs/documents/s19607en/s19607en.pdf.
2. International Pharmaceutical Federation (FIP). *Pharmacy at a Glance 2015-2017*; 2017. The Hague - The Netherlands https://www.fip.org/files/fip/publications/2017-09-Pharmacy_at_a_Glance-2015-2017.pdf.
3. World Health Professions Alliance. All You need to know about spurious medicines. In: *A Practical Handbook for Healthcare Professionals in India*; 2016. http://www.fip.org/files/fip/WHPA_Handbook_India.pdf.
4. Hoppe J, Howland MA, Nelson L. The role of pharmacies and pharmacists in managing controlled substance dispensing. *Pain Med*. 2014;15(12):1996−1998. https://doi.org/10.1111/pme.12531.
5. Varley PR, Zuckerbraun BS. Opioid stewardship and the surgeon. *JAMA Surg*. 2018;153(2):e174875. https://doi.org/10.1001/jamasurg.2017.4875.
6. Gilchrist M, Wade P, Ashiru-Oredope D, et al. Antimicrobial stewardship from policy to practice: experiences from UK antimicrobial pharmacists. *Infect Dis Ther*. 2015;4(Suppl. 1):51−64. https://doi.org/10.1007/s40121-015-0080-z.
7. Cox JA, Vlieghe E, Mendelson M, et al. Antibiotic stewardship in low- and middle-income countries: the same but different? *Clin Microbiol Infect*. 2017;23(11):812−818. https://doi.org/10.1016/j.cmi.2017.07.010.
8. International Pharmaceutical Federation (FIP). Fighting antimicrobial resistance. The contribution of pharmacists. In: *Essential Medicines and Health Products Information Portal*; 2015. http://apps.who.int/medicinedocs/en/d/Js23317en/.
9. Pharmacy Board of Australia. *Guidelines for Dispensing of Medicines*; 2015. http://apps.who.int/medicinedocs/documents/s17807en/s17807en.pdf.
10. The Pharmacy Guild of Australia. *Dispensing Your Prescription Medicine: More than Sticking a Label on a Bottle*; 2016. https://www.guild.org.au/__data/assets/pdf_file/0020/5366/the-dispensing-process.pdf.
11. FIP/WHO. *Joint FIP/WHO Guidelines on Good Pharmacy Practice: Standards for Quality of Pharmacy Services*. World Health Organization; 2011. http://apps.who.int/medicinedocs/en/d/Js18676en/.

12. Lee SWH, Chong CS, Chong DWK. Identifying and addressing drug-related problems in nursing homes: an unmet need in Malaysia? *Int J Clin Pract*. 2016;70(6):512. https://doi.org/10.1111/ijcp.12826.

13. Lee SWH, Mak VSL. Changing demographics in Asia: a case for enhanced pharmacy services to be provided to nursing homes. *J Pharm Pract Res*. 2016;46(2):152−155. https://doi.org/10.1002/jppr.1216.

14. Government of South Australia. *High Risk Medicines*. SA Health; 2018. http://www.sahealth.sa.gov.au/wps/wcm/connect/public+content/sa+health+internet/clinical+resources/clinical+topics/medicines+and+drugs/high+risk+medicines.

15. International Pharmaceutical Federation (FIP). Report of the international summit on medicine shortage. In: *Essential Medicines and Health Products Information Portal*; 2013. http://apps.who.int/medicinedocs/en/d/Js20979en/.

16. Chua SS, Kok LC, Yusof FAM, et al. Pharmaceutical care issues identified by pharmacists in patients with diabetes, hypertension or hyperlipidaemia in primary care settings. *BMC Health Serv Res*. 2012;12:388. https://doi.org/10.1186/1472-6963-12-388.

17. International Pharmaceutical Federation. *FIP Guidelines for the Labels of Prescribed Medicines*; 2001. http://www.fip.org/www/uploads/database_file.php?id=256&table_id.

18. Fitzgerald RJ. Medication errors: the importance of an accurate drug history. *Br J Clin Pharmacol*. 2009;67(6):671−675. https://doi.org/10.1111/j.1365-2125.2009.03424.x.

19. Au D, Wu H, San C, Chua D, Su V, Kirkwood A. Impact of PharmaNet-based admission medication reconciliation on best possible medication histories for warfarin. *Can J Hosp Pharm*. 2016;69(5):348−355. http://www.ncbi.nlm.nih.gov/pubmed/27826152.

20. Sinvani LD, Beizer J, Akerman M, et al. Medication reconciliation in continuum of care transitions: a moving target. *J Am Med Dir Assoc*. 2013;14(9):668−672. https://doi.org/10.1016/j.jamda.2013.02.021.

21. Agency for Healthcare Research and Quality - Patient Safety Network. Medication Reconciliation. Patient Safety Primer. https://psnet.ahrq.gov/primers/primer/1/medication-reconciliation. Accessed on July 27, 2018

22. Mekonnen AB, McLachlan AJ, Brien JE. Pharmacy-led medication reconciliation programmes at hospital transitions: a systematic review and meta-analysis. *J Clin Pharm Ther*. 2016;41(2):128−144. https://doi.org/10.1111/jcpt.12364.

23. Bosma LBE, Hunfeld NGM, Quax RAM, et al. The effect of a medication reconciliation program in two intensive care units in The Netherlands: a prospective intervention study with a before and after design. *Ann Intensive Care*. 2018;8(1):19. https://doi.org/10.1186/s13613-018-0361-2.

24. American Pharmacists Association AS of H-SP. *Improving Care Transitions: Optimizing Medication Reconciliation*; 2012. https://www.pharmacist.com/sites/default/files/files/2012_improving_care_transitions.pdf.

25. World Health Organization. The high 5s project − standard operating protocol for medication reconciliation. In: *Assuring Medication Accuracy at Transitions in Care: Medication Reconciliation*; 2014. http://www.who.int/patientsafety/implementation/solutions/high5s/h5s-sop.pdf.

26. Johnson CM, Marcy TR, Harrison DL, Young RE, Stevens EL, Shadid J. Medication reconciliation in a community pharmacy setting. *J Am Pharm Assoc*. 2010;50(4):523−526. https://doi.org/10.1331/JAPhA.2010.09121.

27. Pharmacy Guild of Australia. *Improving Medication Reconciliation in Community Settings*; 2017. https://www.guild.org.au/__data/assets/pdf_file/0024/27096/Final-QUM-report-27-Feb-2017.PDF.

28. Freund JE, Martin BA, Kieser MA, Williams SM, Sutter SL. Transitions in care: medication reconciliation in the community pharmacy setting after discharge. *Innov Pharm*. 2013;44(2). http://pubs.lib.umn.edu/innovations/vol4/iss2/7.

29. McNab D, Bowie P, Ross A, MacWalter G, Ryan M, Morrison J. Systematic review and meta-analysis of the effectiveness of pharmacist-led medication reconciliation in the community after hospital discharge. *BMJ Qual Saf*. 2018;27(4):308−320. https://doi.org/10.1136/bmjqs-2017-007087.

30. European Directorate for the Quality of Medicines. *Pharmaceutical Care - Policies and Practices for a Safer, More Responsible and Cost-Effective Health System*; 2012. https://www.edqm.eu/medias/fichiers/policies_and_practices_for_a_safer_more_responsibl.pdf.

31. The Free Dictionary. *Patient Education*; 2012. https://medical-dictionary.thefreedictionary.com/patient+education.

32. International Pharmaceutical Federation. *FIP Statement of Policy Strategic Development of Medicines Information for the Benefit of Patients and Users of Medicines*; 2017. https://www.fip.org/www/uploads/database_file.php?id=382&table_id=.

33. Pande S, Hiller JE, Nkansah N, Bero L. The effect of pharmacist-provided non-dispensing services on patient outcomes, health service utilisation and costs in low- and middle-income countries. *Cochrane Database Syst Rev*. 2013;(2):CD010398. https://doi.org/10.1002/14651858.CD010398.

34. American Public Health Association. *The Role of the Pharmacist in Public Health*; 2006. https://www.apha.org/policies-and-advocacy/public-health-policy-statements/policy-database/2014/07/07/13/05/the-role-of-the-pharmacist-in-public-health.

35. International Pharmaceutical Federation. *FIP Statement of Policy - Pharmacy: Gateway to Care. Seoul*; 2017. https://www.fip.org/www/uploads/database_file.php?id=384&table_id=.

36. Joint Commission of Pharmacy Practitioners. *Pharmacists' Patient Care Process*. Joint Commission of Pharmacy Practitioners (JCPP); 2014.

37. Schafer JJ, Gill TK, Sherman EM, McNicholl IR. ASHP guidelines on pharmacist involvement in HIV care. *Am J Heal Pharm*. 2016;73(7):468−494. https://doi.org/10.2146/ajhp150623.

38. Worth T. Counseling patients who are blind or visually impaired. *Pharm Today*. 2014;20(3):26. https://doi.org/10.1016/S1042-0991(15)30949-X.

39. Gerber P. *Counselling Pediatric Patients*; 2009. http://www.canadianhealthcarenetwork.ca/files/2009/10/NovoCE_Dec_E.pdf.

40. Assisted Living Consult. *Guidelines for Pharmacist Counseling of Geriatric Patients*; 2007. http://www.assistedlivingconsult.com/issues/03-04/alc78-Guidelines-719.pdf.

41. American College of Clinical Pharmacy, O'Connell MB, Jackson AN, et al. Cultural competency in health care and its implications for pharmacy Part 3B: emphasis on pharmacy education policy, procedures, and climate. *Pharmacother J Hum Pharmacol Drug Ther*. 2013;33(12):e368−e381. https://doi.org/10.1002/phar.1352.

42. American Society of Health System Pharmacist. ASHP guidelines on pharmacist-conducted patient education and counseling. *Am J Health Syst Pharm*. 1997;54(4):431−434. http://www.ncbi.nlm.nih.gov/pubmed/9043568.

43. Barker A. *How to Handle Angry Pharmacy Customers*. Pharm Times; 2015. http://www.pharmacytimes.com/contributor/alex-barker-pharmd/2015/10/how-to-handle-angry-pharmacy-customers.

44. Brown MT, Bussell JK. Medication adherence: WHO cares? *Mayo Clin Proc*. 2011;86(4):304−314. https://doi.org/10.4065/mcp.2010.0575.

45. Aitken M, Gorokhovich L. Advancing the responsible use of medicines: applying levers for change. *SSRN Electron J*. September 2012. https://doi.org/10.2139/ssrn.2222541.

46. World Health Organization. *The Pursuit of Responsible Use of Medicines: Sharing and Learning from Country Experiences*; 2012. http://apps.who.int/medicinedocs/en/d/Js19894en/.

47. National Coordinating Centre for NHS Service Delivery and Organisation R & D. *Concordance, Adherence and Compliance in Medicine Taking*; 2005. http://www.netscc.ac.uk/hsdr/files/project/SDO_FR_08-1412-076_V01.pdf.

48. Hutchins DS, Zeber JE, Roberts CS, Williams AF, Manias E, Peterson AM. Initial medication adherence—review and recommendations for good practices in outcomes research: an ISPOR medication adherence and persistence special interest group report. *Value Heal*. 2015;18(5):690−699. https://doi.org/10.1016/J.JVAL.2015.02.015.

49. Cramer JA, Roy A, Burrell A, et al. Medication compliance and persistence: terminology and definitions. *Value Heal*. 2008;11(1):44−47. https://doi.org/10.1111/j.1524-4733.2007.00213.x.

50. Brown MT, Sinsky CA. *Medication Adherence: We Didn't Ask and They Didn't Tell*. vol. 20. American Academy of Family Physicians; 2013. https://www.aafp.org/fpm/2013/0300/p25.html.

51. National Institute for Health and Care Excellence. *Medicines Adherence: Involving Patient in Decisions about Prescribed Medicines and Supporting Adherence*; 2009. https://www.nice.org.uk/guidance/cg76/resources/medicines-adherence-involving-patients-in-decisions-about-prescribed-medicines-and-supporting-adherence-pdf-975631782085.

52. Jimmy B, Jose J. Patient medication adherence: measures in daily practice. *Oman Med J*. 2011;26(3):155−159. https://doi.org/10.5001/omj.2011.38.

53. Marcum ZA, Sevick MA, Handler SM. Medication nonadherence: a diagnosable and treatable medical condition. *J Am Med Assoc*. 2013;309(20):2105−2106. https://doi.org/10.1001/jama.2013.4638.

54. Van Wijk BL, Klungel OH, Heerdink ER, de Boer A. Effectiveness of interventions by community pharmacists to improve patient adherence to chronic medication: a systematic review. *Ann Pharmacother*. 2005;39(2):319−328. https://doi.org/10.1345/aph.1E027.

55. Torjensen I. Devising ways to improve medicines adherence. *Pharm J*. 2015. https://doi.org/10.1211/PJ.2015.20200125.

56. Elliott RA, Lee CY, Beanland C, et al. Development of a clinical pharmacy model within an Australian home nursing service using co-creation and participatory action research: the visiting pharmacist (ViP) study. *BMJ Open*. 2017;7(11):e018722. https://doi.org/10.1136/bmjopen-2017-018722.

ANSWERS TO PRACTICE QUESTIONS

1. D

2. D

3. C

Section II

Drug Information

Chapter 9

Drug Information Services and Sources of Information

Matthew P. Van Cuyk[1], Jason C. Cooper[2] and James P. New[2]

[1]Massachusetts General Hospital, Boston, MA, United States; [2]Medical University of South Carolina, Charleston, SC, United States

Learning Objectives

Objective 9.1   Outline features of drug information centers and types of drug information services provided in a hospital.
Objective 9.2   Describe applications of common sources of drug information.
Objective 9.3   Overview of drug information quality on the Internet.

OBJECTIVE 9.1. OUTLINE FEATURES OF DRUG INFORMATION CENTERS AND TYPES OF DRUG INFORMATION SERVICES PROVIDED IN A HOSPITAL

Drug Information Centers

In August 1962, the first drug information center (DIC) was established in the United States at the University of Kentucky.[1] The primary objective of this DIC was to provide comprehensive drug information services and to play an active role in the education of medical, dentistry, nursing, and pharmacy students.

Since 1962, many DICs have been established around the world (Fig. 9.1). For a more complete list of DICs around the world, the Society of Hospital Pharmacists of Australia (SHPA) publishes a document that contains the contact information for these centers. The document the SHPA publishes includes DICs in 51 countries; however, it is not all-inclusive.[2]

By 1974, there were 56 DICs in the United States, which increased to 108 by 1992.[8,9] However, by 2008 the number of centers in the United States dropped to 77.[10] Today, many DICs in the United States are affiliated with large academic teaching institutions, a college of pharmacy, or both. This decrease may be attributed to increased training in pharmacy curricula regarding the necessary drug information skills for pharmacists. Additionally, there has also been an increase in accessibility to valid medical and pharmaceutical Internet databases to help answer various types of drug information questions. Although DICs in many countries began independently at universities or hospitals, some countries, such as the United Kingdom, have a national organization that helps maintain centers throughout the country.[11]

To start a DIC, an individual trained in the provision of drug information and a computer with Internet access will be needed, at a bare minimum. However, ideally, a DIC would have several trained individuals to help maintain the day-to-day functions of the center and access to at least one resource pertaining to each of the different types of reference categories listed later on in this chapter. In regard to the amount of space needed for a DIC, there is no standard amount; however, enough space is required to house computers, references, and supplies, and for the staff and learners to be comfortable in a quiet work environment. Finally, financing a DIC requires enough money for pharmacists to staff the center and provide access to various references. In determining a DIC budget, it is important to keep in mind that text references may cost hundreds of dollars, whereas access to online databases for an institution may cost thousands of dollars.

In addition to more traditional DICs, drug manufacturers have medication information departments that serve as a source of drug information for the products that the manufacturer produces. Another example of a nontraditional DIC would be poison control or toxicology centers. In the United States, there are 55 Poison Control Centers at the time of preparation of this chapter, which can be reached via telephone at 1-800-222-1222 in any state.[12]

Clinical Pharmacy Education, Practice and Research. https://doi.org/10.1016/B978-0-12-814276-9.00009-X

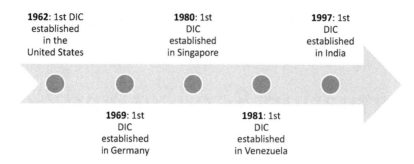

DIC: Drug Information Center

FIGURE 9.1 Examples of first drug information centers established around the world.[1,3–7] *DIC*, drug information center.

DICs participate, in general, in

- Responding to questions
- Formulary management
- Medication use evaluations (MUEs)
- Adverse drug reaction (ADR) reporting
- Communicating newsletters, precepting pharmacy students and pharmacy residents, teaching courses to healthcare professionals in training, and providing in-services to staff.

Responding to Drug Information Questions

One of the primary services provided by DICs, whether it is an academic center, a center associated with a manufacturer, or a poison control center, is to respond to drug/medical questions from healthcare professionals and/or the general public.[10,13] Most academic DICs mainly answer questions from clinicians within their institution; however, others may answer questions from professionals all around their country or state. Others may have policies and procedures in place to respond to questions from patients or the general public. For example, at the Medical University of South Carolina, the Ask-A-Pharmacist web-based service is used to respond to the general public about questions related to their medications (e.g., ADRs, drug–drug interactions). Many retail pharmacies also have their own online services for patients who get their prescriptions filled at that pharmacy to submit a question regarding their medications.

Formulary Management

The cost of healthcare continues to rise. The purchase, use, and monitoring of medications contribute significantly to this increased cost.[15] Although prudent care requires making medical decisions with a patient on an individual basis, streamlining the use of medications for groups of patients has for many years been a method to ensure highly efficacious, safe, and cost-effective utilization.[16–19] As such, many healthcare institutions have a *formulary system* to direct practical use of medications for patients under their care.

A *formulary*, at its essence, is a continually updated list of medications and associated materials approved for use within a particular healthcare institution/country/region. In addition to a list of medications, the formulary consists of policies, guidelines, and other tools designed to support the proper use of these medications. This list should represent the collective clinical judgment of the professionals practicing in that institution. Policies should also be in place to dictate how the use of medications or practices not on the formulary (i.e., nonformulary) should be handled.

The goal of a formulary system is to ensure that the most effective, safe, and cost-effective medications are available for use by practitioners in a particular healthcare facility. At the heart of this review process is the *Pharmacy (or Drug) and Therapeutics (P&T) Committee*. Drug information pharmacists can provide valuable insight to the Committee during the review of medications due to their understanding of evidence-based principles and abilities to find and synthesize information about a drug for Committee members.

Formulary Reviews

A focus of most requests to a P&T Committee involves the review of new medications. Reviews of these agents should be thorough and unbiased including information in the published literature as well as institutional-specific considerations

TABLE 9.1 Formulary Monograph Sections

- General information
  - Brand name
  - Generic name
  - Drug class
- Indications
  - Labeled indications
  - Off-label indications
- Pharmacology
  - Mechanism of action
  - Pharmacokinetics
  - Dosing
- Operations
  - Dosage forms
  - Storage and stability
  - Special handling
- Literature review
  - Clinical trial analysis
  - Grading of evidence
  - Presence in guidelines

- Safety review
  - Contraindications
  - Adverse effects
  - Warnings and precautions
  - Pregnancy and lactation
  - Drug interactions
  - Required monitoring
  - Risk analysis
- Costs
  - Formulary alternatives
  - Reimbursement
  - Pharmacoeconomic analysis
- Conclusion
  - Summary of information
  - Place in therapy
  - Recommendation

(e.g., operational preferences, payment rates, patient acuity). Typically, medications under consideration are reviewed on an individual basis. However, medications that belong to a single class of drugs or treat a similar disease state may require a *class review* to be considered collectively.

An evaluation of a medication can be put together in a drug monograph and submitted to the P&T Committee for review. These monographs should have a standardized format (Table 9.1).

Drug information pharmacists, along with students and residents on rotation, are valuable in creating, evaluating, and editing these monographs. Information is initially gathered on general information (e.g., pharmacology, adverse effects, storage) with the help of common online tertiary databases such as Micromedex, Facts and Comparisons, or Lexicomp. Additionally, the package insert is useful, as this lists the current indications and use of the drug approved by the Food and Drug Administration (FDA). A thorough primary literature review is then necessary to evaluate the available clinical trials for the medication. This can be researched through commonly used secondary databases such as PubMed, SCOPUS, or Medline. Investigation of the studies for the patient population included, outcomes used, and the results obtained should be performed to identify the external validity of the study to one's own institution and patients. The clinical evaluation of efficacy and safety can then be combined with cost and reimbursement to develop general guidance or recommendation for whether or not to add the particular product to the institution's formulary.

Strategies for Maintenance

Once a decision has been made by the P&T Committee, follow-up should be performed to ensure that optimal care is taking place. A MUE or *drug use evaluation* is one tool used to help with continually reviewing a formulary. MUEs are quality improvement tools used to appraise and optimize how medications are managed in the *medication use process* for the purpose of improving patient outcomes.[16,20] MUEs are commonly included as part of the goals/objectives of a pharmacy residency program. These reviews are often led by residents, with the help and guidance of clinicians in that specialized area. Data collection is performed primarily by pharmacy residents, with the ultimate goal of submitting their research for publication. However, the results and information generated are of great importance to the institution in improving their overall efficacy and safety of medication use. These can be presented to the P&T Committee for follow-up and reassessment of previous formulary decisions.

For example, an intravenous immunoglobulin (IVIG) MUE revealed several diagnoses and uses of IVIG in the hospital by various services. Through a literature search, a survey of other similar-sized hospitals, and discussion among specialists who often use IVIG, a list of supported and approved uses was developed. A cost assessment was also performed to estimate expenses saved by adhering to the list. This information was then presented to the P&T Committee and approved. The adopted usage list for IVIG was then built into the electronic medical record where clinicians on designated services could only use IVIG in their patients from the approved list of indications and diagnoses.

Other techniques for optimizing the use of medications on a formulary include the use of generic medications, therapeutic interchange protocols, injectable to oral conversion protocols, automatic discontinuation protocols, and policy and guidelines development.[16–18,21] Use of these tools themselves should also be subject to the continual review and updating required for other parts of the formulary.

Adverse Drug Reactions/Medication Errors

Many DICs affiliated with a hospital may offer services to help track and report ADRs and medication errors.[4,10,13] One tool that is often used for tracking ADRs and medication errors utilizes a trigger tool created by the Institute for Healthcare Improvement (IHI).[22,23] These trigger tools use medications that are commonly administered after an ADR has occurred to reverse the adverse effects of medication (e.g., naloxone for opioids, flumazenil for benzodiazepines, and vitamin K for warfarin). Another method relies on the E-codes available in the supplemental section of the International Classification of Disease 9th and 10th editions.[24,25] These E-codes are used to describe external causes of injury, such as ADRs, which are coded by medical coders. In addition to tracking ADRs, drug information specialists are often tasked with helping to evaluate and set up decision support tools that will alert physicians and pharmacists to drug interactions (i.e., drug–drug interactions, drug–food interactions, drug–allergy interactions, drug–disease interactions).

Education

Many DICs participate in writing or editing newsletters (Fig. 9.2).[4,10,13,26–28] The primary purpose of a newsletter is to educate staff or faculty about new medications recently approved, guideline and policy updates, medication safety issues, and formulary news. In addition to educating readers, data suggest that newsletters may help alter physician prescribing habits in the short term.[26,28,29] Therefore, newsletters may be a useful tool when trying to persuade physicians to use a medication that is on an institution's formulary, which is often the most cost-effective medication.

In-Services for Staff

In addition to writing or editing newsletters, DICs often educate staff or faculty members through in-service programs.[4,10,13] DICs are in a unique position for this service, as they can easily identify the needs of the staff or faculty.[30] If, for example, a DIC notices an influx in questions about a particular disease state or medication, they can prepare an in-service program to educate the appropriate audience. In addition to identifying topics for an in-service program through the questions that a DIC answers, MUEs can be used to identify areas of problematic utilization of a particular medication or class of medications.[31] After these issues and an appropriate alternative or recommendation have been identified, an in-service presentation can be prepared to educate the staff or faculty on the appropriate use of the medication or class of medications.

Precepting Students/Residents on Rotation

Of course, a valuable part of DICs is training students and residents to respond to questions in any type of environment.[13,14] Students and residents are taught about the various tertiary references and secondary databases available for research. An effective and efficient manner of searching, for example, using the modified systematic approach to answering drug information questions, is often taught by using real-life questions pertaining to actual patients. In addtion, case-based scenarios developed from the primary literature or previous calls can be utilized to enforce the modified systematic approach.

OBJECTIVE 9.2. DESCRIBE APPLICATIONS OF COMMON SOURCES OF DRUG INFORMATION

To answer a query using a systematic approach, the order of search follows tertiary to secondary to primary references. This is a general to specific information approach. This section follows the same order.

Tertiary References

Tertiary references/databases are those that contain a collection of information.[32–34] The primary definition of tertiary references is that they do not contain original information. Data and information may be pulled from primary literature sources, but its assembly into one source does/should not declare anything of new or original value.

PHARMACY & THERAPEUTICS

DRUG INFORMATION FOR HEALTHCARE PROFESSIONALS

IS ENDING THE PRESCRIPTION OPIOID EPIDEMIC EVEN POSSIBLE?

Opioids have been used for acute pain relief for more than a century. However, the misuse of prescription opioids in the present day has caused an epidemic.[1-3] As elucidated in a recent article published in the *New England Journal of Medicine*, a key element that highlights the epidemic is the association between an increased prescribing of opioids and opioid-related morbidity and mortality.[1] According to the U.S. Surgeon General, deaths caused by opioid overdose have increased 3-fold since 1999.[3] Overprescribing of opioid analgesics has contributed to the increased use of for medical or nonmedical reasons. It has been estimated that the amount of prescription opioids that was prescribed in 2013 is enough to supply 1 bottle of pills to every adult in the United States.[2] Among all opioid prescriptions, ones written in primary care settings were associated with a higher rate of opioid dependence than those written in a pain clinic setting.[2]

The social and economic burden of opioid misuse and abuse are well-described in the literature. The total societal costs of prescription opioid abuse has been estimated to be $55 billion in 2007. Emergency department and inpatient costs were estimated to be $21 billion in 2009.[4,5] It was only in 2001 that the Joint Commission implemented new pain management standards.[6] These new standards required systematic pain assessment and reassessment during the continuum of care using quantitative measures such as a 10-point pain scale and eliminated "as-needed" or "PRN-range" pain medication orders. The ultimate goal is to optimize opioid prescribing in a safer and more effective way.[6]

In order to tackle the prescription opioid epidemic, the U.S. Department of Health and Human Services (HHS) recommended a multifaceted, harm-reduction approach. In March 2015, the HHS Secretary announced an initiative that focused on 3 priority areas (Table 1).[2]

Table 1. HHS Goals for the Opioid Epidemic
1. Improve prescribing practices
2. Expand access of medication-assisted treatment (MAT) programs
3. Expand the use of naloxone (Narcan®)

To date, federal agencies have implemented policies, grants, and programs to provide resources to counteract the epidemic. The Centers for Disease Control and Prevention (CDC) published guidelines for primary care clinicians on prescribing opioids and provided over $30 million in grants to the states to strengthen Prescription Drug Monitoring Programs (PDMPs).[2] The Substance Abuse and Mental Health Administration (SAMHSA) awarded over $10 million to 11 high-burden states to expand their MAT programs with plans to continue to expand to additional states.[2] These resources are intended to improve the capacity for care of patients with opioid-use

JULY 2017

Ending the Prescription Opioid Epidemic

Barriers to Naloxone Prescribing

Codeine Use in Pediatric Patients

Formulary Update: June 2017

FIGURE 9.2 Part of drug information center newsletter.

Tertiary references are commonly thought of as books, online databases (e.g., Micromedex, UpToDate), and compendiums. Although convenient and easy to use, tertiary texts may be outdated shortly after publication. Therefore, it is always a good idea to check the publication data for a specific book to determine how current the information is. However, because many texts also are now available online or via smartphone apps, databases and references can be updated easily with new information.

Review articles could also be considered tertiary references if they are more narrative in nature. For example, a general review article regarding the current treatment of gout that only summarizes the major information available, but does not put forth any new recommendations, would likely be considered tertiary. However, metaanalyses and systematic reviews that develop a strategy for selection of primary literature, summarize the gathered information, and run statistics to establish new approaches or analysis would be considered more as primary literature due to the generation of original or new material.

It is up to the reader to determine the quality of the information presented in tertiary references. Author bias, misinterpretation, missing data, or other errors may appear in such sources. That is why it is critical to validate and verify the information found in more than one tertiary reference.

When researching drug information questions, it is important first to categorize the question being asked. Once a question is categorized into a specific subject matter (e.g., ADR, drug–drug interaction, etc.), the search for information can begin with tertiary references that are written to cover that particular theme. Categorizing the question also eliminates extraneous tertiary references that would not be helpful to one's search. Table 9.2 is a fairly comprehensive list, broken down by drug information category, of a variety of tertiary references, databases, texts, and compendiums that are available to answer drug information questions. Of note, some of these online databases require a subscription. Please check with your institution to determine availability and access. Additionally, many of these online databases offer mobile applications for smartphones.

Secondary References

Secondary references are usually electronic databases that list primary literature articles via an index or abstracting service.[32,33,35] Indexing services provide basic information of the article such as author, title, publication, and year. Abstracting services, which are more common, provide the citation of the article along with a curtailed description of what the article is about.

Not all indexing and abstracting services are created the same; therefore, it is important to search in various databases to retrieve the most pertinent and up-to-date articles available. For example, PubMed uses medical subject headings (i.e., MeSH terms) to search and find primary literature articles; however, a secondary database such as International Pharmaceutical Abstracts (IPAs) does not use MeSH terms and has its own indexing language. Both databases can be searched using keywords.

Of note, keywords will provide more current articles than using only MeSH terms in a searching strategy, as articles that were most recently published (e.g., last week) may not have had a chance to be indexed and tagged with MeSH terms. This is commonly referred to as the "lag time"—the period between when an article is published in a journal to when it appears in a secondary database. Most major journals (e.g., JAMA, New England Journal of Medicine) do not experience much of a lag time, as their articles are updated and listed in various secondary databases immediately or before publication. However, pharmacy or specialized journals may have more of a lag time because their content is not prioritized in a particular secondary database.

Additionally, most secondary databases use tools such as Boolean operators to search a database. Operators like "AND," "OR," and "NOT" can be combined with general search terms to yield more or fewer articles. For example, creating a searching strategy such as "drug compounding [MeSH]" AND "aspirin [MeSH]" AND "suspensions [MeSH]" would retrieve articles that dealt with all three subjects (i.e., formulations/recipes for compounding an aspirin suspension). Therefore, "AND" is commonly used to limit searches. However, using the operator "OR" will expand a search to include articles that discuss items that might be closely related. For example, if one wanted to find articles about the rate and administration of human immune globulin via the intravenous route, part of the search strategy should include "infusions, intravenous [MeSH]," OR "injections, intravenous [MeSH]" as articles may not differentiate between intravenous injections or infusions. This would offer a broader search at first, and if too many articles were available with the "OR" operator, each MeSH term could be used in its own search and combined with "immunoglobulins, intravenous [MeSH]." Using "NOT" as an operator would eliminate articles that were indexed by a particular subject heading that might be confused with another.

Finally, most secondary databases can use limits when searching and retrieving articles. Common limits such as language, clinical trial design, species (i.e., humans), publication dates (e.g., within last 5 years), and age ranges are available to help narrow down searches to a particular group of patients or within a certain time frame. For more detailed information on how to perform and execute helpful searches within secondary databases, below is a short list of common databases.

Cumulative Index to Nursing and Allied Health Literature

Cumulative Index to Nursing and Allied Health Literature (CINAHL) (https://health.ebsco.com/products/the-cinahl-database/allied-health-nursing) provides indexing of articles from top nursing and allied health literature and includes such

TABLE 9.2 List of Tertiary References by Category

Books/Printed References	Online References
Adverse Drug Reactions	
• Meyler's Side Effects of Drugs: The International Encyclopedia of Adverse Drug Reactions and Interactions • AHFS Drug Information (ASHP) • Drug Information Handbook (Lexicomp) • Drug Facts and Comparisons • Drug-Induced Diseases: Prevention, Detection, and Management	• Facts and Comparisons eAnswers (see Table 9.3) • Lexicomp Online (see Table 9.4) • MICROMEDEX (see Table 9.5) • Clin-Alert Online (http://cla.sagepub.com/) • DailyMed (http://dailymed.nlm.nih.gov/dailymed/index.cfm) • FDA Adverse Event Reporting System (www.fda.gov) • VigiAccess (www.vigiaccess.org/)
Biostatistics	
• Drug Information: A Guide for Pharmacists • Basic & Clinical Biostatistics	• Drug Information: A Guide for Pharmacists (via AccessPharmacy) • Basic and Clinical Biostatistics (via AccessMedicine)
Chemical Structural Information	
• Goodman and Gilman's: The Pharmacological Basis of Therapeutics • Remington: The Science and Practice of Pharmacy • Merck Index	• Goodman and Gilman's: The Pharmacological Basis of Therapeutics (via AccessMedicine) • ChemIDplus (via TOXNET) • PubChem (through PubMed or NLM Drug Information Portal) • USP-NF Online (http://www.uspnf.com/uspnf/login)
Compounding	
• Trissel's Stability of Compounded Formulations • Extemporaneous Formulations for Pediatric, Geriatric and Special Needs Patients • Pediatric Drug Formulations • Handbook of Extemporaneous Formulations • Pediatric Dosage Handbook • Allen's Compounded Formulations	• www.compoundingtoday.com/ (International Journal of Pharmacy Compounding)
Comprehensive Medical Information	
• The Medical Letter • Treatment Guidelines (from The Medical Letter) • Pharmacist's Letter • Prescriber's Letter	• Pharmacist's Letter (http://www.pharmacistletter.com/) • Prescriber's Letter (https://prescribersletter.com/) • eMedicine (http://emedicine.medscape.com/) • DISEASEDEX (see Table 9.5) • UpToDate (http://www.uptodate.com/) • The Medical Letter (http://www.medicalletter.com/) • Treatment Guidelines (from The Medical Letter) (http://www.medicalletter.com/) • DynaMed (www.dynamed.com/home/) • Disease Management Project: Cleveland Clinic (http://www.clevelandclinicmeded.com/medicalpubs/diseasemanagement/)
Critical Care/Emergency Medicine	
• Hall, Schmidt, and Wood's Principles of Critical Care • Fuhrman and Zimmerman's Pediatric Critical Care • Anesthesiology & Critical Care Drug Handbook (Lexicomp) • Tintinalli's Emergency Medicine	• Principles of Critical Care (via Access Medicine) • Tintinalli's Emergency Medicine: A Comprehensive Study Guide (via Access Medicine) • The Atlas of Emergency Medicine (via Access Medicine)
Dermatology	
• Fitzpatrick's Color Atlas and Synopsis of Clinical Dermatology • Lookingbill and Marks' Principles of Dermatology • Clinical Dermatology: A Color Guide to Diagnosis and Therapy	• Fitzpatrick's Color Atlas and Synopsis of Clinical Dermatology (via AccessMedicine) • Fitzpatrick's Dermatology in General Medicine (via AccessMedicine)

Continued

TABLE 9.2 List of Tertiary References by Category—cont'd

Books/Printed References	Online References
Drug Identification	
The Pill Book	• Facts and Comparisons eAnswers (see Table 9.3) • Lexi-Drug ID (see Table 9.4) • IDENTIDEX (see Table 9.5) • Pillbox (NLM) (http://pillbox.nlm.nih.gov/index.html) • Drugs.com (http://www.drugs.com/pill_identification.html) • RxList (http://www.rxlist.com/pill-identification- tool/article.htm) • Medscape (http://www.medscape.com/)
Drug Interactions	
• Drug Interaction Facts • Drug Interactions Analysis and Management (Hansten and Horn's) • Stockley's Drug Interactions	• Facts and Comparisons eAnswers (see Table 9.3) • Lexicomp Online (see Table 9.4) • MICROMEDEX (see Table 9.5) • Medscape (http://www.medscape.com/)
Drug Safety	
	• Facts and Comparisons REMS (see Table 9.3) • LexiComp online (see Table 9.4) • BlackBoxRX (www.blackboxrx.com/)
Enteral/Parenteral Nutrition	
• Handbook of Drug Administration via Enteral Feeding Tubes (ASHP) • Clinical Guide to Parenteral Micronutrition	• American Society for Parenteral and Enteral Nutrition (http://www.nutritioncare.org/)
Evidence-Based Medicine	
• Users' Guide to the Medical Literature: Essentials of Evidence-Based Clinical Practice (JAMA Evidence)	• AHRQ (http://www.ahrq.gov/) • Cochrane Library (http://www.cochranelibrary.com/) • National Comprehensive Cancer Network Guidelines (http://www.nccn.org/professionals/physician_gls/f_guidelines.asp) • National Institute for Health and Care Excellence (https://www.nice.org.uk/guidance)
General Pharmacy References	
• AHFS Drug Information (ASHP) • Drug Facts and Comparisons • Drug Information Handbook (Lexicomp) • Pharmacist's Letter	• Facts and Comparisons eAnswers (see Table 9.3) • Lexicomp Online (with AHFS - see Table 9.4) • MICROMEDEX (see Table 9.5) • Pharmacist's Letter (http://www.pharmacistletter.com/) • Hospital Pharmacist's Letter (https://hospitalpharmacistsletter.com/) • Medscape (http://www.medscape.com/) • UpToDate (http://www.uptodate.com/) • NLM Drug Information Portal (http://druginfo.nlm.nih.gov/drugportal/drugportal.jsp)
Hematology/Oncology	
• Wintrobe's Hematology • Drug Information Handbook for Oncology (Lexicomp) • Hematology: Basic Principles and Practice • Cancer: Principles of Practice of Oncology (DeVita's)	• Chemotherapy Resources (see Table 9.3) • PDQ (Physician Data Query—National Cancer Institute) (http://www.cancer.gov/cancertopics/pdq) • MD Anderson Manual of Medical Oncology (via AccessMedicine) • Memorial Sloan Kettering Cancer Center (http://www.mskcc.org/) • Williams Hematology (via AccessMedicine) • National Comprehensive Cancer Network Guidelines (http://www.nccn.org/professionals/physician_gls/f_guidelines.asp)

Continued

TABLE 9.2 List of Tertiary References by Category—cont'd

Books/Printed References	Online References
Herbal Medications and Dietary Supplements	
• Natural Medicines Comprehensive Database • Handbook of Medicinal Herbs (Duke's) • The Review of Natural Products (Facts and Comparisons)	• Natural Medicines Comprehensive Database (http://naturaldatabase.therapeuticresearch.com/home) • Natural Products Database (see Table 9.3) • Office of Dietary Supplements (http://ods.od.nih.gov/) • Dietary Supplements Labels Database (http://www.dsld.nlm.nih.gov/dsld/) • The National Center for Complementary and Integrated Health (https://nccih.nih.gov/) • Memorial Sloan Kettering Cancer Center: About Herbs, Botanicals, and Other Products (http://www.mskcc.org/mskcc/html/11570.cfm)
Immunology and Vaccines	
• Red Book: 2015 Report of the Committee on Infectious Diseases • Pharmaceutical Biotechnology	• Immunization Resources (see Table 9.3) • Review of Medical Microbiology and Immunology (via AccessMedicine) • CDC (http://www.cdc.gov/vaccines) • Red Book: 2015 Report of the Committee on Infectious Disease (http://aapredbook.aappublications.org/)
Infectious Diseases	
• The Sanford Guide to Antimicrobial Therapy • Red Book: 2015 Report of the Committee on Infectious Diseases • Infectious Diseases (Gorbach's) • Principles and Practice of Infectious Diseases (Mandell's)	• Review of Medical Microbiology and Immunology (via AccessMedicine) • Emerging Infectious Diseases (http://www.cdc.gov/ncidod/eid) • Morbidity and Mortality Weekly Report (MMWR: http://www.cdc.gov/mmwr/) • Infectious Diseases Society of America (http://www.idsociety.org/Index.aspx) • Infectious Diseases (see Table 9.4) • AIDSinfo (http://aidsinfo.nih.gov/) • Red Book: 2015 Report of the Committee on Infectious Disease (http://aapredbook.aappublications.org/) • Cleveland Clinic: Guidelines for Antimicrobial Usage 2012−13 (http://www.clevelandclinicmeded.com/medicalpubs/antimicrobial-guidelines/) • John Hopkins Antibiotics and HIV Guides (http://www.unboundmedicine.com/ucentral)
Injectable Drugs	
• Handbook on Injectable Drugs (Trissel's) • King Guide to Parenteral Admixtures • Pediatric Injectable Drugs (Teddy Bear Book) • Gahart's 2017 Intravenous Medications: A Handbook for Nurses and Health Professionals • Extended Stability for Parenteral Drugs (ASHP)	• King Guide (www.kingguide.com) • Trissel's2 (see Tables 9.3−9.5) • Latexdrugs.com/
Internal Medicine	
• Harrison's Principles of Internal Medicine • Conn's Current Therapy	• Harrison's Online (via AccessMedicine)
International Drug References	
• Martindale: The Complete Drug Reference • Index Nominum	• Martindale: The Complete Drug Reference (see Tables 9.3 and 9.4) • ChemIDplus (via TOXNET) • Lexi-Drugs International (see Table 9.4)

Continued

TABLE 9.2 List of Tertiary References by Category—cont'd

Books/Printed References	Online References
Laboratory Information	
• Guide to Diagnostic Tests • Basic Skills in Interpreting Laboratory Data	• Laboratory Values/Body Measurements (see Table 9.3) • Lab Tests and Diagnostic Procedures (see Table 9.4) • Lab Advisor (see Table 9.5)
Law and Regulations	
	• Code of Federal Regulations Title 21 (http://www.accessdata.fda.gov/scripts/cdrh/cfdocs/cfcfr/cfrsearch.cfm)
Nephrology	
• Drug Prescribing in Renal Failure (Bennett's Tables)	• CURRENT Diagnosis & Treatment: Nephrology & Hypertension (via Access Medicine)
Nonprescription Drugs	
• Handbook of Nonprescription Drugs (APhA)	• Facts and Comparisons eAnswers (see Table 9.3) • Lexicomp Online (limited - see Table 9.4) • MICROMEDEX (limited - see Table 9.5)
Nursing and Allied Health	
• 2017 Nursing Drug Handbook • Mosby's (Elsevier) Nursing Skills • Perry and Potter's Fundamentals of Nursing • Perry and Potter's Clinical Nursing Skills &Techniques	• Perry and Potter Clinical Nursing Skills and Techniques (via www.elsevier.com/) • Mosby's (Elsevier) Nursing Skills (via www.elsevier.com/)
Off-Label Information	
• AHFS Drug Information (ASHP) • Off-Label Drug Facts (Facts and Comparisons) • Drug Facts and Comparisons	• Facts and Comparisons eAnswers (see Table 9.3) • Lexicomp Online (limited - see Table 9.4) • MICROMEDEX (limited - see Table 9.5)
Ophthalmic Medications	
• Ophthalmic Drug Facts • The Wills Eye Manual: Office and Emergency Room Diagnosis and Treatment of Eye Disease	
Pain Management	
• Demystifying Opioid Conversion Calculations (ASHP) • Palliative Pharmacy Care (ASHP)	• Hopkins Opioid Program (http://www.hopweb.org/ - free registration) • Facts and Comparisons E Answers—Opioid Agonist Conversion (clinical calculator)
Patient Education	
• Medication Teaching Manual • Pediatric Teaching Manual	• Facts and Comparisons eAnswers (see Table 9.3) • Lexicomp Online (see Table 9.4) • CareNotes (see Table 9.5) • MedlinePlus (http://www.medlineplus.gov/) • KidsHealth (http://kidshealth.org/) • ToxTown (via TOXNET; http://toxtown.nlm.nih.gov/) • PDQ: Physician Data Query (http://www.cancer.gov/cancertopics/pdq)
Pediatrics	
• Pediatric Dosage Handbook (Lexicomp) • The Harriet Lane Handbook • Red Book: 2015 Report of the Committee on Infectious Diseases • Pediatric Pharmacotherapy (ACCP) • Clinical Handbook of Psychotropic Drugs for Children and Adolescents	• Pediatric and Neonatal Lexi-Drugs Online (see Table 9.4) • Current Diagnosis and Treatment: Pediatrics (via AccessMedicine) • KidsHealth (http://kidshealth.org/) • Pediatric Care Online (AAP Textbook of Pediatric Care) (http://www.pediatriccareonline.org/pco/ub/home) • Red Book: 2015 Report of the Committee on Infectious Disease (http://aapredbook.aappublications.org/)

Continued

TABLE 9.2 List of Tertiary References by Category—cont'd

Books/Printed References	Online References
Pharmacogenomics	
• Concepts in Pharmacogenomics (ASHP)	• Pharmacogenomics (see Table 9.4) • The Pharmacogenomics Knowledgebase (https://www.PharmGKB.org/)
Pharmacokinetics	
• Basic Clinical Pharmacokinetics • Applied Biopharmaceutics and Pharmacokinetics (via AccessPharmacy)	• CredibleMeds.org (list of drugs that affects QT interval) • Applied Biopharmaceutics and Pharmacokinetics (via AccessPharmacy)
Pharmacology	
• Goodman and Gilman's: The Pharmacological Basis of Therapeutics	• Goodman and Gilman's: The Pharmacological Basis of Therapeutics (via AccessMedicine)
Pregnancy and Lactation	
• Drugs in Pregnancy and Lactation (Briggs) • Diseases, Complications, and Drug Therapy in Obstetrics: A Guide for Clinicians • Medications and Mother's Milk • Catalog of Teratogenic Agents (Shepard's)	• Pregnancy and Lactation, In Depth (see Table 9.4) • Briggs Drugs in Pregnancy and Lactation (see Tables 9.3 and 9.4) • REPRORISK (see Table 9.5) • LactMed (via TOXNET) • Medications and Mother's Milk (www.medsmilk.com)
Product Availability/Shortages	

• American Drug Index	• CDER (http://www.fda.gov/Drugs/default.htm)
	   ◦ Approved Drug Products with Therapeutic Equivalence Evaluations (Orange Book)
	   ◦ Drugs@FDA Database
	• FDA Drug Shortages http://www.fda.gov/Drugs/DrugSafety/DrugShortages/default.htm
	• ASHP Drug Shortages (http://www.ashp.org/shortages)

Product Labeling	
• Physicians' Desk Reference (PDR)	• Drugs@FDA • DailyMed (http://dailymed.nlm.nih.gov/dailymed/index.cfm)
Psychiatry	
• Handbook of Psychiatric Drug Therapy • Diagnostic and Statistical Manual of Mental Disorders (DSM-5) • Clinical Handbook of Psychotropic Drugs for Children and Adolescents	• CURRENT Diagnosis & Treatment: Psychiatry (via AccessMedicine)
Therapeutics	
• Goodman and Gilman's: The Pharmacological Basis of Therapeutics • Applied Therapeutics: The Clinical Use of Drugs (Koda-Kimble's) • Pharmacotherapy: A Pathophysiologic Approach (DiPiro's)	• Pharmacotherapy: A Pathophysiologic Approach (DiPiro's) (via AccessPharmacy) • UpToDate (http://www.uptodate.com/) • eMedicine (http://emedicine.medscape.com/) • Merck Manual (http://www.merck.com/mmpe/index.html)
Toxicology, Poisoning, and Environmental Health	
• Goldfrank's Toxicologic Emergencies • Poisoning & Drug Overdose (California Poison Control System) • Tintinalli's Emergency Medicine	• Lexi-Tox (see Table 9.4) • POISONDEX (see Table 9.5) • TOXNET (http://toxnet.nlm.nih.gov/) • Poisoning & Drug Overdose (via AccessMedicine) • Environmental Health and Toxicology SIS (via National Library of Medicine) • OSHA Guidelines • NIOSH Guidelines

Continued

TABLE 9.2 List of Tertiary References by Category—cont'd

Books/Printed References	Online References
Veterinary Information	
• Plumb's Veterinary Drug Handbook • Veterinary Pharmacology and Therapeutics • The Merck Veterinary Manual	• Animal Drugs@FDA (http://www.fda.gov/AnimalVeterinary/default.htm) • DailyMed (http://dailymed.nlm.nih.gov/dailymed/index.cfm)

AccessMedicine (http://accessmedicine.mhmedical.com/), AccessPharmacy (http://accesspharmacy.mhmedical.com/).

topics as nursing (general), patient care, consumer health, alternative medicine, and other health disciplines. Structured subject headings in CINAHL follow MeSH terms and keyword searches, and there are options to limit searches based on the type of journal, publication type, date/range of publication, language, age group, and geographic area of study. This would be a good secondary database to use if one were searching information on patient care issues such as wound care, how to properly move a patient, or how to give an intramuscular injection.

Cochrane Library

The Cochrane Library (www.cochranelibrary.com) has six databases that primarily house systematic reviews and protocols developed by groups and committees within the Cochrane organization. This database is most noted for its systematic reviews which collect and analyze several different trials regarding one particular subject matter and make recommendations for treatment based on the results of the overall analysis. The website can be searched by topic or review group. One might consider this database for searches regarding guidelines, protocols, or thorough reviews of the literature regarding a particular topic (e.g., medications for chemotherapy-induced nausea and vomiting).

EMBASE

EMBASE (www.embase.com) is one of the largest secondary databases available. It allows for access to all the content in MEDLINE, as well as access to more international journals not found in other secondary databases. This would be a go-to database to search for information related to diseases/conditions found in other countries or use of alternative therapies (e.g., traditional Chinese medicine).

Google Scholar

Google Scholar (www.googlescholar.com) is a free, online secondary database that primarily uses keywords (i.e., not MeSH terms) to search for articles. Google Scholar has improved in recent years to eliminate extraneous information not related to published clinical trials; however, there are few limits available to narrow down a search and it may or may not provide access to full-text articles. There may be password restrictions, if one's institution does not subscribe to that particular journal.

International Pharmaceutical Abstracts

Three advantages to IPA are that it is international in its scope, its focus is more about pharmacy and the science of pharmacy, and it contains abstracts/presentations for meetings. IPA is very helpful for searches about drug compounding, intravenous administration rates, and extended stability studies. It is available via EBSCO Health (https://health.ebsco.com/products/international-pharmaceutical-abstracts), but requires a subscription.

PubMed

The National Center for Biotechnology Information, which is part of the US National Library of Medicine (NLM) at the US National Institutes of Health, houses and maintains one of the most commonly used secondary databases in PubMed (https://www.ncbi.nlm.nih.gov/pubmed). It is made up of over 26 million citations from MEDLINE. Citations include those from biomedicine, life sciences, behavioral sciences, chemical sciences, and bioengineering. Free access to the site is available without a need for registration.

TABLE 9.3 Functions Available in Facts and Comparisons eAnswers

Resources Available in Facts and Comparisons eAnswers	
A to Z Drug Facts	Drug Identifier
Boxed Warnings (i.e., Black Box Warnings)	Facts and Comparisons REMS
Briggs Drugs in Pregnancy and Lactation	Immunization Resources IV Compatibility — Trissel's IV Chek
Clinical Calculators	Laboratory Values/Body Measurements
Comparative Data Tables	Manufacturer Index
Don't Crush/Chew List	Natural Products Database (e.g., Review of Natural Products)
Drug and Industry News	Off-Label Drug Facts
Drug Comparison Tables	Patient Assistance Programs
Drug and Disease Interactions Checker	Product Availability
Drug Facts and Comparisons	

TABLE 9.4 Functions Available in Lexicomp Online

Resources Available in Lexicomp Online

5-Minute Clinical Consult	Lexi-Tox (Poisoning/Toxicology; Nuclear, Biological, and Chemical
AHFS DI (Adult and Pediatric)	Agent Exposures)
AHFS Essentials (Adult and Pediatric)	Martindale: The Complete Drug Reference
Briggs Drugs in Pregnancy and Lactation	Natural Products Database
Comparative Efficacy	New Drug Reviews
Drug Allergy and Idiosyncratic Reactions	Patient Education—Adult/Pediatric Medication
Drug Use Evaluations	Patient Education—Disease and Procedure
Geriatric Lexi-Drugs	Pediatric and Neonatal Lexi-Drugs
Infectious Diseases	Pharmacogenomics
Lab Tests and Diagnostic Procedures	Pharmacy and Therapeutics Formulary Reviews
Lexi-Drugs International	Pharmacy and Therapeutics Summary Reviews
Lexi-Drugs Online	Pregnancy and Lactation, In Depth

Other Useful Tools

- Charts/Special Documents (under More
  Clinical Tools—Indexes—specific for each resource)
- Interaction Checker
- IV Compatibility Checker (Trissel's IV Chek)

- Patient Education
- Drug Identification
- Calculators

TABLE 9.5 Functions Available in Micromedex

Resources Available in MICROMEDEX	
Calculators (and other clinically relevant lists)	Lab Advisor (Lab Information)
CareNotes (Patient Education)	Martindale: The Complete Drug Reference
DISEASEDEX Emergency Medicine (Disease Information)	NeoFax
DISEASEDEX General Medicine (Disease Information)	PDR
DRUGDEX Evaluations (Drug Information)	POISINDEX Management (Poisoning and Toxicology)
DRUGDEX Consults (Drug Information)	REPRORISK (Pregnancy and Lactation)
DRUGREAX (Interactions)	• REPROTOX
IDENTIDEX (Drug Identification)	• REPROTEXT
IV Index (Trissels 2 Clinical Pharmaceutics Database)	• Shepard's Catalog
	• TERIS

Primary References

Primary references are simply defined as original research.[32,33,36] Original research is often recognized in the form of a clinical trial, but other forms of original "research" could be case reports, case series, letters to the editor, or conference papers. It is more about being more original than being categorized as bench, lab, or patient research; therefore, something classified as primary literature would depend on the content. For example, review articles, which typically summarize the current literature but do not make original recommendations, are not considered primary literature. They are considered to be tertiary references. Editorials, although they may appear in peer-reviewed journals, may sometimes not be considered primary literature, unless the ideas and observations are completely original and belong only to the author who wrote them. Again, it is up to the reader to interpret the information as to whether or not it is original information; then, it can be classified as primary literature or something else (e.g., tertiary).

The primary advantages of researching the primary literature are that it provides the most up-to-date information on a subject versus tertiary literature. Yet, using primary literature as the sole source for a response may limit the information to one or two particular trials. Other general or background information may need to be found in tertiary literature or review articles.

Most primary references appear in medical journals, which are peer-reviewed. The peer-review process is a review of the proposed publication by experts in that particular field of study.[37] The entire process from first draft to submission may take anywhere between 3 and 12 months but differs between various journals and organizations. However, there are open access journals which may or may not follow the peer-review process. Open access journals may require a fee for publication, but they allow authors who may have been rejected by other journals to publish their results and findings. Therefore, when reviewing open access articles/journals, critical literature evaluation skills are essential to analyze and interpret the data as being useful or not.

Some of the more common peer-reviewed journals are listed here. Many of these journals have other features such as webcasts, podcasts, and videos. Mobile access and tablet applications to journals may also be available. Please check the website for more information or inquire as to mobile/application access via an institutional subscription. In addition, the latest news and articles from many journals can be sent directly to an email account.

New England Journal of Medicine

Renamed the *New England Journal of Medicine* in 1928, the journal can boast that it is the oldest continuously published medical journal, as it has been in circulation since 1812 when it was originally known as the *New England Journal of Medicine and Surgery and the Collateral Branches of Medical Science*. The weekly, peer-reviewed journal is widely international in scope, and access to articles older than 6 months is available for free. The journal and its free-text articles can be accessed at www.nejm.org.

The Lancet

Started in 1823 by an English surgeon, *The Lancet* has expanded into other specialty journals such as *The Lancet Global Health, the Lancet Neurology,* and *The Lancet Infectious Diseases*. The weekly, peer-reviewed journal is one of the best known and most widely used medical journals in the world. The journal can be found at www.thelancet.com, and HINARI-eligible countries (via WHO) may access *The Lancet* free of charge or at a lower cost.

The Journal of the American Medical Association

The Journal of the American Medical Association (JAMA) is a weekly, peer-reviewed, journal published by the American Medical Association. It was started in 1883 and like The Lancet has expanded its readership by including JAMA-specific journals (e.g., JAMA Oncology, JAMA Pediatrics, JAMA Surgery). Access is through www.jamanetwork.com.

Nature

Nature, the parent journal, is a weekly, peer-reviewed publication that was started in 1869 as a "general scientific journal." Today, there are several *Nature* journals specific to topics about chemistry, Earth and the environment, physical sciences, life sciences, and clinical practice. Many of the specific journals (e.g., *Nature Immunology, Nature Chemistry*) are published monthly. Content can be accessed at www.nature.com.

BMJ (Formerly the British Medical Journal)

Started in 1840, *BMJ* is now published online in three editions: a weekly edition for hospital clinicians primarily in the United Kingdom, another weekly edition for general practitioners, and a third monthly edition with a more international audience focused on academic issues. *BMJ* is a peer-reviewed publication and was the first journal to be published completely online in 1995. Access to *BMJ* can be found at www.bmj.com.

Pharmacotherapy: The Journal of Human Pharmacology and Drug Therapy

This monthly, peer-reviewed publication is the official journal of the American College of Clinical Pharmacy (ACCP). Its primary focus is original research articles regarding how medications work in the human body, as well as in-depth review articles on drug therapy. New and unusual case reports of ADRs often appear in this journal. Access can be found at the Wiley Online Library (www.onlinelibrary.wiley.com) by searching *Pharmacotherapy*.

American Journal of Health-System Pharmacy

American Journal of Health-System Pharmacy (AJHP) is the weekly, peer-reviewed publication of the American Society of Health-System Pharmacists (ASHP). One can find drug-related articles about clinical reviews, case reports, and practice research (e.g., MUEs), as well as general pharmacy news about laws, new approvals, and updated guidelines. There is also a Residents' Edition of AJHP that features projects and quality improvement programs completed during pharmacy residency training. The journal can be found at www.ajhp.org.

Drug Information Website Descriptions

Because of the dynamic nature of medical information on the Internet, it would be impractical to include a truly comprehensive listing of all available resources. Utilizing skills in critical appraisal of information sources will ensure that any resource encountered can be properly vetted. However, a short list of reputable and well-organized websites is presented here.

US Food and Drug Administration—*https://www.fda.gov/*

The website of the FDA contains valuable drug information as it pertains to use of medications within the United States. The website contains multiple databases with information specific to product approval and labeling (Drugs@FDA), mandated safety programs (Risk Evaluation and Mitigation Strategies, MedWatch), therapeutic equivalence (Orange Book), and many other resources regarding the clinical and legal use of medications in the United States.

European Medicines Agency—*http://www.ema.europa.eu/ema/*

Similar to FDA, the European Medicines Agency website contains regulatory information regarding the approval and use of medications within the European Union. Information regarding the clinical use and safety of medications as well as herbal products can also be found on this site.

Health Canada Drug and Health Products—*https://www.canada.ca/en/health-canada.html*

Health Canada provides regulatory information regarding the use of medications for Canadian citizens. The site dedicated to drug and health products contains detailed information regarding licensing of health products in Canada, inspections of health products, and alerts based on continual safety monitoring.

Centers for Disease Control and Prevention—*https://www.cdc.gov/*

The website of the Centers for Disease Control and Prevention (CDC) may not initially be thought of as a key place to find drug information. However, many resources contained here provide valuable information regarding the use of medications. The Yellow Book provides information regarding proper vaccination and prophylactic measures that should be considered before traveling to another country. Additionally, vaccination information sheets, vaccine schedules, and guidelines regarding the proper use of vaccines can be found here.

TABLE 9.6 Select Databases Referenced Within the National Library of Medicine Drug Information Portal

MedlinePlus	Consumer-directed health topics; drug information provided by American Society of Health-System Pharmacists
AIDSInfo	Collection of up-to-date guidelines and labeled dosing for medications associated with the treatment of HIV/AIDS
LactMed	Summarized and comprehensive information regarding the use of medications in women who are breastfeeding
LiverTox	Information regarding drug-induced liver injury from a variety of prescription, nonprescription, herbal, or supplement agents
DailyMed	Compilation of FDA-approved drug labels formatted for the Internet
ClinicalTrials.gov	Registry of current and past clinical trials that are both publically and privately supported.
Pillbox	A tool used to aid in the identification of medications
HSDB	Hazardous Substances Data Bank is a toxicology database that provided information regarding data on the toxicity of a chemical including many drugs
PubMed	Secondary database of citations indexed by the US National Library of Medicine
DrugBank	Database of drug information detailed clinical drug data with drug target information on approved products in Canada and the United States
Drugs@FDA	Database of medications approved for use in the United States by the US Food and Drug Administration
European Medicines Agency	Search of the European Medicines Agency website for any drug information regarding human medicines, veterinary medicines, or herbal medicines for human use

Institute for Safe Medication Practices—*https://www.ismp.org/*

Institute for Safe Medication Practices (ISMP) provides a variety of tools to help healthcare institutions increase the safe use of medications. These tools include charts regarding medications that should not be crushed, confused drug names, error-prone abbreviations, high-alert medications, and others. The institute also provides guidelines for healthcare entities to consider in everyday practice such as the safe implementation of smart infusion pumps, practice guidelines for intravenous push medications, and how to create standard order sets. Lastly, they provide several newsletters that bring timely information regarding medication safety to subscribers. ISMP has offices in the United States, Canada, Spain, and Brazil and partners with the International Medications Safety Network.

Drug Information Portal—US National Library of Medicine—*https://druginfo.nlm.nih.gov/ drugportal/drugportal.jsp*

The NLM provides a secondary resource through its Drug Information Portal. This resource provides a comprehensive search of drug information that is contained within the wide variety of health information databases of the NLM (Table 9.6).

OBJECTIVE 9.3. OVERVIEW OF DRUG INFORMATION QUALITY ON THE INTERNET

The quantity of medical information and medical literature is growing exponentially. The technology used to access this information is also on the rise. The use of the Internet, smartphones, tablets, and other devices has radically changed the methods by which information is accessed making a wide array of information accessible to many people.[38] However, with this information evolution, the process by which drug information is evaluated has not changed.

The quality of information on the Internet is up for interpretation. In its nature, it is open and, therefore, anyone with the right technical skills could publish a site available to all. Because of this openness, there is the potential for large quantities of information of varying quality that may be unfiltered when an Internet search is performed. This is especially important when considering health information resources on the Internet.[38−41]

Evaluation of Resources

Critical evaluation of drug information websites should entail the same type of process as for other resources such as books or journal articles. One should identify who may gain financially or through reputation from the site, who pays the

TABLE 9.7 Key Considerations in Evaluating Online Health Information

- Authority
  - Are the authors or editors listed?
  - Do those authors specialize in that field?
  - Do they have any concerning conflicts of interest?
  - Is this information associated with a particular institution or group (e.g., American Academy of Pediatrics)?
  - Have there been any published critiques or vetting of the information provided?
- Accuracy
  - Are citations provided?
  - Do the authors properly cite the information provided?
  - Are those references utilized up to date and pertinent to the question at hand?
- Coverage
  - Is the information presented appropriately for the intended audience?
  - Is the information complete consistent and unbiased?
- Currency
  - When was the last revision made?
  - How frequently is the information reviewed and updated?
- Design
  - Is there a logical and efficient organization to the site?
  - Is an index or search function present?
  - Are there pages intended to help navigate the resource?
- Cost
  - Is the cost prohibitive to the type of work that we will be performing?
  - Is enough additional information granted opposed to utilizing free resources?
  - Does a subscription service make the Internet resource better?

expenses for construction and maintenance of the site, what organizations the site may represent, if there is a statement of policy or principles posted on the site, and if there are editors or "reviewers" whose credentials can be checked.

When evaluating an Internet page with drug information, a reader should consider the *authority*, *accuracy*, *coverage*, *currency*, *design*, and *cost* of the resource (Table 9.7).

There are some helpful resources from various organizations to assist in determining how reliable online health information is. A few are listed below:

- US NLM[39]—https://medlineplus.gov/evaluatinghealthinformation.html
- Medical Library Association[41]—http://www.mlanet.org/page/find-good-health-information
- **The DISCERN Instrument** — DISCERN is a brief questionnaire which provides users with a valid and reliable way of assessing the quality of written information on treatment choices for a health problem. DISCERN can also be used by authors and publishers of information on treatment choices as a guide to the standard which users are entitled to expect.[42,43]
- **Health on the Net (HON)** quality label — The Health on the Net Foundation Code of Conduct (HONcode) for medical and health Web sites addresses Internet's main healthcare issues: the reliability and credibility of information. The HON foundation certification focuses only on human health online content.[40]
- **Flesch Reading Ease** — Flesch Reading Ease test rates text on a 100-point scale. It could be found by copying content in a Microsoft Word document. The higher the score, the easier it is to understand the document. For most standard files, the score to be between 60 and 70. The formula for the Flesch Reading Ease score is: $206.835 - (1.015 \times ASL) - (84.6 \times ASW)$ where: ASL = average sentence length (the number of words divided by the number of sentences) ASW = average number of syllables per word (the number of syllables divided by the number of words).[42,44]

CONCLUSION

Various types of DICs exist, and depending on their set up, each may provide different services to healthcare professionals or the public. However, most DICs have expertise in answering medical- and pharmacy-related questions. DICs have access to a wide variety of tertiary, secondary, and primary databases/sources over and above what individual users can access on their own. These resources are invaluable to the students, residents, and staff of a center when responding to queries related to patients, medications, or therapies, as they allow for the most complete and up-to-date research on the topic at hand. It is important to become familiar with common references/databases to incorporate into the day-to-day practice or research of learners and clinicians.

PRACTICE QUESTIONS

1. Which of the following is/are considered to be ADR trigger tool(s) as defined by the Institute for Healthcare Improvement (IHI)?
   A. Naloxone
   B. Flumazenil
   C. Vitamin K
   D. All of the above
2. Which of the following activities do DICs at hospitals usually NOT directly participate?
   A. Tracking and reporting of ADRs and medication errors
   B. Training healthcare staff on the safe and effective use of medications
   C. Formulary management
   D. Quality control of manufactured medications
3. King Guide is an online source for?
   A. Suppositories
   B. Injectable drugs
   C. Topical preparations
   D. Complimentary drugs
4. Where can you find up-to-date information about drug shortages?
   A. ASHP
   B. Goodman and Gilman's
   C. CredibleMeds.org
   D. MedlinePlus
5. Which of the following is a database maintained by the NLM?
   A. Medications and Mother's Milk
   B. Briggs Drugs in Pregnancy & Lactation
   C. LactMed
   D. Catalog of Teratogenic Agents
6. Which of the following would be the best resource to find information on infection control and vaccinations?
   A. ACCP
   B. ASHP
   C. CDC
   D. Lancet
7. Which of the following would be the best resource to find information regarding medication errors and medication safety?
   A. Nature
   B. EMBASE
   C. OSHA
   D. ISMP

REFERENCES

1. Parker PF. The University of Kentucky drug information center. *Am J Hosp Pharm*. 1965;22(1):42–47.
2. *The Society of Hospital Pharmacists of Australia*. International Register of Drug Information Services; 2017. https://www.shpa.org.au/resources/international-register-of-drug-information-services.
3. Troger U, Meyer FP. The regional drug-therapy consultation service centre - a conception that has been serving patients and physicians alike for 30 years in Magdeburg (Germany). *Eur J Clin Pharmacol*. 2000;55(10):707–711.
4. Chauhan N, Moin S. Indian aspects of drug information resources and impact of drug information centre on community. *J Adv Pharm Technol Res*. 2013;4(2):215–222.
5. Alexandra M, Manosalva N, López Gutiérrez JJ, Cañas M. Drug information centers: an overview to the concept. *Rev Colomb Cienc Quím Farm*. 2016;45(2):243–255.
6. Scala D, Bracco A, Cozzolino S, et al. Italian drug information centres: benchmark report. *Pharm World Sci*. 2001;23(6):217–223.
7. Lim LY, Chui WK. Pharmacist-operated drug information centres in Singapore. *J Clin Pharm Ther*. 1999;24(1):33–42.
8. Thompson D. A personal view of the history and future direction of drug information. *Ann Pharmacother*. 2006;40(2):307–308.
9. Rosenberg JM, Koumis T, Nathan JP, Cicero LA, Mcguire H. Current status of pharmacist-operated drug information centers in the United States. *Am J Health Pharm*. 2004;61(19):2023–2032.

10. Rosenberg JM, Schilit S, Nathan JP, Zerilli T, Mcguire H. Update on the status of 89 drug information centers in the United States. *Am J Health Pharm.* 2009;66(19):1718–1722. https://doi.org/10.2146/ajhp080563.

11. The National Health Service. *UK Medicines Information*; 2017. http://www.ukmi.nhs.uk/.

12. *American Association of Poison Control Centers (AAPCC)*; 2017. http://www.aapcc.org/.

13. Ghaibi S, Ipema H, Gabay M. ASHP guidelines on the pharmacist's role in providing drug information. *Am J Health Pharm.* 2015;72(7):573–577.

14. Bernknopf AC, Karpinski JP, McKeever A, et al. Drug information: from education to practice. *Pharmacotherapy.* 2009;29(3):331–346.

15. Schumock GT, Li EC, Wiest MD, et al. National trends in prescription drug expenditures and projections for 2017. *Am J Health Syst Pharm.* 2017;74(15):1158–1173.

16. Drug and Therapeutics Committees - A Practical Guide. *Drug and Therapeutics Committees - A Practical Guide*; 2003 [Internet]. Available from: http://apps.who.int/medicinedocs/en/d/Js4882e/.

17. Principles of a Sound Drug Formulary System - Endorsed Document. *American Society of Health-System Pharmacists*; 2011 [Internet]. Available from: https://www.ashp.org/-/media/assets/policy-guidelines/docs/endorsed-documents-principles-sound-drug-formulary-system.ashx?la=en&hash=D45C0B8D3E2AB1E80F85267C1DFF116087E89435.

18. ASHP expert panel on medication cost management. ASHP guidelines on medication cost management Strategies for hospitals and health systems. *Am J Health Syst Pharm.* 2008;65(14):1368–1384.

19. Tyler LS, Cole SW, May JR, et al. ASHP guidelines on the pharmacy and therapeutics committee and the formulary system. *Am J Health Syst Pharm.* 2008;65(13):1272–1283.

20. Phillips MS, Gayman JE, Todd MW. ASHP guidelines on medication-use evaluation. *Am J Health Syst Pharm.* 1996;53(16):1953–1955.

21. Hohlfelder B, Stashek C, Anger K, Szumita P. Improvements in a program to Convert IV to oral medications at an academic medical center. *Am J Health Syst Pharm.* 2015;72(23 Suppl. 3):S145–S149.

22. Griffin F, Resar R. IHI Global Trigger Tool for measuring adverse events. *IHI Innov Ser white Pap.* 2007;(September):1–44. http://www.ihi.org/resources/Pages/IHIWhitePapers/IHIGlobalTriggerToolWhitePaper.aspx.

23. Lim D, Melucci J, Rizer MK, Prier BE, Weber RJ. Detection of adverse drug events using an electronic trigger tool. *Am J Health Pharm.* 2016;73:S112–S120.

24. Centers for Medicare & Medicaid Services (CMS). *ICD-9-CM Diagnosis and Procedure Codes: Abbreviated and Full Code Titles*; 2014. https://www.cms.gov/Medicare/Coding/ICD9ProviderDiagnosticCodes/codes.html.

25. *Centers for Medicare & Medicaid Services (CMS). ICD-10*; 2017. https://www.cms.gov/Medicare/Coding/ICD10/index.html.

26. Plumridge RJ, Greenhill GT, Blackbourn J. Drug newsletters and quality assurance of drug usage. *Hosp Pharm.* 1988;23(8), 718, 720–724, 729.

27. Ritchie DJ, Manchester RF, Rich MW, Rockwell MM, Stein PM. Acceptance of a pharmacy-based, physician-edited hospital pharmacy and therapeutics committee newsletter. *Ann Pharmacother.* 1992;26(7–8):886–889.

28. Lyon RA, Norvell MJ. Effect of a P & T committee newsletter on anti-infective prescribing habits. *Hosp Formul.* 1985;20(6):742–744.

29. Phillips L, Landsberg KF. Evaluation of a newsletter in altering physicians' prescribing patterns. *Can J Hosp Pharm.* 1986;39(4):102–104, 108.

30. Parker WA, Heighton V. Drug information services in the provision of pharmacy in-service. *Can J Hosp Pharm.* 2008;30(5):144–145.

31. Keys PW, Lech JG, Duffy MG. Drug audits and in-service education as functions of a drug information center. *Am J Pharm Sci Support Public Health.* 1978;150(3):89–93.

32. Shields KM, Blythe E. Drug information resources. In: Malone P, Mosdell KW, Kier KL, et al., eds. *Drug Information: A Guide for Pharmacists.* 5th ed. New York, NY: McGraw-Hill; 2014. http://accesspharmacy.mhmedical.com/content.aspx?bookid=981&sectionid=54480666(.

33. Wright SG, Lecroy RL, Kendrach M. A review of the three types of biomedical literature and the systematic approach to answer a drug information request. *J Pharm Pract.* 1998;11:148–162.

34. Kee VR, Duba V. Tertiary sources of information. In: Gabay M, ed. *The Clinical Practice of Drug Information.* Burlington, MA: Jones & Bartlett Learning; 2016.

35. Brunetti L, Hermes-DeSantis ER. Secondary sources of information. In: Gabay M, ed. *The Clinical Practice of Drug Information.* Burlington, MA: Jones & Bartlett Learning; 2016.

36. Conrad JL. Primary sources of information. In: Gabay M, ed. *The Clinical Practice of Drug Information.* Burlington, MA: Jones & Bartlett Learning; 2016.

37. Grainger David W. Peer review as professional responsibility: a quality control system only as good as the participants. *Biomaterials.* 2007;28(34):5199–5203. ISSN: 0142–9612 https://doi.org/10.1016/j.biomaterials.2007.07.004.

38. Hwang TJ, Bourgeois FT, Seeger JD. Drug safety in the digital age. *N Engl J Med.* 2014;370(26):2460–2462.

39. Evaluating Health Information. [Internet] Available from: https://medlineplus.gov/evaluatinghealthinformation.html. Accessed on July 27, 2018.

40. @HON. *Health on the Net Foundation*; 2016 [Internet] Available from: http://hon.ch/.

41. MLA. *For Health Consumers and Patients: Find Good Health Information.* Medical Library Association; 2017 [Internet] Available from: http://www.mlanet.org/page/find-good-health-information.

42. Lutz ER, Costello KL, Jo M. A systematic evaluation of websites offering information on chronic kidney disease. *Nephrol Nurs J.* 2014;41(4):355–364. http://www.ncbi.nlm.nih.gov/pubmed/25244890. Accessed May 11, 2018.

43. DISCERN, The DISCERN Instrument. http://www.discern.org.uk/discern_instrument.php. Accessed May 11, 2018

44. Microsoft, Test your document's readability - Office Support. https://support.office.com/en-us/article/Test-your-document-s-readability-85b4969e-e80a-4777-8dd3-f7fc3c8b3fd2. Accessed May 11, 2018

ANSWERS TO PRACTICE QUESTIONS

1. D
2. D
3. B
4. A
5. C
6. C
7. D

Chapter 10

Medical Literature Evaluation and Biostatistics

Christopher S. Wisniewski, Emily P. Jones, Erin R. Weeda, Nicole A. Pilch and Mary Frances Picone
Medical University of South Carolina, Charleston, SC, United States

Learning Objectives:

Objective 10.1 Overview medical literature evaluation and common features of reputed journals.
Objective 10.2 Explain how to interpret and evaluate a typical journal article, including the common biostatistics methods.
Objective 10.2 Utilize clinical expertise to identify the overall validity of a given clinical trial.

OBJECTIVE 10.1. OVERVIEW MEDICAL LITERATURE EVALUATION AND COMMON FEATURES OF REPUTED JOURNALS

Medical literature evaluation (MLE), defined as reading, comprehending, summarizing, and critiquing literature, is a required skill for pharmacists.[1–4] Specific components of this skill set include critically analyzing literature, summarizing basic study design and biostatistics methodology, and differentiating between statistical and clinical significance.[1,2]

These skills are necessary regardless of the setting, as evidenced by the fact that pharmacy organizations recognize MLE competence as an entry-level ability for pharmacists.[5–7] MLE skill is useful in education, practice, and research; anything from answering a simple query using a journal article to preparing a systematic review to clarify a complicated clinical controversy requires MLE skills. In this era of information overload, it is necessary for pharmacists to develop their MLE skills, including selecting, assessing, and interpreting relevant literature. Each time a pharmacy student prepares assignments involving literature review, MLE skills will improve.

Journals

Prior to appraising an article itself, one must first consider the journal. There are many aspects to assess when evaluating a journal's reputation (Table 10.1). The most important is whether the journal has a peer-review process, which is an assessment by outside experts who critique the manuscript prior to publication.[8,9] Advantages associated with peer review include consideration of the article's appropriateness for the journal and the opportunity for the author to receive feedback from other experts in the field in order to improve their work. Peer review does introduce lag time, a delay in publication, and the quality of the review and reviewer is directly proportional, so peer review is not a guaranteed process for quality assurance. Peer review is considered a gold-standard component of the medical literature publication process and is a major qualifying factor for journal reputability, but peer review does not mean that a paper is beyond reproach; regardless of whether peer review has been conducted, careful consideration should be taken when reading an article.

A relatively new concept, seemingly an alternative to peer review, is open access publishing.[10,11] This is a publisher policy which makes articles available free to readers, allowing for duplication, distribution, and use if the source is credited. True open access does not use the formalized peer review because of the theory that poor articles will be identified by the medical community following publication and subsequently ignored.

TABLE 10.1 Considerations in the Evaluation of Journal Reputation

• Purpose of journal (i.e., why is it published)	• Organization association
• Types of medical literature published (i.e., original research or review articles)	• Source (i.e., country of origin) • Editorial board and policies
• Financial support	• Publisher

Identifiers and Metrics

Identifiers are utilized at the journal, author, and object level to aid in attribution and to combat ambiguity. Bibliometrics also applied to the journal, author, and article levels are quantitative measures of scholarly impact that help researchers and organizations make decisions regarding scholarly output. Because no one metric is comprehensive and each has its own limitations and strengths, it is highly recommended that multiple bibliometric performance indicators be applied as a group.[12]

The primary journal identifier is the International Standard Serial Number (ISSN). Used to find serialized publications such as journals, databases, and websites, ISSN is similar to International Standard Book Number, a unique identifier assigned to books.

Metrics have been developed that assess the influence of journals. These metrics may affect researchers' preferences about where to submit manuscripts for publication. There are a variety of journal metrics and each has its own algorithm with its own strengths and limitations (Table 10.2).

The most well-established journal metric, journal impact factor (JIF), reflects the frequency of a journal's publications cited in the literature.[13] This is determined by counting the number of times articles published in the preceding 2 years were cited in the current year and dividing that by the total number of articles published in the journal during those two prior years.[13] For example, the number of times that articles published in a specific journal in 2015 and 2016 were cited in 2017 would be divided by the total number of articles that journal published in 2015 and 2016. SCImago journal rank considers articles published in the previous 3 years, whereas 5-year impact factor considers 5 years. These metrics do not consider the immediate citations received in the same year of publication. Immediacy index, calculated by dividing the number of citations over the number of articles published in the current year, indicates the immediate impact of the journal. Conversely, some journals routinely publish articles that are highly cited for a few years and then ignored. Cited half-life measures the number of years, going back from the current year, that account for half the total citations received by the cited journal in the current year; a long cited half-life means the journal has a good track record of publishing useful articles in the past.

There are several other metrics used to evaluate the dissemination and utilization of research published in a specific journal. Table 10.2 defines these tools and provides some additional information on their value.

The articles themselves have identification tools and are measured via bibliometrics. A digital object identifier (DOI) is a unique alphanumeric code assigned to publications and is regulated by the International DOI Foundation. If known, DOIs allow for easier retrieval of articles and other born-digital publications and act as an online address for the lifetime of the article.[21]

Crossref is an official DOI registration agency that interlinks online content.[22] Many journals publish "online-first" versions of articles before completing the editorial process to provide early access to readers. Crossmark is an option usually found with online articles, by clicking, that will suggest if the version is current or not.[23]

Article-level metrics attempt to estimate the impact of an individual research article. Originally, article-level metrics derived from citations counts because if an article is cited many times, the implication is that the article was useful.[24] Advances in technology have led researchers to investigate using alternative metrics, or altmetrics, for a more comprehensive view of research impact beyond the bounds of traditional, scholarly publications. Altmetrics are defined as "a set of methods based on the social web to measure, track, and analyze the scholarly output."[25] Altmetrics goes beyond traditional citation counts for article-level metrics and uses social web activity to estimate the impact through

TABLE 10.2 Journal Bibliometrics[13–19]

Journal Metric	Measures	Strengths	Limitations	Found In

Journal impact factor (JIF)	Journal prestige within a particular discipline	• An established metric; been in use the longest
		• Depending on the subject, more journals will be indexed in Web of Science than Scopus allowing for more JIF scores
		• Easy to calculate
		• Related metrics include
		  • 5-year Impact Factor
		  • Cited-Half Life
		  • Immediacy Index
			• Need a subscription to Journal Citation Reports
			• Citations are not weighted
			• Scores not universal among all disciplines
			• Includes all self-citations, which raises concerns of skewing impact
			• Takes a minimum of 6 years for a newly published journal to receive a JIF
			• Report on very few open access journals[a]
				Journal citation reports (Web of Science)

Eigenfactor scores	Journal importance	• Freely available • Weighted citations • Algorithm accounts for citation differences of disciplines	• Excludes all self-citations which can have a negative impact on fields with limited researchers where self-citation is necessary • 5-year citation analysis period can be too long for fast-moving fields[13]	Eigenfactor.org
SCImago journal rank (SJR)	Journal influence	• Freely available • Weighted citations • SNIP tool • Report on open access journals • Includes a limited number of self-citations to account for impact measurement issues surrounding reporting them on an all or nothing scale	• Updated twice per year, whereas JIF is updated yearly • Only peer-reviewed citations are counted; can be a limitation for some authors	Scopus SCImagojr.com
CiteScore	Journal impact	• Freely available • Updated monthly • Comprehensive • Transparency • New publications receive CiteScore metrics the year after being indexed by Scopus	• New metric-less research on the metric • Potential conflict of interest	Scopus

SNIP, source normalized impact per paper.
[a]In June 2017, Clarivate Analytics announced a partnership with Impact Story to include 18 million open access articles in Web of Science.[20]

clicks or views, downloads, saves, and online mentions. Like other metrics, altmetrics are not meant to be used as the sole indicator of the impact. However, they should be used in conjunction with other metrics to have a more comprehensive view of the impact.

Research Reporting Guidelines

Over time, individuals have collaborated to develop a standardized research reporting structure for writing manuscripts related to various study designs. The first of these, Consolidated Standards of Reporting Trials (CONSORT), was created in 1996 to address the lack of adequate reporting of randomized controlled trials.[26] These are listed in Table 10.3, along with a brief description.

TABLE 10.3 Manuscript Reporting Guidelines for Study Designs Published in the Medical Literature[27]

Study Design	Description	Reporting Guideline
Case report	Description of clinical course of a single patient	CARE
Observational	Investigate naturally occurring variables and outcomes to identify associations	STROBE
Randomized controlled trial	Establish cause and effect through direct interventional comparison with control for potential confounders	CONSORT
Systematic review	Study and analysis of primary literature identified via a structured process	PRISMA
Clinical practice guidelines	Review and evaluation of evidence summarized to inform clinicians of best practices for patient care	AGREE
Economic evaluation	Outcomes research considering quality and cost of therapy, typically via pharmacoeconomic research	CHEERS

OBJECTIVE 10.2. EXPLAIN HOW TO INTERPRET AND EVALUATE A TYPICAL JOURNAL ARTICLE, INCLUDING THE COMMON BIOSTATISTICS METHODS

Title of the Article

After considering the journal, evaluating the paper begins. The title should be reflective of the work, unbiased, and specific yet concise.[9] Titles should not be declarative sentences, which can overemphasize results, or questions. Including the study design as a subtitle can be helpful. When encountering acronyms, one needs to be wary of duplicate use, rule distortion, and coercion. For example, an article titled "**A**zilimide post**i**nfarct sur**v**ival **e**valuation" used the acronym "ALIVE,"[28] which is a common acronym in the medical literature, distorts the rules by using letters that do not start words in the title, and could be considered coercive because the acronym implies that participants would stay alive if they enrolled in the study. Acronyms do have value, as they can simplify reference to and recall of articles for clinicians, but authors should consider the development of study titles to ensure appropriate use of acronyms.

Authors

Authorship, which is defined as a substantial contribution to a publication, should be considered from two perspectives.[8] As a reader, it is important to evaluate author credentials specifically; profession, degree, training, and practice site.[9] For example, a community pharmacist might not be qualified to write a paper on hospital reimbursement procedures. Reviewing previous publications by the author is another mechanism to determine if an author is qualified to write on a subject. One could use author-level metrics, which measure individual researcher scholarly productivity and impact, when conducting evaluations. The most common author metrics are h-index, g-index, and the i10-index (Table 10.4).[17,29]

From a researcher perspective, when initiating a project that is intended for publication, initial conversation among collaborators should involve the place of authorship. Roles that are generally considered appropriate for authorship are

TABLE 10.4 Author-Level Bibliometrics[17,29]

Author Metric	Strengths	Limitations	Found in
h-index	• Most commonly used	• H-index scores are often different in each database because they are highly sensitive to database coverage • All citations are equal	Scopus Google Scholar Web of Science
g-index	• Accounts for performance or quality	• Fairly new • Not as widely accepted	Publish or Perish tool
I10-index	• Weights highly cited articles	• Only in Google Scholar • Limited to journal offerings within Google Scholar	Google Scholar

study conception and design, statistical analysis, and writing.[8] The first author is the person who completes most of the writing. The last author is the conceiver of the project and takes on a broad oversight role. Authorship is not indicated for people responsible for acquisition of funding or research group supervision.

Unethical practices are found to affect the quality of scientific communications. When authors plagiarize, fabricate, or falsify information, this distorts the integrity of research and introduces a conflict of interest. Conflicts of interest may occur due to funds received or an intention to increase a professional profile. The demand to publish (i.e., publish or perish) also increases research fraud. A common practice is self-plagiarism, which occurs when authors publish the same content in more than one journal without permission from the first journal.[30]

Guidelines found in journals explain the best practices to authors, reviewers, and editors, and journals instruct key points for researchers and authors. The authors should sign a contract with the publisher to avoid any unethical practices in publishing. Standardization of articles is mandated by the research reporting guidelines listed in Table 10.3.[27]

Author identifiers allow researchers to distinguish themselves from others and increase proper attribution of publications; these are especially helpful against combating ambiguity issues such as authors publishing under many name variations (e.g., Smith, J., Smith, J.C., or Smith, John), common names, name changes, and cultural differences in naming. Databases such as Scopus and Web of Science have integrated author identifiers into their records using Scopus Author Identifier and ResearcherID, respectively.[31,32] Open Researcher and Contributor Identification (ORCID) is a nonprofit, globally recognized digital identifier.[33] ORCIDs are free to obtain, and authors can add their Scopus and Web of Science identifier to their ORCID profile and vice versa.

Abstract

The next section of the evaluation, the abstract, is a concise summary of the main points of an article that usually addresses the background, methods, results, and conclusions of a paper. The primary function of the abstract is that it allows a reader to identify if they should read the article; it is also utilized to determine relevance when conducting a literature search.

From a reader perspective, the abstract should be thorough, concise, unbiased, and consistent with the manuscript.[9] Authors are often unable to report all study outcomes in the abstract because of limitations on word count. Furthermore, the authors occasionally publish abstracts that differ from the full paper, particularly in conclusion. For these reasons, no therapeutic decision should ever be made solely based on the information in the abstract, assuming that abstract is associated with a full article.

Introduction

The introduction of a paper provides background on the topic and states the article's purpose.[8] Starting with a brief review of the issue to educate the reader, the introduction then includes a review of the literature and a rationale for how the study will resolve unanswered questions. The introduction should end with a specific objective explaining the goals of the study. As a reader, the introduction is valuable to learn about the area of the study, but one should read this section carefully, being on the lookout for selective references and biased wording.

Methods

The aim, objective, or goal (all of these terms can be used interchangeably) the authors present at the end of the introduction should directly inform the study design that they select. As the consumer of the written research publication, careful evaluation of the study design is needed. The presented aim should lead to a study design that makes sense.

Study Design

Table 10.5 lists common study designs, their use, and advantages and disadvantages organized by the hierarchy (Fig. 10.1) as it relates to the ability to identify cause and effect. This section will describe elements of controlled trials that must be evaluated but could be extrapolated to other study designs.

Study Design Objectives

When conducting controlled trials, there are three ways in which a comparison is made, usually referred to as the objective of the study design. These include superiority, equivalence, and noninferiority.

TABLE 10.5 Study Design Uses, Advantages, and Disadvantages

Study Design	Used to:	Advantages	Disadvantages
Case report	Describe clinical course of a patient	• Quick and inexpensive • Identify treatments for rare disorders • Medication toxicities or adverse effects • Initial step for generating hypotheses	• Small sample size • Results could be arbitrary • Author opinion • Confounders
Cross-sectional	Identify prevalence	• Quick and inexpensive • Multiple outcomes • One-time data collection • No loss to follow-up • Focus on precise populations • Lack ethical difficulties • Hypothesis-generating • Can repeat to show a trend • Oversample subgroups	• Only one point in time • Cannot differentiate cause and effect from association • Transient effect potential • Difficulty determining the sequence of events • Potential for bias (e.g., selection, volunteer, recall) • Low response rate potential • Inaccurate for rare diseases
Case-control	Identify risk factors for diseases	• Efficient for rare outcomes • Quick and inexpensive • Data already exist • No loss to follow-up • Lack ethical difficulties • Consider a large number of variables • Hypothesis-generating	• Retrospective design (e.g., selection of controls, determination of exposure) • Cannot determine cause and effect • Cannot calculate incidence or prevalence • Only one outcome • Confounding variables • Difficulty determining the sequence of events • The potential for bias (e.g., sampling, recall)
Cohort	Identifies incidence or natural history of a condition	• Prospective-demonstrate exposure preceded outcome • Multiple outcome variables • Lack ethical difficulties • Outcomes from rare exposures	• Prospective-expensive • Prospective-a loss to follow-up • Multiple variables cause confounding factors • Prospective-the potential for selection bias • Retrospective-the potential for recall bias • Both-potential for surveillance bias • Not optimal for rare outcomes
Controlled trials	Evaluates efficacy	• Demonstrates exposure preceded outcome • Randomization eliminates potential confounders • Typically one exposure	• Expensive and time-consuming • Potential for loss to follow-up • Ethical constraints • Multiple outcome variables • Inefficient for rare exposures and outcomes
Systematic reviews/ metaanalysis	Identify primary literature via systematic search and evaluate or combine to answer clinical controversies	• Quick and inexpensive • Increases comprehension of the available evidence • Useful for contradictory studies • Data already exist • Lack ethical difficulties • Metaanalysis-increases power	• Compilation of data is only as valuable as data identified and published • Data not generated for reanalysis purposes • The potential for "gray" (i.e., unpublished) literature to introduce publication bias • Language biasconsidering literature for inclusion based on authors' ability to read/write in that language

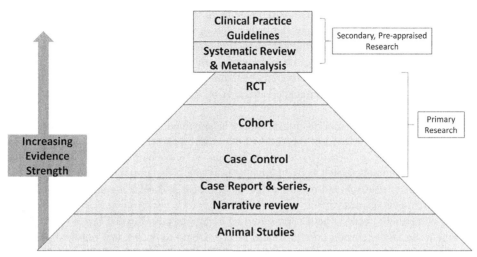

FIGURE 10.1   Hierarchy of study designs in generating evidence.

If the objective of the study is superiority, then the study is trying to prove that something is better than something else. This objective is utilized to demonstrate that a novel intervention is better than either a placebo or active control. Equivalence studies are those studies in which groups are compared with the aim of demonstrating that the effect of one intervention is equal to another, meaning that the amount of response is clinically unimportant. Frequently, equivalence trials in the field of pharmacy are coined bioequivalence and are the design used in trials to compare brand and generic medications. Noninferiority studies look to see if an intervention can produce similar results without being worse than the standard therapy.[34] For example, a medication that is used to prevent rejection in kidney transplant patients and has been used for several years could serve as a control in a study. A novel agent is developed that is similar to the parent compound but causes less gastrointestinal side effects; however, the new medication is thought to be as effective as the standard medication. The noninferiority objective would be appropriate to prove that the new drug is no worse than the standard from an efficacy perspective.

Setting

When considering the study setting, there are three types: inpatient, outpatient, and artificial. The inpatient setting includes hospitalized patients and provides the advantage that patients are located in a predictable setting. This can lead to improved compliance (e.g., patients taking medications as prescribed), less protocol variation, and increased opportunity for evaluation. This setting is ideal to conduct studies that are short and only require observations while the patient is inpatient. The inpatient setting can be difficult if recruiting patients who are admitted for nonelective reasons. For example, studying a new antimicrobial agent for sepsis would seem to be feasible; however, obtaining consent in times of duress is challenging. Additional disadvantages include the inability to predict discharge and coordination with the medical team.

The outpatient setting is used when patients experience interventions in the context of their normal daily activities. This setting has several advantages, mainly that it is more natural and less expensive, but the direct oversight is lost, leading to issues with compliance and patient-driven data collection.

Artificial settings allow for research in a standardized way and are frequently used for convenience and early interventions. These types of settings can achieve the research objective quickly as they are not impacted as much by patients; however, they often do not include what will happen if an intervention is used on patients. This type of environment is often limited to early studies and is not commonly seen in the pharmacy literature.

Readers should be careful when applying the findings of studies across settings. For example, using results from an inpatient study might cause problems when the clinician tries to relate them to nonhospitalized patients due to problems with observation and compliance. It is important to ask how the results of a study in a given setting might be impacted by using the intervention in a different setting before making patient-care decisions.

Patient/Subject Selection

When enrolling subjects, two groups must be established: the population, which includes all objects of a particular kind, and a sample, a subset that will be used to represent the population. During sample selection, researchers want to make sure that they can make generalizations from results and extrapolate them to the population. This requires investigators to get a representative sample and use statistics to measure the results and apply them to the population.

After sample identification and potential participant selection, screening can take place. Investigators use inclusion and exclusion criteria established during protocol development. Inclusion criteria define the characteristics needed for a potential participant to be enrolled. For example, in a study evaluating hypertension, the individual must have higher than a specific blood pressure. Exclusion criteria are characteristics that prevent enrollment in a study; these can be for clinical, safety, or likelihood-to-withdrawal reasons.

Once a subject meets the enrollment criteria, consent must be obtained. When screening patients, it is important for the participant to have a working knowledge of the goals of the study and their own risks and benefits. Rules that direct how one can approach patients are governed by local institutional review boards (IRBs), which are dictated based on international and national requirements related to past human abuses (e.g., Declaration of Helsinki). The IRB is responsible for reviewing all human subject research and ensuring that the protocol and related study activities, including informed consent, are conducted in an ethical manner.[35]

As a reader, it is important to consider whether the sampling techniques used would lead to a sample representative of the population. The inclusion and exclusion criteria should be considered to ensure that enrolled patients will yield valid results and bear similarity to patients that are under one's care. All studies should have IRB approval and require informed consent; if not mentioned, the study should be disregarded.

Patient Handling

Following enrollment, studies are organized to compare participants, usually via intervention and control groups. Interventions in the pharmacy literature are pharmacologic in nature. Goals of therapy, the dosage, dosage form, and regimen, and any concurrent medications allowed should be considered when evaluating an intervention. For example, a suspension must be shaken prior to administration, which may lead to inconsistency in exposure versus a liquid. To overcome this, an investigator could provide the recipient with prefilled syringes to ensure that the correct amount of drug is in each dose. If that suspension interacts with grapefruit juice, did the investigators tell their participants to avoid grapefruit juice? The article should detail these nuances.

Study subjects receiving the intervention are compared with a control group, thus the name controlled trials. Several types of controls are used in the pharmacy literature. Historical controls are previously collected data from patients with similar baseline demographics. A placebo control is an inert entity that is otherwise identical in appearance, taste, and smell to the intervention. Placebo-controlled trials are the minimum requirement for approval by US Food and Drug Administration but should only be used for conditions in which there is not an acceptable therapeutic alternative. An active control is often used when comparing a newer intervention to the standard therapy; both arms receive an active intervention. Active controls are used when forgoing a treatment is unethical or when noninferiority is the objective. Some studies will use no treatment as a control, allowing researchers to show the true efficacy of the intervention.

From a reader perspective, make sure the intervention makes sense, therapeutically and for specific patients one sees. Although using no treatment as a control is the best choice for establishing efficacy, the most common controls are either placebo or active. Placebo controls reduce the risk of bias and are useful to maintain blinding, but may decrease participation or lead to patients overestimating efficacy due to the belief that they received therapy, commonly referred to as the placebo effect. As a clinician, active controls are preferable, but because most of these studies use a noninferiority objective, the true effect of the intervention is difficult to ascertain.

Once patients are selected for inclusion in the study, they will be assigned to the intervention or control groups. There are three strategies for assigning patients: randomization, blinding, and allocation concealment.

Randomization is the principle that elevates controlled trials above observational study designs because randomization gives participants an equal chance of being placed in either group. This minimizes bias by prioritizing similar groups, assuring the only difference between groups is study treatment (i.e., intervention or control).

Blinding prevents subjects or investigators from knowing the treatment status of participants. Blinding reduces bias, limits altered expectations, and increases compliance because patients know there is a chance they are receiving the control. Blinding is especially important for subjective outcomes (e.g., pain), as patients may feel they are benefitting even though they are receiving control. Blinding is less important for objective outcomes (e.g., mortality) where the definition of the outcome is not up to the patient. Double-blind, the gold standard, refers to studies where both the investigator and participant are blinded; other types include open-label (i.e., no blinding), which is acceptable for studies using objective outcomes, single-blind (i.e., one group blinded), and triple-blind (i.e., investigators, participants, and assessors blinded).

Allocation concealment, the third assignment technique, is a procedure where the allocation sequence is not revealed to those assigning participants and thus prevents study personnel from influencing group assignment. Once the randomization sequence has been executed, the enrollee should be assigned to whichever group is next; otherwise, individuals could identify the assignment and push the next patient into the intervention group for the patient to receive therapy instead of control (e.g., placebo).[36] This would cause unequal groups even though technically the randomization sequence was executed correctly.

In randomized trials, patients are followed via either a parallel or crossover methodology. Parallel-group studies enroll patients into treatment or control groups, and they receive only that option. Groups are followed forward in time and then compared against each other. Crossover studies allow participants to serve as their own control by assigning patients to one intervention and then switching them to another intervention later in the trial.

The best-designed studies use all three assignment techniques. While reading an article, check that the assignment techniques investigators use make sense and are appropriate. For example, open-label studies with subjective outcomes likely have decreased value. Parallel study designs are more common in the pharmacy literature than crossover studies. For crossover studies, check that investigators have incorporated a washout period, which is a time that the participant receives no therapy and is considered long enough for the drug to clear from a person's system. This decreases the possibility that the previous therapy would have a continued effect after the new therapy was started.

Data Handling

To understand data handling, three terms must first be defined. Efficacy describes how well an intervention works in an ideal environment, whereas effectiveness describes how well an intervention works in a real-world setting.[37] Finally, attrition occurs when participants are lost to follow-up or withdraw from a study.[38] Attrition occurs if a participant is noncompliant or experiences an adverse event or therapeutic failure while receiving study treatment.

There are three main analyses to handle data: intention-to-treat (ITT), per-protocol (PP), and modified intention-to-treat (mITT).[39–41] In an ITT analysis, all subjects are analyzed even if attrition occurs. In contrast, in PP analysis, patients experiencing attrition are excluded from analysis. An mITT analysis combines principles used in ITT and PP analysis; though the definition differs across studies, most commonly mITT includes patients receiving at least one dose of the study medication.

ITT analysis is advantageous because it preserves randomization[39–41]; thus, the observed treatment effect is more likely a result of the intervention, not an underlying difference in study group characteristics. Another advantage of ITT is that it more closely resembles clinical practice because some patients comply with medication regimens and some do not. Therefore, compared with PP analysis, ITT analysis allows for improved measurement of the effectiveness of a treatment. A disadvantage of ITT analysis is that the treatment effect could be attenuated by noncompliance; an intervention will have a lesser impact in the included noncompliant patients, meaning the effect may be smaller than what would be observed if only compliant patients were analyzed. The key advantage of PP analysis is that it measures efficacy.

Study Outcomes

The outcomes of a study are classified in several ways. First, there is the distinction between primary (i.e., those that measure the most important question in a study) and secondary.[42] Decisions about study methods will be dictated by the expected effect of the intervention on the primary endpoint. In contrast, secondary endpoints are often included to support the primary endpoint.

Endpoints are often considered as surrogate or final health outcomes.[43] Final health outcomes, sometimes called clinically meaningful outcomes, directly measure survival or patient functionality. These outcomes include clinical events (e.g., myocardial infarction [MI]), health-related quality-of-life, and mortality. In contrast, surrogate outcomes are physical signs or laboratory values that serve as an indirect measure of clinically meaningful outcomes. For instance, increased blood glucose is associated with microvascular complications in patients with diabetes.[44] In a study of a medication for diabetes, an endpoint measuring microvascular complications would be considered a clinical outcome, whereas an endpoint measuring the ability of the medication to lower blood glucose would be a surrogate outcome.[43] Surrogate outcomes can be collected faster than clinical outcomes and are used to save time and money.[45] For instance, changes in blood glucose can be measured within 3 months, whereas measuring the microvascular complication of reduced kidney function may require an investigator to follow patients for years. A key disadvantage of a surrogate outcome is that it may not correlate with the final health outcome of interest. There are numerous examples of medications that positively impacted surrogate outcomes but were later shown to have detrimental effects on final health outcomes.[45] If a surrogate outcome is used, the reader should assess if there is an established relationship between the surrogate and clinical outcome.

Studies may utilize a composite endpoint, which combines multiple endpoints into one measure.[42] For instance, in a cardiology trial, the primary endpoint could be a combination of MI, stroke, or cardiovascular death. As compared with designating only one of these events as the primary endpoint, the number of patients experiencing this composite endpoint will be larger. This requires fewer patients and shorter follow-up; however, if a large discrepancy in the occurrence of individual events occurs, composite endpoints may be compromised, especially if the most clinically important event occurs less frequently. Assuming cardiovascular death is most impactful, if the majority of patients in the study are counted as experiencing the composite endpoint because they had a MI, conclusions about the impact of the medication on cardiac death can be difficult to make.

Follow-Up Procedures and Sample Size

To assess the impact of an intervention on outcomes, readers must consider both follow-up and sample size.[46–49] Researchers should choose a length and frequency of follow-up that allows outcomes to be accurately captured.[46] For example, if an antidepressant is not fully effective until 1 month after use, a study that only follows patients for 1 week would not accurately capture the impact of the medication. Readers should also bear in mind that the longer the follow-up, the greater the risk of attrition. Finally, readers should assess compliance with the treatment during follow-up.[47] If compliance was low, the authors should explain (e.g., tolerability of the medication) in order to assist readers in assessing the benefit and risk of the intervention.

To detect differences between treatment and control groups, an adequate sample size is needed.[49] The smaller the difference between treatment and control, the larger the sample size needed to detect this difference. Similarly, when events occur infrequently, more patients will have to be studied to capture these events. Sample size can be limited by cost constraints (as the cost can increase with study size) and other logistical challenges of obtaining data on a large number of participants.

Variables

Variables (i.e., the characteristics measured in a study) are classified as either independent or dependent.[50] Independent variables are those altered by an investigator because of their expected impact on the dependent variable. If an investigator is studying the impact of a low-fat diet on heart disease, diet is the independent variable because it can be manipulated to measure the impact on the dependent variable of heart disease.

The relationship between variables can be distorted by confounders.[51] Confounding occurs when a factor related to the variables of interest meets the following criteria: (1) it impacts the outcome and (2) it is unevenly distributed among treatment and control groups. A confounding variable can lead to an association between the treatment and outcome when one does not exist. For instance, participant exercise performance could influence the results of the heart disease study if subjects in the low-fat diet workout more often than those in the control group. Readers should assess if authors attempted to minimize the impact of confounding either in the design (e.g., assignment techniques) or analysis (e.g., statistical adjustment through techniques such as regression) of the study.[52]

Data

Variables are classified as either nominal, ordinal, continuous, or time-to-event.[50] Nominal data are divided into named, unranked categories that are mutually exclusive. Examples of nominal data include sex, race, or presence of a condition (e.g., diabetes or no diabetes). Ordinal data also fall into categories but differ from nominal data in that these categories are ranked. Stages of disease (e.g., stages I–IV cancer) are often ordinal data. An important characteristic of ordinal data is that the increments between categories are unequal. In the example of cancer stage, stage III has a poorer prognosis than stage II, which has a poorer prognosis than stage I; however, the difference in prognosis between stage III and stage II versus stage II and stage I is not equal. Continuous data do not fall into categories; rather, these data occupy a range of values. Examples of continuous data include blood pressure, blood glucose, weight, and temperature. In studies where outcomes may occur at any point during follow-up, researchers may wish to explore if the intervention leads to differences in the time to the development of the outcome; therefore, time-to-event data are analyzed.[53] Time to the progression of a disease, resolution of symptoms, or death are all examples of such data.

Data are also organized by the manner in which they were generated for comparison purposes. Independent data are derived from separate groups under different conditions, typically via a parallel study design. Paired data are derived from the same person or group under two different conditions. Crossover studies or comparisons of baseline data with the data generated after an intervention are good examples of paired data.

TABLE 10.6 Descriptive Statistics Definitions and Application Based on Data Type

Descriptive Measure	Definition	Type of Data Appropriate for Use
Mean	Average of all values	Normally distributed continuous data
Median	Middle data point in set of ranked data	Ordinal, continuous
Mode	Most frequently occurring value	Nominal, ordinal, continuous
Standard deviation	Average amount each data point is from mean	Normally distributed continuous data
Range	Distance between highest and lowest value	Ordinal, continuous
Interquartile range	Distance between 25th and 75th percentile values	Ordinal, continuous

Descriptive Statistics

Once generated, there are two ways that data are analyzed in clinical trials via statistical analysis. The first, descriptive statistics, present, arrange, and summarize data of a variable. Further classified into measures of central tendency and variability, these groupings show information on the appearance and distribution of a set of data. Measures of central tendency, most commonly mean, median, and mode, are used to numerically measure the distribution of data. When selecting the appropriate measure of central tendency, one must consider the type of data (Table 10.6).

Measures of variability are used to denote the spread of a set of data. Standard deviation, range, and interquartile range are common measures of variability. Again, the type of data dictates the selection of the appropriate measure (Table 10.6).

Inferential Statistics

The other method for analyzing data is through inferential statistics. Used to make interpretations about a set of data, specifically to determine the likelihood that a conclusion about a sample is true, inferential statistics identify differences between two groups or an association of two groups; the former is more common in the pharmaceutical literature. Inferential statistics requires the performance of statistical tests to see if a conclusion is correct compared with the probability that conclusion is due to chance. These tests calculate a P-value that is then compared with the probability that the results are due to chance. This is alpha (α), which is most often 0.05; therefore, a P-value less than 0.05 is typically considered statistically significant.

Power

The other factor of necessity when using inferential statistics is power, the ability to detect a difference if one truly exists. Power is a key aspect of calculating a sample size for a study. Numerically, power is equal to 1 minus beta (β), which is typically between 0.1 and 0.2, meaning power is usually between 80% and 90%. Beyond being influenced by β, power is affected by α, sample size, the magnitude of effect (i.e., hypothesized difference to be detected), and the variance of the outcome variable. Investigators must consider power and sample size to enroll enough participants to detect a difference without wasting resources by over enrolling or treating patients with a potentially ineffective therapy.

Error

Both α and β share a relationship with the potential for error when making a conclusion based on inferential statistics. Type I error is directly related to α and defined as concluding there is a difference when one does not actually exist. The probability of making a type I error is equal to α used in the study; the only reason a type I error could occur is a chance, though because P-values are commonly 0.05 or 5%, 1 of 20 times investigators conclude a difference they may be making a type I error. Therefore, the more times a single set of data is analyzed, the higher likelihood a type I error will occur. Type II error is related to β, which occurs when investigators conclude no difference when one actually exists. The probability of making a type II error is equal to the β used in the study; type II errors occur due to chance or because the required sample size was not enrolled. From a readers' perspective, one must ensure that authors report a power calculation so it can be determined if they make a type II error. Looking for α, β, magnitude of effect, and calculated sample size in the methods of the paper is important.

TABLE 10.7 Summary of Univariate Analysis Test Selection

Data Type	Independent Groups		Paired Groups	
	2	3 or More	2	3 or More
Nominal	Chi-square or Fisher's exact	Chi-square or Fisher's exact	McNemar test	Cochran Q
Ordinal	Mann-Whitney U or Wilcoxon rank sum test	Kruskal-Wallis	Wilcoxon signed rank test	Friedman test
Continuous, normally distributed	Student's t-test	ANOVA	Paired t-test	Repeated measures ANOVA
Continuous, not normally distributed	Mann-Whitney U or Wilcoxon rank sum test	Kruskal-Wallis	Wilcoxon signed rank test	Friedman test

Univariate Analysis

Inferential statistical analysis can be broken into two broad categories: univariate analysis and multivariate analysis. The univariate analysis uses one dependent variable, the outcome, and one independent variable, the intervention. The selection of the appropriate statistical test is determined based on the answers to a few simple questions. First, the reader must answer two questions about the dependent variable: (1) "Are the data nominal, ordinal, or continuous?" and (2) "Are the data paired or independent?". The reader should then ask "How many groups are being compared?" with the only answer options being either two or more than two. Finally, the reader should determine the intention of the statistical test. The two options are either to detect a difference between groups or describe the relationship between two variables. Statistical tests, correlation, and regression, describing relationships between two groups, are beyond the scope of this chapter. Table 10.7 summarizes the statistical tests used to compare groups based on the type of data of the dependent variable (i.e., outcome). For time-to-event data, Kaplan-Meier survival analysis is used to measure the actual length of time to an outcome, generating survival curves that show how long it took for patients to experience the event. These curves are visual only and require the use of a log-rank test to determine if a statistically significant difference exists between them.

Multivariate Analysis

Another way to use statistical analysis is to control for potential confounding factors. Investigators use multivariate analysis, which determines whether two groups or conditions are different while controlling for confounding variables. This occurs in observational studies but may also be required in randomized controlled trials, most commonly to compensate for any potential influence of study sites in multicenter trials. Similar to univariate analysis, the type of statistical test is chosen based on the dependent variable (Table 10.8).

To summarize, important skills from this section include the ability to identify types of variables and data, a grasp of descriptive statistics, the knowledge of power calculation elements, and an understanding of questions that need to be answered to pick a statistical test. Often, the type of data is not explicitly stated in an article, but once determined, the researcher or the reader can easily pick the correct statistical test. Incorporating these concepts into the knowledge base of a pharmacist will provide an important tool that can be used when evaluating medical literature.

TABLE 10.8 Multivariate Analysis Statistical Test Based on Data Type of Dependent Variable

Type of Data of Dependent Variable	Multivariate Analysis
Nominal or ordinal	Logistic regression
Continuous	ANCOVA
Time-to-event	Cox hazards model

Results

In general, the first thing that will appear in the results section of an article is the baseline characteristics of the sample. This may be accompanied by information on enrollment via a flowchart that includes the subjects enrolled, randomized, receiving medication, completing the study, and analyzed. This flowchart should include reasons participants withdrew from the study, which allows the reader to draw conclusions about the intervention after considering attrition.

Baseline characteristics are information collected on participants prior to randomization and can include demographics, disease states, medications, social history, and other variables that impact the study outcome. Baseline characteristics are used to determine if randomization worked by showing differences between groups; the reader should consider whether the groups are equal at baseline. Baseline characteristics are also used to determine the applicability of the sample to the patient population encountered by the reader. Asking whether the sample represents the patients seen by the reader is good practice.

The focus of reviewing results should be on the statistical significance of the outcomes. If the *P*-value is less than α, then a statistically significant difference is detected. Additionally, confidence intervals (CIs), a range of values that include the upper and lower range of possible values for a population based on a sample, are considered. The CI presents an estimate of observed results that will be seen in the population. The CI is typically presented as 95%, which means that with 95% confidence, the true population value is within the CI. As sample size increases, the CI narrows because the investigator is pulling more observations out of the population into the sample. This is largely under the investigator's control, whereas the other major CI influencer, the spread of data, is not. As data become more spread out around a measure of central tendency, the CI will widen.

The CI has two main uses. It is preferable to the *P*-value in presentation of results because it provides information on the effect size in addition to statistical significance. To determine statistical significance from a CI, first consider the type of comparison being made. If a ratio is being calculated, rates of an outcome are divided by one another; if the CI includes 1, then the groups are equal and the result is not statistically significant. Common ratios seen in the medical literature include odds ratios, hazard ratios, and relative risk. For non-ratio data, when groups are being compared via subtraction, the point of no difference is 0; a common example is a comparison of the mean difference between two interventions, which are continuous data (e.g., two antihypertensive agents being evaluated for blood pressure reduction).

Baseline data, enrollment information, and statistical significance will help the reader conduct a power analysis, which is a method to determine if the study has "met power," which means the investigators enrolled enough patients so that if they see no difference, that conclusion is valid. Answering questions via a power algorithm (Fig. 10.2) is a simple way to conduct a power analysis. If the study concludes a significant difference, then power ceases to be a consideration. If no difference is seen, then the reader should determine whether all of the elements of a power calculation were reported. Additionally, reviewing that the conclusion being drawn is related to the outcome used to identify the sample size, usually

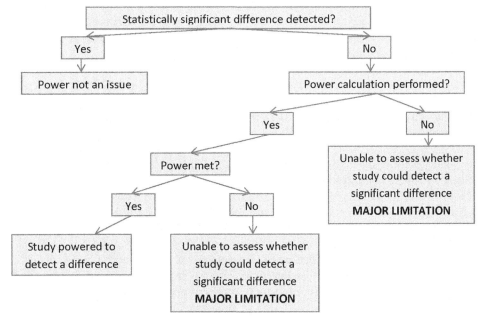

FIGURE 10.2 Power analysis algorithm to appraise power of a study population.

TABLE 10.9 Contingency Table

	Event	No Event
Intervention	A	B
Control	C	D

the primary outcome, is important. This means that results for secondary and safety outcomes are likely to be underpowered; conclusions of no difference for these outcomes are prone to a type II error. Assuming the conclusion is related to the outcome on which the power calculation was based, the reader should check to see if the number of patients or events required to detect a difference were enrolled or occurred, respectively. If the answer is yes, then the study is powered to detect a difference, and the conclusion of no difference is valid. If not, then there may be a type II error, and the conclusion of no difference is invalid.

Once statistical significance is evaluated, and the conclusion is determined appropriate, a reader should consider clinical significance. For continuous and ordinal data, one must consider the range of plausible results for the outcome, the absolute difference, and whether the intervention helps patients meet treatment goals.

For nominal data, measures of association are calculated. Often, authors report the most beneficial value to support their case. Readers need to interpret that value and calculate other values that better represent the difference observed. The first step to calculating measures of association is to develop a contingency table (Table 10.9). One can use a simple example of 20 patients randomized to receive aspirin (n = 10) or placebo (n = 10) to prevent MI over the next 10 years to calculate measures of association. One patient and three patients have MIs in the aspirin and placebo groups, respectively. This is equal to a 10% (1/10) risk in the aspirin group and 30% (3/10) risk in the placebo group.

From risk, one can calculate the four measures of association: relative risk (RR), relative risk reduction (RRR), absolute risk reduction (ARR), and number needed to treat (NNT). RR, sometimes called risk ratio, is the risk associated with exposure on disease state development. It is calculated by dividing the exposed group risk by the unexposed group risk. In this case, 10% divided by 30% is equal to 33%; this means the risk of an MI in the aspirin group is one-third the risk of an MI in the placebo group. RRR is the percent of risk removed by introducing the intervention and is calculated by subtracting RR from 100% because everyone has an equal baseline risk. In this example, RRR is 100% minus 33%, which equals 67%; a person's risk of an MI is reduced 67% by taking aspirin instead of placebo. ARR represents the difference in the percentage of subjects developing an outcome in the control group in comparison with the intervention group. This is calculated by subtracting the risk of the outcome in an unexposed group by the risk in an exposed group. Subtracting the 10% risk in the aspirin group from the 30% risk in the placebo group yields a value of 20%, meaning that 20% of participants were spared an MI due to aspirin. NNT represents the number of patients that need to receive an intervention to prevent one event. Calculated as the reciprocal of ARR, one would divide 1 by 20%, or 0.2, to get a value of 5; therefore, to prevent one MI, five patients need to receive aspirin.

The most valuable measure of association in the determination of clinical significance is dependent on the outcomes and results; however, clinical studies will often present the most appealing value, usually RRR. Readers need to calculate for themselves the measures of association not presented by the authors. A 67% RRR may appear more impressive than a 20% ARR, but the latter is likely more indicative of the clinical value of the intervention. With small sample sizes, these numbers are closer together, but as sample size increases, the relative and absolute differences will become much more disparate.

Beyond efficacy data, safety results must also be considered. All articles should report adverse event data. Because adverse event incidence is often small, readers need to make sure not to draw sweeping conclusions from the results. Adverse events are an excellent example of an opportunity for a type II error because the study would not have been powered to detect a difference in the rates of these outcomes, yet authors might suggest that there was no greater incidence of adverse events for the intervention. This concludes no difference exists when one might because the study was not powered to detect that difference.

Safety results are also important to consider when determining clinical significance. A major consideration of therapeutic decision-making is that the benefits of an intervention outweigh the harm. Considering the NNT and comparing it with a similar calculation specific to adverse effects, the number needed to harm (NNH) is helpful. The NNH is calculated by determining the absolute risk increase (ARI) of an intervention. If two patients taking aspirin developed a gastrointestinal bleed (GIB), whereas only one patient taking placebo had a similar event, the risk of GIB is 20% and 10%

in the aspirin and placebo groups, respectively. ARI is calculated by subtracting the rate of GIB in the control group from the intervention group, in this case, 20% minus 10% equals 10%, meaning that taking aspirin increases the risk of having a GIB by 10%. Similar to NNT, NNH is calculated by taking the reciprocal of the ARI, so 1 divided by 10%, or 0.1, equals 10; 10 patients would need to receive aspirin to cause one GIB.

While NNT and NNH can be valuable for determining the benefit—risk ratio of an intervention and thus clinical significance, it is important to understand that these results have no meaning if a statistically significant difference is not identified and there is no way to define a "good" NNT or a "bad" NNH. Readers should review the difference between the numbers, the severity of the event (e.g., nausea vs. death) and the length of the trial.

Readers may also be required to evaluate the results of systematic reviews or metaanalyses, as the use of these study designs is increasing.[54,55] For metaanalyses, results are often presented using a forest plot, which graphically displays the results of included studies along with a combined effect size.[55] An example forest plot is shown in Fig. 10.3. Each of the six studies in this example has an effect estimate, represented by a block, and corresponding CI, denoted by the horizontal line through the block. The size of the block represents the influence that each study has on the overall results, which is also referred to as study weight. Studies with more precise estimates are given more weight and represented by larger blocks in the forest plot. The diamond is the effect size and corresponding CI when the results of all six studies are combined. One can determine if the results are statistically significant by evaluating if the CI crosses the line of no effect, which is 1 and 0 for the ratio (as shown in Fig. 10.3) and non-ratio data, respectively. By inspecting the forest plot, the reader can quickly determine to what degree the results of individual studies differ and identify studies with the greatest impact on the overall results.

Important steps for readers to take when considering results include looking at the baseline characteristics to make sure randomization worked and that the sample represents the patients seen by the reader. Although performing a power analysis and interpreting statistical significance via P-values or CIs are also an important skill, the most important skill is to take statistically significant results and determine clinical significance. Developing this skill set will take time because there is a great deal of subjectivity associated with clinical significance, but appropriately interpreting results and being able to calculate measures of association will reduce this subjectivity.

Discussion

The discussion section is an opportunity for the authors to provide their interpretation and assessment of the results. This section should summarize key findings, compare and contrast results with previous studies, present strengths and limitations, mention future investigations, and end with a conclusion. As a reader, making sure that authors do not exaggerate the results is important. Common flaws of discussion sections include authors only citing studies with similar

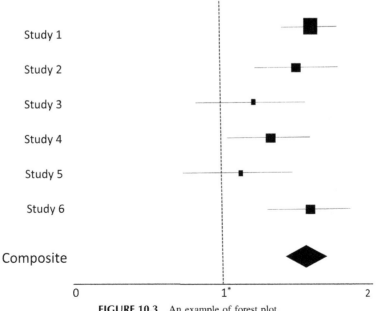

FIGURE 10.3 An example of forest plot.

results, failing to discuss limitations, and making inappropriate conclusions not related to study results. Readers should take caution when reviewing this section, never relying on it to make therapeutic decisions.

Conclusion

The conclusion of the article will be a separate section after the discussion or appear as the last paragraph of the discussion. This is the authors' final determination and clinical recommendation of the evidence presented. The conclusion should focus on primary outcome results and be tied directly to the primary objective of the study. It should not address information not presented within the article itself. As a reader, ensure that the paper and abstract conclusions match, if not in words, at least in intention. To summarize the overall theme of this chapter, one must make their own decisions from an evaluation of the full paper and not just from any one section the authors present, including the conclusion.

Bibliography

The bibliography of the article will follow the conclusion; authors document references used to support the information contained within the article. Any work included in the bibliography should be internally cited within the manuscript. A good reader of the medical literature will scan the bibliography to make sure authors used materials that were from reputable sources and that they did not extensively cite their own work. The bibliography is also a great tool from which to pull cited literature to verify that the documented information is accurate and to gather additional information on the topic.

OBJECTIVE 10.3. UTILIZE CLINICAL EXPERTISE TO IDENTIFY THE OVERALL VALIDITY OF A GIVEN CLINICAL TRIAL

After reviewing every section of an article, one should consider the overall validity. The first consideration is to determine the statistical significance of the results.[8,56–59] If the results are significant, validity should then be considered; if not, the study may prove valuable to review for a future hypothesis generation, but clinical decisions may not be necessary.

Internal validity is the degree to which a study establishes a causal relationship between the treatment and an observed outcome, whereas external validity is the degree to which the results of a study can be generalized to patients outside of the study sample. Both are important considerations when reviewing the medical literature and can be compromised in several ways.[58,60]

Threats to internal validity are detailed in Table 10.10. Most threats, except for experimental mortality, can be removed with randomization. Randomization ensures that threats to internal validity will be present in all study groups; thus, if the results are statistically significant, differences occurred in spite of threats to internal validity. Because of attrition after randomization, ITT analysis is the best way to control for experimental mortality. To assess internal validity, it is important to analyze the method of randomization, appropriateness of blinding, the rate and reasons for experimental mortality, and if scientific misconduct occurred.

Threats to external validity include the Hawthorne effect, which occurs when participants behave differently knowing that they are being observed.[59,60] Examining baseline characteristics of a sample for representativeness of the population is another consideration. Overly strict inclusion and exclusion criteria or inappropriate sampling can cause results of a study to have limited external validity.[56,58–60] Finally, sometimes studies involve complex treatment regimens that cannot be controlled outside of the study environment; in these cases, results seen in the study may not be achievable in the population.[59,60] To analyze external validity, it is important to assess the appropriateness of sampling methods, the inclusion and exclusion criteria of a study, baseline characteristics, and adherence to the study protocol.[56–59]

Assessing the validity of a study helps the reader determine whether the results of a single study are true and can be applied outside of the study sample. There are many threats to internal and external validity, so it is important to take a standardized approach to assessing the possible presence of these threats. Ultimately, assessing validity does not lead to an absolute decision about whether to apply evidence to practice but allows the reader to analyze the degree to which one should consider using the evidence (e.g., will the ultimate recommendation apply to all patients or just patients similar to those studied?).

TABLE 10.10 Threats to Internal Validity[58–60]

Threat	Definition	Example
History	External time-related factors affect the dependent variable and bias results.	Legislation requiring the use of seat belts could confound an experiment designed to determine whether an intervention reduces motor vehicle mortality.
Maturation	Study subjects change over time due to natural progression.	Childhood asthma may resolve on its own or as a result of a specific study intervention.
Testing	Testing subjects multiple times with the same assessment tool may capture improvement not related to the intervention.	Pre- and postassessments of learning that contain the same questions may show improvement simply because the participants were aware of the questions and paid closer attention to those topics.
Instrumentation	Outcomes assessed by measurement tools or devices may change in response to changes in the tool and not related to the intervention.	A new blood pressure cuff is purchased that measures blood pressure more accurately. Study subjects' blood pressure may appear to have improved simply because the tool changed and not as a result of the intervention.
Statistical regression	Subjects selected based on extreme values may show improvement simply because extreme values tend to regress toward the mean and not because the treatment is effective.	A clinical trial for a blood pressure medication only includes patients with excessively high blood pressure. Some patients' blood pressure may improve simply because the value cannot increase any further whether or not the patient receives the medication.
Selection	How subjects are divided into study groups creates groups that are unequal with regard to variables that can affect the study outcome.	A cohort study is performed in two clinics. One is a military-based clinic and the other serves primarily elderly patients. If each clinic serves as a cohort, the groups will not be equal. One group may be mostly young men (i.e., military-based clinic) and is compared with mostly elderly patients.
Experimental mortality	Patients lost throughout the study period (i.e., attrition, withdrawal, dropout) are not lost equally between groups.	A study drug has a terrible side effect, so more patients receiving the treatment drop out of the study. The final group of patients that are analyzed to show the drug is very efficacious; however, that effect will only be realized in patients that can tolerate the terrible side effect and continue taking the medication.

CONCLUSION

As one can see, there is a great deal to consider when reading an article. All studies have some bias, and it is the job of the clinician to determine to what degree that bias will impact their ability to use the information in the study. Over time, considerations described in this chapter will become natural for consumers of the literature. The more reading and interpretation one does, the more flaws they see and the more questions they ask. Using this chapter as a guide for things to consider in MLE will help future and current clinicians as they continue to develop these skills and thus their ability to help their patients.

PRACTICE QUESTIONS

1. JIF considers citations received on a certain year for the articles published with the?
   A. Previous 1 year
   B. Previous 2 years
   C. Previous 3 years
   D. Previous 4 years
2. Which of the following is a metric to calculate the value of a published research paper?
   A. JIF
   B. Eigenfactor Scores

    C. Altmetric

    D. CiteScore

3. Systematic reviews are published in journals in which format?

    A. CONSORT

    B. PRISMA

    C. AGREE

    D. CHEERS

4. Identify a conflict of interest from the following scenarios?

    A. An employee from the sponsoring pharmaceutical company coauthored the article.

    B. An employee from regulatory agency wrote a letter to the editor for a controversial article.

    C. A job title of a clinician at the sponsoring pharmaceutical company was not mentioned in the article.

    D. All the funding sources were mentioned in the article, except the expenses met by the authors themselves.

5. Failing to measure which of the following factors could be considered as a confounding factor in an interventional study on peptic ulcer?

    A. Amount of weight bearing exercise

    B. Smoking status

    C. Marital status

    D. History of blood transfusion

6. The power of the study is used to identify?

    A. Study population

    B. Statistical significance

    C. Clinical significance

    D. Sample size

7. Which of the following you consider as a more serious issue with a paper?

    A. Introduction missed a related reference

    B. Limitations of the study missed a key issue

    C. Results are repeated in the discussion

    D. Conclusion is not in alignment with results

REFERENCES

1. O'Sullivan TA, Phillips J, Demaris K. Medical literature evaluation education at US schools of pharmacy. *Am J Pharm Educ*. 2016;80(1). Article 5.

2. Accreditation Council for Pharmacy Education. *Accreditation Standards and Key Elements for the Professional Program in Pharmacy Leading to the Doctor of Pharmacy Degree (Standards 2016)*; February 2015. Available at: https://www.acpe-accredit.org/pdf/Standards2016FINAL.pdf.

3. Guidance for the accreditation standards and key elements for the professional program in pharmacy leading to the Doctor of Pharmacy degree. In: *Guidance for Standards 2016*. Chicago, IL: Accreditation Council for Pharmacy Education; February 2, 2015. Available at: https://www.acpe-accredit.org/pdf/GuidanceforStandards2016FINAL.pdf.

4. Zellmer WA, Vlasses PH, Beardsley RS. Summary of the ACPE consensus conference on advancing quality in pharmacy education. *Am J Pharm Educ*. 2013;77(3). Article 44.

5. NACDS Foundation-NCPA-ACPE Task Force. *Entry-Level Competencies Needed for Community Pharmacy Practice*. Chicago, IL: Accreditation Council for Pharmacy Education; 2012. https://www.acpe-accredit.org/pdf/NACDSFoundation-NCPAACPETaskForce2012.pdf.

6. ASHP-ACPE Task Force. *Entry-Level Competencies Needed for Pharmacy Practice in Hospitals and Health-Systems*. Chicago, IL: Accreditation Council for Pharmacy Education; 2010. Available at: https://www.acpe-accredit.org/pdf/EntryLevelCompetenciesNeededForPharmacyPractice-HospitalsandHealthSystems.pdf.

7. AMCP-ACPE Task Force. *Entry-Level Competencies Needed for Managed Care Pharmacy Practice*. Chicago, IL: Accreditation Council for Pharmacy Education; 2012. Available at: https://www.acpe-accredit.org/pdf/AMCPACPETaskForce2012.pdf.

8. ICMJE Recommendations: http://www.icmje.org/recommendations/. *International Committee of Medical Journal Editors: Recommendations for the Conduct, Reporting, Editing and Publication of Scholarly Work in Medical Journals [Internet]*. [place unknown]: International Committee of Medical Journal Editors. Available at: http://www.icmje.org. Accessed on July 30, 2018.

9. Kendrach MG, Freeman M, Hughes PJ. Drug literature evaluation I: controlled clinical trial evaluation. In: Malone PM, Kier KL, Stanovich JE, Malone MJ, eds. *Drug Information: A Guide for Pharmacists 5e*. New York, NY: McGraw-Hill; 2013. Available at: http://accesspharmacy.mhmedical.com/content.aspx?bookid=981&sectionid=54480667.

10. Lisegang TJ, Schachat AP, Albert DM. The open access initiative in scientific and biomedical publishing: fourth in the series on editorship. *Am J Ophthalmol*. 2005;139:156–167.

11. Bohannon J. Who's afraid of peer review? *Science*. 2013;342:60–65.

12. Appropriate use of bibliometric indicators for the assessment of journals, research proposals, and individuals. *IEEE Comput Gr Appl.* 2014;34(2):87−88.

13. ClarivateAnalytics. *The Thomson Reuters Impact Factor*; 2017. Available at: http://wokinfo.com/essays/impact-factor//.

14. Kim Y-S, Hong R. *About the Eigenfactor Project*. Eigenfactor's Web Site. Available at: http://www.eigenfactor.org/about.php. Accessed on July 30, 2018.

15. Davis P. *Network-based Citation Metrics: Eigenfactor Vs. SJR*. Scholarly Kitchen Web Site; 2015. Available at: https://scholarlykitchen.sspnet.org/2015/07/28/network-based-citation-metrics-eigenfactor-vs-sjr/.

16. Bergstrom C. Eigenfactor: measuring the value and prestige of scholarly journals. *Coll Res Libr News.* 2007;68(5):314−316.

17. *Research Metrics*. Elsevier Web Site; 2017. Available at: https://www.elsevier.com/solutions/scopus/features/metrics.

18. Zijlstra H, McCullough R. *CiteScore: A New Metric to Help You Track Journal Performance and Make Decisions*. Elsevier Web Site; 2016. Available at: https://www.elsevier.com/editors-update/story/journal-metrics/citescore-a-new-metric-to-help-you-choose-the-right-journal.

19. Davis P. *CiteScore−Flawed but Still a Game Changer*. Scholarly Kitchen Web Site; 2016. Available at: https://scholarlykitchen.sspnet.org/2016/12/12/citescore-flawed-but-still-a-game-changer/.

20. Clarivate Analytics. *Clarivate Analytics Announces Landmark Partnership with Impactstory to Make Open Access Content Easier for Researchers to Use*; 2017. Available at: http://www.prnewswire.com/news-releases/clarivate-analytics-announces-landmark-partnership-with-impactstory-to-make-open-access-content-easier-for-researchers-to-use-300478715.html.

21. DOI Handbook. *International DOI Foundation Web Site*; 2016. Available at: https://www.doi.org/hb.html.

22. Crossref. 2017. Available at: https://www.crossref.org/.

23. Crossmark. 2017. vailable at: https://www.crossref.org/services/crossmark/.

24. Cooper ID. Bibliometrics basics. *J Med Libr Assoc.* 2015;103(4):217−218.

25. Roemer RC, Borchardt R. *Meaningful Metrics: A 21st Century Librarian's Guide to Bibliometrics, Altmetrics, and Research Impact*. Chicago: Assiociation of College and Research Libraries; 2015.

26. Begg C, Cho M, Eastwood S, et al. Improving the quality of reporting of randomized controlled trials. The CONSORT statement. *JAMA.* 1996;276:637−639.

27. Reporting Guidelines. *Equator Network: Enhancing the QUAlity and Transparency of Health Research*; 2017. Available at: http://www.equator-network.org/reporting-guidelines/.

28. Camm AJ, Karam R, Pratt CM. The azilimide postinfarct survival evaluation (ALIVE) trial. *Am J Cardiol.* 1998;81:35D−39D.

29. Kozak M, Bornmann L. A new family of cumulative indexes for measuring scientific performance. *PLoS One.* 2012;7(10):e47679.

30. Herndon NC. Research fraud and the publish or perish world of academia. *J Market Channel.* 2016;23(3):91−96. Available at: http://www.tandfonline.com/doi/full/10.1080/1046669X.2016.1186469.

31. Author Retrieval API. *Elsevier Developers*; 2017. Available at: http://api.elsevier.com/documentation/AuthorRetrievalAPI.wadl.

32. ResearcherID. 2017. Available at: http://www.researcherid.com/Home.action.

33. *ORCiD: Connecting Research and Researchers*; 2017. Available at: https://orcid.org.

34. Christensen E. Methodology of superiority vs. equivalence trials and non-inferiority trials. *J Hepatol.* 2007;46:947−954.

35. US Food and Drug Administration. Institutional review boards frequently asked questions − information sheet. In: *Guidance for Institutional Review Boards and Clinical Investigators*; January 25, 2016. Available at: https://www.fda.gov/RegulatoryInformation/Guidances/ucm126420.htm.

36. Schulz KF, Grimes DA. Allocation concealment in randomized trials: defending against deciphering. *Lancet.* 2002;359:614−618.

37. Cohen AT, Goto S, Schreiber K, Torp-Pedersen C. Why do we need observational studies of everyday patients in the real-life setting? *Eur Heart J Suppl.* 2015;17:D2−D8.

38. Dumville JC, Torgerson DJ, Hewitt CE. Reporting attrition in randomised controlled trials. *BMJ.* 2006;332:969−971.

39. Heritier SR, Gebski VJ, Keech AC. Inclusion of patients in clinical trial analysis: the intention-to-treat principle. *Med J Aust.* 2003;179:438−440.

40. Gupta SK. Intention-to-treat concept: a review. *Perspect Clin Res.* 2011;2:109−112.

41. Ranganathan P, Pramesh CS, Aggarwal R. Common pitfalls in statistical analysis: intention-to-treat versus per-protocol analysis. *Perspect Clin Res.* 2016;7:144−146.

42. Multiple Endpoints if Clinical Trials. *U.S. Department of Health and Human Services Food and Drug Administration*; 2017. Available at: https://www.fda.gov/downloads/Drugs/GuidanceComplianceRegulatoryInformation/Guidances/UCM536750.pdf.

43. Fleming TR, Powers JH. Biomarkers and surrogate endpoints in clinical trials. *Stat Med.* 2012;31:2973−2984.

44. Stratton IM, Adler AI, Neil HA, et al. Association of glycaemia with macrovascular and microvascular complications of type 2 diabetes (UKPDS 35): prospective observational study. *BMJ.* 2000;321:405−412.

45. Weintraub WS, Lüscher TF, Pocock S. The perils of surrogate endpoints. *Eur Heart J.* 2015;36:2212−2218.

46. Hlatky MA. A long-term perspective on short-term outcomes. *J Am Coll Cardiol.* 2014;64:2109−2110.

47. Besch CL. Compliance in clinical trials. *AIDS.* 1995;9:1−10.

48. Moher D, Schulz KF, Altman D. The CONSORT statement: revised recommendations for improving the quality of reports of parallel-group randomized trials. *JAMA.* 2001;285:1987−1991.

49. Röhrig B, Du prel JB, Wachtlin D, Kwiecien R, Blettner M. Sample size calculation in clinical trials: part 13 of a series on evaluation of scientific publications. *Dtsch Arztebl Int.* 2010;107:552−556.

50. De Muth JE. Overview of biostatistics used in clinical research. *Am J Health Syst Pharm.* 2009;66(1):70−81.

51. Brookhart MA, Stürmer T, Glynn RJ, Rassen J, Schneeweiss S. Confounding control in healthcare database research: challenges and potential approaches. *Med Care.* 2010;48:S114−S120.

52. Pourhoseingholi MA, Baghestani AR, Vahedi M. How to control confounding effects by statistical analysis. *Gastroenterol Hepatol Bed Bench*. 2012;5:79−83.

53. Altman DG, Bland JM. Time to event (survival) data. *BMJ*. 1998;317:468.

54. Haidich AB. Meta-analysis in medical research. *Hippokratia*. 2010;14:29−37.

55. Cochrane handbook for systematic reviews of interventions version 5.1.0. In: Higgins JPT, Green S, eds. *The Cochrane Collaboration*; 2011. Available at: www.cochrane-handbook.org.

56. Bryant PJ, McQueen CE, Van Dyke EA. Literature evaluation II: beyond the basics. In: Malone PM, Kier KL, Stanovich JE, Malone MJ, eds. *Drug Information: A Guide for Pharmacists 5e*. New York, NY: McGraw-Hill; 2013. Available at: http://accesspharmacy.mhmedical.com/content.aspx?bookid=981&sectionid=54480668.

57. Morgan GA, Harmon RJ. Sampling and external validity. *J Am Acad Child Adolesc Psychiatry*. 1999;38(8):1051−1053.

58. Slack MK. Establishing the internal and external validity of experimental studies. *Am J Health Syst Pharm*. 2001;58:2173−2184.

59. Morgan GA, Gliner JA, Harmon RJ. Evaluating the validity of a research study. *J Am Acad Child Adolesc Psychiatry*. 1999;38(4):480−485.

60. *Principles of Research Design and Drug Literature Evaluation*. Burlington, MA: Jones & Bartlett Learning, LLC; 2015.

ANSWERS TO PRACTICE QUESTIONS

1. B
2. C
3. B
4. C
5. B
6. D
7. D

Chapter 11

Evidence-Based Practice: Use in Answering Queries and Developing Systematic Reviews

Emily Brennan, Jason C. Cooper and Amanda Davis
Medical University of South Carolina, Charleston, SC, United States

Learning Objectives

Objective 11.1 Define evidence-based practice and explain its framework.
Objective 11.2 Recognize and employ the steps for the modified systematic approach when answering drug information-related questions.
Objective 11.3 Describe the process of preparing systematic reviews using evidence-based practice.

OBJECTIVE 11.1. DEFINE EVIDENCE-BASED PRACTICE AND EXPLAIN ITS FRAMEWORK

Evidence-based practice (EBP) is the integration of best research evidence, clinical expertise, and patient values. EBP is more than theory and skills; it is a way of practicing pharmacy/medicine and therefore should be integrated into the culture of an institution. For these skills and culture to solidify, it is essential that pharmacists learn the concepts of EBP during their education and carry on this practice throughout their professional careers.

The goal of EBP is to achieve optimal patient outcomes by integrating the best research evidence available, along with clinical expertise and patient values/preferences when making patient-care decisions.[1,2] With that in mind, it is important to acknowledge that using a systematic approach to finding the best available research evidence is essential. Overall, five distinct steps create the framework for EBP:

1. Ask: Organizing the clinical question in a structured format is important when developing a literature search. Using a format known as PICO(T) promotes retrieval of articles more closely linked to the clinical question (Table 11.1).
2. Search: Using research databases effectively is dependent on the utilization of concepts and keywords in combination with each other to filter out articles that do not fit the clinical question.
3. Critical Appraisal: Evaluating research articles related to the clinical question of interest can be efficiently completed by focusing on three key questions, which are presented in depth later in this chapter:
   a. *Are the results valid?* The emphasis here is on the design of the study and any limitations that might impact the results.
   b. *Are the results significant?* If the results are valid, it is essential to evaluate whether the results of the study are statistically significant.
   c. *Will these results help determine care for the patient?* Finally, decide how the study's findings can help treat the patient. This may be more related to the clinical relevance of the findings.
4. Implement: Creating a clinical "action plan" based on evidence from the literature is often an underappreciated component of the EBP process. However, achieving and maintaining success without a formal plan that relies on establishing accountability, support of key clinical stakeholders, and a standardized process is very difficult. This is also the ideal step in the process to fully integrate patient values and preferences through shared decision-making.
5. Evaluate: Following implementation, it is important to monitor and evaluate patient and quality outcomes.

TABLE 11.1 PICO(T)—Formulating an Answerable Question

Description	Example
P: Patient/population or problem The patient is a member of a population with a specific health problem. However, factors such as age, sex, and ethnicity should also be considered.	Hospitalized adult patient with recurrent methicillin-resistant *Staphylococcus aureus* bacteremia
I: Intervention The therapy being considered or evaluated.	Linezolid
C: Comparison The "standard care" or comparison therapy.	Vancomycin
O: Outcome The desired outcome should be measurable.	Effective infection clearance
T: Time (if important)	

Many clinicians and healthcare leaders agree that a sixth step, dissemination, also plays an integral role in EBP. This is because dissemination of new knowledge through peer-reviewed publication not only fosters support of the EBP process but also promotes improvements in clinical practice as the literature base for decision-making evolves.

It is also important to think about the use of the EBP in two distinct ways[3]:

- Evidence-based individual decision-making—where the focus is individual clinicians using research evidence when facilitating decision-making to treat individual patients (i.e., a septic patient with urinary tract source and documented penicillin anaphylaxis).
- Evidence-based guidelines—where the focus is using the best research evidence to make recommendations about how to treat a group of patients defined by a specific clinical criterion (i.e., urinary tract infection), rather than an individual patient.

Although the use of best research evidence is an important factor in decision-making for both of these practices, they are not mutually exclusive. Both methodologies play a vital role in improving clinical practice and patient outcomes.

Other Methods Used in EBP

The modified systematic approach explained in depth in this chapter is one of many methods used to promote the integration of research evidence into practice. Another familiar EBP methodology is Critically Appraised Topics (CATs). The Centre for Evidence-Based Medicine at University of Oxford in the United Kingdom has developed standardized templates for CATs in multiple languages that can be used to critically appraise systematic reviews, randomized controlled trials (RCTs), and observational studies on diagnosis and prognosis[4,5] The Centre for Evidence-Based Medicine at University of Oxford in the United Kingdom has also created a downloadable critical appraisal tool, called CATmaker,[5] which supports the step-by-step use of EBP by prompting users to:

- Ask a focused and answerable question
- Search for the best available evidence
- Critically appraise the evidence for validity and clinical relevance
- Apply the results to clinical practice
- Evaluate performance

OBJECTIVE 11.2. RECOGNIZE AND EMPLOY THE STEPS FOR THE MODIFIED SYSTEMATIC APPROACH WHEN ANSWERING DRUG INFORMATION-RELATED QUESTIONS

Use of EBP comes into play in a variety of different ways for clinicians. Healthcare professionals answer a wide variety of questions from their patients, as well as other colleagues. When researching an answer, pharmacists are often sought out for their experience and expertise about specific questions relating to medication use and safety. Whether one is a hospital

TABLE 11.2 Seven Principles of the Modified Systematic Approach[7,9]
1. Secure the demographics of the requester and determine when the information is needed
2. Retrieve the necessary background information from the requester about the question
3. Determine the true informational need and categorize the ultimate question to be answered
4. Develop an appropriate searching strategy and conduct a thorough search
5. Evaluate, analyze, and synthesize the gathered information
6. Formulate and communicate the answer
7. Conduct follow-up, if necessary, and provide documentation

pharmacist stationed in the medical intensive care unit, a retail pharmacist working at an independent or chain drugstore, or a long-term care pharmacist making rounds through a specialized care home, the pharmacist is seen as a valuable source of drug information. For example, a patient receiving warfarin for the first time may experience bruising, and a nurse may want to know the specific monitoring parameters (e.g., blood work, INR) for the patient's specific diagnosis. A medical resident may initially prescribe clindamycin for a mild skin infection in a patient allergic to erythromycin and wants to know if it is safe to do so. A psychiatrist may be treating a patient for depression with selective serotonin reuptake inhibitors and may inquire about starting or stopping other medications to minimize the potential for drug-drug interactions. Whatever the case, the pharmacist should know the best way to search the literature using EBP to answer the question efficiently and effectively.

Pharmacy schools that have a drug information course or teach the concept of providing drug information throughout the curriculum usually employ the use of the modified systematic approach to answering specific drug information questions. This method has been developed by Watanabe[6] in 1975 but has been published and modified to its current format by other noted instructors within drug information practice.[7,8] Basically, it centers on seven principles and employs the basic tenants of using EBP to validate and verify the information researched (Table 11.2).

Secure the Demographics of the Requester

This seems like a fairly simple thing to do, but actually, it is probably one of the most important aspects of the modified systematic approach. Securing the demographics of the requester will set the stage for how to approach the question, what format to use in answering the question, and when the information is needed by the requester.[8,10]

For a question over the phone, the name of the person calling and the number where they can be reached are the first two items that should be collected. Without knowing who is being addressed and how to ultimately communicate the final response to the person calling, the rest of the principles of the modified systematic approach will prove futile. Therefore, it is extremely important to take down the correct information regarding the person's name, their title (e.g., nurse, physician, pharmacist, patient), and contact information (i.e., fax/phone number). A person's title is very important to how the question will be answered because the tone and wording of the answer will vary accordingly. Additionally, some people may wish to receive the information via email and then respond with further questions if the answer is not clear or more information is desired. Email addresses can be cumbersome, especially if they are associated with a private email account. Be sure to repeat email addresses and fax/phone numbers back to the requester to ensure that the right contact information has been collected.

This would also be the best time to ask when the information is needed. Common responses from requesters when this question is posed are "Whenever you can get to it," "As soon as possible," or sometimes, a specific date and time is given. It is important to narrow down the time frame with the first two examples. If the requester says, "Whenever you can get to it," then time may not be of the utmost importance. As long as it is not a scenario where the patient is currently in the hospital, in the clinic, in the counseling area, or waiting for their prescription, one might be able to offer a time in the near future for the answer to be provided (e.g., 24 h, next week). This would allow additional or necessary time for research, especially if the question is a particularly in-depth one (e.g., various secondary databases and primary literature will need to be searched). If the requester indicates that the answer is needed as soon as possible, education of the person making the request may be necessary. Most drug information centers do not provide drug information within 30 min or less because more time is often essential for education, searching, formatting, and editing. In addition, most healthcare professionals who use drug information centers understand that a large amount of work and effort might be required to find the answer to an unusual or peculiar question. Finally, most pharmacies (e.g., hospital, retail) are busy to the point where pharmacists do not have enough extra staff and time to stop and research a question that quickly. Yet, if the patient situation is truly urgent, then measures should be taken by the staff to perform a quick and fairly complete search through tertiary, secondary, and primary literatures with follow-up and additional searching to be performed after the initial information is conveyed to meet the given time frame.

In terms of appropriate health literacy, one would not respond to a patient asking about a possible drug-drug interaction in the same way as one would respond to a physician. It is commonly understood that patients and the general public read at an 8th to 10th-grade level. However, surveys and guidelines from governmental bodies (e.g., Health Literacy Innovations' National Survey of US Medicaid Guidelines,[11] CDC Health Literacy Tools[12]) suggest that medical writings should be geared toward a sixth-grade reading level. In practice, it is very difficult to write patient information at a sixth-grade reading level; however, using shorter sentences, smaller words, plain language, and not using medical jargon can help patients better process and understand the information they receive. Software for editing and creating documents (e.g., Microsoft Word) usually has a tool to show readability statistics (e.g., Flesch-Kincaid Grade Level) on review.

Retrieving Necessary Background Information

Most drug information requests have to do with patient-specific situations. For example, a patient may be experiencing an adverse drug reaction (ADR) to an angiotensin-converting enzyme inhibitor. To help the patient, information needs to be gathered concerning the nature and severity of the reaction, previous drug allergies, and when the medication was taken in relation to the appearance of the ADR. For completeness in providing an accurate and helpful response, other basic information should be collected (Table 11.3).[7,8,10] If working in a hospital or clinic, it may be easy to obtain such information with a medical record number.

To remember the various information needed or questions that should be asked, it may be helpful to develop a call sheet (Fig. 11.1). This can be placed near the phones in a pharmacy or call center and can be easily filled out and completed by staff, residents, and students when receiving requests to provide drug or medical information. Remember, if a valuable piece of information is missed during the initial communication, it is usually appropriate to contact the requester again and ask for further information.

Determining the True Informational Need and Categorizing the Ultimate Question

Once the necessary background information has been collected, the final thing to do before actually starting to research the question would be to come up with the requester's true informational need.[8,10] In other words, what question are they really asking or what do they really want to know? This is extremely important because the "worst" thing about having to research a lengthy and in-depth drug information question is to have to do it again. Therefore, it is a good idea to repeat back to or clarify with the requester the interpretation of the question being asked.

Next, it is necessary to classify the question into one of the following categories (Table 11.4). Categorizing the question will determine a focus for research, as well as offer a concentrated set of references to help answer the question. For example, if a nurse asked if heparin, phenylephrine, and milrinone could be run together via a triple-lumen catheter, categorizing the question to "IV compatibility" would lead to initially using tertiary references such as the *Handbook on Injectable Drugs* (i.e., Trissel's) or the *King Guide to Parenteral Admixtures*. That would also eliminate the need to search

---

TABLE 11.3 Important Background Information to Be Collected

Age, sex, height/weight	Medication history • All over-the-counter and alternative products/supplements • Dose/duration of therapy
Drug/food allergies • Nature of allergy/reaction	Current disease states and diagnoses
Past medical history	Pertinent/current laboratory values
Major organ function (e.g., liver, kidneys)	Diluents/rates of administration (if intravenous)

```
┌─────────────────────────────────────────────────────────────────┐
│                     Drug Information Call Sheet                   │
│                                                                   │
│  Caller Name:                       PharmD   MD   Nurse   Other  │
│                                                                   │
│  Affiliation:                                                     │
│                                                                   │
│  Location:                                                        │
│                                                                   │
│  Phone number:                                                    │
│                                                                   │
│  Email:                                                           │
│                                                                   │
│  When do you need this information:                              │
│                                                                   │
│  Can you tell me more about the situation:                      │
│                                                                   │
│                                                                   │
│                                                                   │
│  Is there anything special that I should know about this patient:│
│                                                                   │
│                                                                   │
│                                                                   │
│  Question:                                                        │
│                                                                   │
│                                                                   │
│                                                                   │
│  Other info (Labs, Medication, Allergies, Medical history):     │
│                                                                   │
└─────────────────────────────────────────────────────────────────┘
```

FIGURE 11.1   Example of a drug information call sheet.

TABLE 11.4 Common Categories for Drug Information Questions

Adverse Drug Reaction	General Information
Compounding	Method of administration
Compatibility of IV medications	Patient education
Contraindications/warnings	Pharmacokinetics
Dietary supplements, herbal and homeopathic medications	Pharmacology
Dosage/schedule	Pediatrics
Dosage form/formulation	Pregnancy/lactation
Drug allergy	Pharmacoeconomics
Drug availability/cost	Reference/citation search
Drug–drug/drug–food/drug–lab/drug–disease interactions	Stability/storage
Drug identification	Therapeutic consult/indications
Formulary management	Toxicology

for references that would not necessarily be helpful or specific enough (e.g., *Facts and Comparisons monographs*, *Goodman and Gilman's: The Pharmacological Basis of Therapeutics*).

At this point, the demographics of the requester have been identified, appropriate background information has been collected, the true informational need has been assessed, and the question has been correctly categorized. Now, it is time to begin the initial stages of answering the question. It all starts with building an appropriate searching strategy.

Developing a Sound Searching Strategy and Conducting a Thorough Search (Validate and Verify)

Tertiary Resources

Once a clinical question is formed, it is time to search for the best evidence. The easiest place to start a search is in tertiary resources. Tertiary resources provide a broad overview of a topic and present information in an easy-to-read format, often with supporting references that lead to primary articles. Examples of tertiary resources include UpToDate, LexiComp, Micromedex, and Facts and Comparisons. Most online tertiary resources will indicate the date when a literature review was last performed on the summary topic and the date when the summary was last updated. These two dates may differ and may not always result in the topic summary being updated (i.e., if no new practice-changing information had been published). If in print, one must look at the publication date and determine how relevant the information might be at the time of research. The most reliable tertiary resources are evidence-based rather than based on expert opinion. Narrative reviews are considered a tertiary resource, whereas systematic reviews are a primary resource (e.g., new statistics/data are generated). Evidence-based summaries will include levels of evidence throughout, and the resource should clearly describe how it determines the quality and levels of evidence.

Secondary Resources

If one cannot find an appropriate or detailed-enough answer to a clinical question in tertiary resources, then secondary resources should be considered. Secondary resources—such as Cochrane Database of Systematic Reviews, PubMed, Scopus, Embase, and Web of Science—compile primary literature such as journal articles, technical reports, and conference papers.

When searching for secondary resources, it is essential to develop a comprehensive search strategy to retrieve all relevant articles that answer the clinical question. There are several techniques that will ensure that a search strategy is well formulated.

First, use subject headings, when available. For example, PubMed includes the MeSH Database. MeSH (Medical Subject Headings) is the National Library of Medicine's controlled vocabulary thesaurus used to index articles in PubMed. Many other databases include subject-heading thesauri, as well. Searching with subject headings ensures that everything indexed on that topic will be retrieved, regardless of what keywords are used in the articles. For example, searching with the PubMed MeSH heading, "Urinary Tract Infections," will retrieve articles that use synonyms (e.g., UTI) as well as narrower terms (e.g., bacteriuria, pyuria, schistosomiasis hematobia) for urinary tract infection. Depending on journal impact factors and other considerations, it may take several months for an article to be assigned subject headings. Therefore, one drawback to searching exclusively with subject headings is that the newest articles may not be retrieved through the search. Using Boolean operators to combine subject headings with keywords will result in a comprehensive search strategy that retrieves both relevant and recently published articles.

Boolean operators (e.g., AND, OR, NOT) are used to connect and define relationships between your search terms (Fig. 11.2).[13]

To frame a search, first list the main concepts within the PICO format (i.e., patient/population/problem, intervention, comparison, outcome). Combine search concepts with "AND" to narrow the number of articles retrieved. List synonyms for each concept and combine synonyms with "OR." Combining synonyms with "OR" will broaden the search and retrieve more results. For the clinical question, "In women with uncomplicated urinary tract infection, what is the effect of nitrofurantoin on clinical cure rate?" a search strategy may look like ("Urinary Tract Infections"[MeSH] OR urinary tract infection) AND ("Nitrofurantoin"[MeSH] OR Macrobid).

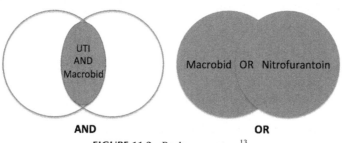

FIGURE 11.2 Boolean operators.[13]

To further focus the search, use subheadings in conjunction with subject headings. Subheadings are used to describe the specific aspects of the subject heading that are pertinent to the article. Not all databases that employ subject headings will use subheadings, but of those that do, most subject headings will be indexed with one or more subheading. A subject heading using a subheading, for example, "Urinary Tract Infections/drug therapy"[MeSH], will be more focused and retrieve fewer, but more relevant, results.

Another search technique is to use quotes and truncation. Put quotes around words to search them as an exact phrase. Put an asterisk at the root of a word to search alternate endings. For example, hospital* would retrieve the words hospital, hospitals, and hospitalized.

The use of subject headings, Boolean operators, quotes, and truncation, will ensure that the search strategy is well formed. After reviewing the results of the search, filters—or limits—can further refine search results. Filters differ among databases. Common filters may include publication dates, article types (e.g., systematic reviews, clinical trials), age, species (e.g., human, other animals), language, and many more. Filters can quickly reduce the search results to a reasonable number of relevant citations. Because searching is complex and vital to EBP, it is imperative to learn the best strategies and consult with a librarian when necessary, to ensure that all relevant articles are being retrieved.

Primary Literature

One must perform a comprehensive search of secondary resources to identify and retrieve primary literature. Primary literature consists of original research, either published or unpublished, such as systematic reviews, RCTs, or case reports. Not all primary literature is created equally. The Hierarchy of Evidence Pyramid illustrates the strength of study design (Fig. 11.3).

Systematic reviews and metaanalyses have the least biased study design and strongest strength of evidence. One systematic review or metaanalysis may synthesize the findings of many RCTs and postulate new conclusions about specific therapies. Therefore, it is easier for the information seeker to read one systematic review rather than appraise the findings of many RCTs. Narrative reviews differ from systematic reviews and metaanalyses in that because they are not rigorously designed; there is more likelihood of bias (Table 11.5).

RCTs, cohort studies, case-controlled studies, cross-sectional studies, case reports, and case series differ in their strength of study design. Generally, it is best to aim for the study design that is highest on the pyramid, but appropriate study design depends on the question. Both the Hierarchy of Evidence Pyramid and Best Study Design chart are meant to be guides to choosing the best study design for a particular question being answered (Table 11.6).

To obtain the primary literature, one must gain access through an institutional license unless the literature is freely available to the public (e.g., open access, public access). Open access articles are free to use without an institutional subscription and are often free of most copyright and licensing restrictions. Public access articles are also free to use without an institutional license and consist of research funded by the United States' National Institutes of Health and other government agencies. PubMed Central is a free database that archives publicly accessible full-text science articles. Those who are affiliated with an institution can gain access to library-subscribed full-text articles or can request articles through their library's interlibrary loan service. The entire search process—from forming the clinical question to developing the search strategy to obtaining full-text articles—is essential to answer the clinical question at hand properly.

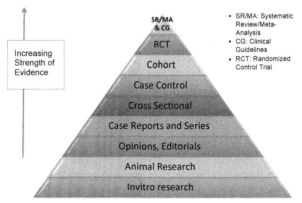

FIGURE 11.3 Hierarchy of evidence pyramid.[14]

TABLE 11.5 Comparison of Types of Review Articles

	Description	Advantages	Disadvantages
Narrative review	Authors' opinions (usually a tertiary reference)	Gain expert's insight, readable, broad scope	Potential bias toward author's opinion, reject alternative viewpoints, rarely reveals its sources of information, may not include the most up-to-date references if the author was not aware of them
Systematic review	Standardized retrieval, appraisal, and summary of the literature (could be tertiary or primary, depending on if new statistics were run and new information was presented)	Narrow clinical focus, best evidence, nonbiased, comprehensive literature critique	Available literature (i.e., publication bias), criterion selection may be too strict (limits generalizability) or too broad (hard to compare studies), search strategy may not be comprehensive
Metaanalysis	Systematic review with the statistical synthesis of data (usually primary b/c new statistics are performed to analyze data and come up with new/alternative recommendations)	Increases the power of the analyses, influence practice earlier	Poor translation to individuals, overinflated findings, limited to previous publications (i.e., publication bias), statistical results may lose meaning if studies that are combined are highly variable

TABLE 11.6 Best Study Design for Question Type

Question Type	Study Design (first being the best)
Diagnosis	Prospective, blind comparison to a gold standard
Therapy	Randomized Controlled Trial → Case Control → Case Series
Prognosis	Cohort Study → Case Control → Case Series
Harm/etiology	Randomized Controlled Trial → Cohort Study → Case Control → Case Series
Prevention	Randomized Controlled Trial → Cohort Study → Case Control → Case Series

Evaluation, Analysis, and Synthesis of Gathered Information

It is important to summarize the research findings in a format that promotes ease of use for the requester. The summary should quickly and straightforwardly provide *actionable steps* to be taken based on the results of the literature search, with supporting evidence for the recommended action. To ensure that the information is always displayed in a concise, consistent format, it may be helpful to develop an evidence summary template. Important items to include in this template would be as follows:

- Clinical question of interest using PICO format
- Therapeutic recommendation
- Evidence-based rationale
- References

When a requestor contacts a pharmacist or drug information center, their goal is to understand "What should I do?" in a specific clinical situation. It is helpful to keep this in mind when responding to their request. It is important to begin responses by formalizing the clinical question and providing an initial therapeutic recommendation. This should be followed by background information from either tertiary and primary references that support the conclusion/recommendation. Finally, some basic monitoring parameters or side effects for the clinician or patient to be aware of and a short summary of the major highlights of the information should be provided at the end of the response. This allows the requestor to quickly know "what to do," as well as being able to view the response in a comprehensive format that can easily be saved for later reference or placed in the patients' chart.

The depth of the evidence-based rationale for a recommended therapy will hinge on two main factors: urgency of the response and patient-specific factors. For example, in urgent situations where timely response is critical, focusing on tertiary data sources and evidence-based guideline recommendations to supply the rationale for decision-making saves time without affecting clinical integrity. However, when making therapeutic recommendations in complex patients, it becomes important to rely on secondary resources and primary literature (i.e., systematic reviews, RCTs) to ensure more precise decision-making. In most cases, though, it is important to balance these two factors against each other when deciding what sources to include in the response.

The content of the evidence-based rationale should highlight the various sources available for the clinical question:

- Tertiary resources and evidence-based guidelines
  The tertiary resources and narrative review articles can be useful sources of evidentiary support when time is a limiting factor for searching the primary literature. Because these sources already provide a broad overview of a clinical topic, the summary is largely completed. Where appropriate, highlight the pertinent evidence cited in these resources and focus on tailoring the summary to the requestor and their potential health literacy needs.

  It is also appropriate to use evidence-based guidelines to formulate a therapeutic recommendation if they exist. However, it is important to review a guideline first to determine how much trust can be placed in its recommendations. Many guideline issuers assign a "strength" or quality of evidence to support their decision-making, so understanding how that assignment was made is critical. Additionally, it is important to look at the development team and any potential conflicts of interest that may exist. The specific criteria for determining the trustworthiness of a guideline are discussed later in this chapter.

- Primary literature
  Secondary resources (i.e., PubMed, Scopus) contain primary literature in the form systematic reviews, metaanalyses, or original research studies (i.e., RCT, observational studies, case studies). The strongest study design for a therapeutic intervention is an RCT, but that does not mean that observational studies cannot assist with decision-making. Regardless of the source, it is essential to critically analyze the publication with three key questions in mind:

  - *Are the results valid?* It is important to critically analyze primary research to identify any significant design limitations, as these limitations impact the level of confidence that can be placed in the results (Table 11.7). For example, when reviewing a RCT regarding the efficacy of lorazepam (Ativan) compared with diazepam (Diastat) as a first-line therapy for pediatric patients in status epilepticus, it is important to evaluate factors such as sample size, blinding, allocation concealment, and loss to follow-up when determining the validity of the study's results.

  - *Are the results significant?* Use the statistical findings of the study to evaluate the significance or importance of the results, with a focus on the size and precision of the treatment effect (e.g., an estimate of effect, 95% confidence intervals, P-values). Common statistics presented as an estimate of effect, used in therapeutic intervention studies

TABLE 11.7 Assessing the Validity of Research Studies

Study Type	Questions for Evaluating the Validity
Systematic reviews and metaanalyses	<ul><li>Did the review address a focused clinical question?</li><li>Was the search detailed and exhaustive?</li><li>Were the studies of high methodological quality?</li><li>Was study inclusion evaluated by multiple authors?</li></ul>
Randomized controlled trials and quasiexperimental studies	<ul><li>Was the sample size large enough to reflect statistical significance (i.e., power calculation)?</li><li>Were the subjects randomized, and if so was it concealed?</li><li>Were the subjects, providers, and outcome assessors blinded?</li><li>Were the groups similar in terms of demographic and prognostic factors?</li><li>Was intent-to-treat analysis of outcomes used?</li><li>Was follow-up complete and sufficient in length to assess for study outcomes?</li><li>Were results reported for all primary and secondary outcomes?</li></ul>
Observational studies	<ul><li>Was the sample size large enough to reflect statistical significance (i.e., power calculation)?</li><li>Was the data collected prospectively?</li><li>Were study participants representative of a defined population (with or without controls)?</li><li>Were all important confounding factors identified and measured?</li><li>Was follow-up complete and sufficient in length to assess for study outcomes?</li></ul>

include the following: relative risk reduction, absolute risk reduction, and number needed to treat/harm. The precision of these findings is based on a range of values presented as a 95% confidence interval. For example, a narrow confidence interval range represents a more precise result.

- *Will these results help determine care for the patient?* A study's results can be generalized to a specific patient most of the time, but it might also be useful to assess whether or not the patient in question would qualify for the study based on its inclusion and exclusion criteria. In addition, how important are the results in terms of clinical significance? For example, if a study only shows a 0.5% improvement in blood glucose (hemoglobin A1C) over 6 months, do those results seem important clinically (i.e., is the benefit big enough)?

Formulate and Communicate the Response[8,10]

One thing to consider as the response is being written is how the requester will use the information. Because most drug information questions are related to one patient, the information provided will most likely be used for that specific scenario without further application. However, if a written response provided to a clinician is included in the patient's chart, then that may become part of the official medical record. It would be important to determine the end result of the information before sending the response to the requester; however, if one has completely followed the systematic approach with the inclusion and proper documentation of references/databases searched, all aspects of research should be covered and easily reproduced if there is ever a question (e.g., clinical, legal) regarding the information provided.

Conversely, drug information centers associated with hospitals tend to receive requests from various departments to create tables and charts that will be used by other healthcare professionals in taking care of a group of patients. For example, the creation of an insulin comparison chart might be used by a diabetic management service as a reference guide to the differences between insulin products (e.g., onset of action, duration of action, product availability). Therefore, for requests that will affect a larger group of patients, extra care must be taken to validate and verify all information and document all references where specific information is located.

Something else to consider would be the format in which the requester would prefer the information (e.g., table, chart, written text). Additionally, should the answer be sent via email or would the requester rather receive a call with a discussion of the information provided? Some of that may be up to the judgment of the person doing the research. For example, if one is researching a question that can best be answered with primary literature and four pertinent studies have been found, it might be best to summarize those in a chart and email the document to the requester. If they have any questions about the summary, the offer should be made to follow up at a later time.

Conduct Follow-Up/Provide Documentation[8,10]

Follow-up for most questions is not always necessary; however, it can be done as a courtesy. Most clinicians will welcome a call 2 or 3 days after the information was given to determine if the information was helpful or not. Follow-up could also be used as self-survey or process improvement tool to assess the overall service and information provided.

As mentioned earlier, appropriate documentation (e.g., citations, databases searched, search terms used) should be recorded in whatever database or archive system is being used to store all of the drug information questions answered by the clinician or service. In addition, if a written response is being provided, the complete answer along with the references and databases used to create the response should be included and provided to the requester. Appropriate documentation of references within the text will come from various medical writing styles (e.g., American Medical Association, Chicago, American Psychological Association); however, the correct way to reference a body of work (e.g., article, book, Internet database) is often standardized. That information can be found within the "how to submit an article" section of most journals, as well as the National Library of Medicine's *Citing Medicine*.[15]

OBJECTIVE 11.3. DESCRIBE THE PROCESS OF PREPARING SYSTEMATIC REVIEWS USING EVIDENCE-BASED PRACTICE

In addition to evidence-based individual decision-making, EBP methods can also be used to answer a specific clinical question for a group of patients (i.e., systematic reviews). Systematic reviews seek to answer a focused clinical question with a comprehensive literature search, strict inclusion and exclusion criteria, and team-based appraisal of evidence. "Researchers conducting systematic reviews use explicit methods aimed at minimizing bias, in order to produce more reliable findings that can be used to inform decision-making."[16] The systematic review process follows the five steps of

EBM (i.e., ask, search, critical appraisal, implement, and evaluate) but with more rigor, thus leading to less likelihood of bias. However, like primary literature, not all systematic reviews are created equally.

The most common types of review articles are systematic reviews, metaanalyses, and narrative reviews. Many other less common review types often get confused with systematic reviews.[17] Often clinicians will decide that they want to write a systematic review until they realize the time and effort that goes into developing one. According to the Cochrane Collaboration, the timeline for a systematic review is 12 months.[18] The Cochrane Collaboration is an international organization that is a leader in developing high-quality, evidence-based health sciences systematic reviews. The Cochrane Library publishes these systematic reviews in the Cochrane Database of Systematic Reviews, which also includes other types of reviews and publications.

The PRISMA (Preferred Reporting Items of Systematic reviews and Meta-Analyses) Statement, which consists of a checklist and flow diagram, was published to standardize the development of systematic reviews.[19] The 27 PRISMA checklist items guide authors through the systematic review process and is recommended for all authors embarking on the review process.[19] Before committing to a systematic review, several things must be accomplished. First, the team of experts who will work on the systematic review should be identified. A team-based approach is essential to establish inter-rater reliability and reduce bias. That team should identify the population/problem, intervention, comparison, outcome, and how benefits and harms will be measured. The specific question being researched should occur in the context of existing knowledge and literature. Therefore, when writing a systematic review, the authors should provide background on the current body of literature and explain what new knowledge their review provides.

The authors should then determine specific inclusion and exclusion criteria. These criteria may relate to details about the study population such as age range, setting, or point in the disease or may relate to study design, published versus unpublished research, and other limitations. The team may consider registering their systematic review in PROSPERO,[20] an international prospective register of systematic reviews, or with the Cochrane Review Group[21] if they are writing a Cochrane Systematic Review. The protocol is published as a placeholder until the full review is completed. The protocol can be compared to the final systematic review to determine if any bias or discrepancies have occurred.[22]

Arguably the most important step in the systematic review process is searching the literature. Authors should collaborate with a librarian to ensure the most comprehensive search possible. Librarians will search a variety of resources, and search strategies should be highly sensitive so that all relevant articles are retrieved. Librarians will combine subject headings and keywords to retrieve everything on the topic including narrower topics and articles electronically published ahead of print. Other relevant articles may be discovered through hand-searching reference lists, reviewing citing articles, and personal communication with key authors. The librarian will keep track of the reproducible search strategy, dates searched, number of results, filters applied, and other details for each database. This comprehensive search strategy is the core of the systematic review and will be described in detail in the methods section of the paper and also published as an appendix.

Once the literature review is complete, references are normally exported into a reference manager such as EndNote[23] or RefWorks.[24] The reference manager will be used to eliminate duplicate citations and to properly cite and format references in the final manuscript. The references will then be screened by at least two team members for inclusion or exclusion. There are many review managers available to facilitate the screening process, such as RevMan[25] or Abstrackr,[26] but Microsoft Excel[27] can be used, as well. The titles and abstracts should be screened first to remove references that are obviously irrelevant. The next step is to retrieve the full text of any potentially relevant articles (the librarian can help with this). At least two authors will independently read the full-text articles to determine if they meet the inclusion and exclusion criteria and vote on whether or not the article should be included in the systematic review. They will then discuss conflicting votes and decide on the final evidence to be included. The PRISMA Flow Diagram, which illustrates the number of records identified, screened, included, and excluded, should be included in the systemic review (Fig. 11.4).[19]

The next step in the systematic review process is to summarize the evidence and interpret the findings. The PRISMA Statement provides a checklist of items to consider when reporting results including (1) study selection, (2) study characteristics, (3) risk of bias within studies, (4) results of individual studies, (5) synthesis of results, (6) risk of bias across studies, and (7) additional analysis.[19] There are many tools available, such as the Cochrane Risk of Bias Tool, to assess considerations such as the risk of bias (i.e., validity or methodological quality of studies).[28] The characteristics of included studies should be detailed in a table and if study methods are too heterogeneous, authors should clearly explain why a metaanalysis cannot be done. Authors should, at a minimum, qualitatively evaluate the included studies and identify what future research is needed to fill existing gaps in knowledge or strengthen the body of evidence. Systematic reviews should be updated regularly or include commentary to explain why this is not possible.[16]

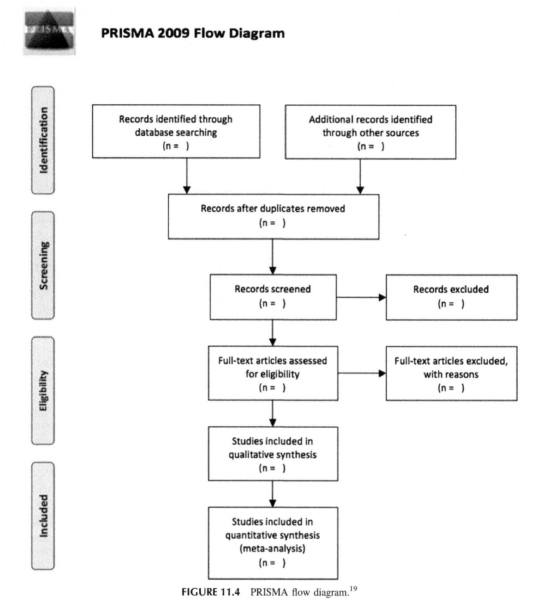

PRISMA 2009 Flow Diagram

Identification

Records identified through
database searching
(n =)

Additional records identified
through other sources
(n =)

Records after duplicates removed
(n =)

Screening

Records screened
(n =)

Records excluded
(n =)

Eligibility

Full-text articles assessed
for eligibility
(n =)

Full-text articles excluded,
with reasons
(n =)

Included

Studies included in
qualitative synthesis
(n =)

Studies included in
quantitative synthesis
(meta-analysis)
(n =)

FIGURE 11.4 PRISMA flow diagram.[19]

CONCLUSION

Overall, when responding to questions from clinicians about patient-specific instances, effective and efficient research, analysis, and use of EBP/medicine are all extremely important tools to have. Use of the modified systematic approach to answering drug information and medical-related questions is a commonly employed process that yields positive results. Development of a proper searching strategy will yield quality resources and data. Results should be validated and verified in more than one source, as various references may be out of date or contain different information. Correct analysis and synthesis of gathered material is also necessary, along with finding and reviewing strong EBP (e.g., RCTs, systematic reviews) when offering recommendations to practitioners. Finally, clear communication of the answer, as well as supporting information, is essential for the pharmacist to provide to the end user for ultimate application to the patient.

PRACTICE EXERCISE

Sarah French, MD (Internal Medicine) calls the Drug Information Center and asks, "What is the recommended dose of nitrofurantoin for urinary tract infections (UTI)?"

1. What would be some background questions to ask Dr. French?
   Age and weight of patient?
   Allergies to medications?
   Current serum creatinine value?
   Other medical comorbidities?
   What is the nature of the UTI (e.g., complicated, uncomplicated)?
   Are there any cultures available?
   Is this a new UTI or recurrent?
   Is the patient currently in the hospital?
   Based on the questions asked, Dr. French indicates that this is a 64-year-old female (80 kg) with end-stage liver disease and acute kidney injury. Her most recent serum creatinine measurement is 3.1 mg/dL, and this is the patient's first UTI (i.e., uncomplicated, mild symptoms with cultures pending). She is currently being treated as an outpatient, and she had a mild skin reaction to Bactrim after being treated for a previous infection.

2. How would you classify this request?
   This would most likely be classified as a therapeutic consult, as Dr. French is asking about a specific patient with a particular set of circumstances. It may also be helpful to get the patient's medical record number, as this would allow direct access to the patient's chart for any new lab values or microbiology results.

3. What is the true informational need/question?
   The original question asked was regarding the recommended dose of nitrofurantoin to treat a UTI. However, the patient has other comorbidities that might influence the overall recommendation for using nitrofurantoin in this patient. Therefore, the true informational need might be more related to how to appropriately treat a UTI in a patient with liver and kidney dysfunction.

4. What would be an appropriate searching strategy to find this information?
   According to the modified systematic approach, a broad to more specific search would be necessary starting with tertiary references (e.g., books, compendiums, online references), followed by more precise searches in secondary databases (e.g., PubMed, Medline). This secondary database search may result in case reports, guidelines, or published studies for this particular patient population (i.e., UTIs in patients with liver/kidney dysfunction).
   First, it would be imperative to estimate the patient's creatinine clearance (CrCl) given her increased serum creatinine measurement. Using the Cockcroft-Gault equation, the CrCl estimation is approximately 23 mL/minute based on the patient's most recent labs. After retrieving information from tertiary sources such as the package insert (via DailyMed), Facts and Comparisons eAnswers, and Micromedex, nitrofurantoin is contraindicated in patients with a CrCl less than 60 mL/min. Therefore, the answer to the original question is that Dr. French would not want to use nitrofurantoin in this patient. In addition, updated Beers Criteria (2015) recommends avoiding use in geriatric patients older than 65 years of age with a CrCl of less than 30 mL/min. Although this patient is 64, it could be assumed that the patient is close enough to also warrant this recommendation, especially as her renal function is so poor.
   At this point, it may be helpful to consult a pharmacotherapy text (e.g., Dipiro's Pharmacotherapy) to get an overview of the treatment of complicated and uncomplicated UTIs. In addition, review articles from major publications (e.g., JAMA, New England Journal of Medicine) may be more up-to-date than printed references.
   Turning to secondary databases next, the use of major MeSH terms in PubMed (e.g., urinary tract infections, renal insufficiency) along with subheadings for "drug therapy" or "complications" may help limit the number of articles retrieved. Search limits in secondary databases could also be used to gather recommendations and guidelines for UTI therapy published within the last 5 years, for example.

5. Perform evaluation, analysis, and synthesis of gathered information
   Based on the information collected for treating uncomplicated/complicated UTIs, it seems that trimethoprim (100 mg PO every 18 h × 3 days [adjusted for renal impairment]), ciprofloxacin (250 mg PO every 18 h × 3 days [adjusted for renal impairment]), and fosfomycin (3 g × 1 dose [no dosing adjustment necessary]) are the current options available. Sulfamethoxazole/trimethoprim is not an option due to the patient having a previous allergy/reaction to Bactrim.

6. Formulate and communicate response
   Using clinical judgment, it may be best to use trimethoprim in this patient initially. Ciprofloxacin resistance is an issue to be considered, as well as the potential for altered mental status when used in geriatric patients. Although fosfomycin is an attractive option due to its one-time dosing, it is usually reserved for resistant UTIs, and it is very expensive. Trimethoprim offers daily (alternative) dosing for 3 days and is relatively cheap. When the results of the urinary cultures are available, therapy can be altered if necessary.

It would be best to begin the answer by restating the clinical question being asked, followed by a specific recommendation to use trimethoprim. This information can be supported by the tertiary and/or primary literature found, as well as providing pertinent data for not using other standard treatments in this particular patient (e.g., contraindicated, drug allergies). Finally, some helpful monitoring parameters should be offered to help the patient determine whether or not the treatment is working. For example, if the urinary discomfort does not subside within 2 days, the patient should follow up with the physician and another medication may need to be tried.

7. Conduct follow-up and provide documentation

If possible, it would be a good idea to get the patients' medical record number or encounter number for their outpatient visit. This way, follow-up could be conducted to view the microbiology results for the patient's urinalysis. At that time, the physician could be called to discuss any changes in therapy needed (i.e., switch to ciprofloxacin or fosfomycin).

REFERENCES

1. Sackett DL, Rosenberg WM, Gray JA, Haynes RB, Richardson WS. Evidence based medicine: what it is and what it isn't. *BMJ Clin Res Ed.* 1996;312(7023):71−72.
2. Sackett D, Strauss S, Richardson W. *Evidence-based Medicine : How to Practice and Teach EBM.* 2nd ed. Edinburgh, Scotland, UK: Churchill Livingstone. 2000.
3. Eddy DM. Evidence-based medicine: a unified approach. *Health Aff (Project Hope).* 2005;24(1):9−17.
4. Sauve S, Lee HN, Meade MO. The critically appraised topic: a practical approach to learning critical appraisal. *Ann R Soc Phys Surg Can.* 1995;28:396−398.
5. Centre for Evidence-Based Medicine. *CATMaker and EBM Calculators - CEBM;* 2017. http://www.cebm.net/blog/2014/06/09/catmaker-ebm-calculators.
6. Watanabe AS, McCart G, Shimomura S, Kayser S. Systematic approach to drug information requests. *Am J Health Syst Pharm.* 1975;32(12):1282−1285.
7. Calis KA, Sheehan AH. Formulating effective responses and recommendations: a structured approach. In: Malone PM, Kier KL, Stanovich JE, Malone MJ, eds. *Drug Information: A Guide for Pharmacists, 5e.* New York, NY: McGraw-Hill Education; 2013.
8. Kirkwood CF, Kier KL. Modified systematic approach to answering questions. In: Malone PM, Kier KL, Stanovich JE, eds. *Drug Information: A Guide for Pharmacists.* 5th ed. New York, NY: McGraw-Hill Education; 2006:29−37.
9. Host TRKCF. Computer-assisted instruction for responding to drug information requests. In: *Paper Presented at: 22nd Annual ASHP Midyear Clinical Meeting; December 1997; Atlanta, GA.* 1997.
10. Brown JN, Choy CK. The systematic approach to responding to drug information requests. In: Gabay M, ed. *The Clinical Practice of Drug Information.* 1st ed. Burlington, MA: Jones & Bartlett Learning; 2016:11−30.
11. Health Literacy Innovations LLC. National Survey of Medicaid Guidelines for Health Literacy.
12. Centers for Disease Control and Prevention. *Health Literacy: Accurate, Accessible and Actionable Health Information for All;* 2017. https://www.cdc.gov/healthliteracy/index.html.
13. Shields KM, Blythe E. Drug information resources. In: Malone PM, Kier KL, Stanovich JE, Malone MJ, eds. *Drug Information: A Guide for Pharmacists.* 5th ed. New York, NY: McGraw-Hill Education; 2013.
14. Petrisor B, Bhandari M. The hierarchy of evidence: levels and grades of recommendation. *Indian J Orthop.* 2007;41(1):11−15.
15. Patrias K. In: Wendling D, ed. *Citing Medicine.* 2nd ed; 2007. https://www.ncbi.nlm.nih.gov/books/NBK7256.
16. Cochrane Collaboration. *About Cochrane Reviews: What Is a Systematic Review? Cochrane Library Website;* 2018. http://www.cochranelibrary.com/about/about-cochrane-systematic-reviews.html.
17. Grant MJ, Booth A. A typology of reviews: an analysis of 14 review types and associated methodologies. *Health Info Libr J.* June 2009;26(2):91−108.
18. Box 2.3.b: Timeline for a Cochrane review. In: Higgins JPT, Green S, eds. *Cochrane Handbook for Systematic Reviews of Interventions Version 5.1.0. The Cochrane Collaboration;* 2018 [updated March 2011]. Available from: http://handbook-5-1.cochrane.org.
19. Moher D, Liberati A, Tetzlaff J, Altman DG. PRISMA Group. Preferred reporting items for systematic reviews and meta-analyses: the PRISMA statement. *PLoS Med.* July 21, 2009;6(7):e1000097.
20. Centre for Reviews and Dissemination. University of York. *Register a Review.* PROSPERO; 2018. Available from: https://www.crd.york.ac.uk/prospero.
21. Cochrane Collaboration. *Proposing and Registering New Cochrane Reviews.* Cochrane Community; 2018. Available from: http://community.cochrane.org/review-production/production-resources/proposing-and-registering-new-cochrane-reviews.
22. Stewart L, Moher D, Shekelle P. Why prospective registration of systematic reviews makes sense. *Syst Rev.* 2012;1:7.
23. *Clarivate Analytics. EndNote.* 2018. http://www.endnote.com.
24. *ProQuest. RefWorks.* 2018. https://refworks.proquest.com.
25. *The Cochrane Collaboration. RevMan 5;* 2018. http://community.cochrane.org/tools/review-production-tools/revman-5.
26. Wallace B, Small K, Brodley C, Lau J, Trikalinos T. Deploying an interactive machine learning system in an evidence-based practice center: abstrackr. In: *Proc. of the ACM International Health Informatics Symposium (IHI).* 2012:819−824.
27. *Windows. Microsoft Excel.* 2018. https://products.office.com/en-us/excel.
28. Higgins JPT, Green S, eds. *Assessing risk of bias in included studies. In: Cochrane Handbook for Systematic Reviews of Interventions Version 5.1.0. The Cochrane Collaboration.* 2018 [updated March 2011]. Available from: http://handbook-5-1.cochrane.org.

Chapter 12

Clinical Guidelines for Decision-Making

Elangovan Gajraj and Leeza Osipenko
NICE Scientific Advice, NICE, London, United Kingdom

Learning Objectives:

Objective 12.1   Overview the rationale for the use of clinical guidelines.
Objective 12.2   Set the framework for the development of a clinical guideline.
Objective 12.3   Introduce the methodology of clinical guideline development.
Objective 12.4   Explain the process of implementation and update of a clinical guideline.

OBJECTIVE 12.1. OVERVIEW THE RATIONALE FOR THE USE OF CLINICAL GUIDELINES

The National Academy of Medicine previously known as Institute of Medicine defines clinical practice guidelines as *"statements that include recommendations, intended to optimize patient care, that are informed by a systematic review of evidence and an assessment of the benefits and harms of alternative care options."*[1] Clinical guidelines recommend how healthcare professionals should care for people with specific conditions. The guidelines can cover any aspect of a condition and may include recommendations for: providing information and advice, prevention, diagnosis, treatment, and longer-term management.[2]

NICE guidelines make evidence-based recommendations on a wide range of topics, from preventing and managing specific conditions, improving health, and managing medicines in different settings, to providing social care and support to adults and children, and planning broader services and interventions to improve the health of communities.

Guideline recommendations set out:

- the care and services that are suitable for most people with a specific condition or need

- the care and services suitable for particular populations, groups or people in particular circumstances or settings

- ways to promote and protect good health or prevent ill health

- the configuration and provision of health and social care services, and/or

- how national and local public sector organisations and partnerships can improve the quality of care and services

Clinical Pharmacy Education, Practice and Research. https://doi.org/10.1016/B978-0-12-814276-9.00012-X

Number of MI publications in Pubmed

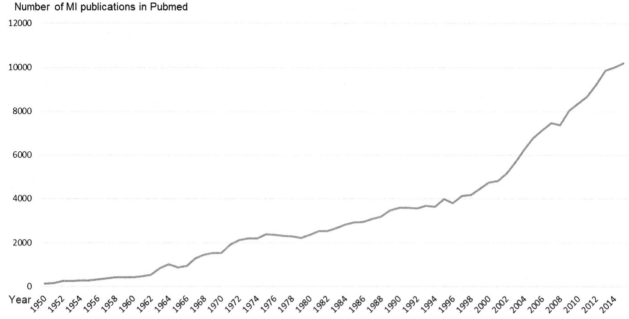

FIGURE 12.1 Number of publications on myocardial infarction on Pubmed.

Clinical practice based on the best available evidence improves the quality of healthcare and results in optimal outcomes for patients. Busy clinicians may be overwhelmed by the quantity of new research. For example, if a diligent cardiologist wanted to keep herself informed of the latest research on myocardial infarction in 1950, she would have to read 150 articles that year. By 2015, she would need to read well over 10,000 articles (see Fig. 12.1). Clearly, this is an impossible task. The conclusions drawn from an individual study may often contradict those resulting from another, oftentimes, without an obvious explanation for the discrepancy. When faced with making a specific clinical decision for a particular patient, the suitability of using the available evidence to inform that decision may not be straightforward to judge.

Developing guidelines helps inform clinical practice by making recommendations based on the totality of the most up-to-date evidence. By addressing a series of clinically relevant questions, the research is translated into information that informs specific clinical decisions. Directing the optimal use of healthcare resources (e.g., labor, diagnostics, hospital beds, drugs) through the use of guidelines improves efficiency. Efficiency, in this sense, means the use of limited healthcare resources in a way that would result in the maximum production of health, however, defined. By standardizing care across patients in different care settings and hospitals across the health system, the guidelines also ensure equity, here defined as equivalent care for equivalent patients.

In addition to the usual arguments underpinning the development of guidelines—quality, efficiency, and equity—it has been argued that "*the spread of guidelines represents a new regulation of medical care … Although the regulation of quality has traditionally been based on the standardization of professional credentials, since the 1960s it has intensified and been supplemented by efforts to standardize the use of medical procedures. The proliferation of collectively produced guidelines since the 1980s represents a growing effort to bring order and coherence to a rapidly expanding and heterogeneous medical domain.*"[3]

Guidelines are an aid to clinical decision-making and not intended to infringe on the discretion of the clinician in treating an individual patient. By their nature, guidelines are summaries of the evidence that will be applicable to most patients but will not cover every patient or clinical situation that a clinician may deal with. Therefore, clinicians are expected to rely on their own judgment when using guidelines to inform decisions made for an individual patient. However, it would be expected that there is a clear justification when the management of a patient deviates from best practice as laid out in a guideline. Guidelines are usually produced by professional bodies, governmental agencies, national, nongovernment agencies, and academic institutions within particular national jurisdiction, though transnational cooperation on guideline production is common.

OBJECTIVE 12.2. SET THE FRAMEWORK FOR THE DEVELOPMENT OF A CLINICAL GUIDELINE

Before Developing a Guideline

Before deciding to initiate the development of a clinical guideline, it would be sensible to assess the need for it. This involves the specification of a clinical problem or a health system issue that can be addressed by a guideline. An objective search of important databases and key clinical evidence sources for relevant existing guidelines should be performed to ensure that no currently available guideline meets the requirements. The involvement of experts in assessing the suitability of an existing guideline to inform clinical practice will allow a judgment to be formed on whether any guidelines identified are relevant to the context to which they will be applied. To aid the process, the quality of existing guidelines can be assessed using an instrument such as AGREE.[4] Guidelines developed in closely related health system contexts, for patients that are similar, will usually be transferable, possibly with some adaptation. This is a judgment that has to be made on a case-by-case basis. When guidelines are adapted, a clear description of guideline adaptation methods is recommended.[5]

> The AGREE instrument is a tool that assesses the methodological rigour and transparency in which a guideline is developed. It is a framework to:
>
> 1. assess the quality of guidelines;
>
> 2. provide a methodological strategy for the development of guidelines; and
>
> 3. inform what information and how information ought to be reported in guidelines

The users of the future guidance should be identified in advance to ensure that they are closely involved in the development process. This ensures that there is a "buy-in" to the final product by people who will be expected to implement the guideline or whose care will be impacted by the recommendations. Equally important, the people who will implement the guideline will also possess the expertise that is required to interpret the evidence and use clinical judgment in developing the guideline, whether from the perspective of a clinician, patient, or health system administrator. Lastly, before starting, it would be wise to consider in advance, the methods and channels that will be used to disseminate the guideline, with some early consideration given to the monitoring of uptake, as well as any training that will be required for implementation by end users. In addition, before commencing the guideline development, a project plan should be put together that specifies timelines and project costs.

Prioritization

It is usually not possible, due to resource constraints, or necessary to create a guideline for every condition. Efforts should be directed to developing guidelines which can have the greatest impact. The process and criteria for selecting and prioritizing topics should be transparent. Some considerations for the prioritization of topics for guideline development include the following:

- High prevalence disease or high use medical intervention
- High associated cost

- Effects on premature mortality and avoidable morbidity
- Evidence that medical care can make a difference in outcomes
- Knowledge of current variations in practice or that practice does not match some known practice parameters
- No existing guidelines of good quality to inform practice
- An expectation that a recommendation, when implemented, will improve health outcomes, reduce inequities, or unnecessary costs
- Implementation of a guideline will not exhaustively use available resources, and barriers to change are not likely to be so high that they cannot be overcome.[6,7]

> Topics on health care are referred to NICE by the NHS. The Department of Health refers topics on public health and social care. The Department of Education can also refer social care guidelines topics.
>
> A decision to select a topic is informed by:
>
> - whether there is existing NICE-accredited guidance on which to base a quality standard that encompasses the whole of the topic
> - the priority given to the topic by commissioners and professional organisations, and organisations for people using services, their families and carers.

To avoid the selection of topics being influenced by stakeholders with a particular interest, the establishment of a process to agree on priorities will be required. The process should specify in advance who will take responsibility for the selection of guideline topics (e.g., the guideline producing organization, policy-makers, health authorities). In practice, it would be sensible to ensure that all relevant stakeholders are involved in the decision and agree with proceeding to guideline development. Criteria for establishing priorities should be applied using a systematic and transparent process, which includes consultation with stakeholders.

Who Is Involved?

A guideline development group should consist of a diverse range of stakeholders who are relevant to the topic. In particular, it is important to not only involve professionals with expertise in the topic but also the end users of guidance who will be responsible for its implementation, as well as patients on whom the guidance will impact. Individuals and groups involved in guideline development should have the range of technical skills that will be required, such as information retrieval, systematic reviewing, health economics, group facilitation, project management, writing, and editing. Careful consideration should be given to the appointment of the Chair of the committee who is responsible for leading and facilitating collaboration between group members and ensuring participation of less vocal members while avoiding imposing personal opinions. As group members will come from a variety of professional and nonprofessional backgrounds, training to understand the technical aspects of guideline development and support should be offered to optimize their ability to participate. Each participant should have a clear idea of the timelines and tasks for their participation, with detailed instructions on the activities, roles, and responsibilities of the group.

It is critical to consider in advance how patients will be involved in the development of guidelines, as the impact of the recommendations will be most keenly felt by them. Involvement of patients can consist of the following:

- incorporating individual patients or patient advocates in guideline development groups;
- a "one off" meeting with patients;
- a series of workshops with patients;
- eliciting the perspective of patients and the public as part of a larger stakeholder input exercise.[7]

Managing Conflict of Interests

Once group members are nominated, any potential conflicts of interests should be identified and addressed. Conflicts of interests of individual group members can cast doubt on the recommendations in the guideline if it is believed that these were the results of interests of, and pressures on, group members, rather than impartially arrived at through the consideration of evidence. Each member of a guideline development group should make a full declaration of competing interests, which should be recorded and addressed. The disclosure should include financial and nonfinancial conflicts of interest, and the methods for resolution of conflicts should be made explicit. A conflict of interest may require the recusal of a member from specific decisions that bring the conflict into operation.

In addition to the individual guideline group members, it is also essential to ensure that the views of the funding body have not influenced the content of the guideline. A guideline should disclose financial support for the development of both the evidence review and the guideline itself.

Key principles for developing guidelines

NICE develops guidelines according to the following core principles:

- Guidance is based on the best available evidence of what works, and what it costs.

- Guidance is developed by independent and unbiased Committees of experts.

- All our Committees include at least 2 lay members (people with personal experience of using health or care services, or from a community affected by the guideline).

- Regular consultation allows organisations and individuals to comment on our recommendations.

- Once published, all NICE guidance is regularly checked, and updated in light of new evidence if necessary.

- We are committed to advancing equality of opportunity and ensuring that the social value judgements we make reflect the values of society.

- We ensure that our processes, methods and policies remain up-to-date.

OBJECTIVE 12.3. INTRODUCE THE METHODOLOGY OF CLINICAL GUIDELINE DEVELOPMENT

Developing a Guideline

The development of a guideline can be broken down into a series of tasks. Guideline development from different organizations may follow a different set of tasks chosen from an exhaustive menu.[5] The individual steps involved in guideline production and a comparison of international guideline development programs vary, but they usually include a core set of activities that can be considered essential to guideline development.[8] A clear process that specifies which of the tasks are included in guideline production should be decided in advance. The guideline development process at National Institute for Health and Care Excellence (NICE) is presented in Fig. 12.2.

Definition and Purpose of Scope

Before embarking on the guideline development, the overall objective(s) of the guideline should be described. This will include the specific health questions the guideline will cover, as well as the population (e.g., patients, public) to whom the guideline is meant to apply. The framework should describe the epidemiology of the disease or condition, the aspects of care, and the settings to be covered by the guideline.[9] The scope of a guideline may include primary or secondary care, prevention, diagnosis, and management. The scope sets the boundaries for what the guideline will make recommendations

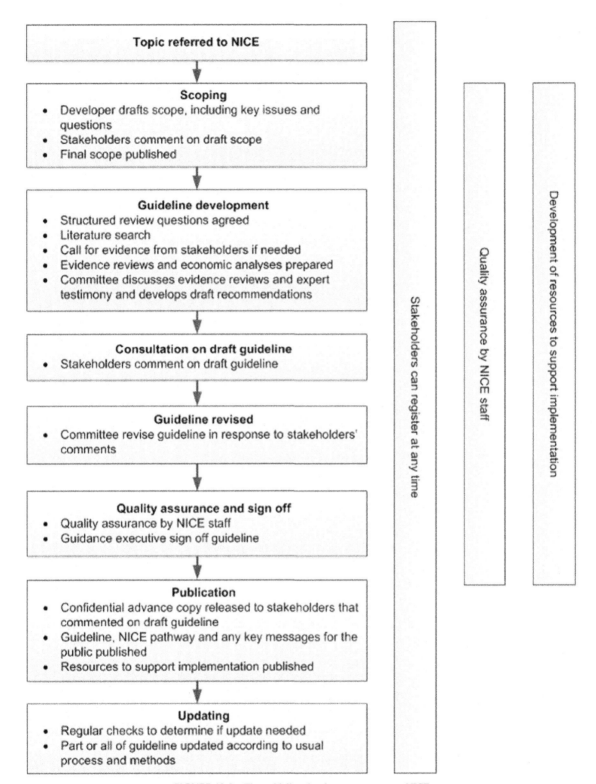

FIGURE 12.2   The guideline development process at NICE.

on and acts as a guide to subsequent steps that are part of the development process. It will also set the limits on the recommendations that will form the output of the development process. Developing the scope will require its own sub-process, which will involve drafting and discussing a scope, consulting on it, and finalizing the scope based on comments received during consultation. Scoping is an important process, as it will determine the boundaries of the guideline, including relevant clinical questions, evidence search, and recommendations.

Purpose of the scope

The scope sets boundaries that ensure the work stays within the referral. The scope:

- defines the population(s) and setting(s) that will and will not be covered
- describes what the guideline will consider
- identifies the key issues and lists the key questions that will be considered
- describes the economic perspective(s) to be used.

The scope will usually include:

- a brief description of the guideline topic
- a brief overview of the context (current policy and practice) in which the guideline will be developed
- a summary of why the guideline is needed and where it will add value
- how the guideline will link to other NICE recommendations and quality standards
- potential equality issues
- health inequalities associated with socioeconomic factors and with inequities in access for certain groups to healthcare and social care, and opportunities to improve health.

Gathering Evidence

Guideline development involves both a technical process (i.e., systematic reviews of relevant evidence) and a social process (i.e., interpretation of the results of the systematic review and development of recommendations).[7]

Developing Clinical Questions

The first step is to develop a series of clinical questions on which guidance will be produced. Within a large disease area, specific questions that relate to clinical practice help focus the search for evidence and provide guidance. For example, the NICE clinical guideline on hypertension in adults asks a series of questions on the management of hypertension such as, "*In adults with primary hypertension, which is the most clinically and cost-effective anti-hypertensive monotherapy (ACEi vs ARB) for first-line treatment, and does this vary with age and ethnicity?*," and, "*In adults with primary hypertension, which is the most clinically and cost-effective combination of anti-hypertensives (A + C or A + D) for second-line treatment, and does this vary with age and ethnicity?*"[10]

At NICE, for each question, the framework is defined using PICO.

> **The PICO framework**
>
> **Population**: Which population should the guideline cover? How can it be best described? Are there subgroups that need to be considered?
>
> **Intervention**: Which intervention, treatment or approach should be used?
>
> **Comparators**: Are there alternative(s) to the intervention being considered in established clinical practice?
>
> **Outcome**: Which outcomes should be considered to assess how well the intervention is working? What is really important for people using services?

Systematic Search for Evidence

Once the review questions are developed, a systematic strategy is used to search for evidence. Systematic searches specify the parameters of the evidence that is being sought, for example, based on the PICO table, but also in terms of the types of study designs, specifying inclusion and exclusion criteria or any other limitations that are relevant. They form the basis of an electronic search of important bibliographic databases using sensitive keywords. Systematic methods must be clearly documented so that they can be rerun by other investigators and the results reproduced. A systematic review will require specialized skills in determining search terms, conducting the search in databases, filtering the results of the search according to predefined criteria, and summarizing and presenting the outcomes.

> **Systematic review**
>
> A review that summarises the evidence on a clearly formulated review question according to a predefined protocol, using systematic and explicit methods to identify, select and appraise relevant studies, and to extract, analyse, collate and report their findings.
>
> **Meta-analysis**
>
> The use of statistical techniques in a systematic review to integrate the results of several studies.
>
> For more details on systematic review and meta-analysis, refer to the Cochrane handbook.

Appraising Identified Research Evidence

Once relevant publications are identified using the search strategy, they need to be appraised for quality and relevance using objective instruments. This allows to clearly describe the strengths and limitations of the body of evidence. NICE has adopted the GRADE approach.[11] This is a validated assessment tool to evaluate the quality of evidence underpinning guideline recommendations. It is used to determine the strength of the recommendations in the guideline. Excluding or including studies that are deemed to be of poor quality, and then looking at the impact on the overall decisions, serves as a sensitivity analysis on the robustness of the conclusions drawn from the evidence and the recommendations.

The GRADE approach to assessing the quality of evidence for intervention studies

- study limitations (risk of bias) – the internal validity of the evidence

- inconsistency – the heterogeneity or variability in the estimates of treatment effect across studies

- indirectness – the degree of differences between the population, intervention, comparator for the intervention and outcome of interest across studies

- imprecision (random error) – the extent to which confidence in the effect estimate is adequate to support a particular decision

- publication bias – the degree of selective publication of studies.

From Evidence to Recommendations

Group decision-making essentially involves three phases: orientation (defining the problem), evaluation (discussion of decision alternatives), and control (deciding which of the alternatives is to prevail).[7]

Ideally, the guidelines group will reach its recommendations through consensus. However, as this situation may not materialize in every case, alternate methods to reach an agreement must be planned for. One option is the use of objective consensus development techniques such as the Delphi method, Nominal Group technique, or more simply as at NICE, by majority voting. Such methods should be clearly established and communicated to group members before commencing on developing recommendations. A savvy Chair of the group, by facilitating decisions and reducing areas of divergence, is an essential ingredient for reaching consensual decisions and avoiding conflict.

When making recommendations, the group will need to be mindful of the future resource implications for implementation of the proposed recommendations. This may be done through the means of explicit incorporation of considerations of cost-effectiveness, as well as affordability and resource implications in the guideline development process. In this case, specific recommendations within the guideline relating to interventions are subject to additional cost-effectiveness analysis before a decision is made to include a specific recommendation in the guideline. At NICE, the need for an economic evaluation depends on the potential overall expected benefit and resource implications of intervention, both for individual people and the population as a whole, and the degree of uncertainty in the economic evidence review and the likelihood that economic analysis will clarify matters. The economic evaluation may not be warranted when:

- clinical efficacy of an intervention is not established
- it is clear that either one of the benefits or costs of the intervention outweighs the other
- when existing cost-effectiveness analysis is suitable for decision-making
- when the costs, benefits, or budget impact is small
- when the evidence or methodology is not suitable for the conduct of an analysis.

When conducting a cost-effectiveness analysis, a clear reference case will be required as a framework to ensure consistency between decisions. At NICE, the reference case used is the same as that specified for appraisals of individual health technologies. In addition, recommendations made through other programs at NICE, based on the assessment of cost-effectiveness, will be incorporated into guidelines to maintain consistency between recommendations across the Institute.

Recommendations in a guideline do not operate within a value-free environment. Values, the relative importance or consequences of a decision (e.g., outcomes relating to benefits, harms, burden, and costs), often influence every recommendation in ways that may not be transparent. Ethical considerations, concepts that determine what is right, also play a role.[12] It is, therefore, useful to integrate such values into guideline recommendations in an explicit fashion. The values used in making recommendations should reflect those of the people affected and whose care will be impacted by the guideline. Judgments should be explicit and should be informed by input from those affected (e.g., citizens, patients, clinicians, policy-makers).

The guideline development group uses the expertise of its members to interpret the available evidence to make recommendations that are actionable by clinicians within the health service. The group needs to take into consideration the health benefits, harms, risks, costs, and values in making recommendations. The wording of the recommendation should make explicit the link to the evidence underpinning it. Recommendations should be worded in clear and unambiguous language as to what action is to be undertaken, who undertakes it, and in what circumstances. Where there is a set of options for management of a condition, these should be laid out as options, with an order of preference, if one exists.

For each recommendation, the guideline should use a rating system that comments on the quality and reliability of the evidence, as well as the strength of the recommendation. The grading of evidence for each recommendation can be based on any validated score for classifying the strength of evidence. Lastly, a series of research recommendations identifying gaps in the available evidence to inform the guideline, which can act as a spur to guide to further research, should be included as part of the document. The research focused on evidence gaps can help inform any further updates or iterations of the guideline. This approach can help plug gaps in knowledge relating to the optimal management of patients and use of interventions and healthcare resources.

Examples of standardised terms for describing the strength of the evidence

No evidence 'No evidence was found from English-language trials published since 1990...'

Weak evidence 'There was weak evidence from 1 (−) RCT'.

Moderate evidence 'There was moderate evidence from 2 (+) controlled before and after studies'.

Strong evidence 'There was strong evidence from 2 (++) controlled before and after studies and 1 (+) RCT'.

Inconsistent evidence. Further commentary may be needed on the variability of findings in different studies. For example, when the results of (++) or (+) quality studies do not agree.

Consultations

Following the development of draft guidelines, these should be consulted on with all stakeholders. In addition, at NICE, a public consultation is undertaken. NICE guidelines are also subject to an external peer review by experts, much as would be expected with any scientific publication. Following consultation, the guideline group should meet to consider the comments received and make any amendments to the guideline as it sees fit. The guideline recommendations are then finalized for publication. At NICE, in an additional step, the guideline is signed-off by senior management before release. This acts as a final check on ensuring that guidelines are in keeping with the Institute's wider remit and the need to meet legal obligations, as well as to help identify controversial recommendations that might elicit a negative response once the public and clinical community are made aware.

Publishing

To facilitate adoption, a guideline should be disseminated widely through multiple channels. Although the use of the Internet would nowadays be considered essential, some regions may require a printed version of the guidance. At NICE, the guideline in its entirety, including the evidence underpinning it, is available in digital format on the NICE website. Electronic documents also include intermediate steps of development that allow the public to follow the various stages of development. Guidelines may need to be simplified and published in a format that is accessible to the lay audience. Production of a shorter version of the guideline limited to key recommendations and actions should be considered.

OBJECTIVE 12.4. EXPLAIN THE PROCESS OF IMPLEMENTATION AND UPDATE OF A CLINICAL GUIDELINE

Implementation

The release of a guideline does not automatically guarantee that its recommendations are put into practice. Firstly, there needs to be a plan for the guideline to be advertised and for people who are working within the health service to be made aware of its existence. The guideline should also provide advice and tools on how the recommendations can be put into practice, with some consideration given to barriers to implementation and suggestions for how these can be overcome. Resources that will aid in the implementation of a guideline include educational tools such as flowcharts and algorithms. A significant barrier to implementation is usually the resource impact of the recommendations. Even when these show cost savings in the long term, implementation of recommendations usually carries an immediate cost, such as when new services need to be developed and new people employed. The use of budget impact and budgeting tools may help managers adequately plan for the financial impact of guideline recommendations.

When releasing a guideline, planning for the monitoring of uptake and impact of the guideline for patient and system outcomes should be incorporated. The development and release of clinical audit and evaluation criteria to accompany the guideline could aid in the monitoring of guideline implementation. Data collection tools, such as audit templates, could accompany the guideline. Separately, additional monitoring for uptake, implementation, and impact of guidelines will help justify the existence of a guideline program. The feedback into the effectiveness of the existing program will help implement necessary changes to the guideline development processes and improve impact.

Reviewing and Updating Guidelines

A guideline is based on evidence collected that is retrospective at the point of the search. Almost from the point of its publication, the evidence on which it is based is out-of-date, as the relentless accumulation of new evidence proceeds. Therefore, a guideline development program should include a process for the review and update of guidelines. Each guideline should have an expiration date, at which point a clearly defined process will determine the requirement for updating recommendations based on new evidence that has become available subsequent to the guideline publication. A guideline may need to be updated as the evidence on the benefits and harms of interventions changes, new interventions become available, or changes occur in the available healthcare resources, health system priorities, or outcomes and values placed on outcomes.

At NICE, the need for updating a guideline is reviewed every 2 years. At 2, 6, and 10 years after a guideline is published, the review is limited to the defined scope, and a search is conducted to identify new evidence. At 4 and 8 years after guideline publication, the areas covered by the guideline, but not within the scope, are also addressed. Following a review, a decision may be taken not to update a guideline based on the lack of new evidence, with a plan to review the evidence at a further time point. When no new evidence is anticipated in the future, the guideline may be moved to a static list, where no further reviews of new evidence or updates are anticipated. However, it is more likely that the guideline will need to be updated. This can be a full update within the scope of the original guideline or a new scope can be developed highlighting new relevant areas which were not within the remit of the original scope. A new scope may also be developed where certain areas are no longer relevant or prioritized. Further outcomes of a review may be a partial update of the guideline, limited to defined sections or recommendations, when the new evidence identified will not require amendments to the whole guideline. A partial update may require a new scope or it can be based on the original scope. Lastly, a guideline may be "refreshed" by adding amendments to the wording of recommendations reflecting the current practice context and, sometimes, to meet current editorial standards.

Key elements of the process for checking whether a published guideline needs updating	
Time since publication	**Key elements of the process**
2 years 6 years 10 years	• Limited to scope of published guideline • Limited evidence review and summary of new evidence • Intelligence gathering from questionnaires, external enquiries, related NICE guidance, updated national policy, medicines licensing information and information on implementation • No consultation
4 years 8 years	• Also considers key areas within the referral of the guideline, but outside the scope of the published guideline • Literature search and summary of new evidence • Intelligence gathering from questionnaires, external enquiries, related NICE guidance, updated national policy, medicines licensing information and information on implementation • Consultation only when 'no update' considered

CONCLUSION

Clinical guidelines are widely used as a means of improving the quality of healthcare delivery. Having a wide range of stakeholders participating in guideline development will improve their relevance and uptake. In particular, care must be taken to include patients in guideline development groups. The first step in creating a guideline is to develop a scope and define specific clinical questions that will be addressed. Guidelines should be informed by a systematic search for evidence. Guideline development groups should have clear processes for reaching consensus on recommendations. Recommendations should be graded according to the strength of the evidence underpinning them. A wide consultation on draft recommendations should be conducted before publication. Guidelines should be accompanied by tools that help end users implement recommendations. Regular reviews and updates of the guideline will ensure that they remain relevant and useful.

REFERENCES

1. Institute of Medicine (US) Committee on Standards for Developing Trustworthy Clinical Practice Guidelines. In: Graham R, Mancher M, Miller Wolman D, et al., eds. *Clinical Practice Guidelines We Can Trust*. Washington (DC): National Academies Press (US); 2011. https://doi.org/10.17226/13058. Available from: https://www.ncbi.nlm.nih.gov/books/NBK209539/.
2. National Institute for Health and Care Excellence. *NICE Guidelines*; 2017. Available from: https://www.nice.org.uk/about/what-we-do/our-programmes/nice-guidance/nice-guidelines.
3. Weisz G, Cambrosio A, Keating P, Knaapen L, Schlich T, Tournay VJ. The emergence of clinical practice guidelines. *Milbank Q*. 2007;85(4):691−727.

4. Brouwers MC, Kho ME, Browman GP, et al. AGREE II: advancing guideline development, reporting and evaluation in health care. *Can Med Assoc J.* 2010;182(18):E839−E842. https://doi.org/10.1503/cmaj.090449.

5. Ansari S, Rashidian A. Guidelines for guidelines: are they up to the task? A comparative assessment of clinical practice guideline development handbooks. In: Zhang H, ed. *PLoS One.* 2012;7(11):e49864. https://doi.org/10.1371/journal.pone.0049864.

6. Oxman AD, Fretheim A, Schünemann HJ, SURE. Improving the use of research evidence in guideline development: introduction. *Health Res Pol Syst.* 2006;4:12. https://doi.org/10.1186/1478-4505-4-12.

7. Eccles MP, Grimshaw JM, Shekelle P, Schünemann HJ, Woolf S. Developing clinical practice guidelines: target audiences, identifying topics for guidelines, guideline group composition and functioning and conflicts of interest. *Implement Sci.* 2012;7:60. https://doi.org/10.1186/1748-5908-7-60.

8. Burgers JS, Grol R, Klazinga NS, Mäkelä M, Zaat J. AGREE Collaboration. Towards evidence-based clinical practice: an international survey of 18 clinical guideline programs. *Int J Qual Health Care.* 2003;15(1):31−45.

9. Woolf S, Schünemann HJ, Eccles MP, Grimshaw JM, Shekelle P. Developing clinical practice guidelines: types of evidence and outcomes; values and economics, synthesis, grading, and presentation and deriving recommendations. *Implement Sci.* 2012;7:61. https://doi.org/10.1186/1748-5908-7-61.

10. National Institute for Health and Care Excellence. *Hypertension in Adults: Diagnosis and Management, Clinical Guideline CG127.* NICE; August 2011. https://www.nice.org.uk/guidance/cg127.

11. Guyatt GH, Oxman AD, Vist GE, et al. GRADE: an emerging consensus on rating quality of evidence and strength of recommendations. *Br Med J.* 2008;336(7650):924−926. https://doi.org/10.1136/bmj.39489.470347.AD.

12. Schünemann HJ, Fretheim A, Oxman AD. Improving the use of research evidence in guideline development: 10. Integrating values and consumer involvement. *Health Res Pol Syst.* 2006;4:22. https://doi.org/10.1186/1478-4505-4-22.

FURTHER READING

A series of 16 reviews on aspects of guideline development have been prepared as background for advice from the WHO Advisory Committee on Health Research to WHO. The articles are available through open access from the Health Research Policy and Systems journal. The first in the series is

Improving the use of research evidence in guideline development: 1. Guidelines for guidelines. Holger J Schünemann, Atle Fretheim, and Andrew D Oxman. Health Research Policy and Systems. 2006;4:13. Available at: http://www.health-policy-systems.com/content/4/1/13.

Eccles and colleagues have reviewed the methods and procedures for guideline development in a series of three papers, available through open access. The first of these papers is

Developing clinical practice guidelines: target audiences, identifying topics for guidelines, guideline group composition, and functioning and conflicts of interest. Eccles et al. Implementation Science. 2012;7:60. Available at: http://www.implementationscience.com/content/7/1/60.

Chapter 13

Drug Information Training for Pharmacists

Dixon Thomas[1], Ivellise Costa de Sousa[2], David J. Woods[3], Ronald A. Herman[4] and Danial E. Baker[5]

[1]Gulf Medical University, Ajman, United Arab Emirates; [2]University Hospital Professor Edgard Santos, Salvador, Brazil; [3]University of Otago, Dunedin, New Zealand; [4]The University of Iowa, Iowa City, IA, United States; [5]Washington State University, Spokane, WA, United States

Learning Objectives:

Objective 13.1   Explain why pharmacists in any work setting require well-founded drug information skills.
Objective 13.2   Review drug information training strategies for pharmacy students.
Objective 13.3   Categorize drug information skills to be covered during training.
Objective 13.4   Plan a week-wise follow-up of learning objectives achieved in drug information training.

OBJECTIVE 13.1. EXPLAIN WHY PHARMACISTS IN ANY WORK SETTING REQUIRE WELL-FOUNDED DRUG INFORMATION SKILLS

Drug information is a service provided by pharmacists in their daily practice. Irrespective of the work settings, community, hospital, consulting, and clinical pharmacists provide drug information services. The level of drug information provided may vary, however. For example, community pharmacists may answer more simple drug-specific questions of their patients (e.g., dosing, generic availability). Hospital pharmacists may answer drug-specific questions (e.g., intravenous administration/compatibility), and pharmacists exclusive clinical practice may answer more patient-specific drug information questions (e.g., alternative therapy due to patient allergy). Drug information pharmacists who have specialized in operating and sustaining a drug information service may tend to answer more complex questions that need a thorough review of the literature. Answering these in-depth, complex questions requires additional time to assess and evaluate patient-specific information and conduct appraisal and analysis of the appropriate literature. The type of drug information training for such positions varies accordingly. To become a clinical specialist in a drug information center (e.g., in a challenging hospital environment), advanced residency training shall be required and may take one to 2 years. Pharmacists, who work as full-time drug/poison information specialists regionally (i.e., not restricted to a hospital), are also commonly contacted by healthcare professionals and the general public to answer drug information questions with varying degrees of complexity,[1] whereas others work for the pharmaceutical industry, health insurance companies, pharmacy benefit management companies, and governmental agencies. Some countries restrict drug information services to the public, determining that incomplete medical information without professional consultation might increase inappropriate self-medication. A consultation with pharmacists shall result in a proper understanding of the medication information.[2]

Pharmacists, being one of the most accessible healthcare professionals, are often approached by the public for their drug information needs. Pharmacists may also contribute to the management of minor ailments, guiding the use of over-the-counter (OTC) drugs and herbal products. They should also be prepared to counsel safe drug use to pregnant women, as well as children and the elderly.[3,4] According to the Consumer Healthcare Products Association website, 93% of US adults prefer to treat their minor ailments with OTC drugs before seeking professional care, and 85% of US parents do the same with their children.[5] OTC drugs allow consumers more accessibility. However, their use is not free from risk.

Drug interactions, cross-reactivity among drugs, toxicity, dosing errors, and continuation of therapy should be considered when counseling patients about their OTC medication use. The provision of accurate and helpful drug information by pharmacists is important, as consumers often forget to discuss their OTC drug use with other healthcare professionals. Identification and appropriate use of references ideally suited for these patient care issues are essential for the busy pharmacist to guarantee proper care of these patients with efficient use of time and resources.

Special attention has also been given to off-label drug use because off-label drug use has been a common practice but often is not supported by strong evidence.[6] Prescribers need to be informed about the availability of drugs for certain indications, as well as details of appropriate dosage regimens. Accepting information from the pharmaceutical company by prescribers shall affect prescribing quality.[7] Unbiased information provided by pharmacists will improve the practice. Informed practice leads to safer and cost-effective drugs use. Information about affordable treatment options reduces healthcare expenses. Consumers and nurses also need reliable information on proper administrations of drugs and how to monitor for adverse events. Drug information training helps pharmacists to promote rational drug use, decrease medication errors, and alleviate adverse effects.

In this era of improved collaborative practice, healthcare professionals share their knowledge and skills across services for the benefit of better patient outcomes. This multidisciplinary approach to patient care increases interactions between other healthcare professionals (e.g., doctors, nurses, dentists) and pharmacists resulting in increased drug information needs. All pharmacists should possess the basic drug information skills to meet the demand of their specific practice.[8]

Drug information skills and general pharmacotherapy knowledge are also useful on an administrative level. Drug information and hospital pharmacists take part in the development and maintenance of the hospital formulary system. Recommendations to include or remove a drug from the formulary need to be supported with sufficient drug information from the literature. The same skills are useful for the development of clinical guidelines within an institution, prior authorization programs, and other drug management programs. Quality assessment of how medications are being used can result in the development of treatment protocols or other guided use strategies for the medications evaluated. This medication use evaluation (MUE) utilizes current knowledge about pharmacotherapy and an assessment of how the medication is being used.

Participating in healthcare research requires drug information skills. Drug information skills equip professionals to conduct better literature searches and evaluations. Pharmacists with enhanced literature searching skills are in a better position to collect comprehensive information from the Internet, databases, and various article-retrieval systems. Critical literature appraisal skills needed to properly analyze and determine if a citation should be included in a research project. Pharmacists skilled in writing publications for various journal articles may contribute to a research team or project by better understanding the submission process and/or writing style for a particular journal. Because of a combination of healthcare and drug-specific knowledge, search and critical appraisal skills, and the writing and online journal article submission expertise, pharmacists are often preferred members of healthcare research teams. Literature evaluation and management skills help to elevate overall evidence-based practice and research.

OBJECTIVE 13.2. REVIEW DRUG INFORMATION TRAINING STRATEGIES FOR PHARMACY STUDENTS

Education starts with information management. Students are taught how to convert received information into knowledge. It is up to them to figure out how to convert that knowledge into wisdom. The abundance of drug information resources available and varying accessibility makes it difficult to manage information without technological skills.[9] Drug information training helps students quickly find relevant information and convert it into an applicable form in clinical practice.[1]

Pharmacy students undergo didactic and experiential education in drug information management. Didactic education is commonly delivered as lectures, interactive learning situations, and structured activities. Experiential education is generally delivered in Advanced Pharmacy Practice Experience (APPE); it is called an internship or clerkship. After graduation, drug information residencies are available to master other skills associated with more advanced drug information-related activities (e.g., formulary management, personnel management, policy/procedure creation, and teaching). Based on the level and type of education program, specific learning objectives need to be developed.

Skills used to provide drug information are taught classically by using the modified systematic approach to answering queries.[10,11] Additional training modalities include journal club discussions, drug profile presentations, therapeutic management presentations, research review, practice research, publishing, and interactions with healthcare professionals or the public. The objectives of these training programs are to ultimately provide unbiased, quality information in a reasonable time frame in an understandable format for the person making the inquiry.

The intentional and unintentional bias of the researchers/authors may result in unreliable articles. With a heavy influence of pharmaceutical marketing, bias within the literature can and does happen.[12] Critical appraisal skills compliment knowledge and attitudes to identify methodological bias that could be associated with conflicts of interests of the authors and the quality of the studies and literature.[13] These literature evaluation skills are required to review the applicability of information in clinical practice.

Other biases regarding the retrieval or dissemination of information may exist. For example, individual pharmacists sometimes heavily depend on sources of information that they are comfortable with and may miss vital information available in other resources. In doing so, pharmacists may unknowingly provide inadequate or wrong information to other healthcare professionals.[14] Yet, if the information being provided has been verified and validated in tertiary, secondary, and primary references, pharmacists should not accept conformity bias to avoid providing clinicians when information is incorrect, biased, or outdated.[15] Healthcare professionals are especially unwilling to expose their lack of understanding on some medical topics.[16] Therefore, confidentiality and good communication skills are important.

The scientific quality of the information being delivered can be ensured by observance and implementation of evidence-based practice (EBP). Drug information centers can and often work as a focal point in the EBP of a hospital. Healthcare professionals need to incorporate data from the literature, as well as their own research. This should be incorporated with experiences from the practice site along with patient observations and values.[17] Drug information pharmacists work to retrieve relevant articles and other up-to-date information at the request of various healthcare professionals within an institution. Additionally, they can contribute to the development and maintenance of evidence-based clinical guidelines and the hospital formulary system to improve medication use practices and overall patient care.[1]

Quality assurance is essential to systematically plan and implement drug information education and training in pharmacy programs. Constructive feedback is used to reassure the student about the skills evaluated and requirements of further training to achieve any unmet learning objectives. The training needs to be comprehensive for achieving these skills, as well as the associated knowledge and attitudes to practice drug information in a variety of settings. The accomplishment of these outcomes also assures that the trainee is self-aware of the need to keep abreast of the current standards in practice.

OBJECTIVE 13.3. CATEGORIZE DRUG INFORMATION SKILLS TO BE COVERED DURING TRAINING

Drug information skills are best improved and attained by using a systematic approach to answer questions. All of the seven steps listed below assess combinations of both general (e.g., communication, clinical, research) and specific (e.g., search, appraisal, writing) identifiable skills.[18]

1. **Secure demographics of the requestor.** It is important to know who is asking the question and who wants to know the answer (not always the same person). The type of person you are talking to may dictate where you will go to find the answer. For example, the information context and level may vary between different health professionals and patients. However, a physician may be more interested in the latest scientific advancement from the primary literature, whereas a patient may require knowing the usual pattern of drug use at different level of understanding.
   a. Requires:
      i.   Communication skills.
      ii. Associated attitudes for developing and maintaining trust of requesters.
   b. Information to be gathered:
      i.   Requestor's name.
      ii. Requestor's location and mobile number.
      iii. Requestor's affiliation (institution or practice), if a healthcare professional.
      iv. Requestor's frame of reference (status—type of profession, nurse, physician, pharmacist, student, etc.).
      v.   The best way to contact the requestor to provide the response.
2. **Obtain pertinent background information.** It is important to obtain this information at the time of the initial contact because it is sometimes difficult to get back in touch with a busy health professional.
   a. Requires
      i.   Communication skills.
      ii. Associated knowledge about pharmacotherapy and medical practices in the work setting.
      iii. Associated attitudes for confidentiality of information and patient benefit.

b. Information to be gathered:
  i. Resources the requestor has already checked—to avoid duplication of effort or validate what the requestor has already read to see what might be missing, misunderstood, or if the information may be outdated.
  ii. Patient-specific information: medical problems, prescription, OTC, and herbal medications, renal function, hepatic function, and other pertinent information.
  iii. Urgency of the request—the time frame for the response.
3. **Determine and categorize ultimate question.** It is important to understand what the requestor wants. The way they phrased the question may give you a clue to what information the person really needs, so listen carefully and then ask good questions of the requestor to identify what really needs to be answered.
  a. Requires
    i. Communication skills.
    ii. Associated knowledge about therapeutics and patient conditions, intervention, comparable therapeutic options, positive and negative outcomes expected (Patient Intervention Comparator Outcome—PICO).
    iii. Associated skills for helping requestors to develop an answerable question while limiting exposure for lack of understanding.
  b. Tips as you gather this information:
    i. On the form where you record your information, have a question background section where you make notes about what the requestor wants.
    ii. Only when you understand what information is needed should you record the question you intend to answer.
    iii. Verify with the requestor that this is indeed the question that you are trying to answer.
    iv. Categorize this question.
      (1). There are numerous examples, but it might be as simple as one of these: adverse drug reaction/contraindication, availability, dosage, drug compatibility/stability, drug interaction, therapeutic use, identification, formulation, or toxicity.
      (2). It is good practice to develop standard templates for appropriate question prompts for specific categories, e.g. for an ADR record dechallenge and rechallenge information and time course of the reaction, etc.
4. **Develop searching strategy and conduct searches.** The time frame for the search, the type of professional requesting the information, and the classification of the question are key to deciding where to search the primary or the tertiary literature and which resource is preferred.
  a. Requires
    i. Literature searching skills.
    ii. Associated knowledge about primary, secondary, and tertiary literature sources of information.
    iii. Range of information available on the internet.
    iv. Associated attitudes for unbiased, quality, and comprehensive search.
5. **Perform evaluation, analysis, and synthesis of collected information.** The information you retrieve must be critically analyzed. Often there is more information obtained that can be easily communicated to the requestor, so you will need to refine what you intend to communicate.
  a. Requires
    i. Critical literature appraisal skills, scientific review skills, and application of knowledge.
    ii. Associated knowledge in clinical practice, especially therapeutics.
    iii. Associated attitudes for unbiased and scientific interpretation of information.
6. **Formulate and provide a response.** Often there is not a clear-cut answer. Therefore, it will be necessary to present the options to the requestor, then make your assessment and emphasize your recommendation in a way that will allow the requestor to make their own decision based on the evidence provided to them in your formal response.
  a. Requires
    i. Medical writing skills, communication skills.
    ii. Associated knowledge regarding background information specific to the question and general pharmacotherapy/scientific knowledge.
    iii. Associated attitudes for tailoring the response to the needs of the requestor.
  b. Research has been done on what a requestor is looking for in your response.[19] They want the answer to be:
    i. Timely and current
    ii. Pragmatic - clinically useful and meaningful and patient focused (these are covered in ix, x and xi)
    iii. Accurate
    iv. Complete, yet concise

    v. Well referenced

    vi. Clear and logical

    vii. Objective and balanced

   viii. Free of bias and flaws

    ix. Applicable and appropriate for the specific circumstances

    x. It anticipates and answers important related questions

    xi. Lastly, it addresses management of patients or situations, if applicable.

7. **Conduct follow-up and documentation.** Documentation of the information provided is very important. Equally important, but often overlooked, there should be a follow-up to document how the recommendation was utilized and the outcome of this intervention.

   a. Requires:

    i. Communication and documentation skills.

    ii. Associated knowledge of relevant policies and practices in the documentation.

   iii. Associated attitudes for client-centered practice, self-development, and adhering to relevant policies and procedures.

In addition to answering queries, key skills to develop and evaluate during training are as follows:

- Critical literature appraisal through journal club review and evaluating news stories
- The ability to asses the benefits and potential harms of treatment and communicate this effectively
- Medical writing skills through writing and editing of drug monographs or other write-ups
- Interpretation skills of clinical practice guidelines and implementation within the practice
- Research skills through participating in practice research
- Communication skills through short educational presentations, reports, and publishing (which could be a newsletter or even a blog).

OBJECTIVE 13.4. PLAN A WEEK-WISE FOLLOW-UP OF LEARNING OBJECTIVES ACHIEVED IN DRUG INFORMATION TRAINING

In academic programs, the curriculum is commonly designed in three steps to provide mastery of learning drug information. (1) In didactic sessions, students learn the basics of references that are available to use and why certain situations would necessitate the use of one over the other. (2) Introductory Pharmacy Practice Experiences allow learners to observe drug information practices in different healthcare settings. (3) APPE drug information rotations are advanced experiences in which students practice drug information under supervision in a real setting, usually in a drug information center that serves a hospital.[20] Pharmacy graduates from other programs without such APPE drug information rotations are usually offered on-the-job training by an experienced pharmacist for the development of overall drug information skills. The following quality checks can be made to assure the development of relevant skills and competencies in drug information practices during the training of pharmacy undergraduates or pharmacists. Scales are used to assure each task is completed satisfactorily. A common example of an evaluation scale is as follows:

ACH—Achieved

SP—Satisfactory progress

NI—Needs improvement

N/A—Not applicable.

Feedback is given on completion of assigned tasks and usually at the end of a rotation. Recommendations are given for any additional tasks if required. A typical 5-week training experience for a hospital-based experience is illustrated in the following tables (Tables 13.1—13.4). Similar types of schedules and objectives can develop each type of learning situations (e.g., pharmacists' practice, drug information center, pharmacy benefits management company, or health insurance company); the key is to provide the student with a guided experience. In these examples each learning objective is followed by its action plans with multiple tasks.

Each task given to the trainee is based on planned objectives. Achievement of each learning outcome should be rated to assure minimum competency for practicing in a hospital setting. A simpler version of this program shall likely be sufficient in community practice.[21] This training also empowers the trainees with the skills for self-learning. With conscious practice and increased experiences, drug information skills will improve over time. Further training (i.e., residencies) shall be required for trainees/pharmacists to work as drug information specialists.

TABLE 13.1 Learning Objectives for Week 1

No	Topic: Drug Information Needs, Resources, and Evidence-Based Practice	
1	Objective 1: Review pharmacy and therapeutic committee (PTC)/formulary management system in the hospital.	
	Action Plans	Review constitution and function of the hospital PTC.
		Interview members of the hospital PTC and clinicians to assess their drug information needs.
		Review hospital formulary list and compare with others (e.g., National, WHO).
		Observe the formulary system (e.g., drug inventory, distribution, dispensing, administration and how the hospital manages potential and actual drug-related problems).
		Present/report about Objective 1.
2	Objective 2: Distinguish between evidence-based and empirical treatment.	
	Action Plans	Review evidence-based practice principles.
		Review evidence-based treatment guidelines within the hospital.
		Explain subjective and objective patient outcome information from clinical case studies reviewed.
		Identify evidence-based and empirical drug use in cases reviewed.
		Present/report about Objective 2.
3	Objective 3: Organize and appraise the quality of drug information sources.	
	Action Plans	Identify quality metrics (e.g., impact factor) in biomedical journals.
		Appraise the quality of information in drug information databases (e.g., Micromedex, Drugs.com, DailyMed).
		Identify search functions available in indexing services (e.g., PubMed, Google Scholar).
		Organize drug information resources available for efficient retrieval of information.
		Review and present modified systematic approach to answering questions.

TABLE 13.2 Learning Objectives for Week 2

No	Topic: Drug Information Service and Literature Evaluation	
1	Objective 4: Answer drug-specific queries by modified systematic approach (continued daily until completion of rotation).	
	Action Plans	Answer drug-specific queries from healthcare professionals using a primary source of information (e.g., original research, journal article).
		Validate information provided using a tertiary source (database/textbook).
		Analyze information and compile into a complete response with proper documentation.
		Respond to feedback from the requestor.
		Discuss in a small group about the drug information experience and strategies to improve the service.
2	Objective 5: Demonstrate responsibility in providing unbiased, quality drug information in a timely manner.	
	Action Plans	Review timeliness of providing drug information service.
		Review conflicts of interest in the resources used.
		Comply with hospital and national policies, as well as regulatory and ethical standards in providing a drug information service.
		Appraise the quality of sources of information used.
		Communicate effectively to healthcare professionals utilizing unbiased, quality drug information as part of evidence-based practice.

Continued

TABLE 13.2 Learning Objectives for Week 2—cont'd

No	Topic: Drug Information Service and Literature Evaluation	
3	Objective 6: Perform critical appraisal of a selected therapy article in journal club that is repeated possibly once per week. (See Appendix 1 for a rubric to assess the journal club presentation).	
	Action Plans	Select a therapy article for critical evaluation.
		Discuss methods of critical evaluation.
		Present and critically evaluate the selected article in a journal club.
		List strengths and weaknesses of the article.
		Justify how the findings from the study are applicable in the local healthcare practice.

TABLE 13.3 Learning Objectives for Week 3

No	Topic: Drug Information Service, Practice Research, and Pharmacotherapy	
1	Objective 7: Conduct retrospective practice research (e.g., drug utilization review, pharmacoeconomics, or pharmacovigilance) or prepare a manuscript for drug information/institution newsletter.	
	Action Plans	Collaborate with other healthcare professionals on planning practice research. Retrospective research from the specified hospital information system is preferred. Otherwise, anarrative review published in an institution's newsletter is acceptable.
		Perform the research to identify issues in healthcare delivery.
		Review literature for similar practice research or topic selected.
		Discuss with different stakeholders possible solutions/ideas or advances in the selected topic through considering local practices (further research or administrative action).
		Complete the research report by Week 5 and submit or send the manuscript for publishing in an appropriate newsletter.
2	Objective 8: Incorporate drug information services to pharmacotherapy services by proactive information.	
	Action Plans	Identify drug-related needs or potential drug-related problems in the patients for whom the queries were answered.
		Collect further information specific to the patient considering subjective and objective information.
		Assess medication-related risk for harm in patients with available information.
		Communicate with the healthcare provider on how to improve pharmacotherapy. Communicate directly with the patient, if necessary.
		Provide/use proper documentation.
3	Objective 9: Perform critical appraisal of a selected therapy topic and give a short (15 min) oral presentation. (See Appendix 2 for a rubric to assess the educational presentation).	
	Action Plans	Select a therapy topic to review.
		Prepare the presentation slides and a handout for this topic.
		Give the educational presentation to a group of fellow students or colleagues and the preceptor.

No additional objectives for week 4; Repeat Objectives 4−6 of Week 2.

TABLE 13.4 Learning Objectives for Week 5

No	Topic: Drug Information Services and Newsletter Communications	
1	Objectives 4–6 continue in Week 5	
2	Objective 10: Author, or at least review, a safety-focused drug therapy monograph that will be submitted to the pharmacy and therapeutics committee for a drug to be considered for addition the formulary.	
	Action Plans	Work with a practitioner that wants to add a drug to the formulary.
		Prepare appropriate monograph using the P&T committee's standard format.
		Identify the primary literature and manufacturer's information that will be necessary to complete the monograph.
		Use knowledge skills to organize the basic information necessary for the P&T committee to assess the efficacy and safety of this proposed addition to the formulary.
		Carefully document all the sources used to prepare the monograph.
3	Objective 11: Prepare the training report.	
	Action Plans	Compile all documents relevant to each task completed.
		Prepare a self-reflection report of the training.
		Revise the report based on feedback.
		Review knowledge, skills, and competencies gained during the training.
		Undergo end of training evaluation by the preceptor.

CONCLUSION

Drug information training is an essential component of pharmacy education. Pharmacists are expected to provide evidence-based recommendations regarding rational drug use to patients and healthcare professionals on a daily basis. Systematic experiential training of drug information skills focuses on search, appraisal, and writing skills. Pharmacists, irrespective of the practice or research setting, need to learn and use strong drug information skills.

REFERENCES

1. Costa de Sousa I, Pereira de Lima David J, Noblat L de ACB. A drug information center module to train pharmacy students in evidence-based practice. *Am J Pharm Educ*. 2013;77(4):80. https://doi.org/10.5688/ajpe77480.
2. Rutter P. Role of community pharmacists in patients' self-care and self-medication. *Integr Pharm Res Pract*. 2015;4:57–65. https://doi.org/10.2147/IPRP.S70403.
3. Dinkins MM. Patient counseling: a pharmacist in every OTC aisle. *US Pharm*. 2010;35(4):9–12. https://www.uspharmacist.com/article/patient-counseling-a-pharmacist-in-every-otc-aisle.
4. Kelling SE, Rondon-Begazo A, DiPietro Mager NA, Murphy BL, Bright DR. Provision of clinical preventive services by community pharmacists. *Prev Chronic Dis*. 2016;13:160232. https://doi.org/10.5888/pcd13.160232.
5. Consumer Healthcare Products Association. *Statistics on OTC Use*. CHPA; August 3, 2018. Accessed on https://www.chpa.org/MarketStats.aspx.
6. Wittich CM, Burkle CM, Lanier WL. Ten common questions (and their answers) about off-label drug use. *Mayo Clin Proc*. 2012;87(10):982–990. https://doi.org/10.1016/j.mayocp.2012.04.017.
7. Fickweiler F, Fickweiler W, Urbach E. Interactions between physicians and the pharmaceutical industry generally and sales representatives specifically and their association with physicians' attitudes and prescribing habits: a systematic review. *BMJ Open*. 2017;7(9):e016408. https://doi.org/10.1136/bmjopen-2017-016408.
8. Ghaibi S, Ipema H, Gabay M. American Society of Health System Pharmacists. ASHP guidelines on the pharmacist's role in providing drug information. *Am J Health Pharm*. 2015;72(7):573–577. https://doi.org/10.2146/sp150002.
9. Fox BI, Flynn AJ, Fortier CR, Clauson KA. Knowledge, skills, and resources for pharmacy informatics education. *Am J Pharm Educ*. 2011;75(5):93. https://doi.org/10.5688/ajpe75593.
10. Watanabe AS, McCart G, Shimomura S, Kayser S. Systematic approach to drug information requests. *Am J Hosp Pharm*. 1975;32(12):1282–1285. http://www.ncbi.nlm.nih.gov/pubmed/1211401.

11. Gershman J. *7 Steps to Respond to Drug Information Requests*. Pharm Times; 18 August 2016. Accessed; 7 August 2018. http://www.pharmacytimes.com/contributor/jennifer-gershman-pharmd-cph/2016/08/7-steps-to-respond-to-drug-information-requests

12. Muth CC. Conflict of interest in medicine. *J Am Med Assoc*. 2017;317(17):1812. https://doi.org/10.1001/jama.2017.4044.

13. Roseman M, Turner EH, Lexchin J, Coyne JC, Bero LA, Thombs BD. Reporting of conflicts of interest from drug trials in Cochrane Reviews: cross sectional study. *BMJ*. 2012;345:e5155. https://doi.org/10.1136/BMJ.E5155.

14. Fejzic J, Emmerton L, Tett SE. Towards concordance in healthcare: perspectives of general practitioners, complementary and alternative medicine practitioners and pharmacists in Australia. *J Clin Pharm Ther*. 2010;35(3):309–321. https://doi.org/10.1111/j.1365-2710.2009.01093.x.

15. Kaba A, Wishart I, Fraser K, Coderre S, McLaughlin K. Are we at risk of groupthink in our approach to teamwork interventions in health care? *Med Educ*. 2016;50(4):400–408. https://doi.org/10.1111/medu.12943.

16. Snyder ME, Zillich AJ, Primack BA, et al. Exploring successful community pharmacist-physician collaborative working relationships using mixed methods. *Res Soc Adm Pharm*. 2010;6(4):307–323. https://doi.org/10.1016/j.sapharm.2009.11.008.

17. Doebbeling BN, Chou AF, Tierney WM. Priorities and strategies for the implementation of integrated informatics and communications technology to improve evidence-based practice. *J Gen Intern Med*. 2006;(21 Suppl. 2):S50–S57. https://doi.org/10.1111/j.1525-1497.2006.00363.x.

18. Hincapie AL, Cutler TW, Fingado AR. Incorporating health information technology and pharmacy informatics in a pharmacy professional didactic curriculum -with a team-based learning approach. *Am J Pharm Educ*. 2016;80(6):107. https://doi.org/10.5688/ajpe806107.

19. Calis KA, Sheehan AH. Formulating effective responses and recommendations: a structured approach. In: *Drug Information: A Guide for Pharmacists*. 4th ed. New York: AccessPharmacy, McGraw-Hill Medical; 2013. http://accesspharmacy.mhmedical.com/content.aspx?bookid=466&sectionid=40064968.

20. Abate MA, Blommel ML. Self-assessment tool for drug information advanced pharmacy practice experience. *Am J Pharm Educ*. 2007;71(1):2. http://www.ncbi.nlm.nih.gov/pubmed/17429502.

21. Lauderdale SA, Kendrach MG, Freeman MK. Preparing students for community pharmacy practice during a drug information advanced practice experience. *Am J Pharm Educ*. 2007;71(2):25. http://www.ncbi.nlm.nih.gov/pubmed/17533434.

Pharmacoepidemiology and Pharmacovigilance

Chapter 14

Essentials of Pharmacoepidemiology

Douglas T. Steinke
University of Manchester, Manchester, Great Britain

Learning Objectives:

Objective 14.1 Outline pharmacoepidemiology and its methodological terminologies.
Objective 14.2 Explain study designs used in pharmacoepidemiology research.
Objective 14.3 Discuss how pharmacoepidemiology influences health improvement.

OBJECTIVE 14.1. OUTLINE PHARMACOEPIDEMIOLOGY AND ITS METHODOLOGICAL TERMINOLOGIES

The classical definition of pharmacoepidemiology is the study of the use and the effects of drugs in large numbers of people.[1] It is a combination of two important components: pharmaco, related to pharmacology or drugs, and epidemiology, the study of determinants and distribution of disease in a population (Fig. 14.1). Therefore, pharmacoepidemiology is a specialized category of the general study of epidemiology where medications are the primary exposure in a population and the determinants of the distribution of the outcome of interest in a large population are investigated. What is also necessary for the study of pharmacoepidemiology is the understanding of clinical practice and the behaviors of clinicians in relation to prescribing and decision making.

In the drug approval process, there are inherent limitations. Randomized clinical trials are used to understand the efficacy of the drug (can the drug work in the body in experimental conditions?) and effectiveness (does the drug provide a desired effect in the real world?), but may be limited by sample size and follow-up time. To clearly understand the drug effects, whether wanted or unwanted, a variety of patient characteristics in a large population are to be observed. It will identify uncommon effects that may not occur immediately, but later in time (e.g., causing cancer). Therefore, a study of the medication used in a *real-world* population, including women, young people, and elderly patients, allows the researcher to follow a patient over several years to identify benefits and adverse drug reactions in a variety of patient characteristics. These studies are conducted usually after the drug has entered clinical practice and are called postmarket surveillance. Pharmacoepidemiological studies not only identify the determinants that may cause bad outcomes but also identify those patients who would most benefit from the medication under study.

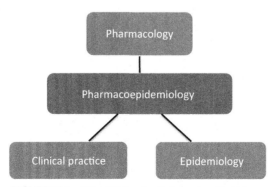

FIGURE 14.1 The components of pharmacoepidemiology.

Clinical Pharmacy Education, Practice and Research. https://doi.org/10.1016/B978-0-12-814276-9.00014-3

Some examples of where pharmacoepidemiological studies may be used include identifying or providing the evidence for best practice that can be used further in evidence-based practice. Drug safety studies may require large populations of patients taking medication in a variety of patient characteristics with varying degrees of disease severity to identify those at most risk of adverse drug reactions. If a drug has a rare adverse drug event, it may need time to be identified and a large number of people to find it.

As a hospital pharmacist, the results and evidence from robust pharmacoepidemiological studies can provide the evidence for therapeutics and formulary choices to plan the best care possible based on research. The evidence from research may show that not everyone will benefit from a particular drug. This may prevent the use of and costs associated with expensive therapies given to patients that may provide suboptimal benefit from the treatment. However, the evidence will also identify the patients that may get effective treatment and perhaps a cure.

In community pharmacy, the evidence from pharmacoepidemiology studies can help provide the best practice for patients who need it the most. The results will help in decision making for clinically effective and cost-effective therapies to use in a particular disease management scheme or evidence to change to a different class of drug.

Link to Pharmacoeconomic Studies

In pharmacoepidemiology, drugs are the primary exposure agent of interest. Drugs cost money to supply to the pharmacy and cost the patient/insurance/government money to buy or provide. Therefore, a cost can be identified. The evidence from pharmacoepidemiological research can, therefore, feed into pharmacoeconomic research providing preferences and effectiveness for such study designs as cost-effective analysis or other analyses.

Methodological Terminology

The following are terms that are often used in pharmacoepidemiology and need to be understood so that the correct interpretation of the data and study design are performed.

Confounding

A confounder is a variable that is associated or has a relationship with both the exposure and the outcome of interest. Fig. 14.2 shows an example of a possible confounder found in the relationship between alcohol use and lung cancer. By itself, this relationship does not make clinical sense; how can drinking alcohol cause cancer? However, when the confounding variable smoking is introduced, the relationship makes more sense; an individual who drinks alcohol is more likely to smoke, and smoking could cause cancer. The variable is related to alcohol use and lung cancer and is part of the causal pathway. Confounding can be controlled for in a study by either matching the confounding variable to ensure equal proportions of the confounder are found in each group or by statistical methods (i.e., multiple variable regression analysis).

Bias

Bias is defined as a difference between groups that favors one group over another.[2] This cannot be controlled by statistical analysis and is a fact of the data. For example, a small group of cancer patients exposed to a particular agent is coded for severity of disease more accurately than another group in a study without the exposure. There is a difference in the coding accuracy between the groups. This would introduce bias to the study of disease severity.

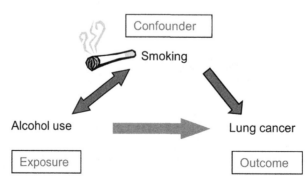

FIGURE 14.2 Illustration showing confounding and the relationship between exposure and outcome.

Incidence

Incidence of disease is defined as the number of newly diagnosed cases of the disease in a population divided by the total population at risk of the disease.[2] New cases of the disease have not had a prior diagnosis of the disease. The calculation of incidence is as follows:

$$I = \frac{\text{Number of people with a new diagnosis of disease}}{\text{Number of people at risk}}$$

Point Prevalence

Prevalence of disease is defined as the number of people with an existing disease (both old and new cases) in a population divided by the total population at risk of the disease.[2] Some of the people could have had the disease for a long time and some may have been diagnosed recently, but all are included. It is the proportion of the population with the disease. This is a useful calculation to quantify the burden of disease in a population. Point prevalence is the number of people with the disease of interest at a specific point in time divided by the number of people in the population at the specific point in time. Point prevalence is calculated using the following equation:

$$\text{Point prevalence} = \frac{\text{Number of people with new and existing disease}}{\text{Number of people at risk at a specific point in time}}$$

Matching

Matching is when one group is made similar to the comparator group by making pairwise matches on a small number of known risk factors. The risk factors are known confounders in the relationship, and the researcher would like to ensure the study is measuring the true relationship between exposure and outcome without being interrupted by other possible risk factors. Matching is usually performed using a small number of variables to ensure that there are sufficient numbers in each group. The more risk factors used in matching, the smaller the number of pairwise matches that can be found in each comparison group. For example, age and sex of the patient are known risk factors for myocardial infarction (MI). As the male subject grows older, they are at increased risk. Matching each individual in the groups by sex and age ensures the groups have a similar distribution of these variables and a more precise final measure of association between the exposure of interest and the outcome. If smoking habits and other lifestyle risk factors are to be matched on, the comparator groups will naturally become smaller with increased number of matching variables.

Drug Utilization

Drug utilization focuses on the various medical, social, and economic aspects of drug use. Medical consequences include the risks and benefits of drug therapy, whereas social aspects can be related to inappropriate use. Economic issues deal with the cost of drugs and treatment for patients and society.[3] This is different to pharmacoepidemiology because drug utilization does not necessarily have to link to a health outcome event. Pharmacoepidemiology always studies both exposure and outcome. Drug utilization is more encompassing and includes social/behavioral factors, which may affect why patients use medications; this is not usually the focus of pharmacoepidemiological research.[3]

Adherence

Adherence and compliance are often used interchangeably. Compliance is the patient's ability to take a medication as prescribed, which sounds like a command to take a medication.[3] If a patient does not take medication as prescribed, they may be thought to have bad medication-taking behavior.[3] Adherence is more complex and multifactorial than compliance. Adherence has issues of patient behavior, patient—doctor relationships, and pharmacist—patient relationships that have to be accounted for or at least identified to fully understand why a patient has decided to take or not to take their medication as directed on the label. Adherence to medication should be taken into account in the analysis of the data because it does relate to the dose of the exposure of interest. Adherence is usually measured as a percentage of time in possession of a medication, assuming the patient is taking the medication the whole time and as directed. Another term that is related to adherence is persistence. This term is used to explain the extent to which the treatment is taken for the recommended duration of therapy.[3] Persistence is used more often in long-term and chronic conditions where taking medication regularly for long periods of time is important to the treatment of the chronic disease.

Disease Severity

Disease severity is another measure that may affect the measure of association in a pharmacoepidemiological study. The patient may have tried many medications as the disease has progressed and is using a new medication as the last hope of treatment. In a study, the new medication may be associated with a bad outcome, not because it is the cause, but because the severity of the disease has caused the patient to fail. For example, a patient with painful arthritis has tried different NSAIDs available and is finally switched to a new analgesic agent but fails (has a joint replacement). The drug should not be associated with the failure of treatment because it was another chance taken before attempting a major invasive intervention.

OBJECTIVE 14.2. EXPLAIN STUDY DESIGNS USED IN PHARMACOEPIDEMIOLOGY RESEARCH

Ecological/Cross-Sectional Studies

For some research questions, the only data available are aggregated at group level instead of the individual patient level. For example, data on cough and cold preparations bought over-the-counter (OTC) in a town's two pharmacies. Here, the total number of packages sold by the pharmacies each day is recorded, but no data are collected on the individual purchases by patients/customers. Analysis of aggregated data of daily purchases can inform decision-makers on what types of products are sold or required and may inform public health if there is a possible outbreak of upper respiratory infection in the area. The data do not necessarily relate it to a particular outcome of interest but can provide information on the use of medications in a particular population. The results of this type of study design can be compared with other areas to investigate if there is a difference in the rate of daily purchases, which further inform area public health officials of the geography of the outbreak. Studies using aggregated data are called *ecological studies*.

There are limitations to ecological study design, namely confounding. Confounding arises because there is a lack of individual patient information. When analyzing aggregated data, information may be lost that could provide an explanation on the use of cough and cold products. For example, there may be a school with young children attending increasing the risk of spreading a cold to a large population (students and parents) or an area of elderly less prone to flu because of vaccination programs. This could lead to an *ecological fallacy* where the researcher makes conclusions at an individual level when only aggregate data are used.[4]

The measures for aggregated data are rates. This is a simple calculation of the number of people that are affected by the total population that are at risk. For example, using the above situation, there were 130 purchases of OTC cough and cold products in 1 day from both pharmacies. The town has a total population of 5145 people. Therefore, the rate of OTC cough and cold purchases is 130/5145 = 0.025 or 25 purchases per 1000 people.

Case–Control Studies

Case–control study designs are used widely in pharmacoepidemiology. They are particularly useful when the outcome of interest is relatively rare. For example, to study the relationship between drug exposure and a specific type of cancer, a case–control design could be used easily.[5] Case–control studies begin with the identification of a sample of patients with the outcome of interest (e.g., death, cancer, or MI); these are the cases. The controls are identified from the same study population that does not have the outcome of interest (e.g., not dead, do not have cancer, and do not have an MI). Within each sample, the researcher then looks back in the medical record to determine the exposure status to a drug of interest (Fig. 14.3). This type of study is retrospective in time because while the data are collected, the outcome and exposure have already happened. The researcher can now calculate the proportion of the case sample and the control sample that was exposed to the drug of interest in the past. We can compare the proportions and calculate the *odds ratio* (OR) (odds of exposure in cases vs. odds of exposure in the controls).[2]

This study design is efficient because the research is not waiting for the outcome to develop after drug exposure. The data collection starts with the outcome and can easily look back in time to see if they were exposed. With this design, the researcher can examine multiple exposures or risk factors of interest for a given outcome, as long as the exposure happened before the outcome. To do this, the case is assigned an index date, which is the date the outcome occurred. Controls (without the outcome of interest) are also given the same index data as their matched case (if matched on a particular variable, e.g., age) or randomly selected case. Exposure status is determined retrospectively from the index date.

Because the study design uses a sample of the study population to allocate the cases and controls, the incidence of disease in the study population cannot be calculated. It is difficult to identify all those that are at risk in the study population. However, the calculated OR could be viewed as a valid estimate of the relative risk (RR) in certain circumstances. These circumstances include the following: (1) cases are representative of the source population; (2) controls should be

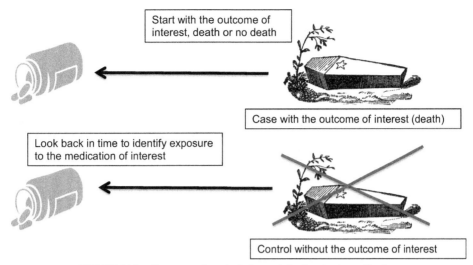

FIGURE 14.3   Case—control study design and timeline for data collection.

selected from the same population; and (3) the controls should be sampled regardless of their exposure status.[2] One way of ensuring that these circumstances are fulfilled is to ensure that eligibility criteria are applied to both cases and controls in the study.

There are some limitations to this study design the researcher should consider. First, the study design is susceptible to bias and confounding, which can have an effect on the final results and interpretation of the study. *Selection bias* may occur if the cases and controls are systematically different from those that are not included in the study. *Information bias* may occur when data are more complete for cases compared with controls, leading to misclassification of disease or outcome or measurement error. *Recall bias* may occur if exposure status is remembered more accurately in cases because the outcome is worse. For example, a life-threatening adverse drug reaction may have exposure to a drug more accurately remembered than those without an adverse drug reaction.[6]

Confounding is a limitation that is found in this study design but can be controlled by matching or statistical analyses. Confounding happens when a variable is related to both the outcome and the exposure. Matching the cases and controls on a confounding variable will ensure that the variable is the same in both groups, decreasing the likelihood of effects on the final results. Statistically controlling the confounding "adjusts" the proportion of the confounder in each group to ensure that they are the same in each group before calculating the final adjusted OR. This is performed using multivariable regression analysis.

Measure of Association for a Case—Control Study

The measure of association for a case—control study is the OR. The calculation of the OR is relatively easy if some simple rules are established and the researcher sets up their results appropriately to identify the exposure and outcome. Table 14.1 shows the calculation of the OR. Interpreting the OR can be remembered by using the result to answer cell "A." For example, there is an increased/decreased risk of the outcome if exposed to the medication.

Case Study: Case—Control Study Design

Prescription-acquired acetaminophen use and the risk of asthma in adults: a case—control study. Kelkar M, Cleves MA, Foster HR, Hogan WR, James, LP, Martin BC. *The Annals of Pharmacotherapy*, 2012;46:1598—1608.

   This study investigates the link between acetaminophen (paracetamol) use and the development of asthma. The authors provide evidence that acetaminophen can cause lung damage, which could lead to asthma. This case—control study design started with the first diagnosis of asthma and looked back to observe acetaminophen use. They used many confounders in the analysis to find the adjusted association. Cases were found to be more ill and used acetaminophen on a chronic basis, whereas controls did not. Some confounders were not found in the data (smoking). The study found that chronic use of high doses of acetaminophen is associated with asthma (OR 1.70 95% CI 1.63—1.98). However, most of the preparations also contain codeine, which may cause respiratory depression and should be taken into consideration when discussing the study results.

TABLE 14.1 Calculation for the Odds Ratio

	Outcome of Interest	
	Yes (Cases)	No (Controls)
Exposed to medication	A	B
Not exposed to medication	C	D

A, exposed and has the outcome; B, exposed and does not have the outcome; C, not exposed and has the outcome; D, not exposed and no outcome; OR, AD/BC.

Cohort Studies

Cohort studies are another popular study design used in pharmacoepidemiology. This type of study is often used when a randomized control trial cannot be undertaken because of requirements for exposure (pregnancy or elderly patients) or the exposure is either impossible or unethical (effects of smoking or taking illegal drugs). The main purpose of the cohort study is to estimate the risk or rate of an outcome among a cohort of individuals.

A cohort study initially starts by identifying a large group of people that are free of the outcome of interest. This is in contrast to the case−control study where the study starts with the identification of people with the outcome of interest. The cohort of disease-free people is now assigned to either exposed or not exposed (e.g., smoking or not smoking) and followed forward in time until the outcome of interest occurs (Fig. 14.4). This may take a long time, so cohort studies may take years or generations until an outcome is identified. The cohort study is prospective in design because it follows people forward in time gathering information along the way. There are particular scenarios where a researcher may say their study is a retrospective cohort study, meaning that samples are collected at the beginning of the study but analyzed when the outcome of interest is identified in the future. This saves a lot of time and money if the analysis is laborious and costly.

For example, the WHO MONICA Project is a large cohort of 10 million people aged 35−64 from 26 countries of Europe, North America, and Western Pacific. Subjects were followed forward in time to a fatal or nonfatal cardiovascular event or stroke. Physical examinations and surveys were performed at regular intervals under a standardized protocol. This study has provided information on risk factors contributing to MI and medications used to control blood pressure and their effects on the mortality rate of acute MI.[7]

Measure of Association for a Cohort Study

Because the cohort study design is prospective, an accurate record of exposure can be recorded, including adherence to any medication and other health effects that occur over time (e.g., flu exposure). The temporal relationship between the exposure and the outcome can also be investigated, which can be important when establishing a causal relationship.[2] A major advantage of cohort studies is that the entire population is at risk because the study population started the study outcome free. Therefore, an accurate *incidence* of the outcome can be calculated for the exposed (I_e) and unexposed (I_0) populations (Fig. 14.5). The incidence is used in the measure of association termed the *relative risk* (RR). The calculation of the RR starts with a similar table as the case−control study, but different information is used because we are interested in the relationship between the incidence of the outcome in the exposed and unexposed.

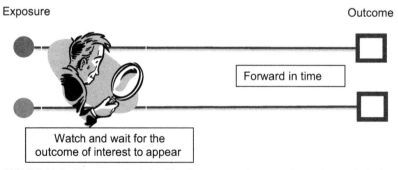

Exposure   Outcome

Forward in time

Watch and wait for the outcome of interest to appear

FIGURE 14.4 The temporal relationship of exposure and outcome in a cohort study design.

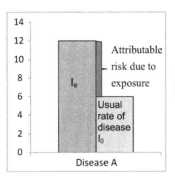

FIGURE 14.5   Explanation of attributable risk in relation to the incidence of disease in the unexposed (I_0).

Knowing the incidence of the outcome of the exposed and not exposed, we can also perform other useful information that can be used in the clinical setting. Attributable risk is the quantification of risk that can be attributed to the exposure alone. It is calculated by taking the absolute value (only positive values) of the difference between the incidences in the exposed and unexposed. The numbers needed to treat or harm can be calculated by taking the inverse value of the AR (1/AR), which will provide the number of individuals who have to receive the treatment for one of them to benefit from the treatment over a specific time.

Case Study: Framingham Heart Study

In 1948, 5209 adult residents of the town of Framingham, Massachusetts, became a cohort of people followed forward in time in the Framingham Heart Study. This long-term cohort study has contributed to much of the knowledge we have today about cardiovascular disease and hypertension.[8] Information we use in clinical practice of the effects of diet, exercise, and medications (particularly aspirin use) were based on the results of this study. The cohort is now in its third generation of participants[9] contributing to study results that now include genetic information. Physical health examinations ended for the original cohort in 2014.

Summary Comparison Tables of Study Designs

Table 14.2 is a summary of the study designs used in pharmacoepidemiology. Table 14.3 is a summary of the advantages and disadvantages of each study design and results given.

Data Used in Pharmacoepidemiological Research

Two types of data are used in pharmacoepidemiological research: primary and secondary data. The type of data appropriate for the study depends on the research question and the study design. Primary data are collected for a specific purpose and

TABLE 14.2 Summary Table of Studies Used in Pharmacoepidemiology

Study Type	Groups	Measure of Association	Purpose
Ecological/cross-sectional study	Sample of population	Prevalence	Assess prevalence Describe population characteristics used in health planning
Case–control study	Cases vs. controls	Odds ratio	Association between disease and historical exposure Useful rare diseases Relatively easy
Cohort study	Exposed vs. unexposed	Relative risk	Association between a risk factor and future outcome Useful rare exposures Expensive

TABLE 14.3 Advantages and Disadvantages for Each Study Design

Study Type	Advantages	Disadvantages
Ecological/cross-sectional study	• Rapid, easy, and cheap • Provides evidence for or against a hypothesis • Can be used in international comparisons	• Only study groups and not individuals • Cannot control confounders • Cannot differentiate cause and confounders • Cannot identify nonlinear relationships
Case—control study	• Identifies rare outcomes • Evaluates multiple risk factors and exposures • Used in diseases with long latent periods • Follow-up is not a problem • Relatively fast, easy, and cheap	• Selection of controls could lead to selection bias • Controls should represent the general population • Retrospective data on exposure may lead to recall bias
Cohort study	• Can measure the incidence and prevalence of disease • Can look at multiple outcomes in a study • Provides a clear temporal association	• Needs a large sample size to look at rare outcomes • Expensive • Long-term commitment of the population to the study • Chance of loss to follow-up

have not been previously used in research. These data can be collected through questionnaires, interviews, focus groups, or medical note extractions. Primary data differ from secondary data in that they offer the researcher increased control over what type of and how much data are collected. For example, if a researcher wanted to find out if patients take their tablets with a meal or not, this question should be asked. These are primary data; they would not be found in any other database or resource. The main disadvantages in collecting primary data are time and cost. Interviews, chart reviews, and questionnaires take time to prepare and analyze. As the sample size of the study increases, the cost of additional people to review notes also increases, which is an additional cost.

Secondary data are preexisting and were collected for another purpose. These may include medical administrative data (e.g., hospital admissions), prescription dispensing data, or data from randomized controlled trials. These types of data have the distinct advantage of being available to the research without waiting for the data to be collected. Secondary data are usually large in sample size and offer generalizability.[10] These strengths have resulted in secondary data being used in a variety of research topics, including drugs utilization, adherence to medication therapy, healthcare interventions, and policy issues. Increasingly, secondary data are becoming more available with computerization of medical records and billing procedures. There are some disadvantages though. Secondary data, however, are usually not collected for the purposes of research, but for other intentions (e.g., billing customers, record keeping, prescription filing) and therefore may not have all the information that is required to complete the study. For example, clinical lab data may not be available at the individual level. With advanced statistical techniques and data management (linking dataset by a unique identifier), many of these disadvantages can be overcome.

Postmarket Surveillance

Postmarketing surveillance (PMS) is defined as the identification and collection of information regarding drugs after their approval for use in a population.[11] The drug approval process in some countries is complicated and lengthy, which may hold drugs back from patients in desperate need of them. PMS is a method of systematically monitoring the safety and effectiveness of new drugs in the real world using a variety of patient types with many different comorbid diseases. The population of potential users after a drug is released is very different from the population studied in the premarking phase of a drug's approval. For example, few clinical trials will include very old patients or patients with two or more comorbidities or women that are breastfeeding.[11]

PMS allows for the long-term monitoring of the effects of drugs. This contrasts the follow-up period of randomized controlled trials that are usually shorter in duration when considering the cost of the trial.[11] The long-term effects, such as tolerance to the drug or adverse drug reactions, use PMS study designs. Especially rare adverse events that may not be identified in clinical trials because of the small sample side, PMS data may include thousands of patients using the medication over a period of time allowing for these rare events to be quantified and studied.

Case Study: Postmarketing Surveillance Study

Postmarketing surveillance study of the safety and efficacy of sildenafil prescribed in primary care to erectile dysfunction patients.[18]

The safety and efficacy of sildenafil use in primary care were studied in a total of 651 men with erectile dysfunction enrolled from primary care in Korea. Patients were followed up, and all adverse drug reactions and efficacy data were collected. 458 patients completed the study. The study found hypertension and diabetes were associated with poor efficacy. A total of 71 adverse events were reported in 56 patients (8.6%). The study concluded that sildenafil prescribed by primary care physicians was well tolerated and improved erectile function in patients with erectile dysfunction.

PMS also allows for other indications for medication use to be observed and evaluated. "Off-label" use or using a medication for another indication not included in the official drug information can be identified and evaluated. Therefore, knowledge gained from PMS allows for the broader application of drugs to special populations, for different indications, and at doses and durations not studied in the prelaunch clinical trials.[11]

Pharmaceutical Policy Issues

PMS can be used to ensure that appropriate and effective pharmaceutical policies are developed to ensure fair and equitable use of drugs in a population. Data on how and where a drug is used after its launch into a large population can inform decision-makers and drug regulators on innovation and service provision, issues of access to drugs, pricing and containment, and rational use of drugs. With additional public health data, such as socioeconomic data, age and sex distributions, and hospital admissions, additional issues of unmet need can be identified and quantified for use at a larger population level.

PMS can provide information about drug safety and effectiveness of drugs that can be used by the public, manufacturers, and government to make informed choices. Rare adverse events from long-term use and in large populations may inform the safe use of drugs. In addition, the effects of nonadherence to therapy can be identified. PMS will continue to be an important "phase" of the clinical approval process of drugs introduction to the market.

OBJECTIVE 14.3. DISCUSS HOW PHARMACOEPIDEMIOLOGY INFLUENCES HEALTH IMPROVEMENT

Identifying the people who need the most pharmaceutical care in a community is a difficult undertaking, but with the right data, services and products can be targeted to the people who need it the most.[12] Developing and producing a pharmaceutical needs assessment will identify those most in need. This may not be what the community wants, but "wants" are based on other factors too. Pharmaceutical needs assessments will direct the services provided to the areas that will benefit most. For example, smoking cessation services to areas of high incidence of asthma and COPD or flu vaccination clinics for the elderly in areas where there is a large aging population. This ensures necessary public health services will be provided where they will maximize the benefit to the most people.

The natural history of a disease can have many areas that might need pharmaceutical interventions to prevent and promote healthy states.[13] Pharmacists can intervene with a patient who is at risk of a disease by providing a smoking cessation program to prevent future COPD or flu vaccinations to prevent the disease, especially in vulnerable populations. This will maintain the health of the population. However, if the intervention is lacking, the disease will progress and may require advanced clinical pharmacy services in a hospital environment during the illness to the point of recovery or death depending on the severity of disease and the patient's circumstances. Therefore, the points of intervention in the natural history of the disease may require unique skills and competencies gained by the pharmacist.

Pharmacoepidemiology by its innate nature assesses and influences decisions in public health. Public health is defined as a discipline concerning itself with improving health or preventing illness in a population, and it is usually implemented by a government or a group accountable to a community.[14] Public health practitioners use data that are readily available, including population health surveys, census data, data on educational attainment, crime and police data, and other sources to determine the health of the population. Pharmacoepidemiology can provide additional information about a population that would not normally be found in the public health data. Pharmacoepidemiology can be used to identify and describe patterns of use or adverse drug reactions, compare the actual use of a medication to the guidelines or expected use patterns, determine factors that promote or inhibit the use of medications, and link usage to outcomes. Pharmacoepidemiology can use postmarket surveillance data to identify medication safety issues and patterns of use in a population.[14] Therefore, the end result will be several sources of information on a population so that the practitioner can make an informed, rational choice for the population.

Vaccination Services and Disease Prevention: an Example of Pharmaceutical Public Health

A widespread outbreak of H1N1 influenza virus in 2009 once again initiated the debate of vaccination of children and adults against the flu virus. Questions like "is it really necessary?" or "isn't it like a bad cold?" were asked by patients without enough information to make an informed decision. Pharmacists became instrumental in providing patients with pertinent information to make informed choices by talking about the risks and benefits of immunization against the virus. Pharmacists may also ease the fears of many patients by providing the facts as well as the significant risks associated with not being vaccinated against flu. Pharmacists are in a unique position to identify those patients that are at most risk of infection, whether the patient is in a hospital or the community pharmacy, ensuring the right patients are targeted for vaccination.[15]

As of 2017, globally, more than 20 countries allow vaccinations in a pharmacy or by a pharmacist. Of these, 13 allow pharmacists to vaccinate independently. This demonstrates the expansion and growing acceptance of pharmacy immunization services around the world.[16] In the United States (USA), all 50 states allow pharmacists to administer vaccinations with appropriate training. Immunization by pharmacists is governed by each state's laws and regulations governing pharmacy practice. Some states require specific education or certification; some limit the types of vaccinations given by pharmacists.[15] Nevertheless, the patient can now make their own informed choice to get a vaccination by a knowledgeable healthcare professional at their convenience. Many community pharmacies are open long hours and provide necessary public health services.

Case Study: Pharmacists Vaccinate Against Cancer

Lowery M. Pharmacists key to widespread HPV vaccination.[19]

Millions of avoidable cancers could be prevented through widespread administration of the human papillomavirus (HPV) vaccination. In the USA, states were encouraged to enact laws allowing pharmacists to administer the HPV vaccination. The reasons behind this recommendation included reducing missed clinical opportunities to recommend and administer the vaccines; increasing parents' and adolescents' acceptance of the vaccines; and maximizing access to HPV vaccination services. Presently, about one-third of girls aged 13–17 years (prevention) and 7% of boys 13–17 years (transmission) have been vaccinated. More young people need to be vaccinated to decrease the risk of cervical cancer even more in the future.

Decision Making

Some drugs are expensive, and new drugs arriving on the market have to be carefully controlled so that the resources of the healthcare system are not used in one particular area. There are innovative methods of treatment being developed that also require new resources, trained people, and money to buy-in the products. Decisions have to be made so that there is rationalizing (not rationing) of the budget to ensure that as many people as possible will benefit from new and existing drugs and procedures. Using data from many sources, including clinical practice and from the literature on the effectiveness of treatment, provides the evidence needed to make informed decisions. With this in mind, it is possible that not everyone will benefit. There are those that have not tried all other treatments and failed or would like a quick fix. However, there may be a large group that requires a moderately priced drug to maintain the status quo of the disease. Guideline development and drug formularies are guidance for practitioners for best practice based on the available evidence that is presented in the literature. Nevertheless, the practice of drug still requires clinical judgment to ensure the right drugs are provided to the right patient safely and effectively.

The people making the decisions realize that they require the evidence to "back up" their decisions. Robust pharmacoepidemiological data, strong study designs, and appropriate use of statistics will give the necessary evidence to ensure that use of the drug is safe and the drug is used in situations where there are positive outcomes. Decision making still needs an understanding of the one variable in this equation—the patient. Knowing the effects of the determinants of health on a patient, other factors must also be considered, which are not always recorded in a database. Communication and analyzing the conversation with the patient will provide additional data to ensure the patient is right for the treatment of choice.

Determinants of Health

When determining the health of a population, it is important to consider the conditions and factors associated with health. These include the wider perspective of living conditions as well as the health-related factors within the individual. The factors are viewed in levels: the individual fixed conditions, lifestyle factors, the social and community level, and finally general socioeconomic, cultural, and environmental conditions (Fig. 14.6).[17]

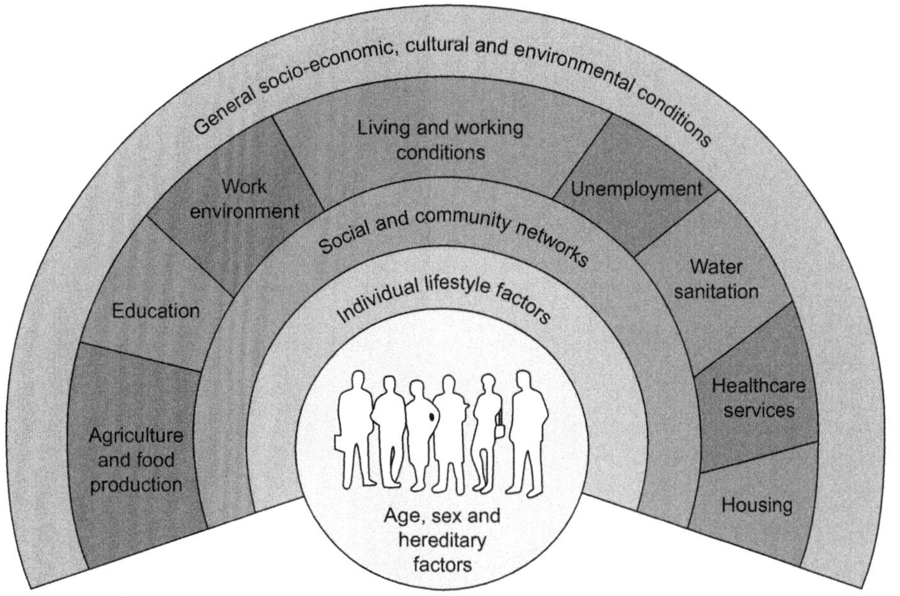

FIGURE 14.6 The determinants of health and the relationship to the individual. *Adapted from Dahlgren, Whitehead. Policies and Strategies to Promote Social Equity in Health. Stockholm, Sweden: Institute for Future Studies; 1991. [Reprinted in 2007].*

For individuals (center of diagram) there are fixed conditions that cannot change and can determine the health of an individual. These include age, sex, and genetics. The next layer includes lifestyle factors that can be changed or modified to prevent or promote health in an individual. These are primarily behavior changes that an individual makes, including smoking cessation, decreasing alcohol consumption, and wearing a seat belt while driving. The next layer contains social and community influences that provide support from friends and family when in unfavorable conditions. The final layer is structural factors that influence health. This layer is not intuitive; it does make sense how housing could affect health. For example, if a housing area has many drafty, damp, and moldy houses, it increases the chances of developing asthma by nature of the environment. Pharmacoepidemiological data are used in this example to evaluate the use of asthma medication in this area and test the hypothesis compared with another area of lesser risk.[17]

CONCLUSION

Pharmacoepidemiology is an emerging field to understand the use of medications in a large population, identify and quantify adverse drug reactions in a population, and to quantify the risk or benefit of taking a medication for a particular disease or condition. Increasingly, secondary data are becoming more available with computerization of medical records and billing procedures. Pharmacoepidemiology has established and robust study designs that provide strong evidence for the drugs in the relationship to outcomes. Pharmacoepidemiology results can be used in conjunction with other data to explain or identify areas of need and improve the health outcomes.

PRACTICE QUESTIONS

1. Why are drug utilization studies not considered as pharmacoepidemiological studies?
   A. Confounding is common
   B. Matching is not possible
   C. Outcomes may not be measured
   D. Biased because multiple factors are involved
2. In pharmacoepidemiological studies, the prevalence of disease in a population is a measure of what?
   A. New cases of a disease
   B. Existing cases of a disease
   C. Both new and existing cases of a disease
   D. Not related to when the disease started

3. The OR is a measure in which of the following research methodologies?
   A. Cross-sectional study
   B. Case—control study
   C. Cohort study
   D. Postmarketing surveillance
4. Which of the following is easier to conduct?
   A. Case—control study
   B. Cohort study
   C. Postmarketing surveillance
   D. Randomized controlled study
5. Framingham Heart Study is an example of?
   A. Case—control study
   B. Cohort study
   C. Postmarketing surveillance
   D. Randomized controlled study

REFERENCES

1. Strom B, Kimmel SE. *Textbook of Pharmacoepidemiology.* Hoboken NJ: John Wiley and Sons Inc.; 2006.
2. Yang Y, West-Strum. *Understanding Pharmacoepidemiology.* New York NY: McGraw Hill; 2011.
3. Elseviers M, Wettermark B, Almarsdottir AB, et al. *Drug Utilization Research: Methods and Applications.* Chichester UK: John Wiley & Sons; 2016.
4. Last JM. *A Dictionary of Epidemiology.* 4th ed. New York NY: Oxford University Press, Inc; 2001.
5. Hitron A, Adams V, Talbert J, Steinke D. The influence of antidiabetic medications on the development and progression of prostate cancer. *Cancer Epidemiol.* 2012;36(4):e243—e250. https://doi.org/10.1016/j.canep.2010.02.005.
6. Hennekens CH, Buring JE. *Epidemiology in Medicine.* Boston MA: Little, Brown and Company; 1987.
7. Bothig S. WHO MONICA Project: objectives and design. *Int J Epidemiol.* 1989;18(3 Suppl. 1):S29—S37.
8. Dawber TR, Meadors GF, Moore Jr FE. National Heart Institute, National Institutes of Health, Public Health Service, Federal Security Agency, Washington, D.C. In: *Epidemiological Approaches to Heart Disease: The Framingham Study Presented at a Joint Session of the Epidemiology, Health Officers, Medical Care, and Statistics Sections of the American Public Health Association, at the Seventy-eighth Annual Meeting in St. Louis, Mo.* November 3, 1950.
9. Mahmood SS, Levy D, Vasan RS, Wang TJ. The Framingham Heart Study and the epidemiology of cardiovascular disease: a historical perspective. *Lancet.* 2013;383(9921):999—1008.
10. Suissa S, Garbe E. Primer: administrative health databases in observational studies of drug effects: advantages and disadvantages. *Nat Clin Pract Rheumatol.* 2007;3(12):725—732.
11. Waning B, Montagne M. *Pharmacoepidemiology: Principles and Practice.* New York NY: McGraw-Hill; 2001.
12. Steinke DT, Burney S, Bennie M, Hudson SA. Using health and population data to help describe the health of a locality: the development and evaluation of a locality health profile. *Int J Pharm Pract.* 2005;14:21—30.
13. Carter J, Slack M. *Pharmacy in Public Health: Basics and beyond.* Bethesda MD: American Society of Health-System Pharmacists; 2010.
14. Beaglehole R. *Public Health at the Crossroads: Achievements and Prospects.* 2nd ed. West Nack, NY: Cambridge: University Press; 2004.
15. Terrie YC. *Vaccinations: The Expanding Role of Pharmacists.* Pharmacy Times 2010; January 14, 2010. Feature focus.
16. Blank C. Pharmacists' role in administering vaccinations on the increase. *Drug Top.* October 3, 2016. http://www.drugtopics.com/vaccination-and-immunization/pharmacists-role-administering-vaccinations-increase.
17. Dahlgren G, Whitehead M. *Policies and Strategies to Promote Social Equity in Health* 14. Stockholm, Sweden: Institute for Future Studies; 2007. https://core.ac.uk/download/pdf/6472456.pdf.
18. Sunwoo S, Kim YS, Cho BL, Cheon KS, Seo HG, Rho MK, et al. Post-marketing surveillance study of the safety and efficacy of sildenafil prescribed in primary care to erectile dysfunction patients. *International Journal of Impotence Research.* 2005;17(1):71—75.
19. Drug Topics. February 12, 2014. http://www.drugtopics.com/associations/pharmacists-key-widespread-hpv-vaccination.

ANSWERS TO PRACTICE QUESTIONS

1. C
2. C
3. B
4. A
5. B

Chapter 15

Pharmacovigilance Systems

Dixon Thomas[1] and Christoph Klika[2]

[1]*Gulf Medical University, Ajman, United Arab Emirates;* [2]*University of Duisburg-Essen, Duisburg, Germany*

Learning Objectives:

Objective 15.1   Introduce the concepts pharmacovigilance, adverse drug event, and adverse drug reaction.
Objective 15.2   Describe the pharmacovigilance framework and the roles of different stakeholders in patient safety.
Objective 15.3   Explain how to report adverse drug events.

OBJECTIVE 15.1. INTRODUCE THE CONCEPTS PHARMACOVIGILANCE, ADVERSE DRUG EVENT, AND ADVERSE DRUG REACTION

Pharmacovigilance (WHO 2002)

The World Health Organization (WHO) defines pharmacovigilance as "the science and activities relating to the detection, assessment, understanding and prevention of adverse effects or any other drug-related problem."[1]

Pharmacovigilance has four general objectives:

- to improve patient care and safety in relation to the use of drugs, and all medical and paramedical interventions;
- to improve public health and safety in relation to the use of drugs;
- to contribute to the assessment of benefit, harm, effectiveness, and risk of drugs, encouraging their safe, rational, and more effective (including cost-effective) use;
- to promote understanding, education, and clinical training in pharmacovigilance and its effective communication with health professionals and the public.

Pharmacovigilance is an essential part of the healthcare system in many countries. As part of national healthcare, pharmacovigilance is regulated through national laws on drug policy. In the European Union (EU), the national laws of member countries have to conform with drug policies made in the EU at the regional level. The pharmacovigilance definitions may vary in some countries in relation to the differences in drug laws. Most of the countries follow more or less the same definitions of the WHO. The WHO in collaboration with the Council of International Organizations of Medical Sciences (CIOMS) and the International Conference on Harmonization (ICH) compiled key terms in pharmacovigilance.[1]

Pharmacovigilance is not just a science of adverse drug reactions (ADRs). It is one of the main sciences dealing with patient safety and includes any drug-related problem that results in adverse events. Pharmacovigilance is an essential part of the drug development process and continues to be important in clinical practice through day-to-day responsibilities of healthcare professionals and postmarketing research. No drug is approved and authorized for use on the market without assessing pharmacovigilance data. Safe and effective use of drugs is fundamental in clinical policy. The question to be asked here is whether the issue of drugs' ineffectiveness should be dealt with by pharmacovigilance. The answer is yes. A drug is supposed to be effective in decreasing the burden of disease; if it fails to do so, harm to the patient is caused by treatment failure, which is a drug-related problem.

Adverse event: Medical occurrence temporally associated with the use of a medicinal product, but not necessarily causally related. Adverse events are commonly called adverse drug events (ADEs).

One of the biggest challenges in pharmacovigilance is to separate the harm caused by the disease from that caused by the drug. When the cause of the reaction could not be associated with the medicinal product, it is an ADE. An ADE after taking a drug may be a complication or altered pathogenesis of the disease itself. There is also the possibility that mysterious genetic or environmental factors are involved. In polypharmacy, the matter becomes more complicated because it is sometimes difficult to identify which drug causes the reaction.[10–19]

Adverse reaction (WHO 1972): A response to a drug that is noxious and unintended, and that occurs at doses normally used in humans for the prophylaxis, diagnosis, or therapy of disease or for the modifications of physiological function.

An adverse reaction, commonly called adverse drug reaction (ADR), has an established causal relationship of a drug or a combination of drugs to the reaction caused. The so-called causality assessment describes the systematic evaluation of reported ADRs to establish a causal link between a drug and the adverse event. The ADR is not necessarily a clinical symptom like a rash; it could also be a significant variation in a laboratory test or other diagnostic measures. An ADR is something that happens when a drug is administered in normal doses to a consumer, not a reaction caused by overdosing (intentional or unintentional). Note that the definition of pharmacovigilance in the EU is different because ADRs include not only overdose but also off-label use, drug abuse, and medication errors.[2] In general, however, ADRs exclude reactions attributed to drug abuse or allergic reactions happening to a particular patient. Some definitions are more inclusive, e.g., the American Society of Health-System Pharmacists defines a significant ADR as any unexpected, unintended, undesired, or excessive response to a drug that

1. Requires discontinuing the drug (therapeutic or diagnostic),
2. Requires changing the drug therapy,
3. Requires modifying the dose (except for minor dosage adjustments),
4. Necessitates admission to a hospital,
5. Prolongs a stay in a healthcare facility,
6. Necessitates supportive treatment,
7. Significantly complicates diagnosis,
8. Negatively affects prognosis, or
9. Results in temporary or permanent harm, disability, or death.

As per this definition, an allergic reaction (an immunologic hypersensitivity occurring as the result of unusual sensitivity to a drug) and an idiosyncratic reaction (an abnormal susceptibility to a drug that is peculiar to the individual) are also considered ADRs.[3]

Side effect: Unintended effect occurring at a normal dose related to the pharmacological properties.

Signal: Defined as reported information regarding a possible causal relationship between a drug and adverse events. Signal detection is an essential element of pharmacovigilance because it helps to identify previously unknown or incompletely documented ADRs. Based on the signal detection, regulators shall decide about possible regulatory actions.[4,5] The strength of the signal depends on the quality of information and the seriousness of the event. In any case, signal detection requires more than one report. To detect signals, pharmacovigilance relies on various sources and methods to establish a causal relationship between drug and an adverse event.

Serious ADE or ADR: Any untoward medical occurrence that at any dose

- results in death
- is life-threatening
- requires inpatient hospitalization or prolongation of existing hospitalization
- results in significant disability or incapacity.

Frequency of ADRs (CIOMS)[1]:

- Very common $\geq 1/10$
- Common (frequent) $\geq 1/100$ and $< 1/10$
- Uncommon (infrequent) $\geq 1/1000$ and $< 1/100$
- Rare $\geq 1/10,000$ and $< 1/1000$
- Very rare $< 1/10,000$

OVERVIEW OF PHARMACOVIGILANCE SYSTEMS

Pharmacovigilance systems are an integral part of healthcare policies in many jurisdictions. In the EU, both marketing authorization holders and member countries are responsible for monitoring the safety of authorized drugs.

Hence, pharmacovigilance in the EU is a system of shared responsibility and cooperation. Furthermore, effective pharmacovigilance systems require cooperation among various actors, such as regulators, pharmaceutical companies marketing a drug, healthcare professionals, and patients.

The cyclooxygenase 2 selective nonsteroidal antiinflammatory drug rofecoxib resulted in many early cardiovascular deaths in the 21st century, resulting in its withdrawal from the market. Improvements in numbers of quality reports and active participation of different stakeholders are essential for consumer safety. Moreover, global data and signal detection are useful in clinical practice throughout the world for patient safety. Advancement in communication in a current pharmacovigilance system shall decrease morbidity and mortality due to ADEs.

To improve the effectiveness of pharmacovigilance systems, ADRs should not be seen as personal failures or lead to the loss of reputation of healthcare professionals. Instead, a culture of care and patient safety should be embedded in national healthcare policies and medical practices in healthcare institutions. As part of this culture, ADR reporting is essential for pharmacovigilance. Gaps between knowledge and action should be decreased, given that response lag by manufacturers, regulators, and healthcare professionals on safety issues potentially result in more casualties.[6] Pharmaceutical products pose significant safety concerns in clinical trials and in clinical practice. Pharmacovigilance is one of the operations in any phase of the clinical trial and even in animal studies. Some safety research is not ethical (e.g., carcinogenicity studies), and thus is not carried out on humans. Once the medicinal product is approved and authorized to the market, the widespread use in bigger populations will help to build more safety data. No pharmaceutical products are without safety concerns; even natural foods can cause unintended effects in populations prone to risk. Healthcare professionals should identify these risk factors and prevent or minimize an actual untoward effect. Having an efficient system of pharmacovigilance in place is essential to consistently monitor and respond to safety concerns about pharmaceutical products.[7] However, some studies have found that underreporting of ADRs is widespread.[8] The main reasons for underreporting are lack of awareness of healthcare professionals regarding the importance of pharmacovigilance, the complexity of reporting, lack of cooperation among healthcare professionals, and technical hindrances.

Pharmacovigilance reports originally focused on reporting ADRs. Currently, with well-established pharmacovigilance systems, especially in industrialized nations, the reports include any drug-related problems. As per the "world medicines situation 2011 pharmacovigilance and safety of medicines," a pharmacovigilance center report includes the following:

- unexpected lack of efficacy;
- quality defects;
- drug abuse;
- medication errors;
- interactions with traditional and herbal drugs; and
- poisoning events.[9]

An ADE could happen due to the poor quality of the product or due to its improper use. It could also happen due to factors that are not under control. The extended focus on additional information is reflected in the EU pharmacovigilance definition, which includes medication errors, for instance.

Mainly, three factors could contribute to ADEs: poor product quality, suboptimal use, and unidentified factors (Fig. 15.1).

FIGURE 15.1 Possible factors resulting in adverse drug events.

Poor Quality Product

Reductions in quality may be intentional or unintentional. The quality of a product can be affected by various mishaps throughout the production cycle, including manufacturing, transportation, and storage. Poor quality assurance in terms of environmental control (temperature, humidity, air pollution, microbial contamination, etc.) can result in poor product quality. This is the case particularly with biological drugs (so-called biologicals). Biologicals are based on living cells and, therefore, are sensitive to change throughout the long and complex process of manufacturing. Adherence to quality standards is vital for ensuring consistent product quality and safety.

Finally, when the product is consumed by the patient, it may have reduced quantities of the labeled products or harmful substances. A good quality product should reach the consumer maintaining its quality and, when given to the patient, should produce intended effects and avoid preventable ADEs. In the United States, product problems should be reported to the FDA when there is a concern about the quality, authenticity, performance, or safety of any medication or device. In the EU, problems can be reported to various regulators in the member countries or directly to the European Medicines Agency (EMA). Problems with product quality include the following:

- suspect counterfeit product;
- product contamination;
- defective components;
- poor packaging or product mix-up;
- questionable stability;
- device malfunctions; and
- labeling concerns.

With drugs, a pharmacist is often the first to recognize a product quality problem. Nurses are often the first to recognize a problem with a medical device. A product problem should be reported through the pharmacovigilance system (e.g., MedWatch).

Suboptimal Drug Use

The scope of a pharmacist's service lies in the optimal use of pharmaceutical products. Rational use of drugs achieves better results. All aspects of drug use should be appropriate for the situation and the patient: right drug, right patient, right dose, right dosage form, right duration, right frequency, right combinations, right lifestyle, diet, etc. Pharmacists, in collaboration with policy-makers and other healthcare professionals, should establish the rational use of drugs.

Medication errors. Medication errors result in ADEs. A higher dose has higher chances of developing an ADE. A lower dose decreases the clinical effectiveness. As a result, the burden of disease is not reduced.

Drug interactions. Drug interactions are not necessarily clinically significant, and sometimes result in beneficial outcomes. However, drug interactions are often harmful and the potential for an ADR increases in the presence of another drug.

Unidentified Factors

ADEs could also happen due to idiosyncratic factors that cannot be explained by pharmacological logic. These ADEs, thus, are difficult to prevent. Confounding factors increase in the presence of comorbidities and multiple medications.

Characteristics of good pharmacovigilance systems include the following:

- Easy to use (reporting forms offline and also online communication like the Yellow Card App in the United Kingdom, accessible manuals for reporting forms, procedures for submission and collection of reports).
- Allows reporting by patients and healthcare providers. Even if healthcare providers and patients are legally allowed to report, easy to use forms and accessible manuals are essential for patients to report.
- Well-structured reports to facilitate analysis.
- Standardized procedures and definitions (e.g., what is a reportable event, follow-up, and processing of case reports).
- Allows analysis of product class level (e.g., erythropoietin) and on an individual product level. Regarding biologicals, reporting of batch numbers is essential given that biologicals are sensitive to change; previously unobserved ADEs may occur only for specific batches of the same drug. However, studies have shown that batch numbers are often not reported even in industrialized nations.
- Procedures for analysis of aggregated information.

- Efficient communication practices improve awareness to report ADRs. Underreporting of ADRs by healthcare professionals and particularly patients is common. All possible means of communication should be utilized, e.g., websites, social media, leaflets, etc. In some countries, regulators cooperate with schools to strengthen the national pharmacovigilance system in the long run.
- Training of healthcare professionals. Training could improve reporting of ADRs (i.e., quantity) and the quality of reported information. E-learning tools and educational materials for healthcare professionals and patients are useful to increase the quantity and quality of ADR reporting.

OBJECTIVE 15.2. DESCRIBE THE PHARMACOVIGILANCE FRAMEWORK AND THE ROLES OF DIFFERENT STAKEHOLDERS IN PATIENT SAFETY

Pharmacovigilance systems are based on the shared responsibilities of different stakeholders, including international organizations, healthcare institutions, policy-makers, and patients. With a view to the effective operation of these systems, different stakeholders should be connected for mutual benefits, and roles and responsibilities should be well defined. In the EU, for instance, the European Network of Centres for Pharmacoepidemiology and Pharmacovigilance aims to improve the science and practice of pharmacovigilance by connecting various stakeholders. Rare ADRs happen sporadically. The rest of the world benefits from reporting of such information. In resource-limited countries, integrating supporting programs are essential for building capacity in pharmacovigilance systems.[20]

Fully developed pharmacovigilance systems and responsible actions of all stakeholders could prevent and manage more ADEs than otherwise. Effective and timely communication between different stakeholders is a key aspect to share and utilize scientific information pertaining to pharmacovigilance. Other specific actions by different stakeholders in pharmacovigilance are provided in the following sections.[11]

Patient/Carers

Patients or their carers report ADEs to healthcare professionals. This includes mostly pharmacists, doctors, and nurses. Patients have limited skills to differentiate between adverse events due to drugs or other factors. Consulting healthcare professionals helps in clarifying what is going wrong.

Healthcare Professionals

Many times, healthcare professionals may not report such events to pharmacovigilance systems due to various constraints, including busy schedules. Depending on the national jurisdiction, in which the pharmocovigilance system operates, they might also fear official inquiries and legal consequences, in case they are held liable for ADEs. The WHO in its guidelines on patient safety states that "the fundamental role of patient safety reporting systems is to enhance patient safety by learning from failures of the healthcare system. Reporting must be safe. Individuals who report incidents must not be punished or suffer ill-effects from reporting." Effective policies on patient safety require sound legal foundations, but there are also social and cultural challenges in healthcare institutions in the daily practice of pharmacovigilance.[21]

National pharmacovigilance systems have different terms and definitions with regard to the notion of healthcare professionals, but the following groups can be included: medical doctors (including general and specialized practitioners), nursing and midwifery professionals, dentists, and pharmacists.

The widespread underreporting of ADRs, among other reasons, is due to ADRs being often seen as a personal failure and associated with a loss of reputation. Apart from social changes in healthcare institutions, effective pharmacovigilance requires a no-blame culture in which healthcare professionals can report ADEs without having to fear legal consequences. The Council of Europe advocates the development of pharmacovigilance systems in which it is not the individual that is blamed but that aims to improve the institutional conditions under which healthcare professionals work.[22] Hence, in addition to the legal foundation of such systems, effective pharmacovigilance also faces social and cultural challenges regarding the daily practice in healthcare institutions.[21]

Healthcare professionals are supposed to be trained to take part efficiently in pharmacovigilance operations. The WHO states that healthcare professionals "maintain health in humans through the application of the principles and procedures of evidence-based practice and caring."[23]

They also have responsibilities to update their knowledge in the field through continuing education. Getting to know newer safety information about pharmaceutical products greatly benefits their patients and increases patient safety. Technical knowledge and skills in assessing patient conditions help healthcare professionals to monitor patient outcomes after medication use. Patients are motivated to report their problems to the healthcare professionals to get clarity on what is going wrong. Nurses and pharmacists usually report any adverse events, which they are not clear about, to the doctors who have higher skills in diagnosing an ADR. Well-educated pharmacists with clinical skills are in a better position than ever before in diagnosing many ADEs by themselves.

Manufacturers

From the viewpoint of trade, as drugs are manufactured and sold by the pharmaceutical companies, they are ultimately responsible for quality and safety of the product. In the pharmacovigilance policy of the EU, for instance, companies holding authorizations to market drugs are responsible for operating a pharmacovigilance system. This system operates in concert with the pharmacovigilance system of the member countries. However, the responsibility of the pharmaceutical companies as the authorization holder does not mean that other stakeholders are not responsible. Manufacturers have to work with healthcare professionals, patients, and regulators to generate safety reports about pharmaceutical products.

Regulators

Drug regulators make laws, guidelines, and policies related to manufacturing, distribution, storage, use, and disposal of pharmaceutical products at all levels of government. At the international level, pharmacovigilance is coordinated by the WHO. At the regional level, the EU has developed a comprehensive pharmacovigilance policy in close cooperation with national regulators. Regulators approve pharmaceutical products to market when the reports suggest its acceptable safety profiles. This can be referred to as market authorization. The regulators continue to monitor the product and mandate the manufacturers to report ADEs from clinical practice. Hence, marketing authorization holders are key actors of pharmacovigilance. Regulators also welcome voluntary reports from healthcare professionals and patients on safety issue experiences related to the products.

Regulators usually establish a pharmacovigilance system with a framework of national, regional, and institutional pharmacovigilance centers. Across levels of government, coordination and networking are crucial for effective pharmacovigilance. Technical and financial support is provided to these centers for generating and communicating quality reports. In the EU, the EMA is at the hub of national regulator's networks. The main task of EMA is to coordinate the evaluation of medicinal products and to advise the EU institutions and the member countries on issues relating to regulation. Following the latest reform of drug policy in the EU, the Pharmacovigilance Risk Assessment Committee (PRAC) has been created in the EMA framework. The PRAC assesses and monitors the safety of medicinal products in Europe.

In most pharmacovigilance systems, like in the United States, regulators also monitor international plants that manufacture pharmaceutical products to be used in the country. Regulators create and maintain pharmacovigilance systems in their countries and coordinate activities of different stakeholders within that country. The national pharmacovigilance systems connect to international pharmacovigilance systems. Pharmacovigilance activities happen through regular communication to manufacturers, healthcare professionals, and patients in the country.

Regulators are committed to train healthcare professionals and encourage clinician and patient reporting of ADEs. Governments/regulators should have sufficient technical and financial recourses to develop and maintain effective pharmacovigilance systems. However, even in industrialized nations, the effectiveness of pharmacovigilance is hampered by the lack of resources and training.[8]

International Organizations and Healthcare Organizations

Organizations like WHO coordinate reporting of drug-related ADEs and generate global information that is shared with different stakeholders. WHO also takes a major role in ensuring the quality of drugs manufactured and used. It has measures to standardize drugs globally by assigning generic names and promoting generic prescribing. Assigning anatomical, therapeutic, and chemical coding and defined daily dose is another strategy to identify and standardize the use of drugs by WHO.

In the EU, the EMA coordinates the evaluation of drugs by national regulators. EMA also maintains the collection of ADR reports in the EudraVigilance database. Through various networks and groups of experts and regulators, EMA contributes to the development of EU health policy in general and pharmacovigilance in particular.

Organizations like ISMP, universities, and healthcare facilities conduct research to generate pharmacovigilance information. The information is communicated to other stakeholders directly or through publishing in appropriate media.

Most of the organizations start their pharmacovigilance centers to perform their operations. Drug and poison information centers in healthcare facilities sometimes coordinate pharmacovigilance operations as an additional service.

These organizations also organize training programs for healthcare professionals or patients/caregivers in different aspects for safe use of pharmaceutical products. Organizations also develop guidelines for the healthcare professionals to implement and monitor the safe use of drugs.

Pharmacists should take care to maintain the quality of a product, prescribers should recommend it appropriately, the nurse should administer it safely, and the patient/caregivers should follow all instructions provided by healthcare professionals. Pharmacists, being specialists of drugs and with clinical expertise, should monitor all stages of drug use for the benefit of the patients.

The notion of patient safety has gained traction in the last few decades to become an issue of high salience in public health and healthcare. Various individual and institutional factors drove the development to patient safety: committed healthcare professionals and developments in public policy making, risk management, and legal systems. Accordingly, policies on patient safety entail multiple challenges for legal systems and the management and culture of healthcare institutions.[21] Pharmacovigilance and reporting of ADEs is a key component of public health and healthcare.

Pharmacovigilance is an essential part of the healthcare system, and ensuring public health through product safety is of great importance in industrialized countries. However, there is significant variation in terms of organization, financing, and responsibility for health. Accordingly, health policy and pharmacovigilance systems vary even in rather homogeneous regions such as Europe, for instance.[8] Given that pharmacovigilance relies on cooperation and coordination at the international level, international organizations are important for developing patient safety policies.

At the international level, the WHO is a key actor in promoting and implementing patient safety policies. In 2002, the 55th World Health Assembly adopted a resolution urging Member States to "pay the closest possible attention to the problem of patient safety."[24] The resolution emphasized the importance of global norms and standards for product safety, ADR reporting, and a culture of safety in healthcare organizations. In the wake of the resolution, two Patient Safety Global Action Summits were held in 2016 and 2017 to facilitate exchange and collaboration between medical experts and policymakers. Such collaboration is needed to address the multiple challenges of pharmacovigilance.

A key issue is the development of legal systems that facilitate the reporting of ADEs. The WHO and the Council of Europe should work toward promoting the development of legal systems facilitating ADR reporting. For many healthcare professionals, reporting of ADRs is seen as a personal failure and associated with a loss of reputation. Apart from the social and cultural challenges in healthcare institutions, effective pharmacovigilance requires a legal system that facilitates reporting. The WHO guidelines for ADE reporting state that patient safety builds on patient reporting and that individuals who report must not face negative consequences.[25] The Council of Europe has issued recommendations to balance the requirements of patient safety through reporting and learning, and the legal protection of patients with confidentiality and legal protection of healthcare professionals.[22] This is referred to as a culture of no blame. Some countries have introduced legislation to facilitate patient reporting in a no-blame culture.[21]

To improve patient safety in nonindustrialized countries, the WHO, together with public and private donors, promotes and implements additional methods of pharmacovigilance to complement spontaneous ADR reporting.[26]

Joint Commission International accreditation of healthcare facilities includes monitoring on the International Patient Safety Goals (IPSGs). IPSGs help accredited organizations address specific areas of concern in some of the most problematic areas of patient safety. The six IPSGs are[27]

Goal 1: Identify patients correctly
Goal 2: Improve effective communication
Goal 3: Improve the safety of high-alert medications
Goal 4: Ensure safe surgery
Goal 5: Reduce the risk of healthcare-associated infections
Goal 6: Reduce the risk of patient harm resulting from falls

OBJECTIVE 15.3. EXPLAIN HOW TO REPORT ADVERSE DRUG EVENTS

ADRs could be clinical or variations in laboratory values. Different trigger tools help in reporting. Standardized forms are used in reporting ADEs. These forms are designed for easy filling and for compliance with the format used in the international pharmacovigilance system. The national and institutional ADE reporting format is standardized in international format. After the ADE data are collected, they are analyzed for causality, severity, preventability, etc. The WHO's International Drug Monitoring Program collects Individual Case Safety Reports (ICSRs) from its member states. Healthcare professionals could report ADEs to regional or national pharmacovigilance centers. If a causal relationship

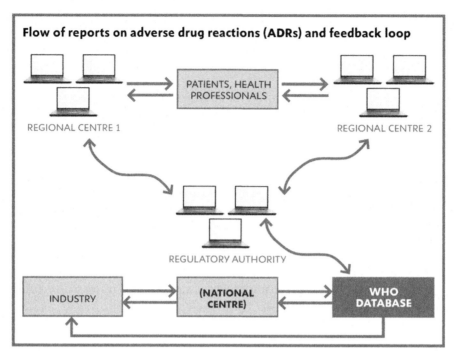

FIGURE 15.2 Flow of reports on adverse drug reaction and their feedback. *Adapted with permission from Pal S, Dodoo A, Mantel A, Olsson S. The World Medicines Situation 2011. Pharmacovigilance and Safety of Medicines. Geneva: World Health Oraganization; 2011. http://apps.who.int/medicinedocs/documents/s18771en/s18771en.pdf.*

is established, it will be considered as an ADR, if not an ADE. Many regulators consider the reporting system to be for ADEs as it is advisable to report any adverse events even if the causal relationship with a drug is not established. Consumers might report adverse experiences after consuming their medication. They are not trained to conclude the causal relationship. All that they are submitting are ADEs until the causal relationship is established by the experts. National pharmacovigilance centers are usually part of the country's drug regulatory agency. The national center will forward these reports to the WHO collaborating center for International Drug Monitoring, Uppsala Monitoring Center (UMC) in Sweden. The flow of reports on ADRs and their feedback is illustrated in Fig. 15.2.

Vigiflow. Vigiflow is software from the UMC for the reporting of ADRs. It helps, especially, developing countries with limited technical resources to report ADRs.

Vigiaccess. Vigiaccess is an open access database from the UMC. Anyone can access it to see the numbers of ADR reports globally.[28]

Spontaneous Reporting on Adverse Drug Reactions

Most countries, industrialized and nonindustrialized alike, rely primarily on spontaneous and voluntary ADR reporting.[26] Spontaneous reporting of suspected ADRs (these are ADEs suspected as ADRs; confirmed as ADRs when causality relationship is established) is a voluntary activity involving any healthcare professionals or consumers. Many safety signals are generated through spontaneous reporting, encouraging voluntary reporting results in a safety culture. All stakeholders communicate through a pharmacovigilance system that reminds everyone of their responsibilities in detecting, preventing, and managing ADEs. With voluntary reporting, the numbers of reports generated are relatively few compared with the actual occurrence of ADEs. The reports could also be incomplete. Most of the reports are based on suspicions based on ADEs that happen following drug use. It is not clear that those cases are truly an ADR to the reported drug. Many factors affect voluntary reporting of suspected ADRs:

- Diffusion of responsibility (many professionals feel someone else shall report the event, and finally no one is responsible for taking it forward).
- Technical insufficiencies for reporting to the pharmacovigilance system.
- Fear of punishment or blame for harming the patients.
- Time constraints in reporting and follow-up if any.

- Institutional policies that discourage reporting of ADEs due to concerns for reputation.
- Lack of training and motivation to healthcare professionals shall decrease abilities to detect ADRs or ignore them.[11]

Examples of databases that collect voluntary reporting:

- WHO International Drug Monitoring Program Vigibase
- US FDA ADR Reporting System for Pharmaceutical Products (FAERS)

Some countries use registries instead of reporting to such databases. These registries from databases could be used further in epidemiological studies. Many hospitals keep their own registries, like a cancer registry, pregnancy registry, ADE registry, etc. Registries are helpful for the organization to analyze the trends in ADEs and become a quality tool to observe the effectiveness of remedial actions to decrease ADEs. Registries are not a good source of rare events as there will be only a few or none. Instead, if these registries connect with international databases that pool events reported from a bigger population, they allow the gathering of more generalizable information. The problem of connecting registries to the international database is its compliance with the formats.

Mandatory Reporting

It is compulsory for manufacturers to conduct postmarketing surveillance of their products in most countries. The pharmacovigilance report should be submitted to regulators at prescribed intervals. When a new drug is approved for marketing, for a few years it is mandatory to report ADEs to the regulators. Manufacturers provide technical and financial support to healthcare facilities to enable reporting. They also facilitate training to healthcare professionals for reporting. Certain national healthcare systems integrate pharmacovigilance reporting into clinical practice. The presence of these types of systems in developed countries results in higher reporting. Such mandatory reporting is present in some of the public health programs (HIV/AIDS, malaria, tuberculosis, etc.) in developing countries. External funding, technical support, and frequent training improve reporting.[11]

EudraVigilance is not exactly voluntary. Marketing authorization holders must report ADRs during drug development after marketing. Reporting obligations are defined in the respective EU legislation and guidance.

Features of a good pharmacovigilance report[29]:

- Description of ADEs
- Suspected and concomitant product therapy details (e.g., dose, dates of therapy)
- Patient characteristics (e.g., age, sex), baseline medical condition, comorbid condition, family history, other risk factors
- Documentation of the diagnosis
- Clinical course and outcomes
- Relevant therapeutic measures and laboratory data
- Dechallenge and rechallenge information
- Reporter contact information
- Any other relevant information

CONCLUSION

Pharmacovigilance is a part of healthcare systems worldwide. The WHO leads pharmacovigilance operations and provides technical support in reporting ADRs. Many countries have well-built pharmacovigilance systems, but actual incidence of ADRs is much higher than what is reported. Underreporting of ADRs is a major problem as well as the quality of reports. The basic objective of pharmacovigilance is the safe use of drugs, patient safety, and, ultimately, safeguarding public health. To achieve this goal, national regulators and international organizations should empower healthcare professionals and the public to report more ADRs.

PRACTICE QUESTIONS

1. Which of the following adverse events is a characteristic feature of an ADR?
   A. Possible clinical symptom
   B. A drug causally related to it
   C. Signal produced before the actual occurrence
   D. Another drug could reverse it

2. Which of the following is a true statement of pharmacovigilance?
  A. The definition of pharmacovigilance is universal
  B. Pharmacovigilance uses a single method in decision making
  C. More than one report is required in signal detection
  D. Drug eruption is considered as serious ADR

3. How does WHO's International Drug Monitoring Program collect reports on ADRs?
  A. ICSRs
  B. ADR report
  C. CIOMS report
  D. ICH report

4. ADR reporting by postmarketing surveillance, especially in Europe, is
  A. Spontaneous reporting
  B. Mandatory reporting
  C. Registry reporting
  D. Voluntary reporting

5. In the new drug development process, pharmacovigilance is part of
  A. Animal studies
  B. Clinical trials
  C. Postmarketing surveillance
  D. All of the above

6. ADEs could happen because of
  A. Poor quality product
  B. Improper use
  C. Unknown reasons
  D. All of the above

REFERENCES

1. *Uppsala Monitoring Center. Definitions*; May 2015. http://www.who.int/medicines/areas/quality_safety/safety_efficacy/trainingcourses/definitions.pdf.
2. European Medicines Agency. *Guideline on Good Pharmacovigilance Practices (GVP) - Annex I - Definitions (Rev 4)*; 2017. http://www.ema.europa.eu/docs/en_GB/document_library/Scientific_guideline/2013/05/WC500143294.pdf.
3. American Society of Health-System Pharmacists. ASHP guidelines on adverse drug reaction monitoring and reporting. *Am J Health Pharm.* 1995;52(4):417–419. https://www.ashp.org/-/media/assets/policy-guidelines/docs/guidelines/adverse-drug-reaction-monitoring-reporting.ashx?la=en&hash=BA21811884B2B15321E4649045740DD4B4D0801B.
4. Inácio P, Airaksinen M, Cavaco A. Language does not come "in boxes": assessing discrepancies between adverse drug reactions spontaneous reporting and MedDRA® codes in European Portuguese. *Res Soc Adm Pharm.* 2015;11(5):664–674. https://doi.org/10.1016/j.sapharm.2014.11.009.
5. Kumar A, Khan H. Signal detection and their assessment in pharmacovigilance. *Open Pharm Sci J.* 2015;2(1):66–73. https://doi.org/10.2174/1874844901502010066.
6. Systems for Improved Access to Pharmaceuticals and Services (SIAPS) Program. *Comparative Analysis of Pharmacovigilance Systems in Five Asian Countries.* USAID and MSH; 2013. http://apps.who.int/medicinedocs/documents/s21335en/s21335en.pdf.
7. Isah AO, Pal SN, Olsson S, Dodoo A, Bencheikh RS. Specific features of medicines safety and pharmacovigilance in Africa. *Ther Adv Drug Saf.* 2012;3(1):25–34. https://doi.org/10.1177/2042098611425695.
8. Kaeding M, Schmälter J, Klika C. *Pharmacovigilance in the European Union : Practical Implementation across Member States*; 2017. http://www.springer.com/gp/book/9783658172756.
9. Pal S, Dodoo A, Mantel A, Olsson S. *The World Medicines Situation 2011. Pharmacovigilance and Safety of Medicines.* Geneva: World Health Organization; 2011. http://apps.who.int/medicinedocs/documents/s18771en/s18771en.pdf.
10. Strengthening Pharmaceutical Systems Program, USAID. *Supporting Pharmacovigilance in Developing Countries The Systems Perspective*; 2009. http://apps.who.int/medicinedocs/en/d/Js18813en/.
11. Olson C. Pharmacovigilance. In: *MDS-3: Managing Access to Medicines and Health Technologies.* Arlington: Management Sciences for Health; 2012, 35.1–35.19.
12. US FDA. *Reporting Serious Problems to FDA - Product Problems*; 2017. https://www.accessdata.fda.gov/scripts/medwatch/index.cfm?action=reporting.home.
13. Almarsdóttir AB, Traulsen JM. Rational use of medicines — an important issue in pharmaceutical policy. *Pharm World Sci.* 2005;27(2):76–80. https://doi.org/10.1007/s11096-005-3303-7.
14. Barrett JS, Patel D, Dombrowsky E, Bajaj G, Skolnik JM. Risk assessment of drug interaction potential and concomitant dosing pattern on targeted toxicities in pediatric cancer patients. *AAPS J.* 2013;15(3):775–786. https://doi.org/10.1208/s12248-013-9489-z.

15. Uetrecht J, Naisbitt DJ. Idiosyncratic adverse drug reactions: current concepts. *Pharmacol Rev.* 2013;65(2):779–808. https://doi.org/10.1124/pr.113.007450.
16. IFPMA. *Pharmacovigilance — Good pharmacovigilance Principles and Considerations for Biotherapeutic Medicines.*
17. Klein K, Scholl JHG, Vermeer NS, et al. Traceability of biologics in The Netherlands: an analysis of information-recording systems in clinical practice and spontaneous ADR. *Rep Drug Saf.* 2016;39(2):185–192. https://doi.org/10.1007/s40264-015-0383-8.
18. Vermeer NS, Straus SMJM, Mantel-Teeuwisse AK, et al. Traceability of biopharmaceuticals in spontaneous reporting systems: a cross-sectional study in the FDA adverse event reporting system (FAERS) and EudraVigilance databases. *Drug Saf.* 2013;36(8):617–625. https://doi.org/10.1007/s40264-013-0073-3.
19. Moore N, Bégaud B. Improving pharmacovigilance in Europe. *BMJ.* 2010;340:c1694. http://www.ncbi.nlm.nih.gov/pubmed/20385717.
20. Olsson S, Pal SN, Dodoo A. Pharmacovigilance in resource-limited countries. *Expert Rev Clin Pharmacol.* 2015;8(4):449–460. https://doi.org/10.1586/17512433.2015.1053391.
21. Tingle J, Bark P. *Patient Safety, Law Policy and Practice. Routledge;* 2011. https://www.routledge.com/Patient-Safety-Law-Policy-and-Practice/Tingle-Bark/p/book/9780415557313.
22. The Council of the European Union. Council Recommendation on patient safety, including the prevention and control of healthcare associated infections. *Off J Eur Union;* 2009, 2009/C 151 https://ec.europa.eu/health/sites/health/files/patient_safety/docs/council_2009_en.pdf.
23. WHO. Definition and list of health professionals. In: *Trasformative Education for Health Professionals;* July 31, 2018. Accessed on http://whoeducationguidelines.org/content/1-definition-and-list-health-professionals.
24. WHO. *Quality of Care: Patient Safety;* 2002. http://www.who.int/medicines/areas/quality_safety/safety_efficacy/ewha5518.pdf.
25. WHO. *World Alliance for Patient Safety;* 2004. http://www.who.int/patientsafety/en/brochure_final.pdf.
26. Pal SN, Duncombe C, Falzon D, Olsson S. WHO strategy for collecting safety data in public health programmes: complementing spontaneous reporting systems. *Drug Saf.* 2013;36(2):75–81. https://doi.org/10.1007/s40264-012-0014-6.
27. Joint Commission International. *International Patient Safety Goals;* 2017. https://www.jointcommissioninternational.org/improve/international-patient-safety-goals/.
28. *Uppsala Monitoring Center.* VigiAccess; 2017. http://www.vigiaccess.org/.
29. US FDA. *Characteristics of a Good Adverse Event Report.* FDA MedWatchLearn; 2017. https://www.accessdata.fda.gov/scripts/MedWatchLearn/good-report.htm.

ANSWERS TO PRACTICE QUESTIONS

1. B
2. C
3. A
4. B
5. D
6. D

Chapter 16

Adverse Drug Events, Medication Errors, and Drug Interactions

Vincent W.L. Tsui[1], Dixon Thomas[2], Shuhui Tian[3] and Allen J. Vaida[4]

[1]Queen Elizabeth Hospital, Hong Kong; [2]Gulf Medical University, Ajman, United Arab Emirates; [3]Beijing United Family Healthcare, Chaoyang District, Beijing, China; [4]Institute for Safe Medication Practices, Horsham, PA, United States

Learning Objectives:

Objective 16.1 Classify and detail adverse drug events.
Objective 16.2 Explain methods for prevention and management of adverse drug events.
Objective 16.3 Classify and detail medication errors.
Objective 16.4 Explain methods for prevention and management of medication errors.
Objective 16.5 Classify and detail drug interactions.
Objective 16.6 Explain methods for prevention and management of drug interactions.

OBJECTIVE 16.1. CLASSIFY AND DETAIL ADVERSE DRUG EVENTS

The World Health Organization (WHO) defines an adverse drug reaction (ADR) as *"a drug-related event that is noxious and unintended and occurs at doses used in humans for prophylaxis, diagnosis or therapy of disease or for the modification of physiological function."* Adverse drug event (ADE) is *"any untoward occurrence that may present during treatment with a pharmaceutical product but that does not necessarily have a causal relation to the treatment."* ADR has a causal relationship for the reaction to a drug. ADR is a type of ADE. Causes of an ADR could be directly attributed to a drug and its pharmacological properties. ADRs were always considered nonpreventable since they occur even if a drug is prescribed, dispensed, or administered appropriately. There is a growing understanding that ADRs may be preventable due to advances in our knowledge of how to prescribe and test drugs for certain patients (i.e., genomics). Many still consider these to preventable medication errors. ADEs that happen due to inappropriate drug use (medication error) or poor control of other contributing factors are considered preventable. ADEs are not necessarily caused by the drug's pharmacology itself. Insulin is known to cause hypoglycemia, but if it is rightly dosed, hypoglycemia is prevented. If the patient skips a meal one day without reducing the dose of insulin they may experience hypoglycemia. This is a preventable ADE occurring due to medication error of wrong drug administration. This incidence should not result in changes of the daily dose as long as meals and dose are scheduled accordingly. This concept highlights that healthcare professionals and consumers must communicate on proper drug administration and just not blame this occurrence as an ADR from the drug. There could be possibilities of many ADRs occurring even if the drug is appropriately prescribed, dispensed, and administered. A general confusion is prevalent in published articles to use ADEs and ADRs interchangeably.[1] Refer to Fig. 16.1. It compares the relationship between medication errors, ADEs, preventable ADEs, nonpreventable ADEs (ADRs), and potential ADEs.[32,33] ADEs have a significant cost both financially and in terms of quality of life. Few studies of ADRs have been conducted in the community, so the effect on primary care is harder to assess, but studies in the hospital environment have shown the following[1]:

- ADRs occur in 10%−20% of patients in the hospital
- ADRs are responsible for 5% of admissions to the hospital
- ADRs might be responsible for 1 in 1000 deaths in medical wards
- ADRs are the most common cause of iatrogenic injury in hospital patients

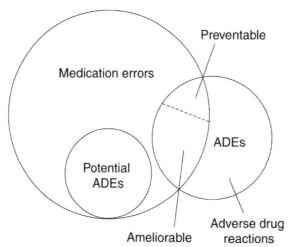

FIGURE 16.1 Relationship among medication errors, adverse drug events (ADEs), preventable ADEs, adverse drug reactions, and potential or preventable ADEs.[33] *Reproduced with permission from BMJ Quality & Safety.*

Classification of Adverse Drug Reactions

Some classification systems exist, but the most widely accepted is to group ADRs as types A to F (Table 16.1). Type A and type F are dose related and commonly occurring, while types B to E are uncommon.[2]

ADRs are also classified by severity into mild, moderate, severe, and lethal (Table 16.2).[4,5]

TABLE 16.1 Classification of Adverse Drug Reactions (ADRs)

Drug Reaction	Examples
Type A: Reactions occurring, given sufficient dose and duration of therapy: common and predictable (dose related or augmented)[2]	
Overdose (usually classified under adverse drug events)	• Hepatic failure with acetaminophen • Metabolic acidosis with aspirin
Side effects	• Nausea, headache with methylxanthines • Oral thrush or vaginal candidiasis with glucocorticoids • Nephrotoxicity with aminoglycosides
Secondary or indirect effects	• Diarrhea due to alteration in gastrointestinal bacteria after antibiotics • Phototoxicity with doxycycline or thiazide diuretics
Drug interactions	• Macrolide antibiotics increasing theophylline, digoxin, or statin blood levels
Type B: Drug hypersensitivity reactions restricted to a small subset of the general population: rare and mostly unpredictable (nondose related or bizarre)[2]	
Intolerance[a]	Tinnitus after a single aspirin tablet
Idiosyncrasy[b] (pharmacogenetics)	• Glucose-6-phosphate dehydrogenase deficiency: hemolytic anemia after oxidative drugs, e.g., dapsone[c] • Thiopurine methyltransferase deficiency: toxicity during azathioprine therapy[c] • Pseudoallergic reaction with nonsteroidal antiinflammatory drugs
Immunologic drug reactions (allergy)	• Anaphylaxis from beta-lactam antibiotics • Photoallergy with quinidine • Immune-mediated thrombocytopenia (with heparin) • Serum sickness (with antivenom preparations) • Vasculitis (with phenytoin) • Stevens–Johnson syndrome (with trimethoprim–sulfamethoxazole) • Drug-induced hypersensitivity syndrome (with allopurinol in HLA-B[a]58:01 individuals)[c]
Type C: Persisting for a relatively long time (dose related and time related or chronic)[3]	
"Continuing" reactions	Osteonecrosis of the jaw with bisphosphonates

Continued

TABLE 16.1 Classification of Adverse Drug Reactions (ADRs)—cont'd

Drug Reaction	Examples
Type D: Becoming apparent sometime after the use of a drug, which may make them more difficult to detect (time related or delayed)[3]	
"Delayed" reactions	Leucopenia with lomustine, which can occur up to 6 weeks after a dose
Type E: Associated with withdrawal of the drug (withdrawal or end of use)[3]	
"End-of-use" reactions	Insomnia, anxiety, and perceptual disturbances following the withdrawal of benzodiazepines
Type F: Unexpected failure of therapy (failure)	
Therapy failure	Therapy failure due to substandard or falsified drug products

[a]Side effects at subtherapeutic doses.
[b]Drug effect not attributable to known pharmacologic properties of the drug and not immune mediated.
[c]This is an example of a type B reaction that is predictable.

TABLE 16.2 Classification of Adverse Drug Reactions (ADRs) Based on Severity

Severity	Description	Example
Mild	No antidote or treatment is required; hospitalization is not prolonged.	• Antihistamines (some): drowsiness • Opioids: constipation
Moderate	A change in treatment, e.g., modified dosage, addition of a drug, but not necessarily discontinuation of the drug, is required; hospitalization may be prolonged, or specific treatment may be required.	• Hormonal contraceptives: venous thrombosis • Nonsteroidal antiinflammatory drugs: hypertension and edema
Severe	An ADR is potentially life-threatening and requires discontinuation of the drug and specific treatment of the ADR. May sometimes even cause disabilities, congenital anomaly, etc.	• ACE inhibitors: angioedema • Phenothiazines: abnormal heart rhythm
Lethal	An ADR directly or indirectly contributes to a patient's death.	• Nonsteroidal antiinflammatory drugs: Stevens–Johnson syndrome. • Desferrioxamine: congestive heart failure

OBJECTIVE 16.2. EXPLAIN METHODS FOR PREVENTION AND MANAGEMENT OF ADVERSE DRUG EVENTS

High-alert medication (also known as high-risk medication): Although most medications have a large margin of safety, a small number of drugs have a high risk of causing injury when they are misused. We call these "high-alert medications" to draw attention to this characteristic so that all involved in their use will treat them with the care and respect that they require. Errors may or may not be more common with these drugs than with the use of any others; however, the consequences of the errors are more devastating. For this reason, special considerations are required. These medications often need to be packaged differently, stored differently, prescribed differently, and administered differently than others. Whenever possible, "forcing function" methods that make it impossible for the drug to be given in a potentially lethal manner should be developed and instituted.[6]

Preventability of Adverse Drug Events

ADE is a negative health outcome. It is estimated that at least 60% of ADEs are preventable.[7] Several interventions have been used to prevent ADEs and can generally be categorized as provider- or system-based interventions. Provider- and system-based interventions should be used together to prevent ADEs optimally.

Provider-based approach—The individual clinician should ideally review the medication list at each patient encounter. Issues to consider range from dosage and directions to drug interactions and side effects.[8,9]

• **Avoid and be vigilant of high-alert drugs**—Several drug classes have been consistently associated with ADRs in studies of hospitalized patients.[10] Clinicians prescribing high-risk drugs should be vigilant of adverse effects and should consider discontinuing these drugs or replacing with drugs that are less likely to cause adverse effects.

- **Discontinue unnecessary drugs**—The risk of ADEs increases with the number of medications taken.[11–13] In addition to potentially harmful drugs, patients are often taking drugs that were previously given for a prior indication and are no longer needed.
- **Avoid drug–drug interactions**—The risk of an ADE due to drug–drug interactions is substantially higher when more medications are being prescribed. Most drug–drug interactions involve commonly used medications. As an example, the risk of bleeding with warfarin therapy is increased with coadministration of nonsteroidal antiinflammatory drugs (NSAIDs), selective serotonin reuptake inhibitors (SSRIs), omeprazole, lipid-lowering agents, and/or amiodarone.[14]
- **Adjust dosing based on age and creatinine clearance**—A common cause of ADEs is a failure to properly adjust doses for age and renal insufficiency. Adjusting appropriately for age is particularly important in pediatric and geriatric populations. Renal impairment can occur at any age but becomes more common with advancing age. For patients with stable renal function, creatinine clearance can be estimated according to published formulas that factor age into the calculation.[15]

System-based approach—Most ADEs are caused by poorly designed systems that either induce errors or make them difficult to detect. Although human error is usually the proximal event leading to an ADE, another fundamental fault is in the system that permits the error to reach the patient.[16]

High-leverage strategies fix the system; low-leverage strategies focus on the individual involved in an error. Because people cannot be expected to compensate for weak systems, error prevention tools that are designed to fix the system have a broader, more lasting impact (high leverage) than those directed at changing human behavior (low leverage).[17]

- **Computerized physician order entry (CPOE)**—CPOE refers to a variety of computer-based systems that facilitate the medication ordering process.[18] Some CPOE systems provide more than prescription-writing capabilities with fixed fields and drop-down menus for drug, dose, route, and frequency. These systems are further enhanced by the integration of clinical decision support systems (CDSSs) of varying sophistication. CDSS includes interactive software designed to assist health professionals in making clinical choices. CPOE with CDSS targets the prescribing stage of the medication use process and improves medication safety in the following ways:
  - Providing a means for standardization of practice
  - Improving the completeness and legibility of orders
  - Alerting clinicians to drug allergies, drug–drug interactions, and cumulative dose limits
  - Updating clinicians with the most current medication information
  - Providing dosage adjustment calculations based on patient characteristics
  - Timely communication of critical changes in a patient's condition, in turn facilitating appropriate adjustments

Several studies have found that CPOE with CDSS significantly prevents medication errors and ADEs. However, some others have reported unintended consequences related to the introduction of CPOE, especially among CPOE systems with limited decision support.[19–21]

- **Electronic medication administration record (eMAR)**—When CPOE has an electronic interface with an eMAR, the need for medication transcription is eliminated, removing errors caused by interpretation and translation. Moreover, eMAR helps organize medication administration schedules and prompts nurses to ensure timely medication administration.
- **Pharmacist interventions**—Pharmacists can play an important role in preventing ADEs through various interventions, such as patient counseling, medication reconciliation, and drug class-specific pharmacist services, e.g., anticoagulation clinics.
- **Others**—**Barcodes** can be affixed to medications and patient wristbands to ensure matching between patients, their eMAR, and their medications at the time of drug administration. **Smart pumps** are used to reduce errors associated with intravenous medication administration through their built-in safety features, such as safety alerts, clinical calculators, dose limits, and drug libraries. **Educational programs** may modestly decrease rates of medication errors and ADEs.[22] ADE reporting systems that include a subsection for ADRs should be established to encourage all professionals to report certain or probable/likely ADRs and other ADEs.

Use of Signals

Early identification of the hazards associated with drugs is the main goal of those involved in pharmacovigilance "signal detection," "signal generation," or "signaling." It refers to a process that aims to find, as soon as possible, any indication of an unexpected drug safety problem. A signal may indicate a new ADR or a change of the frequency of an ADR that is already known to be associated with the drugs involved.[23] Signals are not confirmation for the ADRs. Assessment of signals for a causal relationship between the drug and the reported ADE will confirm the ADRs. Signals are useful in taking measures to prevent and manage newer ADEs.[24]

Causality Assessment of Adverse Drug Reactions

Causality assessment is the method by which the extent of relationship between a drug and a suspected reaction is established, i.e., to attribute clinical events to drugs in individual patients or in case reports.[25] Many systems can be used to make a causality assessment of ADR reports among which the causality categories described by the Uppsala Monitoring Centre (Table 16.3) and the Naranjo algorithm (Tables 16.4 and 16.5) are the most commonly used.[26,27] Both of them have not been validated, and studies evaluating agreement between the two did not give consistent results.[28,29] The adoption of a particular system will be based on the consensus of the causality assessment committee involved. However, in case of analysis of serious ADRs, considerations of both systems should be used to ascertain causality.

TABLE 16.3 WHO—Uppsala Monitoring Centre Causality Categories

Term	Assessment Criteria
Certain	A clinical event, including laboratory test abnormality, occurring in a plausible time relationship to drug administration, and which cannot be explained by concurrent disease or other drugs or chemicals. The response to withdrawal of the drug (dechallenge) should be clinically plausible. The event must be definitive pharmacologically or phenomenologically, i.e., an objective and specific medical disorder or a recognized pharmacological phenomenon, using a satisfactory rechallenge procedure if necessary.
Probable/ likely	A clinical event, including laboratory test abnormality, with a reasonable time sequence to the administration of the drug. Unlikely to be attributed to concurrent disease or other drugs or chemicals, and which follows a clinically reasonable response to withdrawal (dechallenge). Rechallenge information is not required to fulfill this definition.
Possible	A clinical event, including laboratory test abnormality, with a reasonable time sequence to administration of the drug, but which could also be explained by concurrent disease or other drugs or chemicals. Information on drug withdrawal may be lacking or unclear.
Unlikely	A clinical event, including laboratory test abnormality, with a temporal relationship to drug administration, which makes a causal relationship improbable but not impossible, and in which other drugs, chemicals, or underlying disease provide plausible explanations.
Conditional/ unclassified	A clinical event, including laboratory test abnormality, reported as an adverse reaction, about which more data are essential for a proper assessment, or the additional data are under examination.
Unassessable/ unclassified	A report suggesting an adverse reaction that cannot be judged because information is insufficient or contradictory, and which cannot be supplemented or verified.

TABLE 16.4 Naranjo Algorithm: Adverse Drug Reaction Probability Scale

Questions	Yes	No	Do Not Know
1. Are there previous conclusive reports on this reaction?	+1	0	0
2. Did the adverse event appear after the suspected drug was administered?	+2	−1	0
3. Did the adverse reaction improve when the drug was discontinued or a specific antagonist was administered?	+1	0	0
4. Did the adverse reaction reappear when the drug was readministered?	+2	−1	0
5. Are there alternative causes (other than the drug) that could on their own have caused the reaction?	−1	+2	0
6. Did the reaction reappear when a placebo was given?	−1	+1	0
7. Was the drug detected in the blood (or other fluids) in concentrations known to be toxic?	+1	0	0
8. Was the reaction more severe when the dose was increased, or less severe when the dose was decreased?	+1	0	0
9. Did the patient have a similar reaction to the same or similar drugs in any previous exposure?	+1	0	0
10. Was the adverse event confirmed by any objective evidence?	+1	0	0

TABLE 16.5 Naranjo Algorithm: Adverse Drug Reaction Probability Categories

Score	Category
≥9	Definite
5–8	Probable
1–4	Possible
0	Doubtful

OBJECTIVE 16.3. CLASSIFY AND DETAIL MEDICATION ERRORS

The National Coordinating Council for Medication Error Reporting and Prevention (NCCMERP) defines medication errors as those preventable events that may cause or lead to inappropriate medication use or patient harm while the medication is in the control of the healthcare professional, patient, or consumer. Such events may be related to professional practice, healthcare products, procedures, and systems, including prescribing, order communication, product labeling, packaging, nomenclature, compounding, dispensing, distribution, administration, education, monitoring, and use.[30]

In simple terms, the error is a nondeliberate deviation from what is intended, whereas violation is a deliberate deviation. An action that does not go as intended is a so-called error of execution and may be further described as being either a slip, if the action is observable, or a lapse, if it is not. An example of a slip is accidentally pushing the wrong button on a piece of equipment. An example of a lapse is a memory failure, such as forgetting to administer a medication. The intended action is the wrong one: a failure that occurs when the intended action is actually incorrect is clearly a "mistake."[31]

- *Slip*: Drive to the store and head to the office. You know where the store is but are in automatic mode to go to work. You figure a dose of 20 mg/kg as 1400 mg in a 70 kg person but write 140 mg on the order.

A mistake is a failure of planning. This can be either rule based, when the wrong rule is applied, or knowledge based, when a clinician does not take the correct course of action. An example of a rule-based mistake would be getting the diagnosis wrong and so embarking on an inappropriate treatment plan. Knowledge-based mistakes tend to occur when providers are confronted with unfamiliar clinical situations.[31]

- *Mistake*: Drive to the store but go the wrong way because you are not sure of where it is or make the wrong turn. You had a dose of 20 mg/kg and calculated to report 140 mg dose for a 70 kg person.

Root cause analysis is a highly structured systemic approach to incident analysis that is generally reserved for the most serious patient harm episodes.[31]

Types of Medication Errors[32,33]

Medication errors can occur from the clinician who prescribes the medication to the healthcare professional who administers the medication or the patient who self-administers the medication.

Different types of medication errors include (but are not necessarily limited to) the following:

- Prescribing errors
- Omission errors
- Wrong time errors
- Improper dosing errors
- Wrong dose errors
- Improper administration technique errors
- Wrong drug preparation errors
- Fragmented care errors

The Scope of the Problem

In December 1999, the Institute of Medicine (IOM) now called the National Academy of Medicine (NAM) released a report, *To Err Is Human*, that identified medical error as a significant public health problem claiming between 44,000 and

98,000 deaths each year. Medication errors alone were estimated to account for over 7000 deaths annually. This report compellingly summarized the staggering nature and extent of error in healthcare and convincingly thrust medication safety into the forefront as a national priority.[34]

The release in 2006 of another IOM report, *Preventing Medication Errors*, suggested that all stakeholders, including accreditation agencies, state professional boards, and relevant state and federal agencies, should promote medication error reporting more aggressively.[35] Two other studies, namely a 2006 report by the Centers for Disease Control and Prevention and a follow-up in 2016, estimated that 2.4 emergency department visits per 1000 population are due to ADEs and this rate increased to 4 visits per 1000 population in almost 10 years.[36,37]

The medication use process is complex, with many steps, handoffs, and opportunities for error. From ordering, to dispensing, to administering a medication, we must continuously assess the design of systems and processes to refine what we do, how we do it, and the environment in which the work is carried out. In short, preventing errors requires better system design and innovative tools to support safe systems. Much is known about the causes and prevention of medication errors. Yet, our collective challenge to turn this knowledge into practice remains unmet, and harmful medication errors represent a serious concern throughout the world. Other published studies have proven that medication error is a global concern. A systematic review that analyzed 45 studies from 10 middle eastern countries reported the incidence of medication errors across the medication use process.[38] Another systematic review that analyzed 17 studies from six Southeast Asian countries identified medication administration to be the most reported type of medication error (15.2% −88.6%).[39] An Irish study showed that medication error incidents in the acute care setting led to patient harm in 66.6% of the cases.[40] In 2017, WHO launched its third global patient safety challenge, *Medication Without Harm*. WHO has called on all countries and key stakeholders to make strong commitments, prioritize and take early action, and effectively manage three key areas to protect patients from harm, namely high-risk situations, polypharmacy, and transitions of care.[41] In a follow-up article, reminiscent of the call to action from the IOM 2006 report on medication errors, the authors again called on politicians and healthcare leaders to prioritize medication safety. Implementing measures to reduce harm will need to include educating and empowering patients and carers, developing tools to assist frontline healthcare professionals, and engineering new systems of care to create resilience against factors that predispose patients to the risk of medication errors.[42,43]

Despite these calls to action almost two decades ago, healthcare is still struggling to address medication safety across the continuum of care. There exists much information on medication errors as well as prevention methods and strategies, but unfortunately many of these known recommendations are never shared.

Categorization of Medication Errors

The NCCMERP categorizes the severity of error outcomes on a scale known as the medication error index.[44] It considers factors such as whether the error reached the patient and to what degree the patient was harmed. The categories range from A through I (Table 16.6).

TABLE 16.6 Medication Error Index

No Error
(A) Circumstances or events that have the capacity to cause error

Error, No Harm
(B) An error occurred but the medication did not reach the patient
(C) An error occurred that reached the patient but did not cause patient harm
(D) An error occurred that resulted in the need for increased patient monitoring but no patient harm

Error, Harm
(E) An error occurred that resulted in the need for treatment or intervention and caused temporary patient harm
(F) An error occurred that resulted in initial or prolonged hospitalization and caused temporary patient harm
(G) An error occurred that resulted in permanent patient harm
(H) An error occurred that resulted in a near-death event, e.g., anaphylaxis, cardiac arrest

Error, Death
(I) An error occurred that resulted in patient death

OBJECTIVE 16.4. EXPLAIN METHODS FOR PREVENTION AND MANAGEMENT OF MEDICATION ERRORS

Common Causes of Medication Errors

The causes of medication errors are often multifactorial, ranging from human lapses and system loopholes to external factors. The common reasons are as follows[45]:

- Mistakes in writing or filling prescriptions
- Failure to recognize drug interaction
- Failure to properly instruct patient on drug dosage and administration
- Wrong dosage administered
- Similar drug names or medication appearance
- Medical abbreviations
- Failure to properly input prescription onto a computer database
- Poorly designed systems that either induce errors or make them difficult to detect
- Problems with ward-based equipment, e.g., with access or functionality
- Problems with drug supply and storage, e.g., pharmacy dispensing errors or issues with ward stock management
- Staff health status, e.g., fatigue, stress
- Interruptions or distractions during drug administration

Measures to Be Taken to Prevent Medication Errors[46]

Various methods and strategies have been suggested to prevent medications errors, involving both patients and clinical staff (Table 16.7).

Some other measures can be taken to decrease those medication errors,[47,48] such as:

- electronic prescribing and CPOE with CDSSs
- medication error-reporting systems
- alerts about medication errors
- smart infusion pumps
- telemedicine, telehealth, or telepharmacy
- computerized medication box

The Institute for Safe Medication Practices—Sharing and Learning From Errors

The Institute for Safe Medication Practices (ISMP) was formally established in the United States as a nonprofit organization in 1994. However, its reporting program is among the earliest and most aggressive in the battle to prevent medication errors. It also provided error prevention information and encouraged practitioners to submit reports of medication errors so that further recommendations for prevention could be published. Today, collection and analysis of error

TABLE 16.7 Possible Actions by Patients and Clinical Staff to Prevent Medication Errors

Patients	Clinical Staffs
• Find out the name of each of your medications	• Adhere to the "five rights" of medication safety, i.e., administering the right medication, in the right dose, at the right time, by the right route, to the right patient
• Ask questions about how to use the medications	
• Know what your medications are for	
• Read drug labels and follow directions	• Do provide appropriate measurable devices if needed
• Keep all of your healthcare providers informed about your medications and dietary supplements, including vitamins and herbals	• Conduct medication reconciliation with any transition in care, including allergy information and adverse drug reactions
• Keep a list of your medications with you at all times and let your next of kin know	• Consider interventions to reduce medication errors

information from the ISMP National Medication Errors Reporting Program (MERP), Food and Drug Administration (FDA) MedWatch, and many other sources around the world are the foundation on which ISMP's collaborative, educational efforts are based.

ISMP operates three national, voluntary, medication error-reporting programs, namely the ISMP National MERP, the ISMP National Vaccine Errors Reporting Program, and the ISMP National Consumer MERP.

These voluntary reporting programs differ from mandatory external reporting programs in several ways. The reports come directly from frontline practitioners and consumers rather than risk, quality, or safety managers. The narrative descriptions (and pictures) that accompany the reports offer rich content for learning compared with mandatory reports that often prompt for standard information and a succinct description of the event, but not its causes. Communication with the practitioners or consumers who were involved in or detected the event is possible and potentially more helpful than communication with managers screening and completing the mandatory reports. The reports to ISMP are sent for altruistic reasons—because practitioners want to share information that will benefit others, not because there is a mandate to do so.

In November 2006, the International Medication Safety Network was launched. This is a group of safe medication practice centers, including members from the United States and WHO, committed to prevent medication errors and to contribute to safer care. The participants pledged to work together to promote achievement of these essential objectives to encourage and further the development of safe medication practice centers in all countries and to facilitate cooperation among them.[49]

Error-reporting systems represent one of the primary means by which healthcare providers can learn about

- *close calls (near misses)*—errors that occurred but were caught before they reached a patient
- *potential risks*—hazardous conditions hidden in processes
- *actual errors*—errors that occur during the delivery of patient care
- *causes of errors*—underlying weaknesses in systems and processes that explain why an error happened
- *error prevention*—ways to prevent recurrent events and, ultimately, patient harm

Error reporting is a fundamental component of a safety culture, but persuading healthcare workers to submit reports is no easy task given the potential disincentives to reporting. First, people's reactions to making errors are variable, but candid confessions of mistakes are not particularly popular. In fact, people have a natural desire to forget that the incident ever happened. Even if workers are willing to speak up about errors, they may still believe that the extra work is not worth their time if they feel that no good will come from reporting. The workforce is also understandably reluctant to report errors if they are worried that the information will get them or their colleagues in trouble, legally or socially, or impact their job.

It is important to report errors externally as well as internally. External reporting can lead to improved safety in several ways.[50]

- Alerts about new hazards (e.g., complications of a new drug) can be generated from even a few reports.
- Information about the experience of individual hospitals in using new methods to prevent errors can be disseminated.
- Central analysis of many reports can reveal trends and hazards that require attention.
- Central analysis can lead to recommended "best practices" for all to follow.

Many best practices for error prevention exist and are included in ISMP's publications, US FDA warning and alerts, accreditation agencies standards, and in published literature. ISMP has a list of high-alert medications, which are drugs that bear a heightened risk of causing significant patient harm when used in error.[6]

Strategies to prevent errors with high-alert medications include standardizing drug concentrations, controlled storage, automated alerts for prescribing, and the use of checklists and independent double checks.

Using tall man or mixed case lettering and including indications when prescribing medications are strategies to help prevent medication that may look or sound alike.[51,52]

Because medication strengths, e.g., mg, mcg, and doses, e.g., mg/kg, are in metric units, using metric units of measure to express the volume of liquid medications, weigh patients, and document the weight on medical records and prescriptions is another recommendation.

The use of technology to help prevent errors should be employed, such as barcode scanning of medications during the dispensing process and during drug administration; electronic prescribing; workflow system to prepare parenteral medications; infusion devices with smart pump technology; and robotics for storage, dispensing, and preparation of medications.

Finally, having pharmacists available on patient care units in hospitals and counseling patients on their medications in the outpatient setting has shown to prevent errors as well as patient harm.

Although the work of medication safety is the responsibility of many, the coordination of the efforts and assuring communication across all professionals is optimized if the effort stems from one individual. This role is being served with the position of a medication safety officer (MSO). Healthcare organizations, both acute and ambulatory, throughout the world, are adding this position. Either under the direction of an MSO or others, each organization should develop a strategic plan for medication safety and include the importance of sharing and learning from medication errors.

OBJECTIVE 16.5. CLASSIFY AND DETAIL DRUG INTERACTIONS

A drug interaction is said to occur when an agent (the precipitant agent) alters the effect of a drug (the object drug). Drug interactions are generally undesirable because they can result in a decrease in efficacy or increase in toxicity. When doxycycline is taken with iron sulfate, it forms poorly soluble chelates with iron, thus decreasing the absorption of both preparations and the concentration of doxycycline at the site of action. When allopurinol and mercaptopurine are used together, allopurinol inhibits the metabolism of mercaptopurine by xanthine oxidase, mercaptopurine accumulates, and its toxic effects, such as leucopenia and thrombocytopenia, are more likely to develop.

Desirable Drug Interactions

There are also situations in which drug interactions are beneficial, e.g., caffeine, a coanalgesic found in many paracetamol preparations, is included to increase the absorption rate of paracetamol through unclear mechanisms. Contrary to undesirable ones, these drug pairs interact to increase efficacy and/or decrease toxicity (Table 6.8) through various mechanisms.

Drug Interactions Precipitated by Agents Other Than Drugs

Although drug interactions usually involve two drugs, more specifically called drug–drug interactions, the precipitant agent is not always a drug (Table 16.9), but sometimes a herb, food, alcohol, or cigarettes. It would require awareness of social history to recognize them and a holistic approach in counseling to manage them, like diet control and smoking cessation.

Some drug pairs interact in unique ways but much more in a similar manner. Drug interactions are typically classified by mechanism into pharmaceutical, pharmacokinetic, and pharmacodynamic drug interactions.

TABLE 16.8 Examples of Desirable Drug Interactions[53]

Category	Example
Increase Efficacy	
Synergistic	Bactericidal activity in enterococcal infective endocarditis is achieved by the combination of a penicillin, e.g., ampicillin, and an aminoglycoside, e.g., gentamicin, that either alone only inhibits bacterial growth
	Rifampicin, isoniazid, and other antibiotics are used in combination in the treatment of tuberculosis to lower the chance of resistance despite the risk of increased hepatotoxicity
Augmentative	Because of extensive cytochrome P450 (CYP) 3A4 metabolism, lopinavir alone has an exceedingly low plasma concentration so that commercially it is only available in combination with low-dose ritonavir, which inhibits CYP3A4 and increases exposure to lopinavir
Facilitative	Beta-lactamase inhibitors, e.g., clavulanic acid, are used in combination with beta-lactam antibiotics, e.g., amoxicillin, to improve coverage in beta-lactamase producing bacteria
Decrease Toxicity	
Reparative	Constipating aluminum hydroxide is used with laxating magnesium hydroxide in antacids to cancel out the adverse effects of one another
Antidotal	Folic acid is taken, usually at least 24 h after weekly methotrexate, to decrease the gastrointestinal and mucosal adverse effects
Increase Efficacy and Decrease Toxicity	
Complementary	Combinations of thiazide diuretics, loop diuretics, and potassium-sparing diuretics are used to treat refractory edema, lower the doses of individual diuretics, and/or avoid the use of potassium supplements
	Carbidopa is used together with levodopa to inhibit the peripheral conversion of levodopa to dopamine by DOPA decarboxylase, thus minimizing peripheral dopaminergic adverse effects and reserving more levodopa for the central nervous system.

TABLE 16.9 Examples of Drug Interactions With Nondrug Precipitant Agents

Precipitant Agent	Example
Herb	St. John's wort may increase the metabolism of warfarin by inducing CYP2C9 and CYP3A4
Food	Grapefruit juice may decrease the metabolism of carbamazepine by inhibiting CYP3A4
	Tyramine-rich foods may cause a hypertensive crisis in patients taking monoamine oxidase inhibitor
Alcohol	Alcohol may add to the CNS depressant effect of benzodiazepines
	Alcohol may precipitate flushing, tachycardia, breathlessness, and hypotension, called the disulfiram reaction, in patients taking metronidazole
Cigarettes	Smoking may increase the metabolism of theophylline by inhibiting CYP1A2

TABLE 16.10 Examples of Pharmaceutical Drug Interactions

Precipitant Agent	Example
Another drug	Ketorolac is alkaline in solution and incompatible if mixed with an acidic drug, e.g., haloperidol, in continuous subcutaneous infusion[54]
Diluent	Amphotericin B may precipitate with sodium chloride solution
	Ceftriaxone may precipitate with calcium-containing fluids
Container or infusion set	Carboplatin forms precipitate with needles or sets with aluminum parts
	Polysorbate 80 in amiodarone injection may leach di-2-ethylhexyl phthalate from polyvinyl chloride administration sets

Pharmaceutical Drug Interactions (Incompatibilities)

In pharmaceutical drug interactions, also known as pharmaceutical incompatibilities, the precipitant agent affects the object drug before administration. They usually represent physical incompatibilities in parenteral routes and the precipitant agent can be another drug, the diluent, the container, or the infusion set (Table 16.10).

Pharmacokinetic Drug Interactions

In pharmacokinetic drug interactions, the precipitant agent alters the absorption, distribution, metabolism, and/or excretion of the object drug (Table 16.11).

Many drug interactions are attributed to more than one mechanism. For example, it is recognized that the use of salicylates or NSAIDs is a risk factor for methotrexate toxicity.[56] A few mechanisms have been proposed: decrease in renal perfusion, competition for tubular excretion, and displacement from plasma proteins. The significance of each mechanism is not always determined.

Clinically significant protein-binding interactions are particularly uncommon. Taking the example of phenylbutazone and warfarin, while phenylbutazone effectively displaces warfarin from plasma proteins, warfarin has a low extraction ratio in the kidney, which means the body has much capacity to eliminate the free drug displaced. In turn, the interaction is attributed to other mechanisms, e.g., that phenylbutazone inhibits the metabolism of S-warfarin, the more potent enantiomer,[57] or that phenylbutazone increases the risk of gastrointestinal bleeding as an NSAID.

Pharmacodynamic Drug Interactions

In pharmacodynamic drug interactions, the precipitant agent alters the dose—response relationship of the object drug with an agonistic or antagonistic effect (Table 16.12). Sometimes two drugs do not directly alter the effect of one another, but the simple addition of their effects warrants caution, for example, the concurrent use of two drugs that prolong the QT

TABLE 16.11 Examples of Pharmacokinetic Drug Interactions[55]

Subcategory	Common Mechanism	Example
Absorption	Adsorption or chelation	Cholestyramine decreases the absorption of warfarin by complexation
	Changes in gastrointestinal pH	Pantoprazole decreases the absorption of ketoconazole by increasing the gastric pH and decreasing the solubility of ketoconazole
	Induction or inhibition of transporter proteins	Rifampicin decreases the bioavailability of dabigatran by inducing P-glycoprotein and increasing the ejection of absorbed dabigatran
	Changes in gastrointestinal motility	Propantheline decreases the absorption rate of paracetamol in the small intestine by slowing gastric emptying
Distribution	Changes in plasma protein binding	Phenylbutazone increases the concentration of free warfarin by displacing warfarin from plasma proteins
	Induction or inhibition of transporter proteins	Ketoconazole increases the concentration of ritonavir in the cerebrospinal fluid (CSF) by inhibiting P-glycoprotein and decreasing the ejection of ritonavir from the CSF
Metabolism	Enzyme induction	Phenytoin increases the metabolism of quetiapine by inducing CYP3A4
	Enzyme inhibition	Paroxetine decreases the metabolism of tamoxifen to one of its more active metabolites by inhibiting CYP2D6
Excretion	Changes in renal blood flow	Mefenamic acid decreases the urinary excretion of lithium by inhibiting renal prostaglandin synthesis and decreasing renal blood flow
	Changes in urinary pH	Sodium bicarbonate increases the urinary excretion of methotrexate by alkalinizing the urine and increasing the solubility of methotrexate
	Changes in tubular excretion	Probenecid decreases the urinary excretion of ciprofloxacin by competing for tubular excretion

TABLE 16.12 Examples of Pharmacodynamic Drug Interactions

Subcategory	Level	Example
Additive	Receptor-level	Both chlorpheniramine and atropine exhibit anticholinergic properties and may worsen adverse effects such as blurred vision, dry mouth, and constipation
	Effect-level	Both opioids and benzodiazepines can cause drowsiness, and caution is advised with concurrent use
Synergistic	Receptor-level	Amitriptyline inhibits the reuptake of noradrenaline into adrenergic neurons and increases the response to adrenaline
	Effect-level	Thyroxine corrects hypothyroidism and increases the metabolism of clotting factors, thus decreasing the requirement of warfarin
Antagonistic	Receptor-level	Haloperidol blocks dopamine receptors in the brain and antagonizes the effect of levodopa
	Effect-level	Hydrocortisone increases the blood glucose level and diminishes the therapeutic effect of gliclazide

interval, such as citalopram and domperidone. Whether the effects of two drugs are additive, more than additive, or less than additive requires extensive research to establish, but the important point in practice is to recognize the risk of potential synergism in agonistic drug interactions.

Interindividual Variations

Understanding the mechanisms is an essential yet only the first step to manage a drug interaction. It is equally important to recognize that the clinical manifestations are highly variable in individual patients. Some CYP isoenzymes, e.g., 2C9 and

2C19, and some transporter proteins, e.g., P-glycoprotein, are subject to genetic polymorphism, which means variations in the expression of these proteins and therefore pharmacokinetic interactions. As for pharmacodynamic interactions, some outcomes are measurable, e.g., the QT interval, and some are not, like drowsiness. They will require more observation and communication to evaluate. Healthcare professionals must keep these factors in mind when approaching a drug interaction.

OBJECTIVE 16.6. EXPLAIN METHODS FOR PREVENTION AND MANAGEMENT OF DRUG INTERACTIONS

Identification of drug interactions used to be a painful manual process: matching the many drugs on a prescription to the many entries in a reference book. General references, e.g., the *British National Formulary*, list drug interactions under the monographs of individual drugs, whereas more specialized references, like *Stockley's Drug Interactions*, provide monographs of drug pairs. With the help of information technology, drug interaction checkers are available on the Internet and subsequently as applications on handheld devices. Regardless of the tools used, however, some principles are consistently applied:

- Be vigilant with potent enzyme inducers, e.g., carbamazepine, phenytoin, and rifampicin, and potent enzyme inhibitors, e.g., azoles and protease inhibitors (Table 16.13). They can affect more than one isoenzyme and altogether a wide range of drugs to various extents, thus making them common culprits of drug interactions. In particular, carbamazepine, known as an autoinducer, induces its own metabolism. Its half-life starts to decrease 3−5 days after initiation; maximal induction occurs in 3 weeks, and autoinduction may take up to 5 weeks to complete.[58] Coupled with hetero-induction by phenytoin, which takes 1−2 weeks, and that by phenobarbital, which takes 2−3 weeks, the use and therefore dose titration of any concurrent CYP3A4 substrates require extreme caution.

TABLE 16.13 Examples of Potent (Drug Names in Bold) and Moderate Enzyme Inducers and Inhibitors[59]

Isoenzyme	Inhibitors	Inducers
CYP1A2	**Fluvoxamine** Ciprofloxacin Combined hormonal contraceptives	Phenytoin
CYP2C9	Amiodarone Fluconazole 200 mg daily Miconazole	Rifampicin
CYP2C19	**Fluconazole 100 mg daily** **Fluvoxamine** Omeprazole 40 mg daily Voriconazole	Rifampicin
CYP2D6	**Bupropion** **Fluoxetine** **Paroxetine** **Quinidine** **Terbinafine** Duloxetine	
CYP3A4	**Clarithromycin** **Protease inhibitors** **Itraconazole** **Ketoconazole** **Voriconazole** Diltiazem Dronedarone Erythromycin Fluconazole Posaconazole Verapamil	**Carbamazepine** **Phenytoin** **Rifampicin** Bosentan Efavirenz

- Pay attention to drugs with a narrow therapeutic window or requiring specific levels to work, e.g., anticoagulants, antiepileptics, antimicrobials, and immunosuppressants. It is not always easy to put one drug interaction before another, but these drugs are often associated with more pressing concerns.
- Prioritize drug interactions with permanent or detrimental consequences, e.g., organ damage and contraceptive failure, for example; clarithromycin inhibits the metabolism of ergotamine by CYP3A4, and concurrent use of the two is contraindicated because of a high risk of limb ischemia and ergotism.
- Evaluate the evidence of drug interactions. Like that of the efficacy and safety of a drug, the evidence of a drug interaction ranges from extensive research to case reports, from in vitro studies to theories. Although stronger evidence points to the certainty of a drug interaction, weaker evidence gives us insights into rarer ones.
- Always consider patient-specific factors, including liver and kidney function, as well as the history of drug allergies and ADRs. They help to identify patients at risk and determine the feasibility of alternatives.

Risk Ratings of Drug Interactions

When a drug interaction is identified, most practitioners consider its clinical significance next. Unlike the pregnancy risk categories and the common terminology criteria for adverse events in the United States, there is no one single widely accepted grading scale for drug interactions. Many clinical resources, e.g., *Lexicomp* and *Medscape*, have developed their systems of risk ratings (Table 16.14). Each of them involves four to five ratings that indicate the clinical significance of drug interaction and the corresponding action level from modification to no action. Some clinical resources have also assigned ratings to evidence, from extensive to theoretical, and onset, from immediate to delayed.

On top of any one single rating, there is a wide spectrum of strategies to manage a drug interaction. In the example of combined oral contraceptives with phenytoin, contraception is less reliable because phenytoin increases the metabolism of the contraceptive steroids and may allow ovulation to occur. Considering the serious consequences of an unplanned pregnancy, as well as fetal malformation due to antiepileptics with reproductive effects, every possible step should be taken to reduce the risks. Switching to an unaffected contraceptive method, using additional contraceptive precautions, shortening hormone-free interval of 3—4 days, maintaining an ethinylestradiol dose of at least 50 μg daily, and switching to a noninteracting antiepileptic are all possible.[59] Although the luxury of having multiple options is not a must, this scenario has certainly highlighted the many dimensions one can have in managing a drug interaction.

Discontinuation

The first step to prevent and potentially manage a drug interaction is to assess the necessity of drugs involved, which also forms an integral part of a pharmacist's role. For example, if pantoprazole decreases the absorption of ketoconazole, it is simple yet often overlooked to check whether pantoprazole is indicated. Discontinuing it or switching to an H_2-receptor antagonist when necessary would be a better solution than separating the doses of the two drugs considering pantoprazole's long duration of action. In the case that NSAID increases the risk of methotrexate toxicity, avoiding the use of NSAIDs is probably the safest way of management.

Therapy Modification

In the case that both drugs are indicated, the rest is a balance of modifying and monitoring. On the one end of the balance, there is a wide range of modifications to therapy that may manage a drug interaction, including withdrawing one or more

TABLE 16.14 Examples of Risk Rating Systems for Drug Interactions Developed by Clinical Resources

Lexicomp	Medscape	Epocrates	Micromedex	Stockley's
X: Avoid combination	Contraindicated	Contraindicated	Contraindicated	Avoid
D: Consider therapy modification	Serious—use alternative	Avoid/use alternative	Major	Adjust
C: Monitor therapy	Monitor closely	Monitor/modify treatment	Moderate	Monitor
B: No action needed	Minor	Caution advised	Minor	Informative
A: No known interaction			Unknown	No action

TABLE 16.15 Examples of Recommendations on Dose Modification for Drug Interactions

Drug Interaction	Recommendation
Diltiazem decreases the metabolism of simvastatin by inhibiting CYP3A4	Restrict the maximum dose of simvastatin to 20 mg daily[60]
Allopurinol decreases the metabolism of mercaptopurine by inhibiting xanthine oxidase	Decrease the dose of mercaptopurine by 75%[61]
Rifampicin increases the metabolism of lapatinib by inducing CYP3A4	Titrate the dose of lapatinib from 1250 mg daily up to 4500 mg daily or from 1500 mg daily up to 5500 mg daily[62]

drugs, switching to a noninteracting or less-interacting alternative, and adjusting the dosage of the drugs. Clear recommendations from authorities or manufacturers on dose modification may be available for drug interactions that are more significant or better studied (Table 16.15).

Monitoring Without Interventions

On the other end, monitoring is the mainstay of management when there are no alternatives, e.g., monitor the QT interval if two QT-prolonging agents must be used together. It is also possible to decide the course of action through monitoring, like decreasing the dose of lithium with concurrent NSAIDs as guided by the lithium level or decreasing the dose of warfarin with concurrent thyroxine by checking the international normalized ratio. In between the two ends, every factor is considered on a case-by-case basis.

Balance of Strategies

In an example of drug interaction between simvastatin and clarithromycin, simvastatin, an HMG-CoA reductase inhibitor used in the treatment of dyslipidemia, is extensively metabolized by CYP3A4. Clarithromycin, a macrolide, inhibits CYP3A4 and increases the concentration of simvastatin, therefore the risk of toxicity, e.g., myopathy and rhabdomyolysis. Switching to another statin or another macrolide does not appear to eliminate the interaction, not to mention that another macrolide may not be the most appropriate antimicrobial. In this case, given the usual short-term use of antimicrobial therapy, it is prudent to temporarily withdraw simvastatin during the course of clarithromycin.

In another example of drug interaction between tamoxifen and paroxetine, tamoxifen, a selective estrogen receptor modulator used in the treatment of breast cancer, is metabolized by CYP2D6 to antiestrogens that are more active. Paroxetine, an SSRI, inhibits CYP2D6 and may decrease the efficacy of tamoxifen. In reality, it is difficult to ascertain or monitor its impact on the long-term risk of breast cancer recurrence. Given the potential seriousness of this interaction, modifying either drug is a more desirable strategy. As for paroxetine, it is possible to switch to a weak CYP2D6-inhibiting SSRI, such as citalopram and escitalopram, or a non-SSRI antidepressant, e.g., venlafaxine. If the patient does not respond to other antidepressants, the possibility of switching tamoxifen to an aromatase inhibitor can be explored in postmenopausal patients.

In the two examples above, the plan of management would have been very different if it is known, for example, that paroxetine is expected to complete in 2 weeks, or that clarithromycin is used for its long-term immunomodulatory effects. Even when a drug interaction has a standard or straightforward plan of management, there are a few points that every pharmacist must bear in mind:

1. Pay attention to long-term effects when withdrawing one or more drugs, e.g., SSRIs. Always distinguish between temporary and permanent withdrawal. Watch out for unintended discrepancies with any transition in care.
2. Beware of introducing new interactions when switching to alternatives, for example, switching a proton pump inhibitor to an antacid may lessen its impact on the gastric pH but may introduce adsorption or complexation with other drugs.
3. Communicate any changes with patients and carers as far as practicable. They must understand which drug to stop, which one to start, and what doses to take to effect any changes. Often monitoring of signs and symptoms goes beyond laboratory results and requires a prompt response from patients and carers in case of emergency, e.g., when signs of hypoglycemia appear after titrating the doses of antidiabetic drugs.

CONCLUSION

The role of pharmacists in preventing and managing drug-related problems is emphasized. Pharmacotherapy knowledge, in which pharmacists are experts, provides the foundation for classifying and understanding these problems, whereas clinical pharmacy skills give us the tool to prevent and manage them, with a patient-centered approach. Many of the risks and measures are not absolute and present an opportunity for every pharmacist to contribute.

PRACTICE QUESTIONS

1. Antibiotic-induced diarrhea is which type of ADR?
   A. Type A
   B. Type B
   C. Type C
   D. Type D
2. Which of the following is a common type of ADR?
   A. Type C
   B. Type D
   C. Type E
   D. Type F
3. Angioedema caused by ACE inhibitors is usually categorized as?
   A. Mild
   B. Moderate
   C. Severe
   D. Lethal
4. A Naranjo algorithm score of 10 indicates which of the following?
   A. Definite
   B. Probable
   C. Possible
   D. Doubtful
5. Which of the following is a pharmacist intervention to reduce ADEs?
   A. Barcoding of drugs
   B. Anticoagulation clinic
   C. eMAR
   D. CPOE
6. *To Err is Human* was released by?
   A. WHO
   B. Center for Disease Control and Prevention
   C. National Academy of Medicine (previously Institute of Medicine)
   D. Uppsala Monitoring Centre
7. All potential ADEs are?
   A. Preventable ADRs
   B. Ameliorable ADRs
   C. Drug interactions
   D. Medication errors
8. Which of the following best describes the desirable drug interaction between amoxicillin and clavulanic acid?
   A. Synergistic
   B. Augmentative
   C. Facilitative
   D. Antidotal
9. _____ decreases the metabolism of carbamazepine by inhibiting CYP3A4.
   A. St. John's wort
   B. Grapefruit juice
   C. Tyramine
   D. Alcohol

10. Which of the following is a pharmaceutical incompatibility?

    A. Pantoprazole decreases the absorption of ketoconazole by increasing the gastric pH and decreasing the solubility of ketoconazole

    B. Rifampicin decreases the bioavailability of dabigatran by inducing P-glycoprotein and increasing the ejection of absorbed dabigatran

    C. Propantheline decreases the absorption rate of paracetamol in the small intestine by slowing gastric emptying

    D. Ceftriaxone may precipitate with calcium-containing fluids

11. A potent enzyme inhibitor is?

    A. Carbamazepine

    B. Phenytoin

    C. Rifampicin

    D. Fluconazole

12. The drug interaction of diltiazem decreases the metabolism of simvastatin by inhibiting CYP3A4. How is this managed?

    A. Reduce simvastatin dose by 75%

    B. Restrict the maximum dose of simvastatin to 20 mg daily

    C. Titrate the dose by starting at 10 mg by adding 5 mg every week

    D. Stop simvastatin and use clofibrate

REFERENCES

1. Schatz SN, Weber RJ. *Adverse Drug Reactions. CNS/Pharmacy Practice. PSAP.* American College of Clinical Pharmacy; 2015. https://www.accp.com/docs/bookstore/psap/2015B2.SampleChapter.pdf.

2. Classification of adverse drug reactions. In: Pichler WJ, ed. *Drug Allergy: Classification and Clinical Features.* UpToDate. https://www.uptodate.com/contents/drug-allergy-classification-and-clinical-features.

3. Guidance on Adverse Drug Reactions. Medicines and Healthcare Products Regulatory Agency. https://www.gov.uk/government/uploads/system/uploads/attachment_data/file/403098/Guidance_on_adverse_drug_reactions.pdf.

4. *What Is a Serious Adverse Event?* United States Food and Drug Administration; 2016. https://www.fda.gov/Safety/MedWatch/HowToReport/ucm053087.htm.

5. Marsh DE. *Adverse Drug Reactions. Merck Manual Professional Edition*; 2016. http://www.merckmanuals.com/professional/clinical-pharmacology/adverse-drug-reactions/adverse-drug-reactions.

6. ISMP. *High Alert Medications.* http://www.ismp.org/Tools/highAlertMedicationLists.asp.

7. Raut AL, Patel P, Patel C, Pawar A. Preventability, predictability and seriousness of adverse drug reactions amongst medicine inpatients in a teaching hospital: a prospective observational study. *Int J Pharm Chem Sci.* 2012;1(3):1293−1299.

8. Hanlon JT, Schmader KE, Samsa GP, et al. A method for assessing drug therapy appropriateness. *J Clin Epidemiol.* 1992;45(10):1045−1051.

9. Garfinkel D, Mangin D. Feasibility study of a systematic approach for discontinuation of multiple medications in older adults: addressing polypharmacy. *Arch Intern Med.* 2010;170(18):1648−1654.

10. Selected high-risk drugs. In: Zhu J, Weingart SN, ed. *Prevention of Adverse Drug Events in Hospitals.* UpToDate. https://www.uptodate.com/contents/prevention-of-adverse-drug-events-in-hospitals.

11. Cullen DJ, Sweitzer BJ, Bates DW, et al. Preventable adverse drug events in hospitalized patients: a comparative study of intensive care and general care units. *Crit Care Med.* 1997;25(8):1289−1297.

12. Sarkar U, López A, Maselli JH, Gonzales R. Adverse drug events in U.S. adult ambulatory medical care. *Health Serv Res.* 2011;46(5):1517−1533.

13. Mihajlovic S, Gauthier J, MacDonald E. Patient characteristics associated with adverse drug events in hospital: an overview of reviews. *Can J Hosp Pharm.* 2016;69(4):294−300.

14. Holbrook AM, Pereira JA, Labiris R, et al. Systematic overview of warfarin and its drug and food interactions. *Arch Intern Med.* 2005;165(10):1095−1106.

15. *Calculator: Creatinine Clearance (Measured).* UpToDate. https://www.uptodate.com/contents/calculator-creatinine-clearance-measured.

16. Leape LL. Error in medicine. *J Am Med Assoc.* 1994;272(23):1851−1857.

17. ISMP. *Medication Error Prevention Toolbox.* http://www.ismp.org/Newsletters/acutecare/articles/19990602.asp.

18. Kaushal R, Shojania KG, Bates DW. Effects of computerized physician order entry and clinical decision support systems on medication safety: a systematic review. *Arch Intern Med.* 2003;163(12):1409−1416.

19. Ash JS, Sittig DF, Poon EG, et al. The extent and importance of unintended consequences related to computerized provider order entry. *J Am Med Inform Assoc.* 2007;14(4):415−423.

20. Brown CL, Mulcaster HL, Triffitt KL, et al. A systematic review of the types and causes of prescribing errors generated from using computerized provider order entry systems in primary and secondary care. *J Am Med Inform Assoc.* 2017;24(2):432−440.

21. Amato MG, Salazar A, Hickman TT, et al. Computerized prescriber order entry-related patient safety reports: analysis of 2522 medication errors. *J Am Med Inform Assoc.* 2017;24(2):316−322.

22. Trivalle C, Cartier T, Verny C, et al. Identifying and preventing adverse drug events in elderly hospitalised patients: a randomised trial of a program to reduce adverse drug effects. *J Nutr Health Aging.* 2010;14(1):57–61.

23. *Signal Detection.* Drug Safety Research Unit. http://www.dsru.org/consulting-on-risk-management/signal-detection/.

24. *Signal Management.* European Medicines Agency. http://www.ema.europa.eu/ema/index.jsp?curl=pages/regulation/general/general_content_000587.jsp.

25. Pharmacovigilance guide for adverse drug reaction monitoring and causality assessment. *Post Marketing Control Division, Drug Regulatory Authority Bhutan*; 2015. http://dra.gov.bt/wp-content/uploads/2016/05/Pharmacovigilance-guideline.pdf.

26. Causality categories. In: *Safety Monitoring of Medicinal Products: Guidelines for Setting up and Running a Pharmacovigilance Centre.* The Uppsala Monitoring Centre; 2000. http://apps.who.int/medicinedocs/en/d/Jh2934e/15.html.

27. Naranjo CA, Busto U, Sellers EM, et al. A method for estimating the probability of adverse drug reactions. *Clin Pharmacol Ther.* 1981;30(2):239–245.

28. Belhekar MN, Taur SR, Munshi RP. A study of agreement between the Naranjo algorithm and WHO-UMC criteria for causality assessment of adverse drug reactions. *Indian J Pharmacol.* 2014;46(1):117–120.

29. Mittal N, Gupta MC. Comparison of agreement and rational uses of the WHO and Naranjo adverse event causality assessment tools. *J Pharmacol Pharmacother.* 2015;6(2):91–93.

30. *What is a Medication Error?* National Coordinating Council for Medication Error Reporting and Prevention. http://www.nccmerp.org/about-medication-errors.

31. WHO. *Learning from Error. Course — Knowledge is the Enemy of Unsafe Care.* http://www.who.int/patientsafety/education/curriculum/course5_handout.pdf.

32. Gandhi TK, Seger DL, Bates DW. Identifying drug safety issues: from research to practice. *Int J Qual Health Care.* 2000;12(1):69–76.

33. Morimoto T, Gandhi TK, Seger AC, Hsieh TC, Bates DW. Adverse drug events and medication errors: detection and classification methods. *BMJ Qual Saf.* 2004;13:306–314. https://www.ncbi.nlm.nih.gov/pmc/articles/PMC1743868/pdf/v013p00306.pdf.

34. Fathi A, Hajizadeh M, Moradi K, et al. Medication errors among nurses in teaching hospitals in the west of Iran: what we need to know about prevalence, types, and barriers to reporting. *Epidemiol Health.* 2017;39:e2017022.

35. Kohn KT, Corrigan JM, Donaldson MS, et al. *To Err Is Human: Building a Safer Health System.* Washington, DC: National Academy Press; 1999.

36. Aspden P, Wolcott JA, Bootman JL, Cronenwett LR, eds. *Preventing Medication Errors.* Washington, DC: National Academy Press; 2006.

37. Budnitz DS, Pollock DA, Weidenbach KN, et al. National surveillance of emergency department visits for outpatient adverse drug events. *J Am Med Assoc.* 2006;296(15):1858–1866.

38. Shehab N, Lovegrove MC, Geller AI, et al. US emergency department visits for outpatient adverse drug events, 2013-2014. *J Am Med Assoc.* 2016;316(20):2115–2125.

39. Alsulami Z, Conroy S, Choonara I. Medication errors in the Middle East countries: a systematic review of the literature. *Eur J Clin Pharmacol.* 2013;69(4):995–1008.

40. Salmasi S, Khan TM, Hong YH, et al. Medication errors in the Southeast Asian countries: a systematic review. *PLoS One.* 2015;10(9):e0136545.

41. Relihan EC, Ryder SA, Silke B. Profiling harmful medication errors in an acute Irish teaching hospital. *Ir J Med Sci.* 2012;181(4):491–497.

42. Donaldson LJ, Kelley ET, Dhingra-Kumar N, Kieny MP, Sheikh A. Medication without harm: WHO's third global patient safety challenge. *Lancet.* 2017;389(10080):1680–1681.

43. Sheikh A, Dhingra-Kumar N, Kelley E, et al. The third global patient safety challenge: tackling medication-related harm. *Bull World Health Organ.* 2017;95, 546–546A.

44. *Types of Medication Errors.* National Coordinating Council for Medication Error Reporting and Prevention. http://www.nccmerp.org/types-medication-errors.

45. *Medication Errors in Nursing: Common Types, Causes, and Prevention.* Medcomm. https://www.medcomm.com/index.php/articles/common-nursing-medication-errors-types-causes-prevention/.

46. *6 Tips to Avoid Medication Mistakes.* United States Food and Drug Administration; 2015. https://www.fda.gov/ForConsumers/ConsumerUpdates/ucm096403.htm.

47. *Medication errors. Agency for Healthcare Research and Quality*; 2017. https://psnet.ahrq.gov/primers/primer/23/medication-errors.

48. Riaz MK, Riaz M, Latif A. Review - Medication errors and strategies for their prevention. *Pak J Pharm Sci.* 2017;30(3):921–928.

49. *About the International Medication Safety Network.* International Medication Safety Network. https://www.intmedsafe.net/about/.

50. Leape LL. Reporting of adverse events. *N Engl J Med.* 2002;347(20):1663–1668.

51. *FDA and ISMP Lists of Look-Alike Drug Names with Recommended Tall Man Letters.* Institute for Safe Medication Practices. http://www.ismp.org/Tools/tallmanletters.pdf.

52. *ISMP's List of Confused Drug Names.* Institute for Safe Medication Practices. http://www.ismp.org/Tools/Confused-Drug-Names.aspx.

53. Caranasos GJ, Stewart RB, Cluff LE. Clinically desirable drug interactions. *Annu Rev Pharmacol Toxicol.* 1985;25:67–95.

54. Compatibility charts for drugs in WFI. In: Twycross R, Wilcock A, Howard P, eds. *Palliative Care Formulary.* 5th ed. Nottingham: palliativedrugs.com Ltd.; 2014.

55. Mechanisms of drug interactions. In: Preston CL, ed. *Stockley's Drug Interactions.* 11th ed. London: Pharmaceutical Press; 2016.

56. Hoekstra M, van Ede AE, Haagsma C, et al. Factors associated with toxicity, final dose, and efficacy of methotrexate in patients with rheumatoid arthritis. *Ann Rheum Dis.* 2003;62(5):423–426.

57. Banfield C, O'Reilly R, Chan E, Rowland M. Phenylbutazone-warfarin interaction in man: further stereochemical and metabolic considerations. *Br J Clin Pharmacol.* 1983;16(6):669–675.

58. Spina E, Italiano D. Drug interactions. In: Shorvon S, Perucca E, Engel J, eds. *The Treatment of Epilepsy.* 4th ed. Chichester: John Wiley & Sons, Ltd.; 2016.

59. *CEU Clinical Guidance: Drug Interactions with Hormonal Contraception - January 2017.* Faculty of Sexual and Reproductive Healthcare; 2017. http://www.fsrh.org/documents/ceu-clinical-guidance-drug-interactions-with-hormonal/.

60. *Simvastatin: Dose Limitations with Concomitant Amlodipine or Diltiazem.* Medicines and Healthcare products Regulatory Agency; 2012. https://www.gov.uk/drug-safety-update/simvastatin-dose-limitations-with-concomitant-amlodipine-or-diltiazem.

61. *Mercaptopurine 50 mg Tablets: Summary of Product Characteristics.* Electronic Medicines Compendium; 2012. http://www.medicines.org.uk/emc/medicine/24688.

62. *Tykerb (Lapatinib) Tablets, for Oral Use: Prescribing Information;* 2007. Drugs@FDA. https://www.accessdata.fda.gov/drugsatfda_docs/label/2017/022059s022lbl.pdf

ANSWERS TO PRACTICE QUESTIONS

1. A
2. D
3. C
4. A
5. B
6. C
7. D
8. C
9. B
10. D
11. D
12. B

Pharmacoeconomics and Outcomes Research

Chapter 17

Market Access, Pharmaceutical Pricing, and Healthcare Costs

Dixon Thomas[1], Denny John[2], Nermeen Ashoush[3], Federico Lega[4] and Hong Li[5,6]

[1]Gulf Medical University, Ajman, United Arab Emirates; [2]Campbell Collaboration, New Delhi, India; [3]The British University in Egypt, Cairo, Egypt; [4]SDA Bocconi School of Management, Milan, Italy; [5]Shanghai Jiao-Tong University, Shanghai, China; [6]University of Cincinnati, Cincinnati, OH, United States

Learning Objectives

Objective 17.1   Outline market access policies by pharmaceutical and medical technology industries.
Objective 17.2   Overview pricing practices of pharmaceuticals.
Objective 17.3   Explain types of healthcare costs and their estimation.

OBJECTIVE 17.1. OUTLINE MARKET ACCESS POLICIES BY PHARMACEUTICAL AND MEDICAL TECHNOLOGY INDUSTRIES

Market access (MA) can be defined as the set of strategies, activities, and processes that pharmaceutical (pharma) and medical technology (MedTech) companies develop to ensure that their products (drugs, devices, other technologies) are made available and adequately priced in a specific health system. MA supports the ability for a product to achieve at a fair reimbursed price and a favorable recommendation for prescribing through a health system.[1,2]

In this respect, MA is a multidisciplinary field that includes or requires contributions from various business functions, such as managing market channels, stakeholders, key opinion leaders (KOLs), pricing and reimbursement, government affairs, health economics and outcomes research, regulatory, and payer management. Therefore, it is a multidisciplinary field that includes or requires contributions from various other business functions, such as managing market channels, stakeholders, and KOLs.[1]

In the last 20 years, MA has gained considerable attention within the pharmaceutical industry as countries and health systems have started new policies to contain their escalating healthcare expenditures, especially during the last decade due to the global economic slowdown and crisis. Governments and health authorities have adopted stricter measures for new product approvals and introduced several guidelines and actions on clinicians to steer and limit their discretion in prescribing drugs and adopting technologies.

In this new scenario, pharma and MedTech companies have to cope with new challenges posed by decisions and influence exerted from various sources, including government agencies, top management of healthcare organizations, stakeholders, and KOLs.

The pharma and MedTech industries have traditionally built their success on the strategy of "share of voice." The more a company hits the clinicians with its field force, the more sales and revenues are expected. There is a correlation between coverage of the field force and sales; therefore, companies would adopt an aggressive push strategy to ensure their products succeed in the market.[3]

Introduction of a drug/device to the market includes at least three steps. First, a dossier with data on efficacy, safety, and tolerability is submitted to regulatory agencies to get an approval for the authorization of the introduction of the product in the market. Getting market authorization from the regulator is the responsibility of the medical/regulatory affairs division within a pharmaceutical company.

Once the regulatory agency grants market authorization, the MA division prepares a dossier to be submitted for pricing and reimbursement. The national agency that approves price or reimbursement is most of the time different from the regulatory agency that provides market authorization. Sometimes the pricing and reimbursement agency could be independent of the government too but works in an advisory position to the government.

Third, the product is marketed to the targeted physicians, the prescribers, or those that can induce its consumption or utilization. In this stage, the marketing division and other parties within the company proceed with channels to make the product available to customers.

Thus, the introduction of a new product to the market, or revitalizing an old one, is a process involving a few stakeholders—governmental or nongovernmental agencies, pharmaceutical companies, physicians, and in some cases also pharmacies if authorized to prescribe or advise on the use of the product.

However, in the last two decades, the introduction of new products in the market has become a much more complicated and complex process. The MA landscape has evolved primarily due to escalating healthcare costs with difficulties to be reimbursed, safety concerns of newer drugs, aging population, and disease burden that exhaust limited drug/device budgets.

As the institutional environment gets more challenging, healthcare authorities are investigating more in-depth the claim for the value of new products; choices on pricing and reimbursement have become more cautious. For instance, reference pricing and generic substitutions are among the implemented (and accelerating) techniques used to anchor pricing and increase the affordability of new products. Furthermore, pricing or reimbursement agencies (governmental or not) are shifting from cost-sharing approaches to pay for performance (Fig. 17.1).

In this new scenario, pharma and MedTech companies have seen the emergence of a new and diverse set of stakeholders, and a brand new strategy for MA has become fundamental, i.e., specific tools and tactics are needed to support companies to strategize, plan, implement, and monitor engagement activities for the new stakeholders.

The intensity of this new landscape might vary quite a lot from mature markets, such as Europe and North America, consolidating and developing markets (e.g., Latin America, Russia, India, China, Middle East, and some African countries). However, in all these markets, new stakeholders are gaining dominant positions, generating the need for a new "share of voice."

Access and penetration of a market are no longer just a function of the relationship with clinicians and KOLs. Increasingly, MA requires good and deeper interactions with agencies/authorities, hospital managers, hospital pharmacists, leaders of governing authorities, HTA committee members, insurance managers, doctors involved in clinical governance, patient associations, and influential associations (such as "choosing wisely," "slow medicine," etc.).

Specifically, concerned agencies for MA are today a more sophisticated group of stakeholders that shape healthcare policy, establish the rules of conduct for pharmaceutical and MedTech companies to operate in the market, and sometimes are even the payers. Managers and pharmacists of hospitals are exerting greater control over clinician behaviors. Patients today are more aware of treatment modalities, effectiveness, and cost; patients can be very active and demanding, especially if they are charged with co-payments. Pharmacies are key stakeholders that could influence drug access by controlling the availability of the product in the retail or out-of-pocket market. Patient associations and other advocacy groups have the will and need to play an influential role in MA. The innovative new class of drugs needs to be marketed at a reasonable time and should be affordable (e.g., in rare diseases).

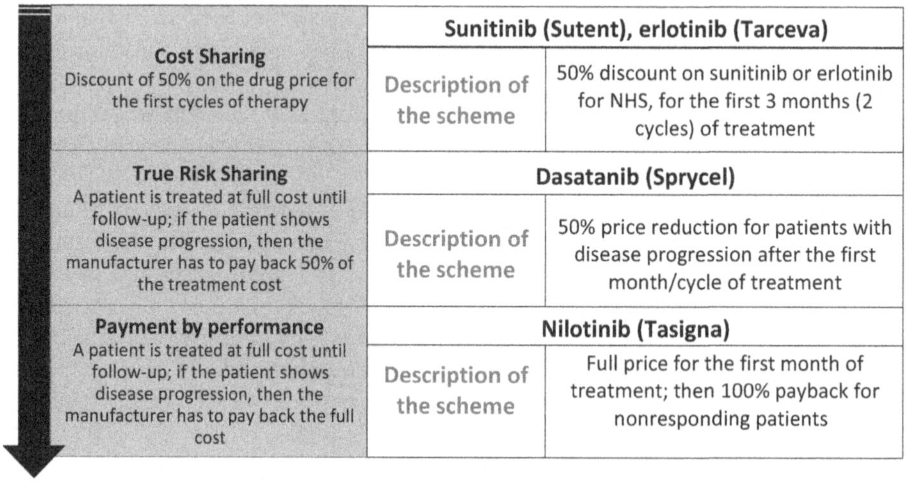

		Sunitinib (Sutent), erlotinib (Tarceva)	
Cost Sharing Discount of 50% on the drug price for the first cycles of therapy		Description of the scheme	50% discount on sunitinib or erlotinib for NHS, for the first 3 months (2 cycles) of treatment
True Risk Sharing A patient is treated at full cost until follow-up; if the patient shows disease progression, then the manufacturer has to pay back 50% of the treatment cost		Dasatanib (Sprycel)	
		Description of the scheme	50% price reduction for patients with disease progression after the first month/cycle of treatment
Payment by performance A patient is treated at full cost until follow-up; if the patient shows disease progression, then the manufacturer has to pay back the full cost		Nilotinib (Tasigna)	
		Description of the scheme	Full price for the first month of treatment; then 100% payback for nonresponding patients

FIGURE 17.1 Evolving landscape in pricing: from cost sharing to pay for performance. *Prepared by using data from Italian Medicines Agency.*

In this scenario, physicians and KOLs are less dominant in the MA value chain. They still are a key "target"; their discretion in prescribing new and expensive products is limited because of

- growing austerity measures,
- the clinical governance tools operated by managers and pharmacists,
- the guidelines to be followed, and
- further restrictions set by health agencies.

The MA landscape in health systems has become quite complex, with intertwined and interlocked relationships among various stakeholders. Pharmaceutical and MedTech companies thus need to identify the right stakeholders that need to be engaged as part of the introduction of the product on the market and to identify the right and tailor-made actions for their engagement. This is why a new "share of voice" is needed.

The MA function is, therefore, the emerging part of the organization of most pharma and MedTech industries. A function that can also work as a link among the more traditional functions, such as R&D, sales, marketing, regulatory affairs, pricing and reimbursement, and medical affairs. MA would become the planner and coordinator of the efforts from all of them, helping the company to build on possible synergies and facilitate coordination in "talking" to stakeholders, rather than having different functions aimed at "share of voice" in an isolated way, with each one talking with multiple stakeholders with probable confusing and mixed messages.

When introducing a new product on the market, a company should do the following:

- consider the implications on the whole healthcare market
- understand the impact of the changing healthcare market
- prepare a positive healthcare environment that supports adoption of the product
- communicate the "value" of the product to the range of stakeholders that influence its introduction and adoption

This paradigm and function of MA are already under implementation in Western markets, with several companies establishing dedicated or cross-functional teams that can handle the multiple facets of MA. In emerging markets, MA is just a beginning. However, the road seems still long to go. Especially in emerging markets, MA still faces several unique challenges:

- Lack of organizational support (e.g., budgetary constraints to develop a new team dedicated to MA)
- Dearth of resources at both global and local offices
- Low level of cooperation between different functional teams (e.g., medical, marketing, etc.)
- Lack of alignment and integration of MA activities among divisions operating in different countries or markets
- Paucity of data critical to MA function (e.g., data on pricing, reimbursement, tenders, formularies, etc.)
- Identification of the right stakeholders and effective engagement with them
- Identification of areas of national importance from a policy-shaping standpoint.[1]

Many of these challenges are also common in developed or mature markets. In any case, futures for pharma and MedTech companies do not envision any change in the dynamics that brought the need for MA:

- burgeoning costs
- limited resources
- attention to performance and outcomes
- higher engagement of multiple stakeholders

For pharma and MedTech companies, this will imply that developing an MA function further is not just being a technical issue, but above all is a change in their organizational culture. Something that will challenge the way how business is conducted today. In this new environment, words such as partnerships and engagement between industry and health systems would have a new and deeper meaning.

OBJECTIVE 17.2. OVERVIEW PRICING PRACTICES OF PHARMACEUTICALS

Pharmaceutical industries and governments use different methods in pricing pharmaceutical interventions. The price of drugs keeps increasing even though governments and health insurance companies take many measures to control costs. Pharmaceutical companies tend to increase prices of marketed products.[4] However, many governments are successful in controlling or even reducing the market prices of essential drugs. For orphan drugs or even life-saving drugs, governments may subsidize partially or fully to improve the availability of the drugs in the market with affordable prices. On the other side, the cost of new drug discovery keeps rising with small success rates.

The pharmaceutical market is a highly regulated market. Pharmaceutical and healthcare markets behave differently in many aspects compared with other businesses. In many jurisdictions, competitive pricing is not allowed above or below certain levels. Ceiling price blocks prices above maximum retail price (the United States is an exception with less price regulation); and discounting below a certain percentage is not allowed to prevent cut-throat competition. Pharmacists need to understand the combination of clinical sciences with business domains. Thus, the pharmaceutical market is not "perfectly" competitive. The intention to make a profit does not overrule a clinical decision to avoid a harmful treatment even though the patient requests it.[5]

The interactions between pharmaceutical manufacturers and consumers are limited to prescription-only products, even the interactions between manufacturers and providers are monitored by governments to avoid unnecessary prescribing for profit.[6] Technically, both sellers and buyers do not have much market power. Thus, they are price takers. Increasing price loses customers, and patients are not in a position to bargain to decrease the price.[5] This is not fully true when a patented proprietary product has market exclusivity (monopoly). Still, a pharmaceutical company has restrictions by most of the governments to fix a reasonable price. In some countries with universal health coverage, the government is the largest buyer on behalf of its citizens. In this case, the government has the market power to bargain for a better price (monopsony).[7] Even with the government's control, the price keeps escalating and the expenses in innovation are high. The pharmaceutical market is strange compared with other markets in a general sense that the consumer is not the customer. Healthcare professionals are influential and, in many cases, dominate the decision on choice of the healthcare product consumed by the patient. Considering the current health insurance system, especially in developed countries, patients do not have the privilege to pay for the products and services they receive. Of course, it is not free, they did spend health taxes/insurance premiums, but in a clinical encounter, to the provider, it is a third party that pays. Above all, patients being less informed about what is going on with disease and health technology are in a poor position to contribute to the decision-making process unless they self-study or the healthcare professionals educate them. Though lots of efforts are in place to enhance patient centeredness in practice, the inherent defects explained in this paragraph limit the privileges of a customer in healthcare. It is not easy for governments to cover the health expenses of citizens, even in developed countries. Regulatory and policy reforms in the United States decreased the percentage of the uninsured.[8]

Supply and Demand Curves

Price, supply, and demand are related to each other. As quantity supplied increases, the demand decreases forcing prices to be decreased. In the reverse case, with the scarcity of the product/service supply, demand increases creating room for increasing prices (Fig. 17.2). Once the innovator drug patent expires, entry of other brands/generic versions increases the supply of the bioequivalent products in the market that decreases demand and thus the price. Having an innovator proprietary product patent is a market monopoly that creates sole demand for the product. Entry of similar products to market with smaller prices creates competition and choice easily changes to cheaper versions as the regulatory system demands similar quality, quantity, and performance across the products. A combination of demand and supply curves joins at a point of equilibrium where it defines the ideal market price and the ideal quantity to keep the demand alive. Overproduction or oversupply disturbs market equilibrium.[5] For hospital managers, bulk ordering increases supply and decreases price, but the supply should not be too much to avoid some products that are not sold before its expiry.

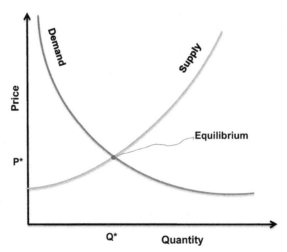

FIGURE 17.2 Supply and demand curves. *Taken from http://braungardt.trialectics.com/sciences/economics/market-mechanism-explained/.*

The price of similar pharmaceutical products (same active ingredient with same quantity) varies between countries and even within a country. Sometimes, the same manufacturer makes similar products and markets them with different brands at different prices. This variation is observed globally irrespective of high-income or low-income countries. Money spent to buy a product from the government, hospital, or a pharmacy varies depending on many factors such as purchase deal, quantity, distribution costs, etc. Deals are also in place between the providers and third-party payers or patients with certain discounts. Thus, there are variations in procurement costs for the providers and purchase price for the patients or third-party buyers.[7] Different countries might use different or a combination of methods in pharmaceutical pricing.[9]

Reference pricing is set by selecting a drug in a therapeutic class as standard price (usually of average or less than average price). The prices of other drugs with similar effectiveness and safety are compared with the standard drug. This method is commonly used by governments and other large third-party buyers. The reference price is also used in reimbursement when a patient buys the standard drug and pays the regular co-pay only. If the patient chooses a higher-priced brand, the amount above the benchmarked price needs to be paid in addition to the regular co-pay. This difference is the brand premium. A combination of reference pricing and brand premium encourages patients to choose cheaper drugs and the pharmaceutical companies to reduce the costs.[7]

In the face of rising healthcare costs across many regions worldwide, decision-makers and regulators have developed a variety of methods to control pharmaceutical and other health technology costs while attempting to maintain access to new innovative health technologies. One commonly used method of directly controlling prices is external price referencing (EPR), which is defined by the World Health Organization (WHO) as "the practice of using the prices of a pharmaceutical product in one or several countries in order to derive a benchmark or reference price for the purposes of setting or negotiating the price of the product in a given country," wherein decision-makers specify a "basket" of countries, whose prices they use to inform their national target price.[10] EPR should be distinguished from internal price referencing, where the prices of identical or therapeutically similar products are used for benchmarking purposes. EPR is frequently practiced worldwide, although countries vary substantially in how they perform EPR. Countries utilize ERP systems primarily to obtain what they believe to be fair and reasonable prices for pharmaceuticals.[11] External reference pricing is also called international price comparison.[12] Government controls the price of products at or below the average price in reference countries. Reference countries should be chosen by studying the pricing policies, production and distribution system, and even the healthcare delivery, reimbursement, taxes, etc., in the health system. These factors influence the cost and a correction should be employed if it is significantly different.[7] External reference pricing is a strategy to control the price of patented products with market exclusivity. Reference pricing practice may vary in different countries.[12]

The advantages of using EPR as a benchmark for decisions within national price control are obvious. First, it seems simple; second, it affords reassurance for most people that prices are not higher than in other countries. Additionally, EPR can be used to drive prices down and can produce cost savings, at least in the short run. Although EPR is not a perfect method, it is used commonly.[13,14]

Selecting reference countries with a similar economic status and health system objectives increases the likelihood of arriving at appropriate levels of reference pricing. Referencing countries that are of lower economic status or have unusual conditions should be avoided. Demanding the same price in lower-priced markets as in higher-income markets could cause innovative pharmaceuticals to become prohibitively expensive for developing countries. In addition, heavily referencing lower-income countries could lead pharmaceutical companies to delay launches in those countries.[14]

The wide use of EPR often has some unintended consequences internationally, which may directly or indirectly affect members of the broader stakeholder community. Worldwide decreases in drug prices may lead to decreases in research and development of new products. WHO has stated that research into innovative pharmaceuticals should be considered a global public good, which is currently driven by price alone.[10] Consequently, the value of pharmaceutical innovation to the healthcare system should always be considered and reflected in drug prices. This perspective requires that systems consider the international implications of their pricing policies. There are also concerns that EPR may cause access disparities through a price increase and launch sequencing and nonentry into certain markets.

OBJECTIVE 17.3. EXPLAIN TYPES OF HEALTHCARE COSTS AND THEIR ESTIMATION

Costing Terms

Economists should distinguish average cost from marginal cost. Average cost is the total cost divided by the number of units produced, whereas marginal cost is the change in total cost that results from the production of an additional unit. In practice, the marginal cost is usually greater than the average cost. Marginal costs can be then distinguished from incremental costs. The incremental cost is the increased cost of one healthcare intervention/program relative to an alternative, whereas marginal cost is the change in total cost that results from the production of an additional unit. The incremental cost differs from the marginal cost in that the former relates to treatment alternatives, whereas the latter refers to more of the same treatment.[15]

Cost Categorization

All the possible sources of costs for a disease, or for increased severity of illness, should be considered to clarify the role of the new intervention that reduces harmful events of the disease. Costs are calculated to determine the resources that are used in the production of a good or service. The most basic cost of a drug or pharmaceutical product is its acquisition cost from a supplier. However, this is a small component of the overall cost. In the field of pharmacoeconomics, the medical costs can be categorized in four ways: direct medical, direct nonmedical, indirect costs, and intangible costs, to provide a comprehensive assessment.[16,17]

1. **Direct costs**: Direct medical costs refer to the costs that are directly related to the resource use associated with a service or commodity needed for providing a healthcare intervention. These are the medically related inputs used directly to provide the treatment. These include
   a. Acquisition cost of the drug (drug price)
   b. Transportation (shipping and insurance)
   c. Supplies and equipment to administer the drug
   d. Supply management (storage facilities, supply personnel)
   e. Medical and allied health consultations
   f. Costs of managing adverse effects of therapy
   g. Hospitalization costs related to adverse events or treatment effectiveness
   h. Laboratory services
   i. Outpatient visits
2. **Direct nonmedical costs** comprise resources supporting the provision of healthcare services but are not medical in nature, such as
   a. Travel
   b. Disease-related time expenditure of affected patients and relatives providing care
   c. Palliative care

$$\text{Direct costs} = \text{Direct medical costs} + \text{Direct nonmedical costs}$$

3. **Indirect costs** are costs associated with lost production capacity because of illness or death and include
   a. Time lost from work for the patient (morbidity costs)
   b. Time lost from work for the caregiver
   c. Premature death (mortality costs)

$$\text{Indirect costs} = \text{Morbidity costs} + \text{Mortality costs}$$

   The majority of pharmacoeconomic analyses focus on the direct costs of medical intervention and services provided within the healthcare system; important costs also arise outside this system. Individuals who undergo treatment are contributing their own time and thus incur an opportunity cost.[18]
   In addition, individuals with the disease will tend to be less productive in the labor market and also in nonmarket uses of their time, including household tasks; productivity losses are also for those whose illnesses lead to premature death. These productivity losses represent an opportunity cost to society (and likely an income reduction to the individual) and should be considered in any assessment of the burden of disease.[18]
   Indirect benefits, which are savings from avoiding indirect costs, are the increased earnings or productivity gains that occur due to medical intervention.

4. **Intangible costs** include the costs of pain, anxiety, or fatigue that occur because of a disease or its treatment. Intangible benefits, which are avoidance or alleviation of intangible costs, are benefits that result from a reduction in pain and suffering related to a medical intervention. It is difficult to measure or place a monetary value on these types of costs.

$$\text{Total costs} = \text{Direct costs} + \text{Indirect costs} + \text{Intangible costs}$$

Intangible costs are usually incorporated in the benefits side and incorporated as utilities assigned to health states that reflect the quality of life (QoL). QoL measures a person's experience of life, including work, recreation, social activities, etc. The impact of a person's health status on their QoL, i.e., their health-related QoL is usually measured in pharmacoeconomic analysis.[19]

Standardized questionnaires measure either the health-related QoL in general or QoL of a specific disease. Short Form 36 (SF 36) and EuroQol tools (EQ-5D or EQ-5D-L) are widely used generic health-related QoL instruments. SF 36 has eight domains: physical functioning, social functioning, role functioning, psychological distress, general health perceptions, bodily pain, vitality, and psychological well-being.[20]

Perspective

The perspective of a study must be determined to specify what costs are important to measure. Perspective is a term that describes which costs are needed based on the purpose of the study. Depending on the group/member making the reimbursement/payment, the following perspectives can be considered: (1) societal, (2) healthcare system, (3) third-party payer, (4) business, (5) government, and (6) participants and families. Common perspectives used in pharmacoeconomics analysis are the perspective of the payer (e.g., insurance company) and societal. The societal perspective is the broadest; it is difficult and time-consuming to estimate all of its cost components. E.g., societal costs include costs to the payer, costs to the provider/institution, other sector costs, costs to the patient, and indirect costs because of the loss of productivity.[21]

When determining costs, it is important to be evaluated in each perspective, irrespective of interventions, therapeutic areas, and patient groups investigated. In pharmacoeconomics, costs are considered from various perspectives (Table 17.1).

Estimating Costs

As a principle, costs should be determined as precisely as possible, including the methods, sources, and results in individual steps of cost estimations. The estimation of costs follows a process:

1. *Identification of resources*: Within the framework of the resources identified for the provision of healthcare services used for treating the disease, the information can be obtained from different sources. The sources are primary data (individual items of a particular service, e.g., drugs, laboratory, radiology, etc.), secondary data (e.g., health insurance data, government surveys), guidelines (e.g., WHO datasets), and expert opinions.
2. *Quantification of resources*: The frequency of use, the proportion of the relevant patient population using each service, and the duration of the service must be determined. The measuring or quantification of resources could be amounts of labor input or outputs (e.g., bed days, time in theater, prescriptions, etc.) and could include patients' or carers' time. Costs of service that are infrequently used and have only a slight impact on the results should be described, but not needed for the calculation. The costing method can use a micro- or the macrocosting approach. The degree of precision of quantification is determined by the perspective and reimbursement system, and the corresponding degree of aggregation of the services.

TABLE 17.1 Perspective and Relevant Costs to Be Considered

Perspective	Medical Costs	Morbidity Costs	Mortality Costs	Transportation/ Nonmedical Costs	Transfer Payments
Societal	All costs	All costs	All costs	All costs	
Healthcare system	All costs				
Third-party payer	Covered costs		Covered costs		
Businesses	Covered costs (self-insured)	Lost productivity (presenteeism/absenteeism)	Lost productivity		
Government	Covered (Medicare, Medicaid)			Criminal justice costs	Attributable to illness
Participants and families	Out-of-pocket costs	Lost wages/household production	Lost wages/household production	Out-of-pocket costs	Amount received

3. *Evaluation of the resources*: If there are prices of healthcare services and if these can be assumed to reflect costs, these can be multiplied by the relevant units of service use to yield total costs, such as x days multiplied by USD per day. For a detailed evaluation of resources, microcosting (bottom-up method) or gross costing (top-down method) is used. For cost identification, in microcosting, all cost components are defined at the most detailed level, whereas in gross costing, cost components are defined at a highly aggregated level. For cost valuation, in the bottom-up approach, cost components are valued by identifying resources used directly employed for a patient, whereas in the top-down approach, cost components are valued by separating out the relevant costs from comprehensive sources.[22] Although analysts favor microcosting, it tends to be costly and runs the risk of being specific to particular contexts. Top-down costing allocates a total budget for specific services such as hospital stays or doctors' visits according to rules. Bottom-up microcosting is considered to overestimate assessed costs, top-down gross costing tends to underestimate them. The choice between microcosting and gross costing depends on the needs of the analysis. Many studies use a mixture of the two, using microcosting for the direct costs of the intervention and gross costing for other costs.[22] Combining these dimensions gives four theoretic approaches: top-down gross costing, top-down microcosting, bottom-up gross costing, and bottom-up microcosting.[35]

Activity-based costing (ABC) is a costing methodology that identifies activities necessary to produce a defined service or product and assigns the cost of each activity resource to processes according to the actual consumption associated with the provision of activity. Models can be implemented relatively quickly because only estimates of two parameters are required: (1) the unit cost of supplying capacity (e.g., cost per minute of a surgeon's time) and (2) the time required to perform a transaction or an activity. The breakthrough of time-driven activity-based costing (TDABC) lies in using time equations to estimate the time spent on each activity.[23] TDABC helps to perform costing in health centers efficiently. It is intended to capture the cost of care delivery for conditions accurately and to control cost in an effort to create value in healthcare.[24] TDABC is more accurate and simpler than traditional ABC because it assigns resource costs to patients based on the amount of time clinical and staff resources are used in patient encounters.[25]

Methods to Measure Indirect Costs

Methods of measuring indirect costs include human capital, friction cost, and willingness to pay (WTP). The human capital method involves factors related to the production of valuable goods or services. Efforts of a talented workforce result in required productivity. It is the investment of a trained workforce that results in better productivity. Productivity losses of an individual due to morbidity or mortality are valued toward the present value of his or her future earnings. Assumptions about future earnings could be wrong. Considering that a worker cannot be replaced even when the employment rates are high is also debatable. It results in an overestimation of indirect costs due to productivity losses. The friction cost method, on the contrary, considers the productivity loss to be avoided when another person is employed and trained to the same talent levels. It assumes that morbidity or mortality will not affect total productivity. The time taken from the discontinuation of the previous employee due to ill health or death until a new employee is trained to comparable productivity is called the friction period. The method is controversial for considering morbidity and mortality to reduce unemployment. The human capital and WTP methods are commonly used.[26]

The WTP method can value both the indirect and intangible aspects of a disease or condition. The WTP method determines how much people are willing to pay to reduce the chance of an adverse health outcome. To elicit WTP values, respondents are presented with a hypothetical scenario describing the benefits of a particular healthcare intervention (e.g., program, pharmaceutical, medical device). Respondents are then asked to value the healthcare intervention in a dollar amount.[11]

A description of the healthcare service or intervention (e.g., medication therapy management program, new drug therapy) should be included in the hypothetical scenario. The scenario intends to provide the respondent with an accurate description of the good or service that he or she is being asked to value. In addition, the scenario should detail the amount of time the person should expect to spend, as well as the benefit (e.g., percent improvement in the condition) of the intervention. After the program or intervention has been adequately described, respondents are then asked to "bid" or place a value on the program or intervention. Bids can be obtained through a variety of formats, such as open-ended questions, closed-ended questions, a bidding game, or a payment card.[27]

1. Open-ended questions, simply ask respondents how much they would be WTP for the program or intervention.
2. Closed-ended questions, respondents are asked whether or not they will pay a specified dollar amount for the program or intervention.
3. Bidding game resembles an auction in that several bids are offered to reach a person's maximum WTP.
4. Payment card provides the respondent with a list of possible WTP amounts (i.e., payment card) to choose from.[27]

Time Adjustment for Cost

Standardization of Cost

If retrospective data are used to assess resources used over the years, more than 1 year before the study these costs should be adjusted before a direct (fair) comparison between medical interventions. Standardization is carried out by calculating the number of units (doses) used per case and multiplying this number by the current unit cost for each medication.[28]

Another method for standardization is to multiply all of the costs from the year the data were collected by the medical inflation rate for that year. Medical Consumer Price Index inflation rates can be found at the Bureau of Labor Statistics' website (www.bls.gov) and have been between 3% and 4% each year since 2005.[29]

Discounting

The time horizon is used to determine a period of time during which the outcomes of analysis will be considered. The time horizon could be expressed as a fixed number of years (or months or weeks) or relative to study variables (e.g., patients' lifetimes). In other words, the time horizon is a point in the future up to which all costs and effects must be accounted for and beyond which everything can be ignored.[30]

If the time horizon of a pharmacoeconomic analysis is several weeks or months, no discounting is required. However, if the time horizon is several years, then costs that occurred at different times must be brought to the same reference time point.[31]

Discounting is needed when costs are determined based on dollars spent or saved in future years. The discount rate is used to estimate the time value of money or benefits. The generally accepted discount rate for any healthcare interventions is between 3% and 5%, but it is recommended that the discount rate should be varied using high and low estimates of various discount rates.[32] To study the effects of varying discount rates on results of the study, a sensitivity analysis could be performed.[33]

The discount factor is equal to $1/(1 + r)^t$, where r is the discount rate and t is the number of years in the future that the cost or savings occur.[34]

CONCLUSION

Pharmaceutical pricing is different from other industries for many reasons. Different types of governmental control regulate the market. Healthcare costs are both direct and indirect. Identifying and valuing costs accurately have challenges, especially with indirect costs. Best practices in estimating costs are essential to build on evidence in value-based decisions.

PRACTICE QUESTIONS

1. Theoretically, as the supply increases, which of the following happens?
   A. Demand increases
   B. Price decreases
   C. Product damage decreases
   D. Quantity in market decreases
2. What is the optimality condition for a public good?
   A. Social marginal benefit is less than social marginal cost
   B. Social marginal benefit is equal to social marginal cost
   C. Social marginal benefit is greater than social marginal cost
   D. None of the above
3. Treatment of an adverse drug reaction is which type of cost?
   A. Direct medical cost
   B. Indirect cost
   C. Intangible cost
   D. Out-of-pocket cost
4. Which type of cost should be considered in case the perspective of the economic analysis is the healthcare system?
   A. Medical costs
   B. Morbidity costs

    C. Mortality costs

    D. Nonmedical costs

    E. All of the above

5. Which of the following methods is not suitable for measuring indirect cost?

    A. Human capital approach

    B. Friction cost

    C. WTP approach

    D. Reference cost

REFERENCES

1. Kumar A, Juluru K, Thimmaraju PK, Reddy J, Patil A. Pharmaceutical market access in emerging markets: concepts, components, and future. *J Mark Access Health Policy*. 2014;2. https://doi.org/10.3402/jmahp.v2.25302.

2. Mikkelsen JS. *White Paper - Market Access for Medical Technology and Pharmaceutical Companies*. Ministry of Foreign Affairs of Denmark; 2012. http://usa.um.dk/en/news/newsdisplaypage/?newsid=3e710ea5-b5cf-490c-b9b2-27250aca4a1d.

3. Mcclearn C, Croisier T. *Big Pharma's Market Access Mission*; 2013. https://www2.deloitte.com/content/dam/insights/us/articles/big-pharmas-market-access-mission/DUP436_Big_Pharma2.pdf.

4. van der Gronde T, Uyl-de Groot CA, Pieters T. Addressing the challenge of high-priced prescription drugs in the era of precision medicine: a systematic review of drug life cycles, therapeutic drug markets and regulatory frameworks. *PLoS One*. 2017;12(8):e0182613. https://doi.org/10.1371/journal.pone.0182613. Mihalopoulos C, ed.

5. Rattinger GB, Jain R, Ju J, Mullins CD. Principles of economics crucial to pharmacy students' understanding of the prescription drug market. *Am J Pharm Educ*. 2008;72(3):61. http://www.ncbi.nlm.nih.gov/pubmed/18698403.

6. Lee I-H, Bloor K, Hewitt C, Maynard A. International experience in controlling pharmaceutical expenditure: influencing patients and providers and regulating industry - a systematic review. *J Health Serv Res Policy*. 2015;20(1):52–59. https://doi.org/10.1177/1355819614545675.

7. Management of Sciences for Health. *MDS-3: Managing Access to Medicines and Health Technologies*. Arlington, VA: Management Sciences for Health; 2012. http://www.msh.org/resource-center/ebookstore/copyright.cfm.

8. Obama B. United States health care reform: progress to date and next steps. *J Am Med Assoc*. 2016;316(5):525–532. https://doi.org/10.1001/jama.2016.9797.

9. Nguyen TA, Knight R, Roughead EE, Brooks G, Mant A. Policy options for pharmaceutical pricing and purchasing: issues for low- and middle-income countries. *Health Policy Plan*. 2015;30(2):267–280. https://doi.org/10.1093/heapol/czt105.

10. World Health Organization. *WHO/HAI Project on Medicine Prices and Availability Review Series on Pharmaceutical Pricing Policies and Interventions Working Paper 1: External Reference Pricing*; 2011. http://haiweb.org/wp-content/uploads/2015/08/ERP-final-May2011a1.pdf.

11. Garcia Mariñoso B, Jelovac I, Olivella P. External referencing and pharmaceutical price negotiation. *Health Econ*. 2011;20(6):737–756. https://doi.org/10.1002/hec.1630.

12. Ruggeri K, Nolte E. Pharmaceutical pricing: the use of external reference pricing. *Rand Health Q*. 2013;3(2):6. http://www.ncbi.nlm.nih.gov/pubmed/28083293.

13. Acosta A, Ciapponi A, Aaserud M, et al. Pharmaceutical policies: effects of reference pricing, other pricing, and purchasing policies. *Cochrane Database Syst Rev*. October 2014. https://doi.org/10.1002/14651858.CD005979.pub2.

14. Rémuzat C, Urbinati D, Mzoughi O, El Hammi E, Belgaied W, Toumi M. Overview of external reference pricing systems in Europe. *J Mark Access Health Policy*. 2015;3(1):27675. https://doi.org/10.3402/jmahp.v3.27675.

15. Pradelli L, Wertheimer AI. *Pharmacoeconomics: Principles and Practice*. SEEd; 2012. https://books.google.ae/books?id=uKoHIfoIYKsC&pg=PA20&lpg=PA20&dq=The+incremental+cost+differs+from+the+marginal+cost+in+that+the+former+relates+to+treatment+alternatives+while+the+latter+refers+to+more+of+the+same+treatment&source=bl&ots=njaJITkZQG&sig=3.

16. IQWiG. *Working Paper Cost Estimation*; 2009. https://www.ispor.org/peguidelines/source/Germany_WorkPaperCostEst.pdf.

17. NHS. *NHS Costing Manual 2*; 2012. https://www.gov.uk/government/uploads/system/uploads/attachment_data/file/216427/dh_132398.pdf.

18. Lipscomb J, Yabroff KR, Brown ML, Lawrence W, Barnett PG. Health care costing: data, methods, current applications. *Med Care*. 2009;47(Supplement):S1–S6. https://doi.org/10.1097/MLR.0b013e3181a7e401.

19. Karimi M, Brazier J. Health, health-related quality of life, and quality of life: what is the difference? *Pharmacoeconomics*. 2016;34(7):645–649. https://doi.org/10.1007/s40273-016-0389-9.

20. Busija L, Pausenberger E, Haines TP, Haymes S, Buchbinder R, Osborne RH. Adult measures of general health and health-related quality of life: medical outcomes study short form 36-item (SF-36) and short form 12-item (SF-12) health surveys, Nottingham health profile (NHP), sickness impact profile (SIP), medical outcomes study short form 6D (SF-6D), health utilities index mark 3 (HUI3), quality of well-being scale (QWB), and assessment of quality of life (AQoL). *Arthritis Care Res (Hoboken)*. 2011;63(S11):S383–S412. https://doi.org/10.1002/acr.20541.

21. Oderda GM. The importance of perspective in pharmacoeconomic analyses. *J Pain Palliat Care Pharmacother*. 2002;16(4):65–69. https://doi.org/10.1080/J354v16n04_07.

22. Hrifach A, Brault C, Couray-Targe S, et al. Mixed method versus full top-down microcosting for organ recovery cost assessment in a French hospital group. *Health Econ Rev*. 2016;6(1):53. https://doi.org/10.1186/s13561-016-0133-3.

23. Akhavan S, Ward L, Bozic KJ. Time-driven activity-based costing more accurately reflects costs in arthroplasty surgery. *Clin Orthop Relat Res.* 2016;474(1):8−15. https://doi.org/10.1007/s11999-015-4214-0.

24. Keel G, Savage C, Rafiq M, Mazzocato P. Time-driven activity-based costing in health care: a systematic review of the literature. *Health Policy (NY).* 2017;121(7):755−763. https://doi.org/10.1016/j.healthpol.2017.04.013.

25. Mandigo M, O'Neill K, Mistry B, et al. A time-driven activity-based costing model to improve healthcare resource use in Mirebalais, Haiti. *Lancet.* 2015;385:S22. https://doi.org/10.1016/S0140-6736(15)60817-0.

26. Jo C. Cost-of-illness studies: concepts, scopes, and methods. *Clin Mol Hepatol.* 2014;20(4):327−337. https://doi.org/10.3350/cmh.2014.20.4.327.

27. Lin P-J, Cangelosi MJ, Lee DW, Neumann PJ. Willingness to pay for diagnostic technologies: a review of the contingent valuation literature. *Value Health.* 2013;16(5):797−805. https://doi.org/10.1016/J.JVAL.2013.04.005.

28. Rascati KL. *Essentials of Pharmacoeconomics.* 2nd ed. Lippincott Williams & Wilkins; 2012. http://www.lwwindia.co.in/book/9788184737264/essentials-pharmacoeconomics-with-point-access-codes.aspx.

29. Bureau of Labor Statistics. *Measuring Price Change for Medical Care in the CPI*; 2018. https://www.bls.gov/cpi/factsheets/medical-care.htm.

30. Claxton K, Paulden M, Gravelle H, Brouwer W, Culyer AJ. Discounting and decision making in the economic evaluation of health-care technologies. *Health Econ.* 2011;20(1):2−15. https://doi.org/10.1002/hec.1612.

31. Frederick S, Loewenstein G, O'Donoghue T. Time discounting and time preference: a critical review. *J Econ Lit.* 2002;40:351−401. https://doi.org/10.2307/2698382.

32. Severens JL, Milne RJ. Discounting health outcomes in economic evaluation: the ongoing debate. *Value Health.* 2004;7(4):397−401. https://doi.org/10.1111/j.1524-4733.2004.74002.x.

33. Briggs AH. Handling uncertainty in cost-effectiveness models. *Pharmacoeconomics.* 2000;17(5):479−500. https://doi.org/10.2165/00019053-200017050-00006.

34. O'Mahony JF, Newall AT, van Rosmalen J. Dealing with time in health economic evaluation: methodological issues and recommendations for practice. *Pharmacoeconomics.* 2015;33(12):1255−1268. https://doi.org/10.1007/s40273-015-0309-4.

35. Tan SS, Rutten FF, van Ineveld BM, Redekop WK, Hakkaart-van Roijen L. Comparing methodologies for the cost estimation of hospital services. *Eur J Health Econ.* 2009;10(1):39−45.

ANSWERS TO PRACTICE QUESTIONS

1. B
2. B
3. A
4. A
5. D

Chapter 18

Pharmacoeconomic Analyses and Modeling

Dixon Thomas[1], Mickael Hiligsmann[2], Denny John[3], Ola Ghaleb Al Ahdab[4] and Hong Li[5,6]

[1]Gulf Medical University, Ajman, United Arab Emirates; [2]Maastricht University, Maastricht, The Netherlands; [3]Campbell Collaboration, New Delhi, India; [4]Ministry of Health and Prevention, Abu Dhabi, United Arab Emirates; [5]Shanghai Jiao-Tong University, Shanghai, China; [6]University of Cincinnati, Cincinnati, OH, United States

Learning Objectives:

Objective 18.1 Discuss the purpose of pharmacoeconomic analyses.
Objective 18.2 Explain pharmacoeconomic analysis approaches.
Objective 18.3 Describe common pharmacoeconomic modeling methods.

OBJECTIVE 18.1. DISCUSS THE PURPOSE OF PHARMACOECONOMIC ANALYSES

Pharmacoeconomics is a branch of health economics that generally focuses on the costs and benefits of drug therapy. All the pharmacoeconomic analyses estimate the cost of various intervention strategies, whereas most (but not all) also include health consequences. With any sort of cost analysis, perspective (cost to whom) matters. Perspectives for pharmacoeconomics analyses include the patient, provider, payer, and the broader societal perspective (including all costs) with the payer or societal perspective being the most common in the published literature.

Economic value may generally be defined as a "comparative analysis of the costs and consequences of a medical intervention or strategy as well as its next best alternative(s)," the value to whom is an important aspect of pharmacoeconomic analyses. Pharmacoeconomic analyses are increasingly used to assess the economic value of pharmaceutical products or medical devices.

The pharmaceutical industry invests enormous amounts of money in developing new health technologies.[1] Even though the success rate of developing newer health technologies is poor, this effort of selecting products that dramatically improve health and others do make incremental gains. After clinical trials, a pharmaceutical product must pass at least two additional regulatory steps. First, the marketing authorization (also called licensing) is granted, for example, in Europe it is the European Medicines Agency (EMA) while in the United States it is performed by the Food and Drug Administration (FDA). The EMA and FDA look at the quality, safety, and efficacy of drugs, by conducting a risk-benefit analysis. Once the pharmaceutical receives marketing authorization (i.e., the benefits outweigh the risks of the intervention), the pharmaceutical industry aims to set a price and achieves coverage and reimbursement. For example, this decision is made at the national level in Europe; however, in the United States, pharmaceutical companies can set a price for the approved drug in the market, but the drug reimbursement status needs to be granted by each health insurance program. In addition to benefit-risk considerations when a decision is made for reimbursement other factors must be taken into consideration such as convenience, affordability, and cost-effectiveness.

In a world with limited healthcare resources, cost containment is becoming important but innovating cheaper products is not common in healthcare. Almost all the time, newer technologies are costlier than the existing products but also provide added benefits over existing products. The questions to consider relate to whether or not the new technology is affordable and an efficient use of resources.

Pharmacoeconomic analyses vary mainly based on the types of outcomes used (Table 18.1). The analyses measuring and comparing the outcomes are considered to be full pharmacoeconomic evaluations.

Clinical Pharmacy Education, Practice and Research. https://doi.org/10.1016/B978-0-12-814276-9.00018-0

TABLE 18.1 Pharmacoeconomic Analysis Based on Types of Costs and Outcomes[1]

Analysis Type	Valuation of Costs[a]	Valuation of Health Outcomes	Calculation
Cost of Illness Analysis (COI)	$	None	At disease level
Budget-Impact Analysis (BIA)	$	None[b] or maximize various[c]	vs.
Cost-Comparison Analysis	$	None	vs.
Cost-Minimization Analysis (CMA)	$	Assume same	vs.
Cost-Consequence Analysis (CCA)	$	Natural units	vs.
Cost-Effectiveness Analysis (CEA)	$	Natural units	÷
Cost-Utility Analysis (CUA)	$	Utilities (e.g., quality-adjusted life years, QALYs)	÷
Cost-Benefit Analysis (CBA)	$	$	÷ or[d] −

[a]Any currency.
[b]That is, determine the impact of an intervention/program on a designated nonfixed budget.
[c]That is, maximize some health outcome within a designated fixed ("capped") budget.
[d]Cost-benefit ratio (÷) or net of costs and benefits (−).
Adapted from US National Library of Medicine, https://www.nlm.nih.gov/nichsr/hta101/ta10107.html.

Burden of Disease and Affordability

- Cost-of-illness analysis (COI): a determination of the economic impact of an illness or condition (typically on a given population, region, or country), e.g., of smoking, arthritis, or diabetes, including associated treatment costs.
- Budget-impact analysis (BIA): determines the impact of implementing or adopting a particular technology or technology-related policy on a designated budget, e.g., of a drug formulary or health plan.

Economic Evaluations Finding Value for Money Spent

- Cost-minimization analysis (CMA): a determination of the least costly among alternative interventions that are assumed to produce equivalent health outcomes.
- Cost-effectiveness analysis (CEA): a comparison of interventions regarding costs in monetary units and outcomes expressed in quantitative nonmonetary health units, e.g., reduced mortality or morbidity.
- Cost-utility analysis (CUA): a form of CEA that compares costs in monetary units with health outcomes regarding their utility and mortality, which is expressed in quality-adjusted life years (QALYs). QALY is a generic outcome measure that takes morbidity and mortality gains into account.
- Cost-consequence analysis (CCA): a form of CEA that presents costs and health outcomes in discrete categories, without aggregating or placing weights on the costs and health outcomes.
- Cost-benefit analysis (CBA): compares costs and health benefits (and risks), all of which are quantified in common monetary units.[1,2]

Pharmacoeconomic Evaluation Purpose

A COI study aims to measure the burden of a disease with regards to costs. This could be useful to prioritize between diseases but does not help in getting an efficient healthcare allocation for coverage and reimbursement decisions of a particular intervention. (A high-cost burden does not mean that treatments are available to reduce this burden.) As affordability is also important for short-run economic purposes, a BIA is often undertaken. By estimating the impact of the new drug on healthcare budgets, this method assesses the affordability of a healthcare intervention if the intervention is used within an environment as compared to not used within an environment.

A full economic evaluation aims to assess the value of money or efficiency of healthcare resources. The preferred type of economic evaluation is CUA because it allows the use of the same health outcome for all interventions and diseases, and thus to help decision makers to allocate resources efficiently.

Full Versus Partial Economic Evaluation

A full economic evaluation compares the costs and health outcomes of at least two interventions. Namely, an intervention of interest compared to its next best alternative(s). We distinguish five full economic evaluations: CBA, CCA, CEA, CUA, and CMA.

A partial economic analysis only evaluates one intervention in isolation or considers only one domain (costs or effectiveness). Under certain circumstances, COI and BIA are considered partial evaluations when they evaluate one disease or intervention in isolation.[3]

Levels of Application

Pharmacoeconomic analyses are useful in both national and local economic settings. In national or population-level decision making, such as the decision to provide access for and fund a drug, CEA and BIA are required components of the process. Other analyses are also used for specific purposes. At a national level related to research funding allocation decisions, COI could help prioritize between diseases. At a more local level, such as a hospital administrator, BIAs and CEAs are used for formulary inclusion decisions. Mini-health technology assessment (HTA) or hospital-based HTA is increasingly used to assess value in a hospital setting. The Danish Centre for Evaluation and Health Technology Assessment (DACEHTA) describes mini-HTA as a management and decision support tool based on reasoning involved in HTAs and may be used where a hospital is contemplating the introduction of new health technology.[4]

Thus, pharmacoeconomic analyses enhance public health decision making for both broader and also at local levels.[5]

OBJECTIVE 18.2. EXPLAIN PHARMACOECONOMIC ANALYSIS APPROACHES

Cost-of-Illness

Using the definition of the International Society of Pharmacoeconomics and Outcomes Research (ISPOR), a COI study or a cost-of-disease study aims to determine the total economic impact (cost) of a disease or health condition in society through the identification, measurement, and valuation of all direct and indirect costs. This form of study focuses on costs but does not address questions relating to treatment effectiveness or efficiency.[6]

COI studies generally measure medical costs; some COI studies also measure nonmedical costs. COI studies aim to assess the economic burden that a specific health problem or groups of health conditions impose on society regarding utilization of healthcare services and productivity losses. This research has the potential of informing policy-makers and decision-makers on the relative impact of diseases at the population level, assisting them in making projections of future healthcare costs and resource allocation decisions. Furthermore, COI studies aid in signaling to innovators the population-level unmet need regarding health losses and the potential for future interventions to reduce this unmet need.

The choice of cost methodology (i.e., top-down vs. bottom-up) for assessing both direct costs and losses in productivity varies depending on the availability of data.[7] For example, epidemiological data availability (i.e., disease prevalence, incidence, and associated mortality) varies by geography and other characteristics. Ideally, COI estimates should use a database linking epidemiological data, resource utilization, health services, and their actual costs (rather than the listed prices), alongside demographic data. Big data and patient registries are rarely available in Central and Eastern Europe, Western Asia and Africa (CEEWAA) countries. Nevertheless, even if these data sources were available, valuation of important cost components, such as patient out-of-pocket expenses and lost productivity of informal caregivers, would be rather difficult, and therefore might be excluded, thus underestimating the true COI.

The challenges on accuracy of methods used for assessing losses of productivity due to an illness are complex due to:

1. The human capital approach (HCA) and friction cost method (FCM) are different in approach. The HCA values the potential lost production because of an illness, whereas the FCM focuses on duration until the person is replaced by another one to continue to contribute to the productivity of the organization. Although appealing, using the FCM requires a tremendous amount of information that is difficulty to collect and subject to change with friction time, for example, on the unemployment rate in the country.
2. Should analyses include losses due to absenteeism or also due to presenteeism? Although the assessment of productivity losses resulting from absenteeism may be relatively uncontentious, this is not the case when presenteeism (i.e., the level of productivity while working) is concerned. These presenteeism-related costs are frequently omitted from COI studies.[7-9]

Budget-Impact Analysis

A BIA is an economic assessment that estimates the financial consequences of adopting a new intervention. It mainly deals with the affordability of new health technologies to a hospital or health system budget with limited resources.[10]

A BIA is usually performed in addition to CEA. A CEA analysis evaluates whether an intervention provides value (i.e., efficiency) relative to an existing intervention (with value defined as cost relative to health outcome). A BIA evaluates whether the high-value intervention is affordable.

A BIA is used to identify the total budget required to fund an intervention. BIA takes the true "unit" cost of an intervention and multiplies it by the number of people who utilize it. Consider the size of the population that utilize the intervention; if it is low, modeling might be required. Also consider if the intervention is replacing an existing standard of care (substitution) or being added to the existing standard of care (combination). There is also the possibility that the standard of care does not exist (e.g., due to patient intolerance of standard care). Modeling is used to fill gaps in data and it is subjected to sensitivity analyses to evaluate the impact of changes in the assumptions used in modeling.[11]

As a BIA is often used for resource allocation purposes, it takes a payer's perspective and uses a short-term time horizon (often 1—3 years). A BIA does not use discounting. Results should be presented on an annual or quarterly basis, or in whatever timeframe is relevant to the decision-maker.

The BIA focus is on the direct costs of specific resources needed to put the intervention into effect, such as supplies, equipment, and staff. Because the BIA uses a short-term time horizon, and overhead costs are fixed in the short term, these overhead costs are ordinarily excluded from BIAs. This distinguishes BIA from cost-effectiveness studies, which includes overhead costs. The overhead can account for a substantial part of the cost of operating a hospital or healthcare system and the CEA.[11]

Some differences between BIAs and CEAs are noted in Table 18.2.

Supply-side thresholds take resource allocation into account, e.g., estimates of the health foregone because an insurance company or other provider spends some of its available budgets on a new intervention and is therefore forced to reduce its funding of older interventions.[12] Budget impact is the difference between COI of new treatment and the existing standard treatment (Figs. 18.1 and 18.2).

TABLE 18.2 Comparison of Budget Impact Analysis With Cost-Effectiveness Analysis

	Budget-Impact Analysis	Cost-Effectiveness Analysis
Perspective	Payer	Societal
Time Horizon	Short term	Long term/Lifetime
Size of Population	Includes	Ignores
Model Inputs	Payer specific	Population average
Model Outputs	Cost	Cost and health outcomes
Discounting	No	Yes
Include Overhead Costs	No	Yes

Adopted from US Department of Veterans Affairs. Budget Impact Analysis. Health Economics Resource Center (HERC). https://www.herc.research.va.gov/include/page.asp?id=budget-impact-analysis.

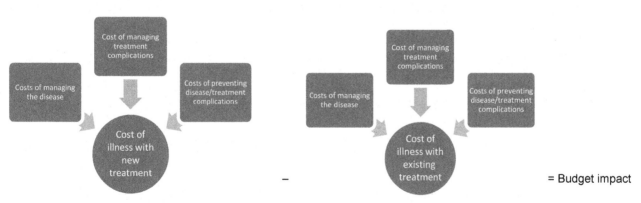

FIGURE 18.1 Framework of budget-impact analysis (difference in the costs of new and existing treatments).

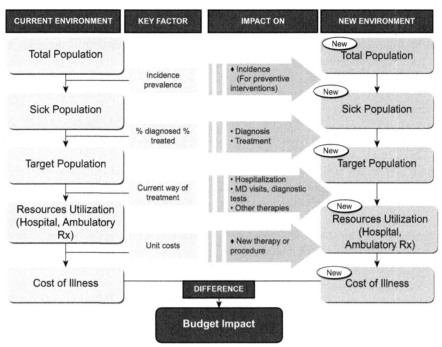

FIGURE 18.2   Budget-impact model. *Adapted from Brosa M, Gisbert R, Rodríguez JM, Soto J. Principios, métodos y aplicaciones del análisis del impacto presupuestario en el sector sanitario.* Pharmacoecon Span Res Artic. *2005;2(2):65−78. https://doi.org/10.1007/BF03320900.*

Cost-Comparison Analysis

As per the definition by ISPOR, a cost-comparison analysis compares only the costs associated with two or more alternative healthcare treatments or interventions. The process of identifying all the costs and their relative importance is often called cost-identification analysis.[6]

Cost-comparison analysis is not commonly used. When COI measures all relevant costs of the disease, including its treatment, cost-comparison analysis is only measuring the costs of different treatment options. Cost-comparison analysis compares the costs of two different treatment mixes (including all medical and nonmedical products and services). When the treatment options have multiple cycles and with complicated dosage regimens, cost-comparison analysis helps in totaling and comparing the differences in costs, e.g., costs of different chemotherapy regimens. In a complex treatment mix, it is essential to identify all the treatment costs, including drugs, devices, nutritional supplements, professional care costs, physiotherapy, acupuncture, etc. Policy-makers usually use COI instead of cost-comparison analysis.

Cost-Minimization Analysis

In the definition of ISPOR, a CMA is a type of pharmacoeconomic analysis comparing only two alternative therapies regarding costs because their health outcomes (effectiveness and safety) are found to be or are expected to be identical.[6]

The CMA considers the costs and health outcomes and compares two alternative therapies, but only in situations assuming the health outcomes are identical. In rare cases where the health outcomes are extremely similar, the decision-makers can prioritize the treatment option that is less expensive. CMA is commonly used to compare between the generic and branded versions of drugs with cost variation. As the generics are considered bioequivalent to the branded version of the same drug, the outcomes of therapy are expected to be identical. CMA could also be used to compare the use of generic and branded versions of drugs in different settings. The costs charged for the same drugs are different in a charity hospital compared to a corporate hospital. If we assume the treatment outcomes with similar drugs to be same in different settings, CMA could be performed. Therapy outcomes are the result of many factors involved in the care process, with drugs being one of the factors. The differences in professional care, nutrition, hygiene, genetic factors, etc. will alter the outcomes. Even the same drug will produce different outcomes depending on rational use approaches. The dose, timing of administration, dosage forms, interactions, etc. will influence the safety and effectiveness of drugs. CMA is criticized for assuming identical outcomes when they are not similar. It is also doubtful that CMA is a full pharmacoeconomic analysis when the health outcomes are assumed to be equal but are not measured to test this equality assumption.[14]

CMA is useful in limited resource settings to decrease the cost when the outcome is the same for interventions of varying costs. Even in developed countries, healthcare budgets are limited. The policy is to provide services and products of acceptable quality, if not the best quality. Generic versions of drugs are preferred over costly brands. Price variation among different brands is significant for some products. Selecting a cheaper bioequivalent brand or generic is a common strategy to minimize costs.

Cost-Benefit Analysis

As per the definition of ISPOR, a CBA is an analytical technique derived from the economic theory that enumerates and compares the net costs of a healthcare intervention with the benefits that arise as a consequence of applying that intervention. For this technique, both the net costs and the benefits of the health intervention are expressed in monetary units.[6]

CBA is commonly used in many economics fields, including healthcare. Even though it is a common method of analysis in public projects, in clinical decision making, it is difficult to assign a monetary value to the clinical outcomes. CEA and CUA are used more commonly in healthcare. CBA is like risk-benefit analysis. Both could be described better as benefit-cost analysis and benefit-risk analysis because the expectation is that benefit outweighs costs. The value of the benefit is worth paying extra costs for the treatment, which is compared with a cheaper version. In CBA costs and benefits are represented in monetary units (e.g., dollar in the United States, pounds in the United Kingdom, etc.) As in CBA, the benefit (outcome) is in monetary units; the comparison is computational and straightforward. The costs and benefits of a healthcare intervention are compared with another standard intervention. This intervention could be a drug (most common), surgical procedure, pharmaceutical care service (e.g., counseling), or even a public health project (e.g., clean drinking water project and decreased expenses for infections averted):

$$\text{Incremental net monetary benefit} = (\text{Benefit of A} - \text{Benefit of B}) - (\text{Cost of A} - \text{Cost of B})$$

The result could be expressed as an incremental net monetary benefit of $10,000, for example. This example would suggest that intervention A is favored over intervention B as the benefits of A versus B less their costs, favor A. The interpretation of this example is that when we value health gains in monetary units, we expect to yield higher health gains in the monetary form of $10,000 for the average patient by opting for intervention A as compared to intervention B.

The difference between cost-benefit analysis and return on investment (ROI) should be understood. Although CBA helps in choosing a better treatment option or a project in comparison with an alternative, ROI measures the value of an investment. CBA is an evaluation and ROI is a valuation.

Return on investment: ROI is a performance measure used to evaluate the efficiency of a project or to compare the efficiency of different projects. ROI measures the amount of return on a project relative to its cost. To calculate ROI, the return (net benefit: benefit minus cost) of a project is divided by the cost of the project, with the result expressed as a percentage[15]:

$$\text{ROI} = (\text{Gain from investment} - \text{Cost of investment})/\text{Cost of investment} \times 100$$

Cost-Consequence Analysis

In the definition of ISPOR, a CCA compares the health intervention of interest to one or more relevant alternatives, listing the cost components and the various outcomes of each intervention separately. This type of economic analysis does not indicate the relative importance of the components listed and leaves it to the decision-maker to form his or her view.

The CCA is relatively difficult to perform as each outcome and its costs need to be separately assessed and evaluated. It is up to the decision-makers to consider the outcomes of their interest.

Cost-Effectiveness Analysis

As per definition by ISPOR, a CEA is a systematic method of comparing two or more alternative programs by measuring the costs and consequences of each. A distinguishing feature of CEA is that the consequences (health outcomes) of all the programs to be compared must be measured in the same common units—natural units related to the clinical objective of the programs (e.g., symptom-free days gained, cases prevented, patients improved, life years gained). If there are just two alternative programs, their difference in cost (incremental cost) is compared to their difference in outcomes (incremental effect) by dividing the former by the latter. This ratio is known as the incremental cost-effectiveness ratio (ICER). If there are more than two alternatives, programs are compared on a systematic pairwise basis using their ICERs.

Many believe that the other full pharmacoeconomic analyses like CBA, CUA, CMA, CCA, etc. are subtypes of CEA. Technically, CEA has differences to other analyses in the denominator of effectiveness (outcome) when calculated. CEA uses natural units of outcomes such as life years gained, symptom-free period, blood pressure, etc.:

$$\text{Incremental cost effectiveness ratio (ICER)} = \frac{\text{Cost}_A - \text{Cost}_B}{\text{Effect}_A - \text{Effect}_B}$$

The result could be written as $45,000 per life year saved. The interpretation of this example is that for every $45,000 invested in intervention A to treat the stated population, we would expect to observe one additional health unit gained (life year in this example) as compared to treating the population with intervention B.

Cost-effectiveness of new health technology (innovative drug) in comparison with an existing health technology (comparator standard drug) could be explained using a cost-effectiveness plane. Effectiveness is on the horizontal axis and cost is on the vertical axis. The "X" in the center represents the cost and effectiveness of the existing health technology. Once the cost and effectiveness of the new technology are measured, they can be spotted anywhere in the four quadrants that help in decision making (Fig. 18.3). Each quadrant is numbered to make things clearer.

First quadrant: If the cost and effectiveness of the new health technology fall within the first quadrant this indicates that the new drug is costlier and less effective compared with the standard drug at X. The new drug shows "strong dominance" in being expensive and with poor outcomes. The fourth quadrant also shows strong dominance. The principle of "strong dominance" leads to easy decision-making: accept or reject.[16] In the case of the first quadrant, it is to reject. There is no sense in paying extra for a new intervention that produces poor outcomes compared to existing standard treatment.

Second quadrant: If the cost and effectiveness of the new health technology is spotted in the second quadrant, a CEA needs to be performed. Here, the strong dominance principle is not used as the new therapy because it is clearly not the standard therapy. The downside is increased cost. Now the question is whether the additional effectiveness is worth paying the additional cost. Is the new therapy value for money spent? Well, the first thing to clarify is that the information from the cost-effectiveness plane or ICER may or may not be used in decision making. This CEA provides only some information, not the complete information required in decision making. Many factors like cultural, political, trade, budgetary, and other administrative factors will influence decision making. CEA is mostly a reasonable attempt to make pharmacoeconomic information clear. The usually used strategy is to draw a line through quadrants 3 and 2. This is called the cost-effectiveness threshold. It is a limit above which the decision will be to reject and below which decision will be

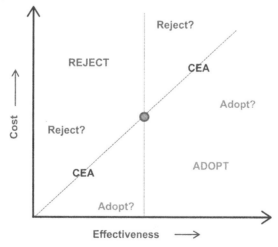

FIGURE 18.3 Cost-effectiveness plane in decision making. *Adapted from National Information Center on Health Services Research and Healthcare Technology (NICHSR). HTA 101: V. Economic analysis methods. NIH.*

to accept. This threshold is selected based on many parameters that affect affordability and expected gains in health. The concept of opportunity cost is really important. A trade-off should be made considering the health gain due to other interventions with the money saved by not buying this new costly drug, with the loss in health if this new drug is not used.[12] Consider the example of a new treatment that cures cancer compared with an existing treatment that could only mitigate the condition. Surely the new treatment will increase life years gained. Because recovering to near normal life is "invaluable," the cost-effectiveness threshold could be higher. A society's cost-effectiveness threshold—which indicates its willingness to pay (WTP) for improvements in health—can also be inferred from its budget for healthcare expenditures. The interventions are to be ranked from lowest incremental cost-effectiveness ratio (ICER) to the highest. Lower ICERs are preferred over higher. Going down in the ranking, at certain points all the available resources will be exhausted and further technologies could not be selected. The cost-effectiveness of the last intervention in the list might be costly and least preferred but comes within the available resource is the society's WTP threshold. It is the highest price the society is willing to pay for the least preferred technology due to higher expenses per quality-adjusted life year (QALY) gain. Healthcare interventions need to be cost-effective and appropriately priced.[17]

Third quadrant: In developing economies with a significant poor class in society, pharmaceutical innovation could focus on to innovate cheaper treatment options often compromising the outcomes. This, of course, creates ambiguity. Decision-makers might need to consider certain thresholds to assist in decision making. Is it still an acceptable level of outcomes for the money spent? The trade-off is what other significant health outcomes could be achieved with this saved money. Decision making becomes even tougher on ethical grounds for accepting new interventions that are worse than existing interventions. The society's cost-effectiveness threshold is called the willingness to accept (WTA) for having fewer outcomes. WTA often exceeds WTP.[18]

Fourth quadrant: Is a situation of reduced cost with increased effectiveness. It is a strong dominant to decide on acceptance of the intervention. The question here is: is it is possible? Such a situation rarely happens in healthcare. As clinical trials are costly and the success rates of new healthcare technology are poor, new intervention is almost always costlier compared to an older intervention.[19] However, this can be possible when we prevent additional costs due to the positive effects of the new treatments.

Cost-Utility Analysis

In the definition of ISPOR, a CUA is a methodology of economic analysis that compares two or more alternative choices regarding both their costs and their outcomes, where the outcomes are measured in units of utility or preference. The purpose of the analysis is to compare, using cost-effectiveness, two or more alternative choices regarding being both clinically meaningful and compared with other economic analyses. CUA can be considered as the "gold standard" methodology for evaluating the cost-effectiveness of healthcare choices.[4]

CUA is considered as a type of CEA and is sometimes called CEA. The only technical difference is that CUA uses QALYs as the denominator in calculating the ICER. Being a universal unit of health outcome, QALYs have been used often. For example, as per NICE, in the United Kingdom £25,000 or up to £30,000 (with conditions) per QALY gained by a new intervention is an acceptable value for money spent to purchase the new intervention. This limit is called the cost-effectiveness threshold. The cost-effectiveness threshold is defined as the "maximum value of money per health outcome that a jurisdiction decides to pay for adopting a technology or an intervention."[20] QALY even though common it is also criticized for its limitations. QALYs gained in geriatrics are not the same as QALYs gained in pediatrics, neither does it differentiate between QALYs gained by a mother of four young children compared with a similarly aged woman with no dependents.

A QALY is a universal health outcome measure applicable to all individuals and all diseases, thereby enabling comparisons across diseases and across programs. QALY is a measure of health benefits of medical interventions, whereas disability-adjusted life years are a measure of the burden of diseases. QALY measures both mortality and morbidity benefits with medical interventions. QALY is the sum of the number of years lived after the intervention with a certain quality of life (regarding utility). Utilities are measured on a scale of zero (representing death) to one (representing perfect health). Some disease conditions are considered worse than death, thus negative utility value could be considered.

The utility is a quantitative expression of an individual's *preference* for, or desirability of, a particular state of health under conditions of uncertainty. Direct elicitation methods to calculate utility are standard gamble (SG), time trade-off (TTO), or visual analog scales. Health-related quality of life measures are not considered as utility measures, e.g., SF-36 and disease-specific instruments. Indirect elicitation methods include, e.g. EQ-5D and SF-6D.

Standard gamble: In the SG method, patients are asked how much of a risk of death they are willing to incur to be cured of the condition.It is a hypothetical choice of taking risks with treatment that has the potential to cause death as an adverse event or cure the disease. A chronic disease state with arthritis and a nonfunctional knee could make the patient choose to undergo knee replacement surgery. Hypothetically, the patient preference is to ask if a probability (p) of 80% is the chance of returning to normal health after surgery (1−p is a 20% chance of immediate death). If the patient accepts to undergo the surgery, the probability of returning to normal health is decreased until a point, e.g., 70% (1−p, the chance of dying is 30%), where the patient is unable to decide yes or no to undergo surgery. In this case, the utility is 0.7. If another patient is *does not* accept to undergo surgery with an 80% chance of returning to normal health, the probability of returning to normal health is increased, e.g., 85% (1−p is 15%), where patient is unable to decide yes or no to undergo surgery. In this case, the utility is 0.85. The point of indifference (not able to decide to undergo surgery or remain in the disease state) is the utility level. The utility (preference) scores for severe cases will be lower compared with not so severe cases.

Time trade-off: In the TTO method patients are asked to rate how much healthy life they are willing to give up to be cured of the condition. It is a hypothetical choice between living with less health for a specific amount of time versus living in perfect health for a shorter period of time. Here the choices are given to a patient to continue staying in ill health for the period of life expectancy or undergo a treatment to be fully healthy for a shorter duration of time followed by death. With the suggested new treatment (for full health), if the reduced life expectancy is 30 years compared with 50 years of continued chronic disease, depending on the patient's preference to accept or reject the new treatment, changes are made. If the patient accepts, the number of years they are expected to live with full health followed by death is *reduced* until the patient is not able to choose yes or no to the treatment. On the other hand, if the patient is not accepting 30 years in full health as an alternative to living 50 years with a chronic disease, the number of years expected to live with full health followed by death is *increased* until the patient is not able to choose yes or no to the treatment. If the number of years where the patient is unable to choose yes or no to the treatment is 35 years, 35/50 = 0.7 is the utility.[16]

Visual analog scales: In visual analog scales, patients are asked to select a score for their present health status. These are patient estimated preference scores for different disease states. In the visual analog scale of 0 (death) to 100 (perfect health), if a patient scores 50, that indicates a utility score of 0.5:

$$\text{Cost-utility ratio} = \frac{\text{Cost}_A - \text{Cost}_B}{\text{QALY}_A - \text{QALY}_B}$$

One year lived in full health (1 utility) is 1 QALY. One year lived with half health (0.5 utility) is 0.5 QALYs. A half year lived with half health (0.5 utility) is 0.25 QALYs.

The result of a CUA could be written as, e.g., $50,000 per QALY gained. The interpretation of this example is that for every $50,000 invested in intervention A to treat the stated population, we would expect to observe 1 additional perfect year of health gained as compared to treating the population with intervention B. Using thresholds of maximum payment per QALY gained is commonly used to ease the decision-making process considering affordability.

Perspectives in Pharmacoeconomic Analysis

Based on differences in the perspectives selected, identification, measurement, and comparison of the costs and consequences change in pharmacoeconomics. The most comprehensive perspective is societal. It includes the perspectives of all stakeholders in healthcare and is thus complex and expensive to consider. The US FDA mandates that any pharmacoeconomic analyses submitted to the regulators should also include a societal perspective. This is called a reference case.[19] When the health insurance companies and employer perform pharmacoeconomic analyses, the payer perspective is used. When studies focus on the services of healthcare providers like hospitals and healthcare professionals, a provider perspective is used. Finally, the important patient perspective covers the viewpoints of the patient. Common perspectives used in pharmacoeconomic studies are payer and societal.[2]

The merits and demerits of pharmacoeconomic analyses approaches are listed in Table 18.3.

Sensitivity Analysis in the Pharmacoeconomic Analysis

Some level of uncertainty is involved in estimations of costs, outcomes, and other variables used in a cost analysis. Certain variables that influence significant changes in the results should be estimated. To address uncertainty, sensitivity analysis should be performed. A sensitivity analysis may find, e.g., that including variables like indirect costs, or assuming the use of generic as opposed to brand-name drugs in a medical therapy, or using a reasonable higher discount rate in an analysis, changes the cost-effectiveness of one intervention compared to another.[1]

TABLE 18.3 Merits and Demerits of Pharmacoeconomic Analyses Approaches

Merits	Demerits
Cost-of-Illness (COI)	
• Easy to calculate	• Not comparing outcomes with costs. • Wary from settings to settings. • Not a universal measure, results vary in different settings.
Cost-Comparison Analysis	
• Easy to calculate	• Not comparing outcomes with costs. • Not a universal measure, results vary in different settings.
Cost-Minimization Analysis (CMA)	
• More useful in resource-limited settings.	• Assumes the outcomes are similar, may not always be true. • Cost-effectiveness analysis is a better alternative even if the outcomes are similar. • Not a universal measure, results vary in different settings.
Budget-Impact Analysis (BIA)	
• Critical analysis dealing with affordability of products and services within a budget.	• Outcomes not measured. • Without cost-effectiveness analysis, BIA has less value in decision-making. • Not a universal measure, results vary in different settings.
Cost-Benefit Analysis (CBA)	
• Compares both costs and outcomes.	• Monetary units for outcomes is not natural, and sometimes unethical. • Not a universal measure, results vary in different settings.
Cost-Consequence Analysis	
• Compares both costs and discrete outcomes. • Decision-makers could find in-depth analysis of each measurable outcome (consequences).	• Difficult to perform (calculate). • Not easy to summarize by the decision-makers. • Not a universal measure, results vary in different settings.
Cost-Effectiveness Analysis (CEA)	
• Compares both cost and outcomes. • Outcomes are measured in natural units. • Combines multiple outcomes.	• Not a universal measure, results vary in different settings. • Does not consider equity considerations.
Cost-Utility Analysis (CUA)	
• Universal unit, QALY. • Gold standard method. • Combines multiple outcomes.	• QALYs may not have the same value in people with different socioeconomic statuses.

Discounting in Pharmacoeconomic Evaluations

Discounting of costs and outcomes is performed if the costs and effectiveness outcomes are considered beyond 12-month time periods. The present value of money, as well as better health, is higher than future costs and outcomes.

OBJECTIVE 18.3. DESCRIBE COMMON PHARMACOECONOMIC MODELING METHODS

The ISPOR book of terms definition is: Modeling refers to the development of a simplified representation of a system (e.g., a population). A particular model may be analytical, visual, or both. In pharmacoeconomics specifically or health economics in general, analytical models can be used to pose and answer questions about interventions that cannot be directly answered by clinical trials due to time and financial constraints. Decision trees are both analytical and visual.[21]

Modeling is especially required when data from research observations are not available. Modeling is not a substitue for generating research data. There are possibilities of it going wrong.

In many situations, the data are insufficient for pharmacoeconomic analysis and related studies to make more informed decision making. In such cases, analytical, diagrammatic models, or mixed models are used to generate clearer information.

Analytical models are mathematical models that use data available from cost-effectiveness studies to prepare further interpretations of the data. Decision trees, the Markov models, and simulation models are commonly used to improve the quality of information in decision making.[19] As the models are based on certain assumptions, there is the possibility that these assumptions may be wrong. Pharmacoeconomic analyses along with modeling supplies information that helps its decision making. This information may be partly considered or fully rejected by decision-makers considering the limitations of such tools in a given context. Thus, these methods are just tools to assist in decision making, and it is not mandatory that the decision should be as per the results of such studies.

Decision Analyses

Decision analyses can be operationalized through decision trees or simulation models. Discrete event simulation models are useful in emergency care or in the transmission of infections. The events must be mutually exclusive. Individuals progress through the model only if they experience a new event (e.g., moving from the ED waiting room to an ED exam room).[22]

State-transition modeling is an intuitive, flexible, and transparent approach to computer-based decision-analytic modeling. A state-transition model can be used to model a cohort of patients, in which case it is called a Markov cohort model. A state-transition model can also be used to model individuals; in this case, it is called a microsimulation (first-order Monte Carlo) model. Most frequently, state-transition models are used in the evaluation of risk factor interventions, screening, diagnostic procedures, treatment strategies, and disease management programs. Discrete event simulation is another rarely used method with flexible frameworks used especially in constrained resources. Because it is used to represent complex systems, it is difficult to develop, implement, and analyze.[23,24]

Regardless of their structural form, there are certain similarities across all healthcare decision analyses:

- all decision analyses require the clinical- and policy-relevant features of the problem, the time frame of the analysis, and the relevant patient population to be specified.
- they all require information on the probability of experiencing a health state or a health event. In decision analysis, these are called "transition probabilities."
- all healthcare decision analyses require information on the payoff(s) associated with a health state or health event. The payoff(s) could be the cost, the health effect, or both.
- due to the limitations of data availability, almost all healthcare decision analyses use inputs from multiple studies (e.g., results from one study evaluating the efficacy of an intervention and estimates of the costs of treating the disease from another study, etc.).[22]

Elements of a Tree (Fig. 18.4)

- There is one decision node at the root.
- The branches of the initial decision tree represent all the strategies that are to be compared.
- There is a series of chance nodes off every strategy branch.
- The outcomes are depicted at the end of each pathway.

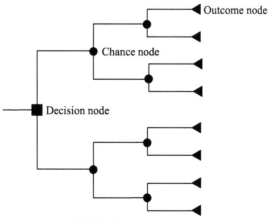

FIGURE 18.4 Decision tree.

Markov Model

Markov models represent disease processes that evolve over time and are suited to model progression of chronic disease; this type of model can handle disease recurrence and estimate long-term costs and life years gained/QALYs.

A Markov model is structured around health states and movements between them. Hence, the natural history of the condition becomes very important in designing the model. Within a model, health is split into distinct categories (or health states) that must be mutually exclusive and cover all the people in the model (i.e., all people must fit into a health state at any given point in time). An individual can only be in one state at a time and will remain in that state for a specified or fixed period of time, i.e., a cycle. At the end of each cycle, the individual/patient can either stay in the same health state (i.e., cycle) or move to another health state.

Let us look at an example. Imagine a simple model in which we have three health states: well, disease, and dead. This model can be shown in the form of a picture using an influence diagram to show the health states and movements between them (Fig. 18.5). If we look into the figure, we notice that three health states are mutually exclusive, i.e., patients can only be well, have the disease, or be dead within the model. Individuals in the model move at the end of each period or cycle along an arrow. For example, if people are in a well healthy state, then they can move to the disease state or the dead state or can be dead within the model. Similarly, people can move from the disease state to the well state or to the dead state or remain in the disease state. Once people are in the dead state, they cannot move from that state to any other state. However, while thinking about the patient journey, one needs to think about how long will people stay in each state, how often will people stay in each state, and the associated costs and outcomes for each state. One way to decide how long each period or cycle is is to consider the "cycle length," i.e., the minimum time people spend in a state (all members of the cohort will spend at least one cycle in the state they begin with). The cycle length is influenced by different factors and is often informed by the smallest clinically meaningful item included as a distinct event. Usually, the cycle should be short enough to consider the changes of clinical effects and resource use in patients between the cycles.

The elements of Markov models are:

- Mutually exclusive and exhaustive.
- The specific cycle length refers to a fixed period of time.
- Transition probabilities depict the transition from one state to another at the end of a single cycle.
- Markov states represent the cost and utility of spending one cycle in that state.

Steps in conducting a Markov model are:

1. Define states and allowable transitions
2. Choose a cycle length
3. Specify a set of transition probabilities between states
4. Assign a cost and utility to each health state
5. Identify the initial distribution of the population
6. Methods of evaluation

The merits and demerits of a decision tree and Markov model are listed in Table 18.4.

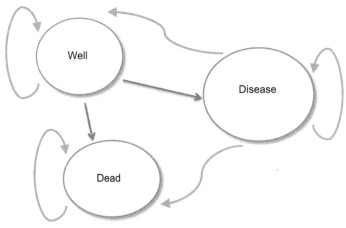

FIGURE 18.5 Markov model.

TABLE 18.4 Merits and Demerits of Pharmacoeconomic Modeling

Merits	Demerits
Decision Tree	
• Used for "one-off" decisions. • Suited for acute care, once-only diseases, short-term diagnostic/screening decisions.	• Less suitable for longer-term outcomes, though possible to add branches, but these are not efficient. • Difficult to handle disease recurrence. • Need to be able to assess full implications of each possibility of the patient pathway.
Markov Modeling	
• Can represent disease processes that evolve over time. • Suited to model the progression of chronic disease. • Can handle disease recurrence. • Estimates long-term costs and life years gained/QALYs.	• No account is taken of history. • Assumes uniform populations are an equal and constant risk. • May overcome these limitations by using a larger number of states. • Alternatively use other methods (individual sampling models, discrete event simulation.)

CONCLUSION

Pharmacoeconomic analyses are useful in assessing the value of pharmaceutical interventions and their affordability. The choice of the method and perspective depends on the purpose of the study. A comparison of merit and demerits helps in differentiating between pharmacoeconomic analyses. Pharmacoeconomic analyses include COI, BIA, cost-comparison analysis, CMA, CEA, CUA, CCA, and CBA. Modeling supports the generation of pharmacoeconomic data.

PRACTICE QUESTIONS

1. Which of the following is also called the burden of disease?
   A. Cost-of-illness
   B. Budget-impact analysis
   C. Cost-minimization analysis
   D. Cost-effectiveness analysis
2. Which of the following analyse find the value of a health intervention?
   A. Cost-of-illness
   B. Budget-impact analysis
   C. Burden of disease
   D. Cost-effectiveness analysis
3. In which of the following are health outcomes measured in monetary units?
   A. Cost-consequence analysis
   B. Cost-effectiveness analysis
   C. Cost-utility analysis
   D. Cost-benefit analysis
4. The top-down or bottom-up method is used to?
   A. Compare costs and outcomes
   B. Measure the costs
   C. Validate the questionnaire
   D. Test uncertainty
5. Which of the following is more difficult to perform regarding fragmentation of data?
   A. Cost-comparison analysis
   B. Cost-consequence analysis
   C. Cost-effectiveness analysis
   D. Cost-utility analysis

6. Which of the following methods involves more ethical issues when valuing health outcomes?
   A. Cost-consequence analysis
   B. Cost-effectiveness analysis
   C. Cost-utility analysis
   D. Cost-benefit analysis
7. Which of the following assess the affordability of healthcare interventions?
   A. Budget-impact analysis
   B. Cost-effectiveness analysis
   C. Cost-benefit analysis
   D. Cost-utility analysis
8. Which of the following is a measure of utility?
   A. Human capital
   B. Friction cost
   C. Standard gamble
   D. Top-down
9. The difference between a Markov model and a decision tree is?
   A. Health states change over time
   B. Relations between intervention and outcomes are shown
   C. Used in acute conditions only
   D. Does not assume uniform population as equals
10. The basic purpose of pharmacoeconomic modeling is to?
    A. Fulfill mandatory requirements by the regulators
    B. Replace the data from research
    C. Fill the gaps in data from research
    D. Create error-free data

REFERENCES

1. National Information Center on Health Services Research and Healthcare Technology (NICHSR). HTA 101: V. Economic analysis methods. NIH.
2. Drummond M. Pharmacoeconomics: friend or foe? *Ann Rheum Dis.* 2006;65(Suppl. 3):iii44−iii47. https://doi.org/10.1136/ard.2006.058602.
3. National Information Center on Health Services Research and Healthcare Technology (NICHSR). Health Economics Information Resources: A Self-Study Course: Module 3. NIH.
4. DACEHTA. *Introduction to Mini-HTA − a Management and Decision Support Tool for the Hospital Service*; 2005. https://www.sst.dk/en/publications/2005/∼/media/47C62A769EBC4E80A153F986C5348F55.ashx.
5. Rabarison KM, Bish CL, Massoudi MS, Giles WH. Economic evaluation enhances public health decision making. *Front Public Health.* 2015:3. https://doi.org/10.3389/fpubh.2015.00164.
6. Berger M, Bingefors K, Hedblom E, Pashos C, Torrance G. *Healthcare Quality, Costs, and Outcomes: ISPOR Book of Terms.* 1st ed. Lawrenceville, NJ: ISPOR; 2003.
7. Greenberg D, Ibrahim MIBM, Boncz I. What are the challenges in conducting cost-of-illness studies? *Value Health Reg Issues.* 2014;4:115−116. https://doi.org/10.1016/j.vhri.2014.08.003.
8. Costa N, Derumeaux H, Rapp T, et al. Methodological considerations in cost of illness studies on Alzheimer disease. *Health Econ Rev.* 2012;2:18. https://doi.org/10.1186/2191-1991-2-18.
9. Akobundu E, Ju J, Blatt L, Mullins CD. Cost-of-Illness studies. *Pharmacoeconomics.* 2006;24(9):869−890. https://doi.org/10.2165/00019053-200624090-00005.
10. Sullivan SD, Mauskopf JA, Augustovski F, et al. Budget impact analysis-principles of good practice: report of the ISPOR 2012 budget impact analysis good practice II task force. *Value Health J Int Soc Pharmacoecon Outcomes Res.* 2014;17(1):5−14. https://doi.org/10.1016/j.jval.2013.08.2291.
11. US Department of Veterans Affairs. Budget Impact Analysis. Health Economics Resource Center (HERC). https://www.herc.research.va.gov/include/page.asp?id=budget-impact-analysis.
12. Bertram MY, Lauer JA, De Joncheere K, et al. Cost−effectiveness thresholds: pros and cons. *Bull World Health Organ.* 2016;94(12):925−930. https://doi.org/10.2471/BLT.15.164418.
13. Brosa M, Gisbert R, Rodríguez JM, Soto J. Principios, métodos y aplicaciones del análisis del impacto presupuestario en el sector sanitario. *Pharmacoecon Span Res Artic.* 2005;2(2):65−78. https://doi.org/10.1007/BF03320900.
14. McBrien KA, Manns B. Approach to economic evaluation in primary care. *Can Fam Phys.* 2013;59(6):619−627.
15. Wright D. *Return on Investment. York Health Economics Consortium*; 2016. http://www.yhec.co.uk/glossary/return-on-investment/.

16. US Department of Veterans Affairs. Cost-Effectiveness Analysis. Health Economics Resource Center (HERC). https://www.herc.research.va.gov/include/page.asp?id=cost-effectiveness-analysis.

17. Neumann PJ, Cohen JT, Weinstein MC. Updating cost-effectiveness — the curious resilience of the $50,000-per-QALY threshold. *N Engl J Med*. 2014;371(9):796–797. https://doi.org/10.1056/NEJMp1405158.

18. Grutters JPC, Kessels AGH, Dirksen CD, van Helvoort-Postulart D, Anteunis LJC, Joore MA. Willingness to accept versus willingness to pay in a discrete choice experiment. *Value Health*. 2008;11(7):1110–1119. https://doi.org/10.1111/J.1524-4733.2008.00340.X.

19. Hiligsmann M, Kanis JA, Compston J, et al. Health technology assessment in osteoporosis. *Calcif Tissue Int*. 2013;93(1):1–14. https://doi.org/10.1007/s00223-013-9724-8.

20. Nimdet K, Chaiyakunapruk N, Vichansavakul K, Ngorsuraches S. A systematic review of studies eliciting willingness-to-pay per quality-adjusted life year: does it justify CE threshold? *PLoS One*. 2015;10(4):e0122760. https://doi.org/10.1371/journal.pone.0122760.

21. Ademi Z, Kim H, Zomer E, Reid CM, Hollingsworth B, Liew D. Overview of pharmacoeconomic modelling methods. *Br J Clin Pharmacol*. 2013;75(4):944–950. https://doi.org/10.1111/j.1365-2125.2012.04421.x.

22. US Department of Veterans Affairs. Decision Analysis. Health Economics Resource Center (HERC). https://www.herc.research.va.gov/include/page.asp?id=decision-analysis.

23. Karnon J, Stahl J, Brennan A, Caro JJ, Mar J, Möller J. Modeling using discrete event simulation: a report of the ISPOR-SMDM modeling good research practices task force-4. *Value Health*. 2012;15(6):821–827. https://doi.org/10.1016/j.jval.2012.04.013.

24. Siebert U, Alagoz O, Bayoumi AM, et al. State-transition modeling: a report of the ISPOR-SMDM modeling good research practices task force-3. *Value Health J Int Soc Pharmacoecon Outcomes Res*. 2012;15(6):812–820. https://doi.org/10.1016/j.jval.2012.06.014.

ANSWERS TO PRACTICE QUESTIONS

1. A
2. D
3. D
4. B
5. B
6. D
7. A
8. C
9. A
10. C

Chapter 19

Interpreting Pharmacoeconomic Findings

Piyameth Dilokthornsakul[1], Dixon Thomas[2], Lawrence Brown[3] and Nathorn Chaiyakunapruk[4]

[1]*Naresuan University, Phitsanulok, Thailand;* [2]*Gulf Medical University, Ajman, United Arab Emirates;* [3]*Chapman University School of Pharmacy, Irvine, CA, United States;* [4]*Monash University Malaysia, Selangor, Malaysia*

Learning Objectives:

Objective 19.1   Describe the influence of pharmacoeconomics in healthcare.
Objective 19.2   Explain how to interpret pharmacoeconomic analysis findings.

OBJECTIVE 19.1. DESCRIBE THE INFLUENCE OF PHARMACOECONOMICS IN HEALTHCARE

Pharmacoeconomics is the scientific discipline that identifies, measures, and compares the value and affordability of pharmaceutical products in the health system and society. *Pharmacoeconomics is commonly defined as the scientific discipline that evaluates the value of pharmaceutical products, services, or programs under individual, firms, government, or societal point of view.*[1] It is a part of health economics and more broadly a part of health technology assessment. It estimates incremental value of pharmaceutical interventions. The term "value" in general refers to the outputs achieved relative to the costs incurred when new is compared with old intervention(s). In healthcare, *value can be defined as the patient health outcomes achieved per money spent.*[2] This is one of the goals of pharmacoeconomics that addresses whether an additional gain from a medical intervention is worth paying extra cost based on three aspects of health outcomes: economic, clinical, and humanistic outcomes (known as the ECHO model).

Selection of drugs, whether included in a national or hospital formulary or consumed by a patient, is not an easy task. Cost and consequences should be considered when evaluating the value of new healthcare interventions compared to old ones. New healthcare interventions, including medical products or pharmacy-related services, are not always safer, effective, and affordable. Commonly, new medical interventions may be safer and/or more effective, but more expensive than existing alternatives. Some interventions can be very expensive causing financial burden to consumers and even the whole healthcare system. Therefore, resources should be wisely spent for sustainability.

Important questions are "Is the drug worth paying for?" and "Is the drug affordable within limited budgets?" To answer these questions, decision-makers need to assess the clinical benefits and costs of newer and existing drugs. It is obvious that clinical benefits and costs of drugs should be assessed in an organized way rather than using an informal assessment, such as "educated guess" or "what we did last time." Pharmacoeconomics provides systematic approaches to assess the clinical benefit and cost of drugs in a comparative manner.[3]

For example, an imaginary expensive lipid-lowering drug (Lipid-remove) was approved in a country. Data from clinical trials show its higher efficacy in lowering low-density lipoprotein cholesterol (LDL-c) than existing lipid-lowering drugs. However, the drug had a higher risk of myopathy and higher cost. The costs and outcomes of Lipid-remove and related hypothetical agents are given in Table 19.1.

Based on the information provided, an important question for health insurance programs is whether Lipid-remove should be included in their benefits packages? Some health insurance companies might decide to add Lipid-remove to their benefits packages but some might not. Without pharmacoeconomic evaluations, the decision might be based on only efficacy data (LDL-c reduction), only safety profile (risk of myopathy), or only cost based on their experience. Those strategies might not be appropriate for decision making because all important information is not appropriately considered collectively.

Clinical Pharmacy Education, Practice and Research. https://doi.org/10.1016/B978-0-12-814276-9.00019-2

Pharmacoeconomics could help decision-makers to systematically consider the efficacy/effectiveness data (LDL-c reduction), safety profile (risk of myopathy), and cost. It could summarize those data into a single measure to inform decision-makers. This will help decision-makers follow a transparent and appropriate decision-making process.

Professional societies, governments, and universities are promoting best use of pharmacoeconomics. Good practice guidelines are available on different topics in pharmacoeconomics. Country-specific pharmacoeconomic guidelines are also available on the International Society for Pharmacoeconomics and Outcomes Research (ISPOR) website (www.ispor.org).[3]

Pharmacoeconomic analyses might be required when more than one healthcare intervention is available that varies in costs and/or outcomes. It is also required if only one expensive intervention is available, as its financial burden (cost of illness) and the budget impact need to be studied.

In addition to the comparative clinical benefits, pharmacoeconomic analyses provide more information that helps in the decision-making process. An analysis might not be needed for an intervention that is safer, more effective, and cheaper than its alternatives. However, when an intervention is not only more effective but also more costly to the comparator, making a decision needs more information about its value and affordability.

TABLE 19.1 A Hypothetical Example of Cost and Consequences

Medication	Status	LDL-c Reduction (%)	Risk of Myopathy (%)	Cost in USD (per year)
Lipid-remove	Newcomer	50	0.5	100,000
Lower-lipid-A	Existing one	40	0.2	80,000
Lipid-reduced-B	Existing one	45	0.1	60,000

LDL-c, low-density lipoprotein cholesterol; USD, US dollar.

According to the hypothetical example shown in Table 19.1, if a health insurance company would like to select either Lower-lipid-A or Lipid-reduced-B for their benefit package, the company does not need to perform pharmacoeconomic analysis because evidence shows that Lipid-reduced-B had a higher efficacy than Lower-lipid-A (45% vs. 40%), lower risk of myopathy (0.1% vs. 0.2%), and lower cost ($60,000 vs. $80,000). It is obvious that Lipid-reduced-B is more cost-effective than Lower-lipid-A.

In general, pharmacoeconomic analysis is needed when a medication of interest, usually a new medication, not only has a higher benefit than a comparator(s) but also has a higher cost or worse safety profile.

Application of pharmacoeconomics ranges from a specific cost-effectiveness of a group of drugs in clinical practice (microeconomics) to a wider cost-effectiveness of a group of public health programs (macroeconomics).[4] As an example, it can range from micro- to macroeconomics as follows:

- cost-minimization in a group of patients;
- cost-effectiveness and budget impact for a health insurer; and
- pricing of pharmaceuticals or resource allocation in a national drug budget.[5]

However, the most common application of pharmacoeconomics is in health insurance reimbursement decisions.

Many countries use pharmacoeconomics as an analytic tool in health technology assessment for new interventions. Australia was the first country to publish a guideline to perform pharmacoeconomic analysis in 1992, and they require pharmaceutical companies to submit pharmacoeconomic data for pharmaceuticals that the companies would like added to the national Pharmaceutical Benefits Scheme (PBS).[6,7] The Pharmaceutical Benefits Advisory Committee (PBAC) in Australia recommends new medications for listing on the PBS. PBAC uses information on comparative clinical effectiveness, safety, and pharmacoeconomics of new medications to be considered for recommendations.[8]

Soon after the publication of the Australian pharmacoeconomic guideline, Canada initiated a health technology assessment agency called "the Canadian Agency for Drugs and Technologies in Health (CADTH)."[7] CADTH has a program called "CADTH common drug review (CDR)," which aims to deliver evidence and reimbursement recommendations to Canada's federal, provincial, and territorial public drug plans to guide their drug funding decisions.[9]

Another well-known health technology appraisal agency that uses pharmacoeconomics as important information for making reimbursement recommendations is the National Institute for Health and Care Excellence (NICE) of the United Kingdom.[10] It was initiated in 1999 with the aim to provide national guidance and advice to improve health and social care. NICE has several centers to develop guidance for improving health and social care, including the Centre for Health

Technology Evaluation, which is responsible for making recommendations for reimbursement using clinical and economic evidence appraisal.

In the United States, there are many health technology assessment agencies that include pharmacoeconomics as one of their works. However, the government agency that is responsible for conducting health technology assessment is "Agency for Healthcare Research and Quality (AHRQ)."[11] AHRQ's mission is to produce evidence to make healthcare safer, higher quality, more accessible, equitable, and affordable. It provides technology assessments for the Centers for Medicare and Medicaid Services to inform its national coverage decision for the Medicare program.

Many other countries have health technology assessment agencies: Sweden, the Netherlands, New Zealand, Belgium, France, Germany, Italy, Spain, Taiwan, Thailand, South Korea, etc.[12–16]

OBJECTIVE 19.2. EXPLAIN HOW TO INTERPRET PHARMACOECONOMIC ANALYSIS FINDINGS

Pharmacoeconomic analyses typically measure both costs and consequences of treatments. There are related studies that measure only costs or only consequences. From Table 19.2, it is clear that full pharmacoeconomic evaluations compare both cost and consequences of at least two interventions.[17]

- Three types of descriptive studies describe certain features of an intervention, but do not compare it with another intervention. An *outcome description study* examines only health outcomes (i.e., blood pressure, hemoglobin A1C, fasting blood sugar, the number of clinical events, quality of life, etc.), and it does not compare an intervention to others. A *cost description study* (e.g., cost of illness describing the costs of an illness) examines only cost with no comparison of an intervention to others. A *cost outcome description study* examines both cost and health outcomes with no comparison of an intervention to others.
- A study that compares only health outcomes of an intervention to other intervention(s) is called an *efficacy or effectiveness study.*
- A study that compares only costs of an intervention to other intervention(s) is called a *cost analysis study.* An example is a budget impact analysis.
- A study that compares both cost and consequences of an intervention to other intervention(s) is classified as *full economic evaluation.* Examples are cost-effectiveness analysis (CEA), cost-benefit analysis (CBA), cost-utility analysis (CUA), cost-minimization analysis (CMA), etc.

For example, a study was conducted to determine hospitalization cost for elective percutaneous coronary intervention in five public cardiac centers using a cross-sectional study.[18] The authors reported that the average hospitalization cost of elective percutaneous coronary intervention ranged from $3186 to $4018. This study can be classified as a *cost description study* because the study examined only hospitalization cost for elective percutaneous coronary intervention with no comparison to other interventions and no examination of health outcomes.

Another study was conducted to determine cost, life years, and quality-adjusted life years (QALYs) of percutaneous coronary intervention with drug-eluting stents compared to bypass surgery for patients with three vessels or left main coronary artery disease.[19] The authors reported that cumulative life years for patients receiving percutaneous coronary intervention and bypass surgery were 4.601 and 4.701 for 5 years of observation, respectively, whereas the cumulative costs of those interventions were $47,641 and $53,260, respectively. This study can be classified as a *full economic evaluation* because it compared both costs and health outcomes for at least two interventions.

TABLE 19.2 Types of Studies Based on the Examination of Costs and Consequences

Categories		Costs and Consequences Examined		
		Health Outcomes Only	**Cost Only**	**Both Health Outcomes and Cost**
Comparison (at least 2 interventions)	No	Outcome description	Cost description	Cost outcome description
	Yes	Efficacy/effectiveness evaluation	Cost analysis	Full economic evaluation

Adapted from Drummond MF, Sculpher MJ, Claxton K, Stoddart GL, Torrance GW. *Methods for the Economic Evaluation of Healthcare Programmes.* 4th ed. Oxford, United Kingdom: Oxford University Press; 2015.

There are at least four types of pharmacoeconomic analyses[17,20]:

- CEA
- CUA
- CMA
- CBA

TABLE 19.3 Types of Pharmacoeconomic Analysis

Type of Pharmacoeconomic Analysis	Cost	Outcomes
Cost-minimization analysis	Monetary value	—
Cost-effectiveness analysis	Monetary value	Health outcomes in a natural unit (i.e., hemoglobin A1C, low-density lipoprotein cholesterol)
Cost-utility analysis	Monetary value	Outcome in a common unit (i.e., quality-adjusted life year)
Cost-benefit analysis	Monetary value	Monetary value

The main difference among these analyses is the unit of health outcomes measured and its implications. Many professionals consider that CUA and CMA are different types of CEA. The CMA assumes that the outcomes are identical for an intervention or its comparator, so if there is a difference in cost, the cheapest intervention could be adopted. CEA is the prototype pharmacoeconomic evaluation that measures the outcomes in natural units, e.g., hemoglobin A1C levels for hypoglycemic agents, LDL-c levels for lipid-lowering agents, life years saved for any intervention affecting mortality rate, etc. The CUA measures health outcomes in a universal unit like the QALY or disability-adjusted life years. Even though technically QALY is used in CUA, some professionals use it as an outcome measure but call the study CEA. The CBA is quite different in the sense that the health outcomes are converted into a currency unit, which is clearly an unnatural unit and sometimes unethical (Table 19.3).

For example, a study was conducted to evaluate long-term cost-effectiveness of insulin detemir compared with insulin glargine in patients with type II diabetes.[21] The authors reported that insulin detemir yielded greater QALYs with higher lifetime cost than insulin glargine. They also reported that health agencies might need to pay 1.7 million US dollars for one additional QALY gained. The study is considered as CUA (some professionals might call it CEA, which is acceptable in common practice) because it measures QALY as the outcome of interest, which is the outcome in a common unit. In fact, when the outcomes are measured in QALY in real practice, the study could be called CUA or CEA. Differentiating CUA with CEA using QALY is only technical and is not observed in real practice.

Because pharmacoeconomic analyses estimate both cost and health outcome and compare such cost and outcome of one intervention with others, there is a specific way to report their findings. In general, pharmacoeconomic analysts report their findings in one common measure "Incremental cost-effectiveness ratio (ICER)."[17,20,22] ICER is calculated by the difference in cost between an intervention of interest and a comparator divided by the difference in health outcomes between the intervention of interest and the comparator (Eq. 19.1). CEA and CUA use the same formula for ICER. When QALY is used as the outcome measure, it could be called CUA or CEA. When natural units such as A1C or LDL-c are used as an outcome measure, it is called CEA.

$$ICER = \frac{\text{Total cost}_{\text{intervention}} - \text{Total cost}_{\text{comparator}}}{\text{Outcomes}_{\text{intervention}} - \text{Outcomes}_{\text{comparator}}} \qquad (19.1)$$

Suppose a medication called "SugarLower" comes on the market as a new glucose-lowering agent, whereas another medication called "GlucoseReduction" is the most effective glucose-lowering agent currently available in the market for patients with type II diabetes mellitus. Estimated total lifetime cost and QALYs for both medications are shown in Table 19.4.

TABLE 19.4 A Hypothetical Example of the Incremental Cost-Effectiveness Ratio

Medication	Status	QALYs	Total Cost per Lifetime (USD)
SugarLower	Newcomer	40	15,000,000
GlucoseReduction	Existing one	38	14,500,000

QALYs, quality-adjusted life years; *USD*, US dollar.

An example of CUA analyzing the value of SugarLower compared with GlucoseReduction. An ICER of the analysis is calculated as shown below:

$$ICER = \frac{15,000,000 - 14,500,000}{40 - 38} = 250,000 \text{ USD/QALY}$$

It could be interpreted that health agencies need to spend an additional 250,000 US dollars for SugarLower to gain one additional QALY compared with GlucoseReduction for patients with type II diabetes mellitus.

An ICER can provide valuable information on how much health agencies need to spend for additional health benefit, but it cannot determine whether the new intervention is worth purchasing. Worthiness is dependent on each context. For example, if a health insurance company (company A) has a willingness-to-pay threshold of 100,000 US dollars for an additional QALY, they might decide not to add SugarLower to their benefits package. On the other hand, another health insurance company (company B) would like to cover SugarLower for their health beneficiaries as the company has a higher willingness-to-pay threshold of 300,000 US dollars per one additional QALY gained. Thus, company B might add SugarLower to their benefits package, while company A would likely not.

An important issue for ICER is that a new intervention does not always come with higher total costs and better health outcomes. Some new interventions come with a lower total cost and a better health outcome and some come with a higher total cost but a worse health outcome. Thus, the ICER should be interpreted correctly in such situations. Therefore, a graphical presentation of ICER findings, which is known as a "cost-effectiveness analysis plane (CEA plane)" could help in the easy interpretation of the results (Fig. 19.1).

A CEA plane provides the relationship between comparative cost and health outcome. The X-axis indicates incremental health outcome (also called incremental effectiveness), whereas the Y-axis indicates incremental cost. The CEA plane is divided into four quadrants. Quadrant 1 has better health outcomes and a higher total cost of a new intervention compared to a comparator. An ICER is needed to be calculated in this quadrant to determine how much health agencies need to spend for additional health outcome gained. The ICER threshold or willingness-to-pay threshold by the health insurance company needs to be compared to the calculated ICER. Most CEAs fall into quadrant 1.

Quadrant 2 stands for worse health outcomes and higher total cost of a new intervention. The intervention that falls in quadrant 2 should not be considered for coverage because it loses some health outcome and increases the total cost of the treatment. The intervention in quadrant 2 is called "dominated intervention" and therefore is a clear reject.

Quadrant 3 stands for worse health outcomes but a lower total cost of a new intervention. The intervention that falls in quadrant 3 is debatable. Some healthcare providers would not consider the intervention in this quadrant because it provides worse health outcomes. Thus, cost should not be a factor to be considered. On the other hand, some healthcare providers consider the intervention in this quadrant because it is the bargain between worse health outcomes and a lower total cost. Other factors should be considered for the intervention in this quadrant.

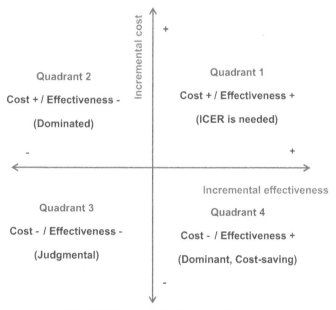

FIGURE 19.1   Cost-effectiveness analysis plane.

TABLE 19.5 ICER of Saxagliptin and a Sulfonylurea in a Study From Thailand

Medication	QALYs	Total Cost (US Dollars)	ICER (US Dollars/QALY)
Saxagliptin	7.552	17,316	76,140
Sulfonylurea	7.528	15,474	

ICER, incremental cost-effectiveness ratio; *QALYs*, quality-adjusted life years; *US*, the United States.

Quadrant 4 stands for better health outcomes and a lower total cost of a new intervention. The intervention that falls in quadrant 4 should be considered for health coverage because it gains some health outcome and decreases the total cost of treatment. The intervention in quadrant 4 is called "dominant intervention" and therefore is a clear acceptance.

According to the hypothetical example in Table 19.4, SugarLower has better QALYs (40 vs. 38 QALYs) and higher cost (15,000,000 vs. 14,500,000 US dollars). SugarLower falls into quadrant 1. Thus, an ICER is needed to determine the value of SugarLower compared with GlucoseReduction.

For instance, a CUA was conducted to determine the value of dipeptidyl peptidase-4 inhibitor monotherapy compared with sulfonylurea monotherapy for type 2 diabetic patients with chronic kidney disease in a study from Thailand.[23] The findings are presented in Table 19.5.

The study indicated that the lifetime cost of saxagliptin was $17,316 with 7.552 QALYs, whereas the cost of sulfonylurea was $15,474 with 7.528 QALYs. Saxagliptin is in quadrant 1 (higher cost with better health benefits). Therefore, an ICER was needed to determine the value of saxagliptin compared with sulfonylurea. The difference in cost was calculated as $17,316 − $15,474 = $1842, and the difference in health benefit was calculated as 7.552 − 7.528 = 0.024 QALY. The ICER was $76,140 per QALY. The willingness-to-pay threshold in the country (Thailand) was 4435 US dollars per QALY gained. The CEA finding showed that saxagliptin was not a cost-effective option because the ICER was higher than the willingness-to-pay.

Another example is a CUA of intravenous immunoglobulin for the treatment of steroid-refractory dermatomyositis in a study from Thailand.[24] It compared the cost and QALYs of intravenous immunoglobulin plus corticosteroid and immunosuppressant plus corticosteroid. The findings are presented in Table 19.6.

The findings indicated that intravenous immunoglobulin plus corticosteroids had better health outcome. Incremental QALY was 1.964. The intervention also had a lower total cost. The incremental cost was $4738. Thus, intravenous immunoglobulin plus corticosteroids fell in quadrant 4 (better health outcomes and lower cost). Thus, there was no need to calculate an ICER. The findings showed that intravenous immunoglobulin plus corticosteroids was the dominant intervention compared with immunosuppressant plus corticosteroid in patients with steroid-refractory dermatomyositis in Thailand.

Pharmacoeconomic Reporting Guidelines

Reporting of pharmacoeconomic evaluation is very important, but often poorly done and this limits the use of pharmacoeconomics by decision-makers. Different guidelines are available for conducting and reporting economic evaluations. One of these is a Consolidated Health Economic Evaluation Reporting Standards (CHEERS) statement, which provides recommendations in a checklist (Table 19.7) to optimize reporting of economic evaluations. As per the CHEERS

TABLE 19.6 ICER for Two Treatment Options in Steroid-Refractory Dermatomyositis in a Study From Thailand

Medication	QALYs	Total Cost (US Dollars)	Incremental QALY	Incremental Cost
Intravenous immunoglobulin plus corticosteroids	6.297	45,385	1.964	−4738
Immunosuppressant plus corticosteroids	4.33	50,124		

ICER, incremental cost-effectiveness ratio; *QALYs*, quality-adjusted life years; *US*, the United States.

TABLE 19.7 Items Present in a Typical Pharmacoeconomic Analysis as per CHEERS Statement 2013[25]

Section	Item No.	Recommendation to Authors of Pharmacoeconomic Studies
Title and Abstract		
Title	1	Identify the study as an economic evaluation or use more specific terms such as "cost-effectiveness analysis," and describe the interventions compared.
Abstract	2	Provide a structured summary of objectives, perspective, setting, methods (including study design and inputs), results (including base case and uncertainty analyses), and conclusions.
Introduction		
Background and objectives	3	Provide an explicit statement of the broader context for the study. Present the study question and its relevance for health policy or practice decisions.
Methods		
Target population and subgroups	4	Describe characteristics of the base case population and subgroups analyzed, including why they were chosen.
Setting and location	5	State relevant aspects of the system(s) in which the decision(s) need(s) to be made.
Study perspective	6	Describe the perspective of the study and relate this to the costs being evaluated.
Comparators	7	Describe the interventions or strategies being compared and state why they were chosen.
Time horizon	8	State the time horizon(s) over which costs and consequences are being evaluated and say why they are appropriate.
Discount rate	9	Report the choice of discount rate(s) used for costs and outcomes and say why they are appropriate.
Choice of health outcomes	10	Describe what outcomes were used as the measure(s) of benefit in the evaluation and their relevance for the type of analysis performed.
Measurement of effectiveness	11a	Single study-based estimates: Describe fully the design features of the single effectiveness study and why the single study was a sufficient source of clinical effectiveness data.
	11b	Synthesis-based estimates: Describe fully the methods used for identification of included studies and synthesis of clinical effectiveness data.
Measurement and valuation of preference-based outcomes	12	If applicable, describe the population and methods used to elicit preferences for outcomes.
Estimating resources and costs	13a	Single study-based economic evaluation: Describe approaches used to estimate resource use associated with the alternative interventions. Describe primary or secondary research methods for valuing each resource item in terms of its unit cost. Describe any adjustments made to approximate to opportunity costs.
	13b	Model-based economic evaluation: Describe approaches and data sources used to estimate resource use associated with model health states. Describe primary or secondary research methods for valuing each resource item in terms of its unit cost. Describe any adjustments made to approximate to opportunity costs.
Currency, price, date, and conversion	14	Report the dates of the estimated resource quantities and unit costs. Describe methods for adjusting estimated unit costs to the year of reported costs if necessary. Describe methods for converting costs into a common currency base and the exchange rate.
Choice of model	15	Describe and give reasons for the specific type of decision-analytical model used. Providing a figure to show model structure is strongly recommended.

Continued

TABLE 19.7 Items Present in a Typical Pharmacoeconomic Analysis as per CHEERS Statement 2013[25]—cont'd

Section	Item No.	Recommendation to Authors of Pharmacoeconomic Studies
Assumptions	16	Describe all structural or other assumptions underpinning the decision-analytical model.
Analytical methods	17	Describe all analytical methods supporting the evaluation. This could include methods for dealing with skewed, missing, or censored data; extrapolation methods; methods for pooling data; approaches to validate or make adjustments (such as half cycle corrections) to a model; and methods for handling population heterogeneity and uncertainty.
Results		
Study parameters	18	Report the values, ranges, references, and, if used, probability distributions for all parameters. Report reasons or sources for distributions used to represent uncertainty where appropriate. Providing a table to show the input values are strongly recommended.
Incremental costs and outcomes	19	For each intervention, report mean values for the main categories of estimated costs and outcomes of interest, as well as mean differences between the comparator groups. If applicable, report incremental cost-effectiveness ratios.
Characterizing uncertainty	20a	*Single study-based economic evaluation*: Describe the effects of sampling uncertainty in the estimated incremental cost and incremental effectiveness parameters, together with the impact of methodological assumptions (such as discount rate, study perspective).
	20b	*Model-based economic evaluation*: Describe the effects on the results of uncertainty for all input parameters, and uncertainty related to the structure of the model and assumptions.
Characterizing heterogeneity	21	If applicable, report differences in costs, outcomes, or cost-effectiveness that can be explained by variations between subgroups of patients with different baseline characteristics or other observed variability in effects that are not reducible by more information.
Discussion		
Study findings, limitations, generalizability, and current knowledge	22	Summarize key study findings and describe how they support the conclusions reached. Discuss the limitations and the generalizability of the findings and how the findings fit with current knowledge.
Other		
Source of funding	23	Describe how the study was funded and the role of the funder in the identification, design, conduct, and reporting of the analysis. Describe other nonmonetary sources of support.
Conflicts of interest	24	Describe any potential for conflict of interest of study contributors in accordance with journal policy. In the absence of a journal policy, we recommend authors comply with International Committee of Medical Journal Editors recommendations.

statement, a typical pharmacoeconomic article shall have the following items. A small description of these items shall give a rough idea of the components present in a typical pharmacoeconomic analysis. The list of items in the statement provides an idea about different parameters found in a typical pharmacoeconomic study. The CHEERS statement focuses on the quality of reporting health economic studies, not the quality of how those studies were conducted.

For consistency, the CHEERS statement checklist format is based on the format of the CONSORT statement checklist.

The **ISPOR CHEERS Task Force Report** provides examples and further discussion of the 24-item CHEERS checklist and the CHEERS statement. It may be accessed via the *Value in Health* link or via the ISPOR Health Economic Evaluation Publication Guidelines—CHEERS: Good Reporting Practices web page.[25]

As the format of reporting guidelines like CHEERS covers key concepts in pharmacoeconomic studies, it familiarizes the reader to such literature.

CONCLUSION

Pharmacoeconomics is the scientific discipline that evaluates the value of drug or pharmacy services. Pharmacoeconomic analyses provide a measure called ICER that is commonly used to assist healthcare decision making. The correct and appropriate interpretations of pharmacoeconomic analysis findings are crucial for any level of healthcare decision making. Pharmacoeconomic reporting guidelines such as CHEERS direct the reports to be in a common format for easy reading of the pharmacoeconomic literature.

PRACTICE QUESTIONS

1. What is pharmacoeconomics?
   A. It is a scientific discipline aiming to evaluate the value of pharmaceutical products.
   B. It is a scientific discipline aiming to estimate the cost of pharmaceutical products.
   C. It is a scientific discipline aiming to assess clinical outcomes of pharmaceutical products.
   D. It is a scientific discipline aiming to assess humanistic outcomes of pharmaceutical products.
2. Which of the following is a feature of pharmacoeconomics?
   A. It provides a systematic approach to assess benefits and costs of pharmaceutical products.
   B. It provides a summative measure that could inform healthcare decision-makers.
   C. It is a tool that evaluates several factors such as efficacy, safety, adherence, and cost simultaneously.
   D. All of the above
3. After a new medication is launched with higher cost, in which of the following situations would you consider pharmacoeconomic evaluations most necessary?
   A. Lower efficacy compared to existing medications.
   B. Higher efficacy compared to existing medications.
   C. Same efficacy compared to existing medications.
   D. None of the above.
4. A study was conducted to determine hospitalization cost of liver transplantation in patients with hepatocellular carcinoma. What type of study is this?
   A. Cost description study
   B. Outcome description study
   C. Cost outcome description study
   D. Economic evaluation study
5. Which of the following is the best description of a full pharmacoeconomic analysis?
   A. It estimates the cost and outcomes of a pharmaceutical intervention.
   B. It compares the outcomes of pharmaceutical interventions.
   C. It compares the cost of pharmaceutical interventions.
   D. It compares the cost and outcomes of pharmaceutical interventions.

Use This Example for Questions 6–9

An insurance company is considering adding insulin glargine to its benefits package. The willingness-to-pay of this company is $4000 per QALY gained. The company decided to conduct a study to determine the cost and effectiveness of insulin glargine and neutral protamine Hagedorn insulin for patients with type 2 diabetes. The findings are presented in the following table:

Medication	QALYs	Total Cost (US Dollars)
Insulin glargine	8.838	24,000
NPH insulin	8.350	22,000

NPH, neutral protamine Hagedorn insulin; *QALYs*, quality-adjusted life years; *US*, the United States.

6. What is this type of pharmacoeconomic analysis?

   A. CMA

   B. CEA

   C. Cost of illness

   D. CBA

7. Which of the following is the ICER of this analysis?

   A. $2000

   B. $−2000

   C. $4098

   D. $−4098

8. Based on a CEA plane, which quadrant did insulin glargine fall into?

   A. Quadrant 1

   B. Quadrant 2

   C. Quadrant 3

   D. Quadrant 4

9. What is the interpretation of this study finding?

   A. Insulin glargine is a cost-effective medication for type 2 diabetes compared with NPH.

   B. Insulin glargine is not a cost-effective medication for type 2 diabetes compared with NPH.

   C. Insulin glargine is the dominant intervention for type 2 diabetes compared with NPH.

   D. Insulin glargine is the dominated intervention for type 2 diabetes compared with NPH.

REFERENCES

1. Berger MK, Bingerfirsm K, Hedblom EC, Pashos CL, Torrance GW, Smith MD. *Health Care Cost, Quality, and Outcomes. ISPOR Book of Terms.* Lawrenceville, NJ, USA: International Society for Pharmacoeconomics and Outcomes Research; 2003.

2. Porter ME. What is value in healthcare? *N Engl J Med.* 2010;363(26):2477−2481.

3. International Society for Pharmacoeconomics and Outcomes Research. *Pharmacoeconomic Guidelines Around the World*; 2017. https://www.ispor.org/PEguidelines/index.asp.

4. Trask LS. Pharmacoeconomics: principles, methods, and applications. In: DiPiro JT, Talbert RL, Yee GC, Matzke GR, Wells BG, Posey LM, eds. *Pharmacotherapy: A Pathophysiologic Approach.* 8th ed. China: McGraw-Hill Education; 2011.

5. Bodrogi J, Kalo Z. Principles of pharmacoeconomics and their impact on strategic imperatives of pharmaceutical research and development. *Br J Pharmacol.* 2010;159(7):1367−1373.

6. Henry D. Economic analysis as an aid to subsidization decisions: the development of Australian guidelines for pharmaceuticals. *Pharmacoeconomics.* 1992;1(1):54−67.

7. Whyte P, Hall C. Working paper 6: the role of health technology assessment in medicine pricing and reimbursement. In: *WHO/HAI Project on Medicine Prices and Availability Review Series on Pharmaceutical Pricing Policies and Interventions.* Australia: World Health Organization and Health Action Internation Project; 2013.

8. Pharmaceutical Benefits Scheme Australian Government Department of Health. *Pharmaceutical Benefits Advisory Committee (PBAC) Membership*; 2017. http://www.pbs.gov.au/info/industry/listing/participants/pbac.

9. *Canadian Agency for Drugs and Technologies in Health. About CADTH*; 2017. https://www.cadth.ca/about-cadth.

10. The National Institute for Health and Care Excellence. *The National Institute for Health and Care Excellence (NICE): About*; 2017. https://www.nice.org.uk/about.

11. Agency for Healthcare Research and Quality. *Technology Assessment Program*; 2017. https://www.ahrq.gov/research/findings/ta/index.html.

12. Levy AR, Mitton C, Johnston KM, Harrigan B, Briggs AH. International comparison of comparative effectiveness research in five jurisdictions: insights for the US. *Pharmacoeconomics.* 2010;28(10):813−830.

13. Gray AM, Wilkinson T. Economic evaluation of healthcare interventions: old and new directions. *Oxf Rev Econ Pol.* 2016;32(1):102−121.

14. Garattini L, Cornago D, De Compadri P. Pricing and reimbursement of in-patent drugs in seven European countries: a comparative analysis. *Health Policy.* 2007;82(3):330−339.

15. International Working Group for HTAA, Neumann PJ, Drummond MF, et al. Are Key Principles for improved health technology assessment supported and used by health technology assessment organizations? *Int J Technol Assess Health Care.* 2010;26(1):71−78.

16. Health Intervention and Technology Assessment Program. *The Health Intervention and Technology Assessment Program (HITAP).* 2017.

17. Drummond MF, Sculpher MJ, Claxton K, Stoddart GL, Torrance GW. *Methods for the Economic Evaluation of Health Care Programmes.* 4th ed. Oxford, United Kingdom: Oxford University Press; 2015.

18. Lee KY, Ong TK, Low EV, et al. Cost of elective percutaneous coronary intervention in Malaysia: a multicentre cross-sectional costing study. *BMJ Open.* 2017;7(5):e014307.

19. Cohen DJ, Osnabrugge RL, Magnuson EA, et al. Cost-effectiveness of percutaneous coronary intervention with drug-eluting stents versus bypass surgery for patients with 3-vessel or left main coronary artery disease: final results from the synergy between percutaneous coronary intervention with TAXUS and cardiac surgery (SYNTAX) trial. *Circulation*. 2014;130(14):1146−1157.

20. Gray AM, Clark PM, Wolstenholme JL, Wordsworth S. Applied Methods of Cost-effectiveness Analysis in Health Care. Oxford, United Kingdom: Oxford University Press.

21. Permsuwan U, Thavorn K, Dilokthornsakul P, Saokaew S, Chaiyakunapruk N. Cost-effectiveness of insulin detemir versus insulin glargine for Thai type 2 diabetes from a payer's perspective. *J Med Econ*. 2017:1−9.

22. Greenhalgh T. *How to Read a Paper: The Basics of Evidence-Based Medicine*. 4th ed. Oxford, United Kingdom: BMJ Publishing Group Limited; 2010.

23. Permsuwan U, Dilokthornsakul P, Thavorn K, Saokaew S, Chaiyakunapruk N. Cost-effectiveness of dipeptidyl peptidase-4 inhibitor monotherapy versus sulfonylurea monotherapy for people with type 2 diabetes and chronic kidney disease in Thailand. *J Med Econ*. 2017;20(2):171−181.

24. Bamrungsawad N, Chaiyakunapruk N, Upakdee N, Pratoomsoot C, Sruamsiri R, Dilokthornsakul P. Cost-utility analysis of intravenous immunoglobulin for the treatment of steroid-refractory dermatomyositis in Thailand. *Pharmacoeconomics*. 2015;33(5):521−531.

25. Husereau D, Drummond M, Petrou S, et al. Consolidated health economic evaluation reporting standards (CHEERS)−explanation and elaboration: a report of the ISPOR health economic evaluation publication guidelines good reporting practices task force. *Value Health*. 2013;16(2):231−250.

ANSWERS TO PRACTICE QUESTIONS

1. A
2. D
3. B
4. A
5. D
6. B
7. C
8. A
9. B

Chapter 20

Outcomes Research

Erin R. Weeda[1], Nicole A. Pilch[1] and Lieven Annemans[2]

[1]*Medical University of South Carolina, Charleston, SC, United States;* [2]*Ghent University, Ghent, Belgium*

Learning Objectives:

Objective 20.1   Define and classify outcomes research.
Objective 20.2   Contrast outcomes research with traditional clinical trial research.
Objective 20.3   Define and explain how to measure health-related quality of life and patient-reported outcomes.
Objective 20.4   Generalize how outcomes research is gaining importance in clinical practice.

OBJECTIVE 20.1. DEFINE AND CLASSIFY OUTCOMES RESEARCH

Patients, clinicians, payers, policy-makers, and the society at large look forward to evidence that novel medications and technologies are beneficial and efficiently implemented in real-world settings. Outcomes research (OR), which is a growing field that combines principles of epidemiology, clinical research, health economics, quality of life assessment, and health policy, is critical in obtaining this evidence.[1] Whereas clinical trials aim to generate knowledge on safety and efficacy, OR studies the benefits, risks, and costs that guide stakeholders in a real-world environment. OR has a focus on patient perspectives and considers the value (e.g., benefits achieved) for money and efforts spent. Patient-reported outcomes (PROs) and clinician-reported outcomes are components of OR.

Because the term OR applies to many research activities, it lacks a consistent definition. This chapter uses the definition proposed by the United States (US) Agency for Healthcare Research and Quality (AHRQ), which is one of the main federal agencies dedicated to improving the safety and quality of healthcare delivery in the US.[2] AHRQ defines OR as follows:

> *Outcomes research seeks to understand the end results of particular healthcare practices and interventions. End results include effects that people experience and care about, such as change in the ability to function. In particular, for individuals with chronic conditions—where cure is not always possible—end results include quality of life as well as mortality. By linking the care people get to the outcomes they experience, outcomes research has become the key to developing better ways to monitor and improve the quality of care.*

According to the AHRQ definition, OR focuses on the "end result" of a healthcare intervention.[2] This end result is measured after the intervention has been implemented in clinical practice, meaning the treatment benefit is assessed in the presence of real-world factors (e.g., patient adherence, access to the intervention, clinician prescribing patterns, etc.). In other words, OR measures effectiveness, or how well the treatment works in clinical practice, rather than the efficacy, or how well the treatment works in an ideal, controlled environment like a traditional clinical trial.[3]

OR has also been defined as *any research that attempts to measure the effectiveness, efficiency, equality, and patient-centeredness of healthcare.*[4]

Characteristics of Outcomes Research

- Focuses on the end result of a healthcare intervention.
- Measures final health outcomes rather than surrogate outcomes.
- Common research method in clinical practice.

Clinical Pharmacy Education, Practice and Research. https://doi.org/10.1016/B978-0-12-814276-9.00020-9

289

- High applicability (granted confounders are considered when interpreting the results) with limitations that are similar to other observational studies.
- Measures quality of care in comparable healthcare systems. Healthcare institutions may use OR to evaluate the quality of care that they are providing in comparison to the care provided by other institutions.
- Considers viewpoints of multiple stakeholders, including patients, policy-makers, providers, payers, and the pharmaceutical industry.
- To capture the perspectives of stakeholders such as payers and the pharmaceutical industry, OR may involve economic analyses. The interdependent relationship between OR and economics led to the development of the International Society of Pharmacoeconomics and Outcomes Research (ISPOR) in 1995. Information and guidance disseminated by ISPOR are highly regarded resources for OR.[5]
- Shares methodology with pharmacoepidemiology (which studies the use of medications at the population level).[6]
- As opposed to the controlled environment of a clinical trial, OR measures the impact of a medication when real-world factors are introduced.

Economic, Clinical, and Humanistic Outcomes

The three main outcomes measured by OR are as follows: clinical, economic, and humanistic (Fig. 20.1).[7,8] Clinical outcomes are medical events (e.g., the rate of myocardial infarction or hospitalization due to heart failure) or physiologic measures (e.g., cholesterol, blood pressure), whereas economic outcomes are disease- or treatment-related resource use and costs. Humanistic outcomes capture the impact of a treatment on patient well-being or health-related quality of life (HRQoL). The interplay between these outcomes is described by the economic, clinical, and humanistic outcomes (ECHO) model.[7,8] Medical research has traditionally relied on the measurement of clinical outcomes; therefore, the ECHO model is unique in that it allows for a more comprehensive approach to assessing the impact of an intervention.

Donabedian's Structure—Process—Outcome Model

Donabedian's structure—process—outcome (SPO) model is used in outcomes studies that are designed to measure or determine the impact of an intervention on quality of care, most commonly at a single institution or within the health system.[9] The model consists of three domains: structure, process, and outcome (Fig. 20.2).

Structure represents the characteristics of the healthcare environment. It consists of the resources that are used to provide care (i.e., the equipment, facilities, and staff). An example of a structural issue would be if a patient was unable to undergo diagnostic imaging because the institution does not have the needed imaging equipment.

Process describes the proportion of patients receiving optimal treatment. For example, it is considered standard practice for patients contacting emergency medical services (EMS) with chest pain to receive an electrocardiogram (ECG) prior to hospital arrival.[10] If only 10% of patients with chest pain transported to the hospital by EMS received an ECG, this could be a process issue.

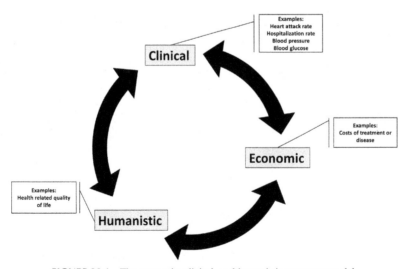

FIGURE 20.1 The economic, clinical, and humanistic outcomes model.

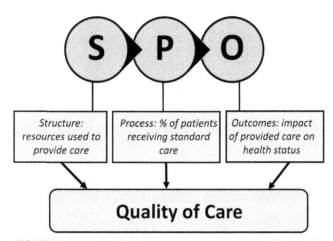

FIGURE 20.2   Donabedian's structure—process—outcome (SPO) model.

Outcomes represent the impact of care on patient health status. These can be measured using the outcomes described in the ECHO model. OR attempts to evaluate and find ways to optimize all three domains in the SPO model to increase quality of care.[9]

Examples of Outcomes Research

Using the above definitions, studies that can be classified as OR span a wide spectrum of clinical areas.[2,4,7,9] An outcomes study might evaluate the rate of hospital-acquired infections after an intervention to increase handwashing among employees at a single hospital. Studies comparing length of stay and costs associated with the use of two antibiotics using billing data from multiple hospitals can also be classified as OR. Other examples include measuring patients' HRQoL while they undergo treatment for cancer, estimating the proportion of patients that achieve their blood pressure goals after receiving education from a pharmacist or calculating 30-day readmission rates among patients that received a novel surgical procedure.

OBJECTIVE 20.2. CONTRAST OUTCOMES RESEARCH WITH TRADITIONAL CLINICAL TRIAL RESEARCH

It has been suggested that "if we want more evidence-based practice, we need more practice-based evidence.[11]" Clinical trials are essential to provide regulatory approval for new medicines. However, these trials use strict selection criteria (e.g., excluding patients with extensive comorbidities) and careful monitoring; thus it is never guaranteed that the observed benefit will hold true in the less-controlled, real-world environment of clinical practice. OR provides a means of measuring the impact of a medication (or other treatment) when real-world factors are introduced.

Overlap Between Outcomes Reasearch and Clinical Trials

As the field of OR progresses, there is increasing overlap between OR and clinical trials. Clinical trials are now incorporating measures that were traditionally components of OR into study protocols. For instance, many clinical trials measure HRQoL as a secondary endpoint.[12] Furthermore, the use of pragmatic trials is increasing, which maintain some qualities of clinical trials (e.g., randomly assigning patients to treatment groups). However, these trials also incorporate methodology used in OR to increase applicability, including the use of less stringent inclusion criteria and simplified study design.[13] An example is "A Pragmatic Trial to Evaluate the Comparative Effectiveness Between Dapagliflozin and Standard of Care in Type 2 Diabetes Patients (DECIDE Study)."[14] Much like a traditional clinical trial, the study design uses randomization to assign patients to either dapagliflozin 10 mg (a glucose-lowering medication for diabetes) or a standard of care arm. Unlike a traditional clinical trial, clinicians are free to replace dapagliflozin with other glucose-lowering drug(s) or use additional medications without restrictions. Patients and the clinicians caring for them are also aware of treatment status (i.e., who receives dapagliflozin and who receives the standard of care). In contrast, patients and clinicians are often unaware of treatment status (i.e., they are "blinded") in traditional clinical trials, as this reduces bias.

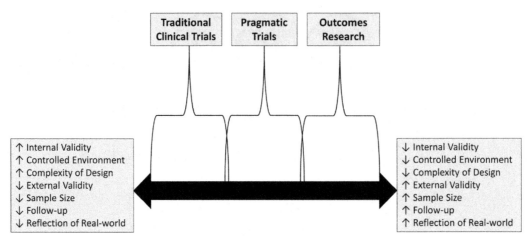

FIGURE 20.3 Relationship between traditional clinical trials, pragmatic trials, and outcomes research.

The relationship between traditional clinical trials, pragmatic trials, and OR is shown in Fig. 20.3.[13] However, for the remaining of this section, we will contrast OR with the objectives and methods traditionally used in clinical trial research.

OR is best distinguished from traditional clinical trials by the questions it attempts to answer (Table 20.1).[3] Traditional clinical trials are designed to show the efficacy of an intervention, often for regulatory purposes.[3] In contrast, OR aims to show that the intervention truly improves health or quality of care in clinical practice. In clinical trial research, endpoints are determined by the viewpoints of clinicians and investigators who try to measure prognosis. In OR, outcomes are determined by taking into account the viewpoints of multiple stakeholders (e.g., patients, providers, and payers). To increase the validity of the study design (i.e., internal validity), clinical trials randomly assign patients to an intervention or control (e.g., placebo) group. In OR, the researchers observe outcomes as patients are treated according to standard practice (i.e., clinicians in discussion with the patients decide on treatment).

TABLE 20.1 Characteristics of Traditional Clinical Trials Contrasted With Outcomes Research

Traditional Clinical Trials	Outcomes Research
Efficacy: Aims to show that the intervention is effective, often to obtain regulatory approval	**Effectiveness:** Aims to show that the intervention improves the quality of care that patients receive and can be delivered in an efficient manner, often within a health system
Outcomes determined by the viewpoints of **clinicians and investigators** who try to select the most valid measure of disease	Outcomes determined by the viewpoints of **multiple stakeholders,** including patients, policy-makers, payers, etc.
Interventional: Patients assigned to treatment groups	**Observational:** Patients treated according to usual clinical practice
Higher **internal validity**	Lower internal validity
Lower applicability	Higher **applicability**
Prospective data collection (i.e., data collection planned prior to the start of the study)	**Data** often **collected from information designed for treatment** rather than research purposes (e.g., billing data or medical charts)
Measure impact of treatment in a **controlled environment** with extensive monitoring	Measure impact of treatment with monitoring **used in routine practice**
Can **exclude patients with extensive comorbid conditions** or medications that may make it unsafe for the patient to receive the intervention	Can **include patients regardless of comorbidity status**
Can **exclude those unlikely to adhere** to therapy	Can **include patients regardless of adherence status**
Limited sample size	**Larger sample size**
Shorter follow-up	**Longer follow-up**

TABLE 20.2 Examples of Surrogate Versus Final Health Outcomes

Surrogate Outcome	Final Health Outcome
Blood glucose control	Microvascular complications of diabetes (e.g., decreased kidney function) prevented
Blood pressure control	Cerebrovascular disease (e.g., stroke) prevented
Controlled lipid profile	Coronary heart disease (e.g., myocardial infarction) prevented
Normal white blood cell count	Cured infection
Elevated CD4 count	Opportunistic infections among patients with human immunodeficiency virus prevented

In clinical trials, internal validity is also increased because investigators decide what data will be collected prior to the start of the study.[3] This allows investigators to plan patient follow-up visits, mostly with a strict follow-up scheme, as well as collect laboratory values as frequently as needed, even if these measures are not routinely collected in clinical practice. In contrast, data used in outcomes studies are often collected from information designed for treatment rather than research purposes. OR may rely on retrospective data already available within medical charts or billing records. Because of this, the researchers do not have access to all applicable outcomes or baseline characteristics.

Clinical trials are also conducted in a more controlled environment than OR.[3] The clinical trial study protocol may require more interaction between patients and physicians (for reasons such as monitoring adverse events) than what is typical in routine care. Furthermore, in an attempt to maximize safety, patients with extensive comorbidities can be excluded from studies of interventions that are not proven to be safe. Those unlikely to adhere to therapy may also be excluded. Because researchers are not intervening in OR, they may include a broader group of patients (e.g., those with extensive comorbidities or poor adherence) who more closely mirror those encountered in clinical practice. Outcomes studies may therefore produce results that can be readily achieved in a healthcare setting.

In contrast to OR, some clinical trials utilize indirect measures of final health outcomes (e.g., laboratory values) referred to as surrogate outcomes (Table 20.2).[15] Because clinical trials are costly to conduct, surrogate outcomes are appealing because they are less costly and easier to measure (e.g., they can be obtained more quickly) than final health outcomes and can often be collected within a relatively short time frame. However, changes in surrogate outcomes do not always correspond to changes in final health outcomes. As OR can measure final health outcomes in an efficient manner, it can be used to confirm that an intervention improves surrogate outcomes and also improves final health outcomes.

OR can play an important role in evaluating the safety of a drug.[3] In clinical trials, a small proportion of patients are exposed to medications for short periods due to cost restraints. This may result in an incomplete understanding of the safety profile of a medication. Perhaps the most notorious example of a medication causing harmful side effects is the thalidomide crisis in Europe, Japan, and Australia.[16] In the 1950s, thalidomide was used by pregnant women for the treatment of nausea. Later, it was discovered that thalidomide use resulted in phocomelia (a congenital disorder where the limbs of an exposed child are largely underdeveloped or absent). Before thalidomide use in pregnant women was banned, ~10,000 children were born with phocomelia. It is possible that a serious adverse effect of a medication, like that observed with thalidomide, would be noticed earlier today due to the increased use of OR.

It is important to remember that OR is best used to compliment traditional clinical trial research rather than replace it. The high internal validity of clinical trial research is often needed for the initial approval of a medication; yet the high applicability and external validity (i.e., reflecting real life) of OR is needed to build confidence in the utility of a medication in clinical practice.

OBJECTIVE 20.3. DEFINE AND EXPLAIN HOW TO MEASURE HEALTH-RELATED QUALITY OF LIFE AND PATIENT-REPORTED OUTCOMES

Patient preferences, along with evidence and clinical experience, make up the three core components of evidence-based medicine.[17] It is imperative to accurately measure and understand the patient perspective in both clinical practice and research. OR allows for the assessment of this perspective.

Defining Health-Related Quality of Life and Patient-Reported Outcomes

HRQoL is defined as *the impact of a health condition or treatment on the physical, psychological, and social aspects of life from the patient's perspective.*[18] An important concept in this definition is that HRQoL incorporates multiple aspects of life, not just the physical aspect (which is frequently the focus in current practice). HRQoL tools are commonly used in prospective trials to show the impact of a treatment on total well-being as it relates to health.

The US FDA defines PROs as *any report of the status of a patient's health condition that comes directly from the patient, without interpretation of the patient's response by a clinician or anyone else.*[18] Tools that can be classified as PROs may measure a patient's symptoms, functional status, or satisfaction with care.

Distinction Between Health-Related Quality of Life and Patient-Reported Outcomes

Although some use HRQoL and PRO interchangeably, others have argued that doing so is incorrect.[19,20] In this chapter, HRQoL and PROs will be presented as two distinct concepts. A key distinction between HRQoL and PROs is their scope.[20] Most HRQoL instruments or tools are completed by patients and are therefore PROs but not all PROs measure HRQoL. Tools used to measure HRQoL are generally broader than other tools used to measure PROs. As such, tools that measure HRQoL may not be sensitive to changes that other PRO tools could detect. On the contrary, some PRO tools may be too focused and thus not capture as many aspects of health as HRQoL tools. For example, a PRO may capture physical functioning, but not psychological or social functioning, whereas there are HRQoL tools available that measure all of these aspects. Currently, HRQoL and other PRO tools are most commonly used in prospective research studies. It is hoped, however, that with the increased recognition of these measures and the advent of technologies to increase access to them (e.g., electronic administration of the tools), PROs/HRQoL will play a bigger role in both routine care and research.[21]

Measuring Health-Related Quality of Life

HRQoL is measured through questionnaires, also known as instruments or tools, which are administered to patients.[22] The instruments consist of questions (also referred to as items) aimed at measuring patient experiences as a result of disease course. A group of these questions that fall under a common theme is referred to as a domain. Domains represent an aspect of health, with the most common domains being physical, psychological, and social functioning.

HRQoL instruments may be generic (i.e., those that can be used across various populations) or disease specific (Fig. 20.4).[22] Those that are classified as generic can be further subdivided into health profile measures and utility measures. *Health profile measures* attempt to capture all aspects of HRQoL. These generally ask patients a series of questions spanning multiple health domains, which are assigned a point value based on how the patient answers. A total score is then calculated either overall or within each domain. *Utility measures* incorporate patient preferences. With these measures, HRQoL is represented as a number between 0 and 1, with 0 representing death and 1 representing perfect health. The key advantage of using a generic instrument is that it allows for comparisons across disease states. For instance, a researcher could evaluate if a medication for asthma improved HRQoL to the same degree as a medication for heart failure. However, while disease-specific instruments make it more difficult to make comparisons across conditions, they are often able to detect smaller changes in the disease course than generic instruments are.

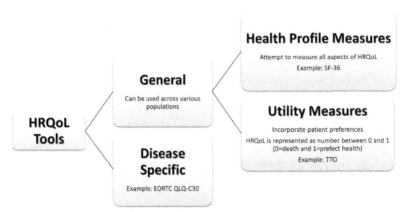

FIGURE 20.4   Categorization of health-related quality of life questionnaires. EORTC QLQ-C30 = European Organization for Research of Cancer Quality of Life Questionnaire Core-30; HRQoL = Health-related quality of life; SF-36 = 36-Item Short Form; TTO = time trade-off.

Generic Instruments: Common Examples

As mentioned above, generic health profile instruments attempt to capture all aspects of HRQoL.[22] A frequently used generic health profile instrument is the 36-Item Short Form (SF-36).[23] This questionnaire consists of the following eight domains: bodily pain, emotional role functioning, general health perceptions, mental health, physical functioning, physical role functioning, social role functioning, and vitality.[24] In addition to covering this comprehensive set of domains, the SF-36 has a minimal time burden associated with its use, as it takes ~7−10 min for participants to fill out the questionnaire.[23] Another common generic instrument is the abbreviated version of the World Health Organization Quality of Life Instrument (WHOQoL-BREF), which consists of 26 items and 4 main domains (i.e., physical health, psychological, social relationships, and environment).[25] In contrast, the WHOQoL-100 instrument has 100 items. The strength of the WHOQoL-BREF is that it is short and was specifically designed to be used across various cultures.

The EQ-5D-5L is a generic instrument that was developed by researchers from several countries in Europe.[26] It contains five dimensions (mobility, self-care, usual activity, pain/discomfort, and anxiety/depression) and assesses the following five levels of functioning: (1) no problems, (2) slight problems, (3) moderate problems, (4) severe problems, and (5) extreme problems. The EQ-5D-5L is available in over 130 languages and can be administered by paper or a variety of electronic devices.

Three commonly used health utility measures are the visual analog scale (VAS), time trade-off (TTO), and standard gamble.[27-32] The VAS is a simple measure, consisting of a line with 0 (representing death) on one end and 1.0 (representing perfect health) on the other.[28] Participants place a mark on the line to represent how they feel about their health state. The VAS has been criticized because it is not a real utility measure based on economic theory.

With the TTO, participants are given two options.[27] The first option is the health state (e.g., a disease state such as heart failure) for a set amount of time followed by death. The second option is living in perfect health for a set amount of time followed by death. Because living in perfect health is desirable, this second option is made shorter than the first. If the respondent prefers to live a shorter time but in perfect health, the questionnaire continues to make the time in perfect health shorter or longer until the participant would consider the two alternatives equal. For example, the instrument may read: would you rather live 40 years with heart failure or 38 years in perfect health? If the participant answers that he or she would rather live 38 years in perfect health, the next question would read: would you rather live 40 years with heart failure or 35 years in perfect health? Depending on the answer, this time in perfect health will then be increased or decreased. If the respondent prefers the 40 years with the disease, then the 35 years will again be increased to 36 years. As such, the time in perfect health would be decreased or increased until the participant finds the two options of equal value. At this point, the amount listed for the perfect health state is divided by the 40 years that was listed for the disease state, which gives a utility value (for instance, if the participant stated that they could not decide between spending 40 years with heart failure or 30 in perfect health, the resulting utility would be 30/40 or 0.75). The more time that the participant is willing to give up to live in perfect health rather than the reduced health state, the less favorably they view the health state. This will be reflected by lower utility values. Finally, the standard gamble produces a utility value by accounting for the probability of death an individual will theoretically accept to no longer experience the pain and suffering of their current condition.[29] Both the TTO and the standard gamble have been criticized due to their complexity.[30]

Disease-Specific Instruments

There are times when it is desirable to measure HRQoL in a way that is more focused on the impact of a particular disease.[33,34] Countless questionnaires have been developed for this purpose, including instruments such as the WHOQoL-HIV, Asthma Quality-of-Life Questionnaire (AQLQ), and the European Organization for Research and Treatment of Cancer Quality of Life Questionnaire Core-30 (EORTC QLQ-C30).[33,34] Disease-specific instruments allow for the inclusion of questions that are commonly used by clinicians to measure a particular disease. For instance, the AQLQ asks the patients questions about wheezing and shortness of breath that may not be applicable to other disease states.[33]

Reliability, Validity, and Responsiveness

When evaluating how well a HRQoL instrument performs, there are three concepts to consider: reliability, validity, and responsiveness.[23] *Reliability* refers to how consistent an instrument is. A tool with high reliability would yield consistent results when applied to similar patients under the same circumstances. *Validity* assesses if a HRQoL instrument adequately captures what it should measure. Finally, *responsiveness* refers to the ability of an instrument to detect important clinical changes in a patient's condition over time. If an instrument has high responsiveness, it is able to detect small changes in the disease course.

Measuring Domain-Specific Patient-Reported Outcomes

As previously stated, many PROs tend to focus on one domain, whereas HRQoL spans multiple domains. PROs may assess symptoms of disease, how well a patient can function (e.g., perform daily tasks such as walking or daily activities including caring for oneself), adherence to treatment, or satisfaction with care. Some PROs are mentioned in this section; however, a more extensive list of PRO measures can be found through the Patient-Reported Outcomes Measurement Information System (PROMIS).[35]

Symptom Measures

PROs that measure specific symptoms such as pain are common. These include scales like the one displayed in Fig. 20.5 or forms such as the brief pain inventory (BPI).[36] The BPI was designed to measure pain reported by cancer patients.[36] It asks patients about pain intensity and how this pain interferes with their life. The BPI is available in both a short (which consists of nine questions) and longer version.[37] Although pain is included in some of the above-mentioned HRQoL tools, it is only one of many domains. Because the BPI focuses on this one aspect, it may provide a more sensitive and detailed description of a patient's pain.

Adverse Event Reporting

When patients are asked questions to assess the presence of adverse events from a medication, this is a PRO.[38] In clinical trials assessing new medications, adverse event monitoring is required. Patients in these trials may be asked to answer questionnaires for the purpose of detecting adverse events that would otherwise be unknown to investigators. Adverse event reporting by the patients is common in cancer chemotherapy. Cancer clinical trials use the Common Terminology Criteria for Adverse Events (CTCAE) to describe the severity of adverse events.[36] CTCAE was initially designed for clinicians and thus contains medical jargon.[39] A revised version of CTCAE for patients uses simple language without losing its original content. For instance, instead of asking about "inadequate oral caloric or fluid intake" as was done in the original CTCAE, the patient-adapted version asks if they are "eating or drinking adequately.[40]"

Patient Satisfaction

PROs can also measure patient satisfaction with care. AHRQ's Consumer Assessment of Healthcare Providers and Systems (CAHPS) program is a predominant means of capturing patient satisfaction in the US.[41] The program administers standardized surveys that can be used to compare patients' experience with care across institutions. This is sometimes referred to as PREMs (Patient-Reported Experience Measures). It was originally designed to measure patients' satisfaction with their health plan but has been expanded to a spectrum of healthcare settings, including hospitals, nursing homes, and physician offices. Results from the CAHPS hospital survey (which asks the patient 32 questions, covering topics such as communication with healthcare providers, discharge instructions, and hospital cleanliness) are publically reported.

Patient or Clinician, Who Should Fill a Questionnaire?

Studies have shown that there is disagreement across questionnaires filled out by healthcare professionals about patient preferences compared with those filled out by the patient themselves.[42] This emphasizes that it is best to collect data about the patient experience directly from the patient. For instance, one study administered HRQoL questionnaires to both patients with prostate cancer and their physicians to fill out on behalf of the patient. The physicians underestimated patient impairment in all domains. Approximately 75% of patients reported fatigue, whereas physicians reported that fatigue was present in only 10% of patients ($P < .001$). Similarly, pain was reported by 43% of patients, but physicians reported that pain was present in <5% of patients ($P < .001$).[42]

Encouraging reporting of patient preferences is a method to improve patient-centeredness in clinical practice and research. This may increase the level of ownership patients take in their medical care. Engagement of patients in the clinical decision-making process is the cornerstone to establishing patient-centered clinical practice.[43]

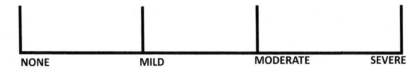

FIGURE 20.5   An example pain scale. A patient selects the vertical line that describes their pain intensity.

OBJECTIVE 20.4. GENERALIZE HOW OUTCOMES RESEARCH IS GAINING IMPORTANCE IN CLINICAL PRACTICE

The cost of healthcare is increasing, and there is a push toward reimbursement of services based on value not volume. Value is subjective. Value can be measured from a patient's perspective (e.g., value = what did the patient get—how much money the patient is willing to pay to get it) versus a healthcare system's perspective, which takes into account the outcomes, the harm, and the resources consumed.[44] A primary concern for healthcare systems is how the insurance companies and payers define value because this determines how the healthcare organization is reimbursed. Each institution is also compared against other like institutions, so if one organization achieves a better perceived value, then other institutions will be forced to follow. Centers are allocating more and more resources into looking at center-specific outcomes and improving value, thus creating an opportunity for OR.

Scenario 1: Outcomes Research in Medical Reimbursement Decisions

Historically, a hospital was paid a certain amount of money as medical reimbursement for performing a surgery to remove the appendix. The operation and length of stay would be covered within reason. Now, depending on how well a surgeon performs this operation (based on their complication rate and expected length of stay for patients), reimbursement between payers may change, even if they perform the same operation at the same center. That means if a patient has to stay an extra 3 days because of a wound infection, the hospital may not get reimbursed for the full expense of that 3 extra days. This is an alternative payment model (APM) or value-based purchasing (VBP) model. These are models in which third-party payers either provide incentives or penalties for measures based on quality and/or costs and may motivate improvement.[45]

Changes in the US demonstrate the refocus of healthcare reimbursement on quality and value versus traditional fee for service. For example, a Merit-based Incentive Payment (MIPS) system is a relatively new term. These came about with the Medicare Access and CHIP (Children's Health Insurance Program) Reauthorization Act of 2015 and are an artifact of the Patient Protection and Affordable Care Act.[46] This is an example of a push for Medicare, the largest provider of public healthcare in the US, to reimburse physicians based on cost and "value" versus the traditional fee for service.[46] The MIPS program provides a penalty or a bonus based on the performance measures and encourages providers to use technology and make improvements while containing costs and optimizing quality.[46] Several other countries are exploring different APM or VBP models trying to figure out which among these will work better: incentives, penalties, or bonuses. This concept is not new in the pharmaceutical industry. Health plans negotiate with pharmaceutical companies to define tiers for medications.[47] This may incentivize medication manufacturers to provide their medication at a lower cost when compared with another medication within the same class or approved indication. OR is essential for measuring value in healthcare and is used widely to help in reimbursement decisions.

Scenario 2: Interpreting OR Data in a Particular Context

The OR data behind metrics should be understood. Suppose a hospital wants to analyze the impact of medications used for empiric coverage of urosepsis because the mortality index for the hospital is increasing. How should this be approached? It is first important to understand the mortality index and how this is measured. Specifically, in looking at the medications used for empiric coverage of urosepsis, the index values are usually based on an equation containing observed mortality over expected mortality. The expected outcome is determined by a model. For example, a previously healthy 30-year-old person presenting to the emergency room with urosepsis has a lower risk of mortality versus an 87-year-old coming from a nursing home with urosepsis. It is important to identify the patients falling into the model and what variables are predicting a higher rate of mortality. In this particular context, the hospital may discover that all of the patients who are dying from urosepsis are not patients who received the wrong empiric medication, but rather they were patients who were underdosed or had a delay in receiving medication. This then makes the answer to the question posed entirely different. Important take-home points when assessing score reports in a particular context are as follows: (1) take a look at the data behind the scores, (2) what methods and definitions are used and what do they mean, (3) what is most relevant (e.g., is a metric that tries to capture overuse of medical imaging or a metric that captures wait time in the emergency room most relevant to patients?), (4) when was the data obtained (data from 10 years ago may not be applicable today), and (5) what is the methodology for reporting (e.g., ranking based on a survey of other physicians or actual data). Thus, score reports should not be interpreted alone. Rather, one should understand how these score reports are calculated to make appropriate clinical decisions.

Scenario 3: Outcomes Research Data in a Healthcare System Performance

OR can be used to analyze the performance of healthcare systems. A classic example is the solid organ transplant services in the US. In January of 2017, the Centers for Medicare and Medicaid services (CMS) adopted new flagging criteria for outcomes, specifically 1-year graft loss and patient mortality.[48] What does that mean? Every 6 months the Scientific Registry of Transplant Recipients releases a transplant program-specific report. This report details all hospital transplants during the reporting period and provides an observed number of graft losses and patient deaths compared with expected number. If a center experiences a higher number of deaths or graft losses than expected and it exceeds some other particular thresholds set by CMS, then the center is at risk of losing funding. This is especially true if the center cannot explain why the observed number of graft losses and patient deaths is higher than expected or explain steps that the center has taken to make improvements and subsequently demonstrate improvements on upcoming reports. If a center loses CMS funding for the transplant program, most other insurance payers will follow suit and also pull their funding. Many third-party health plans only cover centers covered by Medicare. Here is the challenging part! In the case of transplant outcomes, a center is assessed based on 2.5 years' worth of data. So when the next report is released in January of 2018, the data that will be evaluated for 1-year risk of graft loss or mortality are based on outcomes from patients who received transplants from July 1, 2014 through December 31, 2016. This is likely implemented to ensure that most patients have arrived at their 1-year milestone, but the data lag does not demonstrate what may be going on now. Some examples include a center with a new surgical team that was not involved in transplanting the patients included in the data or the center was shut down for 9 months following a hurricane so the denominator is smaller. It is also important to understand what goes into the model. Some mortality models, for example, exclude patients who have had a previous transplant for the organ of interest. Furthermore, a pharmacist member of the team where outcomes are not looking great may be able to suggest an alteration in the immunosuppression regimen used by the center.

OR, along with other measures, is thus useful in analyzing healthcare system performance. However, one must always understand how and in what context data were obtained. For instance, it is known that the infant mortality rate (an OR indicator) is used to measure system performance in the facility, regional, national, or international levels. However, although this measure is universal, it would be unwise to make a decision without accounting for where and how this measure is calculated.

CONCLUSION

In summary, OR places emphasis on patient perspectives and represents multiple stakeholders in healthcare. The most conclusive way to evaluate how a healthcare system functions is by measuring the end result of the interventions. This increases the need for OR to generate real-world safety and effectiveness data. Use of HRQoL and other PRO tools has value in both OR and clinical trials. Patient reporting also improves patient-centeredness in clinical practice. OR is an important tool for improving healthcare across various settings.

PRACTICE QUESTIONS

1. The field of research that attempts to measure the end results of a healthcare intervention is best described as
   A. Clinical trial research
   B. Outcomes research
   C. Pharmacoeconomics
   D. Pharmacoepidemiology
2. The three main types of outcomes measured by outcomes research are
   A. Economic, humanistic, and clinical
   B. Economic, humanistic, and mortality
   C. Efficacy, humanistic, and clinical
   D. Efficacy, humanistic, and morbidity
3. A model used in outcomes studies designed to measure or determine the impact of an intervention on the quality of care provided (usually within a health system) is the
   A. Bismarck model
   B. ISPOR model
   C. PROMIS model
   D. SPO model

4. In a prospective study, an investigator randomizes patients to receive either a cholesterol medication or placebo. The investigator attempts to maintain a high level of internal validity by incorporating numerous follow-up visits into the study protocol and excluding patients with extensive comorbidities and those that are unlikely to adhere to the cholesterol medication. This study design is best described as
   A. Outcomes research
   B. Pharmacoeconomics
   C. Pharmacoepidemiology
   D. Traditional Clinical Trial Research

5. A hospital adds a new antibiotic to formulary. A pharmacist working at the hospital wants to know if this new antibiotic leads to shorter hospital stays compared with an antibiotic that was previously on the hospital formulary. The pharmacist identifies all patients that have received either the old or new antibiotic and examines the patients' length of stay. This study design is best described as
   A. Outcomes research
   B. Pharmacoeconomics
   C. Systematic Review
   D. Traditional Clinical Trial Research

6. A study that maintains some qualities of clinical trials (e.g., randomly assigning patients to treatment groups) but incorporates OR methodology to increase applicability through the use of less stringent inclusion criteria and simplified study design is best described as
   A. Pharmacoeconomics
   B. Pharmacoepidemiology
   C. Pragmatic Trial Research
   D. Systematic Review

7. A HRQoL questionnaire that can be used across all populations and is not designed for a specific medical condition is referred to as a/an
   A. Disease specific
   B. Focused tool
   C. Generic instrument
   D. Pragmatic measures

8. The VAS and TTO instruments represent HRQoL as a number between 0 and 1, with 0 representing death and 1 representing prefect health and are referred to as
   A. Disease specific
   B. Health profile instruments
   C. Utility measures
   D. Pragmatic measures

9. A HRQoL tool that yields consistent results when applied to similar patients under the same circumstances has
   A. High accuracy
   B. High reliability
   C. High responsiveness
   D. High validity

10. Which of the following is an example of decreased healthcare value?
    A. High patient satisfaction scores in the outpatient cardiology clinic
    B. Reduced surgical site infections in orthopedic cases over the past quarter
    C. Earlier time to discharge for internal medicine patients on Saturdays
    D. Higher urinary catheter infection rates if placed in the emergency department

11. Which of the following steps is necessary when considering nationally or internationally published healthcare-related rankings?
    A. Understand the data definitions and what data are included in the ranking
    B. Ensure the time frame in which the data were evaluated is known
    C. Determine how the ranking is achieved
    D. All of the above

REFERENCES

1. Duttagupta S. Outcomes research and drug development. *Perspect Clin Res*. 2010;1:104–105.
2. Outcomes Research Fact Sheet. *Agency for Healthcare Research and Quality*; 2000. Available at: https://archive.ahrq.gov/research/findings/factsheets/outcomes/outfact/outcomes-and-research.html.
3. Cohen AT, Goto S, Schreiber K, Torp-Pedersen C. Why do we need observational studies of everyday patients in the real-life setting? *Eur Heart J Suppl*. 2015;17(Suppl. D):D2–D8.
4. Krumholz HM. Outcomes research: myths and realities. *Circ Cardiovasc Qual Outcomes*. 2009;2:1–3.
5. ISPOR Milestones. *International Society for Pharmacoeconomics and Outcomes Research*; 2015. Available at: https://www.ispor.org/ISPOR-20thAnniv-Milestones-Brochure.pdf.
6. Roger VL. Outcomes research and epidemiology: the synergy between public health and clinical practice. *Circ Cardiovasc Qual Outcomes*. 2011;4:257–259.
7. Kozma CM, Reeder CE, Schulz RM. Economic, clinical, and humanistic outcomes: a planning model for pharmacoeconomic research. *Clin Ther*. 1993;15:1121–1132.
8. Gunter MJ. The role of the ECHO model in outcomes research and clinical practice improvement. *Am J Manag Care*. 1999;5(4 Suppl.):S217–S224.
9. Donabedian A. *An Introduction to Quality Assurance in Health-Care*. New York, NY: Oxford University Press; 2003.
10. O'gara PT, Kushner FG, Ascheim DD, et al. 2013 ACCF/AHA guideline for the management of ST-elevation myocardial infarction: a report of the American College of Cardiology Foundation/American Heart Association task force on practice guidelines. *Circulation*. 2013;127:e362–425.
11. Green LW. Making research relevant: if it is an evidence-based practice, where's the practice-based evidence? *Fam Pract*. 2008;(25 Suppl. 1):i20–i24.
12. Osoba D. Health-related quality of life and cancer clinical trials. *Ther Adv Med Oncol*. 2011;3:57–71.
13. Patsopoulos NA. A pragmatic view on pragmatic trials. *Dialogues Clin Neurosci*. 2011;13:217–224.
14. *A Pragmatic Trial to Evaluate the Comparative Effectiveness between Dapagliflozin and Standard of Care in Type 2 Diabetes Patients (DECIDE Study) (DECIDE)*. Astra Zeneca; 2017. Available at: https://clinicaltrials.gov/ct2/show/NCT02616666.
15. Heneghan C, Goldacre B, Mahtani KR. Why clinical trial outcomes fail to translate into benefits for patients. *Trials*. 2017;18:122.
16. Kim JH, Scialli AR. Thalidomide: the tragedy of birth defects and the effective treatment of disease. *Toxicol Sci*. 2011;122:1–6.
17. Pape TM. Evidence based nursing practice: to infinity and beyond. *J Cont Educ Nurs*. 2013;34:154–161.
18. *Guidance for Industry Patient-Reported Outcome Measures: Use in Medical Product Development to Support Labeling Claims*. U.S. Department of Health and Human Services Food and Drug Administration; 2009. Available at: https://www.fda.gov/downloads/drugs/guidances/ucm193282.pdf.
19. Feeny DH, Eckstrom E, Whitlock EP, Perdue LA. *A Primer for Systematic Reviewers on the Measurement of Functional Status and Health-Related Quality of Life in Older Adults. (Prepared by the Kaiser Permanente Research Affiliates Evidence-based Practice Center under Contract No. 290-2007-10057-I.) AHRQ Publication No. 13-EHC128-EF*. Rockville, MD: Agency for Healthcare Research and Quality; September 2013. Available at: www.effectivehealthcare.ahrq.gov/reports/final.cfm.
20. Rascati KL. *Essentials of Pharmacoeconomics*. Philadelphia: Wolters Kluwer Health/Lippincott Williams & Wilkins; 2013.
21. Schuerenberg BK. A tablet a day. *Health Data Manag*. 2004;12:56–58.
22. Guyatt GH, Feeny DH, Patrick DL. Measuring health-related quality of life. *Ann Intern Med*. 1993;118:622–629.
23. Coons SJ, Rao S, Keininger DL, Hays RD. A comparative review of generic quality-of-life instruments. *Pharmacoeconomics*. 2000;17:13–35.
24. Ware JE, Sherbourne CD. The MOS 36-Item short-form health survey (SF-36®). I.conceptual framework and item selection. *Med Care*. 1992;30:473–483.
25. Development of the World Health Organization WHOQOL-BREF quality of life assessment. The WHOQOL group. *Psychol Med*. 1998;28:551–558.
26. van Reenen M, Janssen B. *EQ-5D-5L User Guide*; 2017. Available at: https://euroqol.org/wp-content/uploads/2016/09/EQ-5D-5L_UserGuide_2015.pdf.
27. Gudex C. *Time Trade-Off User Manual: Props and Self-Completion Methods*. The University of York Centre for Health Economics; 1994. Available at: https://www.york.ac.uk/che/pdf/op20.pdf.
28. Wewers ME, Lowe NK. A critical review of visual analogue scales in the measurement of clinical phenomena. *Res Nurs Health*. 1990;13:227–236.
29. Gafni A. The standard gamble method: what is being measured and how it is interpreted. *Health Serv Res*. 1994;29:207–224.
30. Kuntz KM. Decision modeling for cost-utility analysis. *Value Health*. 2016;19:700–701.
31. Guo J, Konetzka RT, Dale W. Using time trade-off methods to assess preferences over health-care delivery options: a feasibility study. *Value Health*. 2014;17:302–305.
32. Drummond M, Brixner D, Gold M, et al. Toward a consensus on the QALY. *Value Health*. 2009;(12 Suppl. 1):S31–S35.
33. Juniper EF, Guyatt GH, Epstein RS, Ferrie PJ, Jaeschke R, Hiller TK. Evaluation of impairment of health-related quality of life in asthma: development of a questionnaire for use in clinical trials. *Thorax*. 1992;47:76–83.
34. *EORTC QLQ-C30 Scoring Manual*. Brussels: EORTC; 2001. Available at: http://www.eortc.be/qol/files/SCManualQLQ-C30.pdf.
35. *Patient Reported Outcomes Measurement Information System*. National Institute of Health; 2017. Available at: http://www.nihpromis.com/about/overview.
36. Kumar SP. Utilization of brief pain inventory as an assessment tool for pain in patients with cancer: a focused review. *Indian J Palliat Care*. 2011;17:108–115.
37. Cleeland CS. *The Brief Pain Inventory User Guide*; 2017. Available at: https://www.mdanderson.org/documents/Departments-and-Divisions/Symptom-Research/BPI_UserGuide.pdf.

38. Trotti A, Colevas AD, Setser A, Basch E. Patient-reported outcomes and the evolution of adverse event reporting in oncology. *J Clin Oncol.* 2007;25:5121−5127.

39. Basch E, Artz D, Iasonos A, et al. Evaluation of an online platform for cancer patient self-reporting of chemotherapy toxicities. *J Am Med Inform Assoc.* 2007;14:264−268.

40. Basch E, Artz D, Dulko D, et al. Patient online self-reporting of toxicity symptoms during chemotherapy. *J Clin Oncol.* 2005;23:3552−3561.

41. About CAHPS. *Agency for Healthcare Research and Quality, Rockville, MD*; 2016. Available at: http://www.ahrq.gov/cahps/about-cahps/index.html.

42. Litwin MS, Lubeck DP, Henning JM, Carroll PR. Differences in urologist and patient assessments of health-related quality of life in men with prostate cancer: results of the CaPSURE database. *J Urol.* 1998;159:1988−1992.

43. Snyder CF, Jensen RE, Segal JB, Wu AW. Patient-reported outcomes (PROs): putting the patient perspective in patient-centered outcomes research. *Med Care.* 2013;5:S73−S79.

44. Gentry S, Badrinath P. Defining health in the era of value-based care: lessons from England of relevance to other health systems. *Cureus.* 2017;9:e1079.

45. Joynt Maddox KE, Sen AP, Samson LW, Zuckerman RB, DeLew N, Epstein AM. Elements of program design in medicare's value-based and alternative payment models: a narrative review. *J Gen Intern Med.* 2017 (epub).

46. Department of Health and Human Services, Centers for Medicare and Medicaid Services Medicare Program. *Merit-Based Incentive Payment System (MIPS) and Alternative Payment Model (APM) Incentive under the Physician Fee Schedule, and Criteria for Physician-Focused Payment Models*; 2016. Available at: https://www.federalregister.gov/documents/2016/11/04/2016-25240/medicare-program-merit-based-incentive-payment-system-mips-and-alternative-payment-model-apm.

47. Joynt Maddox KE, Sen AP, Samson LW, Zuckerman RB, DeLew N, Epstein AM. Undermining value-based purchasing - lessons from the pharmaceutical industry. *N Engl J Med.* 2016;375:2013−2015.

48. Axelrod DA, Schold J. Measuring what matters. *Am J Transplant.* 2016;16:3315−3317.

ANSWERS TO PRACTICE QUESTIONS

1. B
2. A
3. D
4. D
5. A
6. C
7. C
8. C
9. B
10. D
11. D

Chapter 21

Health Technology Assessment— Policy Objectives and Principles of System Design

Dávid Dankó

Ideas & Solutions, Budapest, Hungary

Learning Objectives

Objective 21.1 Overview of health technology assessment (HTA) from a policy perspective.
Objective 21.2 Describe different paradigms in the assessment of health technologies.
Objective 21.3 Describe a high-level HTA process.
Objective 21.4 Explain HTA system design in current practice.

OBJECTIVE 21.1. OVERVIEW OF HEALTH TECHNOLOGY ASSESSMENT FROM A POLICY PERSPECTIVE

Meaning and Purpose of Health Technology Assessment

Health technology assessment (HTA) is commonly defined as a multidisciplinary approach for the systematic assessment of medical technologies regarding their effectiveness, appropriateness, efficiency, and social and ethical aspects and implications.[1] It is usually conducted by an interdisciplinary group using analytical frameworks, drawing from a variety of methods.[2] By systematically assessing health technologies, HTA fulfills an important decision support role with regard to decisions on a rational allocation of healthcare resources. Thus, it can support health policy in general and, very commonly, pricing and funding decisions in particular. It is supposed to provide responsible bodies and organizations with timely, accurate, and sound information on newly introduced medical technologies. Besides this, HTA can also support decisions on already reimbursed health technologies, for example, pricing and funding reviews.[3]

In principle, HTA can evaluate all medical technologies, including pharmaceuticals, diagnostics, medical devices, surgical procedures, or even public health interventions, such as disease screening or vaccination programs. In most countries, however, HTA is focused mainly on pharmaceuticals (most commonly new active substances). There are three main reasons for this:

- pharmaceuticals are developed, registered, and funded on the basis of evidence generated in clinical trials and, increasingly, real-world evidence;
- they are highly standardized technologies with well-defined intellectual property rights (e.g., patents); and
- they are often associated with high costs or significant impact on public health budgets, which makes payers (budget holders) conscious about the financial implications of pricing or funding decisions.

As discussed below, HTA has often been interpreted as a form of economic analysis focused on cost-effectiveness and budget impact. *Fourth hurdle,*[4] a previously very popular expression, also refers to this suggesting that HTA in general and cost-effectiveness analysis in particular constitute a fourth dimension of critical assessment besides the three main aspects covered in regulatory approval processes: efficacy, safety, and quality. HTA is, however, not limited to, economic analysis.

Clinical assessment is a core component of most HTA systems and many HTA systems consider other aspects in line with the broader academic definition of HTA (e.g., ethical and social considerations).

Traditionally regulatory approval processes and HTA systems have not been interlinked and they have focused on different aspects or comparisons. For instance, a clinical trial design which was approved by regulatory bodies may have been judged as inappropriate or insufficient during a subsequent HTA assessment. An example is the acceptance of placebo-controlled studies for regulatory purposes as opposed to HTA bodies strongly favoring active comparator studies. Similarly, regulatory agencies may grant marketing authorization to a product based on Phase II data which may not be sufficient for HTA bodies to issue positive recommendations. The regulatory and HTA bodies have recognized the necessity of interacting more closely with each other and with technology owners (pharmaceutical companies) by providing harmonized guidance (e.g., early advice) during clinical development.[5,6]

Policy Objectives Related to Health Technology Assessment

Why do healthcare policy-makers or payers (budget holders) rely on HTA? The economist's answer lies in two interrelated concepts in health economics: *supply-induced demand* and *opportunity costs*.[7] A political scientist or a sociologist will add other factors, too.

In simple terms, *supply-induced demand* means that medical professionals and patients will want to use any new health technology that is launched on the healthcare market. The main reason is that new technologies offer, or at least claim, better treatment possibilities and results. In the case of technologies funded by public or private (third-party) payers for patients, low or zero price sensitivity also reinforces supply-induced demand, which means that payers would need ample or even unlimited resources to pay for all healthcare innovations. This is certainly unlikely to ever happen—healthcare budgets are limited even in affluent countries.

Thus, by paying for one health technology, policy-makers and payers will have to forgo the purchase of, or provision of funding to, other health technologies. This situation, whereby the selection of one opportunity rules out the selection of another opportunity for the lack of resources, is called "*opportunity cost*" in economics. Policy-makers and payers execute their role and mandate properly if they minimize opportunity costs in their purchasing decisions by identifying and paying for technologies which have the highest *value* compared with other available and already funded technologies. For this, policy-makers and payers will rely on structured evaluation methods to assess the value of new health technologies in comparison to already available and funded health technologies. This is the economist's explanation for the development and institutionalization of HTA across healthcare systems (Fig. 21.1).

A political scientist will add that structured evaluation methods are likely to increase the transparency and accountability of healthcare funding decisions, which is a significant guarantee for higher-quality health services.[8] From this perspective, the use of HTA decreases the political vulnerability of individual decision-makers through reinforcing institutional decision responsibilities over individual responsibilities. Political science, however, also points out that HTA can also be used or misused for cost containment purposes and/or for limiting patients' access to new health technologies.

OBJECTIVE 21.2. DESCRIBE DIFFERENT PARADIGMS IN THE ASSESSMENT OF HEALTH TECHNOLOGIES

A crucial issue in HTA is that *value* is a concept with several possible definitions. HTA approaches differ significantly in the way they consider and assess the value. These differences have given rise to diverging HTA systems and methodologies around the world. In HTA terminology, these are sometimes referred to as *value frameworks*.[9]

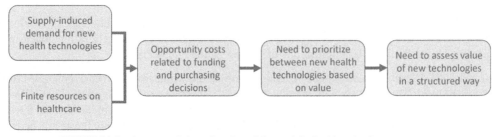

FIGURE 21.1 An economist's explanation of the need for health technology assessment.

ECONOMIC EVALUATION	COMPARATIVE ASSESSMENT	MULTIDIMENSIONAL VALUE ASSESSMENT APPROACHES
• Key metrics: cost-effectiveness, budget impact • Explicit or implicit cost-effectiveness threshold guides reimbursability • Widely uses health economic modeling • Methods set down in health economic guidelines • In some systems, weak consideration for non-economic aspects • *Archetype: United Kingdom* • *Other countries: South Korea, Thailand, Poland, Hungary, Slovakia*	• Emphasis on added clinical benefit against active comparator • Added clinical benefit determines allowable price or funding restrictions • Usually uses standard categories of added benefit • Value appraisal through discussion and deliberative decision-making • Economic considerations are typically introduced during price negotiations • *Archetype: France, Germany, Japan* • *Other example: Italy, Taiwan*	• Multiple assessment criteria are used (both economic and non-economic) • Economic value and clinical value can independently qualify a medicine for funding • Deliberative decision-making processes • Usually strong emphasis on process transparency and accountability • *Multi-criteria assessment: Canada, Australia, Netherlands, Sweden* • *Pragmatic value assessment: initiatives in middle-income countries*

FIGURE 21.2   Main paradigms in health technology assessment.

Most value frameworks can be grouped together into three different *HTA paradigms*[10] (Fig. 21.2):

- The first paradigm, *economic evaluation*, is focused on the costs and benefits of a new technology and is centered around the notion of cost-effectiveness. Budget impact analysis (BIA) is also widely used alongside cost-effectiveness analysis in economic evaluation systems.
- The second paradigm, probably best termed as *comparative assessment* (although often referred to as *comparative effectiveness research* in the US context), is concerned with the added clinical benefit a new medical technology provides over its appropriately chosen comparator.
- The third paradigm encompasses various *multidimensional techniques*, e.g., scoring models and multicriteria decision analysis (MCDA). These are aimed at determining various clinical, economic, societal, and other sources of value for a new technology as well as their relative importance. Based on this, the main objective is prioritization for pricing and funding decisions.

Economic Evaluation

Economic evaluation has been the most widely used paradigm in countries in which the mainstream pharmacoeconomic tradition has developed or which have embraced it. Cost-effectiveness and budget impact are the core concepts in value assessment. *Cost-effectiveness* denotes a positive balance between the health benefits attainable through the new technology and the costs related to its application. If a new technology is cost-effective, it is "value-for-money" so it is worth for payers to consider buying it. The BIA identifies the costs and possible savings related to the application of a new technology and investigates the affordability of the new technology in function of available resources. Here the main question is if payers have enough money to purchase or fund the new technology. Cost-effectiveness and BIAs are interrelated; if a new technology is worth buying, it is still not sure that payers will have the necessary resources to buy it. Vice versa, if funds are available for a new technology, it may still not be worthwhile for investment.

Both cost-effectiveness analysis and BIA are quantitative techniques whose results may be influenced by the methodological choices that designers and users of HTA systems take. The cost-effectiveness of a new technology is usually determined by establishing its *incremental cost-effectiveness ratio* (defined as the incremental cost of providing one quality-adjusted life year [QALY] with the new technology as opposed to the cost of providing one QALY with an already available comparator technology) and by comparing it against a threshold value. Threshold values are often expressed as the multiple of the per capita gross domestic product[11] (e.g., in the United Kingdom or in Poland) or sometimes as the multiple of the minimum wage in a country (e.g., Slovakia). Although many threshold values are asserted as being based on prior value choices by payers, they are ultimately a matter of policy decision and their choice influences the outcomes of cost-effectiveness analyses. For example, "traditional" thresholds such as "X times per capita GDP" are mentioned as access barriers for distinct groups of health technologies such as orphan medicines, targeted combination therapies in oncology—hematology, or some special medical devices (e.g., implants). Because of this, the overwhelming majority of countries applying cost-effectiveness analysis do not use rigid thresholds. Rather, they have opted for differentiated thresholds or they incorporate cost/QALY results into a broader perspective or into a deliberative appraisal process.

The main methodological issue with BIA is the proper identification of relevant costs. We usually distinguish between *direct costs* which are directly related to the use of the new medical technology (e.g., drug administration cost, hospitalization cost) and *indirect costs* which may be medical and nonmedical and are more loosely linked to the technology (e.g., loss of productivity, dietary requirements, rehabilitation need, sick leave payments). Most of the BIAs are in fact just a financial budget sheet that compares cost differences between situations of including or not including a drug. The BIA shall also cover avoided direct and indirect costs, i.e., savings. For example, expenditures related to other medical treatments substituted by the new technology are direct savings, whereas "decreased loss" of productivity (i.e., increase in productivity) is indirect savings.[12]

Perspective is also a key issue in economic evaluation. Relevant costs and benefits are always defined and collected from the perspective of a specific healthcare stakeholder. For example, from a technical payer's perspective, indirect costs incurred by caretaker families are unlikely to be relevant unless the payer compensates the families for their efforts. However, from a policy-maker or societal perspective, these costs become relevant. Most healthcare systems require that cost-effectiveness analyses be performed from a payer perspective but some countries (most prominently Sweden and the Netherlands) also require the presentation of the societal perspective. In the case of BIA, countries usually insist on the payer perspective, and payers do not pay attention to indirect savings in the healthcare system.[13]

Economic evaluation strongly relies on *modeling,* especially when the data are limited. The main purpose of modeling is to extrapolate available clinical and economic evidence (e.g., clinical trial results as well as costs linked to the therapy) to the time frame which is relevant for decision-making. In addition, by incorporating metaanalyses and other sources of evidence, modeling makes it possible to carry out comparisons with comparators which were not originally included in clinical trials. For modeling purposes, the clinical problem or disease is usually "simplified" into a well-defined sequence of health states. For this simplification, decision-tree models, Markov models, and Monte Carlo simulations are the most frequently used techniques. Decision-tree models define mutually exclusive patient pathways between which patients cannot switch. Markov models are based on mutually exclusive health states with transition probabilities between these with time. Finally, Monte Carlo simulations enable patient-level analyses where individual factors of individual patients are incorporated into the analysis.[14] If the disease or condition evolves with time, Markov models or Monte Carlo simulations are preferred. In Markov models, time is represented by discrete periods called "cycles" and patients can move between health states with a certain transition probability, which depends only on the state they are in. Consequently, Markov models have no memory in contrast to Monte Carlo simulations, which can follow any changes in a patient pathway. Here, model inputs are drawn from statistical distributions.[15,16]

Economic evaluation has a highly developed methodological apparatus and its suitability for the comparison of very different technologies are strengths to be pointed out. Possible weaknesses can be its financial focus, resource-intensiveness, and the fact that for the interpretation of its results, policy-makers and payers are supposed to be acquainted with its methodology, which cannot always be the case in smaller or developing healthcare systems. Economic evaluation can exist in a "heavy" form in which a public agency performs both single technology assessments (STA) and comprehensive multiple technology assessments and in a "lighter" form where assessments are triggered by submissions by pharmaceutical companies (STA only).

The reference institution for the economic evaluation approach has traditionally been England's National Institute of Care and Health Excellence. Scotland uses the same approach in a different practical implementation by the Scottish Medicines Consortium. In the United Kingdom, because of the decentralized structure of healthcare budgets, economic evaluation has traditionally been focused on cost-effectiveness analysis rather than BIA but recently the latter has also gained importance. Other countries applying economic evaluation in more or less comprehensive forms include Poland, Hungary, South Korea, Thailand, and Brazil. Some developed healthcare markets such as Australia, Canada, Sweden, and the Netherlands use economic evaluation extensively as one component in a multidimensional decision-making framework. France, which is widely regarded as the "home country" for comparative benefit assessment (see below), introduced cost-effectiveness analysis for special cases (new medicines with high budget impact and claiming high added therapeutic benefit) in 2012.[17] A reverse example is found in South Korea, which generally uses cost-effectiveness analysis but does not require it in special cases if the new technology offers considerable price advantage. For the time being, many developing healthcare systems across Asia, the Middle East, and Latin America only require BIAs of new technologies. This is probably the focus of the assessment that has been on how to contain an already limited budget.

Comparative Assessment

Comparative assessment, sometimes called qualitative assessment or comparative effectiveness research (especially with reference to the United States[18,19]), bears more resemblance than economic evaluation in its approach to the evaluation

France (ASMR framework)	Germany (early benefit assessment system)
Exceptional added clinical benefit (ASMR I)	Major added benefit
Significant added clinical benefit (ASMR II)	Medium added benefit
Moderate added clinical benefit (ASMR III)	Moderate added benefit
Low added clinical benefit (ASMR IV)	Unquantifiable added benefit
No added clinical benefit (ASMR V)	No added benefit

FIGURE 21.3 Value category denominations in France and Germany.

logic of regulatory authorities. In this paradigm, sources of added clinical benefit are in the focus of HTA. The new technology, most commonly a new medicine, is compared in a structured, rigorous way to an already available comparator with special regard to clinical benefit. The comparator is usually the most widely used (gold standard) technology in any given country—for medicines, it can be another medicine, but if no other medicine is available, then it can be any other health technology (surgical procedure, radiotherapy, etc.) or even palliative care. Added clinical benefit should normally come from higher efficacy, but more favorable side effect (adverse event) profiles, convenience of use for patients (e.g., easier or less frequent administration), impact on patient adherence, and evidence about real-world effectiveness may also be considered. Countries using comparative assessment differ in the type of evidence they require to accept new technologies.

Systems of comparative assessment usually apply standard categories of added clinical benefit. Based on the assessment performed, they may categorize new technologies as having "exceptional," "significant," "minor," or "no" added clinical benefit. Exact denominations and definitions of such "value categories" differ from system to system (Fig. 21.3). Formal scoring systems are uncommon. Rather, the value category of a medicinal product is established through collective expert judgment. Some comparative benefit assessment systems have established formal scientific committees for value category designation (e.g., Transparency Commission in France, Technical-Scientific Commission in Italy). These committees usually consist of clinical scientists and pharmacologists and use deliberative processes and techniques to reach their conclusions. These can be recommendations toward policy-makers and payers as well as formal decisions.

The economic viewpoint is included typically indirectly in comparative assessment systems; the added clinical benefit of a new technology (as expressed in the value category) will determine the eligibility of the new technology for public funding ("reimbursability") as well as its maximum allowable price. For example, for new medicines which are granted a designation of exceptional added clinical benefit in France, the marketing authorization owner can claim a reasonable price premium over already funded medicines. On the other hand, medicines with minor or no added clinical benefit must be priced at par with, or even at discount to, already available medicines. Budget impact considerations are usually not part of HTA in such systems—rather they are a part of pricing and reimbursement negotiations between payers and technology owners.

Comparative assessment has the potential to deliver appraisals and recommendations for being more intelligible and relevant for policy-makers and payers than economic evaluation reports. Clinical benefit is explicitly assessed; assessment criteria and the deliberative assessment method can be customized to local health system characteristics. As opposed to these advantages, possible shortcomings can be insufficient standardization and transparency in the application of value assessment criteria and the exclusion of cost-effectiveness aspects of HTA.

Comparative assessment is applied in some major European pharmaceutical markets such as France, Italy, and Germany. Japan, too, has traditionally used an assessment logic similar to the comparative assessment but is currently underway to incorporate economic considerations more emphatically, as France included of cost-effectiveness analysis for selected products.

Multidimensional Value Assessment Approaches

Multidimensional value assessment approaches do not constitute a homogeneous category of HTA methods. Rather, they comprise a set of different techniques which have in common that they acknowledge and assess different dimensions of value for new technologies. Typically, economic and clinical sources of value are considered, but it is also common for multidimensional HTA systems to ponder societal and ethical considerations.

Regarding practical applications, Canada, Sweden, Australia, and the Netherlands all have formal HTA systems which show some elements of "multidimensionality," at least for medicines. The Canadian framework operated by the Canadian Agency for Drugs and Technologies in Health shows a high degree of integration of clinical and economic considerations.

1. Added clinical benefit	Criteria which relate to the performance of a new medicine in its requested indication* along main possible sources of clinical benefit (e.g. efficacy, safety, convenience, adherence, real-world effectiveness etc.)
2. International funding and assessment references	Criteria which relate to 1) relevant health technology appraisals in the requested indication in reference international pharmaceutical markets (both economic evaluation and comparative assessment) and 2) international reimbursement / public funding references.in the requested indication
3. Health policy alignment	Selected criteria which describe how much the new medicine in its requested indication supports the implementation of national (and eventually regional) health policy priorities
4. Social and ethical considerations	Selected social and ethical considerations the new medicine is able to address in the country
5. Budget impact	Net reimbursement outflow that the new medicine is expected to generate in its requested indication in various stages of its adoption (budget impact mitigation effects through managed entry agreements are taken into consideration)

* requested indication = indication in which the manufacturer requests reimbursement / public funding for the medicine

FIGURE 21.4 Example of value dimensions in a pragmatic value assessment system.[21]

In Sweden, societal and ethical considerations are formally incorporated into the HTA framework alongside cost-effectiveness and BIA. In Australia, economic evaluation is dominant, but the HTA system operated by the Pharmaceutical Benefits Advisory Committee allows for "rules of rescue" whereby non-cost-effective products can also be included in the national reimbursement formulary. In the Netherlands, therapeutic benefit, cost-effectiveness analysis, and BIA are all parts of a HTA system, and products must meet the combined requirements to be eligible for reimbursement.

MCDA has recently been adapted as a scientific approach to multidimensional value assessment.[20] MCDA is a set of techniques which apply several assessment criteria with different weights elicited from experts through collective brainstorming or decision-making techniques. Although the MCDA process itself can be reasonably standard, it can be resource-consuming and is better suited for individual decision problems than for continuous pricing and reimbursement decisions. As an alternative, pragmatic value assessment models such as balanced assessment systems[21] (Fig. 21.4) propose standard value dimensions (e.g., added clinical benefit, health policy alignment, social and ethical considerations, affordability, etc.) with customizable sets of decision-making criteria and weights (scores) to facilitate funding and purchasing decisions. These often focus on healthcare systems where there are few capabilities or resources for the deployment of extensive HTA systems. Related to this, resource-intensive quantitative analyses may be substituted through referencing to previous international assessments with the consideration of adoption feasibility. Such pragmatic approaches are best suited to help ranking and prioritization decisions based on multiple policy-relevant criteria. Among practical HTA applications, Taiwan is sometimes mentioned as a resource-conscious, "affordable" system in which comparative effectiveness, budget impact, and cost-effectiveness considerations are analyzed.[22]

OBJECTIVE 21.3. DESCRIBE A HIGH-LEVEL HEALTH TECHNOLOGY ASSESSMENT PROCESS

In any country using HTA, assessment follows a process which can be very precisely defined (like in the United Kingdom, Germany, or Sweden) or less precisely regulated (as in several upper middle-income countries across Central Europe or Latin America using elements of HTA). Fig. 21.5 shows an example for a structured HTA process (embedded into the wider pricing and reimbursement process) for new technologies seeking public funding. It commences with the submission of a dossier by the technology owner followed by technical assessment, then possible consultations (public hearings) with stakeholders, then formal appraisal, then pricing and reimbursement negotiations, and the final decision. It must be noted that such a process can be established in very different organizational setups (i.e., different allocation competences between participating stakeholders and responsible bodies).

A key principle in the HTA process is the separation of the assessment and appraisal.[23] *Assessment* is a technical activity carried out by specialized experts that comprises of the review of the technology owner's submission and the available evidence. The output of the assessment phase is usually an HTA report, which is sent to those participating in the *appraisal* phase. Appraisal is the analysis and consideration of the results of technical assessment, eventually together with other decision-relevant aspects or circumstances which are not covered by the assessment phase. The appraisal phase is often executed by a specialized committee and may conclude with a formal recommendation to the pricing and

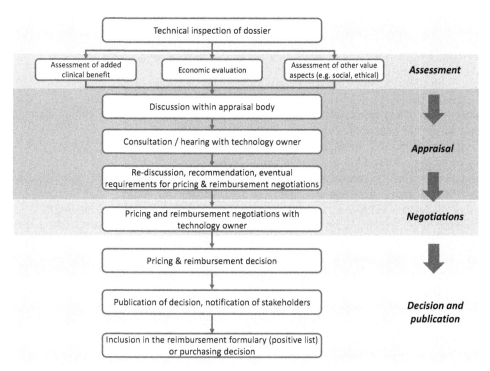

FIGURE 21.5 Example of health technology assessment process for new health technologies seeking public funding in a system applying multidimensional assessment and negotiations with technology owners.

reimbursement decision-making body which then conducts pricing and reimbursement negotiations with the technology owner. Less typically, appraisals can be linked to a formal binding decision which is not followed by any further negotiations. Assessment, appraisal, recommendation, and decision competences are organized in different forms across various healthcare systems.

As mentioned above, the HTA process flows directly into the pricing and reimbursement negotiation process in several healthcare systems. In systems using comparative benefit assessment, appraisal usually takes the form of a value category designation and subsequent pricing and reimbursement negotiations are determined and guided by this. In many countries (e.g., Belgium, Italy, Poland, Hungary), pricing negotiations are geared toward *managed entry agreements* (MEAs) which are contracts between payers and technology owners which contain cost-sharing or risk-sharing elements. Through MEAs payers can attain net prices which are lower than list prices in a confidential way, whereas technology owners can protect their products against international reference pricing mechanisms and parallel exports from systems with low prices to systems with higher prices.

OBJECTIVE 21.4. EXPLAIN HEALTH TECHNOLOGY ASSESSMENT SYSTEM DESIGN IN CURRENT PRACTICE

Although the academic literature of HTA is multidisciplinary and multifaceted, the choice and design of HTA systems has traditionally been a technocratic activity in which HTA systems are designed based on HTA guidelines and best practice recommendations. In this design approach, international best practice is structured, generalized, and codified in a way which gives guidance to designers of HTA systems on what newly implemented systems should look like.[24] This traditional design approach, however, is not without possible risks or drawbacks. As it does not adequately consider the specific local institutional requirements of individual healthcare systems, cultural and political fit may be limited. Furthermore, as best practice recommendations are overwhelmingly based on practices of developed healthcare systems, they may result in resource-intensive implementations in smaller or emerging systems which will not be sustainable for the lack of expertise, available healthcare data, or sufficient funding.

These risks may push a different, institutional design approach into the forefront. From this "institutional" approach, HTA systems can be designed in a rational and structured way which proceeds from context assessment though model design to process design. A high-level overview of this process is shown in Fig. 21.6.

FIGURE 21.6   Health technology assessment design process from an institutional approach.

1. The process starts with context assessment. In this phase, variables of the institutional environment are identified and described. Some of the most commonly analyzed attributes are as follows:
   a. Policy objectives to be fulfilled by the introduction of HTA
   b. Availability of human resources for assessment and appraisal
   c. Level of health economics expertise available (e.g., preexisting knowledge, knowledge of international HTA models)
   d. Availability of health data (e.g., scope and quality of data available for HTA)
   e. Availability of funding for HTA (e.g., amount of annual funding, sustainability of funding)
   f. HTA governance (e.g., existing legal frameworks, level of centralization, political and policy requirements, decision-making styles)
   g. Institutional robustness (e.g., intensity of political cycles, influence from different stakeholders)
   Ideally, the first phase concludes with a comprehensive and dynamic description of the institutional environment in the form of a status report.
2. The second (system architecture) phase addresses high-level conceptual design questions. It includes the choice of the HTA paradigm (economic evaluation, comparative benefit assessment, some multidimensional HTA approach), the perspective of assessment, the timing of assessment (pricing and listing decisions only or also price and reimbursement reviews), principles of HTA governance, technology scope (e.g., pharmaceuticals or broader scope), and eventual data transferability principles.
3. The third (framework design) phase covers a range of delicate technical design decisions. Assessment criteria must be selected, definitions and metrics must be specified, and eventually scores and the weights need to be defined (in systems using multiple criteria). These decision rules will govern if a new technology can be admitted into public funding without conditions or only with certain conditions or it will not be admitted into public funding at all.
4. In the fourth phase, the HTA process is to be designed properly. Milestones and responsibilities as well as the tasks of participating stakeholders must be defined. Internal and external assessment reports must be developed and publicly available information about the HTA process and its outputs (reports, recommendations) must be delineated. In addition, IT systems supporting HTA assessment must be outlined.

CONCLUSION

HTA has become a core system to assist healthcare decision-making under resource constraints in many countries around the world. As mentioned above, a lot of systems have been or are currently deployed in middle-income and emerging healthcare systems, often reflecting on the practices in the United Kingdom, Canada, and Australia. Regardless of the exact architecture that an HTA system takes in any given healthcare system, it is essential that HTA implementation itself should be regarded as a health policy intervention. As such its benefits for policy-makers, payers, and the wider society should exceed the direct and indirect costs that are incurred through its design and implementation. This means that HTA should be cost-effective itself. From a payer perspective, cost-effectiveness of HTA means that the payer benefit (higher quality of decisions) from the increased quality of information should exceed the cost of producing that information. From a societal perspective, health outcomes from improved system efficiency (and possibly higher transparency) through HTA should exceed the direct and indirect costs of HTA. This "*HTA cost-effectiveness requirement*" can be implemented through various system architectures with various scopes and focuses. It is imperative, however, that the chosen architecture should be in line with the determining elements of the local institutional environment.

PRACTICE QUESTIONS

1. Ideally, HTA shall include
   A. Some form of economic assessment
   B. Some form of clinical assessment
   C. Both A and B
   D. Neither A nor B

2. Which of the following assessments is commonly included in HTA but not part of regulatory assessment?
   A. Quality
   B. Safety and efficacy
   C. Cost-effectiveness
   D. Analysis of manufacturing costs
3. What are the most common assessment dimensions in economic evaluation?
   A. Some form of economic assessment
   B. Some form of clinical assessment
   C. Both A and B
   D. Neither A nor B
4. In economic evaluation, which of the following would be considered indirect healthcare costs?
   A. Cost of medication
   B. Costs of administering a medication (i.e., day hospital)
   C. Cost of diagnostics accompanying a medicinal treatment (i.e., blood tests, medical imaging)
   D. Home care and community care payments
5. Which of the following is NOT a source of added clinical benefit in comparative assessment?
   A. New mechanism of action without higher efficacy
   B. More favorable side effect profile
   C. Higher efficacy on the primary endpoint
   D. Easier administration, which does not require hospitalization
6. Which of the following countries embed formalized economic evaluation into a broader HTA framework?
   A. Canada, Sweden, Italy, Spain
   B. Canada, Netherlands, Sweden, Australia
   C. Sweden, Netherlands, United Kingdom
   D. South Korea, Brazil
7. In which phase of the HTA process are "specialized committees" common?
   A. Assessment
   B. Appraisal
   C. Both A and B
   D. Neither A nor B
8. Which of the following should be included in the analysis of the institutional environment of HTA?
   A. Policy objectives to be fulfilled by the introduction of HTA
   B. Availability of funding for HTA
   C. Existing legal frameworks
   D. All of the above
9. In which phase of HTA system design should policy-makers define the scope of technologies that will be subject to HTA?
   A. Context assessment
   B. System architecture
   C. Framework design
   D. Process design

REFERENCES

1. *Swiss Network for Health Technology Assessment*. Berne, Switzerland: SNTH; 2017. Available from: http://www.snhta.ch/.
2. HTAi. *HTAi Consumer and Patient Glossary*. Edmonton, AB: Health Technology Assessment International; 2009. http://www.htai.org/fileadmin/HTAi_Files/ISG/PatientInvolvement/Glossary/HTAiPatientAndConsumerGlossaryOctober2009_01.pdf.
3. Garrido MV, Kristensen FB, Nielsen CP, Busse R. *Health Technology Assessment and Health Policy-Making in Europe*. Copenhagen: WHO; 2008. http://apps.who.int/medicinedocs/en/m/abstract/Js22172en/.
4. Rawlins MD. Crossing the fourth hurdle. *Br J Clin Pharmacol*. June 2012;73(6):855–860.
5. Henshall C, Mardhani-Bayne L, Frønsdal KB, Klemp M. Interactions between HTA, coverage and regulatory processes: emerging issues, goals and opportunities. *Int J Technol Assess Health Care*. 2011;27:253–260.
6. Wonder M, Backhouse ME, Hornby E. Early scientific advice obtained simultaneously from regulators and payers: findings from a pilot study in Australia. *Value Health*. 2013 Sep-Oct;16(6):1067–1073.

7. Richardson JRJ. Supplier-induced demand. *Appl Health Econ Health Policy*. June 2006;5(2):87−98.

8. Banta D, Andreasen PB. The political dimension in health care technology assessment programs. *Int J Technol Assess Health Care*. 1990;6(1):115−123.

9. Oortwijn W. *From Theory to Action: Developments in Value Frameworks to Inform the Allocation of Health Care Resources*. Edmonton, AB: HTAi Policy Forum; 2017. Available from: http://www.htai.org/index.php?eID=tx_nawsecuredl&u=0&g=0&t=1494651646&hash=cee7ed281487daaf3 6f332f416cfbe19ae457293&file=fileadmin/HTAi_Files/Policy_Forum/HTAi_Policy_Forum_2017_Background_Paper.pdf.

10. Dankó D. Health technology assessment in middle-income countries: recommendations for a balanced assessment system. *J Mark Access Health Policy*. 2014;2(1):1−10.

11. Edejer TT, ed. *Making Choices in Health − The WHO Guide to Cost-Effectiveness Analysis*. Geneva: WHO; 2003.

12. Mauskopf JA, Sullivan SD, Annemans L, et al. Principles of good practice for budget impact analysis: report of the ISPOR task force on good research practices—budget impact analysis. *Value Health*. September−October 2007;10(5):336−347.

13. Jönsson B. Ten arguments for a societal perspective in the economic evaluation of medical innovations. *Eur J Health Econ*. 2009;10:357−359.

14. Briggs A, Sculpher M, Claxton K. *Decision Modeling for Health Economic Evaluation*. Oxford: Oxford UP; 2006.

15. Barton P, Bryan S, Robinson S. Modelling in the economic evaluation of health care: selecting the appropriate approach. *J Health Serv Res Policy*. 2004;9(2):110−118.

16. Ademi Z, Kim H, Zomer E, Reid CM, Hollingsworth B, Liew D. Overview of pharmacoeconomic modelling methods. *Br J Clin Pharmacol*. April 2013;75(4):944−950.

17. Rochaix L. *Incorporating Cost-Effectiveness Analysis Into Comparative-Effectiveness Research: The French Experience*. Bethesda, MD: Health Affairs Blog; 2015. Available from: http://healthaffairs.org/blog/2015/04/03/incorporating-cost-effectiveness-analysis-into-comparative-effectiveness-research-the-french-experience-2/.

18. Sox HC. Defining comparative effectiveness research: the importance of getting it right. *Med Care*. June 2010;48(6 Suppl.):S7−S8.

19. Tunis SR, Benner J, McClellan M. Comparative effectiveness research: policy context, methods development and research infrastructure. *Stat Med*. August 2010;29(19):1963−1976.

20. Marsh K, IJzerman M, Thokala P, et al. ISPOR task force. Multiple criteria decision analysis for health care decision making—emerging good practices: report 2 of the ISPOR MCDA emerging good practices task force. *Value Health*. March−April 2016;19(2):125−137.

21. Dankó D, Molnár MP. Balanced assessment systems revisited. *J Mark Access Health Policy*. 2017;5(1):1355190.

22. Chiu WT, Pwu RF, Gau CS. Affordable health technology assessment in Taiwan: a model for middle-income countries. *J Formos Med Assoc*. June 2015;114(6):481−483.

23. Walley T. Health technology assessment in England: assessment and appraisal. *Med J Aust*. 2007;187(5):283−285.

24. Drummond M, Schwartz JS, Jönsson B, et al. Key principles for the improved conduct of health technology assessments for resource allocation decisions. *Int J Technol Assess Health Care*. 2008;24(3):244−258.

ANSWERS TO PRACTICE QUESTIONS

1. C
2. C
3. C
4. D
5. A
6. B
7. B
8. D
9. B

Chapter 22

NICE Guidance and Health Technology Assessment

Leeza Osipenko and Elangovan Gajraj

NICE Scientific Advice, NICE, London, United Kingdom

Learning Objectives:

Objective 22.1 Overview of National Institute for Health and Care Excellence (NICE) guidance development and evidence-based medicine.

Objective 22.2 Explain the purpose, production, and principles of technology appraisal guidance.

Objective 22.3 Detail the NICE technology appraisals process and decision-making.

OBJECTIVE 22.1. OVERVIEW OF NATIONAL INSTITUTE FOR HEALTH AND CARE EXCELLENCE GUIDANCE DEVELOPMENT AND EVIDENCE-BASED PRACTICE

National Institute for Health and Care Excellence (NICE) is a world-renowned organisation and its guidance and guidance production processes are held in high regard internationally.[1] NICE was originally set up in 1999 as the National Institute for Clinical Excellence to reduce variation in the availability and quality of National Health Service (NHS) treatments and care in England. This was primarily achieved through the appraisal of individual health technologies and the development of clinical guidelines. In 2005, after merging with the Health Development Agency, NICE began to develop public health guidance to help prevent ill health and promote healthy lifestyles. In 2013, NICE took on responsibility for developing guidance and quality standards in social care.

NICE is accountable to the Department of Health (the governmental department responsible for health), but operationally the Institute is independent of government. Independent committees are responsible for the development of key NICE guidance and recommendations. Before the establishment of NICE, though mainly at the margins, health authorities and the General Practice fundholders made differing purchasing decisions for healthcare. This resulted in variation in access to certain treatments for patients based on their healthcare provider catchment area—the so-called "postcode lottery." Over time NICE's recommendations have, to a great extent, resolved this problem. The establishment of NICE has also led to the faster uptake of innovative products, not just by the leading treatment centers but nationally.

Evidence-based medicine (EBM) was adopted in the NHS for many years and guided clinical decision-making long before the establishment of NICE. A widely accepted definition states "EBM is the conscientious, explicit and judicious use of current best practice in making decisions about the care of individual patients."[2] The practice of EBM involves integrating individual clinical expertise with the most up-to-date and relevant available clinical evidence from systematic research. In addition, patients should be involved in decisions about their care.

> The National Institute for Health and Care Excellence (NICE) provides national guidance and advice in England to improve health and social care.

Another challenge today is that, with the growth of online resources, healthcare professionals and patients are overloaded with information from many different sources. It is impossible to stay abreast of publications and innovations even in a narrow field. From the information that health professionals actually consider, they need to ensure that it is appropriate and of high quality. Specific research findings may not always be the best source of evidence to inform a particular clinical decision, and there are many areas of medicine where research has not been carried out or is sparse. In addition, trial reporting transparency remains suboptimal despite great advances made in this field over the recent years.[3] NICE helps tackle this problem via NICE Evidence Services that enable access to authoritative clinical and nonclinical evidence and best practice to help professionals from across the NHS, public health and social care sectors make better decisions. The service also works directly with professionals and practitioners to identify evidence and to support the uptake and use of evidence to improve practice and care for people using services. Worldwide, there are many initiatives and organizations helping systematize and organize existing and emerging clinical knowledge (Cochrane,[4] registries, disease- and drug-specific databases, etc.).

> NICE evidence summaries of new medicines Quality-assured summaries of the best available evidence for new medicines, or existing medicines with new indications or a new formulation. They help commissioners, budget holders and groups such as Area Prescribing Committees make informed decisions and aid local planning on the introduction of key new medicines.

> NICE evidence summaries of unlicensed and off-label medicines Quality-assured summaries of the best available evidence for selected unlicensed and off-label medicines. They allow evidence-based prioritisation, treatment and funding decisions to be made in cases where there are no clinically appropriate licensed alternatives.

NICE is an advisory body to the NHS. This means that NICE guidance is not mandatory, but recommendatory in nature. However, for decisions made by the technology appraisal (TA) committees on pharmaceuticals and selected medical devices, a positive recommendation is subject to mandatory funding by the NHS. The NHS Constitution states that patients have the right to drugs and treatments that have been recommended by NICE for use in the NHS, if their doctor believes they are clinically appropriate. Thus, medical professionals are advised to follow NICE guidance but make decisions regarding the treatment of each patient according to patient's condition (e.g., existing comorbidities, fitness level, ability to tolerate treatments), ongoing treatments, unmet need, and best clinical judgment in each given situation.

NICE Guidance

NICE produces six types of guidance which represent evidence-based recommendations:

- guidelines covering clinical topics, medicines practice, public health and social care
- diagnostics guidance
- highly specialized technology guidance
- interventional procedures guidance
- medical technologies guidance
- technology appraisals guidance

All guidance is developed by independent Committees. Draft guidance or interim documents (such as the scope) are consulted on. The consultation process includes registered stakeholders such as competitor companies, professional bodies (e.g., Association of British Pharmaceutical Industries (ABPI), Royal Colleges), patients and patient organizations, clinicians and members of the public (who can register to participate in the consultation process). NICE may also publish a range of supporting documents for each piece of guidance, including advice on how to put the guidance into practice, and on its costs and the evidence it is based on. Tools to support the local implementation of guidance include costing tools or statements and clinical audit tools.

In addition to guidance, NICE also produces quality standards which are a set of specific, concise statements and associated measures. They set out aspirational, but achievable, markers of high-quality, cost-effective patient care, covering the treatment and prevention of different diseases and conditions. Quality standards are based on guidance and advice from NICE and other organizations using NICE-accredited processes.[5] Quality standards help clinicians and organizations improve the quality of care they provide or commission.

Guidance production at NICE follows specific transparent processes and principles. Each guidance program has methods and process guide which can be found on the NICE website.[6] All information relating to the production of guidance (besides commercially sensitive data) is published on the NICE website. NICE committee meetings are being held in public and anyone can register to attend them. All NICE guidance is subject to a review process either at a set time (e.g., every 3 years) or when new evidence emerges (this can be identified by the Institute or notified by any stakeholder). NICE decisions can be appealed. Scientific rigor underpins all guidance production programs, and Committees are presented with the best available systematically identified evidence, which is reviewed by independent academic assessors. Finally, all decision-making at NICE is underpinned by the principles of equality and diversity. NICE's equality scheme describes how the Institute meets these commitments and obligations.[7] The Appraisal Committees also take into account the Institute's guidance on social value judgments described in the Institute's document, "Social value judgments: principles for the development of NICE guidance."[8]

OBJECTIVE 22.2. EXPLAIN THE PURPOSE, PRODUCTION, AND PRINCIPLES OF TECHNOLOGY APPRAISAL GUIDANCE

Technology Appraisals (TAs)

TAs at NICE assess the clinical and cost-effectiveness of health technologies. This is a rigorous process facilitating the decision on the adoption of innovative healthcare technologies into NHS clinical practice. TA recommendations can be issued on

- medicines
- medical devices
- diagnostic techniques
- surgical procedures
- health promotion activities.

The underlying methodology for TA is rooted in the principles of health technology assessment (HTA), which is an independent research about the effectiveness, costs, and broader impact of healthcare (treatments and tests). The reimbursement decision at NICE is informed by cost-utility analysis, with quality-adjusted life years (QALYs), used to measure the benefits of healthcare technologies, which is a key methodological feature of the NICE appraisals.

By combining improvements in survival and quality of life (QoL), QALYs are a uniform unit of benefits, providing a measure that can be used across all types of health interventions—whether a new diagnostic, medicine, surgical, or psychological treatment. The use of QALYs allows the comparison of the value of one treatment against another, leading to consistent decision-making across interventions and disease areas. New interventions are compared to established care, which is standard therapy currently available in the NHS in the given condition. Established care represents the comparator. To estimate QALYs gained with an intervention, it is essential to collect data on QoL and duration of life for patients in the intervention group and in the comparator group. QoL is a number between 0 and 1, called utility, with 1 representing perfect health and 0 representing death (though health states worse than death are possible). There are many generic QoL instruments (e.g., SF-36, SF-D6, EQ-5D, HUI2, HUI3) that measure utilities and many more disease-specific QoL instruments. NICE's preferred instrument is the EQ-5D, which is a standardized five-dimensional instrument. It is completed by the person (or a carer) having a treatment and is easy to use.

> **Cost-utility analysis** - one of the tools used to carry out an economic evaluation. The benefits are assessed in terms of both quality and duration of life, and expressed as quality-adjusted life years (QALYs)

> **Quality-adjusted life year (QALYs)** is a measure of the state of health of a person or group in which the benefits, in terms of length of life, are adjusted to reflect the quality of life. One QALY is equal to 1 year of life in perfect health. QALYs are calculated by estimating the years of life remaining for a patient following a particular treatment or intervention and weighting each year with a quality-of-life score (on a 0 to 1 scale). It is often measured in terms of the person's ability to carry out the activities of daily life, and freedom from pain and mental disturbance.

The cost-effectiveness of a new intervention is established by calculating the incremental QALYs associated with its use, compared with established practice, and the incremental costs. This allows the determination of the incremental cost-effectiveness ratio (ICER), which is the ratio of the difference in costs to the difference in QALYs. The ICER is a cost per QALY, and intuitively it can be understood that an intervention associated with a lower ICER (lower cost per QALY) is to be preferred to one with a higher ICER (greater cost per QALY). However, the appraisal of an individual healthcare technology is not a comparison with other available new technologies. Rather the cost-effectiveness (or ICER) of the technology is compared with a threshold.

The reason that decision-makers are faced with such difficult choices is because NHS in England operates within a fixed budget determined by parliament. The fixed budget necessitates that when a new treatment is recommended, the availability of some currently accessible therapy within the health system has to be withdrawn to fund it.

The concept of the opportunity cost underpins the idea of cost-utility analysis-based decision-making. The opportunity cost of an intervention means that investing in it displaces other treatments, diagnostics, or healthcare interventions somewhere within the system. As long as the cost-effectiveness of the treatment being displaced is worse (higher ICER) compared with what is being adopted, more health (as measured by QALYs) is being gained than what is being foregone, and the system is made more efficient, that is, more QALYs are generated for the same spend.

In actual fact, it is not possible to determine what treatments are, or should be displaced, by the adoption of a new technology. Therefore, NICE uses a threshold of £20,000 to £30,000 per QALY, to decide on whether a new technology is value for money. The threshold represents the cost-effectiveness of the interventions being displaced by the new technology and, in a rational system, should also represent the cost-effectiveness of the least cost-effective treatment currently available in the health system. The threshold, therefore, relates to the opportunity costs, in terms of health, of what is being displaced within the health system, given that it operates within a fixed budget. The threshold is not the willingness to pay for a QALY or the worth of a year of good health.

Methods

TAs, as with many other evaluations at NICE, are based on the PICO (population, intervention, comparator, and outcome) framework. It is a structured approach for developing review questions that divides each question into four components: the population (the population being studied); the interventions (what is being done); the comparators (other main treatment options in established clinical practice); and the outcomes (measures of how effective the interventions have been). The technology being appraised is listed in the scope of an appraisal under 'intervention'. NICE can only make recommendations about the intervention being appraised. A comparator technology is one that is currently used in the NHS and could be replaced by the intervention, if recommended. NICE cannot issue guidance or make recommendations about comparator technologies (unless also listed as an intervention in a multiple technology appraisal [MTA]).

NICE has defined a "reference case" that specifies the elements of HTA and methods considered, by the Institute, to be appropriate for the Appraisal Committee's purpose, and consistent with the objective of maximizing health gain from limited resources.[9] Submissions to the Institute should include an analysis generated using the reference case methods. This does not preclude additional analyses being presented, where one or more aspects of methodology differ from the reference case. However, these must be justified and clearly distinguished from the reference case analysis. Technology Appraisal Committees base their recommendations on a review of clinical and economic evidence. Clinical evidence shows how well the medicine or treatment works. Economic evidence shows how well the medicine or treatment works in relation to how much it costs the NHS—does it represent value for money? The perspective for evaluation of healthcare technologies at NICE is that of the NHS and PSS (Personal Social Services) for costs. This means that the submission should include only resource use and costs associated with the use of the intervention and comparator which are borne by the NHS and PSS and not, for example, by the society or patients themselves. The perspective on outcomes is all direct health effects, whether for patients or, when relevant, carers.

Economic evaluation requires setting a time horizon, which is the period over which the main differences between interventions in benefits and the use of resources in health and social care are expected to be experienced. In most instances, a lifetime horizon (modeling all patients to death) is adopted, which means that the assumptions on the long-term clinical effectiveness of intervention and other parameters are required. This also increases uncertainty for the decision-makers.

Types of Appraisals and Processes

The decision on which process will be used to appraise a technology is made during the topic selection. TA process at NICE has different formats:

- STA - a single technology appraisal which covers one technology for one indication.
- MTA - a multiple technology appraisal, which covers more than one technology for a single indication or one technology for more than one indication (under 10% of all appraisals).[10]
- FTA - a fast-track appraisal, which is a faster version of an STA for highly cost-effective new treatment. This process was launched on April 1, 2017.[11]

The STA process is specifically designed to appraise a single product, device, or other technology for a single indication. The process normally covers new technologies (typically, new pharmaceutical products or newly licensed indications) and enables NICE to produce guidance soon after the technology is introduced in the United Kingdom. NICE seeks relevant evidence from several sources. The company submits the principal evidence. Consultees provide information and selected clinical experts, NHS commissioning experts, and patient experts also give evidence. The Evidence Review Group (ERG), an external academic organization independent of NICE, produces a review of the submitted evidence.

The MTA process is designed to appraise single or multiple products, devices, or other technologies with one or more related indications. NICE seeks relevant evidence from several sources. An independent academic group, the Assessment Group, carries out a systematic review of the evidence and economic analysis. Consultees provide information and selected clinical experts, NHS commissioning experts, and patient experts also give evidence. An overview of the TA development process is presented in Fig. 22.1. The range of participants in a NICE TA process is presented in Fig. 22.2.

The Highly Specialised Technologies (HST) program only considers drugs for very rare conditions (most orphan products, as classified by regulators, are assessed via the TA program at NICE). The methods for the HST program vary from TAs in some instances and can be reviewed on the NICE website.[12]

The majority of topics for the HST program are identified by the National Institute for Health Research Innovation Observatory. They aim to notify the Department of Health of key, new, and emerging healthcare technologies that might need to be referred to NICE against the following time frames:

- new drugs, in development, at 20 months to marketing authorization
- new indications, at 15 months to marketing authorization.

A single HST evaluation can only cover a single technology for a single indication. Cost-utility analysis is required for an HST committee to make a decision.

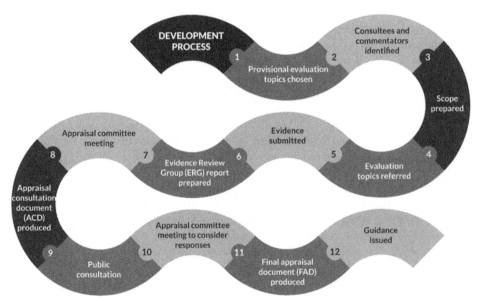

FIGURE 22.1   Overview of NICE technology appraisal development process.

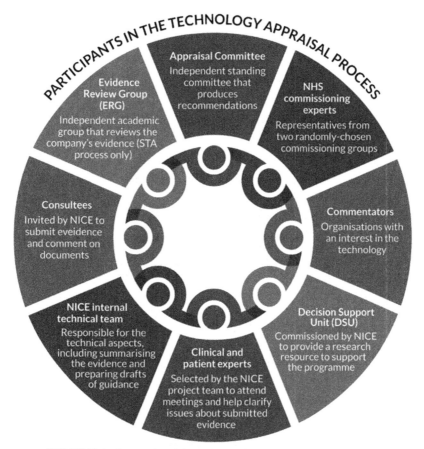

FIGURE 22.2   Range of participants in a NICE technology appraisal process.

OBJECTIVE 22.3. DETAIL THE NICE TECHNOLOGY APPRAISAL COMMITTEE PROCESS AND DECISION-MAKING

Members of a NICE TA Committee are appointed for a 3-year term and are drawn from

- the NHS
- patient and carer organizations
- academia
- pharmaceutical and medical devices industries

The Appraisal Committee considers the evidence and makes a judgment on whether or not the technology should be recommended as a clinically effective and cost-effective use of NHS resources or whether it should only be recommended for specific subgroups of people. The Appraisal Committee submits its recommendations to NICE in either an appraisal consultation document (ACD) or a final appraisal determination (FAD). The Appraisal Committee produces an ACD only if its preliminary recommendations are substantially more restrictive than the terms of the marketing authorization (or equivalent, for example, CE marking for devices) of the technology being appraised or do not recommend the use of the technology. If the Committee produces an ACD, then NICE invites consultees, commentators, and the public to comment on the ACD. After considering these comments, the Committee finalizes its recommendations and submits them to NICE in the form of a FAD. The FAD forms the basis of the guidance that NICE issues to the NHS in England.

The estimation of cost-effectiveness (based on an ICER) is not the only criterion for decision-making, and qualitative criteria such as unmet medical need, patient and clinician's testimony, equity principles, social value judgments are used in deliberations to arrive at the final decision. Below a most plausible ICER of £20,000 per QALY gained, the decision to recommend the use of a technology is normally based on the cost-effectiveness estimate. Above a most plausible ICER of

£20,000 per QALY gained, judgments about the acceptability of the technology as an effective use of NHS resources will specifically take account of the following factors:

- The degree of certainty around the ICER
- Whether there are strong reasons to indicate that the assessment of the change in health-related QoL has been inadequately captured
- The innovative nature of the technology
- The technology meets the criteria for special consideration as a "life-extending treatment at the end-of-life"
- Aspects that relate to nonhealth objectives of the NHS

Above a most plausible ICER of £30,000 per QALY gained, the Committee will need to identify an increasingly stronger case for supporting the technology as an effective use of NHS resources, with regard to the factors listed above. In some situations, at the end-of-life, the Committee can accept a higher ICER of up to £50,000/QALY. For interventions evaluated via the HST program, a higher threshold of £100,000–£300,000/QALY is considered, depending on the QALY gain associated with the intervention.

TA decisions may contain more than one recommendation. NICE classifies its recommendations into five categories:

- Recommended
- Optimized (recommended for only a subgroup of the licensed population)
- Only in research
- Not recommended
- Recommended for use in the CDF (Cancer Drug Fund).[13]

For all NICE appraisals, the Institute acts as a "price taker," with the cost of the health technology determined by the manufacturer. However, where the manufacturer's price results in the intervention not being cost-effective, the manufacturer has the option of offering a pricing agreement designed to improve cost-effectiveness and facilitate patient's access, through a Patient Access Scheme.[14] These discounts are negotiated between the manufacturer and the Department of Health. NICE only ensures that they are operationally viable.

CONCLUSION

NICE issues various types of evidence-based guidance, each of which may be considered specific instances of HTA. Transparent processes have been developed to include various stakeholders, who have defined roles and responsibilities. Cost-effectiveness is estimated using consistent methodology according to a reference case. The decisions are made by the independent Committees. The cost per QALY is compared against a threshold, and the Committee takes into account additional qualitative factors. Technologies for very rare disease are evaluated by a separate program, using a higher threshold. A patient access scheme may be proposed by the manufacturer to lower the effective cost of the technology, improve cost-effectiveness, and improve patients' access to innovative therapies.

REFERENCES

1. Timmins Nicholas, Rawlins Michael, Appleby John. *A Terrible Beauty. A Short History of NICE*; 2018. Available at: http://www.idsihealth.org/wp-content/uploads/2016/02/A-TERRIBLE-BEAUTY_resize.pdf.
2. Sackett DL, Rosenberg WMC, Muir Gray JA, et al. Evidence based medicine: what it is and what it isn't. *BMJ*. 1996;312:71.
3. *Who's Not Sharing Their Trial Results?*; 2018. Available at: https://trialstracker.ebmdatalab.net.
4. *Cochrane*; 2018. http://www.cochrane.org/.
5. *Quality Standards*; 2018. Available at: https://www.nice.org.uk/Glossary?letter=Q#Quality%20standards.
6. *NICE Website*; 2018. https://www.nice.org.uk.
7. *NICE Equality Scheme*; 2018. Available at: https://www.nice.org.uk/about/who-we-are/policies-and-procedures/nice-equality-scheme.
8. Social Value Judgements. *Principles for the Development of NICE Guidance*. 2nd ed. NICE; 2018. Available at: https://www.nice.org.uk/Media/Default/About/what-we-do/Research-and-development/Social-Value-Judgements-principles-for-the-development-of-NICE-guidance.pdf.
9. *Guide to the Methods of Technology Appraisal*. NICE; 2013. Available at: www.nice.org.uk/process/pmg9.
10. *Guide to the Processes of Technology Appraisal*. NICE; September 2014. Available at: www.nice.org.uk/process/pmg19.
11. Process guide addendum. *Fast Track Appraisal*; 2018. Available at: https://www.nice.org.uk/Media/Default/About/what-we-do/NICE-guidance/NICE-technology-appraisals/process-guide-addendum-fast-track.pdf.
12. *Interim Process and Methods of the Highly Specialised Technologies Programme*; 2018. Available at: https://www.nice.org.uk/Media/Default/About/what-we-do/NICE-guidance/NICE-highly-specialised-technologies-guidance/HST-interim-methods-process-guide-may-17.pdf.
13. *Cancer Drugs Fund*; 2018. Available at: https://www.nice.org.uk/about/what-we-do/our-programmes/nice-guidance/nice-technology-appraisal-guidance/cancer-drugs-fund.
14. *Patient Access Schemes*; 2018. Available at: https://www.nice.org.uk/about/what-we-do/patient-access-schemes-liaison-unit.

Section V

Clinical Research

Chapter 23

Clinical Trials

Gunasakaran Sambandan[1] and Adina Turcu-Stiolica[2]

[1]Azidus Laboratories Ltd., Chennai, India; [2]University of Medicine and Pharmacy of Craiova, Craiova, Romania

Learning Objectives:

Objective 23.1 Introduce clinical research methods.
Objective 23.2 Detail methodological aspects in clinical trials.
Objective 23.3 Explain the phases of clinical trials.
Objective 23.4 Discuss the role of pharmacists and newer technologies in clinical research.

OBJECTIVE 23.1. INTRODUCE CLINICAL RESEARCH METHODS

Clinical research involves all research in humans with different study designs. [Clinical means humans and Trials means Experiment][1,2] Clinical research is synonymously used for clinical trials. A clinical trial is any research study that prospectively assigns human participants or groups of humans to one or more health-related interventions to evaluate the effects on predefined health outcomes.[3] As per regulatory requirements, clinical trials are mandatory before drugs are approved and marketed.[4]

First Controlled Clinical Research

There are many records in history for the conduct of studies in humans. In the 18th century (early modern era), one of the first controlled studies was performed by a Scottish physician named James Lind, who is regarded as the "Father of Naval Medicine." Scurvy was considered a dreadful disease among sailors. Sailors with scurvy (gum disease, dry mouth, dry eyes, loss of teeth) were provided with citrus fruits such as oranges and lemons, cider, sulfuric acid, vinegar, salt water and garlic paste, mustard seed, horseradish, balsam of Peru, and gum myrrh. The sailors supplemented with citrus fruits recovered. This was the first controlled study performed across sailors for the treatment of scurvy.[5,6]

Use of Placebo

In the late 19th century, the term placebo was introduced in the field of medicine. In 1863, Austin Flint, a physician, prescribed a placebo (noneffective or fake drug) for his patients with rheumatic fever. The placebo used was a largely diluted tincture of Quassia. He concluded that in more than 90% of patients treated with placebo, there were no significant differences in the results when compared with the ones with active treatment group. Many physicians started with placebo treatment (mint water) for their patients.[5,6]

Use of Randomization

In 1946, 107 patients with acute pulmonary tuberculosis were involved in a clinical trial held in the United Kingdom.[7] As the supply of streptomycin was limited, the patients were randomly selected and assigned to one of the treatment groups. The random selection was indeed blinded to the investigators and coinvestigators.

- Group I—55 patients treated with bed rest plus streptomycin (the active treatment group)
- Group II—52 patients treated with bed rest alone (the control group)

Clinical Pharmacy Education, Practice and Research. https://doi.org/10.1016/B978-0-12-814276-9.00023-4

The observational period for the trial was 6 months. Numbers were randomly assigned to each sex at each center in a closed envelope. The patients on admission were randomized to the groups based on the number on the envelope.[4–6]

In the 20th and 21st centuries, various predetermined randomization techniques for appropriate outcomes are available. In addition, the phases of clinical trials are also developing and may include a larger population for the research purpose of achieving scientific results.

Clinical Research Methods

One of the key objectives of clinical research is to generate health-related information. Randomized clinical trials are considered as the gold standard in generating high-quality medical information, but epidemiologists challenge that clinical trials do not generate real-world data. Studies at real-practice settings with natural bias mimic the results that are normally achieved once a drug is marketed (more realistic outcomes). Pragmatic trials solve this issue by being conducting in real practice settings.[8] The differences of clinical trials and observational studies are compared in Table 23.1, and types of research methods are shown in Figs. 23.1 and 23.2.

TABLE 23.1 Differences Between Clinical Trials and Observational Studies

Clinical Trials	Observational Studies
Experimental	Observational
Data from controlled settings, which is difficult to achieve in real practice	Real-world data are natural confounders
Expensive	Relatively less expensive, retrospective studies are even cheaper than cohort studies
Long duration	Relatively shorter duration when compared to clinical trials
Could be multicentered	Possible in any facility
Mostly sponsored by pharmaceutical companies	Mostly performed by independent agencies, professionals
Populations are covered, but limited in many aspects like pregnant, pediatric, geriatric, etc.	Flexible to perform in different populations
Unethical to study mutagenicity studies	Less ethical concerns as interventions are not required

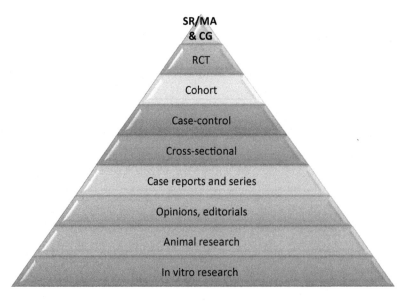

- SR/MA: Systematic review/metaanalysis
- CG: Clinical guidelines
- RCT: Randomized control trial

FIGURE 23.1 Types of research based on quality of evidence generated with higher quality research methods at the top.

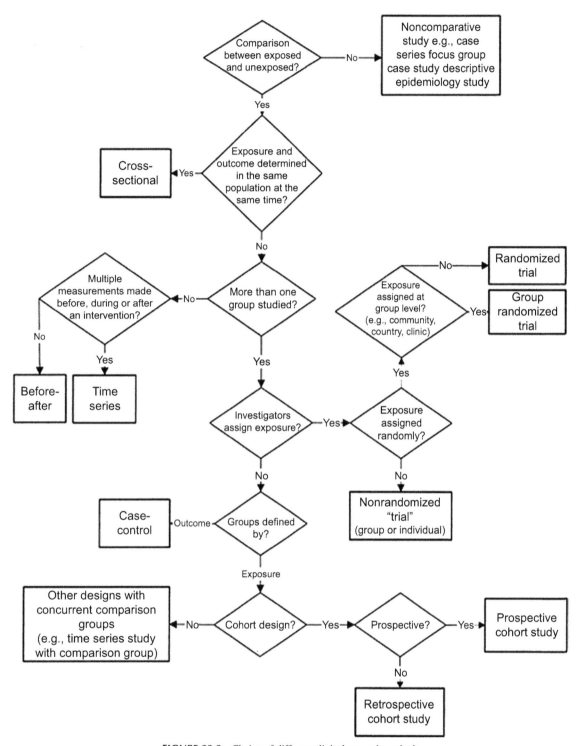

FIGURE 23.2 Choice of different clinical research methods.

OBJECTIVE 23.2. DETAIL METHODOLOGICAL ASPECTS IN CLINICAL TRIALS

Preclinical studies are conducted in lab animals or by other laboratory techniques while clinical trials are conducted in human beings. There are two types of preclinical research: in vitro (the experiment is done in glass or plastic vessels in the laboratory) and in vivo (the experiment is done in the body of a living organism). Preclinical studies are not very large in size but can provide detailed information on dosing and toxicity levels, respecting Good Laboratory Practice by an approved written protocol that clearly indicates the objectives and all methods of how to conduct the study (Fig. 23.3).[15]

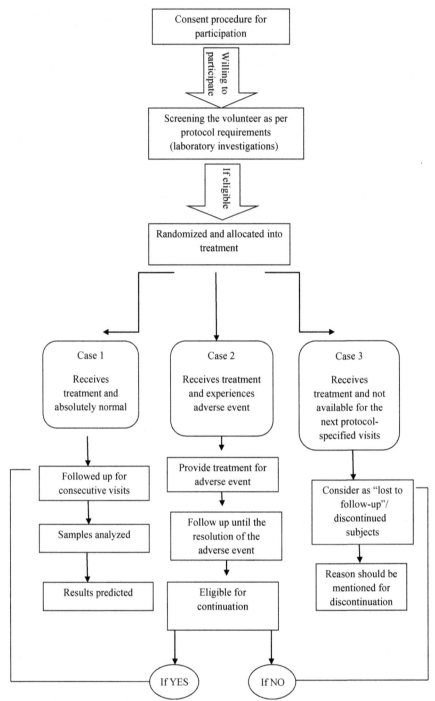

FIGURE 23.3 Clinical trial activity chart.

Randomization

Randomization is used in clinical trials to reduce the possibility of bias. Bias here means the systematic tendency of any aspects of the design, conduct, analysis, and interpretation of the results of clinical trials to estimate a treatment effect deviating from its true value.[7] Therefore, randomized trials are performed to reduce potential bias. Randomization can be generated using various statistical methods. There are various types of randomization: simple randomization, block randomization, stratified randomization, adaptive randomization, and minimization methods are detailed as follows (Fig. 23.4).[9–12]

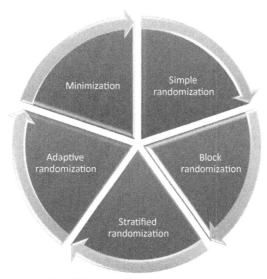

FIGURE 23.4 Types of randomization.

Simple Randomization

In this type, patients/subjects are allocated randomly to different treatment groups. As a simple strategy, this type of randomization could be performed by flipping a coin, or by throwing a dice, or even by shuffling cards. In large clinical research simple randomization generates a similar number of participants among groups, but in a small sample size, this method is problematic. An example is given in Table 23.2; out of 15 patients, 5 of them randomized into group A and 10 randomized into group B. As there is no actual balance in numbers, the outcome variables are therefore imbalanced.[11]

Block Randomization

Here, the sample size or participants are equally distributed all the time using blocks. Blocks are small and balanced with predetermined group assignments. The block size is determined by the researcher and should be a multiple of the number of groups (i.e., with two treatment groups, block size of either 4, 6, or 8). Blocks are best used in smaller increments as researchers can more easily control balance.[11,13]

An example: 2 blocks with 2 treatment groups.

Treatment 1—Control (C); Treatment 2—Treatment (T).

Block 1—CT; Block 2—TC (Table 23.3).

Similarly, 4 treatment groups with 4 blocks can be assigned as randomized in Table 23.4.

T1—A; T2—B; T3—C; T4—D.

B1—ABCD; B2—BCDA; B3—CDAB; B4—DABC.

TABLE 23.2 Example of Simple Randomization

Group A	Group B
1	2
4	3
8	5
11	6
12	7
	9
	10
	13
	14
	15

TABLE 23.3 Example of Block Randomization—Two Blocks

Block	Subject No.	Group A	Group B
B1	1	C	T
B2	2	T	C
B1	3	C	T
B2	4	T	C
B2	5	T	C
B2	6	T	C
B1	7	C	T
B2	8	T	C
B1	9	C	T
B1	10	C	T
B2	11	T	C
B2	12	T	C
B1	13	C	T
B1	14	C	T
B2	15	T	C
B1	16	C	T
B2	17	T	C
B1	18	C	T
B1	19	C	T
B2	20	T	C

The groups generated are usually not comparable for the relevant comorbidities. This reduces the power of the study though a balance in sample size is achieved, and hence stratified randomization is preferred.

Stratified Randomization

Strata means group. Variables such as age, race, gender, and underlying disease (comorbidities) conditions are generally factorized/stratified. In this method, the participants are first divided into strata and then block randomization is applied. A separate block for each combination of covariates is to be generated (Fig. 23.5).

Having many covatiates to stratify complicates randomization. In addition, practically it is difficult to enroll all participants at once to clinical trials, enrollment in trials keeps happening over a period of time. Thus it is difficult to stratify potential participants to different strata before generative blocks. Adaptive randomization has the benefit of enrolling participants one by one with a balance of covariates.[11]

Adaptive Randomization

As the name suggests treatment is adapted depending on the previously assigned treatment. It is also termed "Response Adapted Randomization." This type of randomization is certainly drawing a ball from a basket. The balls of two treatments, say "x" or "y," are chosen on randomization. The investigator decides the treatment (test vs. control) as the outcome would be known immediately. If patient "A" gets "x" treatment and survives and the next patient "B" gets "y" treatment and dies, the consecutive patient would automatically receive "x" treatment. Thus the number of "x" balls would be added to the basket, and this continues until a failure is reached in "x" treatment. Generally, a ratio status of 1:1 (x:y) would be maintained in the beginning and as the treatment continues the ratio might change (3:1). This indicates that the "x" treatment has been carried out in three subjects successfully. However, the decision to choose the treatment may not be possible in a larger sample size study as this method is sometimes disagreeable so is not very often used.[14]

TABLE 23.4 Example of Block Randomization—Four Blocks

Block	Subject No.	Group A	Group B	Group C	Group D
B1	1	A	B	C	D
B2	2	B	C	D	A
B3	3	C	D	A	B
B4	4	D	A	B	C
B1	5	A	B	C	D
B3	6	C	D	A	B
B3	7	C	D	A	B
B2	8	B	C	D	A
B4	9	D	A	B	C
B1	10	A	B	C	D
B1	11	A	B	C	D
B2	12	B	C	D	A
B4	13	D	A	B	C
B2	14	B	C	D	A
B3	15	C	D	A	B
B4	16	D	A	B	C
B1	17	A	B	C	D
B1	18	A	B	C	D
B2	19	B	C	D	A
B3	20	C	D	A	B
B4	21	D	A	B	C
B2	22	B	C	D	A
B3	23	C	D	A	B
B1	24	A	B	C	D
B4	25	D	A	B	C
B1	26	A	B	C	D
B2	27	B	C	D	A
B3	28	C	D	A	B
B4	29	D	A	B	C
B3	30	C	D	A	B
B4	31	D	A	B	C
B4	32	D	A	B	C
B1	33	A	B	C	D
B2	34	B	C	D	A
B1	35	A	B	C	D
B2	36	B	C	D	A
B3	37	C	D	A	B
B4	38	D	A	B	C
B2	39	B	C	D	A
B3	40	C	D	A	B

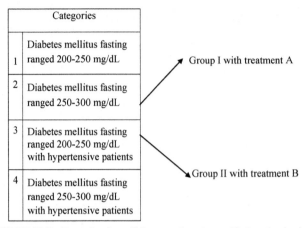

FIGURE 23.5 Example of stratifying covariates in stratified randomization.

Minimization

Minimization is a rather complicated method of adaptive randomization. This is a method that balances the number of patients throughout a stratum. As discussed in "Stratified Randomization" the number of individuals in each stratum are summed up, and the next patient is assigned to a lesser enrolled group. A pattern of this randomization technique is shown in Table 23.5A. Signs of difference as shown in Table 23.5B help in the allocation of the next patients.

A sign of the difference between the two treatments is introduced. Considering the total treatment X has more numbers, allocate the next participant to Y. Also considering the sign of differences, treatment X is greater. Allocate the next

TABLE 23.5A Example of Minimization

Strata	Treatment X	Treatment Y
Sex		
Male	10	8
Female	5	5
Age		
50–64 years	4	6
65 years and above	11	7
Colorectal Cancer		
Stage-1	7	4
Stage-2	2	3
Stage-3	4	4
Stage-4	2	2
Total	15	13

TABLE 23.5B Signs of difference in minimization technique

Strata	Treatment X	Treatment Y	Sign of Difference
Sex			
Male	10	8	+
Age			
65 years and above	11	7	+
Colorectal cancer			
Stage-2	2	3	–
Total	23	18	

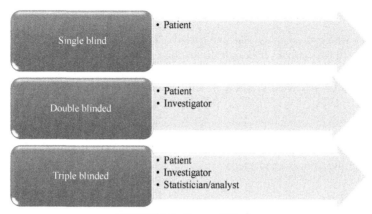

FIGURE 23.6   Types of Blinding.

participant to Y. Such type of randomization can allocate the numbers participating in each treatment group by considering the balance in prognostic factors too. In case if there is an equal allocation between the treatment numbers (e.g., there is a balance in the prognostic variables), mere randomization can be followed. Allocate the next subject in case of such a tie situation to treatment X with a higher assigned probability.

Blinding

The trials are blinded to eliminate bias as well. The tendency for such bias to occur may be unintentional. Nevertheless, blinding should be considered. If blinding is planned, it should be described during the stages of preparation of the protocol. Open label or nonblinded trials are generally adopted in bioequivalence (BE) studies that are conducted to bring generic drugs to the market. In single blinding just the patient is unaware of what they are receiving (investigational product, standard treatment or placebo). In some cases if there are understandable differences between investigational product and standard treatment (e.g. once daily and twice daily dosing), the investigator could figure out which product is used and could not be blinded. In this case the statistician/analyst could be blinded (Fig. 23.6).[10]

Controls

There are different types of control groups predicted for each type of clinical trial.[9]

1. Placebo concurrent control: In this way, a group of people receives a placebo (which does not contain the test drug) and are compared with a test formulation. The fake or dummy drug (placebo) may substantially improve the health condition of the subjects psychologically (he or she realizes the improvement is because of taking a drug). Such an effect is called a "placebo effect."
2. No-treatment concurrent control: In this way, the patients are observed without providing any treatment. However, their outcome will be compared against the interventional test outcome and is thoroughly applicable for nonblinded studies. Study end points should be objective.
3. Dose—response concurrent control: Doses may be fixed and gradually increased. Two such differences in doses (different groups) are compared for a dose—response relationship.
4. Active (positive) concurrent control: Positive control group includes people who are tested with a drug that would give a known response and an expected outcome as that of the test formulation.
5. External (historical) control: The control refers to a group of people who are treated with the same test intervention at the same time but in a different site (external). It can also be historical control, which includes and compares a group of patients treated at an earlier time.[9]

STUDY DESIGNS

Crossover Studies

In crossover studies, the study participants will be switched throughout to all the treatment groups (both test and reference formulations) after a washout period. Being the same set of the population the advantage of crossover studies is that patients act as their own controls. Bioavailability (BA)/BE studies are usually conducted as crossover studies. BE studies can be conducted under fasting and fed conditions. The sampling time points and the duration of BE studies depend on the half-life of the drug of interest. In the case of a feeding study, a high-fat, high-calorie breakfast would be provided to the subjects before administration of investigational product (IP).

Parallel Studies

For drugs with long half-lives where an adequate washout period cannot be given between two treatments, it is preferred to conduct a parallel design instead of a crossover design. In this design, participants do not receive both test and reference formulations. They receive one of the formulations as per the randomization. Usually, this would be a single period study. However, randomization would be generated to know which participant receives a test or a reference.

Steady-State Studies

In steady-state studies, subjects are given multiple doses of IPs so that a steady state can be attained before evaluation of the pharmacokinetic profile of the drug is conducted.

Basket and Umbrella Trials

Clinical trial designs are evolving as a response to precision medicine; the traditional types of clinical trials are not viable in some cases (for example, lung cancer). Over the past several years two clinical trial designs have been proposed and implemented in many oncology trials: basket (or bucket) trials and umbrella trials. The basket and umbrella trial designs avoid overtreatment and save valuable resources by matching the right drug to the right subgroup of patients through genetic biomarkers. Although basket and umbrella trial designs are almost exclusively in oncology trials, we can assume that such designs can be generalized to other therapeutic areas as well. A basket trial is especially meaningful for "rare" diseases, where subjects are difficult to find. Biomarkers are used to identify patients likely to respond to treatment.[27] For example, the umbrella patients with advanced nonsmall cell lung cancer enrolled in an umbrella trial undergo a tumor biomarker analysis that is used to assign them to a phase II study. The differences between these two types of clinical trials are:

- An umbrella trial researches one disease/one cancer type, multiple subgroups identified by the biomarkers, many drugs—many patient groups/arms; a basket/a bucket trial researches many diseases/many cancer types, a single subgroup, one drug.
- An umbrella trial defines cancer as a body location or histology (for example, breast cancer, lung cancer, etc.); a basket trial defines cancer based on the genetic aberrant or biomarker signature (for example, cancer with X-positive biomarker).[28] An umbrella trial allows the researcher to test different drugs and patients with the same disease family and identifies those who respond best to a specific therapy; a bucket trial understands the differences between different types of cancers—all contain the mutation in question.[29]

Adaptive Study Design

In traditional clinical studies, groups of patients receive a predetermined therapy for a fixed period. In an adaptive trial, researchers can see how patients involved in the study are doing while the trial is still running; various aspects of the study design can be changed on the fly or even react to new research insights that happened during the study. New clinical study designs and protocols like these help to transform advances in cancer research into improved options for patients as fast as possible in an effective way.[30]

Registry Trials

Randomized clinical trials provide a foundation of clinical evidence; but they have limitations, including increasingly prohibitive costs of conducting adequately powered studies. Registry trials, which are observational studies, can be used efficiently and effectively to assess hard clinical end points in large patient cohorts; this study design is well suited to hospital settings and registry networks. Despite these advantages, registry studies have disadvantages as well: data quality can be variable and questionable, comparative outcomes research is questionable, and adjustment for possible confounding factors is needed. Potential confounding variables could be removed through randomization in registry-based randomized clinical trials.[31]

OBJECTIVE 23.3. EXPLAIN THE PHASES OF CLINICAL TRIALS

Phases of Clinical Trials

There are five different phases of clinical trials. Clinical trials will start once the preclinical studies give promising results. The five phases of clinical trials are as follows (Fig. 23.7)[16,17]:

- Phase 0
- Phase 1

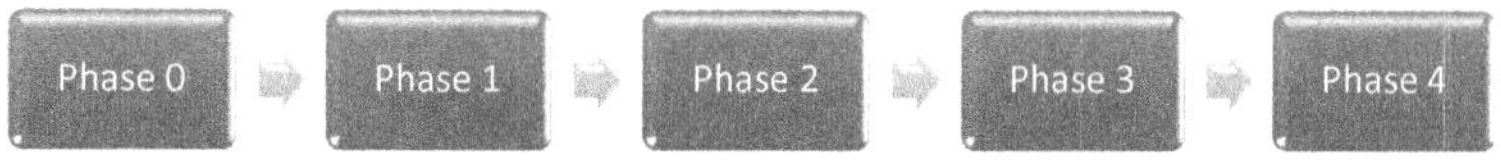

FIGURE 23.7   Phases of clinical trials.

- Phase 2
- Phase 3
- Phase 4

Phase 0

Phase 0 studies are not common. These studies are called microdosing studies. This phase is usually carried with fewer subjects (generally healthy subjects). The phase ascertains the preliminary pharmacokinetic properties of the drug (absorption, distribution, metabolism, and excretion—ADME). It is very difficult to establish the toxicity criteria with such microdosing phenomena. The outcome of the study would rely on or would be compared with preclinical studies done on animals. However, a therapeutic benefit cannot be determined at this phase. Usually, phase 0 studies will be conducted to avoid exposure of the IP to a higher number of subjects in phase 1. Phase 0 studies will provide the preliminary pharmacokinetic information of the lead compound. Microdosing will help in the drug development process without adversely affecting the safety of the subjects.[18]

Phase 1

Usually carried out in a smaller number of people (12—30 numbers) and performed after animal toxicity studies or phase 0 studies are completed. This phase has been carried out with healthy volunteers with exceptions being patients who are being treated for a disease such as cancer and HIV/AIDS. As it is with fewer people, the researchers can monitor the maximum dose required with fewer side effects. These are also called dose escalation studies. Single and multiple doses will be escalated gradually to determine the maximum tolerated dose (MTD).

Safety and tolerability of the drug are determined at this level.

Phase 1 studies are executed in two methodologies:

- Single ascending dose study—SAD
- Multiple ascending dose study—MAD

Single Ascending Dose Study

In a given period of time (e.g., up to 3 months), pharmacokinetic parameters are determined. Three to four volunteers (a small group) receive the lowest single dose (e.g., 1 mg) and are observed for any toxicity/adverse events. If no adverse events and toxicity are established at this dose level of 1 mg, this type of study can be escalated sequentially to a new small group of volunteers with the next higher dose (2 mg). If toxicity is observed at a 1 mg dose, however, the same tested dose (1 mg) is administered to a new set of three subjects and observed for adverse events. This is done until the volunteers experience an adverse event at a defined dose, and the dose before this is considered as the MTD.[17]

Maximum Tolerated Dose

MTD refers to the highest dose of a pharmacological drug, which would produce the desired effect without unacceptable toxicity.[13]

Example of Single Ascending Dose

Considering an X axis as time in hours (h) and a Y axis as the average of volunteers plasma drug concentration in nanogram/milliliter (ng/mL) (Fig. 23.8).

The graph depicts that 1 mg (group I) of drug X has been initiated in a small group of people (in 3—5 numbers). The pharmacokinetic data are predicted. With no toxicity is established at this level, the dose of drug X is further escalated to 2 mg (group II) and 3 mg (group III) with a different group of people. The dose escalation continues as long as the maximum concentration is reached as stated in the protocol. The dose of 4 mg (group IV) is discontinued before the concentration maximum could be reached due to the possible occurrence of unacceptable toxicity. Hence MTD is decided as 3 mg for drug X. Further dose escalation is terminated (Fig. 23.9).

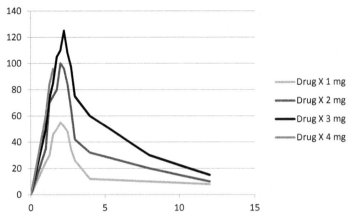

FIGURE 23.8 Example of single ascending dose (Plasma drug concentration on Y-axis and time on X-axis).

FIGURE 23.9 Phase 1—single ascending dose study.

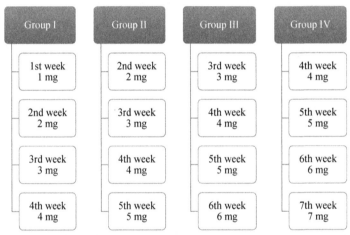

FIGURE 23.10 Phase 1—multiple ascending dose study.

Multiple Ascending Dose Study

A group of people receives multiple doses of a drug to determine pharmacokinetic and pharmacodynamic properties. A second group receives an escalated amount of multiple doses, and the same would be determined at various groups until tolerability is established (Fig. 23.10).[19]

From the figure, dose escalation happens within the group to study the pharmacokinetic parameters. The fate of the drug is determined with multiple dose levels. The escalation of the dose levels among different groups is certainly decided from SAD studies to evaluate the therapeutic drug concentration in the human body.

Example of Multiple Ascending Dose

According to the graphs (X axis: time in hours and Y axis: concentration in ng/mL), the concentration maximum (Cmax) lies around 55 ng/mL (Fig. 23.11A—G) to 180 ng/mL (Fig. 23.11A—G) and the time taken to reach the maximum concentration is 0—4 h. Assessment of the pharmacokinetics parameter using multiple groups assists in determining the toxicity profile.

Phase 2—Therapeutic Exploratory Phase

This phase handles a considerably greater number of patients compared to phase I. The numbers may gradually increase to 100 or more depending on the number of sites. Unlike phase I trials, these trials are intended to treat the patients with an expected indication to find out safety issues as the primary objective. Therefore this is also termed a therapeutic exploratory phase. Safety of the drug is assessed with priority followed by its efficacy.[19] This may be categorized as phase 2a and phase 2b.

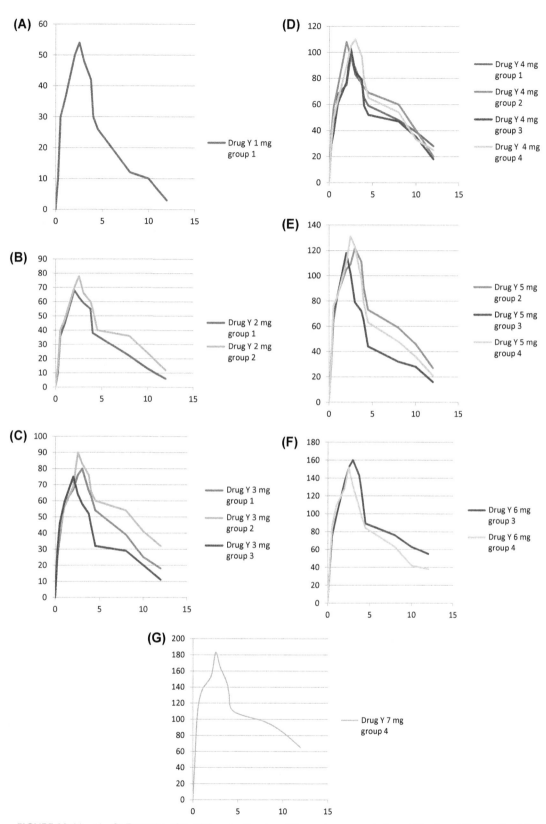

FIGURE 23.11 (A—G) Examples of multiple ascending dose (Plasma drug concentration on Y-axis and time on X-axis).

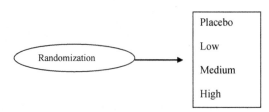

FIGURE 23.12 Proof of concept studies—randomization.

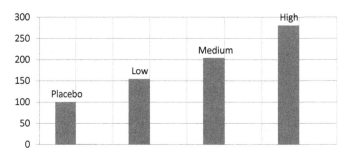

FIGURE 23.13 Responses for different doses.

Phase 2a—Proof of Clinical Concept Studies

These studies are pilot studies, single centric, and a continuation of phase I studies where the tolerated dose level appropriate for desired therapeutic action has been decided. This phase plays a vital role for prolongation of drug development into later phases. Depending on the tolerability, the new intervention can be determined to be included in other phases or not.

These are dose-ranging studies. The study end points and the nature of the population (severity of the disease) should be prefixed. Because the MTD is analyzed in the early phase, dose ranging is fixed among groups as placebo controlled, low, medium, and high (Fig. 23.12).

Certainly, the response to a defined dose can be studied (Fig. 23.13).

The dose-dependent pharmacological activity of the drug (mechanism of action) can be established. Therefore the dosing intervals and frequency of the drug administration can also be predicted for later phases. The therapeutic dose and its toxicity, if any, can be ascertained. The toxicity profile among the diseased population and their concomitant drugs provide a pathway for the continuation of phase 2b pivotal studies.

Phase 2b

These are pivotal studies, and new intervention may be compared with a dummy drug (placebo) or with an intervention already in existence. Thus these can be termed randomized controlled trials (RCTs) (Fig. 23.14).[20]

These are crossover studies and can be performed at multiple sites. As the dose requirements are determined in phase 2a, the efficacy of the dose is established (how well the suggested dose works on receptor mechanisms). The efficacy that has been proved should be determined from the target condition (a drug intended for a specific condition) as these are patient populations.

Phase 3—Therapeutic Confirmatory Phase

In a phase 3 trial, efficacy and safety of the molecule can be determined. These are therapeutic confirmatory phase trials. They are generally carried out in a relatively high number (100—3000) of patients, depending on therapeutic areas, at various centers, hence they are called multicentric trials. These trials are generally carried out for a longer duration (few years) to analyze the exact dosage levels that would prove beneficial to a lesser degree/extent of adverse events. With phase 3 study efficacy, postmarketing studies (phase 4) could study effectiveness. The difference between efficacy and effectiveness is compared in Table 23.6.

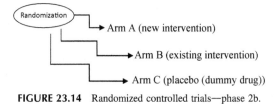

FIGURE 23.14 Randomized controlled trials—phase 2b.

TABLE 23.6 Difference Between Efficacy and Effectiveness

Efficacy	Effectiveness
Results from normal clinical trials (randomized)	Results from normal clinical practice
Efficacy is established in inclusion of population as specified in protocol	Effectiveness is established in inclusion of population as specified in protocol as well as with comorbidity conditions

A new intervention and a standard intervention are randomized among the patients. Sometimes a placebo-controlled trial may also be carried out. The researchers prefer to have a comparison, which could be more than two treatment groups. There are possibilities to study drug—drug interactions due to heterogeneous population selections.[21]

Example

Phase 3 Type 1 Diabetic Study

The possible occurrence of withdrawal cases due to adverse drug reactions could be more than expected. Assuming the clinical end point for a diabetic study would be lowering of (Fig. 23.15):

- HbA1$_C$ (glycosylated hemoglobin),
- fasting blood sugar (FBS),
- postprandial blood sugar,
- triglycerides and cholesterol.

The outcome of this study can be determined from the efficacy of the drug (mechanism of action of the drug on the receptor site, dose—response relationship) and its safety. The data should be statistically significant for expansion of the drug into the marketing phase. These are further categorized as phase 3a and phase 3b studies. *Phase 3a*: These studies are conducted after demonstrating the efficacy but before the submission of a new drug application (NDA). *Phase 3b*: These trials are carried out after NDA but before approval of the drug.

Phase 4—Postmarketing Surveillance

Phase 4 trials are conducted after a drug is approved and comes into a market. These trials will evaluate the effectiveness and safety of the drug in different population groups, not only in patients with intended diseases, but the drug will also be administered to patients with other concurrent diseases in real-world medical practice. Drugs during this phase, which show adverse toxicities, may not further be continued for marketing and could be banned in a given market. These trials are carried out in a patient undergoing clinical care. The statistical effectiveness of a drug on larger patient groups is known to a greater extent, and drug interactions can also be estimated as patients with a secondary illness may participate in the trials.[22]

Sometimes regulatory agencies may also request to conduct long-term postmarketing surveillance (PMS) studies to rule out the long-term adverse events, carcinogenicity, and mutagenic effects of the marketed drug. Data collected after such long-term PMS studies may describe potential long-term adverse reactions in which the drug may be withdrawn from the market.[22]

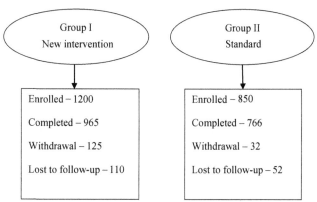

FIGURE 23.15 Example of participant withdrawal from clinical trial.

OBJECTIVE 23.4. DISCUSS THE ROLE OF PHARMACISTS AND NEWER TECHNOLOGIES IN CLINICAL RESEARCH

Pharmacists play important roles in the field of clinical research, and their roles could be:

1. Review of protocols and related documents,
2. Receipt, storage, accountability, dispensing, and return/destruction of IPs, and
3. Blinding/unblinding procedure of codes.

Review of Protocol and Trial-Related Documents

Clinical trial protocols should be prepared or reviewed by the pharmacist to analyze the following:

- The IP vs. control
- Mode of administration
- Dosage form and the dose required for each subject in each period
- Reconstitution solution, if any, in case of injectable
- Indications and uses of the IP
- Adverse effects of an IP
- Contraindications
- Preplanned concomitant medication, if any, to be administered in case of occurrence of adverse events

Pharmacists need to prepare and review protocols as per the pharmacological profile of study drugs. Pharmacists need to make sure that the objectives of a clinical research protocol comply with the pharmacology of the drug and the literature reporting scientific information.

Receipt, Storage, and Accountability of the Investigational Product

A pharmacist has important responsibilities in handling IPs. The number of IPs received, the date of manufacture and expiration, batch/lot numbers of the IPs, and route of drug administration should be accurately checked and documented. The handling and storage conditions (such as humidity, light, and temperature sensitivity) of the IPs as depicted on the label shall be maintained and followed.[32]

Drugs that need special storage conditions, such as narcotic substances or psychotropic substances, shall be preserved in a cupboard or safe, and the same shall be equipped with a security alarm system. The room in which the narcotics are placed should have a controlled access.[33]

Dispensing of the Investigational Product

A randomization schedule generated by the statistician should be used while dispensing. The dosage form and dose required for an individual should be cross-verified against the protocol before dispensing. Dispensing under specific requirements, if any (such as monochromatic light for light liable substances), is also essential for protocol compliance.

The key factors to be observed while dispensing are:

- Unintentional change of IP (test vs. control) that may occur due to overlooking of a randomization schedule to be avoided. Doing so may lead to the withdrawal of subjects from the trial.
- Dispensing extra IPs for the site(s). In case of any damage to packaging, which may be unnoticed during accountability, may once again this will lead to discontinuation of the trial. In some cases, spillage of the drug during intake may also occur.
- The accountability of unused IPs. The amount received should balance with dispensed and undispensed products.[32]

Return/Destruction of Investigational Products

The IPs may be returned to the sponsor after completion of the trial as per their request. Otherwise, the samples may be retained or destroyed as specified in the protocol and applicable regulatory guidelines.[34]

Blinding/Unblinding Procedure of Codes

Blinding of IP is essential in clinical trials for an unbiased result. The blinding procedure should be carried out by a pharmacist. The IPs are coded (i.e., test product is coded "A," and the control product is coded "B"). The blinded codes against IPs are kept in a sealed envelope under controlled access in the pharmacy. The randomization is then generated by the statistician using the blinded codes A or B.[34]

Dispensing the drugs should be performed by a pharmacist and sent across the sites (if multicentric) depending on the code generated against the number of subjects. Any labels for identification of the IP should be made based on the blinded codes only. The unused IP may be returned to the pharmacist.

Unblinding may happen for a subject(s) in case of a medical emergency condition. In such conditions, unblinding may be requested by the investigator to the pharmacist. The details of the subject and the reason for unblinding should be mentioned by the respective on-site investigator. The same should be notified to the sponsor at the earliest.[35]

In case of nonavailability of the pharmacist in such emergency conditions, other team members should be allocated for accessing and breaking the codes. Both blinding and unblinding should be documented by the pharmacist.

Details of the Pharmaceutical Development Used in Clinical Trials

Classical experimental designs were extended to clinical trials. However, before human responses to medical treatments are evaluated, the goal of product development is to design and establish a formulation composition and robust manufacturing process.

Quality by design for pharmaceuticals was introduced with ICH Q8 2009 (International Conference on Harmonization). There is a harmonized pharmaceutical quality system applicable across the lifecycle of the product that is developed following the guidelines:

- Q8—Pharmaceutical Development,
- Q2 (R2)—Pharmaceutical Development Revision,
- Q9—Quality Risk Management,
- Q10—Pharmaceutical Quality System,
- Q11—Development and Manufacture of Drug Substances (chemical/biological entities).[36]

The design of experiments (DOE) is the design of any task that describes or explains the variation of information under conditions that are hypothesized to reflect the variation. Experimental design implies not only the selection of suitable predictors (independent variables) and outcomes (dependent variables), but also planning the delivery of the experiment under statistically optimal conditions given the constraints of available resources. DOE involves making a set of experiments representative with regards to a given question, such as, for example, "What is the value of addition time for a controlled crystallization"—detection of short addition time could occur too late to prevent uncontrolled crystallization and thus impact over particle size distribution. Statistical analysis of crystallization data allows for the determination of the design space.

Researchers should select the system response, factors and their levels, and center point of the design (or the null point). Factors should be controllable and of high measurement precision. Factors could be temperature, agitator tip speed, concentration, and the time during the experiment, and the response could be the particle size.

Analysis of DOE data generates a predictive model:

$$y = \beta_0 + \sum_{i=1}^{k} \beta_i X_i + \sum_{i,j=1}^{k} \beta_{ij} X_i X_j + \sum_{i=1}^{k} \beta_{ii} X_i^2 + \ldots$$

where y is a response (predicted-calculated response value), aim function; Xi is the controllable independent variables, factors; β_0, β_i, β_{ij}, β_{ii} are real regression coefficients; and k is the number of factors. The model can be used to create a design space using narrower ranges and then used in the DOE.

A designed or active experiment is based on using general methodological concepts such as regression and correlation analysis, analysis of variance, randomization, optimal use of factor space, successive experimenting, replication, compactness of information, statistical estimates, etc.[19] It is very important to understand that a model is an approximation that simplifies studies of the reality. A model can never be 100% perfect, but it will be very useful in estimating interactions between factors. It is also very useful to inspect a reliable response contour plot of the investigated system to comprehend its behavior.

CONCLUSION

Key methodological aspects of clinical trials are explained in this chapter. Types of clinical trials and related studies are also discussed. Knowing these details would be beneficial to pharmacists in conducting research as well as to interpret the findings while reading the research.

PRACTICE QUESTIONS

1. Clinical trials prospectively assign human participants to one or more health-related interventions to evaluate the effects on predefined health outcomes. The process of assigning a participant to an intervention by chance (not intentionally select) is called?
   A. Blinding
   B. Placebo
   C. Randomization
   D. Parallel

2. Blinding avoids bias in reporting outcomes of the intervention. Single and multiple blindings are used to reduce this bias. Which of the following studies are usually nonblinded (open label)?
   A. Bioequivalence studies to bring generic drugs to market
   B. Therapeutic exploratory studies to discover new indications
   C. Safety studies to identify adverse drug reactions
   D. Therapeutic studies to prove labeled indication of drugs

3. Which of the following is a microdosing study to find pharmacokinetic properties?
   A. Phase 0
   B. Phase I
   C. Phase II
   D. Phase III

4. A multiple ascending dose (MAD) study is?
   A. Phase 0
   B. Phase I
   C. Phase II
   D. Phase III

5. A therapeutic exploratory phase is?
   A. Phase 0
   B. Phase I
   C. Phase II
   D. Phase III

6. Cross-sectional studies collect data?
   A. Retrospectively
   B. Prospectively
   C. Both retrospectively and prospectively
   D. At a particular point

7. Studies with which of the following characteristics are given more weight in metaanalysis?
   A. More participants
   B. Lower variance or narrow confidence intervals
   C. More participants, lower variance or narrow confidence intervals
   D. All studies are given equal weight

8. In crossover studies, the study participants will be switched throughout to all the treatment groups (both test and reference formulations) after a washout period. For drugs with long half-lives where an adequate washout period cannot be given between two treatments, which method could be adopted?
   A. Cross-sectional design
   B. Case-control design
   C. Blinding design
   D. Parallel design

9. The basket and umbrella trial designs match the right drug to the right subgroup of patients through genetic biomarkers. The main advantage of this is to?

A. Increase the number of participants

B. Avoid overdosing

C. Promote registry trials

D. Permit easy crossover

CROSSWORD EXERCISE

ACROSS:

2	**HIGH FAT HIGH CALORIE** (18) The standard meal consumed as breakfast in bioequivalence studies.
4	**ADAPTIVE** (8) One of the types of randomization.
8	**PHASE FOUR** (9) These types of clinical trials are also called postmarketing surveillance trials.
12	**THERAPEUTIC CONFIRMATORY** (23) Phase 3 trials are also called _____.
14	**HEALTHY** (7) Phase I trials are carried out in _____ population.
15	**PARALLEL** (8) A design allocated to subjects to receive either test or reference investigational products during their participation.
17	**UNBLINDING** (10) The process that may happen in a medical emergency and is initiated by the investigator after dosing of investigational product.
18	**BABE** (4) The studies that are used to bring generics to the market.

DOWN:

1	**RCT** (3) The trial that involves comparison between a new intervention and a placebo.
3	**INVESTIGATIONAL PRODUCT** (22) The technical name of the pharmaceutical form of an active ingredient or placebo being tested or used as reference in trials.
5	**PHARMACIST** (10) A person responsible for drug accountability and retention in clinical trials.
6	**METAANALYSIS** (12) The process in which various data from many trials are pooled together.
7	**DOUBLE BLINDED** (13) The blinding in which the investigator and patients are unknown to trial medications.
9	**JAMES LIND** (9) Father of naval medicine.
10	**EFFICACY** (8) One of the prime objectives to be determined during the phase trials.
11	**HALF LIFE** (8) The sampling time points are determined by the _____ of the drug in bioequivalence trials.
13	**CROSSOVER** (9) The design in which patients receive a test drug in one period followed by a reference in another period after a defined washout time.
16	**ADME** (4) The pharmacokinetic properties of a drug.

REFERENCES

1. U.S. Food & Drug Administration. *Center for Drug Evaluation and Research Guidance for Industry Bioavailability and Bioequivalence Studies Submitted in NDAs or INDs — General Considerations.* March 2014.
2. Song JW, Chung KC. Observational studies: cohort and case-control studies. *Plast Reconstr Surg.* 2010;126(6):2234–2242. https://doi.org/10.1097/PRS.0b013e3181f44abc. PMID: 20697313.
3. World Health Organization. Clinical Trails. Available at: http://www.who.int/topics/clinical_trials/en/.

4. U.S. Food and Drug Administration: Step 3 Clinical Research: Available at https://www.fda.gov/ForPatients/Approvals/Drugs/ucm405622. htm#The_Investigational_New_Drug_Process.

5. Bhatt A. Evolution of clinical research: a history before and beyond James. *Lind Perspect Clin Res.* 2010;1(1):6−10. PMCID: PMC 3149409.

6. NellhaCus EM, Davies TH. *Evolution of Clinical Trials throughout History Marshall Journal of Medicine*; 2017. Available at: http://mds.marshall. edu/mjm/vol3/iss1/9.

7. Anonymous. Streptomycin treatment of pulmonary tuberculosis: a medical research council investigation. *Br Med J.* 1948;2(582):769−782.

8. Patsopoulos NA. A pragmatic view on pragmatic trials: *Dialogues Clin Neurosci.* June 2011;13(2):217−224.

9. International Conference on Harmonization. Choice of Control Group and Related Issues in Clinical Trials E10. Available at: https://www.ich.org/ fileadmin/Public_Web_Site/ICH_Products/Guidelines/Efficacy/E10/Step4/E10_Guideline.pdf.

10. International Conference on Harmonization. Statistical Principles For Cinical Trials E9. Available at: http://www.ich.org/fileadmin/Public_Web_Site/ ICH_Products/Guidelines/Efficacy/E9/Step4/E9_Guideline.pdf.

11. Suresh KP. An overview of randomization techniques: an unbiased assessment of outcome in clinical research. *J Hum Reprod Sci.* 2011;4(1):8−11. PMCID: PMC 3136079.

12. Penn State Eberly College of Science. Design and Analysis of Clinical Trials: Treatment Allocation and Randomization Available at: https:// onlinecourses.science.psu.edu/stat509.

13. Efird J. Block randomization with randomly selected block sizes. *Int J Environ Res Public Health.* 2011;8(1):15−20. PMCID: PMC 3037057.

14. Korn EL, Friedlin B. Outcome-adaptive randomization: is it useful? *J Clin Oncol.* 2011;29(6):771−776. PMCID: PMC 3056658.

15. Food and Drug Administration: Available at https://www.fda.gov/ForPatients/Approvals/Drugs/ucm405658.htm.

16. Umscheid CA, Margolis DJ, Grossman CE. Key concepts of clinical trials: a narrative review. *Postgrad Med.* 2011;123(5):194−204. https://doi.org/ 10.3810/pgm.2011.09.2475.

17. International Conference on Harmonization: General Considerations for Clinical Trials E8: Available at http://www.ich.org/fileadmin/Public_Web_ Site/ICH_Products/Guidelines/Efficacy/E8/Step4/E8_Guideline.pdf.

18. Rani PU, Naidu MUR. Phase 0-Microdosing strategy in clinical trials. *Indian J Pharmacol.* 2008;40(6):240−242.

19. International Conference on Harmonization: Available at: http://www.ich.org/fileadmin/Public_Web_Site/Training/GCG_-_Endorsed_Training_ Events/APEC_LSIF_FDA_prelim_workshop_Bangkok__Thailand_Mar_08/Day_2/Clinical_Trial_Assessment_Industry_perspective.pdf.

20. Reynolds KS. Food and Drug Administration: Available at: https://www.fda.gov/downloads/training/clinicalinvestigatortrainingcourse/ucm340009.pdf.

21. European Medicines Agency. Guideline on the Investigation of Subgroups in Confirmatory Clinical Trials. Available at: http://www.ema.europa.eu/ docs/en_GB/document_library/Scientific_guideline/2014/02/WC500160523.pdf.

22. Haque A, Daniel S, Maxwell T, Boerstoel M. Postmarketing surveillance studies—an industry perspective on changing global requirements and implications. *Clin Therapeut.* April 2017;39(4):675−685.

23. Kumar R, Khan AM, Chatterjee P. Types of observational studies in medical research. *Astrocyte.* 2014;1(2):154−159.

24. Benson K, Hartz AJ. A comparison of observational studies and randomized controlled trials. *N Engl J Med.* 2000;342:1878−1886.

25. Egger M, Smith GD, Phillips AN. Meta-analysis: principles and procedures. *BMJ.* 1997;315:1533−1537.

26. Moher D, Liberati A, Tetzlaff J, Altman DG. The PRISMA group. Preferred reporting Items for systematic reviews and MetaAnalyses: the PRISMA statement. *PLoS Med.* 2009;6(7):e1000097. https://doi.org/10.1371/journal.pmed1000097.

27. Bass MB, Sherman SI, Schlumberger MJ, et al. Biomarkers as predictors of response to treatment with motesanib in patients with progressive advanced thyroid cancer. *J Clin Endocrinol Metab.* 2010;95(11):5018−5027. https://doi.org/10.1210/jc.2010-0947.

28. Jessica M, Baktiar H, Benjamin B. New clinical research strategies in thoracic oncology: clinical trial design, adaptive, baschet and umbrella trials, new end-points and new evaluations of response. *Eur Respir Rev.* 2014;23:367−378. https://doi.org/10.1183/09059180.00004214.

29. Roche. Illuminating Ideas: Innovative Clinical Trial Design. Available at: https://www.roche.com/research_and_development/who_we_are_how_ we_work/clinical_trials/innovative-clinical-trial-design.htm.

30. Mahajan R, Gupta K. Adaptive design clinical trials: methodology, challenges and prospect. *Indian J Pharmacol.* 2010;42(4):201−207. https:// doi.org/10.4103/0253-7613.68417.

31. James S, Rao SV, Granger CB. Registry-based randomized clinical trials − a new clical trial paradigm. *Nat Rev Cardiol.* 2015;12:312−316. https:// doi.org/10.1038/nrcardio.2015.33.

32. International Conference on Harmonization. E6 Guideline for Good Clinical Practice: Available at https://www.ich.org/fileadmin/Public_Web_Site/ ICH_Products/Guidelines/Efficacy/E6/E6_R1_Guideline.pdf.

33. Food and Drug Administration: Electronic Code of Federal Regulations Part 1306. Available at: https://www.ecfr.gov/cgi-bin/text-idx? SID=3ee286332416f26a91d9e6d786a604ab&mc=true&tpl=/ecfrbrowse/Title21/21tab_02.tpl.

34. Food and Drug Administration. Guidance for Industry: Handling and Retention of BA and BE Testing Samples: Available at https://www.fda.gov/ downloads/RegulatoryInformation/Guidances/UCM126836.pdf.

35. Food and Drug Administration. Guidance for Clinical Trial Sponsors. Available at https://www.fda.gov/downloads/regulatoryinformation/guidances/ ucm127073.pdf.

36. Lazic ZR. *Design of Experiments in Chemical Engineering.* Weinheim: WILEY-VCH Verlag GmbH& Co. KGaA; 2004. ISBN 3-527-31142-4.

ANSWERS TO PRACTICE QUESTIONS

1. C
2. A
3. A
4. B

5. C
6. D
7. C
8. D
9. B

CROSSWORD ANSWERS

CROSSWORD:

Chapter 24

Ethics in Clinical Research

Nisha Rajendran[1], Dixon Thomas[2], S. Suresh Madhavan[3] and Ronald A. Herman[4]

[1]Azidus Laboratories Ltd., Chennai, India; [2]Gulf Medical University, Ajman, United Arab Emirates; [3]West Virginia University School of Pharmacy, Morgantown, WV, United States; [4]The University of Iowa, Iowa City, IA, United States

Learning Objectives:

Objective 24.1 Overview untoward drug incidents that influenced the evolution of ethics in clinical research.
Objective 24.2 Explain salient features of laws and guidelines in history to counter unethical research.
Objective 24.3 Detail the constitution and process of review by the research ethics committees.
Objective 24.4 Describe the informed consent process in clinical research.
Objective 24.5 Examples of some unethical practices in current clinical research.

OBJECTIVE 24.1. OVERVIEW UNTOWARD DRUG INCIDENTS THAT INFLUENCED THE EVOLUTION OF ETHICS IN CLINICAL RESEARCH

The term "ethics" was derived from the Greek word meaning "Ethos"[1] (Fig. 24.1). Clinical research should be conducted ethically to protect the rights, safety, and well-being of the study participants.[2] Pharmacists have responsibilities to contribute to the ethical conduct of research no matter where they practice. Training in biomedical research ethics is mandatory for many institutions for their health professionals involved in clinical research. The term Ethos was used to describe the guiding beliefs (norms or customs) of the people. As a guardian of providing safe and cost-effective medications or pharmacy services to consumers, pharmacists must lead in the ethical conduct of clinical research. For many, ethics is a philosophical matter and may be considered as subjective and vary from person to person based on their perceptions or may be relative in nature varying from situation to situation.[3]

Clinical research involves studies conducted in healthy volunteers or patients. There are times when the science of the research might conflict with the well-being of the research subject. The ultimate question then is which is more important, science or ethics? In clinical research, the answer is simple, ethics is the first consideration. The rights of a few should not be sacrificed for the benefit of others. It does not mean that scientific quality in research is not important because poor methodological quality will result in questionable results rendering the study efforts a waste. However, unnecessary exposure of participants to any stimulus (whether it is a drug or a service) is unethical. Thus nonscientific methods are unethical.[4] Therefore, it is the responsibility of an ethics committee to review both the ethical and scientific aspects of a research proposal.[5]

Research has not always been conducted with high ethical standards. Clinical research must always be socially responsible.[6] Historical examples of unethical research practices that focused more on generating scientific knowledge and not on subject safety have led to important changes in how research is conducted today. Other examples of inappropriate conflicts of interest have also forced the development of ethical guidelines and related regulatory requirements. Studying examples of unethical practices from the past is vital to get a thorough understanding of modern ethical practices. The following are summaries of some well-known unethical clinical research from history.

Tuskegee Syphilis Study (1932−72)

Almost 600 underprivileged men (mostly African−American) constituted the Tuskegee Syphilis Study, one of the most notorious of unethical research studies ever conducted.[7] There were even attempts to rationalize the research once it was

Clinical Pharmacy Education, Practice and Research. https://doi.org/10.1016/B978-0-12-814276-9.00024-6

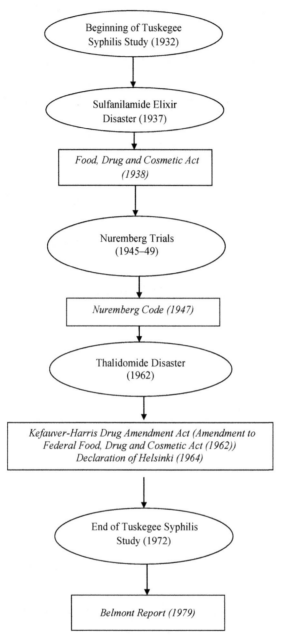

FIGURE 24.1 Evolution of biomedical ethics.

criticized for its unethical nature.[8] It was a United States Public Health Service prospective study in Macon County, Alabama, to study the "natural history" of syphilis. In the trial, around 399 of the participants were infected with syphilis (a sexually transmitted disease), and 201 participants who did not have the disease served as control. The trial was conducted over a period of 40 years, and the study evaluated the progression and complications associated with the untreated disease. The researchers had not explained the purpose of the trial nor treated the participants, though penicillin was available as the recommended drug of treatment for syphilis. It was in 1972 that the study was abandoned at the insistence of the press. By then many of the subjects had died because of the disease and its complications. In addition, a few had transmitted the infection to their spouses, and their children were born with congenital syphilis.[9] The ethical issues identified were as follows:

- Lack of informed consent. Study participants were not told specifically that the study aimed to generate knowledge on syphilis progression. Participants were deceived that they were treated while it was just diagnostic procedures.

- Penicillin was available, but the study participants were not provided with it even though it could cure syphilis. The study protocol prevented participants from receiving penicillin.
- No records were maintained. The actual number of participants who died due to syphilis was never known.
- Although parts of the study appeared in medical journals for many years, the study was not stopped until news in the national press appeared in 1972.[8,10]

Elixir Sulfanilamide Disaster (1937)

The Elixir Sulfanilamide disaster of 1937 was one of the most consequential mass poisonings of the 20th century. Sulfanilamide, an antibacterial drug, was being used safely in the treatment of streptococcal infections. A new elixir formulation with raspberry flavor was prepared using 70% diethylene glycol (DEG) as there was a need for the drug in its liquid form. DEG can be fatal, and unknowingly the company distributed the product across the United States. However, the Food and Drug Regulation (at that time) did not insist on toxicity studies for the new formulation. Hence, the company did not carry out any toxicity studies. Soon after its appearance on the market, the American Medical Association was made aware of the lethal cases from the administration of this elixir, and though immediate attempts were made to recall it, many died. The elixir was produced by a US pharmaceutical company, S. E. Massengill Company. The formulation resulted in the death of 105 patients who consumed the elixir. In reaction to this calamity, the US Congress passed the 1938 Federal Food, Drug and Cosmetic (FD&C) Act, which required proof of safety before the release of a new drug. The 1938 law changed the drug focus of the Food and Drug Administration (FDA).[11,12]

Nuremberg Trials (Nazi Trials 1945–49)

There were several unethical experiments conducted on the prisoners of war in Germany during World War II. Prisoners endured intolerable treatments as they fell victim to many experiments conducted by Nazi doctors.

Numerous inhumane experiments under the disguise of medical research were identified in the Nuremberg war trials[13]:

- Gypsy twins were targeted to understand their genetics and were then brutally killed with phenol injections. Autopsies were performed to compare the similarities among their internal organs. Different chemicals were injected into them to study the color change of their irises.
- Bones were removed and transplanted in prisoners without anesthesia. No concern was given to prisoners who suffered pus infections after the surgery. Some of them developed permanent disabilities after such experiments.
- Jewish females were exposed to a chemical irritant and were mass sterilized leading to dysfunction of the reproductive system. Subsequently, females, as well as male prisoners, were exposed to high intensity X-ray radiation on their reproductive organs.
- High-altitude experiments were carried out to mimic the conditions of altitudes up to 60,000 feet. Such high altitudes were chosen to study the low-pressure limits required for pilots to eject during an emergency. Such low-pressure chambers lacked oxygen, which often led to the death of the victims. On the survivors, the Nazis performed experimentation on the brain (vivisection).
- Many individuals were intentionally burned to see how the wounds would heal.
- Some individuals were dissected while alive so that anatomical drawings of internal organs could be done, and these were published in an anatomy textbook.[13]

Cutter Incident (1955)

The Cutter incident happened in the developmental struggle of a polio vaccine. In April 1955, 10 children died and 200 became paralyzed to varying degrees after receiving polio vaccine in the United States. Cutter Laboratories made the vaccine using Salk's formaldehyde-treatment method that was found to be defective. This incident led to adoption of Sabin's vaccine using an attenuated strain of the virus orally. There were also incidences of polio developed with Sabin's vaccine, and then a different version of Salk's vaccine was marketed. Current strict measures provide better safety profiles of vaccines but are only being produced by a few manufacturers. This has led to vaccine shortages.[14]

Thalidomide Disaster (1962)

Thalidomide is a nonbarbiturate sedative for treating insomnia and was originally marketed by a German manufacturer. From 1961 to 1962, the drug was also used in pregnant women for morning sickness. It was marketed as a safe drug, but about 10,000 cases of phocomelia (shortening or absence of limbs) were reported, and about half of the fetuses died during pregnancy. The disaster occurred mainly in Europe, Japan, and Russia. The drug was not approved in the United States due to lack of safety information. This tragedy led to major concerns about the use of medications in pregnancy and the concept of the fetus as a vulnerable subject.[12,15] Thalidomide is currently available in the global market for the treatment of cancer with an absolute contraindication in pregnancy or women of childbearing age.

The Unfortunate Experiment (1960s–80s)

This was a natural history study of cervical intraepithelial neoplasia 3 in women at the National Women's Hospital, Auckland, New Zealand. Available treatments for the disease were withheld from the patients. The study had an ethics committee approval; however, based on current guidelines the study would be considered wrong factually and ethically. Women with carcinoma in situ (CIS) of the cervix were followed, but not treated, to prove that CIS is not a premalignant disease. The outcomes for women with microinvasive cancer had not previously been reported at the time of the study. More than 100 women with CIS and microinvasive (Stage 1A) cancer of the cervix, vagina, and vulva were not treated for varying lengths of time.[8] These conditions have a substantial risk of developing into higher stages of invasive cancer. This study is popularly known as the "Unfortunate Experiment."[16]

Other Major Issues Reported in Recent Times

Conflict of interest is a major issue affecting ethics in research and drug development. Researchers are responsible for conducting all research experiments with strict ethical standards, including the following: (1) design of the research; (2) fair enrollment of subjects; (3) analysis of results; and (4) the presentation of results. For pharmaceutical industries, the financial benefits of getting a drug approved for commercial use is a leading conflict of interest. For research professionals, receiving payments for conducting studies, paid advocacy for new drugs, and lucrative payments to be consultants are all major conflicts of interest. Other common reported ethical issues are as follows:

- Pharmaceutical companies are influencing health professionals to perform unnecessary research and/or prescribe their drugs.
- Researchers manipulating study results to be published to or remain in the good graces of commercial funders of their research.
- Hiding (failing to publish) negative study results.
- Aggressive marketing by companies of uses that are outside the approved indications of drugs.

OBJECTIVE 24.2. EXPLAIN SALIENT FEATURES OF LAWS AND GUIDELINES IN HISTORY TO COUNTER UNETHICAL RESEARCH

Regulatory initiatives and changes evolved with lessons learned from drug tragedies.

Food, Drug and Cosmetic Act (1938)

After the grief of the Sulfanilamide Elixir tragedy, the United States Congress passed the FD&C Act in June 1938. This legislation created the FDA and required that manufacturers have to apply to the FDA before any new drug could be marketed.[11]

Nuremberg Code (1947)

The cardinal principles of Nuremberg Code can be categorized into three areas[17]:

1. Subject related
2. Investigator related
3. Experiment related

Ten points under these three categories are illustrated in Fig. 24.2.

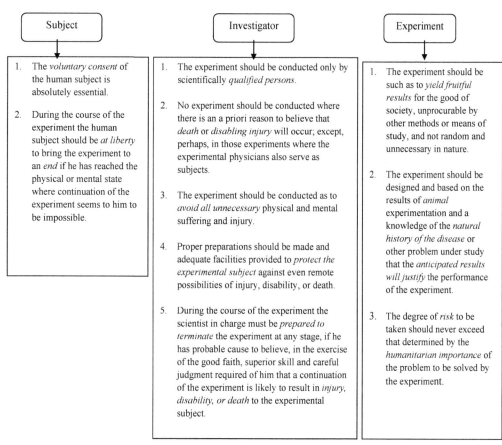

FIGURE 24.2   Cardinal principles of the Nuremberg Code.

The Nuremberg Code provided basic moral, ethical, and legal principles for conducting research, but the problem was that there was no way to enforce these principles. The regulations that established the FDA were able to address the sulfanilamide disaster but did not address the issues related to research for changes to approved drugs undergoing formulation changes.

Kefauver Harris Drug Amendment Act 1962 (Amendment to Federal Food, Drug and Cosmetic Act)

The amendment named after Senator Estes Kefauver states that drug manufacturers must prove the efficacy of drugs and their various formulations before they can be marketed and will report any serious side effects that have been determined. The efficacy of the drug being evaluated should be from subjects willing to consent to participate in adequate and well-controlled trials conducted by expert physicians. It also mentioned that the FDA should approve the marketing application before the drug could be marketed. This amendment was able to address the concerns of research on new drugs and formulations.[18]

Declaration of Helsinki

The World Medical Association met in Helsinki, Finland, in 1964 and developed the primary ethical guidelines for studies involving human beings. Finally, 16 years after the Nuremberg Code, there was a way that made physicians ethically bound to adhere to these principles. This Declaration of Helsinki has been followed by many revisions with the most recent Revision 9 being released in 2013.[19] It is widely used in current practice. Many other guidelines directed at the ethical conduct of research are based on the Declaration of Helsinki.

General Principles

The physician must consider the health of his/her patient as the foremost consideration. It is his/her duty to promote and safeguard the health, well-being, and rights of the patient involved in medical research (Figs. 24.3 and 24.4).

The group of people (vulnerable) in Fig. 24.5 can be involved in medical research, only if a proper justification has been provided for trials that cannot be conducted in nonvulnerable groups. In addition, a trial may have its priority on vulnerable people by improvement of their health condition.

Scientific Requirements and Research Protocols

A research protocol must have adequate details scientifically (trial design and methodology), technically (trial execution), and ethically (safety and well-being of the subjects).

Research Ethics Committees

The committee must be independent of the researcher and should have enough qualified persons to approve the research protocol after a thorough review and should ensure the execution and documentation of the trial that it complies with the protocol and regulatory requirements. The researcher should submit periodic reports regarding the progression of the clinical trials, interim monitoring reports that include serious adverse events (if any), and also a final report to the committee at the end of the study.

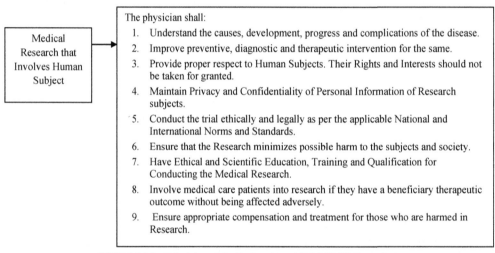

FIGURE 24.3   Principles of the Declaration of Helsinki (2013 version).

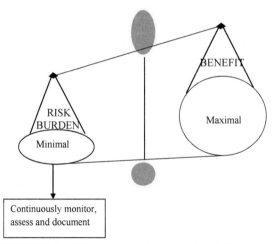

FIGURE 24.4   Risks, burdens, and benefits of clinical research.

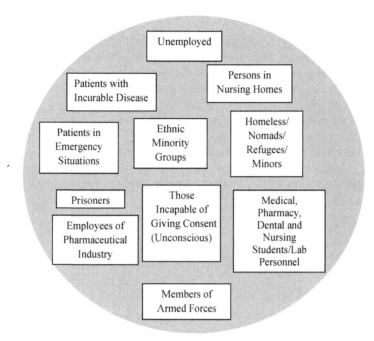

FIGURE 24.5 Vulnerable groups and individuals.

Privacy and Confidentiality

The privacy of the subjects and confidentiality of their medical records must be maintained.

Informed Consent

Subjects should be informed of the elements of informed consent during the process such as objectives, methodologies, details about the trial medications, alternative treatments available, risk/benefit ratio, compensation, insurance policy, etc. The physician/research team shall not influence the participation of the subjects in the trial if he/she has a dependent relationship with the subjects. In such cases, informed consent should be sought by another qualified individual who is independent of this relationship. Similarly, a refusal to participate should not adversely affect the healthcare professional—patient relationship.

Use of Placebo

A placebo shall be used when there is no proven intervention. In addition, in cases of any new intervention that is less efficacious than the best-proven treatment, the use of placebo is necessary to determine the efficacy and safety of that intervention.

In the case of intervention, which is less efficacious when compared to the best-proven treatment, a placebo may again be used as it will not produce any serious risk or harm, as a result of not receiving the best-proven intervention.

Posttrial Provisions

Sponsors, researchers, and government shall allow posttrial provisions for all participants who still need an intervention identified as beneficial in the trial.

Research Registration and Publication and Dissemination of Results

Studies involving humans should be registered in a publicly available database before recruitment of the first subject. All results that are positive, negative, and also inconclusive must be published or otherwise be made publicly available. Periodic updates of research outcomes should be made available to the public by updating the clinical trial registries or databases.

Unproven Intervention in Clinical Practice

In any treatment, when proven interventions do not exist, and other known interventions are ineffective, then an unproven intervention may be used after obtaining informed consent from the subject or his/her legally authorized representative. Such unproven interventional trial may be carried out when the expected outcome is the hope of saving the life of the subject, reestablishing health, or alleviating the suffering of the subject. This unproven intervention can be subsequently involved in research to evaluate its efficacy and safety.[19]

The Declaration of Helsinki provided guidelines about the safe and ethical conduct of research. Members of the World Medical Association required its members to adhere to these basic principles of research. So there was now a mechanism in place to ensure good quality research. However, the Tuskegee exposé and other public reports revealed that additional changes were required. The United States responded with the National Research Act of the US Congress, 1974. This legislation established the National Commission for the Protection of Human Subjects of Biomedical and Behavioral Research (the Belmont Commission) and charged the Commission to

- identify the basic ethical principles for research,
- develop guidelines for research,
- make recommendations about how to implement these changes.[20]

Belmont Report (April 18, 1979)

The Belmont Report defined core ethical principles.[38] The three cardinal principles of biomedical ethics identified in the report are: (1) respect for persons, (2) beneficence, and (3) justice, which are fundamental to understanding current ethical practices.[21]

Respect for Persons: categorizes people into two groups "autonomous individuals" and "individuals with diminished autonomy." Autonomy is respecting competent people for their abilities to take a decision. It is also protecting the autonomy of the vulnerable (e.g., prisoners, psychiatric patients) by preventing the imposition of unwanted decisions. The consent process protects autonomy.[22]

Autonomous individuals are those who are capable of self-thinking and can act individually. Their decision of voluntariness and willingness to participate in a trial should be respected.

Individuals with diminished autonomy are a vulnerable group of the population who seek protection from activities that are harmful, and that would adversely affect them. These groups should not be unduly influenced by participation and should also be respected.[20]

Beneficence is an obligation to provide benefits and to balance benefits against risks.[23] Nonmaleficence means the participants should not be harmed through the conduct of the study.[22] Maximize possible benefits (beneficence) and minimize possible harms (nonmaleficence) to the trial participants. The benefit of participating in a trial is the chance to receive a treatment that may not be available in the market for many years. With randomization, it is unsure whether the participant will receive the expected treatment. To manage this ethical problem, crossover designs allow the placebo group and the treatment group to experience both and are encouraged when the outcome allows this crossover.

No intervention with an expected benefit is without risks. In such cases, the degree of risk determines the continuity or the progress of the trial. Risks should always be weighed against the possible benefits of participating in the clinical trial. The principle of beneficence is to minimize risk or avoid it to the maximum extent possible, thereby protecting the physical, mental, and social well-being of the subjects.

Justice in clinical research demands that all subjects be treated fairly. Thus, equals must be treated equally.[22] Justice refers to the impartial distribution of risk and benefits of participation to different groups of subjects. Recruitments of subjects should also be performed impartially. The vulnerable population should never be coerced or exploited for participation in a trial that would be highly unfavorable regarding justice. Equality in human subjects participating in clinical research is to be ensured.[24] However, not all human subjects are the same; people differ with respect to age, health, gender, race, mental abilities, socioeconomic status, and other characteristics. The subjects with similarities could question if they receive unequal privileges.[24]

Respect for Persons

- Principles of voluntariness, informed consent, and community agreement: Risks and benefits are clear to participants and the decisions are individual.
- Principles of nonexploitation: Appropriate compensation and assured medical treatment for potential harms.
- Principles of privacy and confidentiality: Except when required for legal reasons, personal information should not be disclosed.

Beneficence

- Principles of essentiality: Is it essential to conduct research?
- Principles of precaution and risk minimization: Prevent and minimize risk, the trial should be stopped if required.
- Principles of professional competence: The research team should act with integrity and impartiality.
- Principles of accountability and transparency: Record actions and avoid conflicts of interest.

Justice

- Principles of the maximization of the public interest and distributive justice: Research should be of benefit to society.
- Principles of the public domain: Research findings to be shared with the body of scientific knowledge through appropriate mediums of communication.
- Principles of totality of responsibility: Be responsible in general.

International Council on Harmonization and Good Clinical Practice

To streamline the process of clinical trials, different countries have drafted and finalized their own set of guidelines and laws. When a pharmaceutical company plans to market a drug in different countries, they find it difficult to adopt different regulatory guidelines for drug product registration. To avoid these discrepancies among different drug regulatory agencies across the globe, the European Union, the United States, and Japan initiated a harmonization procedure in consultation with the International Federation of Pharmaceutical Manufacturers and Associations. The regulatory personnel of the European Union, the United States, and Japan planned several international conferences, and in 1990 the International Council on Harmonization (ICH) was founded in Brussels.[2]

In 2017, the following drug regulatory agencies were members of the ICH[26]:

- European Union
- The United States FDA
- Ministry of Health, Labour, and Welfare/Pharmaceuticals and Medical Devices Agency, Japan
- Health Canada, Canada
- Swissmedic, Switzerland
- Ministry of Food and Drug Safety, Republic of Korea
- Agência Nacional de Vigilância Sanitária, Brazil
- China FDA, China

The ICH has released guidelines in the following four categories[27]:

Q—Quality
Harmonization achievements in the quality area include pivotal milestones such as the conduct of stability studies, defining relevant thresholds for impurities testing and a more flexible approach to pharmaceutical quality based on Good Manufacturing Practice (GMP) risk management.

S—Safety
ICH has produced a comprehensive set of safety guidelines to uncover potential risks like carcinogenicity, genotoxicity, and reproductive toxicity. A recent breakthrough has been a nonclinical testing strategy for assessing QT interval prolongation liability, the single most important cause of drug withdrawals in recent years.

E—Efficacy
The work carried out by ICH under the efficacy heading is concerned with the design, conduct, safety, and reporting of clinical trials. It also covers novel types of drugs derived from biotechnological processes and the use of pharmacogenetics/genomics techniques to produce better-targeted drugs.

  E 6. Good Clinical Practice
    ICH enacted Good Clinical Practice (GCP) Guidelines version 1 in 1996. GCP describes the roles and responsibilities of investigators, sponsors, monitors, and the Institutional Review Board (IRB)/Independent Ethics Committee (IEC). It details specific aspects of how clinical trials need to be conducted, the elements of the informed consent document, protocol, and essential documents for the conduct of a clinical trial. A finalized addendum to revision 2 was adopted in November 2016.[28]

M—Multidisciplinary
These are the cross-cutting topics that do not fit uniquely into the quality, safety, and efficacy categories. It includes the ICH medical terminology, the Common Technical Document, and the development of Electronic Standards for the Transfer of Regulatory Information.

Guidance From the Council for International Organization of Medical Sciences in Collaboration With the World Health Organization

Similar to the ICH, the **Council for International Organizations of Medical Sciences (CIOMS)** is an international nongovernmental organization established jointly by World Health Organization (WHO) and UNESCO in 1949. Its members include countries like Belgium, South Africa, Norway, Israel, Republic of Korea, and a few other European countries. CIOMS serves to unify the common ethical guideline interests of the international biomedical community. In 1993, CIOMS released the *International Ethical Guidelines for Biomedical Research Involving Human Subjects* and then updated it in 2002 and 2016. These guidelines relate mainly to ethical justification and scientific validity of research:

- ethical review;
- informed consent;
- vulnerability of individuals, groups, communities, and populations;
- women as research subjects;
- equity regarding burdens and benefits;
- choice of control in clinical trials;
- confidentiality;
- compensation for injury;
- strengthening of national or local capacity for ethical review; and
- obligations of sponsors to provide healthcare services.[29,30]

OBJECTIVE 24.3. DETAIL THE CONSTITUTION AND PROCESS OF REVIEW BY THE RESEARCH ETHICS COMMITTEE

The Belmont Report and resulting US federal regulations, the ICH, and the CIOMS/WHO publication all require that medical research being conducted on human subjects must be written and must be reviewed, approved, and monitored by an ethics committee.

Ethics committees for research are named differently in some countries, but all follow similar principles of operation. Common names are IRB, IEC, research ethics committee, and ethics and scientific committee. The two most common terms, IEC and IRB, are the cardinal authority to oversee the conduct of clinical research studies in accordance with the guidelines and regulatory requirements.[2]

IEC: As the name suggests, it is an independent body consisting of technical and nontechnical members. The prime responsibility of the committee is to protect the rights of study participants included in clinical research and to ensure their safety and well-being. The committee is also responsible for ensuring that the research is carried out according to applicable regulatory guidance and ethical principles.

IRB: This is formed within the members of an organization/institution that holds prime responsibility as stated above.

Composition of the IEC/IRB

They should be constructed with at least five members:

- At least one member of a scientific area (medical scientist, preferably a pharmacologist).
- At least one clinician.
- A legal expert/judge.
- A layperson from the community.
- Ethicist/logician/philosopher.

The committee should have a minimum of five members and a maximum of eight to ten, equally distributed in gender. Each member of the committee plays a vital role in providing the decision of the protocol bearing in mind the regulatory guidance and standards of practice.

The IEC/IRB should have sufficient members and should be unbiased in determining the approval of the study protocol. Members should be knowledgeable in reviewing the protocol and its related documents and be able to function effectively as a team to identify and analyze technical difficulties of the study, if any, and also to ensure that the ethical aspects remain uncompromised to the participants.

In the case of studies that include a vulnerable population, the IRB/IEC can include one or more individuals as members of the ethics committee who are technically sound in handling and working with such a population.[2]

Registration of the IEC/IRB

In the United States, IRBs should be registered with Health and Human Services, the Office of Human Research Protection, and renewal should be done every 3 years.[31] Other countries also have their respective agencies to register IEC/IRBs.

Documents that Need to Be Submitted to the IEC/IRB for Approval

- Protocol and its amendments if any
- Informed consent documents
- Case report forms and other annexes of protocol
- Investigator's brochure/prescribing information or summary of product characteristics
- Curriculum vitae of investigator(s) justifying their qualifications to conduct that particular research
- Undertaking by investigator
- Financial disclosure of investigator
- Insurance and indemnification policies/compensation in case of any trial-related activities
- Form of brochures or any advertisement(s) through which the subjects could be recruited
- Agreement between investigator(s) and study sponsors

After submission of documents to the IEC/IRB, if necessary, the documents can be modified or changed at any stage; the final version after all amendments made must be submitted to the IEC/IRB as well.[2] The final version with changes should be denoted by date for easy accessibility during the conduct of the trials. Fig. 24.6 provides the major criteria that need attention before submitting to the IEC and during its review.

Communications and Functions of the IEC/IRB

The IEC/IRB should have a standard operating procedure in which the following should be described:

- Names of the members of the IEC with their qualifications and their designations in the committee.
- The frequency of meetings to review and approve protocols and for notifying the sponsor/investigator for initiating the conduct of the study.
- The frequency of interim review of trials.

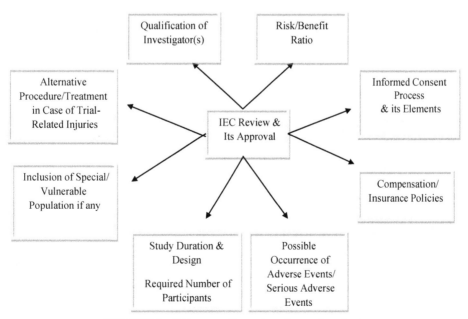

FIGURE 24.6 Ethics committee review of research protocol.

The IEC/IRB must conduct a thorough scrutiny of the informed consent documents. Informed consent communicates risks to subjects, if any, regarding anticipated benefits and the importance of the knowledge that may reasonably be expected to result. The selection of subjects is equitable. Informed consent will be sought from each prospective subject or the subject's legally authorized representative. The consent must be appropriately documented.[2]

The IEC/IRB must ensure that, when appropriate, the research plan makes adequate provision for monitoring the data collected to ensure the safety of subjects. When appropriate, there are adequate provisions to protect the privacy of subjects and to maintain the confidentiality of data. When some or all of the subjects are likely to be vulnerable to coercion or undue influence, such as children, prisoners, pregnant women, mentally disabled persons, or economically or educationally disadvantaged persons, additional safeguards have been included in the study to protect the rights and welfare of these subjects.

A statement must be made about the role of the investigator(s) to notify the IEC/IRB following any serious unexpected event. A statement must also be made that the study would not be conducted unless approved by the IEC/IRB. The IEC/IRB bears the responsibility of conducting spontaneous audits/reviews of ongoing trials at regular intervals and informing the institution/investigator on the actions taken or findings.

Expedited Review Procedure of the IEC/IRB

Expedited reviews may be carried out by the IEC/IRB chairperson or by one or more members of the ethical team designated by the chairperson. Expedited reviews may happen when

1. Research involves minimal risk
2. There is a minor change in an already approved research (which is within a time frame of 1 year or less) protocol.

During such expedited reviews, all functions/authorities of the IEC/IRB may be carried out except for disapproval of research. Disapproval of research may happen only in the nonexpedited review process.

The IEC/IRB may suspend or terminate a research if it is not being conducted as per IEC/IRB requirements or if there is the occurrence of serious unexpected harm to subjects. Such action by the IEC/IRB shall be reported to investigators and regulatory agencies.[2]

OBJECTIVE 24.4. DESCRIBE THE INFORMED CONSENT PROCESS IN CLINICAL RESEARCH

Obtaining informed consent in a trial is one of the most essential steps and should always be a simple process. The informed consent process should be done by extensively detailing all the procedures and risks and benefits involved by participating in the clinical trial. Participants involved in the trial should be respected and never be forced to participate in a trial. Their willingness to participate should be established. The study participants should be given adequate time to understand the consent, and he/she must sign and date the informed consent document. This process should convey the fact that the trial would be conducted in accordance with all the governing regulations, and participation is purely voluntary.

Consent Process

The process should not include the mere signing of the document but should allow a proper interaction between the researcher and the participant. The process should also not coerce any volunteer for their participation. Consent should be presented orally by the investigator. Appropriate time should be given to the subject to read and understand the document.

Aspects such as risk/benefits involved in the trial, the duration of the trial, the occurrence of adverse events due to trial medication, and compensation for participation should be appropriately described in the consent form and discussed. Individual interactions, as well as group discussions, are required. The participant should be free to question the researcher about any trial-related matter. The ability to withdraw at any time from the trial should be known to the participant.

The informed consent document should be easy to understand and technical phrases and words should be avoided. Transparency here defines the occurrence of all adverse events (possibility of risks) and benefits gained from the trial. In case of no study benefits, the same should be mentioned in the informed consent form.

At any point during the trial, whenever new information becomes available that may require a subjects to reconsent, the same information should be included in the revised informed consent form for the IEC/IRB's approval. The subject or his/her legally acceptable representative (LAR) should be informed promptly so that they can decide on their further continuation in the trial.

The following should be explained in the informed consent form[2]:

1. A statement that explains that the trial involves research.
2. The purpose of the conduct of the trial. The duration of the trial (i.e., the subject's expected time of participation in the study, washout period, and randomization procedures).
3. Procedure of the trial (medically invasive procedures, if any, and any other experimental procedures).
4. The foreseeable risks and expected benefits that could happen from the trial.
5. Any alternative procedure/treatment adopted during the course of the trial or during the occurrence of an adverse event(s).
6. Compensation/medical treatments that may be provided in case of trial-related injuries. The expected payment that the subjects would receive and also the expected expenses, which may occur during participation.
7. A confidentiality statement that the records of the subject will be granted direct access only to the ethics committee, sponsors, and regulatory authorities. The records will be kept confidential and will not be made known to the public. The results may be published, but the subject's identity will not be disclosed.
8. A statement that claims participation in the trial is purely voluntary and the subject can withdraw from the trial at any time without penalty or loss of benefits to which the subject is entitled.
9. A statement about whom to contact for trial-related queries and injuries.
10. A statement involving unforeseeable risk to subject and fetus in case of inclusion of pregnant women in the trial.
11. Reasons and circumstances for possible termination of subject's participation by the investigator without his/her consent.
12. Procedure for withdrawal from a study by the subject.
13. An approximate number of subjects participating in the trial.

The statements involving the above elements should be documented and approved by the IEC/IRB. The IEC/IRB is responsible for ensuring the adequacy of the document. The document can then be circulated among the subjects or the subject's LAR.

The document should be provided to the subject in a language that they best prefer. The English version should be translated into vernacular languages for non-English-speaking participants. Utmost care should be taken while translating. The meanings of phrases and sentences should be appropriate, and the similarity between the languages should be maintained.

The document should be signed and dated by the subject or the subject's LAR.[2]

Role of Legally Acceptable Representative

The LAR is an individual or judicial or other body authorized under applicable law to consent on behalf of a prospective subject to the subject's participation in the procedure(s) involved in the research.

An LAR is required for an illiterate person, a pediatric patient, a geriatric patient with diminished cognition, or someone in an unconscious medical condition.

The above subjects can participate in trial interventions with the help of an LAR. The LAR is responsible for ensuring that the subject receives benefits from the trial in a secure way and their rights and interests are protected.[2]

Responsibilities of the Legally Authorized Representative

- The LAR should thoroughly read and explain all the points described in the informed consent to the subject.
- The LAR should not coerce the participant to participate.
- In case of unconscious patients, the LAR can provide consent provided the investigator/LAR feels that the new intervention may yield good results.
- In case of a minor or unconscious person (noncompetent), the LAR can provide consent for such participants.
- The LAR should sign and date the informed consent document on behalf of the subject.
- The LAR should obtain a signature and date from the subject, and if the subject is illiterate, then a thumb impression can be obtained from them.[2]

What if the Legally Acceptable Representative is Illiterate?

Sometimes, even an LAR can be illiterate. In such a situation when the participant and his/her LAR are illiterate, an impartial witness may be chosen who is independent of the trial. This person should not be influenced by anyone (investigators/team members) involved with the trial and must accurately explain the details of the informed consent document. However, he/she can never consent on behalf of the subject as an LAR does. The impartial witness should sign and date the informed consent to document that he/she has fully explained the consent document to the participant. Audiovisual tools could be used in the consent process.[32]

OBJECTIVE 24.5. EXAMPLES OF SOME UNETHICAL PRACTICES IN CURRENT CLINICAL RESEARCH

Research involving humans is highly challenging as it involves the discovery of new interventions. Although ethical aspects are governed and established, there may be some unintentional concerns arising, which may lead to questionable results.

1. *Disclosure of study medications to the patients*: If the trial is being carried out in a randomized, blinded crossover fashion, the disclosure of study medications to the researchers as well as to the patients may lead to the following consequences.

   Situation 1: The investigator/researcher who is interested in a positive outcome may be more likely to "see" these positive outcomes in the patients receiving the new intervention than in those patients receiving the placebo. It may, especially, be seen when the desired outcome of the study is "subjective" (e.g., when the primary objective of the clinical trial is the improvement in pain through changes in the visual analog scale).

   Situation 2: In the case of patients knowing that their study medication is a placebo, the intention to comply with the treatment procedure may diminish and may even force patients to withdraw their participation from the remaining periods. This may result in an unbalanced statistical approach.

   Situation 3: Patients who know that they are being treated with new interventional drugs may be psychologically influenced to feel an improvement in their health conditions, which sometimes may lead to falsification of results.

   To avoid these situations, it is important for the ethics committee to require that, whenever possible, a study is conducted only if the patient and the investigator are both "blinded" to the study intervention that a subject receives. Randomization of the treatment assignments also helps to reduce investigator bias, as does "blinding" the person analyzing as to who received the intervention versus who received the placebo if they are different from the investigator.

2. *Underreporting of adverse events/serious adverse events*: All adverse events and serious adverse events occurring during a trial shall be reported at regular intervals to the ethics committee and sponsor as specified in the regulatory guidelines. Considering a multicenter study, there may be the occurrence of a serious adverse event such as anaphylaxis in only one center. The center may not report all the events as it is not happening in other centers, doubting the causal relationship. Underreporting of such occurrences of serious adverse events even though they occurred only in single study center to the ethics committee may lead to following consequences:

   - Imbalance in risk/benefit ratio.
   - Continuation of the study at the investigator's risk.
   - In either case, the ethics in safeguarding the well-being and health of patients are questioned.

     To avoid such scenarios, the ethics committee should conduct frequent monitoring visits and ensure that the adverse events are reported at regular frequencies.

3. *Misrepresentation of data*: Scientific misconduct may take the form of fabrication or falsification of data or plagiarism. Generally, these are obvious attempts to misrepresent results. Occasionally, there can be an unintentional misrepresentation of results due to poor scientific design of an experiment.[16]

   Situation 1: The laboratory parameters will be assessed as described in the protocol at each visit after administration of the investigational product. The ethics committee should look at study design and analysis to ensure that changes in laboratory parameters are carefully evaluated to ensure accurate reporting of results and any changes in the laboratory parameters in each follow-up visit from the baseline screening values.

   For example, Patient X who is already hyperlipidemic receives an existing diabetic treatment in his first and third period and receives the new interventional diabetic drug treatment in his second and fourth period. Total cholesterol levels of the patient are shown in Table 24.1.

   There is an increase in the total cholesterol levels in Period 2 and Period 4. Is the new drug elevating this? An investigation that looks at cholesterol levels across the entire group would come to a different conclusion compared to examining the cholesterol levels based on treatment groups. Thus, it is important that the ethics committee carefully evaluates the scientific design to ensure appropriate analysis. Failing to do so at this stage may lead to

TABLE 24.1 Changes in Laboratory Parameters

Patient X	Period 1	Period 2	Period 3	Period 4
Total cholesterol Level	275 mg/dL	385 mg/dL	286 mg/dL	370 mg/dL

nonreporting of adverse events/reactions to the ethics committee, raising a concern. It also emphasizes that patients should be followed up at regular intervals factorizing their safety and health concern.

Situation 2: Prescribing information/investigator brochure/summary of product characteristics is a leaflet providing the details of the drug such as its indication, usage, dosage and administration, dosage forms and strengths, contraindications, warnings and precautions, adverse reactions, drug interactions, use in specific populations, overdosage, description, clinical pharmacology, nonclinical toxicology, clinical studies, references, storage, and patient counseling information.

The adverse reaction experienced with drug "X" is reported in such prescribing information/investigator brochure/summary of product characteristics. Such adverse events may be captured in the protocol and informed consent to make the participants aware of the occurrence of events during the conduct of the trial.

An adverse drug reaction mentioned in the product insert or summary of product characteristics could be missed in the informed consent/study protocol. The occurrence of such reaction in the trial is claimed to happen unexpectedly as it is missed out in the protocol/informed consent document. The reporting of the event by the investigator would be "unexpected" but actually, as per its label claim, the event is defined and occurrence is "expected." In such a case, the investigator may provide a wrong causality assessment to the ethics committee and the regulatory agencies.

Situation 3: Consider the same adverse reaction "upper respiratory tract infection" has been added to the protocol and informed consent in its amended version. The amended versions of informed consent should reach the site(s) and should be notified to the patients participating. The amended consent should be signed by all the participants. The amended informed consent document, which has "upper respiratory tract infection," should be appropriately informed to the study participants and be signed by them. If the amended consent document is not provided to the study participants, it may lead to a compromise in safety if the patient is prone to bronchitis or asthma attack.

4. *Scientific misconduct*: Falsification of results or fabrication of data is the most common example of scientific misconduct. Data generated during the trial are essential and should be reported to the regulatory agencies as such. Any fabrication made to such data is highly unethical.[4]

Cases where fabrication may occur include the following:

Situation 1: Considering a hypertensive drug intervention study, the primary objective of the study would be to measure the decrease in the systolic and diastolic blood pressure in such patients.

The blood pressure values (source data) are subjective and can be easily fabricated. Monitoring of studies is essential for auditing the activities of the trial and for ensuring that the data generated are exactly recorded and reported at the end of the trial. The intention to falsify the data values is to provide positive results to the society, which is unacceptable.

Situation 2: Odd values should not be adjusted or ignored. It should be reported as such. Table 24.2 shows the hemoglobin levels of three subjects before and after the study intervention.

Subject B has their hemoglobin value reduced significantly at the end of the trial. The values obtained should be reported as such. The reason for a decrease in the value should be investigated. Appropriate treatment should be given, and the subject should be followed up until a significant increase in hemoglobin level is reached.

The values depicted in the table should be provided in the final report submitted to the regulatory agency. Any alteration of the originally generated out-of-range value to normal value is an offense, and moreover, such laboratory data should have their source data generated (which reflect the out-of-range value) from the hematological analyzer.

TABLE 24.2 Changes in Hemoglobin Levels Before and After the Study Period

Subjects	Hemoglobin Value Before Initiating the Study	Hemoglobin Value After Completion of the Study
A	11	9.5
B	14	7
C	10	8

Cross-verification of the data generated from the machine against the one submitted to the regulatory can be differentiated and questioned for any differences in future regulatory audits. This can help to identify potential misconduct and serves as a deterrent to temptations to either fabricate or falsify data.

5. *Ethical assessment of industry-sponsored clinical trials*: Approximately 70% of the funding of clinical trials now come from pharmaceutical or biotechnology firms. It is not necessarily a bad thing, but given that there are commercial motivations driving such clinical trials, there are important considerations that must be carefully addressed to ensure that this source of funding does not bias the results that are being generated and published. Miller and Shorr report a case analysis where they identified important principles for evaluating industry-sponsored studies. The following seven areas need to be carefully evaluated by the ethics committee: (1) scientific value, (2) scientific validity, (3) fair subject selection, (4) favorable risk/benefit ratio, (5) independent review, (6) informed consent, and (7) respect for enrolled subjects.[33]

Situation 1: Seeding trials are conducted by pharmaceutical companies in the name of research but are intended only for marketing purposes without any strong scientific objectives.[34] Various pharmaceutical companies have been warned by regulatory agencies for providing misleading information arising from this kind of seeding trials. Krumholz and colleagues provide a detailed dissection of the STEPS trial that was used to promote gabapentin and increase prescribing among investigators. The trial was planned and implemented by the marketing arm of the company. It was a phase IV uncontrolled, unblinded trial sponsored by the manufacturer. The stated objective was to study the efficacy, safety, tolerability, and quality of life among gabapentin users when titrating the drug to reduce the frequency of seizures. The authors of the original study did not mention their marketing objectives. However, the Krumholz's article identified the unstated marketing objective of the study to demonstrate efficacy, but an uncontrolled and unblinded study is a very poor design to demonstrate efficacy. They also used very complicated inclusion and exclusion criteria in the design, which would greatly decrease generalizability. The original IRB submission was denied twice because of these design deficiencies.[35]

In an analysis of ADVANTAGE (Assessment of Differences between Vioxx And Naproxen To Ascertain Gastrointestinal Tolerability and Effectiveness), the trial identified the following characteristics of seeding trials:
- there is marketing involved in study conception and design and in data collection and analysis and
- there is nondisclosure of the study's true purpose from IRBs, patients, and investigators.[36]

Situation 2: Sometimes pharmaceutical companies promote the marketing of drugs by providing information to the practicing physicians that reveal only the information that is important for the sale or use of a product, without providing full prescribing information. This "detailing" may come in the form of slick brochures, special "lunch and learn sessions," and continuing education presentations at exotic places. The influence of the pharmaceutical industry in altering prescribing patterns is studied.[37]

CONCLUSION

Ethics is an essential component of clinical research. Unethical studies have been conducted in the past and continue even today in different forms. Governments and other health agencies regulate research with relevant, updated laws and guidelines. However, conflicts of interest involving commercial products or services and the desire for research glory among researchers often get in the way of good science posing a challenge to good ethical practices. Therefore, ethics committees and their recommendations are vital to protect the well-being of research study participants. It also ensures that research involving human participants attains the highest quality standards.

PRACTICE QUESTIONS

1. What was the main ethical issue with the Tuskegee Syphilis study?
   A. No informed consent
   B. No compensation provided
   C. Longer study period
   D. Conducted in Tuskegee
2. The Elixir Sulfanilamide disaster (Massengill massacre) resulted in the Federal Food, Drug and Cosmetic Act in the United States, the key purpose of this bill was to avoid?
   A. Toxic substances in products
   B. Unethical clinical trials
   C. Producing affordable drugs
   D. Decentralizing drug regulations

3. Death and paralysis due to polio vaccine in the United States (1955) is known as?
   A. Cutter incident
   B. Nuremberg trial
   C. Thalidomide disaster
   D. Tuskegee trial
4. The primary ethical guidelines for studies involving human beings prepared in 1964 by the World Medical Association are known as?
   A. Alma-Ata Declaration
   B. Bangkok Declaration
   C. Declaration of Tokyo
   D. Declaration of Helsinki
5. Which of the following best describe the Belmont Report?
   A. Quality of drug products
   B. Avoidance of genotoxicity
   C. Respect for persons, beneficence, and justice
   D. Encouragement of the use of bioinformatics to reduce investigations of drug toxicity in humans

CROSSWORD EXERCISE

UP/DOWN	
1	Legal and financial coverage provided by the sponsor to participants during trial-related injury or death. (9)
3	A dummy drug used during a randomized crossover clinical study that does not produce any therapeutic efficacy. (7)
4	The document in which a subject voluntarily confirms the willingness to participate in a trial. (15)
5	A response to a drug that is noxious and unintended. (15)
7	One of the core principles of the Belmont Report. (7)
8	Subject's participation in a trial should be _____. (9)
9	The code of federal regulation for the protection of human subjects for all clinical research investigations. (6)
11	The ethical principles developed after the Tuskegee Study by the United States government in 1979 for research purposes. (13)
13	Prevention of disclosure of a subject's identity to other than authorized individuals in trials. (12)
15	This should be provided to participants as a financial aid by the sponsor of the trial as per applicable regulatory requirement. (12)
18	The consolidated guidance formed by the European Union, Japan, and the United States for trials that involve human participation. (6)
19	Ethical principles for medical research involving human subjects declared in 1964 by the World Medical Association. (8)

ACROSS	
2	Iniquitous Tuskegee trial carried out with _____ affected men from the 1930s to 1970s. (8)
6	Diethylene glycol, a deadly poison, was added to the formulation of this elixir. (13)
10	The unemployed, prisoners, and pregnant women are termed as particular section of the population in clinical research. (10)
12	An authorized individual under applicable law who consents on behalf of subjects in a trial. (3)
14	An international guideline for Good Clinical Practice (GCP) for trials on pharmaceutical products. (3)
16	Congenital defect due to the drug thalidomide. (10)
17	The person who participates in an informed consent process when the participant/ his or her representative is illiterate. (16)
20	Other name for the Nazi trials that conducted several unethical experiments with prisoners during the Second World War. (9)
21	Greek word for ethics. (5)
22	The foreseeable _____ that may happen during clinical trials should be transparently described on the consent form. (4)
23	A quorum of technical and nontechnical members who are independent and decide upon the approval of protocol and its related documents. (3)

REFERENCES

1. Avasthi A, Ghosh A, Sarkar S, Grover S. Ethics in medical research: general principles with special reference to psychiatry research. *Indian J Psychiatry*. 2013;55(1):86. https://doi.org/10.4103/0019-5545.105525.
2. International Conference on Harmonization. *ICH Harmonised Tripartite Guideline — Guideline for Good Clinical Practice E6(R1)*; 1996. https://www.ich.org/fileadmin/Public_Web_Site/ICH_Products/Guidelines/Efficacy/E6/E6_R1_Guideline.pdf.
3. Carter SM, Rychetnik L, Lloyd B, et al. Evidence, ethics, and values: a framework for health promotion. *Am J Public Health*. 2011;101(3):465—472. https://doi.org/10.2105/AJPH.2010.195545.

4. Sharma OP. Ethics in science. *Indian J Microbiol.* 2015;55(3):341−344. https://doi.org/10.1007/s12088-015-0532-x.

5. Tripathi R. Ethics committee member: reviewing the "Ethics" in clinical research. *Perspect Clin Res.* 2013;4(1):17−20. https://doi.org/10.4103/2229-3485.106371.

6. Resnik DB, Elliott KC. The ethical challenges of socially responsible science. *Account Res.* 2016;23(1):31−46. https://doi.org/10.1080/08989621.2014.1002608.

7. Crenner C. The Tuskegee Syphilis study and the scientific concept of racial nervous resistance. *J Hist Med Allied Sci.* 2012;67(2):244−280. https://doi.org/10.1093/jhmas/jrr003.

8. Paul C, Brookes B. The rationalization of unethical research: revisionist accounts of the Tuskegee Syphilis study and the New Zealand. *Am J Public Health.* 2015;105(10):e12−e19. https://doi.org/10.2105/AJPH.2015.302720.

9. Centers for Disease Control and Prevention. *The Tuskegee Timeline.* CDC; 2015. https://www.cdc.gov/tuskegee/timeline.htm.

10. Heintzelman CA. *The Tuskegee Syphilis Study and its Implications for the 21st Century − SocialWorker.com.* New Soc Work; 2003. http://www.socialworker.com/feature-articles/ethics-articles/The_Tuskegee_Syphilis_Study_and_Its_Implications_for_the_21st_Century/.

11. Wax PM. Elixirs, diluents, and the passage of the 1938 federal Food, drug and cosmetic act. *Ann Intern Med.* 1995;122(6):456−461. http://www.ncbi.nlm.nih.gov/pubmed/7856995.

12. Lex J. Why the watchdog won't bite: U.S. Food and drug administration challenges. *West J Emerg Med.* 2016;17(6):747−748. https://doi.org/10.5811/westjem.2016.9.32492.

13. Yale Law School. *Avalon Project − The International Military Tribunal for Germany. The Avalon Project*; 2008. http://avalon.law.yale.edu/subject_menus/imt.asp.

14. Fitzpatrick M. The cutter incident: how America's first polio vaccine led to a growing vaccine crisis. *J R Soc Med.* 2006;99(3):156. https://www.ncbi.nlm.nih.gov/pmc/articles/PMC1383764/.

15. Paine M. Therapeutic disasters that hastened safety testing of new drugs. *Clin Pharmacol Ther.* 2017;101(4):430−434. https://doi.org/10.1002/cpt.613.

16. Paul C, Sharples KJ, Baranyai J, Jones RW, Skegg DC. Outcomes for women without conventional treatment for stage 1A (microinvasive) carcinoma of the cervix. *Aust New Zeal J Obstet Gynaecol.* February 2018. https://doi.org/10.1111/ajo.12753.

17. Shuster E. Fifty years later: the significance of the Nuremberg Code. *N Engl J Med.* 1997;337(20):1436−1440. https://doi.org/10.1056/NEJM199711133372006.

18. Greene JA, Podolsky SH. Reform, regulation, and pharmaceuticals — the Kefauver−Harris amendments at 50. *N Engl J Med.* 2012;367(16):1481−1483. https://doi.org/10.1056/NEJMp1210007.

19. World Medical Association. World medical association declaration of Helsinki. *J Am Med Assoc.* 2013;310(20):2191. https://doi.org/10.1001/jama.2013.281053.

20. Department of Health. Education, and welfare, national commission for the protection of human subjects of biomedical and behavioral research. The Belmont report. Ethical principles and guidelines for the protection of human subjects of research. *J Am Coll Dent.* 2014;81(3):4−13. http://www.ncbi.nlm.nih.gov/pubmed/25951677.

21. Beauchamp TL, Childress JF. *Principles of Biomedical Ethics.* 7th ed. New York: Oxford University Press; 2013. https://global.oup.com/academic/product/principles-of-biomedical-ethics-9780199924585?cc=ru&lang=en&.

22. Owonikoko TK. Upholding the principles of autonomy, beneficence, and justice in phase I clinical trials. *Oncologist.* 2013;18(3):242−244. https://doi.org/10.1634/theoncologist.2013-0014.

23. Beauchamp TL. Methods and principles in biomedical ethics. *J Med Ethics.* 2003;29(5):269−274. https://doi.org/10.1136/JME.29.5.269.

24. Resnik DB. Unequal treatment of human research subjects. *Med Health Care Philos.* 2015;18(1):23−32. https://doi.org/10.1007/s11019-014-9569-6.

25. Coughlin SS. How many principles for public health ethics? *Open Public Health J.* 2008;1:8−16. https://doi.org/10.2174/1874944500801010008.

26. ICH. *Current Members & Observers.* ICH; 2017. http://www.ich.org/about/members-observers.html.

27. ICH. *ICH Guidelines.* ICH; 2005. http://www.ich.org/products/guidelines.html.

28. ICH. *Integrated Addendum to ICH E6(R1): Guideline for Good Clinical Practice E6(R2)*; 2016. http://www.ich.org/fileadmin/Public_Web_Site/ICH_Products/Guidelines/Efficacy/E6/E6_R2__Step_4_2016_1109.pdf.

29. Council for International Organizations of Medical Sciences (CIOMS). *International Ethical Guidelines for Health-Related Research Involving Humans*; 2016. https://cioms.ch/wp-content/uploads/2017/01/WEB-CIOMS-EthicalGuidelines.pdf.

30. van Delden JJM, van der Graaf R. Revised CIOMS international ethical guidelines for health-related research involving humans. *JAMA.* 2017;317(2):135. https://doi.org/10.1001/jama.2016.18977.

31. Office of the Human Research Protection. *Electronic Submission System FWAs and IRB Registrations.* Health and Human Services; 2017. https://ohrp.cit.nih.gov/efile/Default.aspx.

32. Sil A, Das NK. Informed consent process: foundation of the researcher-participant bond. *Indian J Dermatol.* 2017;62(4):380−386. https://doi.org/10.4103/ijd.IJD_272_17.

33. Miller FG, Shorr AF. Ethical assessment of industry-sponsored clinical trials: a case analysis. *Chest.* 2002;121(4):1337−1342. http://www.ncbi.nlm.nih.gov/pubmed/11948071.

34. Alexander GC. Seeding trials and the subordination of science. *Arch Intern Med.* 2011;171(12):1107−1108. https://doi.org/10.1001/archinternmed.2011.232.

35. Krumholz SD, Egilman DS, Ross JS. Study of neurontin: titrate to effect, profile of safety (STEPS) trial: a narrative account of a gabapentin seeding trial. *Arch Intern Med.* 2011;171(12):1100−1107. https://doi.org/10.1001/archinternmed.2011.241.

36. Hill KP, Ross JS, Egilman DS, Krumholz HM. The ADVANTAGE seeding trial: a review of internal documents. *Ann Intern Med.* 2008;149(4):251−258. http://www.ncbi.nlm.nih.gov/pubmed/18711155.

37. Fickweiler F, Fickweiler W, Urbach E. Interactions between physicians and the pharmaceutical industry generally and sales representatives specifically and their association with physicians' attitudes and prescribing habits: a systematic review. *BMJ Open.* 2017;7(9):e016408. https://doi.org/10.1136/bmjopen-2017-016408.

38. *National Commission for the Protection of Human Subjects of Biomedical and Behavioral Research, The Belmont report: ethical principles and guidelines for the protection of human subjects of biomedical and behavioral research.* Washington, DC: US Government Printing Office; 1979. https://www.hhs.gov/ohrp/regulations-and-policy/belmont-report/read-the-belmont-report/index.html.

ANSWERS TO PRACTICE QUESTIONS

1. A
2. A
3. A
4. D
5. C

CROSSWORD ANSWERS

CROSSWORD

UP/DOWN		ACROSS	
1	Insurance	2	Syphilis
3	Placebo	6	Sulfanilamide
4	Informed consent	10	Vulnerable
5	Adverse reaction	12	LAR
7	Justice	14	WHO
8	Voluntary	16	Phocomelia
9	Part50	17	Impartial witness
11	BelmontReport	20	Nuremberg
13	Confidential	21	Ethos
15	Compensation	22	Risk
18	ICHGCP	23	IEC
19	Helsinki		

Chapter 25

Stakeholders, Resources, and Documents in Clinical Research

Deepak C. Chilkoti

Consultant, Clinical Operations and Pharmacovigilance, Delhi, India

Learning Objectives:

Objective 25.1 Explain responsibilities of stakeholders in clinical research.
Objective 25.2 Overview of the common resources and documents used in clinical research.

OBJECTIVE 25.1. EXPLAIN RESPONSIBILITIES OF STAKEHOLDERS IN CLINICAL RESEARCH

Stakeholders in clinical research have the responsibility to ensure that all the "thirteen" principles of the International Conference on Harmonization Good Clinical Practice (ICH-GCP) are complied with. The Institutional Review Board/ Independent Ethics Committee (IRB/IEC), investigator, and sponsor are the key stakeholders, and other stakeholders such as the regulator, contract research organization (CRO), hospital/clinic, auditor, clinical research coordinator (CRC)/clinical research associate, data and safety monitoring board, subjects, etc. also have important roles during the lifecycle of trial conduct. Most of the following contents under objective 25.1 are extracted from ICH-GCP.[1]

Institutional Review Board/Independent Ethics Committee

IRB/IEC members evaluate the medical, nonmedical, ethical, and legal aspects of trials by collective qualifications and experience of a reasonable number of members (at least five).

Responsibilities

- Rights, safety, and well-being of trial subjects especially those trials that include vulnerable subjects should be safeguarded.
- The IRB/IEC should review the following documents to fulfill its responsibilities: trial protocol(s)/amendment(s), written informed consent form(s), investigator's brochure (IB), subject recruitment procedures (e.g., advertisements), written information to be provided to subjects, information about payments and compensation available to subjects, the investigator's current curriculum vitae, etc.
- Review of a proposed clinical trial by the IRB/IEC should happen within a reasonable time, and the IRB should document its views in writing, clearly identifying the trial and the documents reviewed. IRB minutes should mention the following:
  - approval;
  - modifications required before its approval;
  - disapproval; and
  - termination/suspension of any prior approval.
- The IRB/IEC should review the qualifications and prior experience of the investigator for the proposed trial, as documented by a current curriculum vita before according approval to the investigator.

- The IRB/IEC to ensure that the safety of human subjects is not jeopardized; it should conduct a continuing review of each ongoing trial at intervals depending on the degree of risk, but at least once per year.
- In emergency situations wherein prior consent from the trial subject or the subject's legally acceptable representative cannot be obtained, the IRB/IEC should ensure that the trial documents meet regulatory requirements for such trials and address ethical concerns.
- The IRB/IEC should ensure that, on the informed consent form, information regarding payment to subjects is mentioned. The IRB/IEC should review the amount and method of payment to subjects to assure that neither presents problems of coercion or undue influence on the trial subjects. Furthermore, payments should be made on a prorated basis and not on completion of the trial by the subject.

Investigator

The investigator should comply with the Good Clinical Practice (GCP) and the applicable regulatory requirements during study conduct. The investigator conducting the trial should be qualified by education, training, and experience and should provide evidence of such qualifications through curriculum vitae and/or other relevant documentation. The investigator should be thoroughly familiar with the use of the investigational product, as described in the study documents (protocol, IB, and product information leaflet) provided by the sponsor. The investigator should permit monitoring and auditing by the sponsor, IRB/IEC, and regulatory authority. The investigator should maintain a list of qualified persons to whom the investigator has delegated significant trial-related duties.

Responsibilities of the Investigator

Adequate Resources for the Conduct of the Trial

- The investigator should be able to demonstrate the potential for recruiting suitable subjects within project timelines.
- The investigator should have sufficient time to properly conduct and complete the trial within the agreed trial period.
- The investigator should have an adequate number of qualified staff and adequate facilities for the duration of the trial.
- The investigator should ensure that the site team assisting with the trial is adequately informed about the protocol, the investigational product(s), and their trial-related duties and functions.

Communication With the IRB/IEC

- Before initiating a trial, the investigator should have written and dated approval from the IRB/IEC for the trial protocol, written informed consent form, and subject recruitment procedures (e.g., advertisements).
- The investigator should provide the IRB/IEC with a current/updated copy of the IB.
- During the trial, the investigator should submit to the IRB/IEC all documents subject to review for approval (e.g., consent updates).

Medical Care of Trial Subjects

- For all trial-related medical decisions, a qualified physician, who is an investigator or a subinvestigator for the trial, should be responsible.
- The investigator should inform the subject's primary physician about the subject's participation in the trial if the subject agrees to the primary physician being informed.
- If a subject decides to withdraw prematurely from a trial, the subject is not obliged to give a reason, and the investigator should make all efforts to know the reason while fully respecting subject's rights.

Compliance With Protocol

- The investigator should conduct the trial in compliance with the protocol agreed to by the sponsor, by the regulatory authority, and which was given approval by the IRB/IEC.
- The investigator should not implement any changes of the protocol without agreement by the sponsor and prior review and documented approval from the IRB/IEC of an amendment, except where necessary to eliminate an immediate hazard(s) to trial subjects, or when the change(s) involves only logistical or administrative aspects of the trial (e.g., change in monitor(s), change of telephone number(s)).

Investigational Product(s)

- Responsibility rests with the investigator for investigational product(s) accountability at the trial site. The investigator may assign responsibility for investigational product(s) accountability to a pharmacist who is under the supervision of the investigator.
- The investigational product should be stored as specified by the sponsor and by the applicable regulatory requirement.
- The investigator should ensure that the investigational product is used only in accordance with the approved protocol.
- The investigator, or a person designated by the investigator, should explain the correct use of the investigational product to each subject.

Randomization Procedures and Unblinding

The investigator should follow the trial's randomization procedures, if any, and should ensure that the code is broken only in accordance with the protocol. In case of premature unblinding in a blinded trial due to a serious adverse event or accidental unblinding, the investigator should promptly document and explain it to the sponsor.

Informed Consent of Trial Subjects

Informed consent from trial subjects should be obtained and documented on the IRB/IEC's approved informed consent form. The investigator should adhere to ethical principles having their origin in the Declaration of Helsinki during obtainment of informed consent.

The written informed consent form should be revised whenever important new information becomes available that may be relevant to the subject's consent. Any revised written informed consent form should receive the IRB/IEC's approval opinion in advance of use.

Records/Reports and Progress Reports

- The investigator should maintain adequate and accurate source documents and trial records of the trial subjects. Source data should be attributable, legible, contemporaneous, original, accurate, and complete. Changes to source data should be dated, initialed, traceable, should not obscure the original entry, and should be explained; this applies to both written and electronic changes.
- The investigator should maintain all the essential documents for the conduct of the clinical trial and should take measures to prevent the accidental or premature destruction of these documents.
- Essential documents should be retained until at least 2 years after the last approval of a marketing application in an ICH region and until there are no pending or contemplated marketing applications in an ICH region or until at least 2 years have elapsed since the formal discontinuation of clinical development of the investigational product. These documents should be retained for a longer period, however, if required by the applicable regulatory requirements or by an agreement with the sponsor. It is the responsibility of the sponsor to inform the investigator/institution as to when these documents no longer need to be retained.
- The investigator should make available for direct access all requested trial-related records upon request of the monitor, auditor, IRB/IEC, or regulatory authority.
- The investigator should submit written progress reports of the trial status to the IRB/IEC annually.

Safety Reporting

- All serious adverse events (SAEs) should be reported immediately to the sponsor except those SAEs that the protocol identifies as not needing immediate reporting. The immediate reports should be followed promptly by detailed, written reports.
- Adverse events and/or laboratory abnormalities identified in the protocol as critical to safety evaluations should be reported to the sponsor.

Premature Termination or Suspension of a Trial

- If the trial is prematurely terminated or suspended for any reason, the investigator should promptly inform the trial subjects and should assure follow-up and appropriate therapy for the subjects.

Final Report(s) by the Investigator

- Upon completion of the trial, the investigator should inform the institution and should provide the IRB/IEC with a summary of the trial's outcome, and to the regulatory authority, where applicable, with any reports required with the help of sponsor.

Sponsor

The sponsor is an individual, company, institution, or organization that takes responsibility for the initiation, management, and/or financing of a clinical trial.

Responsibilities of the Sponsor

Quality Assurance and Quality Control

- The sponsor is responsible for implementing and maintaining quality assurance and quality control systems with a written standard operating procedure (SOP) to ensure that trials are conducted, and data are generated, documented, and reported in compliance with the protocol, SOPs, GCP, and the applicable regulatory requirement. Quality control should be applied to each stage of data handling to ensure that all generated data are reliable and have been processed correctly.

Contract Research Organization Selection

- A sponsor may transfer any or all of its trial-related duties and functions that should be specified in writing to a CRO but should ensure continuous oversight of activities done by the CRO, including those that are subcontracted to another party by the CRO. The ultimate responsibility for the quality and integrity of the trial data always resides with the sponsor.

Medical Expertise

- The sponsor should designate appropriately qualified medical personnel internally or appoint outside consultant to advise on trial-related medical questions.

Trial Design

- The sponsor should utilize qualified individuals (e.g., biostatisticians, clinical pharmacologists, and physicians) as appropriate, throughout all stages of the trial process, from designing the protocol and case report forms (CRFs) and planning the analyses to analyzing and preparing interim and final clinical trial reports.

Trial Management, Data Handling, and Record Keeping

- The sponsor should utilize appropriately qualified individuals to supervise the overall conduct of the trial, to handle the data, to verify the data, to conduct the statistical analyses, and to prepare the trial reports.

Investigator Selection

- The sponsor is responsible for selecting the investigator/institution. The sponsor and the investigator/institution should sign the protocol, or an alternative document (e.g., clinical trial agreement that can be bipartite between sponsor and investigator or tripartite between the sponsor, investigator, and institution), to confirm this agreement.

Allocation of Responsibilities

- Before initiating a trial, the sponsor should define, establish, and allocate all trial-related duties and functions within the organization or with external parties (CRO), if involved.

Compensation to Subjects and Investigators

- The sponsor should provide insurance or should indemnify (legal and financial coverage) the investigator/institution against claims arising from the trial, except for claims that arise from malpractice and/or negligence.
- The sponsor's policies and procedures should address the costs of treatment of trial subjects in the event of trial-related injuries.

Financing

- The financial aspects of the trial should be documented in an agreement (e.g., clinical trial agreement) between the sponsor and the investigator/institution.

Notification/Submission to Regulatory Authority(ies)

- Before initiating the clinical trial, the sponsor should submit any required application to the appropriate authority for review, acceptance, and/or permission (as required by the applicable regulatory requirement) to begin the trial.

Confirmation of Review by the IRB/IEC

The sponsor should obtain the following from the investigator/institution:

- The name and address of the investigator's/institution's IRB/IEC.
- A statement obtained from the IRB/IEC that it is organized and operates according to GCP and the applicable laws and regulations.
- Documented IRB/IEC approval of a current copy of the protocol, written informed consent form(s) and any other written information to be provided to subjects, subject recruiting procedures, and documents related to payments and compensation available to the subjects.

Information on Investigational Product(s)

- Before testing the product in the clinical phase, the sponsor should ensure that sufficient safety and efficacy data from nonclinical studies and/or clinical trials are available to support human exposure by the route, at potential dosages, for the duration, and in the trial population to be studied.
- The sponsor should update the IB as significant new information becomes available but not later than 1 year from the initial finalization date of the IB.

Manufacturing, Packaging, Labeling, and Coding Investigational Product(s)

- The sponsor should ensure that the investigational product(s) (including an active comparator(s) and placebo, if applicable) is manufactured in accordance with any applicable good manufacturing practices and is coded and labeled in a manner that protects the blinding, if applicable. In addition, the labeling should comply with the applicable regulatory requirement.
- The sponsor should determine, for the investigational product(s), acceptable storage temperatures, storage conditions (e.g., protection from light), storage times, reconstitution fluids and procedures, and devices for product infusion, if any. The sponsor should inform all involved parties (e.g., monitors, investigators, pharmacists, storage managers) of these determinations.
- The investigational product(s) should be packaged to prevent contamination and unacceptable deterioration during transport and storage.
- In blinded trials, the coding system for the investigational product(s) should include a mechanism that permits rapid identification of the product(s) in case of a medical emergency but does not permit undetectable breaks of the blinding.
- If significant formulation changes are made in the investigational or comparator product(s) during the course of clinical development, the results of any additional studies of the formulated product(s) (e.g., stability, dissolution rate, bioavailability) should be available before the use of the new formulation in clinical trials. Additional studies are needed to assess whether these changes would significantly alter the pharmacokinetic profile of the product.

Supplying and Handling Investigational Product(s)

- The sponsor is responsible for supplying the investigator with the investigational product only after obtaining approval from the IRB/IEC and regulatory authority.
- The sponsor should ensure that written procedures for investigational products address adequate and safe receipt, handling, storage, dispensing, retrieval of unused product from subjects, and the return of the unused investigational product to the sponsor (or alternative disposition at the investigator site if authorized by the sponsor).
- The sponsor should
  - ensure timely delivery of investigational product to the investigator;
  - maintain records that document shipment, receipt, disposition, return, and destruction of the investigational product;

- maintain a system for retrieving investigational products and documenting this retrieval (e.g., for deficient product recall, reclaim after trial completion, expired product reclaim);
- maintain a system for the disposition of unused investigational product and for the documentation of this disposition;
- take steps to ensure that the investigational product(s) are stable over the period of use;
- maintain sufficient quantities of the investigational product(s) used in the trials to reconfirm specifications, should this become necessary, and maintain records of batch sample analyses and characteristics. To the extent stability permits, samples should be retained either until the analyses of the trial data are complete or as required by the applicable regulatory requirement, whichever represents the longer retention period.

Record Access

- The sponsor should ensure that it is specified in the protocol or other written agreement (e.g., clinical trial agreement) that the investigator/institution should provide direct access to source data/documents for monitoring, audits, IRB/IEC review, and regulatory inspection.
- The sponsor should verify that each subject has consented, in writing, to direct access to their original medical records for trial-related monitoring, audit, IRB/IEC review, and regulatory inspection.

Safety Information and Adverse Drug Reaction Reporting

- The sponsor is responsible for the ongoing safety evaluation of the investigational product.
- The sponsor should promptly notify all concerned investigators/institutions and the regulatory authority of findings that could affect the safety of subjects or alter the IRB/IEC's approval opinion to continue the trial.
- The sponsor should expedite reporting of all adverse drug reactions that are both serious and unexpected to all concerned investigator(s)/institutions(s), to the IRB(s)/IEC(s), where required, and to the regulatory authority.
- The sponsor should submit all safety updates and periodic reports to the regulatory authority, as required by applicable regulatory requirement.

Monitoring

- The sponsor should develop a systematic, prioritized, risk-based approach to monitoring clinical trials. The sponsor may choose onsite monitoring, a combination of onsite and centralized monitoring, or, where justified, centralized monitoring. The sponsor should document the rationale for the chosen monitoring strategy (e.g., in the monitoring plan). Onsite monitoring is performed at the sites at which the clinical trial is being conducted. Centralized monitoring is a remote evaluation of accumulating data, performed in a timely manner, supported by appropriately qualified and trained persons (e.g., data managers, biostatisticians). Centralized monitoring processes provide additional monitoring capabilities that can complement and reduce the extent and/or frequency of onsite monitoring and help distinguish between reliable data and potentially unreliable data.

Audit

- Sponsors should perform audits as part of implementing quality assurance. The purpose of a sponsor's audit, which is independent of and separate from routine monitoring or quality control functions, should be to evaluate trial conduct and compliance with the protocol, SOPs, GCP, and the applicable regulatory requirements.

Premature Termination or Suspension of a Trial

- If a trial is prematurely terminated or suspended, the sponsor should promptly inform the investigators/institutions, IRB/IEC, and the regulatory authority of the reason(s) for the termination or suspension.

Clinical Trial/Study Reports

- The sponsor should ensure that the clinical trial reports are prepared and provided to the regulatory agency whether the trial is completed or prematurely terminated. The sponsor should also ensure that in marketing applications the clinical trial reports should meet the standards of the ICH Guideline for Structure and Content of Clinical Study Reports.

Regulator

The regulatory authority (e.g., Food and Drug Administration [FDA], Medicines and Healthcare Products Regulatory Agency) is in charge of protecting public health by assuring the safety and efficacy of drugs, biologics, and medical devices. The regulator achieves this through an extensive review process. In this process, the sponsor works with the regulator to submit an application or investigational new drug/new drug application for the new product. The regulator carefully evaluates the submitted documents, which then leads to either approval or rejection. In addition to the review process, the regulator also performs audits and inspections of any section of clinical research, including sites, sponsors, or IRBs. If the regulator discovers any problems of noncompliance, a warning letter may be sent mentioning corrective action that must be taken immediately by the stakeholder responsible.[2]

Contract Research Organization

A CRO is a person or an organization (commercial, academic, or other) contracted by the sponsor to perform one or more of a sponsor's trial-related duties and functions.

A sponsor may transfer any or all of the sponsor's trial-related duties and functions to a CRO, any trial-related duty and function that is transferred to and assumed by a CRO should be specified in writing.

All responsibilities of a sponsor in this chapter also apply to a CRO to the extent that a CRO has assumed the trial-related duties and functions of a sponsor.

Auditor

The general responsibilities of an auditor include the following:

- Coordinate and conduct internal system audits and external investigative site/vendor audits;
- Create, maintain, and revise departmental standard operating procedures, forms, and templates;
- Host audits by sponsors and regulatory inspectors;
- Coordinate, conduct, and track company-wide regulatory training (ICH-GCP and medical device);
- Develop training materials and applicable tests and guides.

Clinical Research Coordinator

The general responsibilities of the CRC include the following:

- The clinical research coordinator, or CRC, is an essential member of the research team, the stakeholder who conducts the study. This member plays a critical role in organizing a site's participation in the expanding arena of clinical trials.
- The primary function of the CRC is to manage and coordinate the smooth, accurate progress of clinical protocols from the planning stage through study completion by acting as a liaison to other member stakeholders, including the investigator, the subject, the research site, the IRB, and the sponsor. The reason why this role holds such great importance is because the CRC is at the center of the study process.
- The CRC assists in the development, review, and maintenance of conducting a study in accordance with appropriate SOPs, GCP, and regulatory guidelines. This includes assisting in the review of protocols, checking for protocol feasibility, preparing documents for IRB submission, recruiting and screening study participants, obtaining informed consent from study subjects, facilitating continued participation of subjects, and tracking study progress while maintaining compliance.[3]

Clinical Research Associate

General responsibilities of a CRA include the following:

- Coordinating with the ethics committee, which safeguards the rights, safety, and well-being of all trial subjects;
- Managing regulatory authority applications and approvals that oversee the research and marketing of new and existing drugs;
- Identifying and assessing the suitability of facilities to be used as the clinical trial site;
- Identifying/selecting an investigator who will be responsible for the conduct of the trial at the trial site;
- Liaising with doctors/consultants or investigators on conducting the trial;
- Setting up the trial sites, which includes ensuring each center has the trial materials, including the trial investigational medicinal product. Moreover, training the site staff to trial-specific industry standards;

- Monitoring the trial throughout its duration, which involves visiting the trial sites on a regular basis;
- Verifying that data entered onto the CRFs are consistent with patient clinical notes, source data/document verification;
- Collecting completed CRFs from hospitals and general practices;
- Writing visit reports and filing and collating trial documentation and reports;
- Ensuring all unused trial supplies are accounted for;
- Closing down trial sites on completion of the trial;
- Archiving study documentation and correspondence.

Data and Safety Monitoring Board (Independent Data-Monitoring Committee)

A data safety monitoring board or independent data-monitoring committee (IDMC) that may be established by the sponsor to assess at intervals the progress of a clinical trial, the safety data, and the critical efficacy end points and to recommend to the sponsor whether to continue, modify, or stop a trial. The IDMC should have written operating procedures and maintain written records of all its meetings.

Participants (Subject/Trial Subject)

An individual who participates in a clinical trial, either as a recipient of the investigational product(s) or as a control. General responsibilities of participants include the following:[4]

- Respect investigators, research staff, and other participants.
- Read the consent form and other documents. Ask questions if they do not understand something about the study or their rights and responsibilities as a research participant or need more information.
- Carefully weigh the risks and benefits when deciding whether to participate in the study.
- Refrain from signing the consent document until they believe that they understand its content and feel comfortable with their decision to participate.
- Follow directions for proper use, dosing, and storage of self-administered study medications, providing biological samples and preparing for tests, procedures, or examinations.
- Follow directions for abstaining from nonstudy-related medications or other contraindicated medications or procedures.
- Know when the study begins and ends. This is particularly important for an intervention trial that has a follow-up period after the intervention is completed.
- Show up at scheduled appointments on time and inform the staff within a reasonable time if they need to reschedule an appointment.
- Provide truthful answers to questions asked during screening/enrollment and during the study.
- Inform staff if other medical care is needed during the study.
- Inform the staff if there are questions they would rather not answer.
- Report pain, discomfort, nausea, dizziness, and other problems and symptoms they experience during the study.
- Keep information about the study confidential, if asked to do so.
- Keep staff informed when contact information (e.g., phone number, address) changes.
- If they decide to withdraw from the study, inform the staff, and follow the procedures for withdrawal.

OBJECTIVE 25.2. OVERVIEW OF THE COMMON RESOURCES AND DOCUMENTS USED IN CLINICAL RESEARCH

GCP is an international ethical and scientific quality standard for the design, conduct, performance, monitoring, auditing, recording, analyses, and reporting of clinical trials. It also serves to protect the rights, integrity, and confidentiality of trial subjects. It is very important to understand the background of the formation of the ICH-GCP guidelines as this, in itself, explains the reasons and the need for doing so. Most of the information collected for this objective is from the ICH guidelines.[1] Today, the ICH-GCP guidelines are used in clinical trials throughout the globe with the main aim of protecting and preserving human rights. Adherence to the principles of GCPs, including adequate human subject protection, is universally recognized as a critical requirement to the conduct of research involving human subjects.[5] The development of new medicines to improve life is a long and sophisticated process involving many people and significant investments. The ICH-GCP has managed to cope with the challenges of clinical research to a major extent. The conducting of clinical research in accordance with the principles of GCP helps to ensure that the participants in clinical research are not exposed to undue risk and that data generated in the research are valid and accurate. Thus, the GCP not only serves the interest of clinicians and those involved in the research process but also protects the rights, safety, and well-being of subjects and ensures that investigations are scientifically sound and advance public health goals.

Resources for GCP:

- ICH E6 R2 guidelines: www.ich.org/fileadmin/Public_Web_Site/ICH.../Guidelines/.../E6/E6_R2__Step_4.pdf;
- FDA website—Clinical Trials and Human Subject Protection and Office of Good Clinical Practice: https://www.fda.gov/scienceresearch/specialtopics/runningclinicaltrials/default.htm;
- Office of Good Clinical Practice's (OGCP's) mission statement;
- Online Web training by various companies and institutes;
- Colleges and institutes providing clinical research courses—various universities and institutes.

Documents in Clinical Trials

Documents are an essential part of the clinical trial where every activity performed in a clinical trial is captured. These documents are filed timely at the sites of investigator and sponsor as they aid in the proper management of a trial and provide evidence that the conduct of the clinical trial is compliant with the ICH-GCP and all applicable regulatory requirements. Data are recorded in these documents timely, which are usually audited by the sponsor and inspected by the regulatory authority to confirm the integrity of collected data and validity of the trial conducted. A trial master file is established at the beginning of the trial at the investigator's/institution's site and at the sponsor's office where all the documents are placed promptly and maintained throughout the conduct of the trial. Before the final close out of the trial, the monitor reviews both investigator/institution and sponsor files to confirm all documents are placed in appropriate files. These documents should be available for sponsor audits and regulatory inspections.

The sponsor and investigator/institution should record the location where all essential documents, including source documents, are placed. The storage system used during the trial and for archiving (irrespective of the type of media used) should provide for document identification, version history, search, and retrieval. These documents should be supplemented or reduced (if not important and relevant), in advance of trial initiation.

The sponsor should not have control of the CRF data exclusively and should ensure that the investigator has control and continuous access to the data reported to the sponsor. The copy used to replace an original document (e.g., source documents, CRF) should fulfill the requirements for certified copies. The investigator/institution should have control of all essential documents and records generated by the investigator/institution before, during, and after the trial. Details about documents are extracted mainly from the ICH-GCP.[1]

Investigator's Brochure

The IB is the compiled information (data) of clinical and nonclinical studies on the investigational product(s), which is related to the study of the investigational product(s) in human subjects. This brochure contains the relevant and current scientific information that is provided to the investigator and other members involved in the trial before initiation of the clinical trial. This information may aid in recognizing and treating possible overdose and adverse drug reactions.

The purpose is to thoroughly familiarize the investigator with the appropriate use of the investigational product(s), its possible risks and adverse reactions, specific tests, observations, and precautions that may be needed for a clinical trial. A copy of the updated IB is also provided to the IRB/IEC.

The IB is updated whenever any new significant information is available, and the same should be provided to the investigator and IRB/IEC.

Contents of the IB:

- Table of contents
- Summary
- Introduction
- Physical, chemical, and pharmaceutical properties and formulation
- Nonclinical studies
  - Nonclinical pharmacology
  - Pharmacokinetics and product metabolism in animals
  - Toxicology

- Effects in humans
  - Pharmacokinetics and product metabolism in humans
  - Safety and efficacy
  - Marketing experience
- Summary of data and guidance for the investigator
- Confidentiality statement (optional)
- Signature page (optional)

Study Protocol

Study protocol is a document describing the objective(s), design, methodology, statistical considerations, and organization of a trial providing the background and rationale for the trial. The protocol is shared with the investigator to make him/her thoroughly familiar with the appropriate use of the investigational product(s), which is then signed by the investigator for agreement with the sponsor.

The protocol is shared with the IRB/IEC for approval/favorable opinion and is also explained to other responsible members assisting in the trial. The whole clinical trial has to be conducted in compliance with the approved protocol. If there is any noncompliance with the protocol in the study, it is explained and documented by the designated person.

Contents of a trial protocol:

- General information
- Background information
- Trial objectives and purpose
- Trial design
- Selection and withdrawal of subjects
- Treatment of subjects
- Assessment of efficacy
- Assessment of safety
- Statistics
- Direct access to source data/documents
- Quality control and quality assurance
- Ethics
- Data handling and record keeping
- Financing and insurance
- Publication policy
- Supplements

Informed Consent Form

Informed consent is a process in which a subject is informed of each and every aspect of a clinical trial for which the subject confirms his/her voluntary participation. The informed consent form is the document where every aspect of the trial is written, which is signed and dated by the subject voluntarily and the form is documented along with any written information provided to the subject. A copy of the signed and dated written informed consent form and any other written information is provided to the subjects before and during conduct of the trial.

Before conduct of the trial, the IRB/IEC's written approval/favorable opinion is received on the informed consent form (including all translations).

If new information related to the subject's consent is available, the informed consent form should be revised and the written approval/favorable opinion of the IRB/IEC should be taken in advance. The subject or the subject's legally acceptable representative should be informed in a timely manner for the revised information.

The informed consent form must be in a language that is easy to understand by the subject and should be signed before participating in the trial. An impartial witness is required during the discussion of informed consent if a subject or legally acceptable representative is unable to read. The witness has to attest the information in the consent form, and any other written information is correctly explained to the subject or the subject's legally acceptable representative, and apparently understood and freely given by the subject or the subject's legally acceptable representative.

The following should be explained to subjects in informed consent discussion:

- The trial involves research.
- Purpose of the trial.
- The trial treatment(s) and the probability for random assignment to each treatment.

- The trial procedures to be followed, including all invasive procedures.
- The subject's responsibilities.
- Experimental aspects of the trial.
- The reasonably foreseeable risks or inconveniences to the subject and, when applicable, to an embryo, fetus, or nursing infant.
- The reasonably expected benefits. When there is no intended clinical benefit to the subject, the subject should be made aware of this.
- The alternative procedure(s) or course(s) of treatment that may be available to the subject, and their important potential benefits and risks.
- The compensation and/or treatment available to the subject in the event of trial-related injury.
- The anticipated prorated payment, if any, to the subject for participating in the trial.
- The anticipated expenses, if any, to the subject for participating in the trial.
- The subject's participation in the trial is voluntary and that the subject may refuse to participate or withdraw from the trial, at any time, without penalty or loss of benefits to which the subject is otherwise entitled.
- That the monitor(s), the auditor(s), the IRB/IEC, and the regulatory authority(ies) will be granted direct access to the subject's original medical records for verification of clinical trial procedures and/or data. Access should be without violating the confidentiality of the subject to the extent permitted by the applicable laws and regulations and that, by signing a written informed consent form, the subject or the subject's legally acceptable representative is authorizing such access.
- The records identifying the subject will be kept confidential and, to the extent permitted by the applicable laws and/or regulations, will not be made publicly available. If the results of the trial are published, the subject's identity will remain confidential.
- That the subject or the subject's legally acceptable representative will be informed in a timely manner if information becomes available. The information may be relevant to the subject's willingness to continue participation in the trial.
- The person(s) to contact for further information regarding the trial and the rights of trial subjects, and whom to contact in the event of trial-related injury.
- The foreseeable circumstances and/or reasons under which the subject's participation in the trial may be terminated.
- The expected duration of the subject's participation in the trial.
- The approximate number of subjects involved in the trial.

Case Report Form

A CRF, printed or electronic, is designed to collect patient data in a clinical trial; its development represents a significant part of the clinical trial and can affect study success. Site personnel capture the subject's data on the CRF, which is collected during their participation in a clinical trial. The International Conference on Harmonization Guidelines for Good Clinical Practice defines the CRF as a printed, optical, or electronic document designed to record all the protocol-required information to be reported to the sponsor on each trial subject.

Electronic CRFs are largely being used over paper CRFs due to the advantages they offer such as improved data quality, online discrepancy management, faster database lock, etc. Standard guidelines should be followed while designing any format of the CRF. A CRF completion manual should be provided to the site personnel to promote accurate data entry by them. These measures will result in reduced query generations and improved data integrity. A well-designed CRF should represent the essential contents of the study protocol and in an ideal situation; CRF is designed once the study protocol is finalized.[6]

The following points are to be borne in mind while designing a CRF:

- Use consistent formats, font style, and font sizes throughout the CRF booklet
- Select portrait versus landscape versus combination layouts
- Use clear and concise questions, prompts, and instructions
- Visual cues, such as boxes that indicate place and format of data to be recorded, should be provided to the person recording the data as much as possible
- Using the option of "circling of answers" should be limited as it is hard to interpret; instead checkboxes would be appropriate
- Clear guidance about skip patterns like what to skip and what not to skip should be mentioned at appropriate places
- Skips (instructions provided on the CRF page to maintain the connectivity between pages) should be kept to a minimum by the placement of questions to avoid confusions

- Provide boxes or separate lines to hold the answers. This indirectly informs the data recorder where to write/enter the response and helps to differentiate it visually from the entry fields for other questions
- Separate the columns with thick lines
- Provide bold and italicized instructions
- Minimize free-text responses
- Position only specified density of questions on each page
- Page numbering if necessary should be consistent throughout
- Avoid using "check all that applies" as it forces assumptions about the clinical data
- Specify the unit of measurement
- Indicate the number of decimal places to be recorded
- Use standard data format (e.g., dd/mm/yyyy) throughout the CRF
- Use precoded answer sets such as yes/no, male/female, a method of administration of medicine, and severity of adverse event (AE) (mild/moderate/severe) wherever possible
- Do not split modules/sections (a set of one or more related groups of questions that pertain to a single clinical study visit) like, for example, AE section should not be split and laid across pages such that information related to a single AE will have to be collected from different pages
- Use "no carbon required (NCR)" copies to ensure exact replica of the CRF (for paper CRFs)
- Use instructions, including page numbers where data have to be entered (e.g., during a follow-up visit, the investigator is supposed to record whether any AE has occurred and if so, details of the AE have to be recorded in the AE module. Hence, the field corresponding to this question on the module for the particular visit would have the options "yes" or "no." There should be an instruction "if 'yes,' please provide the information on the AEs page (page no. XX)."[6]

Clinical Study Report

A clinical study report is a written description of a trial/study of any therapeutic, prophylactic, or diagnostic agent conducted in human subjects, in which the clinical and statistical description, presentations, and analyses are fully integrated. This is the final report submitted to the regulatory authority with document results and interpretation of the trial. The sponsor should prepare and provide the clinical study reports (as per the standards of the ICH guideline) to the regulatory authority as required by the authority after completion or termination of the trial.[7]

List of contents in clinical study report:

- Title page
- Synopsis
- Table of contents for the individual clinical study report
- List of abbreviations and definitions of terms
- Ethics
- Independent Ethics Committee or Institutional Review Board
- Ethical conduct of the study
- Patient information and consent
- Investigators and study administrative structure
- Introduction
- Study objectives
- Investigational plan
- Study patients
- Efficacy evaluation
- Safety evaluation
- Discussion and overall conclusions
- Tables, figures, and graphs referred to but not included in the text
- Reference list
- Appendices[7]

Clinical Trial Agreement

The financial aspect of the trial should be documented in an agreement between the involved parties, e.g., the sponsor and the investigator/institution, CRO and the investigator/institution, sponsor and the CRO, and investigator/institution and authority(ies) (where required).

CONCLUSION

Though many stakeholders are involved in clinical research, their roles and responsibilities are clearly mentioned in ICH-GCP. Compliance with the guidelines in every aspect, including documentation, is essential.

Case Exercise 1

An informed consent form (ICF) was submitted to the Ethics Committee for their review and approval along with the prediscussed budget sheet. ICF and budget sheet were approved by the EC, and some of the patients consented on the same ICF.

In the ICF the subject travel reimbursement is written as $50, but in the budget sheet, it has been approved as $100. Coordinators discover this later when 12 subjects have already consented.

What should be solution now to keep study GCP compliant?

Solution:

The ICF needs to be changed for the statement of patient reimbursement as $100, and along with the budget sheet, it should be submitted to the EC for their acknowledgment.

As both the documents had already been approved by the EC and there has just been an administrative change, there is no need for reapproval and the same should be informed to the EC.

After changing the document, all the subjects should be reconsented and the whole procedure should be documented in source notes.

Case Exercise 2

In a pharma drug trial, the subject had participated in the study. The subject gave his consent, but is illiterate; the subject had been accompanied by his son (blood relative). On behalf of the subject, all the information in the ICF had been written by his son.

Now, once the subject has given their thumb impression (left hand) on the consent form, where should the son sign—in the LAR column or as an impartial witness?

Solution:

The subject's son should sign as an impartial witness as the subject is well, able to give his consent, and can understand the study procedure.

As per the GCP, the LAR comes into play when the subject is unable to give his consent, like infants, comatose patients, etc. So, in this case, the subject's son would be considered an impartial witness.

REFERENCES

1. International Council for Harmonization. *Integrated Addendum to ICH E6 (R1): Guideline for Good Clinical Practice E6 (R2). Step 4 Version*; 2016. Available at: http://www.ich.org/fileadmin/Public_Web_Site/ICH_Products/Guidelines/Efficacy/E6/E6_R2__Step_4_2016_1109.pdf.
2. Cato A. *Clinical Drug Trials and Tribulations*. 2nd ed. New York: Marcel Dekker; 2002.
3. Woodin KE. *The CRC's Guide to Coordinating Clinical Research*. Boston, MA: CenterWatch; 2004.
4. Resnik DB, Ness E. Participants' responsibilities in clinical research. *J Med Ethics*. December 2012;38(12):746–750. https://doi.org/10.1136/medethics-2011-100319.
5. US FDA. *Clinical Trials and Human Subject Protection*; 2018. Available at: https://www.fda.gov/ScienceResearch/SpecialTopics/Running ClinicalTrials/.
6. Bellary S, Krishnankutty B, Latha MS. Basics of case report form designing in clinical research. *Perspect Clin Res*. 2014;5(4):159–166.
7. ICH. *Structure and Content of Clinical Study Reports E3. Current Step 4 Version Dated 30*; November 1995. Available at: https://www.ich.org/fileadmin/Public_Web_Site/ICH_Products/Guidelines/Efficacy/E3/E3_Guideline.pdf.

Section VI

Pharmacy Education

Chapter 26

Quality Assurance in Pharmacy Education

Dawn G. Zarembski, Michael J. Rouse and Peter H. Vlasses

Accreditation Council for Pharmacy Education, Chicago, IL, United States

Learning Objectives

Objective 26.1 Describe quality assurance of pharmacy curricula in a global perspective.
Objective 26.2 Explain the role of ACPE in accreditation and certification of pharmacy programs.
Objective 26.3 Detail the curriculum mapping process in pharmacy education.

OBJECTIVE 26.1. DESCRIBE QUALITY ASSURANCE OF PHARMACY CURRICULA IN A GLOBAL PERSPECTIVE

Responsibilities of pharmacists are evolving globally to meet public health demands. Once involved primarily with dispensing and compounding medications, pharmacists worldwide are increasingly serving as medication experts working as members of interprofessional healthcare teams.[1] Within individual countries, pharmacy curricula must adapt to address the changing nature of responsibilities for the country's pharmacy workforce as the ability to provide optimal pharmaceutical care depends on the existence of a qualified and competent pharmacy workforce. Governments and academic institutions increasingly need to reevaluate pharmacy education and the methods used to measure, assure, and improve academic quality. Recognizing the need to advance pharmacy education and the quality assurance process, the International Pharmaceutical Federation (FIP), in conjunction with the World Health Organization (WHO) and the United Nations Educational, Scientific and Cultural Organization launched the Pharmacy Education Taskforce (PET) in 2007 to oversee implementation of the 2008–10 Pharmacy Education Action Plan.[2] As defined by PET, "*pharmacy education refers to the educational design and capacity to develop the workforce for a diversity of settings (e.g., community, hospital, research and development, academia) across varying levels of service provision and competence (e.g., technical support, human resources, pharmacist practitioners, pharmaceutical scientists, pre-service students) and scope of education (e.g., undergraduate, post-registration, continuing professional development, practitioner development, life-long learning).*"[3]

Pharmacy Education Planning

The Pharmacy Education Action Plan (hereafter referred to as the Action Plan) advocates for a needs-based approach to pharmacy education (see Fig. 26.1).[1] Central to the Needs-Based Education Model is the vision for pharmacy practice and education, which should be developed through profession-wide consensus. The Action Plan encourages the development of educational systems designed to produce a pharmacy workforce competent to deliver healthcare services that are aligned with the local needs of the country. The Action Plan provides evidence-based guidance and frameworks that can be used to advance pharmacy education and encompasses four domains of action including: (1) development of a vision and framework for education development; (2) development of a competency framework; (3) ensuring a quality assurance system; and (4) building academic and institution capacity.

Within healthcare, the quality assurance process supports and facilitates improvements in practice because educational institutions are expected to modify the education provided in an effort to address advances in knowledge and practice.

FIGURE 26.1 FIP education needs-based education model *Adapted from FIP, Quality Assurance of Pharmacy Education: The FIP Global Framework. 2nd Edition; 2014.*

Framework-Based Quality Assurance Systems Development

Quality assurance systems vary greatly between countries. Although many countries have well-developed quality assurance systems that utilize standards aligned to local healthcare needs, in other countries such systems may be lacking or still emerging. Ideally, each country should have its own national system for quality assurance and standards for pharmacy education that reflect contemporary pharmacy practice and education and meet the country's needs.[4] As the principles and core elements utilized in the quality assurance process are universal, countries seeking to establish or improve their system could utilize an internationally developed and adopted framework for quality assurance of pharmacy education for reference purposes.

The FIP International Forum for Quality Assurance of Pharmacy Education developed a globally applicable framework for quality assurance of pharmacy education that incorporates core principles and elements considered essential for an effective approach to quality assurance.[4]

FIP's Quality Assurance Framework (Framework) provides a template that can be modified to suit local needs and conditions within individual countries and focuses on the elements that need to be included and applied. The Framework addresses three main sections. The *first section*, Prerequisites for Quality Assurance in Pharmacy Education, outlines the prerequisites and foundational elements that need to be identified and will form the basis of the design, development, and implementation of the quality assurance system. For example, individual countries would need to identify the national vision for pharmacy practice and education within their country. Essential to this vision will be the identification of national, societal, and population healthcare needs that form the basis for the pharmacist's responsibilities within the healthcare system. To ensure the vision adequately encompasses the full scope of healthcare needs, a broad array of relevant stakeholders should be identified and engaged in the process. The core healthcare needs and issues of countries are likely to be the same or similar, but differences will certainly exist. These differences are the result of or are influenced by several factors, including population demographics, public health, and morbidity challenges and trends, and national economic and political priorities.

The *second section*, Quality Criteria and Quality Indicators for Pharmacy Education, outlines the criteria that should be addressed to ensure quality. These criteria include the five "pillars" of quality (context, structure, process, outcomes, and impact) of pharmacy education as well as the three "foundations" of competency that should be addressed in pharmacy education (science, practice, and ethics) (see Fig. 26.2).

Once the vision for pharmacy education and practice has been established, the philosophy and purpose of quality assurance can be addressed. The third section of the framework addresses components that should be considered during development of the quality assurance system. An initial step involves establishing the structure, mandate, and purpose of the quality assurance agency. Different models for quality assurance can be considered with the entity charged with

FIGURE 26.2 The pillars and foundations of educational quality *Adapted from FIP, Quality Assurance of Pharmacy Education: The FIP Global Framework. 2nd Edition; 2014.*

oversight of the quality assurance process falling under a governmental agency, a national pharmacy organization, or an independent, autonomous agency. The level of quality assurance, either at the institutional or program-level, should also be established. The composition of the agency's governing/decision-making board or council should be identified, including the criteria for appointment or selection of members and the duration of service. Identification of funding sources to support the agency is essential to ensuring the sustainability of its operations. Policies and procedure need to be established to ensure consistent and fair accreditation decisions that are free from any conflict of interest. The procedures that will be used to evaluate individual pharmacy education programs should form the basis for the decision-making process. The criteria/standards should be clearly articulated, evidence-based, validated, publicly disclosed, and endorsed profession-wide. Periodic updating of the criteria/standards is needed to ensure continued applicability in the face of changes in practice and changing national healthcare needs.

OBJECTIVE 26.2. EXPLAIN THE ROLE OF ACPE IN ACCREDITATION AND CERTIFICATION OF PHARMACY PROGRAMS

Structure and Mission

In most countries, the national government has the responsibility—directly or indirectly—for quality assurance of higher education, including professional degree programs, such as pharmacy. A growing trend, however, is the establishment of independent, autonomous agencies that have a specialized- or programmatic focus of activity. One such example is the Accreditation Council for Pharmacy Education (ACPE), the national agency for the accreditation of professional degree programs in pharmacy and providers of continuing pharmacy education in the United States. ACPE (until 2003 known as the American Council on Pharmaceutical Education) was established in 1932 for the accreditation of professional degree programs in pharmacy, and its scope was expanded in 1975 to include accreditation of providers of continuing pharmacy education (www.acpe-accredit.org). ACPE further broadened its activities to include evaluation and certification of professional degree programs internationally in 2011 and entered into a collaboration with the American Society of Health-System Pharmacists to accredit pharmacy technician education and training programs beginning in 2014. ACPE is a not-for-profit agency, whose mission and sole purpose are to assure and advance quality in pharmacy education.

To address its mission, ACPE routinely interacts with a variety of stakeholders. The 10 members of ACPE's Board of Directors are appointed by the American Association of Colleges of Pharmacy (AACP), the American Pharmacists Association (APhA), the National Association of Boards of Pharmacy (NABP) (three members each), and the American Council on Education (ACE) (one nonpharmacy-related appointment). This structure ensures that the Board includes perspectives and experience from regulators (NABP appointees), practitioners (APhA appointees), and educators (AACP appointees) as well as the public (ACE appointee). In a broader context, ACPE routinely interacts with stakeholders to ensure the organization continues to adapt to the changes within the pharmacy profession in the United States and globally. Engagement with state boards of pharmacy, state and federal governments, and other accreditation agencies ensures ACPE remains informed of regulatory and policy changes. Similarly, changes in education are captured through interactions with pharmacy programs, individual educators, and continuing education providers, whereas changes in practice are identified through interactions with pharmacy practitioner organizations, employers, other health professionals, students, and the public. ACPE works with organizations outside of the profession. In this regard, ACPE, along with several other health disciplines accreditation agencies, formed the Health Professions Accreditors Collaborative to strengthen communication between the healthcare professions and enhance interprofessional education and care. In addition, ACPE, in conjunction with the Accreditation Council for Continuing Medical Education (ACCME) and the American Nurses Credentialing Center (ANCC) provide a process for Joint Accreditation for Interprofessional Continuing Education providers. The joint accreditation process offers providers the opportunity for accreditation by all three providers (ACPE, ACCME, and ANCC) through a single review process and promotes interprofessional continuing education activities that are designed "by the team, for the team" to enhance interprofessional collaborative practice.

US state boards of pharmacy require that domestic licensure applicants be a graduate of an ACPE-accredited pharmacy degree program to be eligible to sit for the North American Pharmacist Licensure Examination (NAPLEX). Accreditation provides a national basis for quality assurance of the education students receive. The value of the accreditation process is multifactorial, serving multiple stakeholders, including the public, students and prospective students, licensing bodies, pharmacy programs and their parent institutions, and the profession. ACPE accreditation provides public recognition that a professional degree program has met the required standards through a series of initial and subsequent periodic evaluations.[5] Graduates of accredited programs meet the educational requirements for licensure and should be educationally prepared for practice. ACPE standards are minimum requirements; programs commonly exceed the minimum requirements by using a continuous quality improvement process. The standards, based on evidence and experience, describe the various elements needed for quality-assured professional education. The standards describe expectations that ACPE has of academic institutions offering the Doctor of Pharmacy degree program. ACPE standards, policies, and procedures also address the expectations that the US Department of Education and state boards of pharmacy have for the quality assurance of professional degree programs.

Many countries have rigorous systems and requirements in place that make it possible for foreign graduates to achieve licensure to practice. For example, in the United States, graduates of foreign pharmacy programs that are not accredited by ACPE are required to pass the Foreign Pharmacy Graduate Equivalency Examination (FPGEE) and TOEFL iBT, an English-language exam, before they are eligible to sit for the license exam. The education of foreign and US graduates may not be equivalent per se, but the evaluation (quality assurance) process—known as the Foreign Pharmacy Graduate Examination Committee Certification (FPGEC)—ensures that a foreign pharmacist's education meets acceptable requirements to allow them to practice as licensed pharmacists.

Standards Development

ACPE's standards are developed with input from a broad range of stakeholders interested in and affected by pharmacy education. The ACPE standards focus on the educational outcomes required of Doctor of Pharmacy programs and the assessment of those outcomes. ACPE's current standards specifically target the Center for the Advancement of Pharmacy Education (CAPE) Educational Outcomes.[6] To promote consistency in care, it is expected that the curriculum will prepare students to provide patient-centered collaborative care as noted in the Joint Commission of Pharmacy Practitioners' Pharmacists' Patient Care Process model.[7] The structural and process-related elements within pharmacy education that are necessary to implement evidence-based outcomes are described within the standards to assist programs with documenting achievement of the standards. In addition, the standards describe areas where programs can experiment and innovate within the didactic and experiential components of their curricula to meet the required educational outcomes. Establishing a commitment to life-long learning and the transition to continuing professional development (CPD) by students and graduates is addressed within the standards, which require that programs impart to graduates the knowledge, skills, abilities, behaviors, and attitudes necessary to demonstrate self-awareness, leadership, innovation, entrepreneurship, and professionalism. The ACPE standards expect that the program will utilize a plan to assess student readiness to enter final year pharmacy practice experiences, provide direct patient care in a variety of healthcare settings ("practice-ready"), and contribute as a member of an interprofessional collaborative patient care team ("team-ready"). To provide evidence of achievement of the standards, programs must provide, at a minimum, documentation related to student achievement throughout the program including: (1) student progression rates; and (2) student performance on standardized examinations both during the didactic curriculum and on the national licensure and state law examinations.

Accreditation Process

The accreditation process is designed to provide a professional judgment as to the quality of a college or school of pharmacy's professional program and to encourage continued improvement thereof. Accreditation concerns itself with both quality assurance and quality enhancement. Recognition does not imply or infer that all Doctor of Pharmacy programs are equivalent beyond meeting the expectations of the accreditation standards. Through the accreditation process, a professional program is evaluated on the extent to which it accomplishes its stated goals and is consistent with the concept that pharmacy is a unique, personal service profession in the health science field. In the application of these standards, literal conformity in every detail is not required beyond meeting the minimum expectations of the standards. The accreditation process assures basic expectations for quality pharmacy education. Many programs exceed the standards in one or more of the various elements.

The accreditation process is based on a structured and systematic system of self and peer assessment with the intention of improving academic quality and providing accountability. In this regard, the accreditation process includes an in-depth self-evaluation ("self-study") conducted by the program seeking initial or continued accreditation. A comprehensive on-site evaluation of the program is conducted by a team of trained evaluators selected by ACPE, the members of which have diverse academic and practice backgrounds and experience. The evaluation team reviews the program's self-study report that includes required documentation and data, and visits the program to evaluate the program's compliance with the standards. The evaluation team provides a written report of its findings and recommendations, which are reviewed by the ACPE Board of Directors. The Board is the decision-making entity and makes all accreditation determinations. Each professional degree program is reviewed comprehensively every 8 years. The Board may act to require additional monitoring, through focused on-site evaluations and/or written interim reports, during the standard accreditation period for any standards that are not adequately addressed. Alternatively, the Board may award a shortened term of accreditation to programs with significant compliance concerns. Programs that fail to address compliance concerns of the Board in a timely fashion may be placed on Probation (which is a public notification) and continued failure to address the issue will result in withdrawal of accreditation; such decisions are, however, subject to appeal by the institution.

ACPE's International Services Program (ISP) offers consultation, training, and degree program evaluation services to stakeholders around the world who seek guidance and assistance related to quality assurance and advancement of pharmacy education. The expertise, global perspectives, staff resources, and formal processes within the ISP support international stakeholders to advance pharmacy education and quality in their respective countries. The activities and programs of the ISP are supported and guided by the International Commission whose international and US-based members are appointed by the ACPE Board of Directors, and the ISP Advisory Group whose expert members are drawn from around the world.

OBJECTIVE 26.3. DETAIL THE CURRICULUM MAPPING PROCESS IN PHARMACY EDUCATION

The role of pharmacists within healthcare is changing and pharmacy curricula need to adapt to these changes as well as changing societal needs and priorities, and evolving quality assurance standards/criteria. To ensure continued relevance and applicability of the curriculum, pharmacy programs must have a clearly defined process for evaluating the curriculum. Typically, the curriculum committee is the entity charged with curricular oversight including ensuring the curriculum aligns with both programmatic outcomes and national quality assurance standards.

A program's curriculum can be viewed through three different lenses: (1) the intended or designed curriculum; (2) the delivered or taught curriculum; and (3) the experienced or learned curriculum.[8] The "intended" curriculum is the curriculum captured on paper. It is the formal, documented curriculum including the course titles, written course content, individual learning objectives, and assessment measures. The "delivered" curriculum encompasses the content delivered by the faculty including the teaching method(s) used in delivery. The "experienced" curriculum describes the curriculum as experienced by the learners. Ideally, all three, the *intended, delivered,* and *experienced* will be aligned.

Curriculum mapping is a technique used to document how curricular content, teaching methods, and assessments are incorporated throughout the pharmacy curriculum in an effort to ensure achievement of programmatic objectives, i.e., competencies of the graduates. The curriculum mapping process evaluates when, how, and what is taught within the curriculum and considers the assessment measures used to evaluate achievement of expected student learning outcomes.[9] Optimally curricular mapping is an ongoing process intended to provide a real-time picture of the curriculum, not a single-point-in-time initiative.

The curricular mapping process provides a means to evaluate the curriculum and interpret curricular data. Curriculum mapping within pharmacy education can be used to identify curricular gaps or excessive redundancies in content to ensure

TABLE 26.1 Example Curricular Mapping Matrix

Intended Student Learning Outcomes	Course A	Course B	Course C	Course D
Outcome 1	Introduced		Reinforced	Mastered
Outcome 2		Introduced		
Outcome 3		Introduced	Reinforced	Reinforced

all programmatic outcomes are adequately addressed throughout the course of the curriculum. Curriculum mapping can also assist in planning for assessment methods to evaluate the curriculum.[10]

The curricular mapping process looks at the intended/delivered curriculum as well as the experienced curriculum. Mapping of course syllabi and the learning objectives for both individual courses and lectures can be used to identify where, when, and how in the curriculum course content is located and delivered. The mapping process should take into consideration the breadth and depth of exposure to curricular content (introduction, reinforcement, and mastery of curricular content addressing knowledge, skills, attitudes, and values) and the type of teaching methods used in the delivery of the content (e.g., passive/lecture based delivery, active learning method, application-based activities) (see Table 26.1: Example Curricular Mapping Matrix). The experienced curriculum should also be mapped using assessment methods including multiple choice examinations, student surveys, Objective Structured Clinical Examinations (OSCEs), and review of student portfolios.

Software programs (e.g., ExamSoft) including electronic testing software can be used to assist in the curricular mapping process in an effort to facilitate data collection and analysis. The ability to search the database using key terms and concepts is essential to ensuring the usability of data gathered. In addition, the database should be accessible to facilitate real-time, dynamic reporting.

Data gathered through the curricular mapping process should be used to document relationships between the curriculum and the intended learning objectives. Analysis of data collected should ensure that the curriculum adequately addresses each of the programmatic outcomes. Areas where gaps or redundancies exist should be reviewed by the curriculum committee. Additionally, the curricular mapping process can be used to identify opportunities for curricular integration. Ideally, the curricular map should facilitate communication among faculty and provide the basis for the identification of needed curricular revisions and continuous quality improvement.

CONCLUSION

Pharmacy education must adapt to the changing needs of the profession. Quality assurance procedures help to assure and advance the quality of pharmacy education. It is essential, however, that all sectors within the profession—primarily those representing education, practice, policy, and regulation communicate and collaborate effectively to advance the profession in line with a common vision.[11] Quality assurance agencies—whether governmental or independent—should likewise collaborate with all stakeholders. The competencies that graduates need for practice must be aligned with the educational outcomes of pharmacy degree programs required by quality assurance agencies, and further aligned with blueprints of national licensure examinations. Licensure examinations must be rigorous and psychometrically valid to ensure that competencies of graduates are appropriately and accurately assessed. Such examinations can also serve as useful indicators of programmatic quality and curricular effectiveness and provide useful data for quality improvement.

The Pharmacy Education Action Plan, developed by FIP's Pharmacy Education Taskforce, encourages the development of educational systems designed to ensure the competency of the pharmacy workforce. Quality assurance systems, such as that utilized by the Accreditation Council for Pharmacy Education in the United States and other countries, are designed to provide assurance of the quality of professional degree programs, to the profession and the public. Individual programs can advance the quality of education provided through continuous quality improvement initiatives such as curricular mapping.

REFERENCES

1. Anderson C, Bates I, Beck D, et al. The WHO UNESCO FIP pharmacy education Taskforce. *Hum Resour Health.* 2009;7:45−53.
2. Anderson C, Bates I, Beck D, et al. The WHO UNESCO FIP Pharmacy Education Taskforce. Enabling concerted and collective global action. *Am J Pharm Educ.* 2008;72:127.
3. *FIPEd Development Team*; 2017. https://www.fip.org/education_taskforce.

4. *Quality Assurance of Pharmacy Education: The FIP Global Framework.* 2nd Edition 2014.
5. *Accreditation Standards and Key Elements for the Professional Program in Pharmacy Leading to the Doctor of Pharmacy Degree;* 2017. https://www.acpe-accredit.org/pdf/Standards2016FINAL.pdf.
6. *Center for the Advancement of Pharmacy Education (CAPE) Educational Outcomes 2013;* 2017. http://www.aacp.org/resources/education/cape/Open%20Access%20Documents/CAPEoutcomes2013.pdf.
7. *The Pharmacists' Patient Care Process;* 2017. https://jcpp.net/patient-care-process/.
8. Ewell PT, Jones DP. *Indicators of "Good Practice" in Undergraduate Education: A Handbook for Development and Implementation.* Boulder, CO: National Center for Higher Education Management Systems; 1996.
9. Harden RM. AMEE Guide No. 21: curriculum mapping: a tool for transparent and authentic teaching and learning. *Med Teach.* 2001;23:123−137.
10. Bouldin AS, Wilkin NE, Wyandt CM, Wilson MC. General and professional education abilities: identifying opportunities for development and assessment across the curriculum. *Am J Pharm Educ.* 2001;65:75S−116S.
11. Bader LR, McGrath S, Rouse MJ, Anderson C. A conceptual framework toward identifying and analyzing challenges to the advancement of pharmacy. *Res Social Adm Pharm.* 2017;13(2):321−331.

Chapter 27

Adult Learning Theories in Pharmacy Education

Kashelle Lockman[1], Dixon Thomas[2] and Lilian H. Hill[3]

[1]*The University of Iowa, Iowa City, IA, United States;* [2]*Gulf Medical University, Ajman, United Arab Emirates;*
[3]*The University of Southern Mississippi, Hattiesburg, MS, United States*

Learning objectives

Objective 27.1   Outline the concepts in adult learning relevant to pharmacy education.
Objective 27.2   Explain applications of adult learning principles in pharmacy education.
Objective 27.3   Describe how to write learning objectives in pharmacy education.

OBJECTIVE 27.1. OUTLINE THE CONCEPTS IN ADULT LEARNING RELEVANT TO PHARMACY EDUCATION

Learning involves acquiring knowledge, skills, and competence. Knowledge is an essential component in deciding, performing, and reviewing actions. Actions are properly implemented with skills (psychomotor skills). Skills are also involved in how knowledge is used (cognitive skills). Values and attitudes contribute to reasoned action and competency to practice. To practice the profession of pharmacy, a student should learn stipulated knowledge, skill, values, and attitudes. Learning starts with receiving or finding information. However, information does not become learning until an individual processes it and makes it his or her own. Additionally, learned information must be used regularly for knowledge retention to occur. Knowledge can also be refreshed and updated as needed. As students progress from being novice to expert, they are able to learn independently because they have acquired the cognitive knowledge and are proficient in the relevant physical, social, and psychological environment of professional practice. However, acquiring professional expertise can take thousands of hours, guided practice, and the willingness to learn from experience.[1]

Adult learning theories evolved over time, with theories specifically explaining how adults learn emerging in the 1970s. Traditional learning theories tend to be individualistic. Examples include a concept of learning as a change in behavior (behaviorism), as personal development (humanism), as a mental process (cognitivism), and as creating meaning from experience (constructivism).

- Behaviorism: Behaviorism focuses on observable behaviors that are shaped by the environment, which is designed by the teacher. Learning is controlled by the positive and negative reinforcements the teacher places in the environment. Behaviors are broken down into smaller tasks, with a focus on stepwise mastery.[2] Behaviorism is operating in pharmacy skills labs: students master taking blood pressure by practicing each required subtask until they develop mastery. Often, these types of skills are evaluated with rubrics in which addition or subtraction of points is the reinforcing locus of control. Sometimes, these are even high stakes, pass or fail behaviors.
- Humanism: The theory of humanism posits that learning occurs to fulfill an individual's potential, to achieve self-actualization. As such, learners are motivated from within. The learning environment must be learner-centered, with educators facilitating students' self-discovery and creativity.[3] Self-directed learning evolved from humanism and is essential to incorporate into pharmacy curricula, so graduates can begin the continual professional development required throughout their careers. An example includes self-discovery and portfolio courses, in which students identify their own learning needs, select their own learning activities to achieve self-written objectives, and document and

reflect on the outcomes. Andragogy, the education of adults, also has roots in humanism. Andragogy holds that adult learners are independent and self-directed, are intrinsically motivated to learn, are practical and problem-focused, have rich experiences to learn from, and value learning when it is congruent with their daily life.[4] Beyond andragogy and heutagogy, the study of self-determined learning seeks to create learners highly capable and competent of autonomous self-directed learning.[5]

- Cognitivism: While behaviorism focuses on learning shaped by the external environment, and what behaviors can be observed, cognitivism focuses on the internal environment of the learner's mind, thought, and memory. Cognitivism requires educators and learners to focus on how dynamic memory and thought processes are effectively changed. As such, reflection and retrieval practice are helpful tools to achieve learning outcomes in the cognitivist framework.[6] Educators must be aware of cognitive load and threats to building long-term memory and critical thinking skills. Metacognition, the awareness of and ability to manage one's own learning and thinking processes, is viewed as essential to successful learning in cognitivism and can be supported through instructional strategies and modeling.[2,7] In pharmacy education, cognitivism can be seen in much of the curriculum, from teaching medication facts to teaching how to reconcile patient-specific factors, including patient preferences, drug-specific factors, and evidence to select a safe and effective medication for a given patient.

Cognitive learning requires thoughtful, focused efforts to relate new and old knowledge and experience. Concept maps help activate higher-order neural networks. Challenging students to create a concept map of their knowledge can help them integrate and reconcile new information and constructs with prior learning to build long-term memory of complex information. Concept maps can mitigate students' tendency to employ rote-learning strategies. This active learning strategy requires students to graphically represent concepts and the interrelationships among them. Instructors can scan a student's concept map to quickly identify and correct any misconceptions held by students.[8]

- Constructivism: Constructivist theory holds that knowledge and understanding is attained through experience and action.[9] It relates to how individuals integrate new knowledge, reconcile it with existing knowledge, and change or expand their mental schemas, meaning "knowledge structures that represent repeated patterns of experiences (cognitive as well as behavioral)".[1] Teaching methods that build on identifying what students already know can help them establish cognitive connections between what they know and what is to be learned. Constructivism is learner-centered and focused on discovery. For example, assign students a drug information question on a clinically controversial topic, followed by a reflective writing prompt and group discussion. This activity would foster students' discovery and reconciliation of contradictions between new information and their previous knowledge and experience on the topic.

Recent adult learning theories are more representative of people living and working together within a sociocultural and historical context. These include situated cognition, social cognitive learning, and communities of practice.

- Situated cognition: Schumacher et al.[6] contend that situated cognition is the ideal theory of learning in medical fields. Situated cognition grew out of constructivism. While constructivism focuses on the individual learner constructing his or her own knowledge, situated cognition maintains that the individual's construction of knowledge hinges on social and cultural interactions of the learner with his or her environment. Learning and knowledge are inseparable from the context, activity, and tools used in that activity; people pharmacists interact within their work, culture, and language. Learning is shaped by social context and the tools used in that setting; learning is seen as an increasingly effective performance across time and situations. A related concept is *scaffolding of learning*, in which pharmacy students are provided support including relevant examples, guides, templates, and other resources. As the student becomes more proficient at the assigned task, the supports are gradually removed. Skills lab makes use of this idea as students learn to handle prescriptions, drugs, bottles, labels, and counting trays. Students receive guidance as they learn to practice each skill independently, but over time they are expected to integrate related skills, become more agile in their performance, and the guidance is gradually reduced. Not surprisingly, pharmacy students who have served as pharmacy technicians have an advantage at first.
- Social Cognitive Learning and Communities of Practice: Communities of practice evolved from social learning theory, the idea that learning is social versus an individual endeavor. In a community of practice, people engage in a network of learning with others in a shared domain of competence or endeavor.[10,11] Newcomers learn from others, but over time they become contributing members and more "senior" members of the group who may in turn learn from new members. There are many online communities of practice in pharmacy education, including the formal communities of practice, such as the American College of Clinical Pharmacy's Practice and Research Networks, and informal, organic communities of practice that emerge on social networks such as Twitter. A related concept is *cognitive apprenticeships* in which apprentices are taught to think about what they are doing as they learn to perform actions; the apprentice serves

under a master who can model appropriate thinking/behaviors/actions and teach what the apprentice should learn and be able to perform. This is related to the clerkship and student/preceptor relationship in which the student learns to perform professional responsibilities under the supervision of a licensed pharmacist.

Practice exercise—structure a group learning activity that requires students to depend on one another:

Create a problem-based learning (PBL) scenario that involves students in solving a group challenge in which the initial information provided is ill-defined. Employ information from authentic practice situations. Students are expected to use questioning, information retrieval strategies, clinical knowledge, and reasoning to make recommendations. PBL requires information analysis and synthesis as well as iterative discussion. Instructors guide the reasoning and deliberative processes involved in students' development of a detailed, stepwise proposal for addressing a patient problem. Instructors challenge the depth and accuracy of their approach, and avoid solving it for them. PBL promotes students' self-directed learning capabilities and part of the instructors' goal is to promote that ability.[12,13] These very skills are needed during training in which students learn they cannot rely on a preceptor's knowledge alone but develop their own methods to figure out the situation. Students must use skills of information retrieval and clinical reasoning to suggest their pharmacy recommendations for patient cases to preceptors.

OBJECTIVE 27.2. EXPLAIN APPLICATIONS OF ADULT LEARNING PRINCIPLES IN PHARMACY EDUCATION

Andragogy, meaning the education of adults, holds that adults learn differently from children (Table 27.1). Malcom Knowles, the father of andragogy, proposed that the defining characteristics of an adult learner are psychological (self-direction, personal responsibility). Adult educators tend not to define adulthood chronologically, but rather as occurring when individuals take on the responsibilities of adult life, e.g., holding a responsible job, supporting oneself, finding a spouse, having children.[4] Many pharmacy students may not meet this definition of adulthood at matriculation. As a concept, andragogy can be used to help pharmacy instructors promote self-direction and a responsible adult self-concept among students through curriculum and instructional design. In addition, pharmacy students should learn about adragogy to become an effective patient educator. To connect well with an adult learner, the pharmacy information being conveyed should be engaging, personally relevant, and immediately useful.[4]

In pharmacy education, curricula must be mapped to outcomes outlined by accrediting bodies to maintain quality standards across educational institutions, preventing learning from being completely student-driven. However, it is possible to incorporate andragogy into instructional design of pharmacy curricula by incorporating the principles outlined in Table 27.2. Students often exhibit more self-directed learning capacity in the informal or hidden curriculum in pharmacy school by choosing which professional organizations to work within and which elective curricular and extracurricular educational activities they will engage in. Self-directed learning could also be encouraged by allowing students to choose among learning activities that support the same learning objectives, such as providing a choice between writing a scholarly paper or preparing a presentation. Examples of smaller assignments include providing a choice between reading a chapter versus watching YouTube videos to prepare for class.

In addition to Knowles, Paulo Freire and Jack Mezirow further shaped adult learning theory. Freire believed education is a tool for social change and focused on shifting power from teachers to learners. In *Pedagogy of the Oppressed*, he proposed a collaborative, horizontal relationship between educators and learners, in which learners contribute to and direct the learning environment. Mezirow advocated that educators have a responsibility to facilitate development of

TABLE 27.1 Assumptions of Pedagogy and Andragogy[4]

Assumption	Pedagogy	Andragogy
Need to know	Teacher/grade-centered	Learner-centered/relevance
Learner's self-concept	Dependence (on educator)	Autonomy and personal responsibility
Role of experience	Educator's wisdom through experience is paramount	Integrating learners' experience is paramount
Readiness to learn	Ready to learn what teacher thinks is important, required knowledge to pass or get desired grade	Ready to learn what is relevant to life and role
Orientation to learning	Subject-oriented	Task- and problem-oriented
Motivation	External (i.e., grades) > internal	Internal > external

TABLE 27.2 Implications of Adult Learning Principles in Pharmacy Education[4]

Principle of Adult Learning[9]	Implication for Pharmacy Education
Adults need to understand why they should learn something.	If pharmacy students fail to see the relevance of content to modern pharmacy practice, they will disengage. For example, modern pharmacy curricula should not include content on medications that are no longer marketed unless the instructor is specifically and explicitly relating that content to a modern pharmacy problem, such as a parallel or recurrent theme in pharmacy practice. Short cases, simulations, and storytelling (pharmacy history, pharmacy law, medical humanities) may improve connection to a topic.
Adults have an adult self-concept and are self-directed individuals.	Adult learners resent situations in which they feel their autonomy is challenged. However, pharmacy students may default to the pedagogical hallmark of passivity in learning environments due to habit. Some students also will not be fully developed self-directed learners at matriculation. Educators should design instruction for pharmacy students that fosters self-directed learning. Creating "flipped classrooms" and incorporating active learning strategies supports self-concept and self-directed learning.
Adult learners are not blank slates; they have knowledge and life experience.	Provide opportunities for pharmacy students to share, apply, or build on their experiences, whether they are work-related (e.g., pharmacy technician or research) or personal experiences with illnesses relevant to course content.
Adult learners are self-directed related to the developmental tasks of his/her social role.	The developmental tasks of a pharmacy technician, student, and pharmacist are vastly different. To overcome the tendency for adults to prefer learning knowledge and skills applicable to their current role and, daily life, pharmacy educators may need to use simulation, shadowing, and career interviews as instructional strategies.
Adult learners are looking for immediate application; learning is relevancy-oriented.	Students will remember the information they believe is significant. Pharmacy educators should consider using pharmacist testimonials, patient testimonials, and simulation to ensure pharmacy students understand the relevance of content. Curriculum and instructional designers should consider the timing of the content. For example, focusing on medication history-taking just prior to an introductory rotation where a student can perform medication histories would be consistent with this principle.
Adults tend to be driven by internal motivation.	Be aware that assessments that foster competition for external rewards may undermine the ability of pharmacy students to remain internally motivated. Ask students to set personal goals and intentions unrelated to external motivators at the beginning of a course or unit. (e.g., evaluate my dad's inhaler technique and provide relevant inhaler education to my dad vs. Make an A on the asthma exam.) Consider using formative, nongraded assessments and reflections to foster internal motivation and focus on personal growth.

learners' critical thinking skills. That is, learners should critically reflect on their own assumptions, including the consequences of those assumptions, and reconcile the validity of held assumptions against alternative assumptions.[14] Discussion, reflective writing, debate, and simulation with standardized patients can be used in the modern pharmacy classroom to facilitate development of critical thinking skills. In an activity based on the Think, Pair, Share strategy, students reflect, write, and discuss their ideas with a partner before sharing them with the larger group. Both Freire and Mezirow were proponents of critical reflection, but Freire thought reflection should be balanced with acting on the world. In modern pharmacy education, those educators embracing learner-centered teaching are a "guide on the side," facilitating student-driven learning, in the spirit of Freire and Mezirow, versus a "sage on the stage," where the professor primarily transfers information to students through lecturing.[14,15]

Pharmacy education should start with the end in mind.[16] Determine which theories and teaching methods will most support pharmacy students achievement of student learning outcomes. The learning objectives are planned to achieve the corresponding learning outcomes. The objectives are mainly planned by the teachers in discussion with students and the outcomes are achieved by the students. In problem-based learning students develop learning objectives. Achievements of learning outcomes to be confirmed with appropriate assessment tools. Sometimes learning objectives and learning outcomes are used interchangeably. Consider characteristics of the audience, such as age/generation, gender, and socioeconomic backgrounds. Although popular in the literature, tailoring instruction to specific learning styles has not been shown to improve learning.[17] Regardless of the learning theory and related instructional methods selected, consider that accumulating evidence shows that learner-centered methods such as retrieval practice, reflection, and flipped classrooms positively impact pharmacy student engagement and learning.[18–20]

Practice exercise—A persistent challenge in educating pharmacy students is retention of information for later application in practice. Imagine a senior pharmacy student in one of his/her final clerkship assignments who is reluctant to search out information about relevant medications relevant to patient cases he/she is responsible for. Instead, he or she appears too dependent on the clinical preceptor for medication information. Using the information in this chapter, think about ways you could help him or her move to become self-directed in his/her learning so that he/she can transition to the next phase of his/her career, in which he/she will be a licensed pharmacist and need to work more independently.

OBJECTIVE 27.3. DESCRIBE HOW TO WRITE LEARNING OBJECTIVES IN PHARMACY EDUCATION

Adult learning suggests that learning must be relevancy-oriented. Learning objectives communicate the relevancy of content to pharmacy students and educators. Learning objectives in pharmacy education are layered. Terminal course-level learning objectives should map to the terminal performance outcomes of the pharmacy curriculum. Likewise, learning objectives written by individual educators for single course sessions or units of instruction within a course should support achievement of, and map to, course-level terminal learning outcomes.[16] To avoid cognitive overload, educators should focus on three to five learning objectives per learning activity. However, students may need to write their own supporting, or enabling learning objectives to ensure they gain the requisite knowledge, skills, or attitudes to meet a learning objective written by an instructor.[16] Students must also write their own learning objectives in self-directed learning courses, such as some professional development, advanced practice pharmacy experience, and portfolio courses. Effective learning is built on a foundation of quality learning objectives aligned with teaching and learning methods as well as assessments.

Use the simple model A-B-C-D to write learning objectives, but also make them SMART (specific, measurable, achievable, relevant, and time-bound).[16] An example objective that encompasses these points would be: "Given an e-learning module, and case discussion, the PHAR 501 student should be able to list five patient-related variables that increase the risk of adverse effects from opioid analgesics." Table 27.3 outlines the construction of objectives.

Desired learning outcomes often encompass multiple domains or dimensions of learning, including cognitive, affective, psychomotor, and interpersonal.[16] Consider the following scenario: You are assigned to teach blood pressure measurement to pharmacy students. As you think through what they should be able to do at the end of your session, you want them to be able to measure a blood pressure, record it, and explain a patient's blood pressure reading to that patient. Measuring blood pressure requires a variety of skills including selecting an appropriate cuff size, inflating and deflating the cuff, and measuring the pulse. These skills are all in the psychomotor dimension of learning, which are manual or physical skills.

TABLE 27.3 Writing Effective Learning Objectives[16]

		Good Examples	Bad Examples
A	Who is your Audience? Be **specific** and write for a singular learner.	• PHAR 501 student • City Pharmacy intern • Midyear attendee	• Students • Learners • Participants
B	What Behavior is desired? It must be observable, **relevant, measurable**, and **achievable** given the resources of your learning activity (**time**, type, etc.).	• Discuss • Identify • Formulate	• Understand • Learn • Know
C	Under what Conditions should the audience achieve this behavior?	• Given a reading, discussion, and role play … • Given access to tertiary databases … • Given a simulated patient with hypertension …	• On completion of this session …
D	To what Degree (extent, measure, or scope) should the behavior be performed? This is an evaluative statement. Assessments should reflect this statement. This statement is often omitted in practice if achievement of an objective will not be evaluated.	• By offering an opinion at least twice • Within 15 min • Without error	• Successfully • Safely • Carefully • At discretion of the examiner • Until finished

Students will also need to have knowledge of what blood pressure is, how to use the cuff and stethoscope, how to interpret systolic and diastolic readings, and some knowledge about communication techniques. These are all in the cognitive dimension. Students will also need to understand the importance of pharmacist-driven blood pressure management, which is an attitude, in the affective dimension. In addition to these dimensions of learning, students will need to respond to patient cues and tailor their interaction to patient needs such as language or literacy barriers. This is the interpersonal dimension and sometimes can encompass knowledge, skills, and attitudes. Objectives should be written and assessed in a single dimension: cognitive, psychomotor, affective, or interpersonal.[16]

Benjamin Bloom created a taxonomy of learning in the cognitive dimension to systematically create learning objectives. The original taxonomy consisted of six cognitive domains. In 2001, these were modified and four knowledge domains were added.[21,22] The knowledge domains include:

- Facts: basic elements one must know to communicate with other pharmacists and solve problems in pharmacy. Examples include facts about medications, medical terminology, pharmacy laws.
- Conceptual knowledge: interrelationships between facts in a larger contextual structure. Examples include knowledge of drug classes and categories, theories, models, structures, principles, and generalizations.
- Procedural knowledge: encompasses protocols, algorithms, techniques, and methods of inquiry and procedures. Examples include how to make an IV, how to dispense a medication in a pharmacy, how to approach a drug information question, how to conduct an opioid conversion, how to interview a patient.
- Metacognitive knowledge: Self-awareness and knowledge of one's own cognition as well as knowledge of cognition in general. Examples include strategic knowledge, and awareness of how one approaches cognitive tasks and problems.[22]

Revised Bloom's Taxonomy

An example of the two-dimensional revision of Bloom's Taxonomy:

Topic: Therapeutic Use of Opioids.

Find each of the following sample behavioral statements in the table below to explore how objectives encompass the knowledge and cognitive domains of the revised Bloom's Taxonomy (Tables 27.4 − 27.7).

1. List patient-related variables that increase the risk of adverse effects from opioid analgesics.
2. Compare the efficacy of opioid analgesics for a given pain complaint.
3. Recommend an opioid analgesic based on patient- and agent-related variables.
4. Determine if opioid conversion is indicated.
5. Outline the opioid conversion process.
6. Propose an opioid stewardship policy for an ambulatory family medicine practice.
7. Interview a patient about his or her pain to collect all elements of symptom analysis.
8. Dissect your own biases in processing opioid prescriptions.
9. Select study strategies for retaining knowledge of opioid pharmacokinetics and pharmacodynamics.

Although Bloom's taxonomy for cognitive learning is the most widely known learning taxonomy, pharmacy educators and students should also be aware of Krathwohl's taxonomy for affective learning and Simpson's taxonomy for psychomotor learning. Affective learning can be the most difficult to incorporate and assess because it encompasses soft skills, but it is in the affective domain that student pharmacists develop a professional identity, empathy, and values needed for interpersonal skills. Affective learning should be integrated across pharmacy curricula.

Teaching and learning methods should align with and support learner achievement of learning objectives. Likewise, formative and summative assessments should evaluate the level and learning domain of a learning outcome.

TABLE 27.4 Blooms Taxonomy for the Opioid Example[22,23]

The Knowledge Dimension[18]	Remember	Understand	Apply	Analyze	Evaluate	Create
Factual knowledge	1					
Conceptual knowledge		2			4	3
Procedural knowledge		5	7			6
Metacognitive knowledge		9		8		

TABLE 27.5 Revised Bloom's Taxonomy for Cognitive Learning: Cognitive Domains[23]

Cognitive Domain Level	Example Action Verbs	Example Supportive Learning Activities
Remember: Access relevant knowledge (facts) from memory	Define, choose, label, list, select, identify, match	Lecture, guided note-taking, online quiz games, flashcards
Understand: Formulate meaning from factual knowledge	Compare, compute, contrast, explain, illustrate, outline, rephrase, summarize, interpret, relate, demonstrate	Guided note-taking, mindmapping or concept mapping, writing summaries, short answer questions, think-pair-share, jigsaw, reflections, infographics
Apply: Use knowledge or skill in a given situation	Apply, construct, develop, identify, interview, manipulate, plan, solve, perform	Send-a-problem, role play, fishbowls, branched e-learning scenarios, cases, simulations, skills lab exercises, formative OSCE
Analyze: Break knowledge into elemental parts and identify how they relate to each other and integrate into a larger structure	Analyze, categorize, classify, compare, contrast, diagram, discover, dissect, examine, distinguish, select	Mindmap or concept map, infographics, branched e-learning scenarios, cases, SOAP notes
Evaluate: Make and defend judgments based on standards or criteria	Assess, choose, contrast, evaluate, interpret, judge, critique, debate, measure, relate, recommend, justify, prioritize, determine, defend	Send-a-problem, debates, branched e-learning scenarios, cases, simulations, drug information exercises, formative OSCE, SOAP notes
Create: Combine elements in a different way to make something original or novel as a logical whole	Construct, create, design, develop, formulate, generate, invent, modify, plan, propose, test, solve, revise, write	Scholarly writing, research projects, cases, simulations, SOAP notes, presentations

OSCE, objective structured clinical examination; SOAP, subjective objective assessment and plan.

TABLE 27.6 Krathwohl's Taxonomy for Affective Learning[24]

Affective Domain Level	Example Action Verbs	Example Supportive Learning Activities
Receive: Becoming aware of a phenomena or situation, being open to different ideas with suspended judgment giving attention to differing ideas	Accept, notice, observe, discern, consider, listen, appreciate, realize	Patient testimonials, readings in medical humanities, activities with simulated patients, debates, role-plays as other disciplines
Respond: Voluntarily responds to a stimulus. At the highest level of responsiveness, this will be self-motivated for self-fulfillment	Engage, participate, discuss, respond, cooperate, practice, contribute	Group projects, simulations, group discussions, experiential rotations, portfolios
Value: Displays an attitude or behavior with sufficient consistency to be perceived as holding it as a value	Recognize, demonstrate, relate	Simulations, discussions, presentations, portfolios
Organize: Placing values in a system or framework and determining relationships among them	Discern, accept, reject, reconcile	Reflective writing, simulations, experiential rotations, portfolios
Internalize: Values are integrated into the person as a whole, evident in character and personality to the degree where behavior can be predicted	Display, perform	Reflective writing, simulations, experiential rotations, portfolios

Learning objectives must therefore be realistic, measurable, and achievable given curricular resources for learning activities and assessments. Although good instructional design starts with the end in mind, including identification of the minimum competencies required for a new pharmacy graduate, objectives may need modification to reflect curricular assets. For example, in a didactic course, it may be unrealistic to have this behavioral statement in a lecture-level objective: Interview a

TABLE 27.7 Simpson's Taxonomy for Psychomotor or Kinesthetic Learning[25]

Psychomotor Domain Level	Example Action Verbs	Example Supportive Learning Activities
Perceiving: Using sensory inputs to guide a motor response	Detect, distinguish, identify	Reading, watching a video, simulation
Set (mind-set): Mental, physical, and emotional readiness to act	Display, begin, proceed	Reading, watching a video (preparing)
Guided response: Imitation, trial and error, practice	Follow, reproduce, copy, replicate	Modeling following by practice in simulations, following a protocol
Mechanism (basic proficiency): Movement with some proficiency, becoming habitual	Assemble, measure, mix, display	Simulations, labs
Complex overt response (mastery): quick, accurate, automatic performance	Assemble, measure, mix, display (increasing mastery)	Simulations
Adaptation: Modification of skills for new situations or changing conditions	Adapt, alter, change, modify, revise, rearrange	Simulations
Origination: Creating new movements or new sequences of movements to address a problem	Arrange, combine, construct, create, design	Simulations

patient about his or her pain to collect all elements of symptom analysis. However, this would be a perfectly reasonable behavioral statement in an objective for an experiential rotation.

Effective pharmacy education centers on well-designed learning objectives that align with assessments and desired outcomes. Learning objectives center both educators and learners on the most relevant knowledge, skills, and attitudes to achieve desired competencies. To meet the needs of patients and healthcare teams in the 21st century, it is essential to design objectives that will support learning in the cognitive, affective, psychomotor, and interpersonal domains.

CONCLUSION

Increasing incorporation of adult learning theory throughout didactic and experiential learning may increase student engagement and improve the effectiveness of curricula. Learning objectives can ensure whether learners recognize the relevancy of designed learning activities. Depending on types of learning activities and cognitive, affective, or psychomotor learning; action verbs for learning objectives change.

REFERENCES

1. Lynch D, Maize D. A primer for the application of cognitive learning principles to pharmacy teaching and learning [serial online] *J Pharm Teach.* 2006;13(1):3–16 (Available from: Education Source, Ipswich, MA).
2. Sink DL. Design models and learning theories for adults. In: Biech E, ed. *ASTD Handbook: The Definitive Reference for Training & Development.* Alexandria, VA: ASTD Press; 2014:181–199.
3. DeCarvalho RJ. The humanistic paradigm in education. *Humanist Psychol.* 1991;19(l):88–104.
4. Knowles MS, et al. *The Adult Learner: The Definitive Classic in Adult Education and Human Resource Development.* 7th Ed. New York: Routledge; 2012:40–46.
5. Blaschke LM. *Heutagogy, Lifelong Learning: A Review of Heutagogical practice and self-determined learning*; 2012. http://files.eric.ed.gov/fulltext/ EJ979639.pdf.
6. Schumacher DJ, Englander R, Carraccio C. Developing the master learner: applying learning theory to the learner, the teacher, and the learning environment. *Acad Med.* November 2013;88(11):1635–1645. https://doi.org/10.1097/ACM.0b013e3182a6e8f8.
7. Torre DM, Daley BJ, Sebastian JL, Elnicki DM. APM perspectives overview of current learning theories for medical educators. *Am J Med.* 2006;119(10):903–907. https://doi.org/10.1016/j.amjmed.2006.06.037.
8. Hill LH. Concept mapping in a pharmacy communications course to encourage meaningful student learning. *Am J Pharmaceut Educ.* 2004;68(5). Article 109.
9. Gredler ME. *Learning and Instruction: Theory into Practice.* Second ed. New York: Macmillan Publishing Company; 1992.
10. Farnsworth V, Kleanthous I, Wenger-Trayner E. Communities of practice as a social theory of learning: a conversation with Etienne Wenger. *Br J Educ Stud.* 2016;64(2):139–160. https://doi.org/10.1080/00071005.2015.1133799.

11. Lave J, Wenger E. *Situated Learning: Legitimate Peripheral Participation*. Campbridge University Press; 1991.

12. Al-Dahir S, Bryant K, Kennedy K, Robinson D. Online virtual-patient cases versus traditional problem-based learning in advanced pharmacy practice experiences. *Am J Pharmaceut Educ*. August 2014;78(4):1—8 [serial online].

13. Williams B. The theoretical links between problem-based learning and self-directed learning for continuing professional nursing education. *Teach High Educ*. January 2001;6(1):85—98 [serial online].

14. University of South Africa. *Principles & Theories of Adult Education*. UNESCO; 2017. http://unesdoc.unesco.org/images/0024/002451/245104e.pdf.

15. Weimer M. Learner-Centered Teaching: Roots and Origins. In: *Learner-Centered Teaching: Five Key Changes to Practice*. Second. San Francisco: Jossey-Bass; 2013:3—27.

16. Chuck H. *ISD from the Ground Up*. American Society for Training & Development; 2011.

17. Newton PM. The learning styles myth is thriving in higher education. *Front Psychol*. 1908;6:2015. https://doi.org/10.3389/fpsyg.2015.01908. Frontiers Media SA.

18. Lockman K, Haines S, McPherson M. Improved learning outcomes after flipping a therapeutics module. *Acad Med*. 2017. https://doi.org/10.1097/ACM.0000000000001742.

19. McLaughlin JE, Roth MT, Glatt DM, et al. The flipped classroom: a course redesign to foster learning and engagement in a health professions school. *Acad Med*. 2014;89(2):236—243. https://doi.org/10.1097/ACM.0000000000000086.

20. Brown PC, Roediger HL, McDaniel MA. *Make It Stick: The Science of Successful Learning*. Cambridge, Massachucetts: The Belknap Press of Harvard University; 2014.

21. Lasley T. Bloom's taxonomy. In: Hunt TC, Carper JC, Lasley TJ, eds. *Encyclopedia of Educational Reform and Dissent*. Thousand Oaks, CA: SAGE Publications Ltd.; 2010:107—109. https://doi.org/10.4135/9781412957403.n51.

22. Krathwohl DR. A revision of Bloom's taxonomy: an overview. *Theory Into Pract*. 2002;41(4):212—218.

23. Anderson LW, Krathwohl DR, eds. *A Taxonomy for Learning, Teaching, and Assessing: A Revision of Bloom's Taxonomy of Educational Objectives*. New York: Addison, Wesley, Longman, Inc.; 2001.

24. Krathwohl DR, Bloom BS, Masia BB. Taxonomy of educational objectives. In: *Book 2: Affective Domain*. David McKay Company Inc.; 1964.

25. Simpson EJ. *The Classification of Educational Objectives, Psychomotor Domain (Report No. ERD-251—265)*. Urbana, IL: University of Illinois, Urbana; 1996 (ERIC Document Reproduction Service No. ED 010 368).

Chapter 28

What to Expect From a Pharmacist Preceptor

Susan S. Vos and Mary E. Ray
The University of Iowa, Iowa City, IA, United States

Learning Objectives

Objective 28.1   Differentiate the roles of a preceptor and clarify the terms preceptor, mentor, faculty, intern, and resident.
Objective 28.2   Describe the qualities of effective preceptors and responsibilities of students.
Objective 28.3   Detail how to develop a productive student—preceptor relationship.

OBJECTIVE 28.1. DIFFERENTIATE THE ROLES OF A PRECEPTOR AND CLARIFY THE TERMS PRECEPTOR, MENTOR, FACULTY, INTERN, AND RESIDENT

Learning is a process. It begins with a foundation of knowledge and should continue throughout a pharmacist's career. A preceptor is a teacher in a clinical setting who will help students grow from a novice into a competent, professional pharmacist. During experiential education in the pharmacy curriculum, student pharmacists are taught by experienced pharmacist preceptors. Many of these individuals have had some sort of training or orientation to become preceptors and should be motivated by a desire to teach the next generation of pharmacists. To have a clear understanding of what a student expects from his/her preceptor, it is important to differentiate the various roles and terms related to being a preceptor.

A *faculty member* is an educator who is employed by a college, school, or university. Responsibilities of faculty members are threefold—research, service, and teaching. Typically, most faculty members have areas of expertise which serve as the foundation for their research and quest for new knowledge. Additionally, faculty members provide service to the greater university and their community (e.g., committee work, serving as a reviewer for a journal, patient care service). A faculty member may teach in a classroom or laboratory as well as in his/her pharmacy practice site. While teaching in a pharmacy practice site, the faculty member would also be a preceptor. A *preceptor* is a pharmacist and educator (or in rare cases another healthcare provider) who provides the practice-based instruction to students at a pharmacy practice site. A preceptor may be employed by a college or school of pharmacy or may be employed by a pharmacy or health system. An *intern* is typically a student or trainee who works with or without payment to gain knowledge and experience related to the practice of pharmacy. And, a *pharmacy resident* is a licensed practitioner who is training under the supervision of an experienced pharmacist preceptor in a specific area of pharmacy practice.

During a student's numerous interactions with a preceptor, because of this relationship (i.e., preceptorship), the preceptor may also become a trusted *mentor and advisor*. Oftentimes, these mentor relationships may extend for the student's career and can provide a mechanism for the learner to receive advice and guidance for a lifetime. This highlights the important facets to consider when communicating and interacting with a preceptor.

Clinical Pharmacy Education, Practice and Research. https://doi.org/10.1016/B978-0-12-814276-9.00028-3

Practice Scenario

You are assigned to complete a practice-based experience in an area of pharmacy you plan to pursue after graduation and licensure. During the experience, you show tremendous growth and perform at a very high level, earning the praise of many of your preceptors. Following the experience you continue to ask your preceptor for advice and guidance regarding your career.

- During the experience, what is your relationship to the preceptor? *During the experience you are in a preceptor–student type of relationship. The preceptor is involved in teaching and facilitating learning for you.*
- Following the experience, what is your relationship to the preceptor? *Following the experience, you are beginning to develop more of a mentor–mentee relationship with the preceptor that may extend your career as you look to this person for guidance and advice.*

The Roles of a Preceptor

Preceptors take on many roles as they provide instruction to students such as providing direct instruction, modeling, coaching, and facilitating.[1] Preceptors can utilize all four roles during a given day or during a type of experience. The four preceptor roles align with Miller's pyramid of learning (Figs. 28.1 and 28.2).[2] The base of Miller's pyramid begins with

FIGURE 28.1 Miller's pyramid of assessment of clinical competence.[2] *Used with permission: Miller GE. The assessment of clinical skills/competence/ performance.* Acad Med. *1990;65:563–567. https://insights.ovid.com/pubmed?pmid=2400509.*

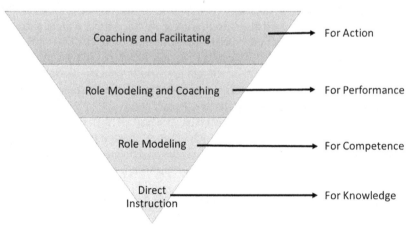

FIGURE 28.2 Roles of a preceptor.[1]

"knows" and "knows how." This knowledge becomes the strong foundation on which experiential learning will build. Correspondingly, preceptors may provide direct instruction only if the foundational knowledge in a specific area is weak.

Further up Miller's pyramid, "shows how" allows the learner to demonstrate what they are able to do. Likewise, preceptors may use modeling to show learners how they want a particular skill carried out. For example, a preceptor may have the student observe a preceptor-to-patient interaction. Once the preceptor feels the student has the knowledge and the ability to perform the skill, the preceptor may utilize a coaching role. The coaching role allows the student to perform the task while a preceptor observes. This allows for confidence building in the student as well as direct and immediate feedback from the preceptor. The topmost point of Miller's pyramid is "does" which corresponds to the preceptor's role of facilitating. When the preceptor serves as a facilitator, the student should be working and learning somewhat independently as the pharmacy laws allow, with the preceptor available as needed.

Often, experiential learning environments have many different levels of learners. For example, there could be an experienced preceptor teaching pharmacy residents as well as students and interns at different levels of their training at the same practice site. This learning model is referred to as layered learning. Layered learning is often used in medical training. The preceptor should clearly delineate the definitions, learning goals, and expectations for each learner in the layered-learning model.

Practice Scenario

You are entering a very specialized field of pharmacy practice for one of your practice-based experiences (e.g., a Pediatric Intensive Care Unit). You have had little to no foundational knowledge in this area prior to your practice-based experience.
- Which role of instruction will your preceptor likely use at the beginning of the experience? *Direct instruction is the likely role the preceptor would use as you may not have a solid foundation in this specialty area of pharmacy practice.*
  Your preceptor asks you to provide education to a patient on the medications while the preceptor observes your performance. Immediately following your patient encounter, the preceptor provides you with direct feedback regarding one strength of your encounter and one area for improvement.
- Which of the four preceptor roles is the preceptor using? *Your preceptor is utilizing the coaching role. The coaching role allows the preceptor to observe and provide immediate instruction and correction as necessary.*

OBJECTIVE 28.2. DESCRIBE THE QUALITIES OF EFFECTIVE PRECEPTORS AND RESPONSIBILITIES OF STUDENTS

Qualities of Effective Preceptors

Professional expertise, empathy, enthusiasm, openness to questions, and giving constructive feedback are just a few of the many attributes that describe effective preceptors. Though awards have been established to recognize preceptors with demonstrated excellence and a long-standing commitment to experiential education, practice, and service,[3] the best judges of qualities of great preceptors, however, are likely students themselves. The Role Model Apperception Tool, designed to assess a clinical trainer as a role model, highlights the importance of both a clinical and caring component of the "3Hs" for positive role modeling: personal (heart), teaching (head), and clinical (hands-on).[4,5] Pharmacy students cite similar role modeling, teaching/coaching, and or facilitating behaviors in award-winning preceptors.[6] A summary of the top qualities cited by learners is found in Table 28.1.

Effective preceptors encourage students to engage fully in learning opportunities to develop their knowledge and skills. Activities should include all those routinely performed by pharmacists, with the level of responsibility commensurate with the student's level of training (beginner, reinforcing, advanced). As identified in Miller's pyramid, the highest level of learning and assessment is to learn by doing. Application of the students' foundational knowledge in real-world patient care settings with other healthcare professional students and practitioners will allow for a smooth transition to practice. Quality preceptors also promote self-directed learning and lifelong learning through the use of strategies such as goal setting, reflection, encouraging creativity in developing new solutions to problems, scholarly inquiry (reading, research, and writing), service-learning, and engagement in activities of leadership and advocacy for the profession.

TABLE 28.1 Selected Qualities of a "good preceptor"

Qualities of Role Model (RoMAT) (Jochemsen) or Modified RoMAT (Bochenek)	Student-Valued Measurable Teaching Behaviors (O'Sullivan)
Clinical ("Hands-On")	**Role Modeling**
Caring Attitude	
• Shows empathy for patients	No equivalent
• Communicates skillfully with patients and their relatives	No equivalent
• Shows enthusiasm for work	• Enthusiasm for patient care
• Interacts in positive way with other healthcare workers	• Works well with other healthcare professionals/colleagues
Effectiveness	
• Possesses excellent clinical reasoning skills	• Very knowledgeable
• Demonstrates professional competence in difficult clinical situations and ability to cope with adversity	No equivalent
Teaching ("Head")	**Teaching/Coaching**
Caring Attitude	
• Shows interest in teaching the rotation[a]	• Teaches students/shares own learning
• Establishes rapport with learners	No equivalent
• Has positive attitude	No equivalent
• Is available to learners	• Goes out of his/her way and always makes time for students
Effectiveness	
• Provides good direction and feedback[a]	• Clear in expectations/provides feedback
• Understands learners' needs and shows commitment to learners' growth	• Interested in student learning and success
• Makes learning stimulating	No equivalent
• Encourages learners to actively participate in discussions and problem-solving exercises[a]	• Answers and asks students questions/has discussions
• Has well-organized and structured rotation[a]	No equivalent
• Is aware of his or her status as role model	No equivalent
Personal ("Heart")	**Role Modeling (Other)**
Caring Attitude	
• Shows patience	• Positive preceptor attitude (e.g., patient, fun, kind)
• Relates to learners as individuals[a]	No equivalent
• Demonstrates honesty and integrity	No equivalent
• Is nice and easy to work with	No equivalent
Effectiveness	
• Is involved with professional pharmacy organizations[a]	• Advocates and has enthusiasm for profession of pharmacy
• Has self-confidence	No equivalent
• Shows leadership qualities	No equivalent
	Facilitating Behaviors
No equivalent	• Flexible, organized, and accommodating to student learning/scheduling • Establishes great working environment • Solicits student input and suggestions • Willing to provide a variety of experiences

[a]Not part of original RoMAT instrument. IIIB pharm organization inquiry was not found to be of importance to pharmacy residents.

Along with recognizing the qualities of an effective preceptor, it is important to recognize the student's responsibilities to ensure that the learning experience is a success. The preceptor will serve as a guide, but the student is ultimately responsible for his or her success. Ongoing communication in the most professional manner possible is key to ensure preceptor expectations are understood. When a student reviews goals with his/her preceptor, learning opportunities can be tailored to meet the needs of the student, preceptor, and practice site to ensure the student can become confident and successful.

Receiving Effective Feedback

One of the greatest responsibilities of a student is to ensure that the preceptor's expectations and feedback are understood throughout the learning experience. One of the biggest mistakes students make is assuming that a lack of negative feedback is a sign that all is going well. Students should ask the preceptor to provide ongoing, routine feedback, as well as a formal midpoint evaluation. The goal is to find out specifically what can be done to improve while there is still time to address concerns. Two types of feedback are highlighted in Table 28.2 and described further below.

Most formal learning experiences include, and most preceptors are quite accustomed to providing feedback that summarizes performance at the end of the experience. This type of feedback is known as summative assessment or summative feedback, which is an assessment *of* learning or measurement of the student's aptitude for accountability purposes. When giving summative feedback, the preceptor takes on the role of an evaluator. This feedback is necessary to determine whether the student is able to progress to the next experience, finish a course of study, or care for patients independently and effectively. The timing of this feedback at the end of an experience, however, does not allow for the student to make modifications to performance that may be below average in real time and learn from their mistakes in a safe environment. A student may be left to discover that they are not performing to a preceptor's satisfaction when it is too late to change the outcome of the experience. This can be very disheartening to the student and quite challenging to the preceptor who does not like to disappoint their trainee.

During the course of the learning experience, there should be many opportunities to learn and to grow in various skill areas. Ideally, the preceptor should proactively offer verbal or written feedback along the way, but if it is not offered, ask for it. This type of feedback, known as formative assessment or formative feedback, is feedback *for* learning, is generally informal, and is intended to serve as a catalyst for further learning. Formative feedback works best when it is (1) embedded in the instructional process and/or workflow, (2) provides specific and actionable feedback, (3) is ongoing, and (4) is timely.[7] Like S.M.A.R.T. (Specific, Measurable, Achievable, Relevant, Timed) goals, a preceptor who functions in the role of a teacher may employ a modified S.M.A.R.T. mnemonic when providing formative feedback to a student: S = Specific, M = Measurable/Meaningful, A = Actionable/Accurate, R = Respectful/Relevant, and T = Timely.[8] By using this approach, discussions involving progress to date, successes, and opportunities for improvement can occur in a timely manner.

Regardless of when feedback is provided, it is important to be open to receiving the feedback; in other words, have a "teachable spirit." As no one is perfect and students are still learning, students should expect to receive some areas of feedback for improvement to allow for growth. When feedback is given that is different from what one might expect, it is important to try to avoid feeling attacked or bad about oneself. Take the opportunity to self-reflect on the performance and be as objective as possible. If questions remain, a discussion to gain more insight with a request for objective examples demonstrating strengths and areas for improvements is recommended. Always be sure to keep the discussion respectful and professional.

Keep in mind the skills learned through the continuing professional development process such as reflection and self-assessment, planning, and evaluation are the foundation for lifelong learning, which is a critical skill for all pharmacists.

TABLE 28.2 Feedback Types During Experiential Rotations

Feedback Type	When?	Goal	Preceptor Role
Formative assessment	Throughout experience	Learning/improvement	Teacher
Summative assessment	End of experience	Measure aptitude/accountability	Evaluator

---

Practice Scenario

You are scheduled to spend time in a hospital pharmacy for 6 weeks with a preceptor that you do not know much about. You are told to show up each morning on time for rounds and to ask the preceptor if you have any questions. You show up on time for rounds each day, attend required meetings with your preceptor, and turn in your assignments on time. You have been asked questions by physicians and have known the answers about one-half of the time (the other half of the time someone else provided them with an answer). Your preceptor has not provided feedback on your assignments. On the final day of the learning experience, you are told that you received an "average" or "competent" rating on the rotation. You feel confused and upset as you had thought you had done everything you needed to do to get a much better grade on the rotation. When you ask for more specific information, you are told that you needed to come in earlier in the morning to prepare more for rounds and have more information about each patient ready for the team, your knowledge base and responsiveness to questions required more attention, and your writing assignments need improvement.

- What type of feedback did you receive? *In the case above, you received only summative feedback or "assessment of learning." It was provided only at the end of the experience and intended to measure your aptitude in various skill areas.*
- What role did the preceptor play in the above scenario? What is the student's responsibility in acquiring effective feedback? *The preceptor served more as an evaluator throughout this experience than a teacher. Ideally, the preceptor should have provided more clear expectations for you regarding what was expected prior to and during daily patient care rounds. Formative feedback through a variety of mechanisms would be helpful. This can often be accomplished by setting aside even a small amount of time each day for discussion.*

For example, the preceptor might have considered attending rounds with you to provide feedback in real time regarding your skills and contributions to the patient care team. Additionally, having your written work corrected and returned with feedback would have allowed you to view and incorporate suggestions into future assignments.

However, the responsibility does not rest solely with the preceptor to ensure a better outcome for you. You should never assume all is going fine but rather should ask specifically about your performance at minimum once each week. It is best to work with your preceptor to develop a plan for improvement as soon as an issue is identified. In the end, it is important to recognize that until you are able to demonstrate competence, you should not receive a passing grade.

OBJECTIVE 28.3. DETAIL HOW TO DEVELOP A PRODUCTIVE STUDENT–PRECEPTOR RELATIONSHIP

The most productive student–preceptor relationship can be established when both parties actively participate in fostering its development through planning, communication, and the conveyance of respect throughout the spectrum of the experience: prior to, during, at the end of, and following the experience.

Prior to the Experience

Ideally, the preceptor prepares for the student's arrival by completing preceptor training from the pharmacy program, planning a schedule and activities for learning including interactions with as many other healthcare professionals as possible. Preceptors should also acquire space for the student to work and keep belongings, inform other staff of the student's arrival and the role they will play in the student's education, and communicate with the student regarding how to prepare for the experience. At the start of the experience, policies such as arrival time, dress code, and other expectations should be reviewed, leaving no room for ambiguity on the part of the student. Perhaps most importantly, the preceptor should start each experience with renewed passion for teaching and an open mind regarding the student's individual capabilities and learning needs.

The student should also have a solid foundation in understanding the expectations for the learning experience, of the preceptor, and the practice site. As identified by Holt and colleagues, altruism, honesty and integrity, respect for others, professional presence, professional stewardship, and dedication and commitment to excellence are the tenets of professionalism that should be the foundation for every student and pharmacist.[9]

Before each experience, the student should professionally communicate with the preceptor. This communication could include a short introduction and the student's curriculum vitae or resume. Students should reflect on their own strengths and weaknesses while identifying what they hope to learn or gain from the experience. From the very start, the student should have a clear understanding of the schedule and the preceptor's expectations for the experience.

During the Experience

As discussed earlier, the preceptor should strive to provide the student with formative assessment opportunities to offer low-stakes feedback and the opportunity to grow before the final evaluation. When assignments are given, the preceptor should offer explicit instructions to prevent confusion. Additionally, the best preceptor serves as both coach and cheerleader as he/she guides the student through the experience, offering both constructive feedback and praise as needed. Students should accept feedback as a constructive way to improve and not take feedback personally.

The student should be present both physically and mentally each day and should have an organized approach to solving problems. For each problem encountered, students may consider using the SOAP (Subjective, Objective, Assessment, Plan) approach to thinking through the problem. Subjective information includes the observations or data the patient shares with the pharmacist. For example, it may include symptoms or feelings expressed by the patient or the person asking the question. Objective information is data that can be measured or quantified. This may include laboratory values or numbers that have been quantified related to the problem. Assessment is a way to state the problem that was identified, in other words, the diagnosis of what is wrong. Finally, the plan is the student's recommendation to solve the problem. Using the SOAP approach is a quick way to communicate an issue with a preceptor whether it is written or verbal communication. A newer, but similar method to SOAP is pharmacists' patient care process (PPCP).

The preceptor is present to assist with learning and reasoning through problems appropriately. It is also of the utmost importance to receive feedback during the experience to make performance improvements and ultimately learn. If a preceptor does not provide feedback, ask for it in a way that is positive. Such as, "I would really appreciate your advice on how I can improve in this activity." In addition, every patient deserves the best performance in every encounter, regardless of the situation. As a student and learner, it is ok to say, "I don't know, let me look it up and get back to you." It is never ok to guess when it comes to caring for a patient.

During the practice experience, students may be introduced to multiple members of an interdisciplinary or interprofessional healthcare team. Interprofessional education occurs when two or more professionals learn with, from, and about each other to allow for collaboration and improved health outcomes for patients.[10] Interprofessional education and practice involves students and preceptors in exhibiting competency in having mutual respect and shared values of other professions, knowledge of roles of each health professional, communication with patients, families, communities, and other professionals (both health and other fields), and team dynamics and relationship-building skills to care for patients.[11] Students should clearly understand the role of each individual of a healthcare team and take time to develop communication styles and team building skills during each practice-based experience to embody the competencies of interprofessional education and practice.

At the End of the Experience/Following the Experience

At the conclusion of the experience, the preceptor will have feedback for the student regarding their overall performance. As part of this evaluation, students may be asked to complete a self-assessment as a way to create a dialog back and forth between preceptor and student, which serves as an opportunity to strengthen the quality of the relationship. If both the preceptor and the student have been proactive throughout the rotation in fostering the relationship, nothing said during the final evaluation will be a surprise. If a surprise does reveal itself, let it serve as a valuable lesson regarding the importance of soliciting feedback from the preceptor throughout the experience.

Lastly, it is important to recognize what to do after the practice-based learning has occurred through gratitude and reflection. Gratitude practices allow the student to show appreciation to his/her teacher. One of the recommended ways this can be done is through a simple handwritten note of thanks. Reflecting and documenting achievements during the experience or journaling is a way to reflect on what has been learned and to track meaningful encounters with patients, preceptors, and other healthcare providers. Kolb describes a method involving reflection in the experiential learning cycles. It can begin with describing what happened in an experience. The next step is an analysis or reflective observation of what happened, including the meaning this experience had on the students' learning. Making generalizations about the experience is the next step. Finally, the student identifies future action through planning and the experiential learning cycle continues.[12]

Ready for Practice

The critical outcome for all experiential learning is creating students who are ready to enter professional practice as a pharmacist (i.e., practice-ready), prepared to work on a team (i.e., team-ready), and ready and willing to teach the next generation of pharmacists (i.e., preceptor-ready). Practice-ready and team-ready graduating students are competent to contribute to patient care by working in collaboration with other healthcare providers. Maintaining a forward-thinking, visionary approach to learning and development will ensure that you are ready to practice the profession of pharmacy and become a future preceptor on graduation.

Practice Scenario

You are about to have your first practice-based experience in a hospital setting. Before the experience, you researched information about the hospital and communicated with the preceptor regarding where to report on the first day.

- What steps did this student miss in preparing for a practice-based experience? *One critical step missed was to self-assess and identify your strengths and weaknesses. A second step in self-assessment is to plan and identify what you would like to learn throughout the experience as it relates to this specific practice area.*

CONCLUSION

What to expect from a preceptor is different from what is expected from faculty teaching in a classroom. How to adapt to experiential education sites, preceptors, and the healthcare team is to be planned well in advance. Preceptor roles vary depending on where the student stands on performance level for a particular task. Understanding the roles and responsibilities of the preceptors and interns is pivotal in establishing a productive relationship.

REFERENCES

1. American Society of Health-System Pharmacists. *Accreditation Standards for PGY1 Pharmacy Residencies*; 2017. https://www.ashp.org/-/media/assets/professional-development/residencies/docs/pgy1-accreditation-standard-2016.ashx?la=en&hash=82D0575273AD83E720B114D62B7926FD35792AFD.
2. Miller GE. The assessment of clinical skills/competence/performance. *Acad Med*. 1990;65:563−567.
3. American Association of Colleges of Pharmacy. *Master Preceptor Recognition Program: 2016-2017 Program Criteria and Selection Procedures*; 2017. http://www.aacp.org/advocacy/WhatDoesAACPAdvocateFor/BudgetandAppropriations/Documents/Master%20Preceptor%20Program%20Application%20Information%20FINAL%2020160926.pdf.
4. Jochemsen-van der Leeuw HGAR, van Dijk N, Wieringa-de Waard M. Assessment of the clinical trainer as a role model: a role model apperception tool (RoMAT). *Acad Med*. 2014;89:671−677.
5. Bochenek SH, Fugit AM, Cook AM, Smith KM. Pharmacy residents' perception of preceptors as role models. *Am J Health Syst Pharm*. 2016;73(Suppl. 3):S94−S99.
6. O'Sullivan TA, Lau C, Patel, et al. Student-valued measurable teaching behaviors of award-winning pharmacy preceptors. *Am J Pharm Educ*. 2015;79(10). Article 151.
7. Norcini J, Anderson B, Bollela V, et al. Criteria for good assessment: consensus statement and recommendations from the Ottawa 2010 Conference. *Med Teach*. 2011;33:206−214.
8. DiVall MV, Alston GL, Bird E, et al. A faculty toolkit for formative assessment in pharmacy education. *Am J Pharm Educ*. 2014;78(9). Article 160.
9. Holt SL, Lau MS, Wong FL, et al. Tenets of professionalism for pharmacy students. *Pharmacotherapy*. 2009;20(6):757−759.
10. World Health Organization (WHO). *Framework for Action on Interprofessional Education & Collaborative Practice*. Geneva: World Health Organization; 2017. http://apps.who.int/iris/bitstream/10665/70185/1/WHO_HRH_HPN_10.3_eng.pdf.
11. *Interprofessional Education Collaborative Expert (IPEC) Core Competencies for Interprofessional Collaborative Practice: 2016 Update*; 2017. https://hsc.unm.edu/ipe/resources/ipec-2016-core-competencies.pdf.
12. Kolb DA. *Experiential Learning: Experience as the Source of Learning and Development*. New Jersey: Prentice Hall; 1984.

Section VII

Pharmacokinetics/
Pharmacogenomics/Nutrition

Chapter 29

Clinical Pharmacokinetics

Mohammad Kowser Miah[1], Imam Hussain Shaik[1], Firuz Gamal Feturi[1], Alshabi Ali[2] and
Raman Venkataramanan[1,3,4]

[1]*University of Pittsburgh, Pittsburgh, PA, United States;* [2]*Clinical Pharmacy Department, College of Pharmacy, Najran University, Najran, Saudi Arabia;* [3]*Thomas Starzl Transplantation Institute, University of Pittsburgh, Pittsburgh, PA, United States;* [4]*University of Pittsburgh Medical Center, Pittsburgh, PA, United States*

Learning Objectives:

Objective 29.1 Explain the basic concepts in clinical pharmacokinetics.
Objective 29.2 Discuss factors affecting pharmacokinetics of a drug.
Objective 29.3 Outline pharmacometrics.

OBJECTIVE 29.1. EXPLAIN THE BASIC CONCEPTS IN CLINICAL PHARMACOKINETICS

Clinical Pharmacokinetics and Terminology

Pharmacokinetics (PK) deals with the time course of a drug in the body following drug administration. Pharmacokinetic parameters describe various processes such as the absorption, distribution, metabolism, and excretion of a drug. Clinical PK is the application of PK principles for the safe and effective management of drug therapy in an individual patient. It is the blood that transports drugs to various organs in the body. The organs that clear the drug can eliminate it only if it is brought to that organ by the blood. Measurement of the time course of the drug concentrations in the blood is useful to determine the overall ability of the body to remove a drug. Pharmacokinetic principles help establish a relationship between drug concentrations measured in easily accessible body fluids (blood, plasma, urine, and saliva) and therapeutic effects and/or toxicities associated with a drug. For pharmacokinetic assessments, drug concentrations are typically measured in plasma or blood samples collected at various times after drug administration.

Drug concentration monitoring, e.g., in plasma is based on the concept of kinetic homogeneity. It means when plasma concentration of the drug increases, drug concentration in most of the other tissues increases proportionally. Same way when the concentration decreases in plasma, concentration in tissues also decrease proportionally. While pharmacokinetics describes the time course of absorption, distribution, metabolism, and excretion of drugs, pharmacodynamics relates drug concentration to drug response.

Routes of Drug Administration: Drugs are normally administered via different routes. Generally, the routes for drug administration are divided into two classes: intravascular route and extravascular route. When a drug is administered directly into the systemic circulation (blood circulation), it is called intravascular administration. On the other hand, when a drug is administered outside the vascular system, not directly into the systemic circulation, it is called extravascular drug administration. An extravascular route could be oral, sublingual, nasal, rectal, intramuscular, subcutaneous, or topical. If a drug is administered via extravascular route, it has to reach the blood, and the drug must cross various biological membranes to reach the systemic circulation before it travels to the site of action to elicit a pharmacological effect. Sometimes drugs can be administered directly at the site of action, called site-specific drug delivery. Site-specific drug delivery is e.g., used for local topical drug delivery and for local delivery of highly toxic drugs such as anticancer drugs to minimize unwanted/off target effects.

Clinical Pharmacy Education, Practice and Research. https://doi.org/10.1016/B978-0-12-814276-9.00029-5

All drugs undergo a series of processes after administration by different routes. Drugs are absorbed, distributed, metabolized, and finally excreted from the body. One of the basic concepts in pharmacokinetics is linear and nonlinear pharmacokinetics.

Linear Pharmacokinetics: If a drug follows linear PK (first order kinetics), the plasma drug concentration varies proportionately with the dose, but the pharmacokinetic parameters of that drug would remain constant, when the dose is changed. Dose normalized plasma concentration - time profiles will be superimposible. Most drugs that we currently use follow linear PK.

Nonlinear Pharmacokinetics: When plasma drug concentration changes disproportionate to the drug dose, and when a pharmacokinetic parameter varies depending on the administered dose, it is referred to as nonlinear PK. Nonlinear PK is the results of one or more saturable processes during drug absorption, distribution, metabolism, or elimination. Once elimination is saturated the quantity eliminated per unit time is same as this is the maximum ability of the body to eliminate the drug. For example, phenytoin follows linear PK at lower doses; however, at higher dose it follows nonlinear PK. See Table 29.1 for the differences between linear and nonlinear kinetics.

Absorption: Absorption is a process by which a drug molecule moves from the site of administration to the site of measurement (normally blood or plasma). The absorption can be a simple diffusion across a concentration gradient which is a passive process or involve a transporter or a specialized carrier which is an active process. Absorption normally starts immediately after drug administration and continues till the entire drug that can be absorbed is absorbed. Soon after drug administration, the absorption rate is much higher than the elimination rate. When the absorption rate is higher than the elimination rate, the drug level will increase in the body. At the time of maximal blood concentration (C_{max}), the absorption rate is equal to the elimination rate. After C_{max}, the elimination rate is higher than the absorption rate and the drug level will decrease in the body. Absorption is followed by distribution and/or elimination.

Distribution: Distribution is a reversible process of movement of drugs from and to the site of measurement. Distribution is influenced by multiple factors such as permeability of the drug in various tissues, blood flow, and binding of the drug to plasma or tissue proteins. In some cases, distribution of the drug is mediated by drug transporters. The distribution of a drug can be selectively altered by specific formulations such as liposomal formulations, nanodelivery systems, or targeted delivery systems such as antibody−drug conjugates.

Metabolism: Metabolism is a process of bioconversion of one chemical to another by various enzymes. A majority of the drugs undergo metabolism in the liver, but some drugs may be metabolized in the gut also. Other organs such as kidneys, lungs, and brain also contain drug metabolizing enzymes but their contribution to the overall metabolism of the drug is limited. Localized metabolism may affect the tissue levels of the drug and its metabolites, which may potentially influence the local concentration of a drug and its efficacy and/or toxicity.

Excretion: Excretion is the irreversible loss of unchanged drug from the body through bile, urine, sweat, etc. Elimination includes both metabolism and excretion. A fraction of the dose administered can be excreted unchanged (fe) via kidney and the remaining fraction of the dose may undergo metabolism (1 − fe). Drugs mainly excreted unchanged through urine like metformin have a high fe, whereas drugs like amiodarone that are mainly metabolized by liver have a high fm (1-fe).[1−4]

TABLE 29.1 Linear and Nonlinear Kinetics

Linear Pharmacokinetics	Nonlinear Pharmacokinetics
Pharmacokinetics parameters are dose independent	Pharmacokinetics parameters are dose dependent
Follows first order kinetics	Follows mixed order kinetics
Does not involve saturable process	Saturable processes are involved
Plasma concentration−time profiles are superimposable at wide dose ranges, when dose normalized	Plasma concentration−time profiles are not superimposable at wide dose ranges, when dose normalized

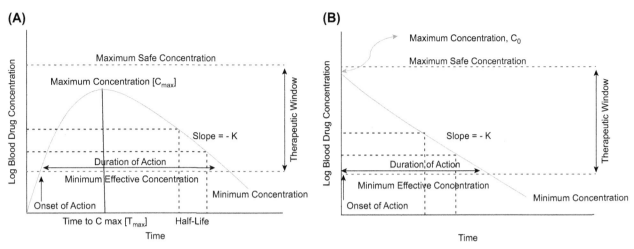

FIGURE 29.1   Blood/plasma drug concentration versus time profile of a drug after oral (A) and IV (B) administration.

Fig. 29.1 represents a typical plasma concentration versus time profile of a drug after oral (A) and IV (B) administration. Information about the PK parameters, T_{max}, C_{max}, AUC, MIC, MEC, and TW can be visualized.

Eqs. (29.1) and (29.2) can be used to describe the plasma concentrations of a drug after oral and intravenous single dose administration, respectively, at any time (t) after drug administration.

$$C = \frac{F \cdot D \cdot k_a}{V_d(k_a - k_e)} \times (e^{-k_e \cdot t} - e^{-k_a \cdot t}) \tag{29.1}$$

plasma concentration of a drug after oral administration

$$C = C_0 \times e^{-K_e t} \tag{29.2}$$

plasma concentration of a drug after IV dose

here, D = dose; F = fraction absorbed; C = plasma concentration at time t; C_0 = plasma concentration at time 0 (immediately after IV administration); V_d = volume of distribution; K_a = absorption rate constant; K_e = elimination rate constant; and $e^{-Ke \cdot t}$ = fraction or percent of the drug that remains in the body at a certain time after dose (t). This means $1 - e^{-Ke \cdot t}$ is the pecent or fraction of the drug excreted after time t.

Maximum Concentration: Maximum concentration (C_{max}) is the highest concentration of the drug observed within a dosing interval. It is also called the peak concentration (C_{peak}). After IV bolus administration, $C_{max} = C_0$ (g/L), where C_0 is the drug concentration immediately after the completion of IV bolus dose. After oral administration, C_{max} can be observed from the concentration−time profile and it can be estimated using the following equation:

$$C_{max} = \frac{F \times D}{V_d} e^{-K_e T_{max}} (g/L) \tag{29.3}$$

where, F is the fraction of drug absorbed, D is the dose, V_d is the volume of distribution, K_e is the elimination rate constant, and T_{max} is the time to C_{max} (Fig. 29.1A).

Minimum Concentration: Minimum Concentration (C_{min}) is the lowest concentration of a drug within a dosing interval. It is also called trough concentration (C_{trough}), when drugs are administered repeatedly. The value of C_{min} can be obtained from the concentration−time profile after IV administration (Fig. 29.1B) and can be calculated using the following equation:

$$C_{min} = C_0 e^{-K_e T_{last}} (g/L) \tag{29.4}$$

where, C_0 is maximum concentration, K_e is elimination rate constant, and T_{last} is the time of the last blood sample collected within a dosing interval (Fig. 29.1B).

Time to Maximum Concentration: Time to Maximum Concentration (T_{max}) is the time taken for the drug concentration to achieve its highest value within a dosing interval. The value of T_{max} can be observed from the concentration−time profile and it can be calculated using the following equation:

$$T_{max} = \frac{\ln \frac{K_a}{K_e}}{(K_a - K_e)} \, (hr) \tag{29.5}$$

where, T_{max} is the time taken to reach maximum concentration, K_a is the absorption rate constant, and K_e is the elimination rate constant.

Minimum Effective Concentration: Minimum effective concentration (MEC) is the minimum concentration needed to elicit desired therapeutic effect. It is expressed as gm/L (Fig. 29.1A and B).

Maximum Safe (Tolerable) Concentration: Maximum safe concentration (MSC) is the maximum concentration with no undesired effects and beyond which toxicity is observed. It is also called minimum toxic concentration. It is expressed as g/L.

Therapeutic Window: Therapeutic window (TW) can be defined as the range of drug concentrations that provide therapeutic response without significant adverse effects. Drug concentrations above MSC are associated with toxicity, and the drug concentration below MEC does not provide adequate therapeutic effect leading to therapeutic failure. The ratio between MSC and MEC is called the therapeutic index (TI). The TI is a measure of the safety of the drug. The larger the TI, the safer the drug.

Half-Life: Half-life ($T_{1/2}$) is the time taken for the drug amount or concentration to decline to half of its original value. Most of the drugs follow first order kinetics. Mathematically, it is calculated using the following equation:

$$T_{1/2} = 0.693/K_e \text{ or } 0.693 \times V_d/CL \tag{29.6}$$

where, 0.693 is the natural log of 0.5 meaning half, K_e is the elimination rate constant, CL is the clearance, and V_d is the apparent volume of distribution. $T_{1/2}$ is typically represented in minutes to hours. Half-life is useful to determine how long it will take the body to eliminate the entire drug, to determine the duration of drug action, and to determine the dosing interval and the time to reach steady state for medications administered chronically.

Elimination Rate Constant: Elimination rate constant (K_e) describes drug loss by all elimination processes and the unit of elimination rate constant is per unit time (sec^{-1}, min^{-1}, h^{-1}). Mathematically, K_e can be calculated from the slope of the terminal disposition phase of the ln plasma concentration versus time profile and by the equation

$$K_e = [\ln(C_1) - \ln(C_2)]/(T_2 - T_1) \tag{29.7}$$

where, C_1 and C_2 are plasma/blood concentrations at time T_1 and T_2, respectively.

Area Under the Curve: The area under the curve (AUC) represents total systemic drug exposure after a dose. The AUC is calculated from the concentration−time profile data by the trapezoidal rule, where AUC is divided into discrete set of rectangles. Each rectangle represents the area for that interval and the sum of area of trapezoids represents AUC up to the last sampling time. The AUC from last sampling time point to ∞ is calculated as shown below and the unit of AUC is amount/volume/time; ng/mL.h. AUC is calculated using the following equation:

$$AUC_{0-\infty} = \sum \frac{(C_n + C_{n+1}) \times (T_{n+1} - T_n)}{2} + \frac{C_{last}}{K_e} \tag{29.8}$$

Clearance: Clearance is the term used to describe the ability of the body to eliminate a drug from the body. The unit of clearance is the volume of blood or plasma that is cleared of the drug per unit time (mL/h, mL/min, L/h, etc.). Clearance is normally described as blood clearance, plasma clearance (depending on where the drug concentration is measured), and may be based on total drug concentrations or free (unbound) drug concentrations. For example, clearance of phenytoin is 10 L/h, and this means that in 1 h, an equivalent of 10 L of blood gets cleared of phenytoin (amount of the drug removed from body is equivalent to what is present in 10 L of blood).

Normally, more than one organ is involved in the elimination of drugs. Although the most important organ that is involved in drug elimination is the liver, kidney also contributes to the removal of many drugs. Additionally, lung and intestine can also contribute to the total clearance of a drug. Clearance is an additive process that includes contribution from all the organs. Total body clearance of a drug is the sum of hepatic clearance, renal clearance, and clearance by other organs.

$$CL_{total} = CL_h + CL_r + CL_{other} \tag{29.9}$$

where, CL_{total} = total body clearance, CL_h = hepatic clearance, CL_r = renal clearance, and CL_{other} = clearance by other organs.

Clearance of a drug by a particular organ depends on the blood flow to the organ and the ability of the organ to extract the drug. Extraction ratio (E) is a term used to describe fraction of drug being removed by a specific organ during a single passage. ER is measured from the concentration of drug in the incoming artery (C_a) and the concentration of drug in the outgoing vein (C_v) leaving that organ and with the organ blood flow (Q). ER is dependent on the hepatic blood flow (Q), intrinsic clearance (CL_{int}), and fraction of the drug unbound in plasma (f_u).

$$E = \frac{Q \times (C_a - C_v)}{Q \times C_a} = \frac{C_a - C_v}{C_a} \tag{29.10}$$

$$CL_{organ} = Q_{organ} \times \frac{(C_a - C_v)}{C_a} = Q_{organ} \times E = (Q \times f_u \, CL_{int}) / (Q + f_u \, CL_{int}) \tag{29.11}$$

A drug is considered to be a high extraction ratio drug if E is greater than 0.7, on the other hand if E value is less than 0.3, the drug is considered a low extraction ratio drug. If E is between 0.3 and 0.7, the drug is considered intermediate extraction ratio drug. Lidocaine and propronolol are examples of drugs with high hepatic extraction ratio. As most of the drug is cleared in one passage through liver, clearance is depended on hepatic blood flow. From Eq. (29.11), also it is clear that if the entire drug is being removed by a particular organ during single pass (high extraction ratio), CL equals to the hepatic blood flow. Clearance of a drug can be estimated from area under plasma concentration time curve and dose by using Eqs. (29.12) and (29.13).

$$CL = \frac{Dose}{AUC}, \text{ for IV adminstration} \tag{29.12}$$

$$CL = \frac{F \, Dose}{AUC}, \text{ for extravascular administration} \tag{29.13}$$

where, F is the fraction bioavailable. Typically, when the drug is given by extravascular route, the value of F is unknown and the apparent clearance calculated as dose/AUC is CL/F.

Volume of Distribution: Volume of distribution (V_d) defines the volume of fluid which would be required to contain the amount of drug in the body based on plasma concentration measurements. The volume of distribution does not represent a true physical volume, rather it is a hypothetical volume which is different than the actual human body volume. V_d does not provide any indication about the types of tissue or organ into which drug has accumulated or distributed.

$$V_d = \frac{\text{Amount of Drug at time 0}}{\text{Plasma drug concentration at time 0}} \ldots Dose/C_p^0, \text{ where } C_p^0 \text{ is the concentration at time zero} \tag{29.14}$$

When a drug is administered into the blood, depending on the characteristics, a certain portion of the drug binds to the plasma proteins (albumin, α-1-acid glycoprotein, or blood cells) and the remaining drug stays as free drug in the plasma. It is only the free drug, which is not bound to the blood cells or plasma proteins, which can cross cell membrane and distribute into the other organs or tissues. So, if a drug is 100% bound to plasma proteins, the volume of distribution will be equal to the plasma volume (3 L) or if certain portion binds to plasma and blood cells, the volume of distribution might be equal to total blood volume (5.5 L). On the other hand, if some of the drug is free in the plasma and distributes to the tissue but remains only in the extracellular water, the volume of distribution might be equal to total water content in the body (42 L). If a drug is highly taken up in the tissues, V_d values could be a large number. For example, digoxin (a cardiac drug) is highly distributed into tissues and has a volume of distribution of about 400 L, which is almost 10 times of the total human body volume (70 kg human).[5] Table 29.2 represents the commonly used medications with their clearances class, volume of distribution, total clearance, half-life, and route of administration. Total volume of distribution is physiologically related as follows:

$$V_d = V_p + V_{tw} \times \frac{f_u}{f_{ut}} \tag{29.15}$$

here, V_p = volume of plasma, V_{tw} = volume of water outside the plasma, f_u = free fraction of the drug in plasma, and f_{ut} = unbound fraction of drug in the tissue.

TABLE 29.2 Route of Administration, Clearances, Volume of Distribution and Half-Life of Top 15 Drugs Prescribed in the United States (2017)

Drug	Route of administration	Clearance CL or CL/F[a]	Volume of distribution Vd (or) Vd/F[a]	Half-life (t1/2)
Lisinopril	PO	3 L/h	0.5 L/Kg [b]	12 h
Levothyroxine	PO	11.8 ± 5.5 L/h	0.043 L/Kg [b]	6−7 days
Atorvastatin	PO	37.5 L/h	5.44 L/Kg [b]	14 h
Metformin HCL	PO	36 ± 7.92 L/h	9.34 ± 5.11 L/Kg [b]	6.2 h
Simvastatin	PO	52.59 L/h	67.5 L/Kg [b]	5.8 h
Omeprazole	PO, IV	30−36 L/h	0.3 L/Kg	0.5−1 h
Amlodipine Besylate	PO	40 L/h	21 L/Kg	30−50 h
Metoprolol	PO, IV	0.05L/h	3.2−5.6 L/Kg	3−4 h
Acetaminophen	PO	19 L/h	0.8 L/kg	2.4 h
Albuterol	Inhaler	263 L/h	9 ± 2.4 L/Kg [b]	6 h
Hydrochlorothiazide	PO	21 L/h	4.19 L/Kg	5.6−14.8 h
Losartan Potassium	PO	36 L/h	0.5 L/Kg [b]	2 h
Gabapentin	PO	11.4 L/h	0.83 L/Kg [b]	5−7 h
Sertraline HCL	PO	96 L/h	20 L/Kg	26 h
Furosemide	PO, IV	11.64 L/h	0.2 L/Kg [b]	2 h

[a]Vd/F and CL/F may be high due to low F.
[b]Values converted based on 70 kg body weight.

Multiple Dosing: Drugs are administered to achieve a desired plasma concentration within the TW. In some disease conditions, drug therapy continues for a long period of time or even lifelong, such as the case with antidiabetic or antihypertensive drugs. For these chronic conditions, multiple dosing of the drug is required. In case of multiple doses, accumulation of the administered drug occurs depending on the half-life and dosing interval until steady-state plasma concentration is achieved, where the rate of input equals to the rate of output. For example, assume a drug has a half-life of 8 h. If a second dose is administered 8 h after administration of the first dose, 50% of the previous dose will still remain in the body. Whereas, if we administer the second dose 16 h after administration of the first dose, only 25% of the previous dose will remain in the body. So, accumulation is dependent on drug half-life and dosing interval and calculated by the following equation:

$$R_{acc} = \frac{1}{1 - e^{-K\tau}} \tag{29.16}$$

where, R_{acc} = accumulation ratio, K = elimination rate constant, and τ = dosing interval. If the accumulation ratio is 1, that means there is no accumulation. On the other hand, $R_{acc} > 1$ indicates accumulation. At steady state, there will be no accumulation because the drug input is equal to the drug output. The time to reach steady state depends on the half-life of the drug, such that 3.3 half-life is required to achieve 90% steady state and 5 half-life is required to achieve 97% steady state. In case of multiple dosing, steady-state plasma concentration does not mean a fixed concentration of drug is present in the plasma. At steady state, plasma level fluctuates between maximum $\left(C_{max}^{\infty}\right)$ and minimum $\left(C_{min}^{\infty}\right)$ plasma concentrations and the plasma concentration time profile will be identical from one dose to the next. The relationship between $\left(C_{max}^{\infty}\right)$ and $\left(C_{min}^{\infty}\right)$ is as follows:

$$C_{min}^{\infty} = C_{max}^{\infty} \times e^{-K\tau} \tag{29.17}$$

One important PK parameter at steady state is the average steady-state concentration $\left(C_{avg}^{\infty}\right)$, though $\left(C_{avg}^{\infty}\right)$ does not give any indication about the degree of fluctuations. Eq. (29.18) dictates the relationship among $\left(C_{avg}^{\infty}\right)$, $\left(C_{min}^{\infty}\right)$, and $\left(C_{max}^{\infty}\right)$ as follows:

$$C_{avg}^{\infty} = \frac{C_{max}^{\infty} - C_{min}^{\infty}}{\ln \dfrac{C_{max}^{\infty}}{C_{min}^{\infty}}} \tag{29.18}$$

In case of oral dosing, $\left(C_{avg}^{\infty}\right)$ could be calculated from dose (D), fraction bioavailable (F), clearance (CL), and dosing interval (T) as indicated by Eq. (29.19)

$$C_{avg}^{\infty} = \frac{F\left(\dfrac{D}{\tau}\right)}{CL} = AUC/\tau \tag{29.19}$$

In clinical practice, we want to achieve steady state as early as possible, and minimize the fluctuations between minimum and maximum drug concentrations. Once a steady state plasma concentration is achieved but if a patient is not responding to the drug, increasing the dose or decreasing the dosing interval or both together are options to increase plasma concentration of the drug. Once a dose is changed, it will take approximately 4–5 half lives to achieve new steady state plasma concentration. If a drug has longer half-life, more time will be required to achieve desired steady state as compared with a drug with shorter half-life. For example, half-life of phenobarbital is 4 days, so 20 days would be required to achieve a steady state (5 half lives). To avoid this delay in achieving steady state, maintenance dose is preceded by a loading dose to achieve and maintain steady state quickly.

Loading Dose: A loading dose is the initial dose of the drug that is given to achieve target plasma concentration faster. Fig. 29.2 illustrates the blood concentration vs time curve after multiple IV dose of a drug (MD) without a loading dose, and with a loading dose (LD). As shown in the figure, a loading dose is given to reach the desired concentration faster.

Maintenance Dose: Maintenance dose is the dose of drug that is to be administered to keep the plasma concentration of a drug within a certain level at steady state. When we only administer a maintenance dose, it will take a long time to

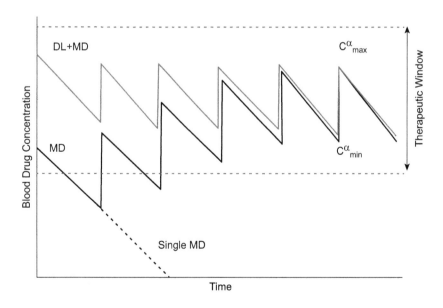

DL = Loading Dose, MD = Maintenance Dose

FIGURE 29.2 Plasma concentration–time profile after loading and maintenance dose.

reach steady state. Whereas, when we provide a loading dose followed by maintenance dose, desired plasma level is achieved earlier. Fig. 29.2 shows the scenario of loading dose with maintenance dose for IV bolus injection. The relationship between loading dose and maintenance dose is expressed by following equation:

$$D_L = D_M \times R_{acc} \tag{29.20}$$

Additionally, required loading dose can be calculated from desired maximum plasma concentration at steady state (C_{max}^{∞}) and volume of distribution

$$D_L = V \times C^{\infty}{}_{max} \tag{29.21}$$

Pharmacokinetic Models

Movement of the drug within the body and out of the body is a very complex process because a drug passes through a series of biological processes before it enters or exits from the body. The major processes which a drug goes through in the body are absorption, distribution, metabolism, and elimination. The best way to explain drug behavior within the body is with the use of mathematical models and equations. The most commonly used models for pharmacokinetic estimations are referred to as compartmental models. Compartmental models describe the movement of a drug within and out of the body. There are one, two, and multicompartment models. Each compartment does not necessarily represent any specific organ or tissue, rather they represent a group of tissues or organs with similar time course of drug concentrations. The compartmentality of a drug is determined by the number of compartments required to explain the plasma concentration−time profile of that particular drug. Imagine an example, where a drug X easily distributes into blood, liver, and kidney, but distribution of same drug (X) into the brain happens very slowly. We can combine blood, liver, and kidney into one compartment, but the brain will be in a separate compartment. The compartment that includes blood and highly perfused organs (such as liver, lung, and kidney) is called the central compartment. And compartment that includes slowly perfused organs or tissues (brain, adipose tissue) is called the peripheral compartment.

One Compartment Model

In case of a drug that can be described by a one compartment model, the entire body is considered as a single unit and the drug instantaneously distributes throughout the body. In a one compartment model, drug irreversibly exits from the

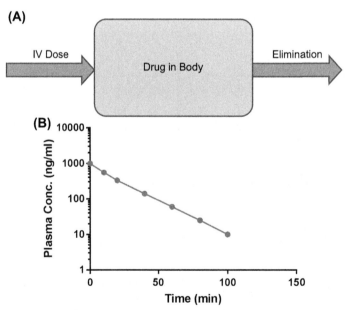

FIGURE 29.3 (A and B) One compartment model.

(A)

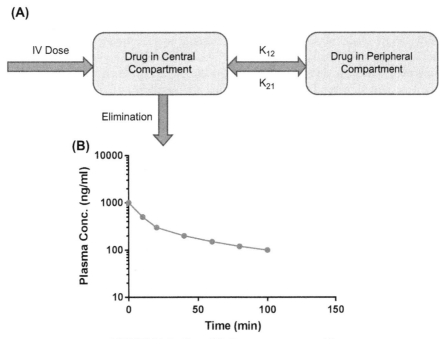

FIGURE 29.4   (A and B) Two compartment model.

compartment (Fig. 29.3A). The plasma concentration versus time profile on a semilog plot shows a straight line if drug follows one compartment model (Fig. 29.3B).

Fig. 29.3A represents a one compartment model. Drug enters into the body from administration site. Drug is irreversibly eliminated from the body. Additionally, Fig. 29.3B represents plasma concentration time profile a drug following one compartment model in semilog graph after IV administration.

Two Compartment Model

Fig. 29.4A represents a two compartment model. Drug enters the central compartment from administration site. Drug is either irreversibly eliminated or distributed into the peripheral compartment. The drug in peripheral compartment can redistribute to central compartment; K_{12} and K_{21} are the rate constants from central to peripheral and peripheral to central compartment, respectively. Fig. 29.4B represents a plasma concentration time profile of drug following two compartment model on a semilog graph after IV administration, a curvilinear profile showing distribution followed by elimination. E.g., digoxin after IV administration exhibits a rapid decline in plasma due to distribution to cardiac tissue. Digoxin has high affinity to skeletal and cardiac tissues compared to plasma. The cardiac tissue to plasma digoxin concentration ratio is 70:1.

OBJECTIVE 29.2. DISCUSS FACTORS AFFECTING PHARMACOKINETICS OF A DRUG

Absorption

Several factors can influence the rate and extent of absorption of drugs. These can be categorized as physicochemical, physiological, and formulation factors. Physicochemical factors include solubility in aqueous system, lipophilicity, size and structure, ability to form hydrogen bonds, polar surface area, chemical stability, and susceptibility to enzymatic reactions. Physiologic factors include gastric pH, gastric motility, intestinal motility, fluid volume, surface area, food–drug interactions, drug–drug interactions, intestinal metabolism, and intestinal uptake and efflux transporters. Formulation factors include disintegration and dissolution/release of drug from dosage form.

The biopharmaceutics classification system (BCS) classifies drugs based on their permeability and aqueous solubility into four classes. Class I, drugs are highly soluble and highly permeable. These drugs are normally completely absorbed from GI tract and show physicochemical properties for optimum oral bioavailability. Normally, dissolution from solid dosage form is the rate-limiting step in the overall concentration time profile of Class I drugs. The overall bioavailability of these drugs can be affected by chemical degradation, complexation, or presystemic/first pass metabolism. The in vivo performance of a dosage form of a Class 1 drug can be readily assessed in vitro, leading to potential biowaiver. Acetaminophen, piroxicam, midazolam, and propranolol hydrochloride are drugs that are highly water soluble and have high permeability. They are well absorbed from the GI tract and are classified as Class I drugs.

Class 2 drugs show low solubility, but high permeability. These drugs show rapid absorption from solution or from a readily absorbable dosage form. Formulation strategies can help in overcoming the lower aqueous solubility of the drugs and in improving the dissolution rate of the product. The in vivo performance of a dosage form of a Class 2 drug can be readily assessed in vitro, leading to potential biowaiver. Most of the immunosuppressive drugs such as tacrolimus, sirolimus, mycophenolic acid, and cyclosporine fall into this category. Drugs in this class show moderately rapid absorption ($T_{max} \sim 1-4\,h$). Improved and consistent absorption of cyclosporine from the microemulsion compared with olive oil formulation and tacrolimus extended release formulation compared with immediate release tablet that demonstrated the significance of the formulation in the improved PK of Class 2 drugs. Similarly, lipid-lowering agents such as simvastatin, rosuvastatin, and other statin drugs belong to BCS Class 2.

Class 3 drugs show high aqueous solubility and low permeability. Intestinal permeability is the rate-limiting step in the absorption of these drugs. Class 4 consists of poorly soluble and poorly permeable drugs. These drugs are poorly bioavailable after oral administration and are typically used for local action.

A recently proposed Biopharmaceutics Drug Disposition Classification System (BDDCS) is a complimentary system to BCS that predicts the importance of transporters in determining drug disposition, as well as in predicting drug—drug interactions. Both BCS and BDDCS use solubility as one of the two classification criteria, but in BDDCS, predictions are based on extent of drug metabolism. Class 1 drugs are highly soluble and highly metabolized; Class 2 drugs are poorly soluble and highly metabolized indicating involvement of efflux transporter in gut and both uptake and efflux transporters in the liver; Class 3 drugs are highly soluble and poorly metabolized predicting involvement of uptake transporters; and Class 4 drugs are poorly soluble and poorly metabolized predicting significance of uptake and efflux transporters. Class 2 drugs such as tacrolimus, sirolimus, and cyclosporine were predicted to have predominant effect of efflux transporters, and the experimental results have proven these predictions to be true.

The overall systemic availability of a drug after oral administration can be calculated by the following equation:

$$F = f_a \times f_g \times f_h \qquad (29.22)$$

where f_a is the fraction of the drug absorbed, f_g is the fraction of the drug going through gut and reaching portal circulation, and f_h is the fraction of drug passing through liver during first pass and reaching systemic circulation.

f_a will be less than one if the drug is either incompletely absorbed or degraded/metabolized or effluxed while passing through the gut. F_g will be less than 1 if a drug is metabolized in the gut wall. F_h will be less than 1 if the drug is metabolized in the liver. If the drug is completely soluble and permeable, not complexed or degraded or effluxed or metabolized in gut, and not metabolized or effluxed in liver, F will be close or equal to unity. Poor oral bioavailability of immunosuppressive drugs such as tacrolimus, sirolimus, and cyclosporine is attributed primarily to metabolism and efflux of these drugs in the gut wall.

Distribution

Distribution of a drug in the body is influenced by many factors. The apparent volume of distribution is a hypothetical volume which refers to volume of plasma required to occupy the total amount of drug in the body at the concentration observed in plasma. The volume of distribution is influenced by blood or plasma volume, total body water, and binding to plasma and tissue proteins. The volume of distribution is represented by Eq. (29.15). Immunosuppressive drugs such as tacrolimus, sirolimus, and cyclosporine show very large volume of distribution indicating extensive binding to different tissues and lower levels in circulation. In contrast, large molecules such as biologics and antibodies show a small volume of distribution and are predominantly restricted to plasma or blood.

Metabolism

Metabolism is the process of converting one chemical into another by removal of specific group or addition of a molecule or both to make it easily excretable. If a drug is eliminated only by metabolism, metabolic clearance accounts for total body clearance. For a drug metabolized by the liver only, hepatic clearance will represent metabolic as well as total body clearance. Hepatic clearance CL_h of the drug can be influenced by hepatic blood flow Q, the intrinsic metabolic capacity of the liver for that drug CL_{int}, and the fraction unbound in plasma f_u as follows:

$$CL_h = \frac{Qf_uCL_{int}}{Q + f_u \times CL_{int}}(mL/min) \tag{29.23}$$

For high hepatic intrinsic clearance drugs, the equation transforms to

$$CL_h \approx Q(mL/min) \tag{29.24}$$

indicating that the highest clearance of the drug by the liver corresponds to blood flow to the liver and changes in the blood flow to liver significantly change hepatic clearance. For low intrinsic clearance drugs, the equation simplifies to

$$CL_h = f_u \times CL_{int}(mL/min) \tag{29.25}$$

indicating that changes in f_u and CL_{int} will significantly influence the hepatic clearance and changes in hepatic blood flow may have limited to no effect on the hepatic clearance of the drug.

Hepatic blood flow, intrinsic clearance, and unbound fraction in plasma can be altered by physiological, pathological, and pharmacological factors. Treatment with enzyme inducers such as rifampin, phenobarbital, phenytoin, and carbamazepine increases intrinsic clearance, whereas inhibitors such as ketoconazole, ritonavir decrease intrinsic clearance. Several drug—drug interactions have been reported with cytochrome P450 3A4 enzyme substrate immunosuppressive drugs such as tacrolimus, sirolimus, and cyclosporine with both inducers and inhibitors of these enzymes warranting extreme caution while taking multiple medications. Altered physiological states such as liver disease can lead to decreased albumin concentrations and decreased plasma protein binding leading to increased free fraction and clearance. Subsequent to liver transplantation the increase in albumin levels in patients decreases unbound fraction of the drugs such as mycophenolic acid in plasma resulting in decreased overall total body clearance.

Clearance of the drug can be influenced by age, gender, diet, co-medications, and environmental and genetic factors. It is well known that clearance of immunosuppressants such as tacrolimus, sirolimus, cyclosporine, and mycophenolic acid is higher in pediatric patients than in adults requiring higher dose on a milligram/kg basis to achieve similar exposure and clinical outcomes.

For a drug metabolized by liver, the fraction of bioavailable drug after first pass can be calculated using the equation:

$$F = 1 - E \tag{29.26}$$

where E is the fraction of the drug extracted in the liver in a single passage, by incorporating Eq. (29.9) for E, Eq. (29.20) transforms to

$$F = 1 - \frac{CL}{Q} \tag{29.27}$$

Substituting Eq. (29.12) for CL;

$$F = 1 - \frac{Dose_{IV}}{AUC_{IV} \times Q} \tag{29.28}$$

Therefore, with information on IV dose and corresponding AUC and assuming physiologic liver blood flow of 1.5 L/min, theoretical bioavailability of the drug can be predicted after IV administration and the deviation from the predicted values can be attributed to incomplete absorption, degradation of the drug in gut or metabolism or efflux for over prediction, and saturable hepatic metabolism for under prediction.

Further modifying the above equation by incorporating Eq. (29.17) into Eq. (29.21), F can be related to blood flow, intrinsic clearance, and f_u as follows:

$$F = \frac{Q}{Q + f_u \times CL_{int}} \tag{29.29}$$

For very low clearance drugs (low intrinsic CL_{int}), F approaches 1. Whereas for drugs with high intrinsic clearance, the equation transforms to

$$F \approx \frac{Q}{f_u \times CL_{int}} \qquad (29.30)$$

Increase in blood flow increases F, increase in F_u and CL_{int} decreases F.

Excretion

Excretion is irreversible removal of drug from the body. Kidneys are the primary organs for elimination of unchanged drug from body. Renal clearance CL_r of the drug can be estimated by the following equation:

$$CL_r = \frac{\text{Cumulative amount excreted in urine}}{AUC_{Plasma(o-\infty)}} \qquad (29.31)$$

or

$$CL_r = \frac{\text{Amount excreted in urine over a time period}}{\text{Plasma concentration of drug at mid point of urine collection}}$$

The above equation can be used to calculate CL_r of the drug whether the drug was given by intravascular or extravascular route.

A drug is excreted through kidneys by glomerular filtration and/or active secretion and may undergo tubular reabsorption. The renal clearance can be represented by the following equation:

$$CL_r = (CL_{filtration} + CL_{secretion})(1 - F_{Reabsorption}) \qquad (29.32)$$

where $CL_{filtration}$ is the filtration clearance, $CL_{secretion}$ is the secretion clearance, and $F_{Reabsorption}$ is the fraction reabsorbed from the tubules.

Certain drugs are excreted in the bile. If the unchanged drug or a metabolite of drug is excreted in bile, and this metabolite can be converted into the parent drug in gut and absorbed back into systemic circulation leading to a process of enterohepatic circulation, which leads to increase exposure of the drug in patient. Mycophenolic acid, an immunosuppressant, and indomethacin, an NSAID, undergo conjugation and the conjugates secreted in bile are cleaved in gut and reabsorbed back into systemic circulation.

OBJECTIVE 29.3. OUTLINE PHARMACOMETRICS

Pharmacometrics is the science of understanding and mathematically explaining the relationship between dose–concentration effects with the application of pharmacology, biology, mathematics, and biostatistics principles. In general term, pharmacometrics encompasses modeling and simulation for PK, pharmacodynamics (PD), and disease progression. Pharmaceutical and Biotech companies and regulatory agencies all over the world have invested heavily in the development of proper expertise to analyze data generated during drug development process from preclinical to clinical stages to understand drug exposure and disease progression for better efficacy with minimum toxicities. The purpose of this segment of the book chapter is to provide a general idea about types of modeling and simulation and their application in real-world research.

PKPD modeling and simulation could be divided into two major categories: (1) population pharmacokinetic modeling and simulation (PopPK) and (2) physiologically based pharmacokinetic modeling and simulation (PBPK).

Population Pharmacokinetic Modeling and Simulation

In conventional PK, data are analyzed either by compartmental or noncompartmental approaches. In both cases, extensive samples are collected over a considerable period of time based on drug clearance, half-life, and the dosing interval. Then standard two-stage approach is applied to analyze the data. In the first stage, the PK parameters are calculated at individual level and in the second stage, individual PK parameters are combined together to estimate population parameters in addition to standard deviation (SD) or variance of the parameters in the population. However, this method has certain limitations; it typically uses a small number of subjects; the calculated SD or variance is based on the population studied without accounting for the variability that may arise in a typical patient population. Another issue with conventional PK analysis is the need to collect a lot of samples after a given dose in each patient to estimate various PK parameters. In general, the intense sample collection leads to additional complications including need for withdrawal of large blood volume and increased cost of sample analysis. Moreover, intense sampling becomes inconvenient for some special population such as children and pregnant women. For these reasons, application of limited or sparse sampling strategy is becoming more popular in pediatric and pregnancy research, where sparse sampling implies the collection of smaller number of samples from each individual. The use of sparse or limited sampling to obtain population PK parameters was the main incentive behind development of population PK analysis approaches. In population pharmacokinetic approach, sparse or limited sampling could be used to estimate same PK parameters as we do in conventional PK analysis with extensive sampling from a large number of patients in the clinical setting. In therapeutic drug monitoring (TDM) programs, we only collect limited samples per dosing interval, and these data cannot be readily used to estimate PK parameters by conventional approach, but by applying PopPK approach, we can use those data to estimate PK parameters in patients who actually use the drug. Additionally, collecting less number of samples is convenient for the patients, and it reduces the time and cost involved in the drug research and development. Currently, various software are available for PopPK analysis such as NONMEM, MONOLIX, and Phoenix NLME, etc.

Application of Sparse or Limited Sampling in PopPK

Population PK modeling and simulation is applied in normal clinical practice to improve patient care. First, a population PK model is developed for a drug using a patient population, where typical values for the PK parameters of a drug are calculated. Several patient covariates are incorporated into the model and a final model is developed.[13,14] Once the model is developed, this developed model could be used to predict drug exposure and response in a different disease, different patient population, and with different dosage regimen. In practice, very limited numbers of samples are collected from each patient; measured plasma levels are given as an input into the developed population model to generate a model for individual patient. Finally, individualized model is used to predict drug exposure and effects relationship for different dosage regimen.

Practical Example

Vancomycin is a commonly used medication to treat gram-positive cocci (*Staphylococcus aureus* and *Staphylococcus epidermidis*) as well as in empirical antibiotic therapy in patients with malignant hematological diseases. However, PK of vancomycin shows a high interindividual variability, primarily associated with patents age and disease condition. Additionally, PK of vancomycin is different in oncology patients as compared with other patient populations. Very limited data are available about the variability in vancomycin PK in pediatric and oncology patients. A population pharmacokinetic model in pediatric patient was developed using patient's TDM samples and major covariates affecting the PK of vancomycin were identified. Then this developed model was used to calculate individual patient-tailored dose to achieve target plasma levels for better therapeutic effect. Following equation was used to calculate patient clearance, and resultant clearance value was used to calculate final individualized dose.

$$\text{Clearance} = 4.37 \times (\text{body weight} \div 20.7)^{0.67} \times (\text{creatinine clearance} \div 191)^{1.03}$$

where, 4.37 is the reference clearance, 20.7 is the reference body weight, and 191 is the reference creatinine clearance.

Traditional dose of vancomycin (60 mg/kg/day) results in only 15% of the children achieving target AUC/MIC. Whereas, based on PopPK simulated trial using the above-mentioned factors for vancomycin clearance calculation, children receiving a dose of 90 mg/kg/day have a risk of under dosing in only 20%. This example shows the importance of population PK modeling and simulation for individualized patient dosing.[15]

PHYSIOLOGICALLY BASED PHARMACOKINETIC MODELING AND SIMULATION

Pharmaceutical scientists have been using modeling and simulation technique for a long time. Quantitative structure activity relationship and quantitative structure property relationship models have been very useful in the drug development process. Unfortunately, the predictive powers of these modeling approaches are not always good, and their predictability is mainly depended on the compounds' characteristics that were used to develop the model. On the other hand, mechanistic models are predefined and can explain the underlying mechanism for variability in the PK parameters as well as can extend the known to unknown for prediction. Physiologically based pharmacokinetic models integrate the physicochemical properties of a drug along with the drug-independent properties of biological system to provide a mechanistic representation of the compounds in a specific biological system, enabling prediction or simulation of the plasma concentration time profile. Additionally, PBPK provides physiological representation at the organ level. This modeling technique is very useful to predict drug concentration—time profile in an organ or tissue, where collection of real biological sample is practically impossible such as brain, fetus, and other organs.[16]

Generally, whole body PBPK model connects all the major organs such as heart, lung, kidney, brain, gut, pancreas, liver, skin, bone, and adipose tissue (Fig. 29.5) in the selected species. Each of the organs represents a single compartment in the PBPK model. These organs are linked by artery and vein in such a way that they represent their exact blood flow from in and out of an organs. In a PBPK model, we can populate drug-metabolizing enzymes, transporters, proteins, volume of the organ, and blood flow for each of the organs to predict the impact of various disease states or different patient populations or drug—drug interactions.

Application of PBPK modeling and simulation: PBPK modeling is very useful in drug development and research. Due to the improvement of computational power, companies are developing robust PBPK modeling software with advanced applications and features. Mostly known PBPK software include Simcyp, PKSIM, Gastroplus, ADMEWORKS,

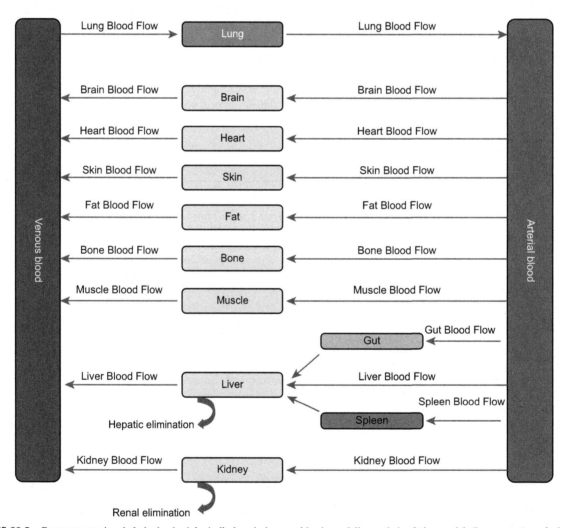

FIGURE 29.5 Compartments in whole body physiologically based pharmacokinetic modeling and simulation model. *Representation of whole body PBPK model. Organs are connected with corresponding arterial and venous blood flow; liver and kidney are the two major drug-eliminating organs.*

DDI simulators, etc can be usedto simulate pharmacokinetic profiles in virtual patients, to predict possible drug–drug interaction, extrapolate data from preclinical models to human, simulate human plasma concentration time profile from in vitro data, predict drug exposure from one patient population to another.

CONCLUSION

In summary, pharmacokinetic parameters are very important to estimate how much drug has to be administered to achieve a desired drug exposure for optimal therapeutic effects, avoiding unwanted side effects and/or therapeutic failure. Additionally, pharmacokinetic parameters help us to understand the mechanisms responsible for interpersonal and/or intrapersonal variability in drug exposure. Pharmacometrics is an emerging field in the area of PK, where mathematical modeling is used to describe/interpret pharmacokinetic data.

PRACTICE QUESTIONS

1. Which of the following is a feature of Nonlinear Kinetics?
   A. Pharmacokinetics parameters are dose independent
   B. Follows first order kinetics
   C. Does not involve saturable process
   D. Dose normalized plasma concentration–time profiles are not superimposable
2. Extraction ratio for a drug is dependent on
   A. Q
   B. fu
   C. CLint
   D. All of the above
3. The time to reach steady state plasma drug concentration is dependent on;
   A. Half-life
   B. Volume of distribution
   C. Clearance
   D. Loading dose
4. Which of the following is a factor that increases volume of distribution?
   A. High water solubility
   B. High plasma protein binding
   C. High distribution to tissues
   D. High extraction ratio
5. Which of the following should be considered while assessing hepatic drug metabolism?
   A. Drug interaction
   B. Plasma protein binding
   C. Extraction ration
   D. All of the above
6. In multiple dose administration, approximately how many doses are required to achieve steady state plasma concentration?
   A. 1
   B. 2
   C. 4
   D. 8
7. One of the patients stabilized at steady state plasma concentration of a drug is experiencing toxicity due to recently developed renal insufficiency. Which of the following strategy will decrease the plasma drug concentration to a new steady state?
   A. Decrease the dose
   B. Increase the dosing interval
   C. Decrease the dose and increase the dosing interval
   D. Any of the above

REFERENCES

1. Rowland Malcolm, Tozer Thomas N. *Clinical Pharmacokinetics and Pharmacodynamics: Concepts and Applications.* 4th ed. 2010.
2. Yacobi A, Skelly Vinod JP, Shah P, Benet LZ. *Integration of Pharmacokinetics, Pharmacodynamics, and Toxicokinetics in Rational Drug Development.* 2013.
3. Gibaldi Milo. *Biopharmaceutics and Clinical Pharmacokinetics.* 4th edition 1991.
4. Shargel Leon, Andrew BCYu. *Applied Biopharmaceutics & Pharmacokinetics.* 7th ed. 2016.
5. Currie GM, Wheat JM, Kiat H. Pharmacokinetic considerations for digoxin in older people. *Open Cardiovasc Med J.* 2011;5:130–135.
6. Glare PA, Walsh TD. Clinical pharmacokinetics of morphine. *Ther Drug Monit.* 1991;13(1):1–23.
7. https://www.drugbank.ca/drugs.
8. McAllister Jr RG, Kirsten EB. The pharmacology of verapamil. IV. Kinetic and dynamic effects after single intravenous and oral doses. *Clin Pharmacol Ther.* 1982;31(4):418–426.
9. Ochs HR, Grube E, Greenblatt DJ, Knüchel M, Bodem G. Kinetics and cardiac effects of propranolol in humans. *Klin Wochenschr.* 1982;60(10):521–525.
10. Holford NH. Clinical pharmacokinetics and pharmacodynamics of warfarin. Understanding the dose-effect relationship. *Clin Pharmacokinet.* 1986;11(6):483–504.
11. Donna C, Bergen MD. Pharmacokinetics of phenytoin: reminders and discoveries. *Epilepsy Curr.* 2009;9(4):102–104.
12. Punyawudho B, Ramsay ER, Brundage RC, Macias FM, Collins JF, Birnbaum AK. Population pharmacokinetics of carbamazepine in elderly patients. *Ther Drug Monit.* 2012;34(2):176–181.
13. Sharma Shringi, Caritis Steve, Hankins Gary, et al. Population pharmacokinetics of 17α-hydroxyprogesterone caproate in singleton gestation. *Br J Clin Pharmacol.* 2016;82:1084–1093.
14. Pillai VC, Han K, Beigi RH, et al. Population pharmacokinetics of oseltamivir in non-pregnant and pregnant women. *Br J Clin Pharmacol.* 2015;80(5):1042–1050.
15. Zhao W, Zhang D, Fakhoury M, et al. Population pharmacokinetics and dosing optimization of vancomycin in children with malignant hematological disease. *Antimicrob Agents Chemother.* 2014;58(6):3191–3199.
16. Kalluri HV, Zhang H, Caritis SN, Venkataramanan R. A physiologically based pharmacokinetic modelling approach to predict buprenorphine pharmacokinetics following intravenous and sublingual administration. *Br J Clin Pharmacol.* 2017;83(11):2458–2473.

ANSWERS TO PRACTICE QUESTIONS

1. D
2. D
3. A
4. C
5. D
6. C
7. D

Chapter 30

Therapeutic Drug Monitoring

Toluwalope Junaid[1], Xuemei Wu[1], Harisudhan Thanukrishnan[1] and Raman Venkataramanan[1,2,3]

[1]University of Pittsburgh, Pittsburgh, PA, United States; [2]Thomas Starzl Transplantation Institute, University of Pittsburgh, Pittsburgh, PA, United States; [3]University of Pittsburgh Medical Center, Pittsburgh, PA, United States

Learning Objective:

Objective 30.1   Describe the concept and need for therapeutic drug monitoring.

OBJECTIVE 30.1. DESCRIBE THE CONCEPT AND NEED FOR THERAPEUTIC DRUG MONITORING

Drug Dosing and Personalized Drug Therapy

Dosing of medications can be fixed (also called "flat" dosing) or variable. Fixed dosing refers to the use of a single dose for all patients regardless of any subject-specific variables such as age, body weight, body surface area, or disease conditions. With variable dosing on the other hand, such factors are usually considered and the dose is adjusted for. For example, weight-based dosing means the required dose for a patient depends on the patient's body weight, whereas body surface area–based dosing means the patient's dose depends on the patient's body surface area, which is a better measure of the overall metabolic capacity in a person. Personalized dosing requires considering and adjusting for more variables such as the pharmacodynamics (response-based/logical dosing) and pharmacokinetics of the product. Personalization may be based on the genotype and/or the phenotype of the patient. Genotyping is the process of determining differences in the genetic make-up (genotype) of an individual by examining the individual's DNA sequence using biological assays and comparing it with another individual's sequence or a reference sequence. It reveals the alleles an individual has inherited from their parents. Genotyping has advantages of being an easy test, can help identify starting dose, is useful for several drugs once done, and can be part of an individual's medical record. Limitations of genotype-based dosing include cost, complex algorithms necessary to decipher complex interactions with multiple genotypes, and potential for compensatory pathways that can mask the impact of a given genotype when multiple enzymes are involved. Furthermore, genotyping error can occur, which poses a major risk of lifelong mismanagement of health issues of the patient as genotypes are lifelong test results.

A phenotype (from Greek "phainein" and "typos," meaning "to show" and "type," respectively) is the composite of an organism's observable characteristics or traits such as its morphology, development, biochemical or physiological properties, phenology, behavior, and products of behavior. Phenotypic measure is determined by various pharmacokinetic properties such as absorption, distribution, metabolism, and excretion of a product. In case of drugs that are primarily eliminated by the kidney, the phenotypic surrogate measure that can be used is a measure of glomerular filtration rate (creatinine clearance). Drugs that are metabolized more commonly require monitoring unlike drugs that are primarily renally excreted (without being significantly metabolized). Phenotypic measures take into account genetic and other factors contributing to variability in drug exposure in a patient.

Clinical Pharmacy Education, Practice and Research. https://doi.org/10.1016/B978-0-12-814276-9.00030-1

Optimizing the Use of Medications: Therapeutic Drug Monitoring

Therapeutic drug monitoring (TDM) is a clinical practice that involves measuring concentrations of a drug in a patient's blood or plasma at designated intervals to provide guidance on individualized dosage regimen and adjustment of drug dosage to maintain a suitable concentration of the drug in the patient's circulation.[1] TDM is required to ensure that therapeutic levels for maximal effectiveness and minimal side effects are achieved in each individual patient.

For a drug to produce its desired therapeutic benefit, it must be present in adequate concentration at the site of action. If the drug concentration is too low (ineffective) or too high (toxic), there will be therapeutic failure. The minimum effective concentration (MEC) of a drug is the lowest concentration of the drug required to achieve the therapeutic benefit. On the other hand, the maximum therapeutic concentration or minimum toxic concentration (MTC) is the concentration at which a drug produces unwanted side effects. In between the MEC and the MTC is the concentration range at which the drug produces optimal therapeutic outcome. This is the therapeutic window, illustrated in Fig. 30.1.

The therapeutic range or therapeutic window of a drug is the concentration range in plasma or blood at which the drug has been determined to be efficacious with minimal toxic effects in most people. Depending on the interval between the MEC and MTC, the therapeutic window of a drug may be narrow or wide.

The therapeutic window is the range of concentrations at which the drug is effective with acceptable side effects.

Goal of Therapeutic Drug Monitoring

There are two main goals of TDM. First is to maximize the effectiveness of the drug and therapeutic benefit. The second is to minimize drug toxicity and adverse effects.

Why Is Therapeutic Drug Monitoring Necessary

TDM is helpful to detect and prevent suboptimal treatment and avoid drug toxicity in patients. If a drug is used at a concentration below the lower limit of its therapeutic range, the drug will be ineffective. If used at a concentration above the upper limit of the therapeutic range, the drug will be toxic. Although the therapeutic window is wide for some drugs, some drugs have a narrow therapeutic window and must be monitored to prevent therapeutic failure (undertreatment or toxicity). Consequences of therapeutic failure may be serious. For example, in patients on immunosuppressive drugs following organ transplantation, inappropriate drug concentrations may result in organ rejection or increased susceptibility to infections due to increased immunosuppression.

TDM is useful for individualization of drug dosage and therapy. Due to exogenous and endogenous factors such as variations in drug metabolism, individual patients may respond differently to similar doses of certain drugs with same dose producing variable drug exposure. This interindividual variability necessitates adequate monitoring of such drugs to maximize effectiveness and prevent toxicity.

TDM helps with monitoring and detection of drug and disease-based interactions. In patients with conditions requiring polypharmacy or when changes in a patient's clinical state necessitate changing drugs or adding new drugs, drug–drug interactions need to be monitored to ensure proper adjustment of drug doses to maximize effectiveness. For example, in patients on digitalis therapy, concomitant use of quinidine necessitates adjustment of digoxin dose because quinidine decreases renal clearance of digoxin thereby predisposing the patient to digoxin toxicity. Another example is verapamil which also impairs digoxin clearance, and coadministration requires decreased digoxin dosing.

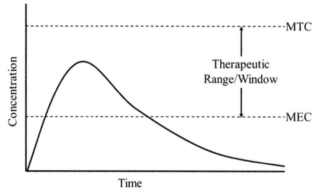

FIGURE 30.1   Plasma concentration Vs time curve. *MEC*, minimum effective concentration; *MTC*, maximum therapeutic concentration.

Furthermore, in practice, TDM is warranted in certain clinical scenarios. Patients who do not respond appropriately to treatment or whose responses raise the suspicion of drug toxicity will require TDM for proper dose adjustments. Similarly, patients on long-term therapy and those with major organ failure (such as hepatic or renal impairment) may also benefit from TDM to prevent toxicity. Other benefits of TDM are that it is a simple method to monitor patient compliance and it can be useful for differentiating adverse effects of drugs from disease symptoms.

Drugs that Require Therapeutic Drug Monitoring

Examples of commonly used drugs that require TDM are described in Table 30.1. Typical characteristics of drugs that require TDM include narrow therapeutic range; significant interindividual pharmacokinetic variability; nonlinear pharmacokinetics (drugs following saturation metabolism); drugs whose therapeutic effect cannot be readily assessed by clinical observation; drugs whose plasma levels (or metabolite plasma levels) correlate directly with the pharmacological or toxic effects; and drugs used for treating life-threatening conditions. On the flip side, drugs that do not require TDM are usually those with a wide therapeutic range; irreversible action (i.e., hit and run drugs such as MAO inhibitors, Omeprazole, Reserpine, Guanethidine); clinically quantifiable pharmacological effects which can be monitored by clinical end points such as blood pressure, heart rate, blood sugar, urine volume, and body temperature; drugs whose plasma levels do not correlate with therapeutic or toxic effects; and drugs used to treat less complicated or non life-threatening diseases.

Measurement of Systemic Drug Levels

The principle of TDM is to estimate the concentration of a drug and/or its metabolites in a patient's body fluids. An ideal method should distinguish between compounds of similar structure, drug versus metabolites, detect small amounts of drug/metabolite(s), be simple enough to use as a routine assay, be unaffected by other drugs administered simultaneously, and is rapid in turnaround time.

Laboratory Techniques Used for Therapeutic Drug Monitoring

TDM assays can be specific or nonspecific. Examples of each are listed in Table 30.2, and comparisons of the assays are shown in Table 30.3. Specific assays separate and detect metabolite and parent drugs, providing better pharmacokinetic parameter estimation of a drug and information on its metabolites. Nonspecific assays typically tend to identify a class of compounds and may provide an overestimation of the actual drug concentrations.

Samples Used for Therapeutic Drug Monitoring

TDM typically involves measurement of drug concentrations in patient's biological fluids. These include the following:

1. Plasma/serum: this is more commonly used as drug concentrations are relatively easy to measure in plasma or serum.
2. Whole blood: more physiologically relevant but less commonly used due to need for generally more technically demanding assay.
3. Saliva: sample collection is noninvasive. Useful for measuring concentration of unbound drug; however, it may be inaccurate due to drug binding to salivary proteins or oral debris. Can be used for detecting drugs such as phenytoin, lithium, and amitriptyline.
4. Breath: Commonly used for detecting alcohol.

Timing of Sample Collection

Sample collection time(s) and the frequency of sampling for TDM vary depending on the pharmacokinetics of the drug being monitored and the purpose of TDM (see Table 30.4). Factors that determine the frequency of sampling include the half-life of the drug; length of drug use; change in dose; change in drugs; change in patient's hepatic or renal function; and clinically mandated factors such as rejection or toxicity.

Clinical Interpretation of Therapeutic Drug Monitoring Reports

If there are alterations in serum drug concentration, either lower or higher than expected, or if a patient fails to respond to therapy despite adequate serum drug concentration, then drug dosage adjustment is required. The common causes of alterations in serum drug concentration in clinical practice are listed in Table 30.5.

TABLE 30.1 Examples of Drugs That Require Therapeutic Drug Monitoring (TDM)

Drug	Biological Matrix	Assay Method[a]	Therapeutic Range	Consequences of No TDM	When to Measure[c]	What to Measure
Antiepileptics[2]						
Carbamazepine	Serum Plasma	LC-UV LC-MS GC-TSD FPIA EMIT MECC	4–12 mg/L[b]	↓Lack of therapeutic response ↑Lethargy, dizziness, headache, blurred vision, nystagmus, diplopia, ataxia, incoordination, sedation, nausea, vomiting, cardiac disturbances, osteomalacia, etc.	Trough level	Parent drug and active metabolite: carbamazepine-10,11-epoxide
Phenytoin	Serum Plasma	FPIA EMIT GC-TSD LC-UV MECC	10–20 mg/L	↓Lack of therapeutic response ↑Confusion, ataxia, coma, nystagmus, diplopia, cognitive and behavioral dysfunctions, exacerbation of seizure frequency, folate and vitamin D deficiency, etc.	Trough level	Parent drug
Phenobarbital	Serum Plasma	RIA FPIA EMIT GC-TSD LC-UV MECC	10–40 mg/L	↓Lack of therapeutic response ↑Sedation, drowsiness, slowness, ataxia, coma, nystagmus, diplopia, cognitive and behavioral dysfunctions, exacerbation of seizure frequency, folate and vitamin D deficiency, etc.	Trough level	Parent drug
Valproic acid	Serum Plasma	FPIA EMIT GC-FID LC-FLD LC-UV	50–100 mg/L	↓Lack of therapeutic response ↑Nausea, vomiting, diarrhea, sedation, stupor, tremor, malaise, thrombocytopenia, hepatotoxicity, platelet aggregation defects, etc.	Trough level	Parent drug
Topiramate	Serum Plasma	GC-MS GC-FID GC-NPD FPIA EMIT	5–20 mg/L	↓Lack of therapeutic response ↑Psychomotor slowing, trouble concentrating, speech and language difficulties, somnolence, fatigue, etc.	Trough level	Parent drug
Primidone	Serum Plasma	GC-TSD GC-MS FPIA EMIT LC-UV MECC	5–10 mg/L[d]	↓Lack of therapeutic response ↑Sedation, drowsiness, slowness, ataxia, coma, nystagmus, diplopia, cognitive and behavioral dysfunction, exacerbation of seizure frequency, folate and vitamin D deficiency, etc.	Trough level	Parent drug and active metabolite: phenobarbital
Lamotrigine	Serum Plasma	LC-UV EMIT	2.5–15 mg/L	↓Lack of therapeutic response ↑Somnolence, dizziness, sedation, diplopia, skin rash, Stevens-Johnson reaction, toxic epidermis necrolysis, etc.	Trough level	Parent drug

| Oxcarbazepine | Serum Plasma | LC-UV GC-MS EMIT | 3–35 mg/L[e] | ↓Lack of therapeutic response ↑Psychomotor slowing, trouble concentrating, speech and language difficulties, dizziness, somnolence, diplopia, fatigue, nausea, vomiting, ataxia, abnormal vision, gait disturbances abdominal pain, tremor, dyspepsia, abnormal gait, etc. | Trough level | Active metabolite: eslicarbazepine |
| Levetiracetam | Serum Plasma | LC-UV GC-NPD EMIT | 12–46 mg/L | ↓Lack of therapeutic response ↑Drowsiness, somnolence, dizziness, fatigue, asthenia, ataxia, abnormal gait or incoordination, agitation, hostility, anxiety, apathy, emotional lability, depersonalization, depression, etc. | Trough level | Parent drug |

Antibiotics

Gentamicin[3]	Serum Plasma	FPIA EMIT	25–30 mg/L (peak)[f] <1 mg/L (trough)[f]	↓Lack of therapeutic response ↑Nephrotoxicity, ototoxicity (dizziness, vertigo, tinnitus, roaring in the ears, hearing loss), neuromuscular blockade, etc.	Peak level Trough level	Parent drug
Amikacin[4]	Serum Plasma	GC-MS FPIA EMIT	40–60 mg/L (peak)[f] <5 mg/L[f]	↓Lack of therapeutic response ↑Nephrotoxicity, ototoxicity (dizziness, vertigo, tinnitus, roaring in the ears, hearing loss), neuromuscular blockade, etc.	Peak level Trough level	Parent drug
Tobramycin[3]	Serum Plasma	FPIA EMIT	25–30 mg/L (peak)[f] <1 mg/L (trough)[f]	↓Lack of therapeutic response ↑Nephrotoxicity, ototoxicity (dizziness, vertigo, tinnitus, roaring in the ears, hearing loss), neuromuscular blockade, etc.	Peak level Trough level	Parent drug
Vancomycin[5]	Serum Plasma	LC-UV LC-FLD LC-MS FPIA EMIT	15–20 mg/L	↓Lack of therapeutic response ↑Nephrotoxicity, ototoxicity, skin rashes and anaphylaxis, red-neck syndrome, chills and fever; phlebitis and pain at site of injection, etc.	Trough level	Parent drug

Immunosuppressants[6]

| Tacrolimus | Whole blood | HPLC-MS MEIA ELISA FPIA EMIT ECLIA | 5–15 ng/mL | ↓Organ rejection ↑Nephrotoxicity, CNS toxicity (headache, seizure, tremors, altered mental status and motor function), hyperglycemia, hypertension, infections, hyperlipidemia, electrolyte abnormalities, anemia, diarrhea, nausea, pruritus, alopecia, etc. | Trough level[8] | Parent drug |

Continued

TABLE 30.1 Examples of Drugs That Require Therapeutic Drug Monitoring (TDM)—cont'd

Drug	Biological Matrix	Assay Method[a]	Therapeutic Range	Consequences of No TDM	When to Measure[c]	What to Measure
Sirolimus[7]	Whole blood	LC-UV LC-MS MEIA Competitive CLIA	5–10 ng/mL	↓Organ rejection ↑Infection, thrombocytopenia, leukopenia, hypertriglyceridemia, etc.	Trough level[g]	Parent drug
Everolimus[8]	Whole blood	LC-UV LC-MS ELISA FPIA	3–8 µg/L	↓Organ rejection ↑Renal dysfunction, infections, thrombocytopenia, hyperlipidemia, hypercholesterolemia, leukopenia, neurological disorder, anemia, gastrointestinal disorder, etc.	Trough level[g]	Parent drug
Mycophenolate mofetil (MMF)	Serum Plasma	LC-MS EMIT	MPA AUC:30–60 mg h/L MPA trough level: 1–3 µg/mL	↓Organ rejection ↑Infection	AUC[g] Trough level[g]	Parent drug MMF and metabolites: MPA and MPAG
Cyclosporine	Whole blood	LC-MS FPIA EMIT RIA ECLIA	100–400 ng/mL	↓Organ rejection ↑Nephrotoxicity, neurotoxicity (tremors and seizures), hypertension, electrolyte abnormalities, infections, hyperlipidemia, gingival hyperplasia, hirsutism, hepatotoxicity, etc.	Trough level[g]	Parent drug
Antipsychotics						
Clozapine	Serum Plasma	LC-MS GC-MS LC-UV RIA	350–600 ng/mL	↓Lack of therapeutic response ↑Confusion, delirium, seizure, obsessive/compulsive symptoms, etc.	Trough level	Parent drug
Lithium[9]	Serum	ISE RSM SM	0.8–1.2 mEq/L for acute mania 0.6–0.8 mEq/L for prophylaxis of mania and/or depression	↓Lack of therapeutic response ↑Tremor, confusion, sedation, slurred speech, vomiting, lethargy, nausea, diarrhea, muscle weakness, polyuria, polydipsia, seizure, hyperreflexia, cardiovascular collapse, etc.	Trough level	Parent drug
Antifungals[10]						
Voriconazole	Serum Plasma	LC-UV LC-MS LC-FLD EMIT	For prophylaxis, >0.5 µg/mL; For therapy >1–2 µg/mL	↓Lack of therapeutic response ↑Severe hepatopathy, unexplained neurological symptoms, etc.	Trough level	Parent drug and its metabolites voriconazole N-oxide
Posaconazole	Serum Plasma	LC-UV LC-MS LC-FLD	For prophylaxis, >0.5 µg/mL; For therapy, >0.5 –1.5 µg/mL	↓Lack of therapeutic response	Trough level	Parent drug

Drug	Specimen	Method	Therapeutic range	Clinical effect / Toxicity	Sampling time	Analyte
Itraconazole	Serum Plasma	LC-UV LC-MS LC-FLD	For prophylaxis, >0.5 µg/mL; For therapy, >1–2 µg/mL	↓Lack of therapeutic response		Parent drug
Antineoplastics						
Methotrexate	Serum Plasma	LC-UV EMIT FPIA	<10 µM^h <1 µM^h <0.1 µM^h <0.05 µM^h	↓Lack of therapeutic response ↑Nausea vomiting, mucositis, rash, hepatotoxicity, leukoencephalopathy, myelosuppression, nephrotoxicity, etc.	20 h postinfusion 44 h postinfusion 68 h postinfusion 92 h postinfusion	Parent drug
Busulfan	Serum Plasma	LC-MS LC-FLD GC-MS GC-ECD	1000–1400 µmol/L·min for 6 h dosing interval; 4000–5600 µmol/L·min for 24 h dosing interval	↓Engraftment failure ↑Hepatic veno-occlusive, central nervous system toxicity, interstitial pneumonia, mucositis, etc.	AUC	Parent drug
Antiarrhythmics						
Digoxin	Serum Plasma	MEIA LC-MS FPIA ECLIA EMIT	0.8–2 µg/L	↓Lack of therapeutic response ↑Decreased heart rate, ECG change, arrhythmias, anorexia, nausea, vomiting, diarrhea, visual disturbances, etc.	Trough level	Parent drug
Lidocaine	Serum Plasma	LC-UV LC-MS GC-MS GC-NPD FPIA EIA	1.5–6 mg/L	↓Lack of therapeutic response ↑Confusion, dizziness, slurred speech, diplopia, tremor, severe nausea, vomiting, seizure, obtundation, hypotension, respiratory depression, sinus bradycardia, sinus arrest, atrioventricular conduction disturbances, etc.	Trough level	Parent drug and active metabolites: monoethylglycinexylidide and glycinexylidide
Antipyretic						
Acetaminophen	Serum Plasma	LC-MS GC-MS EMIT FPIA	10–20 mg/L	↓Lack of therapeutic response ↑Skin rash, drug fever, mucosal lesions, hepatic necrosis, renal tubular necrosis, hypoglycemic coma	Peak level (1 h after a dose)	Parent drug
Antiinflammatory						
Salicylate	Serum Plasma	LC-UV LC-MS GC-MS FPIA	150–300 mg/L	↓Lack of therapeutic response ↑Tinnitus, headache, vertigo, hearing loss, central hyperventilation, respiratory alkalosis, metabolic acidosis, hyperglycemia, hypoglycemia	Peak level (1–3 h after an oral dose)	Salicylic acid

Continued

TABLE 30.1 Examples of Drugs That Require Therapeutic Drug Monitoring (TDM)—cont'd

Drug	Biological Matrix	Assay Method[a]	Therapeutic Range	Consequences of No TDM	When to Measure[c]	What to Measure
Bronchodilator						
Theophylline[11]	Serum Plasma	GC-MS FPIA EMIT CEDIA PETINIA	Asthma: 10–20 mg/L COPD: 5–15 mg/L Apnea or bradycardia in neonates: 5–10 mg/L Ventilator weaning of neonates: 5–20 mg/L	↓Lack of therapeutic response ↑Nausea, vomiting, diarrhea, headache, irritability, nervousness, insomnia, tremor, hyperglycemia, hyperkalemia, hypotension, cardiac arrhythmias, cerebral hypoxia, hyperthermia, seizures, brain damage and death, etc.	Peak level	Parent drug

Key: ↓ correlates to subtherapeutic levels, ↑ correlates to supratherapeutic levels. *AUC*, area under the blood/plasma concentration versus time curve; *CEDIA*, cloned enzyme donor immunoassay; *COPD*, chronic obstructive pulmonary disease; *ECD*, electron capture detection; *ECLIA*, electrochemiluminescence immunoassay; *EMIT*, enzyme multiplied immunoassay; *FID*, flame ionization detector; *FLD*, fluorescence detector; *FPIA*, fluorescence polarization immunoassay; *GC*, gas chromatography; *HPLC*, high-performance liquid chromatography; *ISE*, ion-selective electrode; *MECC*, micellar electrokinetic capillary chromatography; *MEIA*, microparticulate enzyme immunoassay; *MPA*, mycophenolic acid; *MPAG*, mycophenolic acid glucuronide; *MS*, mass spectrometry; *NPD*, nitrogen–phosphorus detector; *PETINIA*, particle enhanced turbidimetric inhibition immunoassay; *RIA*, radioimmunoassay; *RSM*, reflectance spectrophotometry; *SM*, spectrophotometry; *TSD*, thermionic specific detection; *UV*, ultraviolet absorbance detection.

[a]Immunoassays typically tend to identify a class of compounds and overestimate concentrations. Specific Assays, such as GC and HPLC/UPLC, can separate and detect metabolite and drugs, which can provide better pharmacokinetic parameter estimation and also get information on the metabolites.

[b]Active 10,11 epoxide metabolite contributes to clinical effects.

[c]Trough level was usually sampled immediately before next dose, peak level was usually sampled at the end of infusion or 1 h after IM for injection.

[d]Represents the concentration of Primidone; its active metabolite phenobarbital also contributes largely to clinical effects and its concentrations should also be monitored.

[e]Represents the concentration of active monohydroxy-derivative metabolite, eslicarbazepine.

[f]Represents the concentrations of once-daily aminoglycosides dosing regimen.

[g]TDM should be done daily after the first week post transplantation, 3–4 times per week in the early transplant period, and every 6 months once stable. Therapeutic ranges may differ in different transplant centers, type of organ transplanted, and different period of post transplantation. In transplantation, patients are maintained at the higher end of the therapeutic range initially, and then the desired concentration is often lowered over time to minimize nephrotoxicity and overimmunosuppression.

[h]For high doses of methotrexate (HDMTX) and intermediate dose methotrexate (MTX) therapy greater than and equal to 100 mg/m², serum concentration monitoring is necessary. Patients with elevated MTX concentration require increased leucovorin doses administered for a sufficient period for the MTX concentration to fall below 0.05 µM.

TABLE 30.2 Therapeutic Drug Monitoring Assays

Nonspecific Assays	Specific Assays
Immunoassays (radio/enzyme):	Chromatography (gas/liquid):
• Radioimmunoassay (RIA)	• Gas Chromatography (EC, FID, NPD, MS)
• Enzyme-linked immunosorbent assay (ELISA)	• HPLC-UV
• Enzyme Multiplied Immunotechnique (EMIT)	• UPLC-UV
• Fluorescence polarization immunoassay (FPIA)	• HPTLC-UV
• Nephelometric inhibition immunoassay (NIIA)	• UPLC-Mass spectrophotometry
• Particle-enhanced turbidimetric inhibition immunoassay (PETINIA)	• HPLC-Fluorescence spectrometry
	• HPLC-Mass spectrometry

EC, electron capture detection; *FID*, flame ionization detection; *HPLC*, high-performance liquid chromatography; *HPTLC*, high-performance thin-layer chromatography; *MS*, mass spectrometry; *NPD*, nitrogen–phosphorus detection; *UPLC*, ultra performance liquid chromatography; *UV*, ultraviolet.

TABLE 30.3 Comparison of Therapeutic Drug Monitoring Assays

Immunoassay

- Lowest complexity test (convenient for smaller hospitals)
- Least expensive in terms of capital equipment
- Nonspecific; high variability between different sample batches and also within same run
- More expensive kits (primary cost)
- Typically for measuring one drug at a time

HPLC

- Generally specific
- Only cost-effective if test volumes are low
- Relatively slow
- Technically demanding

LC-MS/MS—UPLC-MS/MS

- Highest expense in capital equipment
- Can analyze several drugs and metabolites simultaneously
- Much less variability than immunoassay or HPLC
- Direct reagent costs considerably lower than immunoassay
- Technically demanding

HPLC, high-performance liquid chromatography; *LC-MS*, liquid chromatography–mass spectrometry; *LC-MS/MS*, liquid chromatography–tandem mass spectrometry; *UPLC-MS/MS*, ultra-performance liquid chromatography tandem–mass spectrometry.

TABLE 30.4 Guidelines for Sampling Time

Drug Type/Purpose	When to Sample
Drug with short half-life	Sample before dose Obtain samples for measurement of peak and trough concentration levels (Fig. 30.2)
Drug with long half-life	Time point in the dosing interval that is correlated with exposure or area under the plasma concentration versus time curve, typically trough concentrations Obtain single sample
Drug with low clearance	Just before next dose
For assessment of drug toxicity	Any time
For adjustment of dose	Just before next dose
To diagnose suboptimal therapy	Trough level
To detect noncompliance	Trough level

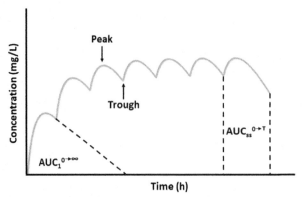

FIGURE 30.2 Plasma concentration Vs time curve. *AUC*, area under the curve - is a measure of drug exposure.

TABLE 30.5 Common Causes of Alterations in Serum Drug Concentration

Drug Concentration Lower Than Expected in Serum

- Noncompliance
- Dosing error
- Decreased bioavailability due to drug or disease conditions
- Increased clearance due to metabolizing enzyme induction due to another drug or dietary supplement
- Increased clearance of renally eliminated drug due to physiological changes

Drug Concentration Higher Than Expected in Serum

- Dosing error
- Increased bioavailability
- Reduced renal clearance
- Metabolizing enzyme inhibition
- Poor hepatic or renal function

Patient Fails to Respond to Therapy Despite Adequate Drug Concentration in Serum

- Tolerance (impaired receptor sensitivity)
- Drug interactions
- Change in pathophysiology

Limitations of Therapeutic Drug Monitoring

TDM has shortcomings such as inconsistencies in drug assays used including specificity, sensitivity, accuracy, precision, reproducibility, and limit of detection/quantification. Other limitations of TDM include variations in laboratory reporting methods of assay results; inconsistencies in validity of suggested target ranges depending on other drugs used; limited accessibility to equipments; limited trained/skilled personnel; and high costs.

CONCLUSION

TDM is crucial in clinical practice, to maximize drug effectiveness and minimize toxicity in each individual patient, typically for drugs with narrow therapeutic index.

Case Studies

Case 1: Adjustment of Drug Dosage in a Patient at Risk of Drug Toxicity Due to Drug—Drug Interactions
Source: Jain et al.[12]

Scenario
Mr. A is HIV positive and has been taking the antiretroviral drug Kaletra (combination of lopinavir 133.33 mg and ritonavir 33.3 mg). He takes three capsules of Kaletra twice per day and has undetectable HIV RNA (<50 copies/mL). He was diagnosed with end-stage liver disease, requiring liver transplantation.

Case Studies—cont'd

Therapeutic Drug Monitoring and Clinical Management

Mr. A's Kaletra was temporarily discontinued and, following liver transplantation, he was started on oral Tacrolimus 5 mg twice daily (70 mg weekly). This achieved a 12-h trough Tacrolimus blood concentration of 10.6 ng/mL (therapeutic range, 9.5−11.9 ng/mL). Two weeks later, his Kaletra was restarted. Two days later, Mr. A developed neurologic symptoms including altered mental status. When checked, his trough Tacrolimus blood concentration had increased to 78.5 ng/mL (toxic). Tacrolimus was discontinued. Over the next few days, his neurologic symptoms subsided and his Tacrolimus concentration had dropped to 6.4 ng/mL (subtherapeutic) by 22 days later. Tacrolimus was restarted at 0.5 mg weekly (140× reduction in dose), achieving a mean daily Tacrolimus blood concentration of 12.9 ng/mL (range, 8.9−19.7 ng/mL) while Mr. A continued both medications. His HIV RNA remained undetectable.

Case Discussion

Mr. A needed antiretroviral therapy (Kaletra) to reduce his HIV viral load, as well as immunosuppressant (Tacrolimus) to minimize his risk of organ rejection post transplantation. Tacrolimus has a narrow therapeutic window, thus requires frequent monitoring of its concentration to optimize therapy. Low Tacrolimus concentrations can induce organ rejection, whereas high concentrations can lead to toxicity and immunosuppression-related complications, such as infection. In a patient like Mr. A, who already has immunosuppression from HIV and subsequent increased susceptibility to opportunistic infections, Tacrolimus dosing needs to be appropriately titrated to prevent overimmunosuppression. In this case, Mr. A's concurrent use of Kaletra necessitated a 140-times reduction in his Tacrolimus dose (reduced from 70 mg weekly to 0.5 mg weekly) to achieve a suitable therapeutic level of Tacrolimus.

Case 2: Therapeutic Drug Monitoring-Based Dose Management of Amiodarone When Coadministered With Rifampicin
Source: Oude Munnink et al.[13]

Scenario

Mr. B, a 69-year-old man, has been on amiodarone (AM) (200 mg/day) for about a year, to control arrhythmogenic right ventricular cardiomyopathy. He had comorbid chronic left knee arthritis for which he had knee replacement surgery. His orthopedic prosthesis became infected; hence, Mr. B is initiated on therapy with rifampicin (900 mg/day).

Therapeutic Drug Monitoring and Clinical Management

The potential for drug−drug interaction (DDI) between AM and rifampicin is anticipated; however, no alternate drugs were found suitable for Mr. B. Monitoring of AM and its active metabolite desmethylamiodarone (DAM) was indispensable for continuation of therapy. At baseline, the cumulative AM + DAM concentration was 1.72 mg/L (ref range: 1−4 mg/L) with a metabolic ratio (DAM/AM) of 0.8. Suddenly, 10 days after initiating rifampicin, the cumulative AM + DAM was found to be 0.83 mg/L (reduced by 52%) with metabolic ratio of 1.6. To avoid risk of arrhythmias due to subtherapeutic concentration, AM dose was increased to 600 mg/day. Yet, 1 week later the cumulative AM + DAM concentration was 0.65 mg/L (reduced by 62% from baseline despite threefold dose increase). Consequently, AM dose was further increased to 900 mg/day resulting in therapeutic cumulative AM + DAM concentration of 1.52 mg/L and metabolic ratio <1.

Case Discussion

Two challenges existed in predicting DDI between AM and rifampicin: (1) Induction of Cytochrome P 450 (CYP) enzymes by rifampicin varies with the CYP3A4 effect delayed more than CYP2C8. AM is metabolized by both CYPs, whereas metabolism of DAM is CYP3A4 dependent. (2) Furthermore, AM and DAM have very long half-lives of 50 and 60 days, respectively. Hence, drug monitoring for AM in presence of rifampicin was vital for a timely and appropriate increase in dose. The total duration of coadministration in Mr. B was 90 days, and during this period AM concentrations were maintained within therapeutic range by therapeutic monitoring. Mr. B did not experience any event of arrhythmias.

REFERENCES

1. Kang JS, Lee MH. Overview of therapeutic drug monitoring. *Korean J Intern Med.* 2009;24(1):1−10.
2. Patsalos PN, Berry DJ, Bourgeois BF, et al. Antiepileptic drugs−best practice guidelines for therapeutic drug monitoring: a position paper by the subcommission on therapeutic drug monitoring, ILAE commission on therapeutic strategies. *Epilepsia.* 2008;49(7):1239−1276.
3. Prescott Jr WA. A survey of extended-interval aminoglycoside dosing practices in United States adult cystic fibrosis programs. *Respir Care.* 2014;59(9):1353−1359.
4. Galvez R, Luengo C, Cornejo R, et al. Higher than recommended amikacin loading doses achieve pharmacokinetic targets without associated toxicity. *Int J Antimicrob Agents.* 2011;38(2):146−151.
5. Martin JH, Norris R, Barras M, et al. Therapeutic monitoring of vancomycin in adult patients: a consensus review of the American society of health-system pharmacists, the infectious diseases society of America, and the society of infectious diseases pharmacists. *Clin Biochem Rev.* 2010;31(1):21−24.

6. Kahan BD, Keown P, Levy GA, Johnston A. Therapeutic drug monitoring of immunosuppressant drugs in clinical practice. *Clin Ther*. 2002;24(3):330−350. discussion 329.

7. Kahan BD, Napoli KL, Kelly PA, et al. Therapeutic drug monitoring of sirolimus: correlations with efficacy and toxicity. *Clin Transplant*. 2000;14(2):97−109.

8. Mabasa VH, Ensom MH. The role of therapeutic monitoring of everolimus in solid organ transplantation. *Ther Drug Monit*. 2005;27(5):666−676.

9. Mose T, Damkier P, Petersen M, Antonsen S. Therapeutic drug monitoring of lithium: a study of the accuracy and analytical variation between laboratories in Denmark. *Ther Drug Monit*. 2015;37(4):466−471.

10. Andes D, Pascual A, Marchetti O. Antifungal therapeutic drug monitoring: established and emerging indications. *Antimicrob Agents Chemother*. 2009;53(1):24−34.

11. Tachi T, Hase T, Okamoto Y, et al. A clinical trial for therapeutic drug monitoring using microchip-based fluorescence polarization immunoassay. *Anal Bioanal Chem*. 2011;401(7):2301−2305.

12. Jain AB, Venkataramanan R, Eghtesad B, et al. Effect of coadministered lopinavir and ritonavir (Kaletra) on tacrolimus blood concentration in liver transplantation patients. *Liver Transpl*. 2003;9(9):954−960.

13. Oude Munnink TH, Demmer A, Slenter RHJ, Movig KLL. Amiodarone rifampicin drug-drug interaction management with therapeutic drug monitoring. *Ther Drug Monit*. 2018;40(2):159−161.

Chapter 31

Pharmacogenomics and Precision Medicine

David F. Kisor, Carrie Hoefer and Brian S. Decker[†]

Manchester University College of Pharmacy, Natural and Health Sciences, Fort Wayne, IN, United States

Learning Objectives

Objective 31.1   Define terms and explain basic concepts in pharmacogenetics/pharmacogenomics.
Objective 31.2   Explain the relationship of pharmacogenomics with pharmacokinetics and pharmacodynamics.
Objective 31.3   Describe pharmacist competencies in genomics/pharmacogenomics and their roles in precision medicine.

OBJECTIVE 31.1. DEFINE TERMS AND EXPLAIN BASIC CONCEPTS IN PHARMACOGENETICS/PHARMACOGENOMICS

Pharmacogenomics, as a component of overall genomics and precision medicine, requires the use of terms that are new to many pharmacists and student pharmacists. Table 31.1 presents the terms as used throughout this chapter. Although the terms are not entirely standard across all disciplines, the terms presented here are commonly used.

Optimization of patient care related to drug therapy includes providing a given patient with efficacious treatment while minimizing or avoiding the risk of adverse drug reactions/events.[1] The advent of pharmacogenomics as a component of data in clinical decision-making is facilitating optimal therapy from the start, avoiding "trial and error" therapeutics.[2]

The concept of genetic-related adverse drug reactions was discussed in 1957, and the term "pharmacogenetics" was applied in 1959 as researchers at the time were starting to investigate drug—gene interactions.[3,4] The broader term "pharmacogenomics" was born out of the recognition that likely many genes are involved in an individual's response to medication.[5] Rapid expansion of pharmacogenomic research, as a component of overall genomic research, occurred as the Human Genome Project (HGP), initiated in 1990, progressed to formal completion in 2003.[6] The HGP was intended to improve the basic science research infrastructure related to human genetics, have the human DNA sequence serve as the connection of human biology and the biology of model organisms, and to promote ongoing advancement in analytical biochemistry.[7] The advancement in analytical technology, which has continued post-HGP, has led to efficient and cost-effective approaches to the genotyping and sequencing of human DNA (Fig. 31.1).[8] The terms pharmacogenetics and pharmacogenomics have the abbreviations PGt and PGx, respectively.[9] PGx will be utilized as the common term in this chapter, except where explicitly cited.

Relative to PGx, the interactions of interest affect drug effectiveness as well as adverse drug reactions, with pharmacogenes involving drug metabolism, transport, interaction with receptors, enzymes, and/or alteration of biochemical signaling pathways.[10] When considering the influence of a drug—gene(s) interaction, it helps to recognize the consequence related to pharmacokinetics (PK) and/or pharmacodynamics (PD). As the majority of currently identified drug—gene interactions are related to drug metabolism, mainly considering the cytochrome P450 drug-metabolizing enzymes, it is important to understand what information is provided when PGx testing is undertaken.[11]

---

† Deceased. This chapter is dedicated to Dr. Brian S. Decker.

Clinical Pharmacy Education, Practice and Research. https://doi.org/10.1016/B978-0-12-814276-9.00031-3

TABLE 31.1 Terms and Definitions Utilized in Genetics/Genomics/Pharmacogenomics

Term	Definition
Allele(s)	Versions of the same gene inherited from each parent.
Biomarker (genomic)	Measurable indicators of normal biologic processes, pathogenic processes, and/or response to therapeutic or other interventions.
Gene	Regions of the genome (DNA) that contain the instructions to make proteins.
Genome	The entire DNA of an organism.
Genotype	The specific pair of alleles inherited at a locus on a given gene.
Heterozygous	Having two different alleles for the same trait.
Homozygous	Having identical alleles for the same trait.
Indel	Inserted or deleted DNA either as single nucleotides or spanning regions of DNA involving many nucleotides.
Intermediate metabolizer (IM)	Enzyme activity which is less than normal metabolizer activity and is more than poor metabolizer activity.
Monogenic trait	Features derived from a single gene.
Mutation	An alteration in DNA sequence between individuals.
Normal metabolizer (NM)	Full enzyme activity
Nucleoside/nucleotide	One of the structural chemicals of DNA, including adenine (A), cytosine (C), guanine (G), and thymine (T), and of RNA, including adenine (A), cytosine (C), guanine (G), and uracil (U). Nucleoside linked to a phosphate group.
Precision medicine	Utilization of patient-specific information and biomarkers to make more informed choices regarding the optimal therapeutic treatment regimen for a given patient.
Pharmacodynamics (PD)	The relationship between drug exposure and response.
Pharmacogenetics (PGt)	A single gene involved in response to a drug. Pharmacogenomics will be used as the preferred term, which encompasses pharmacogenetics.
Pharmacogenomics (PGx)	The study of many genes, and potentially the entire genome, involved in response to a drug.
Pharmacokinetics (PK)	The relationship of time and drug absorption, distribution, metabolism, and excretion.
Phenotype	An individual's expression of a physical trait or physiologic function due to genetic constitution and environmental and other factors.
Polymorphism	A mutation in DNA in a given population that may be observed at greater than 1% frequency.
Poor metabolizer (PM)	Enzyme activity which is less than IM activity. No too little enzyme activity.
Rapid metabolizer (RM)	Enzyme activity which is more than NM activity and is less than ultrarapid metabolizer activity.
Reference sequence number (refSNP, rs#, rs)	A unique and consistent identifier of a given single nucleotide polymorphism.
Single nucleotide polymorphism (SNP)	A variant DNA sequence in which a single nucleotide has been replaced by another base.
Theragnostics	Treatment approaches which combine therapeutics and diagnostics.
Ultrarapid metabolizer (UM)	Enzyme activity which is more than RM activity.

Genetic Variations

The nucleotide bases adenine (A), cytosine (C), guanine (G), and thymine (T) in ordered sequence comprise genes.[10] There are approximately 20,000 genes in the human genome, with the total sequence of DNA base pairs of the "double helix" being 3.2 billion. Variations in genes can be a consequence of a change in the sequence of the nucleotides with as little as

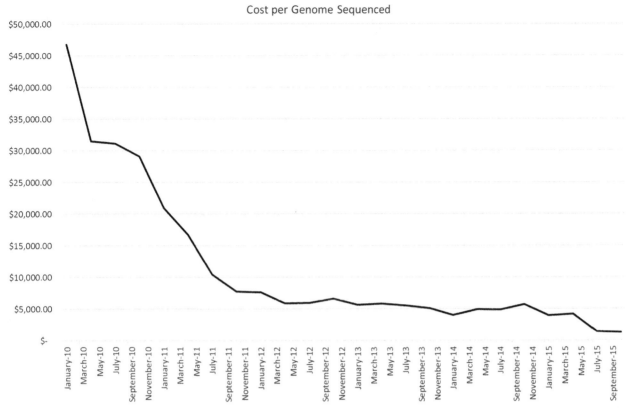

FIGURE 31.1 Decreasing costs of genetic testing either whole genome sequencing (shown above) or genotyping are leading to more economical applications of pharmacogenomics in the clinical setting.[8]

one base change resulting in altered gene product function/activity.[10] These single base changes, called **single nucleotide polymorphisms** (SNPs, "snips"), are the most common form of DNA variation.[10] Other forms of DNA variation include insertions and deletions ("indels"), which result in "shifting" of bases and altered sequences of amino acids and variant gene products.[10] Other DNA changes can also occur, such as the occurrence of gene duplication, where a number of copies of a given normal function gene (i.e., copy number variants (CNVs)) result in increased function. Broader discussion of genetic variation is beyond the scope of this chapter.

As SNPs are the most common form of DNA variation, defining the exact location of a given SNP in the DNA is noted by a reference sequence number or "rs" number.[12] An rs number is a consistent reference to a SNP that can be referred to across publications so the reader knows exactly what change is being discussed. The US National Center for Biotechnology Information houses an archived database of SNPs.[12] The database, dbSNP, is available for query and is the most comprehensive SNP database. As an example, the database can be searched for SNPs related to the gene *CYP2C19*. One such SNP is rs4244285, also known as c.681G>A, among other names, and defines the single change of A replacing G at position 681 of the coding region of the *CYP2C19* gene.[13] This SNP results in a no-function gene product CYP2C19 enzyme.[13] Examples of other SNPs and related rs numbers can be found below. By convention, a gene is noted in the text by italicized font (e.g., *CYP2C19*), whereas the gene product is not italicized (e.g., CYP2C19).

Nomenclature

In PGx relative to pharmacokinetic pharmacogenes, a "star (*)" nomenclature has been adopted to denote specific DNA changes.[14] For instance, rs4244285 is noted as *CYP2C19*2* in the star nomenclature. An international working group has recommended moving away from the star nomenclature, with specific recommendations.[15] However, PGx databases, such as the Pharmacogenomics Knowledgebase (PharmGKB) and guidelines from organizations (e.g., the Clinical Pharmacogenetics Implementation Consortium [CPIC] and the Dutch Pharmacogenetics Working Group [DPWG]), utilize the star nomenclature to a great extent.[16,17] Therefore, it is important to understand this nomenclature as PGx testing results, related to PK, are typically translated using the star nomenclature (e.g., A at rs4244285 is reported as *CYP2C19*2*).

To help clinicians avoid the pitfalls of nomenclature differences, standard metabolism phenotypes related to drug-metabolizing genes have been defined.[18] There are *five* defined metabolizer phenotypes including, from greatest metabolism to least metabolism,

- ultrarapid metabolizer (UM),
- rapid metabolizer (RM),
- normal metabolizer (NM),
- intermediate metabolizer (IM), and
- poor metabolizer (PM).

These phenotypes have been related to clinical application of PGx through guidelines, such as those from CPIC and the DPWG.[17,19] The metabolic phenotypes are related to an individual's genetics, being the basis for the inherent differences in maintenance dose requirements.[20] Other terms have been adopted for drug transporter genes and genes related to PD.[18] Individual rs numbers and metabolic phenotypes are referred to in the examples presented throughout this chapter.

Pharmacogenomic Testing in Pharmacotherapy

In the 2000s and 2010s, PGx testing costs have decreased dramatically and Illumina Scientific, a manufacturer of genotyping and sequencing instrumentation, has stated that the cost of sequencing an individual's whole genome (WGS) will drop to approximately $100 (USD).[21] To put this in perspective, the cost of WGS in 2001 was over $95 million (USD).[9] Even with lower technology costs, broad application of PGx in the clinical is still a major undertaking and there are many obstacles for transition to full implementation.[22–27]

Pharmacogenetic testing became prevalent with the discovery of monogenic (single) drug–gene interactions. With monogenic drug–gene interactions, clinicians order a pharmacogenetics test on an as needed reactionary basis; a clinician may order a test when effectiveness or an adverse drug reaction is of concern.[28] With the advancement of technology, and reduced costs, pharmacogenomic testing is more plausible in the clinic. Patients can now have numerous genes assayed at the same time, leading toward a preemptive approach that could guide clinicians in the care of individual patients over the remainder of their lifetime.[28–30] The preemptive approach could include genotyping/sequencing individuals when they are young (even at birth) and these results could be stored securely and queried throughout the patient's lifetime.[28–30] This preemptive approach would only include germline (inherited) DNA mutations, and any mutations occurring somatically (not inherited) may need to be tested later in life depending on the disease state (e.g., cancer).[11]

OBJECTIVE 31.2. EXPLAIN THE RELATIONSHIP OF PHARMACOGENOMICS WITH PHARMACOKINETICS AND PHARMACODYNAMICS

Many factors should be considered while clinically addressing a patient's drug therapy, with PGx being one of them.[31] PGx is important to consider as DNA variants can influence many physiologic-related processes, such as drug metabolism, and drug transport, resulting in ineffectiveness and/or adverse drug reactions. PK is the time course of drug absorption, distribution, metabolism, and excretion (ADME), i.e., the movement of a drug into and out of the body.[32] PGx can influence PK by altering the ADME of a given drug.[10] Therapeutic drugs are most often administered by the per-oral route and need to be absorbed and undergo other processes (e.g., distribution) to produce their intended effect. Orally absorbed drugs are characterized by their bioavailability, with a drug being bioavailable when it moves from the gastrointestinal lumen to systemic circulation having escaped gastrointestinal wall and "first-pass" metabolism by the liver.[10,32] For some drugs, active transport is required to facilitate movement across the enterocytes of the small intestine to bring drug to portal vein blood flow to the liver.[10] Both influx (taking drug up into intestinal epithelial cells) and efflux transporters (moving drug back to gastrointestinal lumen) can be altered by genetics, affecting the amount of drug that ultimately reaches systemic circulation.[33] Although a large majority of drugs cross the gastrointestinal wall via passive diffusion, influx and efflux transporters also influence drug movement (absorption) from the gastrointestinal lumen to portal blood flow.[10,33]

Additionally, the enterocytes of the gastrointestinal lumen and hepatocytes in the liver contain drug-metabolizing enzymes that can metabolize a drug before it reaches the systemic circulation.[10] Here, genetics can influence (i.e., reduce or increase metabolism) at these sites, affecting the amount of drug that reaches the systemic circulation. A number of drug-metabolizing enzymes in the gastrointestinal wall and liver are members of the cytochrome P450 superfamily and include CYP3A4/CYP3A5, CYP2C9, CYP2C19, and CYP2D6, among others.[34,35]

With the administration of a drug, via per-oral or any other route, numerous processes are set in motion. As discussed, on per-oral administration drug absorption leading to systemic exposure is required to elicit the desired effect. As drug is distributed to various tissues of the body, it is also undergoing processes which result in a drug being "removed" from the body.[10,32] Many drugs require metabolic conversion to be eliminated from the body. Here, typically, a given drug is modified chemically to be more water soluble, thus promoting urinary excretion of drug metabolites. There are two types of drug metabolism: Phase I metabolism, which refers to chemical reactions such as oxidation, reduction, or hydrolysis, and Phase II metabolism, which refers to conjugation reactions such as glucuronidation, sulfation, acetylation, and methylation. Extensive research has revolved around Phase I-metabolizing enzymes such as the cytochrome P450 enzymes, but both phases of metabolism can be altered by genetics.[36] PGx can influence the metabolism of drugs by increasing the metabolic rate, which in turn clears the drug from the body faster (RM or UM). There can also be a decreased metabolic rate of drugs causing greater exposure as drug accumulation occurs (IM or PM). Typically, the majority of the general population are "normal" metabolizers of most drugs; however, genetic-related alteration in the metabolism of some drugs can result in inefficacy or serious adverse reactions (ADR). For instance, a given active drug may never be efficacious in a patient who is an UM, whereas the given active drug may result in an ADR in a PM.[37] Conversely, the administration of a prodrug to an UM may result in toxicity, whereas therapeutic failure may occur in a PM.[37] Other drug elimination processes include drugs or its metabolites being excreted from the body in the urine, bile, etc.[33] Influx and efflux transporters related to drug distribution and/or excretion, as noted above, can be influenced by genetics.

The clinical utility of PGx lies with how it influences drug response, either through PK or the PD of the drug. PD is the relationship between drugs and the mechanisms of their actions or the pharmacological response/effect in a given patient.[38] The variability in PD is usually greater than the PK variability and defining the drug response phenotype has become one of the most difficult components of PGx.[11]

The PD effects involve drug targets such as receptors, enzymes (nondrug metabolizing), and certain transporters (e.g., serotonin reuptake).[10] Drug targets are proteins and therefore can have altered function due to underlying DNA variation, such as SNPs. These polymorphisms can lead to decreased binding ability, a decrease in affinity for the drug receptor, and a decrease in the efficacy of the drug.[38] To add to the complexity, multiple drugs can act as either agonists or antagonists and enhance or inhibit the ability of the drug to elicit its effect(s).

Overall, drug response is likely due to multiple genetic factors that influence PK and/or PD. The influences of genetics on drug effects, related to inefficacy and/or toxicity, have now been noted in more than 140 package labels of drugs approved by the USFDA.[39] Below, specific examples of drug−gene interactions involving PK and/or PD are presented.

Example Drug−Gene Interactions

The following drug−gene pairs represent "model" interactions that are illustrative and can be used to understand similar pharmacogene effects across many drug−gene pairs.

Drug-Metabolizing Enzyme Pharmacogenes

CYP2C19-clopidogrel—For the specific indication of acute coronary syndrome postcoronary artery stent placement, clopidogrel is indicated as a component of antiplatelet therapy.[40] As a prodrug, clopidogrel needs to be converted into an active metabolite to elicit its antiplatelet effect. This conversion is facilitated by CYP2C19, the protein enzyme product of *CYP2C19*.[40−42]

More than 30 *CYP2C19* variants produce enzymes with different activities.[41] Table 31.2 provides example *CYP2C19* variants and related enzyme product activities.

The combination of alleles, called diplotypes, in Table 31.3 represented using the star nomenclature, leads to the assignment of metabolic phenotype designations. The CPIC undertook a survey process to identify standard terms for

TABLE 31.2 Example *CYP2C19* Variants and Resulting CYP2C19 Activity

CYP2C19 Variant (Base Change)/rs Number	Star Nomenclature Allele Designation	Enzyme Product Activity
c.681G>A/rs4244285	*2	No activity
c.636G>A/rs4986893	*3	No activity
c.-806C>T/rs12248560	*17	Increased activity

TABLE 31.3 CYP2C19 Diplotypes, Related Phenotypes, and Potential Therapeutic Consequences of Clopidogrel Use in ACS With PCI

CYP2C19 Diplotype (Star "*" Nomenclature)	Metabolic Phenotype	Clopidogrel Therapeutic Consequence in ACS With PCI of Stent Placement
*1/*1	Normal metabolizer (NM)	Clopidogrel use indicated
*1/*2	Intermediate metabolizer (IM)	Alternative to clopidogrel indicated
*2/*3	Poor metabolizer (PM)	Alternative to clopidogrel indicated
*1/*17	Rapid metabolizer (RM)	Clopidogrel use indicated
*17/*17	Ultrarapid metabolizer (UM)	Clopidogrel use indicated

consistency in reporting phenotypes.[18] Table 31.3 presents the various metabolizer phenotype examples relative to *CYP2C19* diplotypes. Considering clopidogrel in the setting of ACS and PCI with stent placement, the CYP2C19 phenotype has therapeutic implications (Table 31.3).

The resultant therapeutic consequence is a result of altered PK where the metabolism/conversion of the prodrug clopidogrel into its active metabolites is decreased.[43] The antiplatelet activity is altered, and patients with an IM or PM status are at increased risk of adverse cardiovascular events, including stent thrombosis and death.[42] The USFDA placed a boxed warning in the clopidogrel package labeling describing the reduced efficacy of the drug in PMs. The statement includes information about testing patients to identify their metabolic phenotype.[43]

CYP2D6-codeine—Tragic adverse drug reactions in children related to codeine use have been tied directly to PGx.[44] A number of deaths and serious ADRs to codeine in children have been attributed to individuals with an UM phenotype.[45,46]

Codeine is the prodrug of the active analgesic morphine. The conversion of codeine into morphine is mediated by CYP2D6, with UMs converting more codeine into morphine following a given dose. As there are more than 110 *CYP2D6* alleles resulting in more of a continuum of drug metabolism variation from the PM through UM phenotypes, an "activity score" system has been established to assign metabolism phenotypes.[41,47] Activity scores of each allele are summed to provide the overall activity score. Alleles with an activity score greater than 1, as is seen with gene duplication, are considered to have increased function; those with an activity score of 1 are normal function; those with an activity score of 0.5 are decreased function alleles; and those with an activity score of 0 are no-function alleles.[47] Table 31.4 provides examples of *CYP2D6* alleles *CYP2D6* diplotypes, the related overall activity score and the metabolic phenotype. It should be noted that other approaches to defining the activity of CYP2D6 are being considered in an effort to better qualify genetic influence.

The frequency of alleles in a given population varies considerably. Table 31.5 presents the most frequent variant allele, including gene duplication for different populations.[48]

TABLE 31.4 *CYP2D6* Allele Activity Scores, *CYP2D6* Diplotypes, CYP2D6 Metabolic Phenotypes, and Therapeutic Consequences Related to Codeine Therapy

CYP2D6 Allele— Activity Score	CYP2D6 Diplotype (Star "*" Nomenclature)—Overall Activity Score	Metabolic Phenotype	Codeine Therapeutic Consequence
*1—1 *2—1	*1/*1—2	Normal metabolizer (NM)	Codeine use as provided in package labeling
*4—0 *9—0.5	*4/*9—0.5	Intermediate metabolizer (IM)	Codeine use as provided in package labeling
*5—0 *6xN—0	*5/*6xN—0	Poor metabolizer (PM)	Alternative to codeine indicated due to potential inefficacy
*1—1 *2x3—3	*1/*2x3—4	Ultrarapid metabolizer (UM)	Alternative to codeine indicated due to potential toxicity

TABLE 31.5 Population Frequencies of Example *CYP2D6* Alleles

Population	CYP2D6 Allele—Activity Score	Frequency (%) in Population
African	*17—0.5	19.98
African American	*17—0.5	18.22
Caucasian	*4—0	18.50
Middle Eastern	*41—0.5	20.37
East Asian	*10—0.5	42.31
South/Central Asian	*10—0.5	19.76
Americas	*4—0	11.28
Oceanian	*1xN—>1	11.83

TABLE 31.6 Example Thiopurine Methyltransferase (TPMT) Gene Diplotypes, Related Phenotypes, and Potential Therapeutic Consequences of Mercaptopurine Use

TPMT Diplotype (Star "*" Nomenclature)	Metabolic Phenotype	Mercaptopurine Therapeutic Consequence
*1/*1	Normal TPMT activity	Mercaptopurine standard initial dose as indicated
*1/*2	Intermediate TPMT activity	Reduced dose as indicated by guidelines
*2/*3A	Low TPMT activity	Extremely reduced dose and decreased frequency of administration as indicated by guidelines

The use of codeine has been decreasing for a number of reasons, including the potential for serious adverse drug reactions, including death.[46] In April of 2017, the USFDA provided a safety announcement stating that codeine and the analgesic tramadol were contraindicated for use in children under the age of 12 years. This population is at increased risk of respiratory depression and death.[49]

TPMT-Mercaptopurine—"Rational drug design" led to the discovery of mercaptopurine (6-MP), with the drug eventually becoming a component of treatment for acute lymphocytic leukemia (ALL).[50] The drug, used as maintenance therapy in combination with methotrexate, represents the foundation drug therapy in childhood ALL.[51] Exposure to 6-MP thioguanine metabolites can result in severe, life-threatening myelosuppression. The exposure to 6-MP is related to a number of variables, including genetics.[52] Thiopurine methyltransferase (TPMT), the protein product of *TPMT*, is responsible for metabolizing 6-MP to form the thioguanine metabolites. In fact, individuals who are homozygous, with two nonfunctional *TPMT* alleles, are expected to experience severe myelosuppression with risk of death.[52] Individuals who carry one no-function *TPMT* allele along with a functional *TPMT* allele have an intermediate risk of myelosuppression.[52] Table 31.6 presents example *TPMT* diplotypes related to myelosuppression risk.

The recognition that the exposure to 6-MP was a pharmacokinetic-based, genetically mediated issue has resulted in a standard of care of preemptive *TPMT* genotyping to minimize the risk of myelosuppression.[52]

The previous examples involve pharmacogenes that are related to drug metabolism with direct dosing/drug selection consequences. Other pharmacogenes of interest, in the pharmacokinetic context, include drug transporters.

Transporter Pharmacogene

SLCO1B1-Simvastatin—Beyond drug-metabolizing gene products (e.g., CYP2C19, CYP2D6, TPMT, etc.), drug transporters as products of PK pharmacogenes also affect drug response.[33] The gene *SLCO1B1* codes for the influx (uptake) transporter organic anion transporter 1B1 (OATP1B1, also called SLCO1B1). OATP1B1, among other transporters, works to move simvastatin and other statins into tissues. Relative to the liver, OATP1B1 moves simvastatin to its site of action where inhibition of HMG CoA reductase results in decreased cholesterol production, thus exerting its pharmacologic and therapeutic effects.[53] Additionally, the liver is the main site of statin metabolism.[54] Decreased transport of simvastatin into hepatocytes has been related to increased risk of myopathy. Variants of *SLCO1B1* impart an increased risk of muscle pain

TABLE 31.7 Example *SLCO1B1* Alleles, Example Diplotypes, Related Phenotypes, and Potential Simvastatin Therapeutic Consequences

SLCO1B1 Allele—Function Status	Example Diplotype	Transporter Phenotype	Simvastatin Therapeutic Consequence
*5—decreased	*1a/*5	Decreased function	Utilize desired dose
*15—decreased	*1b/*15	Decreased function	Utilize a lower dose or consider a different statin
*17—decreased	*5/*17	Poor function	Utilize a lower dose or consider a different statin

(myalgia) and damage, including myopathy and in severe cases rhabdomyolysis.[53] Normal function forms of *SLCO1B1* include *1a and *1b, and the *14 and *35 variants appear to impart increased function. Table 31.7 presents example variant alleles of *SLCO1B1* that have been associated with simvastatin-induced muscle pain and damage.

A combination of a normal function form (e.g., *1a) and an increased function variant (e.g., *14) results in an increased function phenotype where the desired dose can be utilized. Simvastatin exposure in the face of a decreased or poor function phenotype is greater than that for the other statins and the current recommendations for therapeutic considerations apply to this statin with a strong recommendation.[53]

Research has also identified relationships between pharmacodynamic (PD) pharmacogenes and certain drugs. Examples of PD pharmacogenes include those that code for receptors (e.g., beta adrenergic, opiate) and enzymes (nondrug metabolizing; e.g., glucose-6-phosphate dehydrogenase [G6PD] and vitamin K epoxide reductase [VKORC1]). Two specific examples of drug-PD pharmacogene interactions are presented below.

Pharmacodynamic Pharmacogenes

G6PD—Rasburicase—G6PD is necessary to help protect red blood cells from oxidative stress and prevent excessive formation of methemoglobin.[55] Increased oxidative stress can lead to hemolytic anemia, resulting in cardiovascular, renal, liver, and other organ system complications.[55–57] Additionally, red blood cell hemolysis in G6PD deficiency can lead to methemoglobinemia.[58] In this setting, neither oxygen nor carbon dioxide is carried as iron in hemoglobin is in the ferric state rather than the ferrous state.[57,58] Methemoglobinemia may result in death in severe cases.[57–59] There are well over 150 *G6PD* variants and, unlike the previous examples, *G6PD* variants are not designated using the star "*" nomenclature. Individuals with a normal phenotype are not at increased risk of hemolytic anemia, whereas those with a deficient phenotype of any kind are at risk of acute hemolytic anemia. A "variable" phenotype may be identified in some individuals and requires further testing to ascertain risk.[60]

Numerous drugs and chemicals can elicit complications in patients with G6PD deficiency due to a *G6PD* variant or variants.[60] Rasburicase is indicated for use in managing plasma uric acid concentrations in patients with hematologic or solid tumor cancers who are receiving drugs that can cause lysis of cells.[61] Tumor lysis can result in elevated plasma uric acid concentrations, which can cause acute kidney injury.[61] Rasburicase administration in the presence of G6PD variants can result in hemolytic anemia and methemoglobinemia. Rasburicase is contraindicated in persons with a phenotype of "deficient" (of any kind). There are many potential diplotype combinations, which can result in the various phenotype designations. Table 31.8 presents examples of the rasburicase—*G6PD* interaction. Additionally, tables related to drugs to be avoided or monitored in patients who are G6PD deficient are provided in the literature.[60]

TABLE 31.8 Example G6PD Gene Diplotypes, Related Phenotype, and Potential Rasburicase Therapeutic Consequence

Example Diplotype	Phenotype	Rasburicase Therapeutic Consequence
B/Sao Boria	Normal	Utilize drug as indicated
Chatham/Chatham	Deficient	Contraindication to the use of the drug—consider alternative
Villeurbanne/Villeurbanne	Deficient	Contraindication to the use of the drug—consider alternative

TABLE 31.9 *VKORC1* and *CYP2C9* Genotypes and Diplotypes, Related to Predicted Daily Warfarin Dose Requirements

VKORC1	*CYP2C9* Diplotype					
	*1/*1	*1/*2	*1/*3	*2/*2	*2/*3	*3/*3
GG	5−7	5−7	3−4	3−4	3−4	0.5−2
AG	5−7	3−4	3−4	3−4	0.5−2	0.5−2
AA	3−4	3−4	0.5−2	0.5−2	0.5−2	0.5−2

VKORC1—Warfarin—There are a number of genes that have been found to affect warfarin dosage requirements. These include variants of *CYP2C9*, and *CYP4F2* and *VKORC1*, the former of which is a PK-related pharmacogene and the latter two of which are PD-related pharmacogenes. The *CYP2C9* variants, *2 and *3 are the most common, result in decreased clearance of warfarin, potentially leading to decreased dose requirements.[62] Here, considering the vitamin K epoxide reductase complex subunit 1 gene (*VKORC1*), individuals with adenine (A) replacing guanine (G) at c.-1639 (c.-1639G>A; rs9923231) are more sensitive to warfarin. According to the product package labeling, individuals who are homozygous for the A allele, regardless of *CYP2C9* diplotype, have a reduced warfarin dose requirement.[63] Dosing algorithms can be applied in this case, along with other information, including genetics to calculate the appropriate dose.[64−66] Table 31.9 shows the impact of both VKORC1 and CYP2C9 on initial warfarin dose (mg/day) recommendations. Algorithms can refine initial dosing and have been recommended for various populations.[64,67]

Numerous other drug—gene interactions have been identified beyond the examples here. Groups such as CPIC and the DPWG continue to develop and publish evidence-based guidelines that provide clinicians with clear ways forward when considering PGx as a component of clinical decision-making. Pharmacists continue to lead the way in the application of PGx across practice settings.

OBJECTIVE 31.3. DESCRIBE PHARMACIST COMPETENCIES IN GENOMICS/ PHARMACOGENOMICS AND THEIR ROLES IN PRECISION MEDICINE

Beyond the science of PGx are components related to pharmacist clinical use and application of DNA data. Pharmacist competencies have been developed to address the areas of basic genetic knowledge, genetics and disease, pharmacogenetics and PGx, as addressed above, and ethical, legal, and social implications (ELSI).[68,69] These competencies have been updated from the original set provided by the American Association of Colleges of Pharmacy in 2002.[70] The pharmacist competencies are provided along with other healthcare profession's competencies through the Genetics/Genomics Competency Center (G2C2) of the US National Human Genome Research Institute.[69] In total, these competency statements across the health professions distinguish individual professional expertise.[69] There are four domains of competencies for pharmacists, including the following:

1. Basic genetic concepts;
2. Genetics and disease;
3. Pharmacogenetics/PGx; and
4. ELSI.

Competency domains 1 and 3 were presented earlier to some extent. These competency domains, as well as domains 2 and 4, are addressed briefly here.

Basic Genetic Concepts

Competency domain 1 is related to demonstration of an understanding of basic genetic/genomic concepts and nomenclature. This includes the pharmacist understanding the role of many factors that influence genetics related to the manifestation of disease. The pharmacist must appreciate genetic variations that facilitate strategies related to disease prevention, diagnosis, and treatment. Included in this competency is the expectation that pharmacists realize the differences in PGx testing methodologies. Finally, competency domain 1 relates to the use of the family history over at least three generations in assessing disease risk and selection of drug therapy.[69]

Genetic and Disease

A genetic predisposition to a disease or "genetic susceptibility" is the increased likelihood of developing a specific disease based on an individual's genotype.[71] The genetic basis for many diseases such as cystic fibrosis, hemophilia, sickle-cell anemia, neurofibromatosis, and Huntington's disease has long been established.[72,73] Moreover, the more recent discovery of mutations in the BRCA1 and BRCA2 genes, which are the strongest susceptibility genes for breast and ovarian cancer, has become critical indicators for the prevention, treatment, and prognosis of these cancers in clinical medicine.[74–76] Underlying these advances is the elucidation of the human genome which has led to remarkable progress in determining the genetic basis for more complex, multifactorial diseases.

The patterns of inheritance of genetic diseases can be classified into two broad categories: single gene or monogenic and multifactorial.[77,78] The monogenic or Mendelian pattern which is the simplest pattern of genetic inheritance encompasses autosomal recessive, autosomal dominant, sex-linked, and mitochondrial genes.[72] In autosomal recessive disease inheritance, a trait is expressed in individuals who have two copies (homozygous) of the gene.[72,73,77] Autosomal recessive diseases include cystic fibrosis, alkaptonuria, and phenylketonuyria.[72,77] The autosomal dominant inheritance pattern results in a disease phenotype in individuals who inherit one copy (heterozygous) or two copies (homozygous) of the gene.[72,73,77] Autosomal dominant diseases are Marfan syndrome, a chrondrodysplasia and osteogenesis imperfecta.[72,77] Disease genes can also be transmitted by the X or Y chromosome and are termed sex-linked.[72,73,77] However, an X-linked gene cannot be transmitted from a father to a male son.[72,73,77] Sex-linked diseases include Rett syndrome, Klinefelter syndrome, Duchenne muscular dystrophy, and hemophilia.[72,77] Disease traits can also be transmitted by a cell's mitochondria. The mitochondria, which play a key role in energy metabolism for cells, contain multiple copies of a circular double-stranded DNA. Interestingly, this mitochondrial DNA is only maternally inherited. As a result, mitochondrial disease traits are only passed on to the offspring from the mother.[72,73,77] Mitochondrial diseases include Leigh syndrome, Leber hereditary neuropathy, and fatal infantile neuropathy.[72,77] Though many important diseases are monogenic, the majority of common disease are multifactorial or polygenic.[78–80] Furthermore, multifactorial disease inheritance is inherently more complex as it is phenotypically expressed by a combination of multiple genetic and environment interactions.[78,79] Important multifactorial diseases with known genetic markers include type 1 and 2 diabetes mellitus, hypercholesterolemia, breast, ovarian, and colorectal cancer, familial Alzheimer's disease, schizophrenia, premature coronary heart disease, hypertension, Crohn's disease, and ankylosing spondylitis.[79,81,82]

A critical tool in discovering the genetic markers for these complex, multifactorial diseases is the *genome-wide association study* or GWAS.[82–84] Prior to the development of GWAS, determining specific genetic markers or SNPs for common diseases was limited to searching for the genes predicted to be associated with the disease based on disease's pathophysiology.[72,81,83] This "candidate gene" approach provided some important breakthroughs in finding the specific SNPs for disease but was limited because knowledge of the specific pathophysiology of a disease was not always known.[72,81,83] However, with the technological advances in genetic analysis and the concomitant reduction in the cost of this testing, it has become possible to test an individual's entire genome.[81] Currently, GWAS uses complex SNP arrays to genotype hundreds of thousands of SNPs in large numbers of individual for the multifactorial disease of interest.[81] In addition, with the high throughput analysis now possible with GWAS, genetic markers for a disease can be determined without knowledge of its specific pathophysiology. The use of GWAS has led to advances in the potential genetic underpinnings of an increasing list of multifactorial diseases. However, GWAS has its limitations, including a relative insensitivity to rare variants, the requirement for large sample sizes, the risk of genotyping errors and possible bias in the selection of the individuals for the GWAS.[83] Despite these limitations, however, GWAS will remain a powerful tool to determine the genetic signals that underlie the genetic predisposition to disease.

Pharmacogenetics/Pharmacogenomics

As stated earlier, PGt/PGx for pharmacists relates to understanding the influence of populations relative to polymorphisms and associations of polymorphisms with response to medications. Additionally, pharmacists need to recognize the availability of evidence-based guidelines, such as those from CPIC and the DPWG, which can be applied to patient care.[68,69]

Ethical, Legal, and Social Implications

Perhaps no other competency domain is as common across healthcare professions.[69] This speaks to healthcare professionals, respecting patient privacy and utilizing patient information with confidentiality. Pharmacists as well as other healthcare professionals understand the need for patient privacy. Although one pharmacist ELSI competency statement points to privacy, emphasis should be placed on security of the DNA data.[68] Here, it is important to understand that genetic data relate to family members, not to the patient only.

Although testing may be intended to provide PGx information, incidental findings may relate to the predisposition of disease. For example, apolipoprotein E (Apo E) variants may be related to certain statin effectiveness in types of familial hypercholesterolemia; however, an APO E variant are also related to the risk of late onset Alzheimer's disease.[69] Clearly, incidental finding of PGx testing must be put in context, and the pharmacist must carefully consider how to utilize this type of data.

Legislation has been enacted at various government levels to help prevent discrimination of individuals relative to healthcare and employment based on genetic information. In the United States, the Genetic Information Nondiscrimination Act was adopted in 2008.[85] State governments have expanded the Federal law to provide further protection of individuals based on their genetics.[86] The previous examples address only a couple of the noted ELSI components of the pharmacist's competency statements in genomics, and the reader is directed to the G2C2 for more detailed information.[69]

Growth and Future Direction of Pharmacogenomics

As PGx testing has previously focused on single drug—gene interactions and has moved to testing multiple genes in panel-based testing, it is envisioned that whole genome sequencing will eventually be a standard of clinical care, moving beyond the research realm of GWAS. This will allow for identification of rare variants that were not tested for in single gene or gene panel tests. Further implementation of PGx will occur and will be placed in a broader context of precision medicine with the potential application of theragnostics, where diagnosis and treatment(s) include molecular biomarkers.[87,88] Drug development is moving to include PGx, and drugs and molecular tests are being marketed together as "companion diagnostic" products.[89]

In specific genetic diseases, applications of biotechnology in genetic medicine, such as gene editing with CRISPR-CAS9, will lead to important treatment advances.[90] In 2012, the European Medicines Agency approved the first gene therapy using an adeno-associated virus vector (Glybera) to treat lipoprotein lipase deficiency, a very rare genetic disease.[91] Similarly, specific gene therapies, such as the first product approved by the US Food and Drug Administration, in 2017, tisagenlecleucel, for childhood and young adult leukemia will provide options that were not available before, giving hope to patients and their families.[92] PGx, however, will have broader application than the above-mentioned advances, and pharmacists can lead the way in PGx implementation.

CONCLUSION

Better understanding of relationships between genes and drug response through technological advancements has resulted in the more precise individualization of therapy. Pharmacogenomic testing is becoming more affordable. PGx, related to PK and PD parameters, are used to improve drug therapy. With defined genomic/pharmacogenomic competencies and teamwork, pharmacists can take the lead in contributing to efficacious and safe treatment being provided to patients early in therapy.

PRACTICE QUESTIONS

1. The conceptual difference between pharmacogenetics and PGx include
   A. Risk for adverse drug reactions are inherited in one case, but not the other.
   B. One refers to "trial and error" therapeutics, whereas the other refers to evidence-based therapeutics.
   C. One refers to a single gene related to drug response, whereas the other involves more than one gene related to drug response.
   D. One refers to precision medicine, whereas the other refers to personalized medicine.
2. The most common form of DNA variation is termed
   A. Insertion
   B. SNP
   C. Frame shift
   D. CNV

3. Patients who have the "least" or lowest metabolism rate, who are receiving an active drug, are at increased risk of an adverse drug reaction. These individuals are considered
   A. PMs
   B. IMs
   C. RMs
   D. UMs

4. Codeine, a prodrug, would be most likely to produce an ADR in which of the following patients?
   A. UM
   B. PM
   C. IM
   D. RM

5. Clopidogrel, a prodrug, would be least likely to provide therapeutic benefit in which of the following patients?
   A. UM
   B. PM
   C. IM
   D. RM

6. The pharmacogene, *SLCO1B1*, represents which of the following?
   A. A PK drug-metabolizing pharmacogene.
   B. A pharmacodynamic drug receptor pharmacogene.
   C. A pharmacodynamic transporter pharmacogene.
   D. A pharmacokinetic transporter pharmacogene.

7. A deficiency in which of the following are considered pharmacodynamic pharmacogenes?
   A. *CYP2C19*
   B. *G6PD*
   C. *TPMT*
   D. *CYP2C9*

8. All of the following are PGx competency domains for pharmacists, except
   A. Basic genetic concepts
   B. Diagnosis and genetic risk
   C. Pharmacogenetics/PGx
   D. Ethical, legal, and social implications

9. A tool that can be used to identify multiple SNPs that may be related to complex multifactorial diseases is
   A. Candidate gene study
   B. Insertion/deletion analysis
   C. Intron exploration
   D. Genome-wide association study

10. PGx/genomics with associated testing of DNA may have many consequences. Which of the following are implications beyond the strict scientific aspects of testing?
    A. Ethical, legal, and social
    B. Biological
    C. Physicochemical
    D. Mathematical

REFERENCES

1. Reiss SM. Integrating pharmacogenomics into pharmacy practice via medication therapy management. *J Am Pharm Assoc.* 2011;51(6):e64−74. https://doi.org/10.1331/JAPhA.2011.11543.

2. Relling MV, Gardner EE, Sandborn WJ, et al. Clinical Pharmacogenetics Implementation Consortium guidelines for thiopurine methyltransferase genotype and thiopurine dosing: 2013 update. *Clin Pharmacol Ther.* 2013;93(4):324−325. https://doi.org/10.1038/clpt.2013.4.

3. Motulsky AG. Drug reactions, enzymes, and biochemical genetics. *J Am Med Assoc.* 1957;165(7):835−837.

4. Vogel F. Modern problems in human genetics [Moderne problem der humangenetik]. *Ergeb Inn Med U Kinderheilk.* 1959;1959(12):52−125.

5. Kalow W. Pharmacogenetics and pharmacogenomics: origin, status, and the hope for personalized medicine. *Pharmacogenomics J.* 2006;6:162−165. https://www.ncbi.nlm.nih.gov/pubmed/16415920.

6. Lander ES. Initial impact of the sequencing of the human genome. *Nature.* 2011;470:187−197. https://doi.org/10.1038/nature09792.

7. Olson MV. The human genome project. *Proc Natl Acad Sci USA*. 1993;90:4338−4344.

8. U.S. National Human Genome Research Institute. *DNA Sequencing Costs: Data*; 2017. https://www.genome.gov/sequencingcostsdata/.

9. U.S. Food and Drug Administration. *Guidance for Industry: E15 Definitions for Genomic Biomarkers,Pharmacogenomics, Pharmacogenetics, Genomic Data and Sample Coding Categories*; 2017. https://www.fda.gov/downloads/drugs/guidancecomplianceregulatoryinformation/guidances/ucm073162.pdf.

10. Kisor DF, Kane MD, Talbot JN, Bright DR, Sprague JE. *Pharmacogenes: Scientific Background and Clinical Applications*. Fort Wayne, Indiana: Manchester University; 2017. https://www.manchester.edu/pharmacogenes/book.

11. Relling MV, Evans WE. Pharmacogenomics in the clinic. *Nature*. 2015;526:343−350. https://doi.org/10.1038/nature15817.

12. U.S. National Center for Biotechnology Information. *SNP FAQ Archive*; 2017. https://www.ncbi.nlm.nih.gov/books/NBK44417/.

13. Scott SA, Sangkuhl K, Stein CM, et al. *Clinical Pharmacogenetics Implementation Consortium Guidelines for CYP2C19 Genotype and Clopidogrel Therapy: 2013 Update. Supplemental Data*; 2017. https://cpicpgx.org/guidelines/guideline-for-clopidogrel-and-cyp2c19/.

14. Robarge JD, Li L, Desta Z, Nguyen A, Flockhart DA. The star-allele nomenclature: retooling for translational genomics. *Clin Pharmacol Ther*. 2007;82(3):244−248.

15. Kalman LV, Agundez JAG, Appell ML, et al. Pharmacogenetic allele nomenclature: international workgroup recommendations for test result reporting. *Clin Pharmacol Ther*. 2016;99(2):172−185. https://doi.org/10.1002/cpt.280.

16. *The Pharmacogenomics Knowledgebase (PharmGKB)*; 2018. https://www.pharmgkb.org/. Accessed on August 6, 2018.

17. *The Clinical Pharmacogenetics Implementation Consortium (CPIC)*; 2018. https://cpicpgx.org/.

18. Caudle KE, Dunnenberger HM, Freimuth RR, et al. Standardizing terms for clinical pharmacogenetic test results: consensus terms from the Clinical Pharmacogenetics Implementation Consortium (CPIC). *GeneticsMed*. 2017;19(2):215−223. https://doi.org/10.1038/gim.2016.87.

19. Swen JJ, Nijenhuis M, de Boer A, et al. Pharmacogenetics: from bench to byte−an update of guidelines. *Clin Pharmacol Ther*. 2011;89(5):662−673. https://doi.org/10.1038/clpt.2011.34.

20. Westervelt P, Cho K, Bright DR, Kisor DF. Drug−gene interactions: inherent variability in drug maintenance dose requirements. *P T*. 2014;39(9):630−637.

21. Herper M. *Illumina Promises To Sequence Human Genome For $100 − But Not Quite Yet*. Forbes; 2017. https://www.forbes.com/sites/matthewherper/2017/01/09/illumina-promises-to-sequence-human-genome-for-100-but-not-quite-yet/#35b8d0f7386d.

22. Klein ME, Parvez MM, Shin JG. Clinical implementation of pharmacogenomics for personalized precision medicine: barriers and solutions. *J Pharm Sci*. 2017;106:2368−2379. https://doi.org/10.1016/j.xphs.2017.04.051.

23. Alexander KM, Divine HS, Hanna CR, Gokun Y, Freeman PR. Implementation of personalized medicine services in community pharmacies: perceptions of independent community pharmacists. *J Am Pharm Assoc*. 2014;54(5):510−517. https://doi.org/10.1331/JAPhA.2014.13041.

24. Bright DR, Kisor DF, Smith A, Conaway M, Yu M. Implementation of a pharmacogenetics management service for post-myocardial infarction care in a community pharmacy. *Pers Med*. 2015;12(6):563−573. https://doi.org/10.2217/pme.15.7.

25. Weitzel KW, Alexander M, Bernhardt BA, et al. The IGNITE network: a model for genomic medicine implementation and research. *BMC Med Genom*. January 5, 2016;9:1. https://doi.org/10.1186/s12920-015-0162-5. https://bmcmedgenomics.biomedcentral.com/articles/10.1186/s12920-015-0162-5.

26. Arwood MJ, Chumnumwat S, Cavallari LH, Nutescu EA, Duarte JD. Implementing pharmacogenomics at your institution: establishment and overcoming implementation challenges. *Clin Trans Sci*. 2016;9(5):233−245. https://doi.org/10.1111/cts.12404. http://onlinelibrary.wiley.com/doi/10.1111/cts.12404/full.

27. *The Personalized Medicine Coalition. The Personalized Medicine Report*; 2017. http://www.personalizedmedicinecoalition.org/Userfiles/PMC-Corporate/file/The_PM_Report.pdf.

28. Ji Y, Skierka JM, Blommel JH, et al. Preemptive pharmacogenomic testing for precision medicine: a comprehensive analysis of five actionable pharmacogenomic genes using next-generation DNA sequencing and a customized CYP2D6 genotyping cascade. *J Mol Diagn*. 2016;18(3):438−445. https://doi.org/10.1016/j.jmoldx.2016.01.003.

29. Dunnenberger HM, Crews KR, Hoffman JM, et al. Preemptive clinical pharmacogenetics implementation: current programs in five United States medical centers. *Annu Rev Pharmacol Toxicol*. 2015;55:89−106. https://doi.org/10.1146/annurev-pharmtox-010814-124835.

30. Kisor DF, Sprague JE. The application of drug-dosing guidelines based on preemptive genetic testing. *Spec Pharm Times*; May 29, 2013. https://www.specialtypharmacytimes.com/publications/specialty-pharmacy-times/2013/may_june-2013/the-application-of-drug-dosing-guidelines-based-on-preemptive-genetic-testing.

31. Bottorff MB, Bright DR, Kisor DF. Should pharmacogenomics evidence be considered in clinical decision making? Focus on select cardiovascular drugs. *Pharmacotherapy*. September 2017;37(9):1005−1013. https://doi.org/10.1002/phar.1979.

32. Murphy JE. *Clinical Pharmacokinetics*. 5th ed. Bethesda, MD: American Society of Health-System Pharmacists; 2012.

33. Shugarts S, Benet LZ. The role of transporters in the pharmacokinetics of orally administered drugs. *Pharm Res (N Y)*. 2009;26(9):2039−2054. https://doi.org/10.1007/s11095-009-9924-0.

34. Paine MF, Hart HL, Ludington SS, Haining RL, Rettie AE, Zeldin DC. The human intestinal cytochrome P450 "Pie". *Drug Metab Dispos*. 2006;34(5):880−886.

35. Shimada T, Yamazaki H, Mimura M, Inui Y, Guengerich FP. Interindividual variations in human liver cytochrome P-450 enzymes involved in the oxidation of drugs, carcinogens, and toxic chemicals: studies with liver microsomes of 30 Japanese and 30 Caucasians. *J Pharmacol Exp Ther*. 1994;270:414−423.

36. Crettol S, Petrovic N, Murray M. Pharmacogenetics of phase I and phase II drug metabolism. *Curr Pharm Des*. 2010;16(2):204−219.

37. Elliott LS, Henderson JC, Neradilek MB, Moyer NA, Ashcraft KC, Thirumaran RK. Clinical impact of pharmacogenetic profiling with a clinical decision support tool in polypharmacy home health patients: a prospective pilot randomized controlled trial. *PLoS One*. 2017;12(2):e0170905. https://doi.org/10.1371/journal.pone.0170905. http://journals.plos.org/plosone/article?id=10.1371/journal.pone.0170905.

38. Rowland M, Tozer TN. *Clinical Pharmacokinetics and Pharmacodynamics*. 4th ed. Baltimore, MD. Lippincott: Williams & Wilkins; 2010.

39. U.S. Food and Drug Administration. *Table of Pharmacogenomic Biomarkers in Drug Labeling*; 2017. https://www.fda.gov/drugs/scienceresearch/researchareas/pharmacogenetics/ucm083378.htm.

40. Johnson JA, Roden DM, Lesko LJ, Ashley E, Klein TE, Shuldiner AR. Clopidogrel: a case for indication-specific pharmacogenetics. *Clin Pharmacol Ther*. 2012;91(5):774–776. https://doi.org/10.1038/clpt.2012.21.

41. https://www.pharmvar.org/gene/CYP2C19.

42. Scott SA, Sangkuhl K, Stein CM, et al. Clinical Pharmacogenetics Implementation Consortium guidelines for CYP2C19 genotype and clopidogrel therapy: 2013 update. *Clin Pharmacol Ther*. 2013;94(3):317–323. https://doi.org/10.1038/clpt.2013.105.

43. *Plavix®(clopidogrel Bisulfate Tablet, Film Coated). Dailymed*; 2017. https://dailymed.nlm.nih.gov/dailymed/drugInfo.cfm?setid=01b14603-8f29-4fa3-8d7e-9d523f802e0b.

44. Lam J, Woodall KL, Solbeck P, et al. Codeine-related deaths: the role of pharmacogenetics and drug interactions. *Forensic Sci Int*. 2014;239:50–56. https://doi.org/10.1016/j.forsciint.2014.03.018.

45. Crews KR, Gaedigk A, Dunnenberger HM, et al. Clinical Pharmacogenetics Implementation Consortium guidelines for cytochrome P450 2D6 genotype and codeine therapy: 2014 update. *Clin Pharmacol Ther*. 2013;95(4):376–382. https://doi.org/10.1038/clpt.2013.254.

46. Vuilleumier PH, Stamer UM, Landau R. Pharmacogenomic considerations in opioid analgesia. *Pharmacogenom Pers Med*. 2012;5:73–87. https://doi.org/10.2147/PGPM.S23422.

47. Gaedigk A, Simon SD, Pearce RE, Bradford LD, Kennedy MJ, Leeder JS. The CYP2D6 activity score: translating genotype information into a qualitative measure of phenotype. *Clin Pharmacol Ther*. 2008;83(2):234–242.

48. Crews KR, Gaedigk A, Dunnenberger HM, et al. *Clinical Pharmacogenetics Implementation Consortium Guidelines for Cytochrome P450 2D6 Genotype and Codeine Therapy: Supplemental Material*; 2017. https://cpicpgx.org/guidelines/guideline-for-codeine-and-cyp2d6/.

49. FDA Drug Safety Communication. *FDA Restricts Use of Prescription Codeine Pain and Cough Medicines and Tramadol Pain Medicines in Children; Recommends against Use in Breastfeeding Women*; 2017. https://www.fda.gov/Drugs/DrugSafety/ucm549679.htm.

50. Elion GB. The purine path to chemotherapy. *Science*. 1989;244(4900):41–47.

51. Schmiegelow K, Nielsen SN, Frandsen TL, Nersting J. Mercaptopurine/Methotrexate maintenance therapy of childhood acute lymphoblastic leukemia: clinical facts and fiction. *JPediatrHematolOncol*. 2014;36(7):503–517. https://doi.org/10.1097/MPH.0000000000000206.

52. Relling MV, Gardner EE, Sandborn WJ, et al. Clinical Pharmacogenetics Implementation Consortium guidelines for ThiopurineMethyltransferase genotype and ThiopurineDosing. *Clin Pharm Ther*. 2011;89(3):387–391. https://doi.org/10.1038/clpt.2010.320.

53. Ramsey LB, Johnson SG, Caudle KE, et al. The clinical pharmacogenetics Implementation Consortium guideline for SLCO1B1 and simvastatin-induced myopathy: 2014 update. *Clin Pharmacol Ther*. 2014;96(4):423–428. https://doi.org/10.1038/clpt.2014.125.

54. García MJ, Reinoso RF, Sánchez Navarro A, Prous JR. Clinical pharmacokinetics of statins. *Methods Find Exp Clin Pharmacol*. 2003;25(6):457–481.

55. Hecker PA, Leopold JA, Gupte SA, Recchia FA, Stanley WC. Impact of glucose-6-phosphate dehydrogenase deficiency on the pathophysiology of cardiovascular disease. *Am J Physiol Heart Circ Physiol*. 2013;304(4):H491–H500. https://doi.org/10.1152/ajpheart.00721.2012.

56. Abid S, Khan AH. Severe hemolysis and renal failure in glucose-6-phosphate dehydrogenase deficient patients with hepatitis E. *Am J Gastroenterol*. 2002;97(6):1544–1547.

57. Genetics Home Reference. *Glucose-6-phosphate Dehydrogenase Deficiency*; 2017. https://ghr.nlm.nih.gov/condition/glucose-6-phosphate-dehydrogenase-deficiency.

58. Reading NS, Ruiz-bonilla JA, Christensen RD, Cáceres-Perkins W, Prchal JT. A patient with both methemoglobinemia and G6PD deficiency: a therapeutic conundrum. *Am J Hematol*. 2017;92(5):474–477. https://doi.org/10.1002/ajh.24683.

59. Rehman HU. Methemoglobinemia. *West J Med*. 2001;175(3):193–196.

60. Bubp J, Jen M, Matuszewski K. Caring for glucose-6-phosphate dehydrogenase (G6PD)–Deficient patients: implications for pharmacy. *PT*. 2015;40(9):572–574.

61. Relling MV, McDonagh EM, Chang T. Clinical Pharmacogenetics Implementation Consortium (CPIC) guidelines for rasburicase therapy in the context of G6PD deficiency genotype. *Clin Pharmacol Ther*. 2014;96(2):169–174. https://doi.org/10.1038/clpt.2014.97.

62. Johnson JA, Caudle KE, Gong L, et al. Clinical Pharmacogenetics Implementation Consortium (CPIC) guideline for pharmacogenetics-guided warfarin dosing: 2017 update. *Clin Pharmacol Ther*. 2017;102(3):397–404. https://doi.org/10.1002/cpt.668.

63. *Warfarin Sodium Tablets. Dailymed*; 2017. https://dailymed.nlm.nih.gov/dailymed/drugInfo.cfm?setid=558b7a0d-5490-4c1b-802e-3ab3f1efe760.

64. Alzubiedi S, Saleh MI. Pharmacogenetic-guided warfarin dosing algorithm inAfrican-Americans. *J Cardiovasc Pharmacol*. 2016;67:86–92. https://doi.org/10.1097/FJC.0000000000000317.

65. Gage BF, Eby C, Johnson JA, et al. Use of pharmacogenetic and clinical factors to predict the therapeutic dose of warfarin. *Clin Pharmacol Ther*. 2008;84:326–331. https://doi.org/10.1038/clpt.2008.10.

66. Klein TE, et al. Estimation of the warfarin dose with clinical and pharmacogenetic data. *N Engl J Med*. 2009;360:753–764. https://doi.org/10.1056/NEJMoa0809329.

67. Hamberg AK, Friberg LE, Hanséus K, et al. Warfarin dose prediction in children using pharmacometric bridging–comparison with published pharmacogenetic dosing algorithms. *Eur J Clin Pharmacol*. 2013;69:1275–1283. https://doi.org/10.1007/s00228-012-1466-4.

68. Roederer MW, Kuo GM, Kisor DF, et al. Pharmacogenomics competencies in pharmacy practice: a blueprint for change. *J Am Pharm Assoc (2003)*. 2017;57(1):120−125. https://doi.org/10.1016/j.japh.2016.08.014.

69. *National Human Genome Research Institute. The Genetics/Genomics Competency Center*; 2017. http://genomicseducation.net/competency.

70. *History of the Pharmacist Competencies in Pharmacogenomics*; 2017. http://genomicseducation.net/files/Pharmacist-Comp.pdf.

71. National Institutes of Health. *What does It Mean to Have a Genetic Predisposition to a Disease?* https://ghr.nlm.nih.gov/primer/mutationsanddisorders/predisposition.

72. Korf BR, Irons MB. *Human Genetics and Genomics*. 4th ed. John Wiley and Sons; 2013.

73. Read A, Donnai D. *New Clinical Genetics*. 2nd ed. Scion Publishing Ltd.; 2012.

74. Nicoletto MO, Donach M, DeNicolo A, Artioli G, Banna G, Monfardini S. BRCA-1 and BRCA-2 mutations as prognostic factors in clinical practice and genetic counseling. *Cancer Treat Rev*. 2001;27:295−304.

75. Teng L, Zheng Y, Wang H. BRCA1/2 associated hereditary breast cancer. *J Zhejiang Univ - Sci B*. 2008;9:85−89. https://doi.org/10.1631/jzus.B0710617.

76. McCarthy AM, Armstrong K. The role of testing for BRCA1 and BRCA2 mutations in cancer prevention. *JAMA Intern Med*. 2014;174:1023−1024. https://doi.org/10.1001/jamainternmed.2014.1322.

77. Strachan T, Read A. *Human Molecular Genetics*. 4th ed. Garland Science. Taylor and Francis Group; 2011.

78. Galton DJ, Ferns GA. Genetic markers to predict polygenic disease: a new problem for social genetics. *Q J Med*. 1999;92:223−232.

79. Lowe WL, Reddy TE. Genomic approaches for understanding the genetics of complex disease. *Genome Res*. 2015;25:1432−1441. https://doi.org/10.1101/gr.190603.115.

80. Kathiresan S, Srivastava D. Genetics of human cardiovascular disease. *Cell*. 2012;148:1242−1257. https://doi.org/10.1016/j.cell.2012.03.001.

81. Price AL, Spencer CC, Donnelly P. Progress and promise in understanding the genetic basis of common diseases. *Proc R Soc B*. 2015;282:1821. https://doi.org/10.1098/rspb.2015.1684.

82. Jostins L, Barrett JC. Genetic risk prediction in complex disease. *Hum Mol Genet*. 2011;20:R182−R188. https://doi.org/10.1093/hmg/ddr378.

83. Wang TH, Wang HS. A genome-wide association study primer for clinicians. *Taiwan J Obstet Gynecol*. 2009;48:89−95. https://doi.org/10.1016/S1028-4559(09)60265-5.

84. Visshcer PM, Brown MA, McCarthy MI, Yang J. Five years of GWAS discovery. *Am J Human Gen*. 2012;90:7−24. https://doi.org/10.1016/j.ajhg.2011.11.029.

85. U.S. Equal Employment Opportunity Commission. *Genetic Information Discrimination*; 2017. https://www.eeoc.gov/laws/types/genetic.cfm.

86. *Genomics Law Report. A New Law to Raise GINA's Floor in California*; 2017. https://www.genomicslawreport.com/index.php/2011/12/07/a-new-law-to-raise-ginas-floor-in-california/.

87. Ozdemir V, Williams-Jones B, Glatt JG, Tsuang MT, Lohr JB, Reist C. Shifting emphasis from pharmacogenomics to theragnostics. *Nat Biotechnol*. 2006;24:942−946.

88. Pene F, Courtine E, Cariou A, Mira JP. Towardtheragnostics. *Crit Care Med*. 2009;37(1 Suppl.):S50−S58. https://doi.org/10.1097/CCM.0b013e3181921349.

89. U.S. Food and Drug Administration. *FDA Guidance. Principles for Codevelopment of an in Vitro Companion Diagnostic Device with a Therapeutic Product*; 2017. https://www.fda.gov/downloads/MedicalDevices/DeviceRegulationandGuidance/GuidanceDocuments/UCM510824.pdf.

90. Xiao-Jie L, Hui-Ying X, Zun-Ping K, Jin-Lian C, Li-Juan J. CRISPR-Cas9: a new and promising player in gene therapy. *J Med Genet*. 2015;52(5):289−296. https://doi.org/10.1136/jmedgenet-2014-102968.

91. European Medicines Agency. *Glybera*; 2017. http://www.ema.europa.eu/ema/index.jsp?curl=pages/medicines/human/medicines/002145/human_med_001480.jsp&mid=WC0b01ac058001d124.

92. Kaiser J. Modified T cells that attack leukemia become first gene therapy approved in the United States. *Science*; August 30, 2017. http://www.sciencemag.org/news/2017/08/modified-t-cells-attack-leukemia-become-first-gene-therapy-approved-united-states.

ANSWERS TO PRACTICE QUESTIONS

1. C
2. B
3. A
4. A
5. B
6. D
7. B
8. B
9. D
10. A

Chapter 32

TPN Primer for the Pharmacist: Approach to Nutrition Therapy

Mark Decerbo[1,2]

[1]Roseman University of Health Sciences, Henderson, NV, United States;
[2]University of Nevada School of Medicine, Reno, NV, United States

Learning Objectives:

Objective 32.1 Explain the need of parenteral nutrition.
Objective 32.2 Plan administration, calculation, and preparation of parenteral nutrition.

OBJECTIVE 32.1. EXPLAIN THE NEED OF PARENTERAL NUTRITION

Parenteral nutrition (PN) is a critical therapeutic modality used for a number of indications in neonates, children, and adults in which the pharmacist can play a major role in ensuring appropriate patient outcomes. PN is a complex medication containing as many as 40 separate components and is associated with numerous medication errors as well as significant adverse events, including death, and is therefore classified as a high-risk medication by the Institute for Safe Medication Practices (ISMP). Because of this, it is essential that the practicing pharmacist has a deep understanding of the provision of PN support, including appropriate indications for PN, selection of an appropriate formula, steps for safe initiation, approach to daily monitoring, need for modification to the prescribed PN formula, and awareness of potential complications. To achieve this, pharmacists are required to possess an advanced knowledge of pathophysiology, volume status, protein and energy requirements, macronutrients, and micronutrients to optimize the appropriate use of PN across all patient populations.[1,2]

Determine if Parenteral Nutrition Needed

The centerpiece of nutrition support is to use the least invasive and most appropriate method of feeding, which may not always be PN. The provision of macronutrients (e.g., protein/amino acids, carbohydrate, fat) and electrolytes directly via the intravenous route is fraught with potential issues, not the least of which are risks associated with central venous catheter placement. Because of this, PN is the overall the least preferred method of providing nutrition support, with enteral nutrition generally preferred. However, for appropriate patients, PN is the only viable means to provide nutrition and can therefore be seen as a potential life-saving measure. Due to the increased risk of complications with PN therapy, the pharmacist should first carefully assesses whether PN is appropriate for a given patient prior to proceeding with preparation of the formula.

General contraindications for PN include a functioning gastrointestinal (GI) tract, an inability to obtain venous access, a terminal prognosis which does not warrant aggressive care, and anticipated treatment for less than 5 days in a patient without severe malnutrition. Conversely, PN is generally indicated with the inability to absorb nutrients from the GI tract (which can occur in such conditions as short bowel syndrome, massive small-bowel resection, severe diarrhea, radiation enteritis, and untreatable malabsorption), complete bowel obstruction, intestinal pseudoobstruction, inability to obtain enteral access for enteral feeding, GI hemorrhage, high output enterocutaneous fistula where enteral access distally cannot be established, severe catabolism with expected duration of nill per oral (NPO) status ×5–7 days, and pancreatitis where jejunal feeds cause intolerable abdominal pain.[3,4]

Clinical Pharmacy Education, Practice and Research. https://doi.org/10.1016/B978-0-12-814276-9.00032-5

Assessing the Patient

An assessment of malnutrition is a multifactorial process encompassing weight change, recent oral intake, functional capacity, symptoms, as well as a physical exam looking for presence of fat loss, muscle wasting, and edema. Recognition of malnutrition is key, as it is associated with an increased incidence of nosocomial infections, a higher rate of surgical complications, higher hospital costs, increased mortality, and increased length of stay. Prior to initiating PN, a nutrition assessment is therefore necessary to determine nutrient needs due to the patient's underlying condition(s). Factors that predispose to weight loss and malnutrition must be identified and generally fall into one of four categories: (1) Medical illnesses (sepsis, chronic disease, recent surgery/trauma), (2) Psychosocial factors (poverty, alcoholism, drug abuse, disability), (3) GI disorders (anorexia, dysphagia, persistent nausea/vomiting/diarrhea, inflammatory bowel disease, pancreatitis, GI fistulas), and (4) Medications (chemotherapy, appetite suppressants).[5,6]

Generally, a patient is considered malnourished if there is an established lack of enteral intake $\times 7-10$ days, 5% weight loss over 1 month, or 10% weight loss over 6 months. Scoring tools, such as the Subjective Global Assessment, Mini-Nutritional Assessment, and Prognostic Inflammatory and Nutritional Index, have been developed to predict nutritional status. More commonly, however, are laboratory assessments which can also be used to investigate the presence of malnutrition through an examination of acute phase proteins. These hepatic proteins can be useful nutritional markers but are not foolproof and may not truly reflect current nutritional status. The most commonly used markers are transferrin, albumin, and prealbumin, all of whom have differing half-lives (albumin 18–22 d, prealbumin 2–4 d, transferrin 7–10 d), and all of whom which can be falsely increased or decreased by associated factors. Volume depletion and renal failure can falsely elevate, whereas volume overload and iron deficiency, liver disease, pregnancy, cancer, trauma, and alcohol abuse can falsely suppress via general inflammation leading to an increase in TNF and Eicosanoids, which in turn leads to capillary leak and resultant low hepatic proteins. Despite these limitations, serum albumin level remains an important marker with studies showing progressively lower serum albumin correlated with increased ICU stay, increased hospital days, and even increased mortality. Approach to nutritional assessment in hospitalized patients with obesity is mentioned in the guidelines.[7]

A patient's current weight and weight history is therefore critical to consider when first addressing a patient's nutritional status. This information will assist the pharmacist in establishing the degree of malnutrition which may exist, and such can be measured against a variety of standards, including Ideal Body Weight, Ideal Creatinine Excretion, Upper Arm Anthropometry, and Body Mass Index. In addition to assessing degree of malnutrition, the patient's true weight will also form the basis by which caloric needs and protein requirements are calculated. If a falsely high weight is used, whether from operator error, patient history, or other variables such as volume status, such can lead to the overprovision of calories and the attendant risks and metabolic complications associated with overfeeding. The opposite is also true, with a falsely low reported weight leading to underfeeding, which can contribute to metabolic stress and morbidity and mortality in severely malnourished patients.[8]

Determining calorie and protein needs in malnourished patients is difficult, as matching caloric expenditure to caloric provision can be imprecise. Calorie requirements often increase in relation to stress, trauma, burns, and fever, whereas a decrease in needs may be seen in sedated and ventilated patients. Providing either more or fewer calories than that which is required by the patient can lead to poor outcomes. Overall, however, when determining the appropriate needed calorie level in patients, providing lower calorie levels initially appears to decrease risks associated with overfeeding, so long as an acceptable minimal level of calories is supplied. Indirect calorimetry is considered the gold standard when determining a patient's caloric expenditure; however, a wide variety of formulas and calculations are frequently used in practice to estimate the true amount of calories and protein which should be provided to the patient via their PN treatment. These predictive equations for energy needs each come with advantages and disadvantages, with the most commonly used equations being the: Harris–Benedict Equation, Ireton Jones Equation, Penn State Equation, and Mifflin St. Jeor Equation.[9–11] Regardless of which calculation is used by the pharmacist to estimate nutrient requirements, there is a notably convincing lack of evidence linking a given calorie and protein amount to patient outcomes, and the debate among healthcare professionals over the "best" equation to use continues in modern day practice. In general, most acutely ill patients require between 25 and 30 kcal/kg/day, with most critical care patients targeted to receive around 25 kcal/kg/day. Notable exceptions to this rule of thumb include obese patients (defined as $\geq 130\%$ of their IBW), who are generally limited to 15–20 kcal/kg/day of their adjusted body weight, and patients at risk for refeeding syndrome (RFS) who are targeted to receive 15–25 kcal/kg/day.[12]

OBJECTIVE 32.2. PLAN ADMINISTRATION, CALCULATION, AND PREPARATION OF PARENTERAL NUTRITION

Once a decision has been made to appropriately proceed with PN, and a total goal number of calories have been calculated, the pharmacist must next verify the type of line/venous access which is present in the patient, either peripheral or central. Central PN is defined as nutrients provided intravenously which are delivered into a high flow vein, usually the superior vena cava adjacent to the right atrium. This is most commonly achieved through placement of a peripherally inserted central catheter line in the patient, although several other types of central access, each with their own advantages and disadvantages, are available. Conversely, peripheral PN, commonly referred to as PPN, is defined as nutrients provided intravenously which are delivered into a peripheral vein, usually of the hand or forearm via a peripheral line (short or midline).

PPN is utilized when central venous access is not possible and/or desired but is fraught with inherent nutritional limitations. It is optimally used only in select patients, namely those who require short-term (less than 10−14 days) nutrition support due to patency issues with this type of access. Additionally, patients being considered for PPN must generally possess adequate cardiac and renal function, as high volumes of PN must often be used to meet the patient's macronutrient goals, as the final protein concentration of the admixture must be <4.25%, whereas the final dextrose must be <10%. Lastly, due to risk of thrombophlebitis and the risk for loss of venous access due to hypertonicity, calculated osmolarity of the PPN formulation must never exceed an osmolarity of 900 mOsm/L, generally requiring <1800 kcal to be delivered via the formula, which may limit the appropriateness of this type of therapy. PPN can also be used adjunctively to diet in a transition period where a patient's oral intake is improving but is still suboptimally meeting the desired macronutrient balance.[13]

When administering PPN, the patient's peripheral line should be changed every 2−3 days, so as to minimize loss of patency and/or infection risk. The pharmacist can recommend several interventions in an attempt to maximize patency of the line, including addition of hydrocortisone and/or heparin the PN formula, as well as application of a transdermal nitroglycerin patch placed close to the catheter site. Drug−nutrient interactions should be avoided or monitored.[14] Even with all the aforementioned interventions, peripheral line patency may not be maintained, thus necessitating the potential need for central PN. Of note, there are several premixed commercially available fixed concentration PPN products containing dextrose and amino acids in varying strengths which are appropriate for peripheral use. Available with or without electrolytes, these products can play an important role in facilities and institutions in which the technical ability to make custom PN products is limited, as such ensure the potential for some, albeit limited, ability to provide some measure of nutritional support.

Central PN is provided via a venous catheter to large diameter veins with high rates of blood flow. Because of this, central PN allows infusion of formulations with osmolarities greater than 900 mOsm/L and are the route of choice for patients with cardiac or renal impairment, patients with poor peripheral venous access, and those who require PN for >10−14 days.[13]

Once the pharmacist has confirmed that the appropriate vascular access is present, they must next confirm and/or calculate the appropriate dose of each macronutrient for the individual patient, considering all current diagnoses, existing other therapies, and the targeted number of kcals/day. The doses of macronutrients used in PN should be mainly targeted at supporting protein synthetic response, while also addressing caloric support and metabolic management. Inappropriate provision of nutrients to a given patient can be dangerous, a fact which is complicated by the body's response to starvation and stress. In these conditions, metabolic responses are altered. Stressors can cause a breakdown in protein stores along with an accompanied increase in fat oxidation and energy expenditure. By accelerating loss of protein stores, patients are at higher risk for malnutrition. When designing the appropriate PN formula for a PN patient, the pharmacist must therefore carefully consider appropriate amounts of protein, carbohydrate, and fat by which to provide via the admixture. The process of calculating a patient's needed protein and caloric requirement is fairly straightforward, based primarily on a correct patient weight, along with analysis of the patient's degree of ongoing metabolic stress and body's ability to process macronutrients.[8] When ordering the PN solution, the following macronutrients should always be ordered as "amount per day" expressed as grams per day. Other methods, such as "amount per kg" or "% per PN bag," have let to sometimes catastrophic errors and should be avoided.

Protein

Amino acids, commercially supplied in numerous formulations (standard, hepatic failure, pediatric, renal) of varying percentages, provide 4 kcal/g. With acute metabolic stress, there is a significant increase in the amount of protein breakdown, thereby resulting in an increased amount of urea production. Patients requiring PN generally therefore have increased requirements, with protein/amino acids typically supplied in a range depending on the degree of stress and amount of catabolism which may be present. These ranges differ between adult and pediatric patients and are calculated on a gram per kilogram of euvolemic body weight basis. Neonates generally require between 2.5 and 3.0 g/kg/day, infants require 2.0—3.5 g/kg/day, and children require 1.5—2.0 g/kg/day. In adults, critical care, burn, surgery, and dialysis patients usually require protein administration in the range of 1.2—2 g/kg/day, extending up to 2—2.5 g/kg/day in severely catabolic states. Acute renal failure can require protein supplementation in the range of 1.5—1.6 g/kg/day due to protein losses through the glomeruli or hemodialysis; however, in renal failure patients who are not being dialyzed, protein restriction to as low as 0.8 g/kg may be needed to avoid elevating BUN to such a degree that complications arise.[15] Optimal degree of protein administration in patient with liver disease is somewhat controversial. Although dietary protein is converted by colonic bacteria into ammonia, intravenous amino acids in PN will not increase ammonia generation in the colon. Therefore, in patients with hepatic impairment, protein goals are generally suggested to be between 1.0 and 1.5 g/kg, with a reduction to 0.8 g/kg only if hepatic encephalopathy resistant to medication management is present.[16]

Carbohydrate

Dextrose, providing 3.4 kcal/g and commercially supplied in solutions of varying percentages, is the only carbohydrate utilized in PN. In stressed patients, there is an increased need for glucose accompanied by impaired insulin secretion and sensitivity, leading to the potential for hyperglycemia. Therefore, in most PN formulations which are infused over 24 h, carbohydrates are generally provided in varying amounts up to a maximum of 60% of total kcals/day. Initial dextrose in these PN solutions should generally not exceed 7.2 g/kg/day (5 mg/kg/min). This parameter is known as the glucose infusion rate (GIR) and is used as a benchmark to minimize the risks of overfeeding with dextrose, which are primarily the occurrence of fatty liver and hyperglycemia. In circumstances where patients are receiving a cyclic PN solution, that which is infused over less than 24 h per day, patients may exceed the above GIR when additional calories for weight maintenance or gain are desired. Conversely, due to the risk associated with hyperglycemia in the critically ill patient, dextrose in this population is generally limited to no more than 5 mg/kg/day. In patients with history of diabetes, insulin therapy should be initiated for blood glucose more than 140 mg/dL. In patients without diabetes, insulin therapy is indicated if blood glucose is above 180 mg/dL or in patients with persistent requirement for correction insulin.[17]

Fat

Injectable lipid emulsions (ILE), formerly known as intravenous lipid emulsions (IVFE), arise from various oil sources, including soybean oil, olive oil, fish oil, safflower oil, and medium chain triglycerides. Irrespective of the selected commercially available product, lipids should generally provide 20%—30% of total daily kcals or <2.5 g/kg/day in acute care patients, whereas critical care patients are generally limited to 0.4—0.75 g/kg/day. Exceptions exist, the most notable being precluding concomitant conditions, such as concurrent treatment with propofol and/or clevidipine infusions. These medications can decrease a patient's need for supplemental lipid in the PN solution, as the vehicle for both medications provides essential fatty acids and calories. Additionally, hypertriglyceridemia, with the risk for acute pancreatitis when markedly elevated, can also serve to limit the amount of lipid provided to the patient as well. In all cases, however, if a patient is to be on PN for greater than 3 weeks, a minimum of 2%—4% of total calories should come from IVFE to prevent essential fatty acid deficiency. Of the various commercially available lipid products, naturally occurring Vitamin K varies depending on the manufacturer and concentration, with safflower oil containing less vitamin K than soybean oil. Vitamin K typically increases proportionally with increasing lipid concentrations and must be considered by the pharmacist when used in a patient on concomitant warfarin therapy.[18]

Micronutrients

Micronutrients are generally defined as essential nutrients (vitamins, electrolytes, trace elements) required daily in small (milligram, microgram) amounts. Vitamins are a vital component of any PN admixture and should generally be supplemented based on daily recommended doses for adults and children. To achieve this, vitamins are usually commercially supplied as standardized doses formulated to meet daily requirements and prevent toxicity. These prespecified formulations generally meet the needs of the majority of patients, with modifications possible for select situations. Of note, thiamine is perhaps the most important vitamin to consider, as it is not only one of the first vitamins to manifest with symptoms of acute deficiency but has been implicated as a cause of death in several patients receiving thiamine-deficient PN therapy. Of the deaths, each patient developed lactic acidosis and died within 5 weeks of initiation of treatment with thiamine-deficient TPN. Thiamine is essential for two enzymes needed for aerobic metabolism, and without sufficient amounts, pyruvate cannot enter the Krebs cycle, resulting in pyruvate accumulation and conversion into lactate. For these reasons, prevention and recognition of thiamine deficiency is critical.[19,20]

Trace minerals, similar to multivitamins, are commercially formulated in quantities expected to match patient needs. These are especially important in providing adequate PN formulations in long-term PN patients, as deficiencies can result when there is no oral intake and trace minerals are withheld from the PN formulation. Although infused in minute quantities, if not carefully monitored in these patients, they can have detrimental effects through accumulation and resultant toxicity. It is vital that the pharmacist understand dosages available, patients' conditional requirements, and the importance of increasing or decreasing supplemental amounts based on patient-specific factors. Perhaps the most commonly employed trace element is zinc, which can commonly manifest via delayed wound healing and impaired immunity. Although the standard PN dose of zinc is 2.5–5 mg/day, patient with high GI losses may require upward of 12–17 mg/L of fluid lost, providing a concrete example of the importance of patient-specific trace mineral dosing.[19,20]

Electrolytes

Electrolytes in PN formulations are added according to anticipated patient requirements, demonstrated laboratory deficiencies, metabolic response to medications, and recommended daily intakes. Although there are various published recommendations which provide typical ranges for parenteral electrolyte content, a patient's age and renal function are the two main determinants of the daily dosage of electrolytes. Electrolyte needs can also vary widely based on losses from wounds, surgical drains, fever, emesis, GI suctioning, and diarrhea and must therefore be replaced either in the PN solution itself or as separate electrolyte riders. Electrolytes must be ordered as the complete salt form rather than the individual ion, with ingredients ordered as "amount per day" in units of mEq, mmol, mcg, or mg.

Parenteral Nutrition Preparation

Appropriate PN preparation requires the pharmacist to collect and monitor a multitude of information. Prior to proceeding with the actual compounding of the formula, the pharmacist should undertake a review to ensure that the following standards are met. If not, additional information and clarifications may be required to be obtained prior to proceeding any further. Sterile compounding of PN preparations is shown in Fig. 32.1.

FIGURE 32.1 Sterile compounding of parenteral nutrition. *Courtesy of Baxter Healthcare Limited.*

Required elements of the PN allow for order review:

- Patient information
  - Name, identifiers, date of birth, age, allergies, height, dosing weight, and diagnoses
- Indication for PN
- Route and access device for PN
- Prescriber contact information
- Date and time PN order submitted
- Date and time PN order to be administered
- Volume, rate of infusion, and infusion schedule for PN
- Method of ILE delivery (separate infusion or total nutrient admixture [TNA])
- PN ingredients for adults listed as amounts/day
- PN ingredients for neonates/pediatrics listed as amounts/kg/day
- PN ingredients
  - A dose for each macronutrient
  - A dose for each electrolyte salt
  - A dose for each multivitamin
  - A dose for each individual vitamin
  - A dose for each trace element
  - A dose for each nonnutrient medication, if ordered

Following receipt of all ordered components of the PN, the pharmacist must ensure that all ingredients are compatible with each other, and that the PN preparation is expected to be stable from the time of compounding through the end of the infusion. From a formula standpoint, the pharmacist must determine if all ordered components of the PN solution can be physically supplied based on desired final volume of the solution. This can be especially difficult in volume restricted patients, at times impossible to deliver the desired macronutrients and additives based on stated fluid restrictions.[13]

From a stability standpoint, certain components in PN admixtures may be incompatible. This most often occurs in orders where highly concentrated PN admixtures are ordered. There is a well-known physiochemical incompatibility between calcium and phosphate salts, which can react to produce dangerous insoluble products known as precipitates. Minimizing the amount of calcium or phosphate can reduce the risk of precipitation, but this is not always practical based about patient-specific needs. Numerous other factors may affect calcium and phosphorus compatibility as well, including temperature, pH of the final PN solution, selection of salt used, and final concentration of macronutrient additives. For this reason, acetate salts can be used in PN solutions, but never carbonate salts, which are known for the propensity to insolubilize calcium. When supplying calcium, the gluconate salt must be used preferentially over chloride salts, as it is least dissociated into its free form when mixed in PN solutions. Because of the multitude of factors which affect solubility, calcium phosphate limits must be evaluated with every PN formulation. Given the multiple variables that impact calcium−phosphate solubility, the use of simple equations to calculate calcium−phosphate limits which do not consider all factors should be avoided. Practitioners may instead consult published graphs or use validated software programs for specific products which provide adequate guidance when determining if the specific PN formulation is at risk for precipitation.[13,21]

In terms of effect of macronutrient concentration, PN solutions are primarily ultimately admixed in one of two different manners, due to the inherent instability of lipid emulsion. Although dextrose and protein are always admixed in the same container with one another, IVFE may need to be administered separately or have its dose adjusted to be stable in a TNA. Also known as a 3-in-1, a TNA is a PN formulation containing ILE as well as the other components of PN (carbohydrate, amino acids, vitamins, minerals, trace elements, water, and other additives) in a single container, whereas a 2-in-1 contains carbohydrates and amino acids (along with the other aforementioned components) except for lipid which is given as a physically separate infusion. In these cases, to ensure stability when using a TNA, in the absence of any manufacturer data, TNA should have a final concentration of amino acid formulations $\geq 4\%$, dextrose $\geq 10\%$, and soybean oil−based lipid emulsion $\geq 2\%$. These stability parameters may vary depending on the amino acid formulation and specific IV lipid emulsion from other oil sources. Ideally, TNAs should remain stable for up to 30 h at room temperature (25°C) or for 9 days refrigerated (5°C) followed by 24 h at room temperature. In the absence of formulation-specific emulsion stability data, it is recommended that a 2-in-1 admixture be compounded and a lipid be administered as a separate infusion.[22]

Lastly, the PN formulation must be assessed for potential incompatibilities with nonnutrient medications which have been included in the order. Nonnutrient medications must be included in PN only when supported by pharmaceutical data describing physicochemical compatibility and stability of the additive medication, as well as clinical data confirming the expected therapeutic actions of the medication. Adding medications without the above-proven data can lead to unnecessary patient risks and is generally only considered routinely safe for regular insulin and H2 receptor antagonists. Hyperglycemia is the most common complication of PN, and for this reason, regular human insulin is commonly added to PN to aid in regulation of blood glucose. Other insulin products, while commercially available, are not compatible with PN solutions, and should be avoided. For a patient requiring insulin, most practitioners target the addition of 1−2 units per 10 g dextrose to the PN formulation. As needed, this amount should be increased daily by adding 75%−100% of the prior day's sliding scale insulin to the subsequent PN formulation. The timing and frequency of blood glucose monitoring while on PN must be based on the patient's clinical status and performed in a manner appropriate for the PN infusion schedule (24 h infusion vs. cyclic PN).[14]

H2 receptor antagonists are additionally often added to the PN admixture in patients requiring GI stress ulcer prophylaxis, of which famotidine and ranitidine are most common. Both are stable in 3-in-1 admixtures of various formulations and may be added without hesitation. However, it is not uncommon for potentially incompatible medications to be ordered as part of the PN solution, the most common of which is intravenous iron. Often required for issues related to the underlying need for PN therapy, iron has been shown to destabilize lipid formulations and thus should be preferentially supplemented separately when using 3-in-1 solutions. Whenever an incompatible medication is ordered, infusion of the PN admixture will need to be interrupted so the incompatible medication can be infused. After the PN infusion is stopped, the line should be flushed with a fluid compatible with the medication such as saline or dextrose. The medication may then be infused, and after the medication has been administered, the line is flushed again with the compatible fluid before the PN infusion is resumed.[14]

Serious consequences associated with the use of PN are well-known and can generally be divided into either short-term or long-term risks. In the short term, primary PN-associated risks include those presented by the placement of a central line, infection, and RFS. First described following the Second World War, RFS is one of the most dramatic and life-threatening side effects described in PN patients. Occurring primarily in severely malnourished patients who receive aggressively high amounts of calorie and carbohydrates in their PN therapy, RFS results from hormonal and metabolic changes. These changes induce rapid onset hypophosphatemia, hypomagnesemia, and/or hypokalemia which can lead to cardiac and respiratory failure and death. Strategies to reduce the risk of developing RFS include appropriate screening to identify at risk patients, aggressive prophylactic thiamine repletion, aggressive electrolyte repletion, as well as a gradual introduction of nonprotein kcals when initiating PN in severely malnourished patients, with patients titrated to caloric goal over a minimum 5−7 days.[23,24]

In the long-term, complications have been commonly reported with the excessive provision of macronutrients and/or total calories over time. These primary long-term complications of PN include fatty liver, cholestasis, metabolic bone disease, and electrolyte/vitamin/mineral deficiency or toxicity. In the long-term PN patient, it is important to be aware of, monitor for, and attempt to address these adverse effects. Approximately 1 in 5 deaths in patients on long-term PN is due to liver failure, and excess caloric provision from either dextrose or lipid sources is thought to be the cause. With dextrose overfeeding, the excess dextrose causes hyperinsulinemia, which in turn enhances glucose conversion into fat within the liver. Because of this, recommendations for decreasing rates of TPN included liver disease include limiting dextrose to 4 g/kg/day. Although essential fatty acid deficiencies contribute to the development of hepatic complications in patients on long-term PN, it is equally important to avoid overfeeding with lipids, generally limiting such to 30% of total daily calories through supplementation of no more than 1 g/kg/day. At signs of liver dysfunction, lipids can be further reduced while ensuring no deficiencies result. Lastly, supplementation with carnitine, taurine, glutamate, and choline may also help to decrease the long-term liver effects seen with PN, as can a trial of cyclic PN, in which PN therapy is infused over periods of 8−16 h per day, rather than the standard 24 h.[25]

PN should be discontinued once the patient has been transitioned to either PO or enteral nutrition, although in some patients, such as those with short-gut syndrome, therapy will be lifelong. Generally, once oral intake has advanced to approximately 50% of estimated kcals needs, the PN formula can be weaned or discontinued. Attention to glycemic control is critical in those patients who were treated with insulin as part of their PN formulation and/or those who developed new onset hyperglycemia while on PN therapy. In clinical practice, when discontinuing PN, formulations are routinely tapered off to prevent rebound hypoglycemia. In adults, such a process is most likely unnecessary, especially if the patient is receiving carbohydrates through their oral diet. Nevertheless, this tapering can be practically accomplished by cutting the infusion rate of the PN solution by 50% over the final 1−2 h of infusion prior to turning off completely. If the infusion of an ILE being given separately from the 2-in-1 infusion needs to be discontinued, no rate reduction prior to turning off is necessary.

Prior to dispensing the final completed PN product to the patient or third-party service, the pharmacist should undertake a series of steps to ensure that both safety and quality measures are in place. The original PN order with patient-specific label and compounding formulation label should again be verified, with all patient-specific and auxiliary labels affixed to the PN container. The pharmacist should next visually inspect the PN container and contents for evidence of precipitation or lipid destabilization (cracking, creaming, oiling out of the emulsion) or physical leaks to the bag, with the PN formula remade if any of the aforementioned issues are observed. Next, the pharmacist should place the prepared PN admixture under the appropriate storage conditions (refrigeration, out of light) while on the way to delivery.[13]

CONCLUSION

PN can be a life-saving modality, but as with all medical interventions, diligent monitoring and correct administration are required to be successful. PN is a valuable and necessary medical treatment for many patients, but when used suboptimally through knowledge deficits or oversight can present a host of risks to the patient. By focusing on the core essentials of PN management from the pharmacist's perspective, this form of nutrition support can be applied successfully to optimize patient outcomes.

PRACTICE QUESTIONS

1. ISMP classified PN as
   A. Nonprescription medication
   B. Sterile preparation
   C. High-risk medication
   D. Simple solution
2. Harris—Benedict Equation is used for calculating
   A. Water requirement
   B. Energy requirement
   C. Protein requirement
   D. Vitamin A requirement
3. Peripheral PN should be preferably used
   A. For administration more than 2 weeks
   B. For preparations with osmolarity above 900 mOsm/L
   C. When central line cannot be used
   D. When dextrose concentration is less than 25%
4. Which nutrient deficient in PN shall result in lactic acidosis and death?
   A. Zinc
   B. Folate
   C. Iron
   D. Thiamine

REFERENCES

1. Mirtallo J, Canada T, Johnson D, et al. Safe practices for parenteral nutrition. *JPEN J Parenter Enteral Nutr*. 2004;28(6):S39—S70. http://www.ncbi.nlm.nih.gov/pubmed/15568296.
2. Kochevar M, Guenter P, Holcombe B, Malone A, Mirtallo J. ASPEN board of directors and task force on parenteral nutrition standardization. A.S.P.E.N. Statement on parenteral nutrition standardization. *J Parenter Enter Nutr*. 2007;31(5):441—448. https://doi.org/10.1177/0148607107031005441.
3. Bankhead R, Boullata J, Brantley S, et al. A.S.P.E.N. Enteral nutrition practice recommendations. *J Parenter Enter Nutr*. 2009;33(2):122—167. https://doi.org/10.1177/0148607108330314.
4. Ayers P, Adams S, Boullata J, et al. A.S.P.E.N. parenteral nutrition safety consensus recommendations. *J Parenter Enter Nutr*. 2014;38(3):296—333. https://doi.org/10.1177/0148607113511992.
5. Soeters PB, Reijven PLM, van Bokhorst-de van der Schueren MAE, et al. A rational approach to nutritional assessment. *Clin Nutr*. 2008;27(5):706—716. https://doi.org/10.1016/j.clnu.2008.07.009.
6. Jensen GL, Compher C, Sullivan DH, Mullin GE. Recognizing malnutrition in adults. *J Parenter Enter Nutr*. 2013;37(6):802—807. https://doi.org/10.1177/0148607113492338.
7. Choban P, Dickerson R, Malone A, Worthington P, Compher C. American Society for Parenteral and Enteral Nutrition. A.S.P.E.N. Clinical guidelines: nutrition support of hospitalized adult patients with obesity. *J Parenter Enter Nutr*. 2013;37(6):714—744. https://doi.org/10.1177/0148607113499374.

8. Blackburn GL, Bistrian BR, Maini BS, Schlamm HT, Smith MF. Nutritional and metabolic assessment of the hospitalized patient. *J Parenter Enter Nutr.* 1977;1(1):11−21. https://doi.org/10.1177/014860717700100101.

9. Ireton-Jones C, Jones JD. Improved equations for predicting energy expenditure in patients: the ireton-jones equations. *Nutr Clin Pract.* 2002;17(1):29−31. https://doi.org/10.1177/011542650201700129.

10. Mifflin MD, St Jeor ST, Hill LA, Scott BJ, Daugherty SA, Koh YO. A new predictive equation for resting energy expenditure in healthy individuals. *Am J Clin Nutr.* 1990;51(2):241−247. http://www.ncbi.nlm.nih.gov/pubmed/2305711.

11. Stucky C-CH, Moncure M, Hise M, Gossage CM, Northrop D. How accurate are resting energy expenditure prediction equations in obese trauma and burn patients? *J Parenter Enter Nutr.* 2008;32(4):420−426. https://doi.org/10.1177/0148607108319799.

12. Institute of Medicine. *Dietary Reference Intakes for Energy, Carbohydrate, Fiber, Fat, Fatty Acids, Cholesterol, Protein, and Amino Acids.* Washington, D.C: National Academies Press; 2005. https://doi.org/10.17226/10490.

13. Boullata JI, Gilbert K, Sacks G, et al. A.S.P.E.N. clinical guidelines: parenteral nutrition ordering, order review, compounding, labeling, and dispensing. *J Parenter Enter Nutr.* 2014;38(3):334−377. https://doi.org/10.1177/0148607114521833.

14. Boullata JI, Barber JR. A perspective on drug-nutrient interactions. In: *Handbook of Drug-nutrient Interactions.* Totowa, NJ: Humana Press; 2004:3−25. https://doi.org/10.1007/978-1-59259-781-9_1.

15. Marsen TA, Beer J, Mann H. German IDPN-Trial group. Intradialytic parenteral nutrition in maintenance hemodialysis patients suffering from protein-energy wasting. Results of a multicenter, open, prospective, randomized trial. *Clin Nutr.* 2017;36(1):107−117. https://doi.org/10.1016/j.clnu.2015.11.016.

16. Silva M, Gomes S, Peixoto A, et al. Nutrition in chronic liver disease. *GE Port J Gastroenterol.* 2015;22(6):268−276. https://doi.org/10.1016/j.jpge.2015.06.004.

17. Gosmanov AR, Umpierrez GE. Management of hyperglycemia during enteral and parenteral nutrition therapy. *Curr Diab Rep.* 2013;13(1):155−162. https://doi.org/10.1007/s11892-012-0335-y.

18. Driscoll DF. Pharmaceutical and clinical aspects of lipid injectable emulsions. *J Parenter Enter Nutr.* 2017;41(1):125−134. https://doi.org/10.1177/0148607116673187.

19. Sriram K, Lonchyna VA. Micronutrient supplementation in adult nutrition therapy: practical considerations. *J Parenter Enter Nutr.* 2009;33(5):548−562. https://doi.org/10.1177/0148607108328470.

20. Buchman AL, Howard LJ, Guenter P, Nishikawa RA, Compher CW, Tappenden KA. Micronutrients in parenteral nutrition: too little or too much? The past, present, and recommendations for the future. *Gastroenterology.* 2009;137(5):S1−S6. https://doi.org/10.1053/j.gastro.2009.09.001.

21. Allwood MC, Kearney MC. Compatibility and stability of additives in parenteral nutrition admixtures. *Nutrition.* 1998;14(9):697−706. http://www.ncbi.nlm.nih.gov/pubmed/9760591.

22. Barat AC, Harrie K, Jacob M, Diamantidis TG, Mcintosh NL. Effect of amino acid solutions on total nutrient admixture stability. *J Parenter Enter Nutr.* 1987;11(4):384−388. https://doi.org/10.1177/0148607187011004384.

23. Mehanna HM, Moledina J, Travis J. Refeeding syndrome: what it is, and how to prevent and treat it. *BMJ.* 2008;336(7659):1495−1498. https://doi.org/10.1136/bmj.a301.

24. Walmsley RS. Refeeding syndrome: screening, incidence, and treatment during parenteral nutrition. *J Gastroenterol Hepatol.* 2013;28:113−117. https://doi.org/10.1111/jgh.12345.

25. Dibb M, Teubner A, Theis V, Shaffer J, Lal S. The management of long-term parenteral nutrition. *Aliment Pharmacol Ther.* 2013;37(6):587−603. https://doi.org/10.1111/apt.12209.

ANSWERS TO PRACTICE QUESTIONS

1. C
2. B
3. C
4. D

Section VIII

Conclusion

Chapter 33

Advanced Clinical Pharmacy Practitioner

Erick Sokn[1], Sam Calabrese[1], Douglas Scheckelhoff[2], Dixon Thomas[3] and Jason A. Roberts[4,5]

[1]Cleveland Clinic, Cleveland, OH, United States; [2]American Society of Health-System Pharmacists, Bethesda, MD, United States; [3]Gulf Medical University, Ajman, United Arab Emirates; [4]The University of Queensland, Brisbane St Lucia, QLD, Australia; [5]Royal Brisbane and Women's Hospital, Herston QLD, Australia

Learning Objectives:

Objective 33.1 Review the impact of pharmacist-provided interventions.
Objective 33.2 Overview innovative pharmacy practice models.
Objective 33.3 Explain the development of competencies in pharmacy workforce leadership.
Objective 33.4 Detail continuing education needs of pharmacists.

OBJECTIVE 33.1. REVIEW THE OUTCOMES OF PHARMACIST-PROVIDED INTERVENTIONS

Pharmacists are versatile members of the healthcare team. Residency training is becoming a common method for pharmacists to advance their skills and knowledge following pharmacy school,[1] allowing pharmacists to be increasingly involved throughout the medication use process. This trend continues from a long history of improving patient care. In one of the most widely cited reviews of pharmacist impact on patient care, the 2011 Report to the US Surgeon General described published studies noting pharmacist services having a positive impact on healthcare access, reduction of healthcare disparities, and improved outcomes with diabetes, hypertension, dyslipidemia, congestive heart failure, and cost-effectiveness of medication use.[2] These benefits and many others have been described in all pharmacy practice areas. An initiative that led to 80% of nursing homes in Singapore choosing to benefit from pharmaceutical care was jointly awarded the 2018 Pharmacy Practice Improvement Award by the International Pharmaceutical Federation (FIP). The award, given to the Pharmaceutical Society of Singapore (PSS), was shared with the American Pharmacists Association (APhA) for a model of care that maximizes the opportunity for pharmacists to contribute to vaccine coverage.[37]

Inpatient Practice

Pharmacists practicing in hospitals are commonly involved in medication dispensing, medication reconciliation, medication order review, monitoring, dosing, and patient counseling (Fig. 33.1).[3] Pharmacists are consistent members of medical rounding teams, where therapeutic decisions are discussed and implemented. Participation on rounding teams has been shown to decrease adverse drug events, with the potential to reduce hospital length of stay.[3–5] Through medication dosing and order verification practices, pharmacists improve both international normalised ratio (INR) control with warfarin therapy and dosing of vancomycin and aminoglycosides.[3] Pharmacist involvement in antimicrobial stewardship programs aims to improve antibiotic selection, dosing, and duration of therapy, reduce the emergence of antibiotic resistance, and decrease costs associated with antimicrobial use.[6] Medication reconciliation and discharge counseling

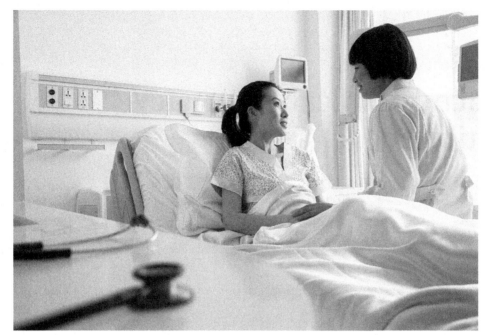

FIGURE 33.1 Patient counseling at bedside.

have been shown to decrease the risk of hospital readmission within 30 days of discharge.[7–9] In some cases, pharmacy services have even been associated with decreased hospital mortality rates.[10]

Ambulatory Practice

Patients spend the majority of their time in ambulatory clinic practice settings. Pharmacists in these settings, like their counterparts in inpatient practices, can work closely with the medical team to devise and adjust short- and long-term therapy plans for a wide range of conditions. By managing medication dosing and monitoring, pharmacists have improved hypertension and diabetes control, improving the quality of life for patients.[11–17] In many cases, pharmacist interventions leading to improved quality also lead to decreased overall costs of care.[11,15,16] Pharmacists are also commonly involved in medication adherence initiatives, utilizing motivational interviewing and other techniques to improve patients' abilities to use prescribed medications effectively.[16] Additionally, pharmacists have successfully decreased the unnecessary use of medications, especially in elderly patients.[17] With demonstrated benefits in a wide variety of clinical conditions, pharmacists have numerous opportunities to improve care in ambulatory settings.

Community Pharmacy Practice

Community pharmacy practice comprises the majority of licensed pharmacists, wherein pharmacists review the appropriateness of prescribed medications as part of the dispensing process for ambulatory patients. Also, various other cognitive clinical services can be performed that can be funded by the patient, health insurance, or government, depending on the country. Given their availability, many surveys of patient and physician perceptions of pharmacist roles and impact are driven by services provided by community pharmacists. Clinical interventions in community practice settings often focus on comprehensive medication use reviews and patient counseling to decrease poly-pharmacy, improve dosing, and improve patient adherence. These programs are collectively referred to as Medication Management Services, officially recognized in the United States by the Centers for Medicare and Medicaid Services as a reimbursable pharmacist-provided service in community pharmacies. Similar recognition is provided in other countries. Medication therapy management programs, which may include pharmacist prescribing, identify drug therapy problems (such as needing additional medication therapy to treat an established condition) leading to improved disease control, and cost savings for health systems.[18]

OBJECTIVE 33.2. OVERVIEW INNOVATIVE SPECIALTY PHARMACY PRACTICE MODELS

With successful demonstration of improved patient care outcomes, pharmacists are a valuable resource for health systems. In the United States, a pharmacist's scope of practice (what they are legally allowed to do as a licensed pharmacist) is determined by each state. As such, how a pharmacist interacts with patients and medical teams, including the degree of autonomy granted, may differ by practice location. Related to a pharmacist's scope of practice is the ability to receive payment for some types of nondispensing pharmacy services, based in some cases on whether the pharmacist is deemed a healthcare provider and thus has "provider status" and is allowed to submit for reimbursement of services provided.

Prescriptive Authority

As described previously, pharmacists have been shown to improve patient care quality. As their interventions rely on the knowledgeable use of medications, prescriptive authority is a natural progression for pharmacists with advanced training or demonstration of appropriate skills and knowledge. Many types of prescriptive authority exist for pharmacists.[19]

Policy- or protocol-driven prescribing allows a limited amount of action by the pharmacist based on previously approved clinical decisions. Examples include formulary interchanges in a hospital or initial response to elevated INR in patients receiving warfarin. Decisions are mapped out in detail, and pharmacists assess clinical situations to determine which plan to implement.

A broader application of clinical knowledge is used in collaborative practice, wherein a written agreement outlines criteria for patients the pharmacist may address, responsibilities of the pharmacist, training requirements for the pharmacist, and broad guidelines to ensure consistent care.[20] Under collaborative practice agreements, more flexibility is afforded to pharmacists in determining appropriate actions than is typically seen in protocol-driven prescribing. In the United States, nearly all states allow collaborative practice agreements.[21]

In both protocols and collaborative practice examples, pharmacist prescribing is tied to an agreement with a group of physicians (dependent prescribing). Independent prescribing, as is available in some healthcare systems such as the United Kingdom, does not require prior agreements with physicians to permit assessment and treatment.[22] Independent prescribing is also available to some US practices, such as inpatient services achieved through privileging.[23] As the Centers for Medicare and Medicaid Services defined "medical staff" to apply to pharmacists at the discretion of each hospital, it created an opportunity to apply medical staff bylaws in defining pharmacists' scope of practice and thereby "privilege" a pharmacist to prescribe in some cases. Through privileging, the hospital can review the credentials of nonphysician clinicians and permit independent action within the scope of practice outlined by the state.[23] Regardless of the method used, prescriptive authority is critical for pharmacists to exercise their clinical expertise to deliver care efficiently.

Pharmacist Providers

Although prescriptive authority provides the ability for pharmacists to practice at a high level, establishing pharmacy services requires some type of financial benefit to offset the salary of the pharmacist (through reimbursement in fee-for-service models or improved clinical outcomes in outcome-driven payment models). Without recognizing pharmacists as care providers, many healthcare institutions may struggle to recognize and support pharmacist roles, opting instead to utilize physicians, nurse practitioners, or physician assistants to meet patient needs easily addressed by pharmacists. Achievement of provider status in the United States is recognized by many pharmacy leaders as a high priority for the profession given its significant impact in supporting advanced pharmacist roles.[24]

OBJECTIVE 33.3. EXPLAIN THE DEVELOPMENT OF COMPETENCIES IN PHARMACY WORKFORCE LEADERSHIP

Evolution of the role of pharmacists and pharmacy technicians continues in nearly all parts of the world. In most settings, there is a shift away from pharmacist involvement in traditional compounding, preparation, and dispensing roles toward practicing as clinical pharmacists in patient care roles, usually as part of the healthcare team. The primary difference between one country and another is the status of this transition. Some countries are well along the pathway and have a significant portion of pharmacist time spent in a clinical role providing patient care, while others might be far more restrictive, just beginning this transition.

The reason for the shift is similar regardless of location: traditional preparation and dispensing roles are replaced by automation and technology and the availability of commercial products, plus the growing role of support personnel such as pharmacy technicians. There is also significant supporting evidence of the value that pharmacists bring as clinical pharmacists in these new roles, improving patient outcomes, safety, and lowering cost. In most US hospitals, in addition to monitoring drug therapy in patients, clinical pharmacists also have total responsibility for managing certain medications. In these cases, the pharmacist is responsible for and has the authority to select and order the initial dosage of medication, order necessary laboratory tests associated with the medication, and then to adjust the dosage and frequency of the medication based on the laboratory results. Examples of medications where this commonly occurs are vancomycin, aminoglycoside antibiotics, and other medications that require dosage adjustment based on the renal status of the patient. In ambulatory clinics, pharmacists perform similar roles, working more independently and receiving patient referrals from physicians. Examples of where pharmacists manage patients in this setting include anticoagulation clinics (managing warfarin therapy) and medication therapy management clinics.

These changes have a profound impact on undergraduate and postgraduate pharmacist training and how they maintain their competence once in practice. Pharmacy education has shifted in many locations toward a much more clinically focused curriculum, with less emphasis on preparations, compounding, and manufacturing. There has also been more focus on graduate training, such as pharmacy residencies, and demonstrating competence through board certification.

Influential pharmacy leaders spearhead changes in pharmacy practice and training needs. Leadership can be described in many ways. To some, it is focused on providing a compelling vision for pharmacy services that others may aspire to achieve and influencing others to achieve set goals.[25] For others, leadership focuses on demonstrating advanced skills and the impact that inspire others to advance their knowledge and skills. However it is defined, some leadership qualities stand out as critical for all pharmacists, not just those in formal management positions. The American Society of Health-System Pharmacists, for example, believes that leadership in assuring safe and effective medication use is a professional obligation for all pharmacists.[26] Indeed, the changing landscape of healthcare requires individuals capable of identifying new opportunities, ensuring pharmacists are trained and available to meet the opportunities, and that healthcare partners recognize the role pharmacists can play in advancing patient care. There are several leadership qualities, particularly useful for successful pharmacy leaders.

Vision

For many pharmacists, practice is about helping improve the health conditions for patients. For the effective advancement of these goals, a clear and defined purpose that can unify diverse pharmacists' interests in a common direction is essential. To be effective, the vision must be compelling and resonate with the pharmacists' core personal values.[27] It must provide a view of pharmacy practice that encourages continual growth and advancement of pharmacist skills and must be reflected in the daily actions of pharmacists and leaders throughout the organization. Although vision statements are often looked at as management tools, any pharmacist, with or without a formal leadership position, can be the source of a compelling vision if he or she identifies the motivation for pharmacy practice and strives each day to act in a way consistent with that motivation.

Communication Skills and Relationship Building

Advanced communication skills, both written and verbal, are often considered essential skills for pharmacy managers. Having a compelling vision is only effective if that vision can be effectively shared with others to foster alignment of purpose. Furthermore, given the role of pharmacists as part of the healthcare team, effective communication of ideas, concerns, and suggestions to other team members (such as physicians and nurses) is critical for establishing effective clinical practices. In practice, communication skills are needed when making recommendations on rounds, when counseling patients on the use of a new medication, when sharing the results of pivotal research with colleagues, when proposing a new pharmacist-run service to senior leaders, and when teaching students and residents how to improve clinical reasoning. For communication to be effective, pharmacists need to build strong relationships up and down the leadership structure, and across our care teams.[28] The relationships that are built with members of a team will have an impact on credibility, integrity, and overall value of the team. At all levels, formal and informal, pharmacists must develop effective relationships in conjunction with excellent verbal and written communication skills not only to perform core functions but also to provide leadership in medication use within the medical team.

Emotional Intelligence

Emotional intelligence consists of capabilities in self-awareness (how we feel and our feelings' impact on our surroundings), self-management (how we respond to our feelings), social awareness (how we respond to others' emotions), and social skill (how we combine our awareness of others to develop their skills and influence their actions).[29] To lead others, we must first understand ourselves and be conscious of our reactions and the way others perceive us. In healthcare, work is understandably emotional—either in helping others cope with a new diagnosis and identify a care plan or in addressing the stress of complex and challenging decisions made by the healthcare team. As a result, all pharmacists benefit from developing emotional intelligence. In practice, emotional intelligence supports leadership by allowing pharmacists to recognize and empathize with motivators for patients and coworkers. Through that empathy, pharmacists can build on common goals and influence others.

Challenge the Status Quo/Change Management

In pharmacy practice advancement, a team that has become accustomed to the day-to-day work can become blind to new opportunities. For pharmacists, the ability to challenge the status quo by seeking to understand the reasons behind the team's processes is key to effective leadership. As healthcare priorities shift, a need to critically evaluate why services are or are not employed affords the greatest opportunity to adapt to new patient care needs. Revisiting old ideas and questioning current practices, when done to assess applicability to current needs, can be an effective way to identify improvement opportunities. When opportunities are identified, managing the change appropriately for a team is a key component of successful leadership. The ability to convey a change and the reasons for the change to a team is part of this navigation, as well as assisting individuals through letting go of the old and embracing the new. John Kotter outlines the eight steps required for change management in his article "Leading Change: Why Transformational Efforts Fail."[30] In this article, he describes the important steps a leader must take to ensure successful change.

Resilience

Resilience is a necessary leadership skill in multiple ways. For starters, workload in healthcare is often perceived to be increasing—the expectation to do more with less is prevalent as a means to address declining reimbursement relative to costs in the United States. Resilience in some cases is a matter of addressing physical, emotional, and spiritual energy so that pharmacists can address the demands and stresses of the job.[31] Resilience is extremely important in a fast-paced emotional environment to ensure appropriate performance. Stephen Covey addresses this in his classic book "The 7 Habits of Highly Effective People." His seventh habit describes the need to Sharpen the Saw, or take time to focus on oneself to reenergize for the complex work environment.[32] For leaders, resilience also means accepting setbacks, such as denials for new service opportunities, and quickly pivoting to new or remaining opportunities. The ability of pharmacists to maintain focus during busy days and quickly move on from setbacks allows greater flexibility and thus greater success in identifying effective ways to improve patient care.

OBJECTIVE 33.4. DETAIL CONTINUING EDUCATION NEEDS OF PHARMACISTS

Most countries and jurisdictions have a regulatory framework for licensing pharmacists, usually after completing the required training and passing a licensure examination. Many also recognize the importance of the pharmacist maintaining their skills and keeping current with new information over their 40 or more year career. Usually, this comes in the form of a minimum requirement for continuing education to keep and maintain a pharmacist license. It is common that the minimum requirement will be stated as the number of education hours one must receive each year, usually leaving the selection of specific topics, format, and other details to the pharmacist. Although this method may ensure that the pharmacist receives additional education on a regular basis, it has many shortcomings because usually a passive process (listening to a lecture) does not require that the pharmacist demonstrate competence or proficiency after attending the program. Also, there is nothing to prevent the pharmacist from choosing to attend educational programs that may not be related to their professional practice, which defeats the intended purpose and does not help in maintaining competence.

Some locations rely on a different model for continuing education known as Continuing Professional Development or CPD. CPD is a model where the pharmacist performs an ongoing self-assessment and identifies their areas of proficiency and where they have knowledge gaps based on what they do in day-to-day practice. The pharmacist then chooses educational programs that are targeted at closing educational gaps, and then the CPD process starts all over again. If performed correctly, this more individualized process should result in the desired outcome of improving and maintaining the pharmacist's ongoing competence to practice as a pharmacist.

Regardless of the process and what is legally required, pharmacists should strive to take advantage of the many educational opportunities now available in various formats. It is a fundamental responsibility of being a professional.

Certificate Programs

Certificate programs are another form of continuing education or skill development that usually involves completion of a course or series of courses with a specific focus. The length of certificate programs varies, depending on the area of focus, but is typically at least 15 h of instruction and can be 80 h or more. They are notably different from professional, undergraduate, or postgraduate degree programs because of their limited focus and shorter duration. Certificate programs can be conducted live or online and may or may not involve completion of an examination or project to demonstrate a mastery of skills through the program. Examples of certificate programs in pharmacy include immunization, sterile compounding, antimicrobial stewardship, medication therapy management, pharmacy informatics, medication safety, and others.[33] It is important to distinguish a certificate program from certification.

Certification

Certification demonstrates expertise in pharmacy practice specialties and requires successful completion of an extensive examination validated as a measure of knowledge in an area of practice. Certification also requires having a pharmacy degree and meeting the minimum number of years of practice. Most practice areas available for board certification are clinical specialties, but other nonclinical areas are also developing. There is usually specific continuing education required to maintain certification once it is achieved. In the United States, the Board of Pharmacy Specialties (BPS) is the primary organization providing certification for pharmacists, and more than 20,000 individuals are certified worldwide by BPS in eight specialties. The specialty areas kept increasing. Examples of specialties available in 2018 include ambulatory care pharmacy, cardiology pharmacy, critical care pharmacy, geriatric pharmacy, infectious diseases pharmacy, nuclear pharmacy, nutrition support pharmacy, oncology pharmacy, pediatric pharmacy, pharmacotherapy and psychiatric pharmacy.[34] Many organizations provide review courses to help prepare pharmacists for the certification exam and may also provide approved continuing education to maintain certification.

Residency Training

Pharmacy residency training builds on PharmD education and outcomes to contribute to the development of clinical pharmacists responsible for the medication-related care of patients with a wide range of conditions. The program is available for graduate pharmacists and begins with a general pharmacy practice residency that lasts at least 12 months and is referred to as a Post Graduate Year 1 (PGY1) residency. After the PGY1 residency, the individual may choose to pursue specialty training with an additional year or more in a specialty area, and this is known as a Post Graduate Year 2 residency.[35]

It should be noted that residency-training programs are postgraduate programs and are different from experiential training associated with most pharmacy curricula, such as Advanced Pharmacy Practice Experiences or APPEs. The APPEs usually involve rotations, but as a student who is not yet graduated and is not licensed to practice, their role in providing patient care will be more limited, and they will not be able to practice independently.

Residency programs are designed to meet standards, demonstrating best practices for resident training and provision of pharmacy services. The American Society of Health-System Pharmacists (ASHP) provides accreditation of programs in the United States and around the world that evaluates the residency program and pharmacy services against an established residency standard. In 2018, there are more than 2000 programs that are accredited by ASHP, mostly in the United States, but there is a growing number of other countries. Many consider residency training to be a critical component in advancing the practice, demonstrating a high level of pharmacy services, and in training clinical pharmacists for future practice.[36]

CONCLUSION

The pharmacy profession and pharmacists have advanced to deliver specialized patient care services. These successful healthcare service models advance the profession. The pharmacy workforce needs to demonstrate leadership along with other professional competencies to positively influence patient care. Continuing education, certification and residency, and other higher education are methods to advance professional practice.

REFERENCES

1. *ASHP Match Statistics*; 2017. https://natmatch.com/ashprmp/stats.html.
2. Giberson S, Yoder S, Lee MP. *Improving Patient and Health System Outcomes through Advanced Pharmacy Practice: A Report to the U.S. Surgeon General*. Office of the Chief Pharmacist. U.S. Public Health Service; December 2011.
3. Kaboli P, Hoth A, McClimon B, et al. Clinical pharmacists and inpatient medical care: a systematic review. *Arch Intern Med*. 2006;166:955−964.
4. Leape LL, Cullen DJ, Clapp MD, et al. Pharmacist participation on physician rounds and adverse drug events in the intensive care unit. *JAMA*. 1999;282:267−270.
5. Bjornson DC, Hiner WO, Potyk RP, et al. Effect of pharmacists on health care outcomes in hospitalized patients. *Am J Hosp Pharm*. 1993;50:1875−1884.
6. Goff D. Antimicrobial stewardship: bridging the gap between quality care and cost. *Curr Opin Infect Dis*. 2011;24(Suppl. 1):S11−S20.
7. Warden BA, Freels JP, Furuno JP, et al. Pharmacy-managed program for providing education and discharge instructions for patients with heart failure. *Am J Health Syst Pharm*. 2013;71:134−139.
8. Pal A, Babbott S, Wilkinson ST. Can the targeted use of a discharge pharmacist significantly decrease 30-day readmissions? *Hosp Pharm*. 2013;48(5):380−388.
9. Dedhia P, Kravet S, et al. A quality improvement intervention to facilitate the transition of older adults from three hospitals back to their homes. *J Am Geriatr Soc*. 2009;57(9):1540−1546.
10. Leguelinel-Blache G, Nguyen T-L, Louart B, et al. Impact of quality bundle enforcement by a critical care pharmacist on patient outcome and costs. *Crit Care Med*. November 2017. https://doi.org/10.1097/CCM.0000000000002827.
11. Beney J, Bero L, Bond CM. Expanding the roles of outpatient pharmacists: effects on health services utilization, costs, and patient outcomes (review). *Cochrane Database Syst Rev*. 2009;1:1−40.
12. Bunting BA, Smith BH, Sutherland SE. The Asheville Project: clinical and economic outcomes of a community-based long-term medication therapy management program for hypertension and dyslipidemia. *J Am Pharm Assoc*. 2003;48(1):23−31.
13. Bunting BA, Cranor CW. The Asheville Project: long-term clinical, humanistic, and economic outcomes of a community-based medication therapy management program for asthma. *J Am Pharm Assoc*. 2006;46(2):133−147.
14. Cranor CW, Bunting BA, Christensen DB. The Asheville Project: long-term clinical and economic outcomes of a community pharmacy diabetes care program. *J Am Pharm Assoc*. 2003;43(2):173−184.
15. Scott DM, Boyd ST, Stephen M, et al. Outcomes of pharmacist-managed diabetes care services in a community health center. *Am J Health Syst Pharm*. 2006;63:2116−2122.
16. Altavela JL, Jones MK, Ritter M. A prospective trial of a clinical pharmacy intervention in a primary care practice in a capitated payment system. *J Manag Care Pharm*. 2008;14(9):831−843.
17. Ramalho de Oliveira D, Brummel AR, Miller DB. Medication therapy management: 10 years of experience in a large integrated health care system. *J Manag Care Pharm*. 2010;16(3):185−195.
18. Trapskin K, Johnson C, Cory P, et al. Forging a novel provider and payer partnership in Wisconsin to compensate pharmacists for quality-driven pharmacy and medication therapy management services. *J Am Pharm Assoc*. 2009;49:642−651.
19. Emmerton L, Marriott J, Bessell T, Nissen L, Dean L. Pharmacists and prescribing rights: review of international developments. *J Pharm Pharmaceut Sci*. 2005;8(2):217−225.
20. Academy of Managed Care Pharmacy. *Practice Advisory on Collaborative Drug Therapy Management*; 2017. Available at: http://www.amcp.org/WorkArea/DownloadAsset.aspx?id=14710.
21. Murawski M, Villa KR, Dole EJ, et al. Advanced-practice pharmacists: practice characteristics and reimbursement of pharmacists certified for collaborative clinical practice in New Mexico and North Carolina. *Am J Health Syst Pharm*. 2011;68:2341−2350.
22. Tonna AP, Stewart D, West B, et al. Pharmacist prescribing in the UK − a literature review of current practice and research. *J Clin Pharm and Ther*. 2007;32:545−556.
23. Jordan T, Hennenfent J, Lewin JJ, et al. Elevating pharmacists' scope of practice through a health-system clinical privileging process. *Am J Health Syst Pharm*. 2016;73:1395−1405.
24. American Pharmacists Association. *Provider Status: What Pharmacists Need to Know Now*; 2013. http://www.pharmacist.com/provider-status-what-pharmacists-need-know-now.

25. Nahata MC. Balancing leadership and management. *Am J Pharm Educ.* 2001;65:295–296.

26. American Society of Health-System Pharmacists. *ASHP Statement on Leadership as a Professional Obligation*; 2017. https://www.ashp.org/-/media/assets/policy-guidelines/docs/statements-leadership-as-professional-obligation.ashx?la=en.

27. Woodward B. The journey to professional excellence: a matter of priorities. *Am J Health Syst Pharm.* 1998;55:782–789.

28. Eschenbacher L. *Pharmacy Clinical Coordinator's Handbook.* Bethesda, MD: American Society of Health-System Pharmacists; 2016.

29. Goleman D. Leadership that gets results. *Harv Bus Rev.* 2000:78–90.

30. Kotter JP. Leading change: why transformation efforts fail. *Harv Bus Rev.* January 2007:85.

31. Schwartz T, McCarthy C. Manage your energy, not your time. *Harv Bus Rev.* October 2007. https://hbr.org/2007/10/manage-your-energy-not-your-time.

32. Covey S. *The Seven Habits of Highly Effective People.* New York: Simon and Schuster; 1989.

33. American Society of Health-System Pharmacists. *Professional Certificate Programs*; 2017. https://www.ashp.org/Professional-Development/Professional-Certificate-Programs.

34. Board of Pharmacy Specialties. *About BPS*; 2017. https://www.bpsweb.org/about-bps/.

35. American College of Clinical Pharmacy. *What Is a Residency and How Do I Get One?* ACCP; 2017. https://www.accp.com/stunet/compass/residency.aspx.

36. American Society of Health-System Pharmacists. *How to Start a Residency Program*; 2017. https://www.ashp.org/-/media/assets/professional-development/residencies/docs/how-to-start-residency-what-you-really-need-to-know.ashx?la=en.

37. FIP, Press Release. *Singaporean nursing home service, US vaccine care model and Belgian "family pharmacist" concept win global pharmacy practice improvement and health campaign awards.* Glasgow; September 4, 2018.

Appendix I

Case Studies With Pharmacist Interventions

Asawari Raut[1], Saba Naeem[2], Siby Joseph[3] and Seeba Zachariah[2]

[1]Bharati Vidyapeeth, Pune, India; [2]Gulf Medical University, Ajman, United Arab Emirates; [3]St. Joseph's College of Pharmacy, Cherthala, India

CASE 1: DRUG-INDUCED ELECTROLYTE DISTURBANCES

A 42-year-old male came to the hospital with complaints of fever, excessive weakness, and giddiness. He was a known case of IgA mesangioproliferative nephropathy (for 3 years). His hemoglobin was 8 g/dL (normal: 12—16 g/dL), total leukocyte count was 2800 million cells/cmm (normal: 4000—10,000 million cells/cmm), red blood cells were 2.79 million/cmm (normal: 4.7—6.1 million cells/cmm), and platelet count was 2,89,000/cmm (normal: 3.5—4.5 million cells/cmm). Serum electrolytes analysis revealed that he had hyponatremia (serum sodium: 118 mEq/L, normal 135—145 mEq/L) and hypokalemia (serum potassium: 2.9 mEq/L, normal: 3.5—5.5 mEq/L). He was admitted for febrile neutropenia along with pancytopenia and electrolyte abnormalities.

Medical history revealed that, 3 years ago, he was diagnosed with nephropathy and was prescribed tablet torsemide 20 mg/day. On suspecting poor prognosis (increased peripheral edema, giddiness, elevated serum creatinine), the dose of torsemide was increased to 40 mg/day and tablet metolazone 5 mg/day was added to his therapy. Two months before hospitalization, tablet azathioprine 100 mg/day was started for immunosuppressive action against the autoimmune type of renal nephropathy.

On admission to the hospital, febrile neutropenia, pancytopenia, and electrolyte abnormalities were managed with IV fluids and blood transfusion. Diuretics and azathioprine were stopped. Electrolyte correction was done successfully, and the patient was discharged on low dose torsemide 10 mg/day. He was asked to come for a follow-up after 7 days with electrolyte and blood count reports. The patient's blood counts resolved within 3 weeks and are maintained on torsemide 40 mg/day with constant electrolyte monitoring.

How Is the Relationship Between the Suspected Drug and the Reported Reactions Established?

For systematic adverse drug reaction (ADR) assessment, a stepwise collection of information is necessary. The information collected can be compiled and assessed using the standard scales.

Information obtained from the patient: A detailed review of the patient's demographic details of complaints, medication history, social history, allergies, and use of over-the-counter (OTC) medications would help in ADR assessment. Medication review can be conducted for assessing the appropriateness of dose and regimen. The patient interview can help to assess adherence to the therapy. For a better assessment, medication adherence scales can be used. Azathioprine can cause hematological disturbances.[1] There is a high possibility that pancytopenia was associated with azathioprine.

Evidence: A literature search reveals that around 5% of the population on azathioprine may have myelosuppressive adverse effects.[3,4] However, the onset of pancytopenia with azathioprine may vary with duration of treatment. It may show an onset within 2–11 weeks of therapy or as prolonged as 2–3 years of treatment. In this patient, there is no other possible drug/disease condition that may lead to pancytopenia. The blood counts showed a gradual increase on dechallenge of azathioprine, suggesting that pancytopenia was a drug-induced effect.

Correlating the observed findings with patient data: Electrolyte disturbances are a well-known side effect of diuretics.[2] The patient was on a combination of two diuretics for 2 years (it was not clear from the patient history when the second diuretic was added to the first), and such prolonged diuresis can probably be associated with electrolyte disturbances. However, his coexisting renal impairment may also lead to electrolyte disturbances.

Electrolyte disturbances are common with metolazone. Excessive diuresis leads to loss of electrolytes from the body. In this patient, the additive effect of two diuretics can be related to hyponatremia and hypokalemia. Withdrawal of diuretics along with administration of IV fluids helped to correct his sodium and potassium levels.

How Are the Causality and Severity of the ADR Determined?

Standard causality assessment scales can be used to assess the causal relationship between the suspected drug and the reported reaction. In this case, the World Health Organization (WHO) causality assessment scale was used to assess the causality and Hartwig scale was used to assess the severity. Pancytopenia is "Probable" ADR due to azathioprine. Hyponatremia and hypokalemia are "Probable/Likely" ADRs due to metolazone and torsemide, because rechallenge data are lacking and the time relationship is not clear.

What Type of Adverse Drug Reaction Is It Likely to Be (Type A or Type B)?

Acute pancytopenia can be due to myeolosuppression by azathioprine. Eexcessive diuresis and subsequent electrolyte disturbances are directly related to the dose of diuretics. So, pancytopenia, hyponatremia, and hypokalemia are "type A" adverse drug reactions.[5]

What Follow-Up Actions Need to Be Taken in This Case?

Rechallenge with azathioprine may be fatal and should be avoided in such cases. The physician's clinical judgment plays an important role in the tailoring of diuretic doses. A follow-up of blood counts and serum electrolytes should be done. As the patient is still suffering from an autoimmune nephropathy, corticosteroids can be added instead of azathioprine as an alternative.[6]

Patient education: The patient should be made aware of the ADRs associated with his therapy. Benefits of regular monitoring of the blood counts and electrolytes need to be emphasized. He should be informed that during immunosuppressive therapy, even a mild infection should be reported to the concerned physician, as it may be an early sign of blood count abnormalities. This would prevent similar reactions to the same/similar drug in future.

Education of healthcare professional: Effective patient counseling and regular monitoring of parameters, which may be affected due to drugs, can help to improve the quality of patient care.

CASE 2: ANTIPSYCHOTIC DRUG-INDUCED METABOLIC ENCEPHALOPATHY

A 43-year-old male was hospitalized for metabolic encephalopathy and one episode of seizure. He was a known case of schizophrenia for 2 years, for which he was taking olanzapine 2 mg/day, a fixed-dose combination of trihexyphenidyl 2.5 mg/trifluoperazine 2.5 mg once daily, and procyclidine 2.5 mg/day. When admitted, he was excessively agitated and had dry skin, dry mucosal membranes, and intermittent high fever spikes. He was found to be disoriented to time/place and people, and his blood pressure was constantly elevated >140/90 mmHg.

All the antipsychotics were stopped on admission, and he was treated symptomatically for metabolic encephalopathy. On the fourth day of hospitalization, the patient was reinitiated with all the previously mentioned antipsychotics. On readministration, there were two episodes of fever spikes and elevated blood pressure (150/110 mm/Hg). The patient was found to be aggressive and irritated. The psychiatrist advised to stop procyclidine, and the patient was observed for 2 days, wherein he did not have any mood disturbances and was vitally stable.

Could These Signs and Symptoms Be ADRs? How Can They Be Assessed?

Correlation of patient information: Collection of relevant patient information is the key step in ADR detection. Demographic details and medical and medication history play an important role. Assessment of adherence to antipsychotic therapy may help to find medication errors. The information obtained should be critically assessed to establish the association of reactions with suspected drugs. This patient's adherence to antipsychotic medication can be assessed using the 8-item Morisky medication adherence scale (MMAS-8).[7] The brief psychiatric rating scale (BPRS-E), which is an expanded version, can be used to assess psychiatric symptoms.[7]

The patient was taking procyclidine, trihexyphenidyl/trifluoperazine, and olanzapine for 2 years. This suggests prolonged exposure to the drugs. Olanzapine is an atypical antipsychotic.[8] Atypical antipsychotics have a benefit of reduced risk of causing extrapyramidal symptoms and tardive dyskinesia in comparison to conventional antipsychotics.[9] However, they may cause anticholinergic side effects.[9] The symptoms of dry mucosal membranes, hyperthermia, irritation, and drowsiness are suggestive of anticholinergic effects. Procyclidine and trihexyphenidyl are drugs used in parkinsonism with moderate to strong anticholinergic effects.[10] The combination of these drugs can lead to additive anticholinergic toxicity.[10] Thus, the observed findings could be related to procyclidine and trihexyphenidyl.

However, hyperthermia and dehydration can be associated with dryness of mouth and skin. In addition, irritation, agitated behavior, disorientation, and elevated blood pressure could be associated with the patient's clinical condition. Thus, the patient's condition could be pathological and drug induced. Systematic ADR assessment is required in such cases.

The highlight of this case is the onset of fever, mood disturbances, and elevated blood pressure on reinitiation of the antipsychotics. This can be considered as a rechallenge that showed a positive response, but the effects may not be completely drug induced. However, they may have a role in potentiating the observed effects.

Evidence: Procyclidine is an anticholinergic drug. In addition, 30%−50% of the patients taking trihexyphenidyl, an antiparkinsonian drug, experience anticholinergic effects.[11] Thus, these drugs can have additive anticholinergic side effects such as dry mucosal membranes, agitated behavior, and drowsiness. A systematic adverse drug assessment with coherent clinical assessment is required in such cases. The WHO causality assessment scale was used in this case, and it was found that procyclidine and trihexyphenidyl were possibly associated with the reactions.

What Follow-Up Actions Need to Be Considered in This Case?

Patient education: In psychiatric conditions, it is always better to counsel the patient's caretakers about drug therapy, side effects, and monitoring parameters. A patient information leaflet can be very useful in such cases, which would focus on the administration of these medications, side effects, probable drug interactions, and monitoring parameters.

Healthcare professionals: The patient should be monitored for the various side effects associated with antipsychotics and anticholinergics, especially when multiple antipsychotics that can have additive anticholinergic side effects are being given.[12] Patient education plays an important role in avoiding serious adverse effects. The patient should be instructed to observe and report early signs of an ADR immediately. The patient can be given a list of the most common anticholinergic side effects, so they can report to the doctor as soon as they notice any. In addition, the patient should be informed about any interactions with OTC anticholinergic drugs, and special care should be taken to obtain any such information while taking medication history.[12] Published case reports or any other information about adverse effects of neuropsychiatric drugs can be reviewed to understand this case better.

CASE 3: DRUG-INDUCED LIVER INJURY

A 21-year-old male was admitted for acute febrile illness, thrombocytopenia (platelet count: 97,000 cells/cmm), and excessive nausea. He was a known case of childhood epilepsy and mental retardation. The blood count was normal, except reduced platelet count and elevated liver enzymes (AST: 312 IU/L, ALT: 111 IU/L). The patient was tested negative for typhoid, dengue, and malaria. No signs/symptoms of viral/bacterial infection were evident. Medication history revealed that, 6 months ago, the patient was started with carbamazepine 500 mg/day, sodium valproate 200 mg/day, and a fixed-dose combination of risperidone 2 mg/trihexyphenidyl 2 mg once daily.

Sodium valproate and carbamazepine were stopped on admission to the hospital. The patient was administered IV paracetamol (under monitoring), IV fluids, and antiemetics. On the third day of hospitalization, he was afebrile and did not complain of nausea. Platelet counts were resolving (1,23,000 cells/cmm), and the patient was stable. The patient was continued on trihexyphenidyl/risperidone along with levetiracetam 500 mg twice a day. On follow-up, the patient was stable with resolving platelet counts and liver enzymes.

Could the Signs and Symptoms Be ADRs? How Is the Relationship Between the Suspected Drug and the Reported Reaction Established?

Information obtained from the patient: Collection of relevant information is the key step in ADR detection. Demographic details, medical and medication history, and social history play an important role. Assessment of adherence to anticonvulsants and antipsychotics therapy may help to find medication errors. MMAS can be used to assess adherence to all the drugs the patient is taking.[13] Onset, progression, and duration of fever and nausea, use of OTC medications, history of allergy, or past illnesses would be useful in ADR assessment.

In this case, the patient was started with anticonvulsants and antipsychotic therapy 6 months ago. Use of any OTC medications/history of other illness/previous allergies was not found. This information can be used to rule out the association of any other drugs/diseases with elevated liver enzymes, nausea, and thrombocytopenia. The patient's complaints can be associated with drugs or due to infection pathology. In such cases, literature survey and systematic ADR assessment would help to discover the drug's association with the patient's clinical condition.

Evidence: Sodium valproate is a highly hepatotoxic drug.[14] The Food and Drug Administration (FDA)'s black-box warning suggests that hepatotoxicity usually occurs during the first 6 months of therapy with valproic acid or its derivatives.[15] Fever (2%), thrombocytopenia (26%−30%), and nausea (31%) may occur with sodium valproate. Similarly, nausea (29%) and hepatic impairment are well-documented adverse effects of carbamazepine.[16] Thrombocytopenia may occur in the initial few days of treatment with carbamazepine and resolves on drug withdrawal.[17] Nausea is observed in 5%−10% of patients with risperidone. Prevalence of risperidone-induced hepatotoxicity is not well established.[18]

How Are the Causality and Severity of the ADR Determined?

ADR assessment using standard scales would help to assess the causality and plausibility of the observations with suspected drugs. The WHO causality assessment scale rates hepatotoxicity as a "Probable" ADR due to both sodium valproate and carbamazepine. Although impractical in most clinical situations, further details such as serum concentration of sodium valproate and carbamazepine are needed to strengthen the causal relationship between the ADR and suspected drug.[19] The symptoms resolved on dechallenge, suggesting that there is an association between medications and reactions.

What Follow-Up Actions Need to Be Considered in This Case?

As the patient was on both sodium valproate and carbamazepine, it is difficult to say which drug caused hepatotoxicity. In such cases, rechallenge with a less than therapeutic dose of one drug first, and then an increase to a therapeutic level if there is no elevation in liver enzymes, can confirm which drug caused hepatotoxicity in this patient.

Patient education: The patient needs to be educated about his drug therapy. Counseling of caretakers is important in this patient. They should be made aware of the benefits along with the potential toxicity of drugs prescribed for neuropsychiatric conditions. A mentally challenged patient in this case may not take an active role in decision making.

Education of healthcare professionals: Healthcare professionals should be educated about the importance of monitoring of important parameters before and after initiation of medications with wide side effect profile. Liver function tests and blood counts should be monitored regularly.

Dissemination of information: Use of case reports or case series can be used as a tool to indicate the various incidences of serious adverse effects associated with neuropsychiatric drugs. Exchange of information on reported adverse effects among healthcare professionals may result in cautious use of drugs.

CASE 4: PHENYTOIN TOXICITY

An 8-month-old male infant weighing 5 kg was brought to the hospital with three seizure episodes in the past 12 h (tonic−clonic movements of all four limbs with uprolling of eyes) and mild fever for a day. He has a normal development history and no history of any major illness. The child had received all immunizations to date and had no known allergies. He was playful, responsive, vitally stable, and accepted oral feeds. On admission, he was administered intravenous (IV) paracetamol (10 mg/kg/dose) and IV phenytoin at 5 mg/kg/day 12 hourly. However, the child had recurrent seizure episodes on the day of admission. Hence, levetiracetam was added to the therapy at a dose of 10 mg/kg/day 12 hourly. The fever subsided within a day, and no further seizure episodes were observed. However, magnetic resonance imaging (MRI) reports suggested a seizure focus in the left parietal lobe, thereby confirming focal seizures. Hence, anticonvulsant therapy was required. Phenytoin and levetiracetam were continued at 5 and 10 mg/kg/day, respectively. On the 10th day of admission, the child had nine episodes of vomiting, sudden in onset, and the mother complained of poor oral feed. The medication chart and drug dosing were reviewed and it was found that phenytoin was given at a higher dose for 4 days. The child was switched to oral phenytoin after 3 days of admission. As per the child's weight, he required 25 mg/day of phenytoin, divided into two doses.[16] Phenytoin syrup available had a concentration of 30 mg/5 mL. Hence, the required dose was 2 mL/dose twice daily. However, the child was administered 3 mL/dose, which is equivalent to 36 mg/day. Thus, an overdose of phenytoin was detected, and suitable dose modifications were done. No further episodes of vomiting were observed, and the child started accepting oral feeds the next day. The physicians and nurses were informed about the medication error, and the parents were counseled for drug dosing and monitoring of side effects.

Phenytoin-induced vomiting is a common side effect.[20] However, an overdose of phenytoin can lead to psychiatric and neurologic side effects such as ataxia, slurred speech, and coordination problems, which can be fatal.[21] Drug dosing and administration of narrow-therapeutic index drugs such as phenytoin should be carefully monitored.[22] The total phenytoin reference range for children and adults is between 10 and 20 mcg/L.[23] The principle "Treat the patient, not the numbers," should be considered when planning therapeutic drug monitoring of antiepileptic drugs.[24] Two patients may react differently to the same therapeutic concentration.[24] As phenytoin is a drug that undergoes saturation kinetics in overdose, there is an increased chance for drug accumulation and toxicity.[25] So patient education is an unavoidable measure.

CASE 5: VANCOMYCIN DILUTION ERROR

A 3-year-old toddler was brought to the hospital with complaints of fever for 1 day, periorbital swelling (right eye), and decreased appetite for 2 days. The child was found to be tachycardic with heart rate (122 beats/min), hypotensive (60 mmHg systolic BP), anemic (hemoglobin 7.2 g/dL; normal: 11−15 g/dL), had elevated total leukocyte count (14,300 cells/cmm; normal: 3000−10,000 cells/cmm), and low erythrocyte count (2.19 million cells/cmm; normal: 3.5−4.5 million cells/cmm). Suspecting sepsis, a blood culture report, and MRI of the orbit were advised on admission to the hospital. Investigation reports confirmed the presence of *Acinetobacter* species in the blood and orbital cellulitis with mild proptosis of the right eye. Antibiotic sensitivity testing suggested susceptibility to vancomycin. A 6-week therapy of vancomycin was planned at a dose of 60 mg/kg/day divided into four doses. The weight of the child was 8.3 kg, thus requiring a dose of 500 mg/day (125 mg/dose, four times/day). On the 14th day of vancomycin therapy, thrombophlebitis was observed on the right hand and on the 16th day the child's serum creatinine levels showed an elevation from a baseline value of 0.4 mg/dL on the day of admission to 0.73 mg/dL (normal range: 0.6−0.8 mg/dL). Because vancomycin is nephrotoxic,[26] the dosing and dilution were checked, and a gross dilution error was found. There is no standardized definition for nephrotoxicity due to vancomycin. Thus, vancomycin monitoring guidelines define nephrotoxicity as a 50% increase in serum creatinine over 2−3 consecutive measurements.[27] However, the Acute Kidney Injury Network states how morbid smaller increases over baseline, like 0.3 mg/dL, in serum creatinine can be.[27] In the future, other biomarkers, like kidney injury molecule-1, may be used, which increases as renal tubules are damaged.[27] Vancomycin (250 mg/vial) is available as a powder for suspension, to be diluted in 10 mL of distilled water to get 250 mg/10 ml and further diluted as per patient requirement (5 mL of the reconstituted solution needed to be diluted in 20 mL 0.45% normal saline).[28] However, the vancomycin powder was diluted in 5 mL of distilled water and administered with 20 mL 0.45% normal saline, subsequently causing an overdose in the patient. Thus, instead of 125 mg/dose, the patient was administered 250 mg/dose. This error in dilution for 6 days by a trainee nurse led to suspected acute kidney injury and thrombophlebitis. The error was corrected, nurses were counseled, vancomycin was administered every 12 h instead of every 6 h at 60 mg/kg/day, and thrombophlebitis was managed with topical ointment consisting of benzyl nicotinate and heparin. Ointment with this combination is often used to manage thrombophlebitis.[29] The serum creatinine normalized after 3 days and thrombophlebitis resolved in a week.

Thus, in the pediatric population, although dose calculation may be correct, gross errors can occur during dilution of the drug, which may lead to toxic outcomes. Therefore, healthcare professionals should be cautious while administering drugs requiring dilution and should follow the product monograph guidelines for drug administration. Moreover, vancomycin is a drug that may cause red man syndrome if it is administered quickly.[30] It should be administered over 1 hour.[31] This should be emphasized to nurses, otherwise, even the right dose may lead to adverse events.

CASE 6: IRRATIONAL EMPIRICAL ANTIBIOTICS

A 63-year-old female was admitted with a femur fracture and required open reduction internal fixation surgery. The patient had diabetes for 15 years with no other major illness and was vitally stable. Due to fracture-associated immobility, the patient was catheterized for passage of urine. On the third day of catheterization, the patient developed symptoms of urinary tract infection (UTI), i.e., burning micturition, fever, and back pain.[32] Due to prevailing UTI, she could not be posted for surgery. Diabetic patients are at a higher risk of UTI due to multiple reasons, like incomplete bladder emptying due to autonomic neuropathy, a lower immunity, and poor metabolic control.[33] While culture reports were awaited, the patient was administered an intravenous injection of ceftriaxone 2 g/day and a tablet of norfloxacin/tinidazole (400/600 mg) once a day as empirical therapy for 3 days. The patient complained of seven episodes of diarrhea, excessive nausea, and decreased appetite on the third day of empirical therapy, which was suspected to be antibiotic induced. The urine culture reports showed the presence of *Klebsiella* species with the colonization of >100,000 cells, thus confirming UTI. However, an antibiotic sensitivity report suggested resistance to cephalosporins and fluoroquinolones. For the management of diarrhea, the drugs were withdrawn, and the patient was given oral fluids and probiotic. According to the antibiotic sensitivity report, she was given piperacillin/tazobactam 4.5 g thrice a day for 7 days. The UTI resolved within 5 days of therapy with piperacillin/tazobactam and the patient was posted for surgery. This case highlights the irrational use of antibiotics empirically, which induced side effects and unnecessary increment in the overall cost of therapy.

For hospital acquired catheter-associated UTI, empirical antibiotic therapy should be started considering the resistance patterns in the hospital antibiogram. A quinolone, third generation cephalosporin or gentamycin can be considered based on the hospital data and patient's medical history.[34] Infectious Diseases Society of America (IDSA) guidelines recommend the use of trimethoprim/sulfamethoxazole for empirical treatment of uncomplicated UTI.[35,36] Thus, in this patient, the choice of antibiotics given empirically was not accurate.

CASE 7: UNTREATED INDICATION

A 36-year-old male came to the hospital with complaints of excessive weakness, decreased appetite, and malaise for 15 days. He was a known case of rheumatoid arthritis for 1 year. Medication history revealed that he was on hydroxychloroquine 200 mg/day. He was pale, hypotensive (blood pressure: 90/50 mmHg), and tachycardic (116/min). His blood count reports suggested severe iron deficiency anemia with hemoglobin 5.4 g/dL (normal: 14−16 g/dL), red blood cells 3.1 million cells/cmm (normal: 4.5−6.5 million cells/cmm), and hypochromic microcytic red blood cells. His medical records, dating back to the time of diagnosis of rheumatoid arthritis, showed baseline hemoglobin 10.6 g/dL, and hypochromic red blood cells with mild anisopoikilocytosis morphology suggestive of the coexisting anemic condition before the initiation of hydroxychloroquine. The anemia worsened on administration of the drug. Thus, coexisting anemia was left untreated at the time of diagnosis of rheumatoid arthritis. His condition was managed with blood transfusion and oral hematinics. The patient was counseled for potential side effects of antirheumatic agents and the importance of blood count monitoring along with dietary changes for improving the iron stores and preventing anemia-associated complications. Iron-rich food sources include red meat, poultry, and fish, which are heme sources, and pulses, grains, and fruits, which are non-heme sources.[37]

At the initiation of chronic drug therapy, the baseline parameters should be considered, and regular monitoring should be done. Several drugs can cause different types of anemia, such as megaloblastic anemia, aplastic anemia, sideroblastic anemia, and marrow aplasia.[38] Hydroxychloroquine can cause aplastic anemia, agranulocytosis, thrombocytopenia, and leukopenia.[39] The patient should be counseled about the drug therapy and its monitoring. Irrespective of blood count reports, hematinics should be adjuvants to immunosuppressants to avoid the hematological side effects. Hematinics include iron, folate, vitamin B12, riboflavin, and vitamin A.[40] Monitoring is required to prevent iron overload. Iron overload is defined as serum ferritin concentrations higher than 300 mcg/L in men and higher than 200 mcg/L in women.[41]

CASE 8: DRUG INTERACTION-INDUCED HYPOGLYCEMIA

A 55-year-old diabetic and hypertensive male was brought to the emergency department with complaints of excessive sweating and sudden loss of consciousness. On regaining consciousness, the patient was drowsy and disoriented. He was found to be hypotensive with blood pressure 90/60 mmHg and bradycardic with heart rate 58 beats/min. His blood glucose levels were 34 mg/dL, thereby confirming a hypoglycemic episode. A glucose level of <54 mg/dL is sufficiently low to indicate serious, clinically important hypoglycemia.[42] He has been a known case of hypertension for 7 years, diabetes mellitus for 5 years, and was recently diagnosed with acute bacterial sinusitis 2 days ago. He was on the tablet metoprolol 25 mg once daily, the tablet aspirin 75 mg once daily, the tablet metformin 500 mg twice daily, and the tablet levofloxacin 750 mg once daily for 5 days. On the day of hypoglycemic attack, the patient apparently took all the prescribed medicines within an hour after lunch and started to experience excessive sweating and nausea within 2 h of intake of drugs. Drug—drug interactions might have occurred between aspirin—metformin and levofloxacin—metformin, causing an additive effect on reducing the blood glucose levels.[16] The probable mechanism may be increased effectiveness of oral hypoglycemic agents due to aspirin and levofloxacin. There had been case reports of hypoglycemia from patients who took levofloxacin while on oral hypoglycemics.[43] The patient's condition was managed with 25% dextrose (IV) and the offending drugs were withdrawn. The blood glucose levels normalized (103 mg/dL) within 12 h of management, and all the medicines were reinitiated on the next day with a warning to separate timings to ingest interacting drugs. The patient was counseled for blood glucose monitoring, the new dosing regimen (avoid interacting drugs together), and identification, prevention and treatment of hypoglycemia.

This case highlights the effect of drug—drug interactions that may lead to fatal events like severe hypoglycemia, which can be avoided with appropriate drug regimen and patient counseling. Metformin is otherwise known as a euglycemic agent because it does not directly stimulate insulin secretion. Therefore, the risk of hypoglycemia is much lower than other oral hypoglycemic agents.[44] Concomitant use of drugs like levofloxacin and aspirin with metformin can increase the risk of hypoglycemia. If concomitant use of these agents are unavoidable, blood glucose levels should be closely monitored.[45]

REFERENCES

1. Chisholm MA, Lance CE, Williamson GM, Mulloy LL. Development and validation of an immunosuppressant therapy adherence barrier instrument. *Nephrol Dial Transplant*. 2005;20(1):181—188. Serial online. Available from: https://academic.oup.com/ndt/article/20/1/181/1818575.

2. Mendyka BE. Fluid and electrolyte disorders caused by diuretic therapy. *AACN Clin Issues Crit Care Nurs*. 1992;3(3):672—680. Serial online. Available from: https://www.ncbi.nlm.nih.gov/pubmed/1524938.

3. Connel WR, Kamm MA, Ritchie JK, Lennard-Jones JE. Bone marrow toxicity caused by azathioprine in inflammatory bowel disease: 27 years of experience. *Gut*. 1993;34:1081—1085. Serial online. Available from: https://www.ncbi.nlm.nih.gov/pmc/articles/PMC1374358/pdf/gut00559-0087.pdf.

4. Berg PA, Lohse AW, Tiegs G, Wendel A. *Autoimmune Liver Disease. Immunosuppressive Therapy of Autoimmune Hepatitis*. Kluwer Academic Publishers; 1997:109. Serial online. Available from: https://books.google.ca/books?id=9F-0lddLZZ8C&pg=PA109&lpg=PA109&dq=5%25+azathioprine+myelosuppression+myelosuppression+adverse+effects+side&source=bl&ots=pPgCS_br6w&sig=jIxxDlUsY0WD_AHbtARzyWWahoQ&hl=en&sa=X&ved=0ahUKEwjruq6qgbjXAhVE4GMKHYXMDMwQ6AEIbTAJ#v=onepage&q=5%25%20azathioprine%20myelosuppression%20myelosuppression%20adverse%20effects%20side&f=false.

5. Iasella CJ, Johnson HJ, Dunn MA. Adverse drug reactions: type a (intrinsic) or type B (idiosyncratic). *Clin Liver Dis*. 2017;21(1):73—87. Serial online. Available from: https://www.ncbi.nlm.nih.gov/pubmed/27842776.

6. Pozzi C. Steroids help preserve kidney function in type of kidney disease. *J Am Soc Nephrol*; July 2010. Serial online. Available from: https://www.eurekalert.org/pub_releases/2010-07/ason-shp071310.php.

7. Sweileh WM, Ihbesheh MS, Jarar IS, et al. Antipsychotic medication adherence and satisfaction among Palestinian people with schizophrenia. *Curr Clin Pharmacol*. 2012;7(1):49—55. Serial online. Available from: https://www.ncbi.nlm.nih.gov/pubmed/22299769.

8. *Atypical Antipsychotic Drugs Information*. USFDA; 2016. Serial online. Available from: https://www.fda.gov/Drugs/DrugSafety/PostmarketDrugSafetyInformationforPatientsandProviders/ucm094303.htm.

9. Muench J, Hamer AM. Adverse effects of antipsychotic medications. *Am Fam Physician*. 2010;81(5):617—622. Serial online. Available from: http://www.aafp.org/afp/2010/0301/p617.html.

10. Horn JR, Hansten PD. *Anticholinergic Drug Interactions*. Pharmacy Times; July 2015. Serial online. Available from: http://www.pharmacytimes.com/publications/issue/2015/july2015/anticholinergic-drug-interactions.

11. Trihexyphenidyl. *Human Health Effects*. Toxnet; 2017. Serial online. Available from: https://toxnet.nlm.nih.gov/cgi-bin/sis/search/a?dbs+hsdb:@term+@DOCNO+3196.

12. Lieberman JA. Managing Anticholinergic Side Effects. *Prim Care Companion J Clin Psychiatry*. 2004;6(suppl. 2):20—23. Serial online. Available from: https://www.ncbi.nlm.nih.gov/pmc/articles/PMC487008/.

13. Getnet A, Woldeyohannes SM, Bekana L, et al. Antiepileptic drug nonadherence and its predictors among people with epilepsy. *Behav Neurol*; 2016, 6 pp. Article ID 3189108. Serial online. Available from: https://www.hindawi.com/journals/bn/2016/3189108/cta/.

14. Powell-Jackson, Tredger, Williams. Hepatotoxicity to sodium valproate: a review. *Prog Rep Gut*. 1984;25:673—681. Serial online. Available from: http://gut.bmj.com/content/gutjnl/25/6/673.full.pdf.

15. Depakene (valproic acid) capsules, oral solution. *FDA Approved Labeling Text. Boxed Warning*.; October 2011. Serial online. Available from: https://www.accessdata.fda.gov/drugsatfda_docs/label/2011/018081s046_18082s031lbl.pdf.

16. Micromedex® 2.0, (electronic version). *Truven Health Analytics, Greenwood Village, Colorado, USA*; 2017. Available at: http://www.micromedexsolutions.com/.

17. Tohen M, Castillo J, Cole JO, Miller MG, de los Heros R, Farrer RJ. Thrombocytopenia associated with carbamazepine: a case series. *J Clin Psychiatry*. 1991;52(12):496–498. Serial online. Available from: https://www.ncbi.nlm.nih.gov/pubmed/1752850.

18. Risperdal (Risperidone). *Highlights of Prescribing Information*; 2007. Serial online. Available from: https://www.accessdata.fda.gov/drugsatfda_docs/label/2016/020272s077,020588s065, 021346s055, 021444s051lbl.pdf.

19. Miller JJ. *Serum Levels of Psychiatric Drugs*. Psychiatric Times; November 2014. Serial online. Available from: http://www.psychiatrictimes.com/cme/serum-levels-psychiatric-drugs/page/0/3.

20. Phenytoin. *Epilepsy Society*; February 2014. Serial online. Available from: https://www.epilepsysociety.org.uk/phenytoin#.WgeEjnRrzIU.

21. Verma R, Kumar S, Biyani S, Singh A. Available from: Opsoclonus – Myoclonus syndrome induced by phenytoin intoxication. *J Neurosci Pract*. 2014;5(suppl 1):S109–S110. Serial online. Available from: https://www.ncbi.nlm.nih.gov/pmc/articles/PMC4271371/.

22. Blair K. *Medicines Management in Children's Nursing*; 2011, 105 p. Serial online. Available from: https://books.google.ca/books?id=XxY8yf7KH9cC&pg=PA105&lpg=PA105&dq=carefully+monitor+narrow+index+drug+phenytoin&source=bl&ots=_pzPlIdEbl&sig=EYyx Gv2_0j5dvOsfjsdqip_dvGM&hl=en&sa=X&ved=0ahUKEwj5qPvUh5fYAhUW82MKHWALB0MQ6AEIOzAC#v=onepage&q=carefully%20monitor %20narrow%20index%20drug%20phenytoin&f=false.

23. Galjour JL, Bentley S. *Phenytoin Level. Reference Range*; November 2014. Serial online. Available from: https://emedicine.medscape.com/article/2090306-overview.

24. Wu MF, Lim WH. Phenytoin: a guide to therapeutic drug monitoring. *Proc Singapore Healthc*. 2013;22(3):198. Serial online. Available from: http://journals.sagepub.com/doi/pdf/10.1177/201010581302200307.

25. Hwang WJ, Tsai JJ. Acute phenytoin intoxication: causes, symptoms, misdiagnoses, and outcomes. *Kaohsiung J Med Sci*. 2004;20(12):580–585. Serial online. Available from: https://www.ncbi.nlm.nih.gov/pubmed/15696787.

26. Review of vancomycin-induced renal toxicity: an update. *Ther Adv Endocronol Metab*. 2016;7(3):136–147. Serial online. Available from: https://www.ncbi.nlm.nih.gov/pmc/articles/PMC4892398/.

27. Lomaestro BM. Vancomycin dosing and monitoring 2 years after the guidelines. *Medscape*. 2011;9(6):657–667. Serial online. Available from: https://www.medscape.com/viewarticle/747418_10.

28. Vancomycin 500MG AND 1000MG. *Powder for Concentrate for Solution for Infusion*. MHRA; August 2011. Serial online. Available from: http://www.mhra.gov.uk/home/groups/par/documents/websiteresources/con131955.pdf.

29. MC0112003. *A Comparative Study to Assess the Effectiveness of Glycerin with Magnesium Sulphate versus Heparin – Benzyl Nicotinate (Thrombophob) Ointment on Management of Thrombophlebitis Among Patients Admitted in Intensive Care Units (ICU) of Selected Hospital in Belgaum, Karnataka*. Belagavi: KLE Academy of Higher Education and Research; 2014. Serial online. Available from: http://182.48.228.33:8080/jspui/bitstream/123456789/1462/1/10.pdf.

30. Sivagnanam S, Deleu D. Red man syndrome. *Crit Care*. 2002;7(2):119–120. Serial online. Available from: https://www.ncbi.nlm.nih.gov/pmc/articles/PMC270616/.

31. Grammer L, Greenberger PA. *Patterson's Allergic Disease*. 11th ed.; 2017. Serial online. Available from: https://books.google.ca/books?id=pNZCDwAAQBAJ&pg=PT5&lpg=PT5&dq=patterson%27s+allergic+diseases+8th+edition&source=bl&ots=eBrkN2riTG&sig=fPiBS_zuAw 684JRVlClbj7wFlHQ&hl=en&sa=X&ved=0ahUKEwj9uJrf45fYAhVC7GMKHXHLAegQ6AEISTAG#v=onepage&q=patterson's%20allergic%20 diseases%208th%20edition&f=false.

32. Yamamoto S. Prevention and treatment of complicated urinary tract infection. *Urological Science*. 2016;27(4):186–189. Serial online. Available from: http://www.sciencedirect.com/science/article/pii/S1879522616303785.

33. Nitzan O, Elias M, Chazan B, Saliba W. Urinary tract infections in patients with type 2 diabetes Mellitus: review of prevalence, diagnosis, and management. *Diabetes Metab Syndr Obes*. 2015;8:129–136. Serial online. Available from: https://www.ncbi.nlm.nih.gov/pmc/articles/PMC4346284/.

34. Brusch JL. Urinary tract infection (UTI) and Cystitis (bladder infection) in females treatment & management. *Medscape*; October 2017. Serial online. Available from: https://emedicine.medscape.com/article/233101-treatment.

35. Le TP, Miller LG. Empirical therapy for uncomplicated urinary tract infections in an Era of increasing antimicrobial resistance: a decision and cost analysis. *Clin Infect Dis*. 2001;33(5):615–621. Serial online. Available from: https://academic.oup.com/cid/article/33/5/615/465468.

36. Olmstead S, Meiss D, Ralston J. *Probiotics and Antibiotic-associated Diarrhea*. Klaire Labs. ProThera; 2007. Serial online. Available from: http://www.klaire.com/images/probioticsantibiotic.pdf.

37. Santoyo-Sanchez A, Aponte-Castillo JA, Parra-Pena RI, Ramos-Penafiel CO. Dietary recommendations in patients with deficiency Anemia. *Revista Médica Del Hospital General De México*. 2015;78(3):144–150. Serial online. Available from: https://www.sciencedirect.com/science/article/pii/S0185106315000463.

38. Girdwood RH. Drug-induced Anemias. *Drugs*. 1976;11(5):394–404. Serial online. Available from: https://www.ncbi.nlm.nih.gov/pubmed/782836.

39. Plaquenil. *Hydroxychloroquine Sulfate*. USP; 2006. Serial online. Available from: https://www.accessdata.fda.gov/drugsatfda_docs/label/2007/009768s041lbl.pdf.

40. McKew S, Rajab J, Bates I. *Hematological Diseases. Hunter's Tropical Medicine and Emerging Infectious Disease*. 9th ed.; November 2012 (Chapter 5). Serial online. Available from: https://www.sciencedirect.com/science/article/pii/B9781416043904000059.

41. Adams PC, Reboussin DM, Barton JC, et al. Hemochromatosis and iron-overload screening in a racially diverse population. *NEJM*. 2005;352(17):1769–1778. Serial online. Available from: https://www.scopus.com/record/display.uri?eid=2-s2.0-20244372858&origin=inward&txGid=26d488c6de263e489c0386a9cbaed0c4.

42. Davis SN, Lastra-Gonzalez G. Diabetes and low blood sugar (hypoglycemia). *JCEM*. 2008;93(8). Serial online. Available from: https://academic.oup.com/jcem/article/93/8/E2/2623144.

43. Micheli L, Sbrilli M, Nencini C. Severe hypoglycemia associated with levofloxacin in type 2 diabetic patients receiving polytherapy: two case reports. *Int J Clin Pharmacol Ther*. 2012;50(4):302–306. Serial online. Available from: https://www.ncbi.nlm.nih.gov/pubmed/22456302.

44. Bodmer M, Meier C, Krahenbuhl S, Jick SS, Meier CR. Metformin, sulfonylureas, or other antidiabetes drugs and the risk of lactic acidosis or hypoglycemia. A nested case-control analysis. *Diabetes Care*. 2008;31(11):2086–2091. Serial online. Available from: https://www.ncbi.nlm.nih.gov/pmc/articles/PMC2571051/.

45. Hypoglycemic Drug Interactions. *The Rx Files: Q&A Summary*; 2001. Serial online. Available from: http://www.rxfiles.ca/rxfiles/uploads/documents/diabetes-QandA-Hypoglycemic-DIs.pdf.

Appendix II

Sample Evaluation Tools in Pharmacy Experiential Education

Susan S. Vos[1], Mary E. Ray[1], Ronald A. Herman[1] and Dixon Thomas[2]

[1]The University of Iowa, Iowa City, IA, United States; [2]Gulf Medical University, Ajman, United Arab Emirates

Below are some examples of checklists, other evaluation forms, and data collection forms that are useful in experiential education. The data collection forms are useful in collecting and analyzing patient information in real-life settings. Most preceptors and colleges/schools of pharmacy have their evaluations and assessment tools that include both summative and formative feedback strategies. The checklists can be useful when students prepare to present cases, journal articles, drug information, or other in-service type presentations. Checklists are relatively easier to fill compared to detailed evaluation forms. The detailed evaluation forms capture more information about the performance of the students. These evaluation tools could be mapped with program outcomes to ensure achievement of learning outcomes. Wordings need to be adjusted as per the educational outcomes expected, whether introductory or advanced.

- Patient Case Presentation Checklist
- Drug Information Question Checklist
- In-Service Presentation Checklist
- Journal Club Evaluation Checklist
- Case Presentation Evaluation
- Journal Club Evaluation
- Educational Presentation Evaluation
- Medication History/Patient Interview Collection Form
- Patient Data Collection Form
- Overall evaluation form for the advanced pharmacy practice training experience (aligned with CAPE educational outcomes)

PATIENT CASE PRESENTATION CHECKLIST

Criteria	Checklist
Patient presentation • Patient identification, chief complaint, history of present illness, medication history, social history, family history, review of symptoms, vital signs, physical exam, laboratory results • Detail of chronology of events leading to presenting to healthcare facility	
Discussion of patient-specific disease states • Etiology, Epidemiology • Pathophysiology • Risk factors • Signs and symptoms	

Drug therapy
- Indications and rationale for patient's drug therapy
- Problem list with drug therapy
- Appropriateness of current regimen
- Pharmacology of drugs
- Dosing regimen including pharmacokinetic considerations
- Potential adverse effects of drugs
- Potential drug interactions
- Other options and alternatives

Monitoring
- Monitoring parameters
- Follow-up

Patient information and counseling
- Purpose(s) of drug therapy
- Important instructions for use
- Side effects and precautions
- Self-monitoring parameters

Presentation style
- Organization
- Voice projection, correct pronunciation
- Ability to answer questions—can support with evidence from the literature
- Ability to present without "reading" notes
- Distracting mannerisms

Audiovisual
- If handouts are used, they are organized and appropriately referenced
- If overheads or slides are used, they are clear and free of errors

Comments:

DRUG INFORMATION QUESTION CHECKLIST

Criteria	Checklist
Define and understand the question • Classify the question asked (therapeutics, pharmacology, adverse drug reaction, drug interaction, pharmacokinetics, dosing, toxicology, IV compatibility, availability, etc.) • Classify the background and contact information of the requestor (i.e., nurse, physician, etc.)	
Obtain the necessary background information • Demographic information of the requestor and patient (if applicable) • Appropriately framed question • Time line for responding to the questions	
Search for the answer • Start with tertiary references and then proceed to secondary references then to primary references	
Evaluate, organize, and interpret the facts • Evaluate the literature to formulate an answer	
Formulate an answer • The response should be clear, complete, and concise with the arguments to support your recommendations. All references have to be listed • The time the response delivered to the requestor and the name of the person who received the message should be noted	

Comments:

IN-SERVICE PRESENTATION CHECKLIST

Criteria	Checklist
The handout/slides are clear and concise without typos and/or crowding of information	
The presentation is organized (content order flows well and makes sense)	
The learning objectives are directed toward the audience's outcomes	
All information provided supports the presentation objectives	
The information provided was accurate	
Transitions between topics and/or speakers are carried out in a smooth fashion	
The major points are summarized at the end of the presentation	
References are provided and are cited correctly	
The student functioned independently and did not require an unreasonable amount of guidance in research or preparation	
The student accepts questions and comments in a nondefensive manner	
The student answers questions satisfactorily	
The student appears confident	
The student displays enthusiasm	
The student speaks at an appropriate volume and rate	
The student uses language appropriate to the audience	
The student has good eye contact with the audience	
The student has appropriate stance and posture while avoids distracting mannerisms	
The length of presentation and time spent presenting was appropriate to the topic	
Comments:	

JOURNAL CLUB EVALUATION CHECKLIST

Criteria	Checklist
Overview • Brief summary • Why did you select this article • Are the authors experienced in the area • Does the abstract adequately describe the manuscript	
Describe the purpose of the study and the hypothesis • Clearly stated the purpose and author's hypothesis • Existing standard of care about the topic generating the study	
Describe the characteristics of the study population • Inclusion/exclusion criteria • Date study conducted, country(ies), center(s) • Age, gender, other drugs being taken, co-morbid conditions of the research subjects	
Describe the study design • Type of study (i.e., randomized, blinded, controlled metaanalysis, etc.) • Study population • Study group allocations, drug doses, regimens, duration (if applicable) • Outcome measures of the study • In your opinion, is the study design appropriate • Analyze the statistical analysis. Explain the statistical tests used and are they appropriate for the data being evaluated • Is the sample size adequate	

Describe the results of the study ● What is/are the outcome measure(s) for the study ● What are the study's endpoint(s) and if they are, or are not, clinically meaningful to patients ● Explain how practice would change based on the study's results ● How can you apply the results to clinical practice	
Analyze the discussion and conclusion section **Is the author's interpretation of their results consistent with their actual findings** ● Whether the study was ethical or not ● Limitations and strengths of the study ● Discussed whether or not the student agrees or disagrees with the investigators conclusions and why ● How does this study compare to other similar studies already in the literature	
Identified potential sources of bias ● Sources and methods used for controlling or adjusting for bias ● How to overcome/control for bias in the study ● Comment on the author's use of references. (Did they cite themselves frequently? Is other pertinent literature cited?)	

CASE PRESENTATION EVALUATION

Score		Criteria
1	Needs significant improvement	The student is not meeting the competency and substantial effort is needed to meet the competency. The student rarely performs the competency within expectations and requires constant guidance and supervision. Must provide comments to indicate deficiencies.
2	Needs improvement	The student is developing skills in this competency; however, some minor improvement(s) are needed to meet the competency. The student sometimes performs the competency within expectations and requires regular guidance and supervision.
3	Meets expectation	The student has adequately demonstrated this competency. The student frequently performs the competency within expectations and requires minimal guidance and supervision from the preceptor.
4	Exceeds expectation	The student has demonstrated excellence in this competency. The student consistently performs the competency above expectations and requires minimal guidance and supervision from the preceptor. Must provide comments to justify rating.
NO	Not observed/no opportunity	The student has not had the opportunity to demonstrate this competency.

For each item below, rate the student's performance using the above rating scale.
(Question 1 of 4—Mandatory)

	Rating
Case history (HPI or current clinical situation) clear and concise	
Past medical history (other conditions, their status, relevance to current situation) clear and concise	
Medication history (complete list, accurate regimens, how patient actually uses) clear and concise	
Knowledge of patient (describes more than chart knowledge of specifics of patient history, indication that patient was interviewed and student has collected additional information)	
Drug therapy problems identified and detailed (problem is labeled and described)	
Goals of therapy (goal for each condition under discussion is stated)	
Therapeutic alternatives given (for each condition/issue discussed, the student gave all reasonable choices for treatment)	

Rational choices for therapeutic intervention (recommendation and rationale given for decision)	
Intervention plan (what was done or is planned to implement recommendations)	
Monitoring plan (parameters and intervals given)	
Follow-up schedule (interval and parameters to be assessed for next patient encounter)	
Overall quality of the information presented	

Comments:

JOURNAL CLUB EVALUATION

Score		Criteria
1	Needs significant improvement	Student had demonstrated excellence in this competency.
2	Needs improvement	Student meets competency.
3	Meets expectation	Student is developing skills in this competency; however, some minor improvement(s) are needed to meet the competency.
4	Exceeds expectation	Student is not meeting the competency and substantial effort is need to meet the competency.
NA	Not assessed	Not able to assess.

For each item below, rate the student's performance using the above rating scale.

	Rating
Stated the study objective in his/her own words.	
Described how the study objective and hypotheses are relevant to community pharmaceutical care.	
Stated the study design and how it was relevant to the clinical setting in which the study was performed.	
Described the advantages, disadvantages, and limitations of the study design with respect to community pharmaceutical care.	
Described the patient/subject population studied, including how they were selected and adequacy of sample size.	
Described the study intervention, including all groups studied and details of the specific intervention in different groups if applicable.	
Listed the main outcome measures of the study and how they were analyzed.	
Explained how the major study endpoints are relevant to the population studied.	
Presented the main results of the study with comparison to the original hypotheses.	
Described the study conclusions as presented by the authors.	
Stated their evaluation and clinical significance of study results.	
Anticipated how results of the study might differ in the population of patients cared for in the rotation site.	
Identified limitations to applying the study results in the population of patients cared for in the rotation site.	
Comments:	

EDUCATIONAL PRESENTATION EVALUATION

Presenter: _____   Date: _____

Topic:_____   _____

3	Nicely done, complete or thorough discussion.
2	Adequate job, but limited insight or assessment.
1	Lacking, incomplete understanding, or unclear discussion.
0	Poor job, missing element or unable to answer questions.

1. Introduction was able to gain the interest of the audience.	3 2 1 0
2. Provided adequate background for the importance of this topic.	3 2 1 0
3. Main points of the presentation were clearly identified. (Learning Objectives)	3 2 1 0
4. Smooth transitions were used throughout the presentation.	3 2 1 0
5. Conclusion brings finality to the topic.	3 2 1 0
6. Handout summarized key points in a brief, easy to follow format.	3 2 1 0
7. Handout documented key resources for this topic.	3 2 1 0
8. Slides and/or overheads nicely prepared.	3 2 1 0
9. Sufficient evaluation of the literature conducted and presented.	3 2 1 0
10. Able to adequately answer audience questions.	3 2 1 0
11. Delivery of the presentation (voice projection, variation, posture and gestures).	3 2 1 0
12. Length of the presentation (should be 15 minutes, with up to 15 minutes Q&A).	3 2 1 0
TOTAL SCORE FOR PRESENTATION (MAX IS 36 PTS)	

Evaluator: _____

MEDICATION HISTORY / PATIENT INTERVIEW COLLECTION FORM

Date: _____

□ Male   □ Female   Age: _____

Source of information (e.g., patient, family member, etc.): _____

Chief Complaint or Reason for visit to pharmacy or healthcare setting: _____

_____

Past Medical/Surgical History: _____

_____

_____

_____

*Medication History (include all prescription, over the counter, supplements and herbal products used by the patient); use additional page if necessary.

Medication (name, strength, dose, route, frequency)	Last taken	How long have they taken?	Indication/Purpose/Comments	Last Filled

Medication Allergies:

Medication name: _____ Reaction: _____

Medication name: _____ Reaction: _____

Medication name: _____ Reaction: _____

Immunization Record (date/year of last dose if known):

Influenza, Hepatitis, Pneumonia, Tetanus, Zoster, other?

_____

_____

_____

Alcohol/Tobacco Use and Quantity:

PATIENT DATA COLLECTION FORM

Name or Initials:			
Age:	Ht:	Wt:	BMI:
Allergies:			
CC:			

HPI:

PMH:	Home Meds:
	1.
	2.
	3.
	4.
	5.
	6.
	7.
	8.
	9.
	10.

FH:	SH:

Imaging:

Date	Imaging	Interpretation

Labs:

Na									
K									
Cl									
CO_2									
BUN									
Scr									
Glu									
GFR									
PO_4									
Mg									
Ca									
TG									
LDL									
HDL									
WBC									
Bands									
HgB									
HCT									
AST									
ALT									
Alk P									
T.Bili									
ALB									
aPTT									
INR									
CK									
MB									
Trop									
I/O									

Microbiology:

(Columns: Sensitivity / Growth / Site / Date / Notes:)

Problem List:
1.
2.
3.
4.
5.
6.
7.
8.

Medications:
Indication—Dosage—Monitoring

Routine
1.
2.
3.
4.
5.
6.
7.
8.
9.
10.
11.
12.

PRN
1.
2.
3.
4.
5.

Continuous Infusions
1.
2.
3.
4.

Progress Notes:

OVERALL EVALUATION FORM FOR THE ADVANCED PHARMACY TRAINING EXPERIENCE

APPE Student Evaluation Form

Student Name: _____ Reg. No: _____ Dates: _ -

Rotation: _____ Rotation Site: _____

Preceptor: _____ □ Pass the Rotation □ Rotation to be repeated

Final Score Out of 100: _____

Instructions:

1. Please complete this form for the midpoint (12th Day) and final evaluation (25th Day) of the student.
2. The student should submit a daily log electronically and the preceptor should provide feedback specific on learning outcomes.
3. If the student *does not progress to expected level of performance* for any of the required educational outcomes at the mid-point evaluation, please notify the student's Faculty Incharge before the 13th day of rotation and provide a written explanation in the comments section of this evaluation form which identifies areas of student improvement.
4. From the applicable evaluation elements, the total score should be converted to 100. More than 70% of the total score is required for passing the rotation.
5. The preceptor should ensure this form is completed with both student and preceptor signatures and is discussed in detail with the student before it is printed or emailed. Contact the College office if you have any questions.
6. Disclaimer: This form is developed using similar forms in other universities as a model, it could be tailored to the program and healthsystem requirements.

LEVEL OF PERFORMANCE EXPECTATIONS AND SCORING KEY

Perform consistently as expected		Perform occasionally as expected	Unable to perform as expected		Not Applicable
5	4	3	2	1	NA
Student performs consistently as expected or exceeds expectation. Student works independently, requiring **no assistance** or guidance from the preceptor.	Student performs more often, not ideally consistent. Shows clear signs of progress.	Student performs occasionally, is progressing, but not yet achieved the educational outcomes. Student requires **moderate assistance** and guidance from the preceptor.	Student attempting & showing only minor signs of progression. Student requires **significant assistance** and guidance from the preceptor.	Student attempts only when repeatedly prompted by preceptor. Shows no signs of progress.	Not enough evidence to evaluate as the assessment item is not applicable.

I. Educational Outcome on Drug, Therapeutic and Practice Information Skills (Learner)

Criteria and Student Performance	Perform consistently as expected		Perform occasionally as expected		Unable to perform as expected		Not Applicable
1. Knowledge of pathophysiology	Consistently explains pathophysiology in detail.	Student performs more often, not ideally consistent. Shows clear signs of progress.	Explains pathophysiology in adequate detail on some occasions.	Student attempts with significant assistance by preceptor. Shows some signs of progress.	Unable to explain pathophysiology in adequate detail.		NA
Mid evaluation	☐ Progressing		☐ Needs improvement		☐ Not progressing		☐
Final evaluation	5	4	3	2	1		☐
2. Knowledge of pharmacology, pharmacokinetics	Consistently demonstrates extensive knowledge of drug action and pharmacokinetics.	Student performs more often, not ideally consistent. Shows clear signs of progress.	Demonstrates adequate knowledge of drug action and pharmacokinetics on some occasions.	Student attempts with significant assistance by preceptor. Shows some signs of progress.	Unable to demonstrate adequate knowledge of drug action and pharmacokinetics.		NA
Mid evaluation	☐ Progressing		☐ Needs improvement		☐ Not progressing		☐
Final evaluation	5	4	3	2	1		☐
3. Knowledge of therapeutics (Pharmacotherapy discussion/ presentation)	Consistently demonstrates adequate knowledge of current, evidence-based pharmacotherapeutics. Able to explain well advanced pharmacotherapy in a related area.	Student performs more often, not ideally consistent. Shows clear signs of progress.	Demonstrates adequate knowledge of current, evidence-based pharmacotherapeutics on some occasions. Explains advanced pharmacotherapy in related area though not at optimum levels.	Student attempts with significant assistance by preceptor. Shows some signs of progress.	Unable to demonstrate adequate knowledge of current, evidence-based practices. Not able to explain advanced pharmacotherapy in a related area.		NA

	Progressing		Needs improvement		Not progressing	
	☐		☐		☐	☐
	5	4	3	2	1	
Mid evaluation	☐		☐		☐	☐
Final evaluation	5	4	3	2	1	NA
4. Interpretation of the evidence and application of conclusions (Journal Club)	Consistently demonstrates overall competency and ability to identify and critically evaluate published research. Often employs such data into patient care decision-making.	Student performs more often, not ideally consistent. Shows clear signs of progress.	On some occasions, demonstrates competency and ability to adequately identify and critically evaluate published research.	Student attempts with significant assistance by preceptor. Shows some signs of progress.	Unable to demonstrate competency and ability to identify and critically evaluate published research.	NA
Mid evaluation	☐		☐		☐	☐
Final evaluation	5	4	3	2	1	
5. Self-directed learning, innovative practice development	Consistently demonstrates ability to learn by self with minimum guidance. Participate in continuing education event, especially the presentations by other students in the same cohort.	Student performs more often, not ideally consistent. Shows clear signs of progress.	On some occasions, demonstrates ability to learn by self with moderate guidance. Moderate participation in continuing education event, especially the presentations by other students in the same cohort.	Student attempts with significant assistance by preceptor. Shows some signs of progress.	Unable to demonstrate ability to learn by self. Poor participation in continuing education event, especially the presentations by other students in the same cohort.	NA
Mid evaluation	☐		☐		☐	☐
Final evaluation	5	4	3	2	1	
Total						

COMMENTS AND SPECIFIC FEEDBACK

Educational Outcome: Drug, Therapeutic and Practice Information Skills

II. Educational Outcome on Patient Care (Caregiver, Problem solver, Health promoter)

Criteria and Student Performance	Perform consistently as expected		Perform occasionally as expected		Unable to perform as expected	Not Applicable
	5	4	3	2	1	
6. Conducts patient interviews and seeks other sources (family, medical record, care providers) to obtain patient medication and medical information	Consistently and reliably obtains thorough and complete medication histories from multiple sources, including individuals and medical charts.	Student performs more often, not ideally consistent. Shows clear signs of progress.	On some occasions obtains accurate and complete medication histories from multiple sources.	Student attempts with significant assistance by preceptor. Shows some signs of progress.	Unable to obtain accurate and complete drug histories and/or overlooks the opportunity to seek appropriate information from individuals and medical charts.	NA
Mid evaluation	☐ Progressing		☐ Needs improvement		☐ Not progressing	☐
Final evaluation	5	4	3	2	1	☐
7. Identification of actual and potential drug-related problems (DRPs)	Consistently identifies and justifies actual and potential DRPs accurately.	Student performs more often, not ideally consistent. Shows clear signs of progress.	On some occasions identifies and justifies actual and potential DRPs accurately. At times requires prompting.	Student attempts with significant assistance by preceptor. Shows some signs of progress.	Unable to identify and justify actual and potential DRPs accurately. Requires significant and repeated amount of prompting.	NA

	☐ Progressing		☐ Needs improvement	☐ Not progressing		
	5	4	3	2	1	
Mid evaluation						☐
Final evaluation						☐
8. Statement of desired therapeutic outcomes (patient-specific goals of therapy, including International Patient Safety Goals, infection control)	Consistently, thoroughly and accurately states desired outcomes in detail.	Student performs more often, not ideally consistent. Shows clear signs of progress.	On some occasions states desired outcomes of therapy in adequate detail. At times requires prompting.	Student attempts with significant assistance by preceptor. Shows some signs of progress.	Unable to state desired outcomes of therapy in adequate detail. Requires significant and repeated amount of prompting.	NA
	☐ Progressing		☐ Needs improvement	☐ Not progressing		
	5	4	3	2	1	
Mid evaluation						☐
Final evaluation						☐
9. Identification of viable therapeutic alternatives for each DRP identified (including drug and non-drug measures)	Consistently identifies viable drug and non-drug therapeutic alternatives for managing DRPs.	Student performs more often, not ideally consistent. Shows clear signs of progress.	On some occasions identifies most viable drug and non-drug therapeutic alternatives for managing DRPs. At times requires some prompting.	Student attempts with significant assistance by preceptor. Shows some signs of progress.	Unable to identify viable drug and non-drug therapeutic alternatives for managing DRPs. Requires significant and repeated amount of prompting.	NA
	☐ Progressing		☐ Needs improvement	☐ Not progressing		
Mid evaluation						☐

Final evaluation	5	4	3	2	1	☐
10. Development of an individualized and evidence-based pharmacotherapeutic recommendation for each DRP	Consistently develops an appropriate pharmacotherapeutic plan that is evidence-based and individualized for most DRPs.	Student performs more often, not ideally consistent. Shows clear signs of progress.	On some occasions, develops an appropriate pharmacotherapeutic plan for most DRPs. At times requires prompting for evidence or individualization.	Student attempts with significant assistance by preceptor. Shows some signs of progress.	Unable to develop an evidence-based and individualized pharmacotherapeutic plan for most DRPs. Requires significant and repeated amount of prompting.	NA
Mid evaluation	☐ Progressing		☐ Needs improvement		☐ Not progressing	☐
Final evaluation	5	4	3	2	1	☐
11. Monitoring parameters for efficacy and potential toxicities of current therapy	Consistently and accurately states and monitors efficacy parameters and possible toxicities of current therapies. Can consistently describe common limitations of these parameters (e.g. prioritizes practical monitoring parameters for the pharmacist). The monitoring is always executed in patient care activities.	Student performs more often, not ideally consistent. Shows clear signs of progress.	On some occasions, accurately states and monitors efficacy parameters and possible toxicities of current therapies. On most occasions can describe common limitations of these parameters, but sometimes offers impractical or incorrect parameters.	Student attempts with significant assistance by preceptor. Shows some signs of progress.	Unable to state monitoring efficacy parameters and possible toxicities of current therapies. Cannot consistently describe common limitations of these parameters and often identifies impractical parameters. Requires significant and repeated amount of prompting.	NA
Mid evaluation	☐ Progressing		☐ Needs improvement		☐ Not progressing	☐
Final evaluation	5	4	3	2	1	☐

12. Adjustment of pharmacotherapeutic plan (Case presentation with all elements in patient care process)	Consistently and accurately anticipates potential risks or unintended failure of pharmacotherapeutic plan and considers appropriate alternative therapy.	Student performs more often, not ideally consistent. Shows clear signs of progress.	On some occasions anticipates potential risks or unintended failure of pharmacotherapeutic plan and considers appropriate alternative therapy. At times requires prompting.	Student attempts with significant assistance by preceptor. Shows some signs of progress.	Unable to anticipate potential risks or unintended failure of therapeutic plan and formulate appropriate alternative therapy. Requires significant and repeated amount of prompting.	NA
Mid evaluation	☐ Progressing		☐ Needs improvement		☐ Not progressing	☐
Final evaluation	5	4	3	2	1	☐
Total						

COMMENTS AND SPECIFIC FEEDBACK
Educational Outcome: Patient Care

III. Educational Outcome on Communication Skills (Communicator, Educator)

Criteria and Student Performance	Perform consistently as expected		Perform occasionally as expected		Unable to perform as expected	Not Applicable
13. Conducts patient and/or family education	Consistently takes time to provide adequate pharmacotherapeutic education to assigned patients (and family members when appropriate). This often includes provision of written materials (calendars, info sheets).	Student performs more often, not ideally consistent. Shows clear signs of progress.	On some occasions, provides adequate pharmacotherapeutic education to assigned patients (and family members when appropriate) that is sometimes initiated by the student, but also prompted by the preceptor. It sometimes includes providing written materials.	Student attempts with significant assistance by preceptor. Shows some signs of progress.	Unable to provide adequate pharmacotherapeutic education to assigned patients and does not take any initiative to interact with patients or families.	NA

	Progressing		Needs improvement	Not progressing		
Mid evaluation ☐	☐		☐	☐		☐
Final evaluation ☐	5	4	3	2	1	☐
14. Communication with other members of the healthcare team	On most occasions proactively and professionally approaches members of the healthcare team (not only physicians, but also nurses and other care providers) and efficiently and reliably relays patient information and consistently participates in collaborative pharmacotherapeutic decision-making.	Student performs more often, not ideally consistent. Shows clear signs of progress.	On some occasions, proactively and professionally interacts members of the healthcare team and communicates with them accurately. Consistently and reliably collaborates with other team members (not only physicians) on most relevant patient care issues.	Student attempts with significant assistance by preceptor. Shows some signs of progress.	Unable to approach members of the healthcare team and communicate with them. Unable to consistently collaborate with other team members on many relevant patient care issues.	NA
Mid evaluation ☐	Progressing ☐		Needs improvement ☐	Not progressing ☐		☐
Final evaluation ☐	5	4	3	2	1	☐
15. Professional presentation skills (e.g. case presentations, journal club, other presentations)	On most occasions, demonstrates ability to organize, develop, and deliver adequate oral presentations that display great degree of preparation. Actively engages the audience and presents material in a clear and organized manner. Answers all questions effectively.	Student performs more often, not ideally consistent. Shows clear signs of progress.	On some occasions, demonstrates ability to organize, develop, and deliver adequate oral presentations that display moderate degree of preparation. Partly engages with the audience and presents in a moderately clear and organized manner. Can address some questions.	Student attempts with significant assistance by preceptor. Shows some signs of progress.	Unable to organize develop, and deliver adequate oral presentations and/or is not well prepared for them. Presents the material in an inadequate, confusing, or superficial manner and is mostly unable to answer questions.	NA
Mid evaluation ☐	Progressing ☐		Needs improvement ☐	Not progressing ☐		☐
Final evaluation ☐	5	4	3	2	1	☐

16. Chart documentation (Patient instructions, ADR, Medication Error, Drug Information, SOAP notes, Other Pharmacist interventions documented)	On most occasions, timely, completely and concisely documents relevant findings of patient assessments or education, pharmaceutical care recommendations in appropriate format.	Student performs more often, not ideally consistent. Shows clear signs of progress.	On some occasions, timely, completely and concisely documents relevant findings of patient assessments or education, pharmaceutical care recommendations in appropriate format.	Student attempts with significant assistance by preceptor. Shows some signs of progress.	Unable to make appropriate and relevant documentation of pharmacist activity. Documentation is unclear or contains irrelevant information.	NA
Mid evaluation	☐ Progressing		☐ Needs improvement	☐	☐ Not progressing	☐
Final evaluation	5	4	3	2	1	☐
Total						

COMMENTS AND SPECIFIC FEEDBACK
Educational Outcome: Communication Skills

IV. Educational Outcome on Management of Pharmacist Roles and Responsibility (Manager, Includer)

Criteria and Student Performance	Perform consistently as expected		Perform occasionally as expected	Unable to perform as expected		Not Applicable
17. Medication information management, innovation & entrepreneurship	On most occasions, effectively and efficiently searches online resources. Responds to all patient, team or preceptor questions in a timely fashion with evidence-based data that is usually retrieved at the bedside or point of care.	Student performs more often, not ideally consistent. Shows clear signs of progress.	On some occasions, effectively and efficiently searches online resources to acquire evidence-based information for most purposes. At times, provides preceptor or team members with copies of such information or identified resources.	Student attempts with significant assistance by preceptor. Shows some signs of progress.	Unable to access suitable resources or retrieve relevant information. At times prepares inappropriate responses or fails to follow through on information requests. Does not use a patient work-up tool.	NA

	□ Progressing		□ Needs improvement	□ Not progressing		□ □
	5	4	3	2	1	
Mid evaluation						
Final evaluation						
18. Patient care organization	On most occasions, effectively manages patient volume assigned by the preceptor. Proactively participates in discharge planning of outgoing patients and efficiently assumes care of newly admitted patients. Demonstrates evidence of use of a patient work-up tool.	Student performs more often, not ideally consistent. Shows clear signs of progress.	On some occasions, effectively manages patient volume assigned by the preceptor. Proactively participates in discharge planning of outgoing patients and efficiently assumes care of newly admitted patients. Demonstrates evidence of use of a patient work-up tool.	Student attempts with significant assistance by preceptor. Shows some signs of progress.	Unable to manage patient volume assigned by the preceptor. The number and/or complexity of patients in care is stable or decreases as the rotation progresses. Is unfamiliar with patient history of care. Does not use a patient work-up tool – unaware of patient needs in the practice site.	NA
Mid evaluation						
Final evaluation						
	5	4	3	2	1	
19. Patient care management, innovation to improve practice	On most occasions, provides daily update to preceptor on patient progress, medical plan and discharge plan, efficacy and safety monitoring assessment and maintains accurate records of current drug therapy for all patients. Visits the patients routinely daily. Consider cultural issues in practice.	Student performs more often, not ideally consistent. Shows clear signs of progress.	On some occasions, daily update to preceptor on patient progress, medical plan and discharge plan, efficacy and safety monitoring assessment and drug therapy for all patients in care. Sees some of patients daily. Considering cultural issues in practice only occasionally.	Student attempts with significant assistance by preceptor. Shows some signs of progress.	Unable to provide preceptor update on patient progress, medical plan and discharge plan. Does not fulfill efficacy and safety monitoring assessments or maintain accurate records of patients' current drug therapy. Does not use a patient work-up tool. Ignore cultural issues in practice.	NA
Mid evaluation						

Final evaluation	5	4	3	2	1	□
Total						

COMMENTS AND SPECIFIC FEEDBACK

Educational Outcome: Management of Pharmacist Roles and Responsibility

V. Educational Outcome on Professional Conduct (Professionalism, Self-aware)

Criteria and Student Performance	Perform consistently as expected		Perform occasionally as expected	Unable to perform as expected		Not Applicable
20. Respect	Consistently addresses preceptor with courtesy and respect at practice. Proactively seeks to learn more about the preceptor's experiences and practice development.	Student performs more often, not ideally consistent. Shows clear signs of progress.	On some occasions, addresses preceptor with courtesy and respect at practice.	Student attempts with significant assistance by preceptor. Shows some signs of progress.	Consistently addresses preceptor without courtesy and demonstrates behavior lacking in respect at practice.	NA
Mid evaluation	□ Progressing	4	□ Needs improvement 3	□ Not progressing	2	□
	5					
Final evaluation	5	4	3	2	1	□

21. Reliability, motivation, and response to feedback	On most occasions completes assigned tasks on time with little or no assistance. Consistently demonstrates initiative to engage in professional roles or proactively look for ways to assist with other appropriate tasks. Acknowledges own limitations. Encourages and evaluates constructive criticism and modifies response to feedback.	Student performs more often, not ideally consistent. Shows clear signs of progress.	On some occasions completes assigned tasks own time with moderate assistance. On some occasions demonstrates initiative to engage in professional roles or proactively look for ways to assist with other appropriate tasks. On some occasions, encourages and evaluates constructive criticism and modifies response to feedback.	Student attempts with significant assistance by preceptor. Shows some signs of progress.	Unable to complete assigned projects and tasks on time and requiring extensive assistance. Unable to demonstrate initiative to engage in professional roles or proactively look for ways to assist with other appropriate tasks. Lacks insight into own limitations and is unable to either receive constructive criticism or modify behavior in response to feedback.	NA
Mid evaluation	☐ Progressing		☐ Needs improvement		☐ Not progressing	☐
Final evaluation	5	4	3	2	1	☐
Total						

COMMENTS AND SPECIFIC FEEDBACK

Educational Outcome: Professional Conduct

VI. Educational Outcome on Professional Collaboration and Teamwork (Collaborator)

Criteria and Student Performance	Perform consistently as expected		Perform occasionally as expected	Unable to perform as expected		Not Applicable
22. Collaboration with other members of the healthcare team	Consistently forms respectful work relationships with all team members (not only physicians) to improve patient care and promote drug knowledge. Listens to and proactively seeks learning opportunities from all team members.	Student performs more often, not ideally consistent. Shows clear signs of progress.	On some occasions, respectfully interacted with the majority of team members for patient care decision-making. At times offered drug education or gained drug-related information from team members.	Student attempts with significant assistance by preceptor. Shows some signs of progress.	Unable to form effective work relationships with team members. Provided most patient care in isolation of other patient care providers.	NA
Mid evaluation	☐ Progressing		☐ Needs improvement	☐ Not progressing		☐
Final evaluation	5	4	3	2	1	☐
23. Collaboration with other pharmacy students and members of the pharmacy staff	Consistently forms respectful work relationships with pharmacy staff and other students. Supports the learning experience of others during the rotation.	Student performs more often, not ideally consistent. Shows clear signs of progress.	Forms moderate work relationships with pharmacy staff and other students. At times requires prompting by preceptor to initiate these interactions.	Student attempts with significant assistance by preceptor. Shows some signs of progress.	Demonstrates inability or unwillingness to interact with other pharmacy members not directly participating with rotation activities.	NA
Mid evaluation	☐ Progressing		☐ Needs improvement	☐ Not progressing		☐
Final evaluation	5	4	3	2	1	☐
Total						

COMMENTS AND SPECIFIC FEEDBACK
Educational Outcome: Professional Collaboration and Teamwork

VII. Educational Outcome on Advocate for Patient Care and Pharmacy Practice (Advocate, Leader, Innovator)

Criteria and Student Performance	Perform consistently as expected		Perform occasionally as expected	Unable to perform as expected		<u>Not Applicable</u>
24. Pharmacist in patient advocacy	Proactively and consistently is a source of information and referral to community resources for patients/caregivers. Voices patient considerations in decision-making.	Student performs more often, not ideally consistent. Shows clear signs of progress.	On some occasions, considers patient factors in decision-making. At times has served as a source of information and referral to community resources for patients/caregivers.	Student attempts with significant assistance by preceptor. Shows some signs of progress.	Does not demonstrate consideration of patient factors in decision-making and is unable to provide health or community resource information.	NA
Mid evaluation	☐ Progressing		☐ Needs improvement	☐ Not progressing		☐
Final evaluation	5	4	3	2	1	☐
25. Leadership, innovation, research aptitude, innovation & entepreunership	Proactively and consistently communicates existing and innovative roles of pharmacists to patients and healthcare team and highlights utility of pharmacist knowledge and skills at this and other practice sites through drug-related activity/service. Takes initiative in research relevant to the area of practice.	Student performs more often, not ideally consistent. Shows clear signs of progress.	On some occasions, takes opportunity to communicate and highlight pharmacist knowledge and skills at this and other practice sites by performing drug-related activities and services. Needs significant assistance in developing a research plan relevant to the are a of practice.	Student attempts with significant assistance by preceptor. Shows some signs of progress.	Unable to highlight pharmacist roles to patients or healthcare team. Unable to propose research relevant to the area of practice.	NA
Mid evaluation	☐ Progressing		☐ Needs improvement	☐ Not progressing		☐
Final evaluation	5	4	3	2	1	☐
Total						

COMMENTS AND SPECIFIC FEEDBACK

Educational Outcome: Advocate for Patient Care and Pharmacy Practice

From the applicable evaluation elements, the total score should be converted to 100.

Grand Total out of 100:

A	B+	B	C+	C	F
90-100%	85-89%	80-84%	75-79%	70-74%	<70%

SPECIFIC FEEDBACK FOR STUDENT SUPPORT AND IMPROVEMENT OFFERED BY PRECEPTOR:

Student Strengths:

Student Areas for Improvement in Future Rotations:

Student Signature _____

Date

Verified by Faculty incharge _____

Date

Preceptor Signature _____

Date

Received by training coordinator _____

Date

Index

Printed in the United States
By Bookmasters